AF527880

Emerging Indian State

Emerging Indian State

Socio-economic Profile of Gujarat

A Select Bibliography

SEEMA SHUKLA

RAWAT PUBLICATIONS

Jaipur • New Delhi • Bangalore • Guwahati • Kolkata

ISBN 978-81-316-0996-5

© Author, 2019

No part of this book may be reproduced or transmitted in any form or by any means, electronic or mechanical, including photocopying, recording or by any information storage and retrieval system, without permission in writing from the publishers.

Published by
Prem Rawat for **Rawat Publications**
Satyam Apts, Sector 3, Jawahar Nagar, Jaipur 302 004 (India)
Phone: 0141 265 1748 / 7006 Fax: 0141 265 1748
E-mail: info@rawatbooks.com
Website: www.rawatbooks.com

New Delhi Office
4858/24, Ansari Road, Daryaganj, New Delhi 110 002
Phone: 011 23263290

Also at *Bangalore, Guwahati* and *Kolkata*

Typeset by Rawat Computers, Jaipur
Printed and bound in India

Contents

Foreword

India has been experiencing pressure to increase its strength in higher education. The gross enrolment ratio is being watched carefully. The number of students seeking admissions for Post-Graduate, M.Phil. and Ph.D. have been increasing steadily. Research supervisors are searching for newer topics for research. In case of our country India, until 1970, most research topics dealt with country level questions. From 1970 onward, regions became important. Collection and availability of data at state, district and lower levels improved gradually. Social scientists and humanities scholars and teachers began conducting state and regional level analysis. In the decades that followed, there was a fair amount of research material available at state level. This has given rise to the need for regional level bibliographies. However, very little work has been done in this regard.

One more trend needs to be noted in the above context. In the post 1960 era, most universities in the country introduced higher education in mother tongue. Unfortunately, teachers and scholars missed out on creating knowledge in regional languages. Good translation work also lacked significantly. National Knowledge Commission 2006, in its report, states, 'High quality translation is vital for increasing access to knowledge in many critical areas, and strengthening people's participation in education and the creation and dissemination of knowledge. However, the current facilities for translation are inadequate. There is both latent unrecognized demand and uneven availability of complete information.' Consequently, a vicious circle set in. Most of the students who got their degrees in regional languages, relied mainly on the teachers' notes, limited texts and guides that were available. When some of them became teachers, they in turn took recourse to same material while teaching and so on. When such teachers became M.Phil. and Ph.D. supervisors, they struggled to direct the students in proper direction for topics and references. Most of them did not have any idea as to what type of research work was being done and published. In this context too, a need for bibliographies on the work done at regional level arose.

Pressure toward academic excellence is also mounting. Teachers and students have begun to search for good research material. Library science has scope to step in here to aid them. Bibliography is a well-developed subject area. There are very good quality bibliographies available focussing on subject, area and time. A good bibliography becomes an important guiding aid for teachers and research supervisors to select research topics and reference material.

Gujarat has been less fortunate in the matter of good bibliographies, especially in social sciences. The state has been rich in terms of social science research institutions. There are three research institutions recognised by the Indian Council of Social Science Research (ICSSR) besides a few others. And of course, the state does have a few good universities as well, since 1950. All these institutions put together have produced significant and reasonable research output in post-independence times. It also includes limited work in regional languages as well. Large number of studies on socio-economic issues, works on history, sociology, anthropology, political science and social work have also been attempted. However, hardly any good bibliography is available on research and documentation work done on Gujarat.

A welcome attempt has been made to address the lacuna suggested above with the help of ICSSR research project funding. Keeping in view the needs of students, teachers and researchers, Dr Seema Shukla, Assistant Librarian at Centre for Social Studies (CSS), first institute in Gujarat to be recognised by the ICSSR, has tried to compile a bibliography on Gujarat focussing largely on socio-economic issues. As a good researcher, she has tried to address the questions like what is available, what is not available, what is in demand, and tried to build possible response. She did not get affected by initial discouragements and setbacks and forged ahead with nerve. She collected material with the help of a small team and compiled systematically. She has compiled a good bibliography on Gujarat. She could have limited her work to research material created in English and that would have been convenient too, but she went ahead to collect and compile material in Gujarati also. She has published it as a separate volume.

The present bibliography on Gujarat has a special feature. It is in the form of a Union Catalogue where the reader is able to get the location of the material. Eight university libraries, 14 research institute libraries and 3 libraries in Mumbai have been the source for material on Gujarat. Gujarat was part of erstwhile Bombay State before 1960 and hence historical research material is contained in selected libraries in Mumbai. Entries in the bibliography are classified into 18 subjects. In addition, multiple accesses are facilitated by year, author and word index. Bibliography is preceded by a brief introductory note which is very useful to the user of the bibliography. The bibliography contains in all 6414 entries including books, reports and articles in books, journals and occasional publications.

The bibliographer has put in commendable efforts to accomplish the work and deserves appreciation. I have personally gained by getting involved in the project by providing occasional advice. The bibliography will prove immensely useful for all those who are interested in knowing research and documentation done on Gujarat. Students looking for topics for research will be greatly enabled by this work. The work is timely and will help boost research work in the state and it will also help researchers in India and outside. The present work may encourage other librarians in the states to undertake similar and more comprehensive work of preparing bibliographies.

Dharampur, Gujarat
25 June, 2018

Sudarshan Iyengar
Former Vice Chancellor,
Gujarat Vidyapith, Ahmedabad

Acknowledgement

A huge task, such as this, could not have been accomplished without the support of many individuals sitting at key positions in various institutional Libraries and a proactive team, who collected the data. First of all I thank ICSSR, New Delhi for giving financial support for this reserch project. At the Centre for Social Studies, Surat, where I work, successive Directors have provided necessary support and colleagues encouraged me to pursue this research project.

I would like to acknowledge my sincere thanks to officials and various individuals at different universities and research institutions. I would like to acknowledge and thank Ms Bharti Desai, Dr Batuk Gohel, Dr Shishir Mandalia, Dr Mayank Trivedi, Dr Ankuya, Mr Nilesh Soni, Dr Yogesh Parekh, Dr Anil Kumar, Ms Heema Soni, Dr Shailesh Yagnik, Ms Meenal Sheth, Ms Tejasvini Joshi, Ms Sarita Das, Ms Manjula Pai, Mr Krishna Yeri, Dr Ganapati, Mr Harish Rathawa, Mr Dabhi, Mr Manish Vyas, Mr Pankaj Mahadik, Ms Swati, Ms Anjali Kareker, and Mr B.K. Ahire. I also specially thank Mr Achyut Yagnik, Director, SETU Ahmedabad and Dr S.S. Kalamkar, Director, Agro-Economic Research Centre for their help and guidance. Special mention needs to be made of Professor Sudarshan Iyengar who took more than casual interest and guided me at every stage of the Project.

I also sincerely thank Mr Jayant Meghani, Dr Nimesh Oza, Bhargav Jani, Dr Niharika Udani and Ms Alpa Bhatt.

I was fortunate to have a good team. Barring a few exceptions, each one of them, especially the girls, worked very diligently and hard to collect the data. I thank all of them heartily. At the CSS, I thank Ashokbhai, Ashish and Nitinbhai, for their final processing help and I also thank Gaurang and Nehali, who were hired for the work of data entry and processing.

I acknowledge and profusely thank Professor Urmila Thakar for going through the entire draft and offering frank and critical comments. Similarly, I thank Dr P.R. Goswami, the ICSSR appointed reviewer for reviewing the report thoroughly and making very valuable suggestions. The quality of the work has improved because of the review of these two senior professionals.

I sincerely thank Rawat Publications, Jaipur who agreed to publish this work.

It has been a pleasure to undertake this project. There would be limitations and they reflect my inadequateness and I alone am responsible for them.

Seema Shukla

Introduction

The state of Gujarat holds an important position in India. Gujarat of today is one of the economically advanced states. Research scholars have been studying history, culture, religion and various socio-economic aspects of Gujarat since long. There has been a felt need for sourcing research material on Gujarat. In my relatively short span of working as Assistant Librarian at the Centre for Social Studies, Surat, I have come across a number of inquiries about bibliography on Gujarat that could help the interested research scholar to source appropriate material for study. The present work on Gujarat is a modest attempt to respond to the need.

Having taken up the task of building a bibliography on Gujarat, it became imperative to define clearly the need first. Simple inquiries of the kind that I have mentioned above cannot be sufficient to embark on a project like this. One needs to investigate whether such works exist already and what is being attempted is not duplication. My initial research revealed that there are a few bibliographies that have been compiled at national level and they contain works on Gujarat. It has also been found that there are at least two bibliographies on Gujarat that are available to research scholars. These are as mentioned below;

1. Satyaprakash, Compil. and Ed. *Gujarat: A Select Bibliography*. Gurgaon: Indian Documentation Service, 1976.

This Bibliography comprises of 2451 entries including articles, research papers, notes, news and book reviews from 199 Journals and a daily 'The Times of India', which covers years from 1962 to 1976. The information in the Bibliography is arranged alphabetically. The information is arranged according to subject and author. It does not contain subject and author indexes.

2. Simpson, Edward. *Society and History of Gujarat Since 1800: A Select Bibliography of the English and European Language Sources*. Hyderabad: Orient Blackswan, 2011.

This Bibliography is a good attempt in preparing research database on Gujarat. This Bibliography includes more than 6,500 entries that are arranged alphabetically. Well-known company like amazon has the following to say about the book.

> "This book consolidates scholarship on Gujarat in English and other European languages, notably, Dutch, German, French, Italian and Portuguese. It draws

together well-known sources, as well as rare and under-exploited research material. Detailed bibliographical references are provided for books, chapters, periodical literature, dissertations, project reports, other materials published since 1800; anonymous works and select government publications, such as gazetteers and census reports, are also included. The titles considered spread across the disciplinary boundaries of history, political and development studies, literature and the liberal arts, sociology, cultural and social anthropology .... Annotations pointing to some of these connections are provided, especially when titles are uninformative, argument, data or provenance notable, or when serendipity has demanded .... The book also contains a substantial introduction based on new and original research on the key themes in the literature on Gujarat and how these themes spill into popular politics and life in the region at present"[1].

While focusing on these two specific works, one may ask that how one more bibliography on Gujarat would help the researchers. The need arises on two counts. One, there is always scope for updating the information as research work continues. For instance, Satyaprakash's work referred to above covers a period between 1962 and 1976. Hence, there is obvious scope to cover the period from 1976 onwards. Two, each person compiling bibliography has different objectives. Such effort leaves some areas which may be important from the point of some different types of inquiry. On both these counts the scope for compiling a fresh bibliography remains promising. Simpson's bibliography covers a vast area, but it still leaves some gap. For instance, it has not treated various subjects separately. If a researcher wants to find information on Narmada Project related aspects in the Bibliography and if he or she is not aware of the name of the author, then it becomes difficult to trace the information. The researcher has to go through all the entries from beginning till end to locate the information. A subject index would have improved the usability immensely.

Purpose or Objectives

As a Librarian at the CSS, I had some specific inquiries. Most inquiries pertain to socio-economic problems, development, and planning aspects of Gujarat. It was found that to locate articles that appear in edited books, volumes and journals is not an easy task. The intended search could be for both published and unpublished documents. Further, it was realized that researchers are also seeking information on the locations where the sourced material can be accessed. Thus, a specific need was identified for preparing a fresh bibliography. More specifically, the objectives were the following:

- To collect and compile research and scholarly published and unpublished material on socio-economic aspects of Gujarat and present it as a bibliography and a union catalogue
- To guide the researchers to the information sources[2]
- To introduce a range of subjects and references to the students studying Gujarat
- To help the Librarians across the state and elsewhere in locating the material on Gujarat and help them to provide a reference material for teaching bibliography as subject to Library science students
- To collect and present the bibliography also in Gujarati as a separate volume

Scope

The need for a bibliography was felt because the researchers' inquiries pertain more about socio-economic, political, cultural aspects. Inquiries also pertain to problems related to planning and development and hence an attempt has been made to focus on those areas. Thus, the bibliography mainly covers socio-economic, political, cultural, and planning and development studies on Gujarat. However, subjects generally falling under humanities including history have been considered on merit of their being analytical in social science perspective. It has been mentioned already that Simpson's work has covered a vast ground in historical studies. In that sense, the present work complements the former. Time and resource constraints would also limit the scope of any ambitious work in preparing comprehensive bibliographies. The present one claims to be no exception. The coverage within the specified areas has also been kept limited about which more will be said later when limitations of the work are discussed.

Methodology

Two aspects are discussed in this section. One, sources consulted and information, and second method of compilation.

Gujarat has number of universities and research institution libraries. These libraries contain both published and unpublished material. For sourcing material, they have been searched first for this documentation. Thus, the present work of bibliography is based mainly on the information collected from selected university and research libraries. Gujarat has a special history and hence we have also included three libraries that are in Mumbai (then the capital of erstwhile Bombay State that included parts of present Gujarat, Maharashtra, and Karnataka). These are, Mumbai University Library, Asiatic Society Library and Bharatiya Vidyabhavan Library.

It was indeed desirable that one includes all the university libraries and social research institution libraries. However, it has not been possible to do so. In the case of university libraries, it should be mentioned that the universities that have come to exist relatively recently have been excluded from the present study. A test check was undertaken and it was found that the new universities were yet to acquire research publications in any significant way. The new universities had not obtained the old material and their main focus has been to collect good text and reference books for students. In case of social science research institutions too we could not collect information from all because in few cases the library staff for various reasons regretted their inability to cooperate. Thus, we have collected information from the following institutions.

University Libraries	: 7 Conventional and 1 Agriculture
Socio-economic Research Institutions	: 14
Libraries in Mumbai	: 3

A total of 25 libraries have been consulted to source the material. The list is given in Annexure 1.

Ideally, a good bibliography should include all units within the subject. It is called a bibliographic unit which includes books, journal articles, reports, manuscripts, sound and video recordings, individual web pages and/or entire web sites, computer programs or printouts, films, charts, etc. We have not been able to source complete material in case of all subjects. There are limitations and they will be discussed as we detail out the method of data collection. The work is limited to books, journal articles, reports, and unpublished micro material. The other forms including electronic and based on internet have not been included due to paucity of time and resources. Further, most institutional libraries have not been able to maintain the material in the method in which they could be easily identified and coded. It would have consumed a lot of time of the Principal Investigator to carry on special search of such material in selected libraries. The Principal Researcher being a full time working librarian could not get such time.

Method of Data Collection and Limitations

Persons, who were trained mostly in Library Science were hired to collect data. A total of 28 persons were engaged, for time period ranging from 1 month to 6 months. A data sheet containing specific details was constructed and the investigators were instructed to collect data in data sheets.

Permission was sought from each library and institution head to help to collect the data. Some institutions failed to cooperate. We did not pursue very hard. Once the permission was granted, data has been collected from checking the material on stacks and racks, electronic data base such as Online Public Access Catalogue (OPAC) and websites wherever available.

For sourcing material, the key words selected were 'Gujarat' or name of any location in Gujarat. The set of such words found in title, sub-title, chapter in a book or an article in journal, report and/or any such published and unpublished material was selected to be included in the bibliography. We have also tried to include such units where indication mentioned above was not available but was found by sifting through material. Obviously, this process has had limitations.

In this bibliography, only articles from selected research and other journals have been included. List of journals that have been consulted are given in Annexure 2. In selecting articles from journals, letters to editors, discussion notes, book reviews, and opinions have not been included. Since the Principal Investigator has not been present everywhere and data has not been collected by her only, such items may have got included inadvertently. Few other limitations in data collection may also be listed.

The last date for including data was set as December 2013. Only in case of the Library of the Centre for Social Studies, where the Principal Investigator works, available data for March 2014 have also been included.

The name of the author/s may have been misspelt or due to lack of complete attention on the part of the Investigator. It has not been possible to cross check each and every unit entry. There may be some cases where either the starting page numbers or ending page number or both of an article selected from a journal or a book or a report are missing. Once the data was collected and brought to the Principal Investigator by the investigators, it has not been possible to revisit the places to rectify such omissions due to lack of resources and time.

In case of some entries, persons who have edited, compiled or translated may have been shown as authors as due care in specifying has not been taken by the data collectors. The Principal Investigator has tried to check and mend in a few cases. However, in some cases the mistake may have remained.

In a few cases it has not been possible to get the year and/or place of publication. This may have happened due to negligence or non-availability. In all such entries we have notified them by using [ ] sign.

The main method of collecting data has been by sifting through each rack in the library stacks. It is possible that at the time collection the book/report/journal was issued to a reader and hence not found on rack, it is also possible that it was misplaced or lost. There may be some loss of material.

In case of some libraries it was not possible to send investigators to collect data, and the collection has not been listed in computer. In such cases, we have relied on the library staff there and if they have missed some data, we also have missed.

Government publications have been generally not included. Annual or serial publications containing administrative data and publications containing statistics have not been included. The main reason for not including the Census, Sample Survey results and other Annual Reports and statistical abstracts published periodically are well-known sources. They do not contain any analytical studies on any subject. Most researchers and scholars are necessarily by training aware about existence of such data. Had they been included the number of entries would have risen by a few hundred occupying space and costing money for collection and printing. However, government's departmental and sponsored studies on special aspects including district and state Gazetteers have been included.

Organisation

Organising material is very important part of any bibliography. We have tried to organise the material suitably for subjects and targeted users. We have tried to adhere to broad principles of organised bibliography. The compiler has used some discretion with respect to subjects about which explanations are given. The bibliography has thus been arranged in 18 chapters, each devoted to a subject on whom researchers are most likely to search for entries. The entries have been organised alphabetically and using these two sequences user may be able to locate the work if the broad subject and the author is known to her/him without taking help of any other index. In this sense, it is a classified bibliography and hence it is logical and easy to understand for users. The details of organisation are given below:

- Each entry has been given alphabetically starting with surname (family name).
- Each chapter in the bibliography has been given in three part sequence.
- Book, Chapter in edited book
- Journal article
- Working paper, Report and other material

- Articles 'a' 'an' 'the', appearing in the title of book, journal, report and other documents, have been removed. However, where they appear in sub-titles, they have been retained.
- Edited volumes containing two or more articles on Gujarat contain the entry of the articles and that of the volume too. For example, Fascism in India: Faces, Fangs, and Facts, contains 44 chapters on Gujarat. Hence, there are 44+1, 45 entries. This has been done because in case a researcher does not have prior knowledge about the title or author of a particular chapter in the volume, but conducts search through editor's name, he or she should be able to identify the volume.

Format of Units or Entries

Book

Author. *Book title: Sub-title*. Place: Publisher, year. Pages. Abbreviation of Libraries.

Chaturvedi, Vinayak. *Peasant Pasts: History, politics, and nationalism in Gujarat*. Ranikhet: Permanent Black, 2007. p. 307. CSSL, SGUL.

Desai, M.B. and Vakil, C.N. *Rural economy of Gujarat*. Bombay: Oxford, 1948. p. 352. AAUL.

Sharma, S.S., Raju, K.V., and Sarkar, Sabyasachi. *Grwoing rural-urban disparity in Gujarat*. New Delhi: Serials, 2009. p. 114. CEPTL, GVL.

Chapter in Edited Book

Author. Chapter title: Sub-title. In *Edited book title*. Ed. by name of editor. Place: Publisher, year. Pages. Abbreviation of Libraries.

Iyengar Sudarshan. Voluntary initiatives for tribal development in Gujarat. In *Tirbal Situation in India: Issues in development, with special reference to Western India*. Ed. by Vidyut Joshi. Jaipur: Rawat, 1998. pp. 175–214. CSSL, GVL, SGUL, UML.

Journal Article

Author. Article title. *Name of Journal*. Volume Number, Issue Number, year. Pages. Abbreviation of Libraries.

Haque, M. Anthropology of Padhar in Ranagadh, Gujarat. *Man in India*. 64,3,1984. pp. 294–303. CSSL, UML.

Report and Other Documents

Acharya Akash. *Access and utilisation of health care services in urban low income settlements in Surat, India*. Surat: Centre for Social Studies, 2008. p. 29. Working Paper No. 5 CSSL.

Note: In any entry if there are more than three authors, the name of the first author is followed by et al. For example:

Pandey, C.N. et al. *Medicinal Plants of Gujarat*. Gandhinagar: Gujarat Ecological Education Research (GEER) Foundation, 2005. p. 410. CEEL, EDIL.

Chapter Scheme and Content

The data collected was sifted carefully and it was classified. The subjects on which material are available are fairly diverse and a comprehensive classification would have led to very large number of chapters. An attempt has been made to stick to broad classification so that more than one specific area is merged to the nearest broad area. With this careful merging, the information has been classified into following 18 subjects:

1. *General*. Two considerations have gone in creating the general category. One, the studies and works that defy any specific classification scheme are included here. Two, areas in which there are very few entries and they cannot form a viable logical group have been included in general. For instance, media studies have been included in general.
2. *Sociology*: Anthropological studies, studies on society, religion, social movements, protest movements, social security, welfare, displacement, resettlement and rehabilitation etc. Tribal studies in general about status and development etc. have been included in this chapter. However, specific tribe or ethnic groups have been included in separate chapter.
3. Communalism, sectarian and other conflicts, violence and conflict resolution have been included here.
4. Ethnicity, identity and social groups
5. Gender and women
6. Culture and diaspora
7. Politics, governance, democracy and human rights
8. Economics, economic growth and development
9. Finance and cooperation
10. Labour, employment and migration
11. Environment, natural resources, and disaster related studies
12. Industry
13. Trade and transport
14. Agriculture, forest and forestry, and animal husbandry
15. Poverty
16. Education, human development
17. Health and well-being
18. History, geography, archaeology and tourism

In addition to subject classification and alphabetical entries the user has been given multiple access facility by giving three more indexes. They are following:

1. Year index
2. Author index
3. Keyword index

A clarification for the year index is necessary. Since the bibliographical material contains material belonging to 19th and early 20th century also, it was thought proper to provide year index to access data easily. The present Gujarat state came into existence in 1960 and hence the year has been taken as the cut off year. For all the information that is available for the time period that precedes 1960, year index has been given. The following two Indices are self-explanatory.

Union Catalogue and Location of Material

A special feature of this bibliography is that we have tried to help the users with additional information with respect to location of the material. Generally, it is not necessary for a bibliography to contain information on location of the material. But in the field of Library Science, preparing and presenting union catalogue has been a useful recent practice. The dictionary identifies union catalogue as a noun and defines thus. Union Catalogue is a catalogue containing bibliographical records that indicate locations of materials in more than one library or in several units of one library[3]. From the definition it is obvious that various types of union catalogues can be prepared. They can be place specific, library specific, time specific etc. A lot of work has been done on how the concept of Union Catalogue has evolved. Since the focus of the present work is not union catalogue, definition suffices.

The idea of turning the present bibliography into a union catalogue also occurred when the data collection work began. Since, the data collection team visited various libraries, the location became known. Then it was easy to present the data in which for each entry the location is specified by naming the location in abbreviated form. The present bibliography now contains abbreviation of the library from where the material was located. A list of libraries and the abbreviations are given in Annexure 3. When the Principle Investigator reflected upon the advantages of preparing a union catalogue following benefits became obvious. This is not an exhaustive list of benefits, but only illustrative.

Single or multiple locations of the sourced material could be made available easily to the users.

Different editions available in different locations got identified. In cases where only year of publication was available, it came to our notice that same title was published during different years, may be at times by different publishers.

It became possible to assess which libraries specialised in material on socio-economic aspects of Gujarat.

Users would be able to know what material is available to them nearest to their place of work and residence.

The user from outside Gujarat will be able to know in which specific library the material is available and she/he can plan their library consultation work accordingly.

The union catalogue is also very useful for librarians. They would know about the availability or otherwise and they can arrange the inter library loan more efficiently.

The librarian may also decide whether to buy and add a book or other material in her/his own library or arrange for borrowing.

Troubles, Trouble Shooting and Limitations

Once the data started pouring in the classification process, a number of problems cropped up. One of the serious problems was incomplete information. Despite fairly rigorous training and some direct and some distant supervision, the investigators failed in some cases. An effort was made to make up by revisiting some of the libraries again. The revisits were very helpful, but in some cases the gaps remained. The second difficulty was more professional. The classification into broad subjects had to be based on the titles only. Barring the Principal Investigator's own library, the material from all other libraries had to be classified only on the basis of titles. Obviously, when authors give title to their work they do not keep librarians in their minds! The difficulty was faced and resolved to the extent possible. Some expert consultations were also done in case of some titles. But it is hoped that most classification is correct.

Another set of problem pertains to confusing and misleading information about authors, contributors, and editors. Some illustrations are provided below:

1. An edited book in which various authors have contributed has been brought out as a book by one author. For example, 'Rural Sociology of India' by A.R. Desai is an edited book. But the title page and the inner page show A.R. Desai as author as nowhere it is mentioned that he is the editor. In all such cases we decided to give the name then put [ ] to be read as edited by.

2. Some old volumes did not contain year of publication. In such cases too in place of year [ ] is given. A user, if has a book and comes to know about the year of publication, she/he can insert the year in the bracket. If the researcher is careful and helpful, she/he may pass on the information to the complier of the bibliography so that it can be incorporated in the next addition or future work.

3. There has also been surname, family name confusion. For example whether Devadas Pillai is the surname or Pillai alone could not be known for certain. It was decided to enter the surname as Devadas Pillai. It would also help the user if she/he knew the name.

4. Information about page numbers was also confusing. Some gave normal numerals say pages 1–150. In some cases roman numbers have been used.

5. Some books, chapter in a book or journal article include many subjects in the title. For instance, Urbanisation, employment generation, and poverty under the shadow of globalisation: The case of Gujarat, India by Amitabh Kundu, in Dynamics of development in Gujarat. Ed. by Indira Hirway, S.P. Kashyap and Amita Shah. This chapter has many subjects, but a careful look tells that it deals with economic development. Thus, it has been classified in the subject on which contains main discussion. We have found a way out in this. The key word index would help the user to locate the study and she/he may decide to use.

6. Some old volumes are being reprinted also by different publishers. The title and the cover have been retained as such. In such cases, we have given the entry in the following way:

Ovington, J. Voyage to Surat: in the year 1689. Ed. by H.G. Rawnlison. New Delhi: Asian Educational, 1994. [London: Oxford, 1929].

Information given in the bracket shows its first publication details. Such information is useful to the user.

With this introductory note we are presenting the bibliography in the following chapters. It contains 6415 entries in all.

Notes

1. For those interested in details may refer (http://www.amazon.in/Society-History-Gujarat-since-1800/dp/8125041885 Accessed on October 22, 2014).
2. The spirit here is the one that is stated in the RUSA guidelines of the American Library Association, "As appropriate to the audience, the author(s) may select to use a more common term to describe the final bibliography, such as "pathfinder," "finding aid," or "research guide." p. 1.

   http://www.ala.org/rusa/resources/guidelines/guidelinespreparation Accessed on 23 October 2014
3. Refer http://dictionary.reference.com/browse/union+catalog

Annexures

Annexure 1

List of Selected Libraries

1. Adivasi Academy, Mandaar, At Post Tejgadh, Chhota Udepur, Dist. Vadodara-391156. www.adivasiacademy.org.in

2. Agro-Economic Research Centre, H.M. Patel Institute of Rural Development, Opp. Nanadalaya Temple, Post Box No. 24, Sardar Patel University, Vallabh Vidyanagar-388120, Dist. Anand.

3. Anand Agriculture University, Anand-388110. www.aau.in

4. Asiatic Society Library, Town Hall Library, Shahid Bhagat Singh Marg, Fort, Mumbai-400001. www.asiaticsociety.org

5. Bhartiya Vidyabhavan, 3rd Floor, Munshi Sadan, Bhartiya Vidyabhavan Chowk, Kulpati K.M. Munshi Marg, Mumbai-400007. www.bhavans.info (OPAC)

6. Bhavnagar University Library, Maharaja Krishnakumarsinhji Bhavnagar University, Sardar Vallabhbhai Patel Campus, Gauri Shankar Lake Road, Bhavnagar-364001. www.mkbhavuni.edu.in (OPAC)

7. Centre for Environment Planning and Technology, CEPT University, Kasturbhai Lalbhai Campus, University Road, Navrangpura, Ahmedabad-380009. www.cept.ac.in (OPAC)

8. Centre for Environmental Education, Nehru Foundation for Development, Thaltej Tekra, Ahmedabad-380054. www.ceeindia.org

9. Centre for Social Studies, South Gujarat University Campus, Udhana-Magdalla Road, Surat-395007 www.css.ac.in (OPAC)

10. Entrepreneurship Development Institute of India, (Via Ahmedabad Airport), P.O. Bhat-382428, Dist. Gandhinagar. www.ediindia.org (OPAC)

11. Gujarat Institute of Desert Ecology, Mundra Road, Post Box No. 83, Bhuj-370001. www.gujaratdesertecology.com

12. Gujarat Institute of Development Research, Gota, Ahmedabad-380060. www.gidr.ac.in

13. Gujarat University Library, Navrangpura, Ahmedabad-380009. www.gujaratuniversity.org.in (OPAC)
14. Gujarat Vidyapith Library, Gujarat Vidyapith, Near Income Tax Office, Ashram Road, Ahmedabad-380014. www.gujaratvidyapith.org
15. Hansa Mehta Library, M.S. University of Baroda, Station Road, Vadodara-390002. www.hmlibrary.ac.in (OPAC)
16. Indian Institute of Management Library, Vastrapur, Ahmedabad-380015. www.iimahd.ernet.in/library (OPAC)
17. Institute of Rural Management, Anand, Post Box No. 60, Anand-388001. www.irma.ac.in (OPAC)
18. Mudra Institute of Communications, Shela, Sarkhej-Sanand Highway, Ahmedabad-380058. www.mica.ac.in (OPAC)
19. SETU: Centre for Social Knowledge and Action. Punyashlok, Near Liberty Bus Stand, Ahmedabad-380009.
20. Sardar Patel Institute of Economic and Social Research, Thaltej Road, Near Door Darshan, Ahmedabad-380054. www.spiesr.ac.in
21. Sardar Patel University Library, Sardar Patel University, Vallabh Vidyanagar-388120. www.spuvvn.edu (OPAC)
22. Saurashtra University Library, Saurashtra University, Rajkot-360005 www.saurashtrauniversity.edu (OPAC)
23. South Gujarat University Library, Veer Narmad South Gujarat University, Udhana-Magdalla Road, Surat-395007. www.vnsgu.ac.in (OPAC)
24. Tribal Research and Training Institute Library, Gujarat Vidyapith Campus, Near Income Tax Office, Ashram Road, Ahmedabad-380014. www.trti.gujarat.gov.in
25. University of Mumbai Library, University of Mumbai, Vidyanagri, Kalina, Santacruz(E), Mumbai-400032. www.mu.ac.in (OPAC)

Annexure 2

List of Journals

- Administrator
- Adivasi Gujarat
- Agriculture and Agro-Industries Journal
- Agricultural Economics Research Review
- Agricultural Situation in India
- American Anthropologist
- Annals of Agricultural Research
- Anvesak

- Arhta-Vikas
- Arth Vijnana
- Asia Pacific Journal of Rural Development
- Asian Biotechnology and Development Research
- Asian Economic Review
- Asian Journal of Horticulture
- Asian Survey
- Bhavan's Journal
- Bulletin of the Anthropological Survey of India
- Bulletin of the Deccan College Research Institute
- Calcutta Historical Journal
- Changing Villages
- Conservation and Society
- Contributions to Indian Social Science
- Contributions to Indian Sociology
- Cooperative Perspective
- Current Agriculture
- Demography India
- Deccan Geographer
- Decision
- Development in Practice
- Eastern Anthropologist
- Economic and Political Weekly
- Economic Research Review
- Economic Scene
- Environment and Urbanization
- Environmental Awareness
- Farmer
- Folklore
- Gandhian Perspectives
- Gender and Development
- Gender, Technology and Development
- Geographical Review of India
- Gujarat Agriculture University Research Journal
- Gujarat Journal of Extension Education
- Gujarat Police Journal
- Handloom Journal
- Health, Policy and Planning
- Historical Review
- Humanscape

- IASSI Quarterly
- India Past and Present
- Indian Anthropologist
- Indian Archives
- Indian Co-operative Review
- Indian Dairyman
- Indian Economic Journal
- Indian Economic Panorama
- Indian Economic and Social History Review
- Indian Economic Journal
- Indian Educational Review
- Indian Farming
- Indian Food Industry
- Indian Forester
- Indian Highways
- Indian Historical Quarterly
- Indian Historical Review
- Indian Journal of Agricultural Economics
- Indian Journal of Agricultural Sciences
- Indian Journal of Agricultural Marketing
- Indian Journal of Adult Education
- Indian Journal of Agricultural Sciences
- Indian Journal of Agronomy
- Indian Journal of Dairy Science
- Indian Journal of Economics
- Indian Journal of Fisheries
- Indian Journal of Gender Studies
- Indian Journal of Horticulture
- Indian Journal of Industrial Relations
- Indian Journal of Labour Economics
- Indian Journal of Malariology
- Indian Journal of Marketing
- Indian Journal of Nutrition Dietetics
- Indian Journal of Political Science
- Indian Journal of Public Administration
- Indian Journal of Regional Science
- Indian Journal of Secularism
- Indian Journal of Social Research
- Indian Journal of Social Science
- Indian Journal of Social Work

- Indian Journal of Soil Conservation
- Indian Labour Journal
- Indica
- International Journal of Development Studies
- International Journal of Geoinformatics
- International Journal of Rural Management
- Islamic Perspective
- Journal of Agricultural Development and Policy
- Journal of Agrometeorology
- Journal of Asian Studies
- Journal of Commerce and Management Thought
- Journal of Development Studies
- Journal of Economic Development
- Journal of Educational Planning and Administration
- Journal of Entrepreneurship
- Journal of Family Welfare
- Journal of Gujarat Research Society
- Journal of Health Management
- Journal of Human Ecology
- Journal of Indian Education
- Journal of Indian History
- Journal of Indian Ocean Studies
- Journal of Indian School of Political Economy
- Journal of Indian Water Resources Society
- Journal of Numismatic Society of India
- Journal of Peasant Studies
- Journal of Region, Health and Health Care
- Journal of Rural Development
- Journal of Scientific and Industry Research
- Journal of Social and Economic Development
- Journal of South Asian Development
- Journal of the Anthropological Society of Bombay
- Journal of the Anthropological Survey of India
- Journal of the Bombay Branch of the Asiatic Society
- Journal of the Indian Society of Remote Sensing
- Journal of the M.S. University of Baroda
- Journal of the Oriental Institute
- Journal of the University of Bombay
- Journal of Tropical Forestry
- Khadi Gramodyog

- Labour and Development
- Madhya Pradesh Journal of Social Sciences
- Man and Development
- Man and Environment
- Man in India
- Manpower Journal
- Margin
- Modern Asian Studies
- Modern Review
- Muslim India
- Nagarlok
- National Geographical Journal of India
- National Medical Journal of India
- Occupational and Environmental Health
- Past and Present
- Political Science Review
- Prajna
- Productivity
- Psychology and Developing Societies
- Quarterly Review of Historical Studies
- Radical Journal of Health
- Research and Development Journal
- Review of Development and Change
- Rural India
- Seminar
- Social Action
- Social Change
- Social Change and Development
- Social Scientist
- Social Welfare
- Sociological Bulletin
- South Asia Research
- South Asian Bulletin
- South Gujarat University Journal
- Southern Economic Review
- Southern Economist
- Studies in History
- Think India
- Third Concept
- Trends in Social Science Research
- Tribal Research Bulletin

- Urban India
- Vanyajati
- Vidya: The Journal of Gujarat University
- Vikalp: Alternatives
- Vishleshan
- VNSGU Journal of Humanities and Social Sciences
- Voices for Change
- Wastelands News
- Water and Energy International Quarterly
- Wamana
- World Development

Annexure 3

Abbreviations Used for Library Names

AAL	Adivasi Academi Library
AAUL	Anand Agriculture University Library
AERCL	Agro-Economic and Research Centre
ASL	Asiatic Society Library
BUL	Bhavnagar University Library
BVL	Bhartiya Vidyabhavan Library
CEEL	Centre for Environmental Education Library
CEPTL	Centre for Environmental planning and Technology Library
CSSL	Centre for Social Studies Library
EDIL	Entrepreneurship Development Institute Library
GIDEL	Gujarat Desert Ecology Library
GIDRL	Gujarat Institute of Development Research Library
GUL	Gujarat University Library
GVL	Gujarat Vidyapith Library
HML	Hansa Mehta Library
IIML	Indian Institute of management Library
IRMAL	Institute of Rural Management, Anand Library
MICAL	Mudra Institute of Communications, Ahmedabad Library
SETUL	SETU Library (Centre for Social Knowledge and Action Library)
SGUL	South Gujarat University Library
SPIESRL	Sardar Patel Institute of Economics and Social Research Library
SPUL	Sardar Patel University Library

SUL	Saurashtra University Library
TRTIL	Tribal Research and Training Institute Library
UML	University of Mumbai Library

While abbreviating the names of the Libraries from where we have collected data, we have used popular names of four Libraries and not their formal names. These libraries are:

1. Instead of Maharaja Krishnakumarsinghi Bhavnagar University Library, we write in short form, Bhavnagar University Library (BUL).
2. Instead of M.S. University of Baroda Library, we write in short form, Hansa Mehta Library (HML).
3. Instead of Veer Narmad South Gujarat University Library, we write in short form, South Gujarat University Library (SGUL).
4. Instead of Bhaikaka Library, we write in short form, Sardar Patel University Library (SPUL).
5. Gujarat Vidyapith has copyright section, from where we have collected some data. Against such entry we have written the short form as *GVL.

1

General, including Media and Others

Books/Chapter in Books

Agrawal, Binod C. *Television in Kheda: a social evaluation of site.* New Delhi: Concept, 1986. p. 78. SGUL, SPIESRL.

Bokil, Milind S. *Weaving carpets for development designs: a study of Gujarat Khet Vikas Parishad.* Ahmedabad: Gujarat Khet Vikas Parishad, 1992. p. 54. IRMAL.

Brown, W. Norman. Jaina manuscript from Gujarat illustrated in early Western Indian and Persian styles. In *India and Indology: selected articles.* Ed. by Rosane Rocher. Delhi: Motilal Banarsidass, 1978. pp. 232–242. SPUL.

Chatterjee, Ashok. *Rising: Utthan: an Indian quest for dignity & hope set in Gujarat.* Delhi: Business Standard, 2011. p. 204. CSSL.

Desai, Rakesh, ed. *Society and literature: Narmad in critical discourse.* Surat: Veer Narmad South Gujarat University, 2011. p. 408. CSSL.

Dhamija, Jasleen. *Crafts of Gujarat: living traditions of India.* Ahmedabad: Mapin, 1985. p. 167. IRMAL, SGUL.

Fischer, Eberhard and Shah, Haku. *Rural craftsmen and their work: equipment and techniques in the Mer village of Ratadi in Saurashtra, India.* Ahmedabad: National Institute of Design, 1970. p. 227. CSSL.

Forbes, Alexander Kinloch and Rowlinson, H.G. *Ras mala: hindoo annals of the province of Goozerat in western India.* Vol. 2. Delhi: Low Price, 1997. p. 459. UML.

Hasan, Mushirul. *Wit and wisdom: pickings from the Parsee punch* (Cartoons). New Delhi: Niyogi, 2012. p. 164. CSSL.

Jain, Jyotindra. Painted panels and scrolls from Western Indian villages: their mythology and rituals. In *Cultural heritage of the Indian village.* Ed. by Brian Durrans and Richard Blurton. London: British Museum, 1991. pp. 119–134. GVL.

Joseph, Prince C. *Sociolinguistic study of a minority language in Gujarat.* Annamalai Nagar: Centre of Advanced Study in Linguistics, Annamalai University, 2002. p. 262. AAL.

Joshi, O.P. *Art and aesthetics in tribes of Gujarat.* Jaipur: RBSA, 2006. p. 180. CSSL, TRTIL.

Joshi, Uma, Pandya, Rameshwari and Mathur, Anuradha. *Folk media and communal harmony.* Delhi: Swastik, 2010. p. 290. GVL.

Mehta, S.S. *My own image or a historical study of the ancient literature of Gujarat.* Bombay: [ ], 1916. p. [ ]. BVL.

Mitra, Sudipta. *Gir forest and the saga of the Asiatic Lion.* New Delhi: Indus, 2005. p. 254. CSSL.

Munshi, Kanaiyalal M. *Gujarat and its literature.* Bombay: Bharatiya Vidya Bhavan, 1967. p. 292. IRMAL.

Munshi, Kanaiyalal M. *Gujarat and its literature*. Calcutta: Longmans, Green, 1935. p. [ ]. BVL.

Murdeshwar, Anand K. "Administrative problems relating to nationalisation". In *Kutch State*. Ed. by Anand K. Murdeshwar. Bombay: Popular, 1957. pp. 246–298. HML.

Pavarala, Vinod and Malik, Kanchan K. *Other voices: the struggle for community Radio in India*. New Delhi: Sage, 2007. p. 318. CSSL.

Pramar, V.S. "Architectural study of rural/urban relations in Gujarat". In *Cultural heritage of the Indian village*. Ed. by Brian Durrans and Richard Blurton. London: British Museum, 1991. pp. 91–100. GVL.

Pramar, V.S. *Social history of Indian architecture*. New Delhi: Oxford, 2005. p. 256. CSSL.

Shah, Haku. Votive Terracottas of Gujarat. In *Cultural heritage of the Indian village*. Brian Durrans and Richard Blurton. London: British Museum, 1991. pp. 143–166. GVL.

Tamakuwala, Shital Jimmy. *Gender, media and interface*. New Delhi: Concept, 2013. p. 226. CSSL.

Vittal, N. *Red tape guerrilla: a game of tactics*. New Delhi: Vikas, 1996. p. 273. CSSL.

Journal Articles

Bhagat, Niranjan. Garvi Gujarat. *Seminar*. 470, 1998. pp. 47–51. CEPTL, CSSL, GVL, IRMAL, MICAL, UML.

Bhatt, L.J. Planning psychological research in Gujarat. *Journal of the Gujarat Research Society*. 20, 1/77, 1958. pp. 15–18. GVL.

Chatterjee, Ashoke. NID experience (Ahmedabad). *Seminar(Our Institutions)*. 335, 1987. pp. 19–25. CSSL, GVL, UML.

Divatia, H.U. Research in Gujarat. *Journal of the Gujarat Research Society*. 1, 1, 1939. pp. 1–5. GUL.

Frater, Judy. Apna vishay. *Seminar*. 570, 2007. pp. 21–25. CSSL, MICAL, UML.

Guzder, Cyrus. Is secularism good for business? *Seminar*. 513, 2002. pp. 68–72. CSSL, MICAL, UML, SPUL.

Iyengar, Sudarshan. Gujarat experience. *Seminar*. 499, 2001. pp. 45–49. CSSL, IRMAL, MICAL, UML.

Jayswal, Mitesh M. and Salvi, Priti. Paradigm shift in brand communication accentuating the perception of the youth of Gujarat regarding product placement in Hindi movies. *Indian Journal of Marketing*. 37, 6, 2007. pp. 3–11. IRMAL.

Joshi, Rakesh Mohan. Gujarat electricity board's turn around. *Administrator*. 50, 1, 2007. pp. 99–120. CSSL.

Kamdar, K.H. Research work in Baroda state. *Journal of the Gujarat Research Society*. 1, 1, 1939. pp. 33–38. GUL.

Kumar, Neeraj and Patel, J.G. Analysis of regional droughts intensity and frequency over North Gujarat. *Journal of Agrometeorology*. 14, 1, 2012. pp. 95–96. IRMAL.

Martin, Max. English elite Gujarat through the eyes of the media. *Voices for Change: Journal on Communications for Development*. 7, 1, 2003. pp. 57–60. IRMAL.

Nilkanth, Vidyaben. New institute of learning and research in Gujarat. *Journal of the Gujarat Research Society*. 9, 2, 1947. pp. 133–137. GUL.

Panda, Smita Mishra. Kutchch Nav Nirman Abhiyan an evolving network of NGOs in Gujarat India. *Gender, Technology and Development*, 6, 2, 2002. pp. 313–317. IRMAL.

Pandya, C.B. Gujarat state archives: its problems and prospects. *Indian Archives*. 32, 1, 1983. pp. 31-[ ]. HML.

Sengupta, Smita. Problems of changing land use pattern in the urban fringe of Ahmedabad. *Geographical Review of India*. 50, 1, 1988. pp. 77–83. HML.

Shastri, H.G. Epigraphic Sanskrit in Gujarat in the ancient period. *Journal of the Oriental Institute*. 44, 1–4, 1994–1995. pp. 37–44. GVL.

Shukla, Sonal. Cultivating minds: 19th century Gujarati women's journals. *Economic and Political Weekly*. 26, 43, 1991. pp. WS-63-WS-66. CEPTL, CSSL, IIML, IRMAL, SPIESRL, UML.

Suchitra. What moves masses: Dandi march as communication strategy. *Economic and Political Weekly*. 30, 14, 1995. pp. 743–746. CEPTL, CSSL, IIML, IRMAL, MICAL, SGUL, SPIESRL, UML.

Yagnik, Achyut. My mother tongue. *Seminar*. 470, 1998. pp. 58–62. CEPTL, CSSL, IRMAL, MICAL, UML.

Working Papers, Reports and Other Materials

Blankenberg, Floris. *Implementation of biogas plants in Gujarat, India*. Enschede: Twente University of Technology, 1983. p. 102. Working Paper No. 3. CSSL.

Iya, K.L.N. Development of post and telegraph service in Ahmedabad. In *Ahmedabad*. Ahmedabad: Rotary Club of Ahmedabad, 1940. pp. 71–80. CSSL.

Kumbhar, B.L. *Baseline survey for Sarbhon project on rural crafts and nutrition centre (Taluka Bardoli, Dt. Surat)*. Ahmedabad: Gujarat Institute of Arca Planning, [ ]. p. 159. CSSL.

Streefkerk, Hein. *On the production of knowledge field work in South Gujarat 1971–1991*. Amsterdam: Centre for Asian Studies, Amsterdam (CASA); VU University Press, 1993. p. 49. CASA Comparative Asian Studies 11. CSSL, GIDRL.

2

Sociology, Civil Society, Anthropology, Social Movements

Books/Chapter in Books

Aandahl, Guro. Slum dweller's room to manoeuver in Ahmedabad. In *Issues in urbanization: study of Ahmedabad city*. Ed. by Jan Hesselberg. Jaipur: Rawat, 2002. pp. 84–127. SPIESRL.

Abels, Monika. Field observations from rural Gujarat. In *Researching families and children: culturally appropriate methods*. Ed. by S. Anandalakshmy et al. New Delhi: Sage, 2008. pp. 211–232. HML, IIML.

Acharya, Shrawan Kumar and Parikh, Sonal. Slum improvement through partnership initiatives: review of the slum-networking project in Ahmedabad. In *Issues in urbanisation: study of Ahmedabad city*. Ed. by Jan Hesselberg. Jaipur: Rawat, 2002. pp. 38–83. SPIESRL.

Amin, R.K. *Radio rural forums in Gujarat: an observation study*. Vallabh Vidyanagar: Saradar Vallabhbhai Vidyapeeth, 1966. p. 63. AAUL, SPUL.

Anand, Mulk Raj. Beauty as a way of life in the Kutch village. In *Art, culture and natural history of Kutch*. Ed. by S.K. Bhowmik. Vadodara: Government Press, 1976–77. pp. 13–24. CSSL, TRTIL.

Andrade, C. Preston. Spatial efficiency of rural service centres in Junagarh district of Gujarat. In *Regional planning and national development*. Ed. by R.P. Misra, D.V. Urs and V.K. Natraj. New Delhi: Vikas, 1978. pp. 442–452. HML.

Anker, Richard and Anker, Martha. *Reproductive behaviour in households of rural Gujarat: social, economic and community factors*. New Delhi: Concept, 1982. p. 140. CSSL, GIDRL, HML, IIML, IRMAL, TRTIL.

Arakeri, A.V. Swaminarayan sampraday: a study of syncretism. In *Portrait of anthropological research*. Ed. by Debabrata Mandal, Tilak Bagchi and Ashok Mukhopadhyay. New Delhi: Sarup, 2008. pp. 26–47. GVL.

Bagchi, Tilak. Nature man and crafts of Kachchh. In *Portrait of anthropological research*. Ed. by Debabrata Mandal, Tilak Bagchi and Ashok Mukhopadhyay. New Delhi: Sarup, 2008. pp. 427–435. GVL.

Bahadur, K.P. *Castes, tribes and culture of India. Vol. VII: Western Maharashtra and Gujarat*. New Delhi: Ess Ess, 1981. p. 202. CSSL, GUL, TRTIL.

Bajpai, Gita. *Agrarian urban economy and social change: the socio-economic profile of select districts of Gujarat 1850–1900*. Delhi: Daya, 1989. p. 198. AAUL, CSSL.

Baks, Chris. Bureaucracy and citizens. In *Winners and losers: styles of development and change in an Indian region*. Ed. by S. Devadas Pillai and Chris Baks. Bombay: Popular, 1979. pp. 302–319. CSSL, HML, SPIESRL.

Ballabh, Vishwa, et al. *Organising for rural development: experience of an action research project in Gujarat, India*. Anand: Institute of Rural Management, 2001. p. 88. IIML.

Basu, D. N, Roy, Raghu and Nikhil, Pallavi. *Impact of agricultural development on demographic behaviour*. New Dehli: Abhinav, 1979. p. 163. CSSL.

Bhanot, I.V. and Gandotra, M.M. Baroda fertility study: a Brien report. In *Studies in demography*. Compil. by Ashish Bose, P.B. Desai, and S.P. Jain. London: George Allen, 1970. pp. 473–482. SPIESRL.

Bhatia, Reena and Balakrishnaiah, B. Preservation and promotion of crafts: role of NGOs in Gujarat – a case studies. In *Networking with NGOs for development: Indian perspective*. [Ed.] by Rameshwari Pandya. New Delhi: Serials, 2006. pp. 188–204. CSSL.

Bhatt, Anil. *Development and social justice: micro action by weaker sections*. New Delhi: Sage, 1989. p. 208. CSSL, SGUL.

Bhatt, Ela R. Empowering the poor through micro-finance: the SEWA bank. In *Social change through voluntary action*. Ed. by M.L. Dantwala, Harsh Sethi and Pravin Visaria. New Delhi: Sage, 1998. pp. 146–161. CSSL.

Bhattacharyya, Manjula. Medieval bhakti movements in Gujarat. In *Medieval bhakti movements in India: Sri Caitanya quincentenary commemoration volume*. Ed. by N.N. Bhattacharyya. Delhi: Munshiram Manoharlal, 1989. pp. 97–105. CSSL.

Bhingradiay, Punita and Kamala, R. Intergenerational study on the situation of the elderly in rural Saurashtra. In *Studies in gerontology: intergenerational perspectives*. Ed. by K.L. Sharma. Jaipur: Rawat, 2007. pp. 142–151. CSSL, HML.

Boman-Behram, B.K. Social relationship between the Parsis and other communities. In *Sugar in the milk: Parsis of India*. Ed. by Nancy and Ram Singh. Madras: Institute for Development Education, 1986. pp. 52–67. CSSL.

Borradaile, Harry and Nathoobhoy, Munguldass. *Borradaile's Gujarat caste rules. Vol. 2*. Bombay: Nirnaya Sagar, 1884–87. p. 982. ASL.

Bose, Pradip Kumar. Stratification among tribals in Gujarat. In *Social inequality in India: profiles of caste class, power and social mobility*. Ed. by K.L. Sharma. Jaipur: Rawat, 1995. pp. 411–426. CSSL, GUL, GVL, HML, SPIESRL.

Breman, Jan. Agrarian change and class conflict in Gujarat, India. In *Rural development and population: institutions and policy*. Ed. by Geoffrey Mcnicoll and M. Cain. New York: Oxford, 1990. pp. 301–323. HML.

Breman, Jan. Extension of scale in fieldwork: from village to region in Southern Gujarat. In *Conversations between economists and anthropologists*. Ed. by Pranab Bardhan. Delhi: Oxford, 1989. pp. 127–136. CEEL, CSSL, TRTIL.

Breman, Jan. Pauperization of a tribal caste. In *Aspect of changing India*. Ed. by S. Devadas Pillai. Bombay: Popular, 1976. pp. 255–261. CSSL, SPIESRL.

Breman, Jan. Practice of poor relief in rural South Gujarat. In *Long road to social security: assessing the implementation of national social security initiatives for the working poor in India*. Ed. by K.P. Kannan and Jan Breman. New Delhi: Oxford, 2013. pp. 293–334. CSSL.

Breman, Jan and Hommes, Enno W. Social change in South Gujarat. In *Winners and losers: styles of development and change in an Indian region*. Ed. by S. Devadas Pillai and Chris Baks. Bombay: Popular, 1979. pp. 3–17. CSSL, HML, SPIESRL.

Centre for Social Studies. *Caste, caste-conflict and reservation*. New Delhi: Ajanta, 1985. p. 212. CSSL, SETUL.

Centre for Social Studies. Resettlement and rehabilitation in Gujarat. In *Dam and the nation: displacement and resettlement in the Narmada valley*. Ed. by Jean Dreze, Meera Samson and Satyajit Singh. Delhi: Oxford, 1997. pp. 215–235. CSSL.

Chakrabarti, Anindita. Soteriological journeys and discourses of self-transformation: the Tablighi Jamaat and Svadhyaya in Gujarat. In *Gujarat beyond Gandhi: identity, conflict and society.* Ed. by Nalin Mehta and Mona G. Mehta. London: Routledge, 2010. pp. 60–87 or pp. 184–209. BVL, CSSL, GIDRL, IRMAL, UML.

Chandra, Ramesh. Ahmedabad district and Ahmedabd city. In *Cities and towns of India.* Ed. by Ramesh Chandra. New Delhi: Commonwealth, 2004. pp. 19–33. BUL.

Chanana, Charanjit. Physical environment and social context: an approach to planning for rural settlements in Gujarat. In *Rural settlements in South Asia.* Ed. by Charanjit Chanana. New Delhi: MERB Bookshelf, 1980. pp. 108–137. CSSL, GVL.

Chatterjee, Shankar. Case about implementation of NREGA from Gujarat. In *Implementation of rural development programmes.* New Delhi: Serial, 2011. pp. 62–67. SPUL.

Chatterjee, Shankar. Gokul Gram Yojana: a unique scheme in Gujarat. In *Implementation of rural development programmes.* New Delhi: Serials, 2011. pp. 140–170. SPUL.

Chaturvedi, H.R. and Mitra, S.K. *Citizen participation in rural development.* New Delhi: Oxford and IBH, 1982. p. 127. CSSL, SGUL.

Chaturvedi, Vinayak. *Peasant pasts: history, politics, and nationalism in Gujarat.* Ranikhet: Permanent Black, 2007. p. 307. CSSL, SGUL.

Chavda, Vijaysingh. *Gujarat in transition.* Vadodara: Sanket, 2007. p. 290. HML.

Chavda, Vijaysingh. Social and religions reform movement in Gujarat in the nineteenth and twentieth centuries. In *Social and religious reform movement in the Nineteenth and Twentieth centuries.* Ed. by S.P. Sen. Calcutta: Institute of Historical Studies, 1979. pp. 197–228. IIML.

Chitralekha. Hindu extremists in rural and adivasi Gujarat: Sardarpura and Palla. In *Ordinary people, extraordinary violence: naxalites and Hindu extremists in India.* New Delhi: Routledge, 2012. pp. 208–248. IIML.

Choksi, Nishaant. *Tribal literature of Gujarat.* Mysore: Central Institute of Indian Languages, 2009. p. 185. TRTIL.

Chopra, P.N., ed. *Religions and communities of India.* New Delhi: Vision, 1982. p. 316. CSSL, GUL.

Clarke, Marieke. *We are the original people: the story of a development project in an adivasi village in South Gujarat in India.* Delhi: Ajanta, 1991. p. 257. CSSL, IIML, IRMAL.

Cort, John E. Murtipuja in Svetamber Jain, temples. In *Religion in India.* Ed. by T.N. Madan. Delhi: Oxford, 1992. pp. 212–223. CSSL.

Crowell, Daniel W. Kutch and DWCRA. In *SEWA movement and rural development: the Banaskantha and Kutch experience.* New Delhi: Sage, 2003. pp. 160–168. IIML, UML.

Dalvadi, Shreya. Integrating street vendors in city planning: the case of Vadodara. In *Street vendors in the global urban economy.* Ed. by Sharit K. Bhowmik. New Delhi: Routledge, 2010. pp. 87–119. CSSL.

Dar, Muhammed Ibrahim. *Literary and cultural activities in Gujarat.* Bombay: Ismail Yusuf College, 1960. p. 62. GVL.

Das, Biswaroop. *Socio-economic study of slums in Surat city.* Surat: Centre for Social Studies, 1994. p. 211. CSSL, SPIESRL.

Dave, H.T. *Life and philosophy of Shree Swaminarayan, 1781–1830.* Bochasan: Akshar Purushottam Sansthan, 1967. p. 184. SETUL.

Dave, Manjula. *Urban ecology and levels of development.* Jaipur: Rawat, 1991. p. 211. CSSL.

Dave, Parul, Hakim, Mushira and Dalaya, Veena. *Tribal project on child care at Sampoi, Jhalod, Panchmahals*. Dahod: Project Administrato's office Adijati Pet Vistar Yojana, 1981. p. 28. TRTIL.

Dave, Sureshchandra and Soni, Ramanlal. *Shamlaji: a holy place of pilgrimage*. Shamlaji: Yogindrabhai N. Mafatlal, 1981. p. 58. TRTIL.

Dayal, Parmeshwari. *Aftermath of war: an impact-study of war on the borders of Gujarat and Rajasthan*. Ahmedabad: Peace Research Centre, 1985. p. 228. GVL.

D'Costa, Wilfred. In the cauldron of communal conflicts! Shrinking political space and vulnerability of minorities. In *Poverty and vulnerability in a globalising metropolis Ahmedabad.* Ed. by Amitabh Kundu and Darshini Mahadevia. New Delhi: Manak, 2002. pp. 349–372. CEPTL, CSSL.

D'Costa, Wilfred and Das, Bhabani. Life and living of the vulnerable in Ahmedabad city. In *Poverty and vulnerability in a globalising metropolis Ahmedabad.* Ed. by Amitabh Kundu and Darshini Mahadevia. New Delhi: Manak, 2002. pp. 179–206. CEPTL, CSSL.

Deobhankar, Mukund and Rajaram, N.S. *Dangs and after: missionaries, media and politics*. Gujarat: Vishva Sumvad Kendra, 1999. p. 218. HML.

Desai, A.R., ed. *Rural sociology in India*. Bombay: Popular, 1969. p. 966. AAUL, CSSL, GUL, GVL, HML, IIML, SGUL, SPIESRL, TRTIL.

Desai, Anjana. Differential perception of resident to environmental quality of an urban area: the case of Ahmedabad. In *Urbanization and environmental problems.* Ed. by S.D. Maurya. Allahabad: Chugh, 1989. pp. 249–265. SPIESRL.

Desai, Anjana. Myth of low income housing: case of Ahmedabad. In *Population and housing problems in India*. Vol. II. Ed. by S.D. Maurya. Allahabad: Chugh, 1989. pp. 28–37. CSSL, GUL.

Desai, Anjana. Problems of rural development: a case of Dangs district in South Gujarat. In *Geography and rural development.* Ed. by R.N.P. Sinha. New Delhi: Concept, 1992. pp. 221–228. GVL.

Desai, Anjana P. and Rawal, Ami U. Growth and decline of small town in Gujarat: a tale of two towns in Mehsana district. In *Urbanisation: trends, perspective & challenges*. Ed. by Jaymala Diddea and Vimla Rangaswamy. Jaipur: Rawat, 1993. pp. 179–185. SGUL.

Desai, D.K. *Our roots: genealogical research studies of families of Jhalod, India and families from Maharashtra, 1582–2008*. Ahmedabad: Smriti Ajitkumar Dagur, 2008. p. 254. IIML.

Desai, Govindbhai H. *Hindu families in Gujarat: being an account of their domestic social and economic life*. Baroda: State press, 1932. p. 472. ASL, CSSL.

Desai, Hakumat and Desai, Kiran. *Pardi annakhed satyagraha: adivasi assertion for rights.* Surat: Centre for Social Studies, 1997. p. 136. CSSL.

Desai, Harshad and Maheria, Chandu. Dalit assertion for self-esteem: from Sambarda to Swamannagar. In *Development and deprivation in Gujarat: in hounour of Jan Breman*. Ed. by Ghanshyam Shah, Mario Rutten and Hein Streefkerk. New Delhi: Sage, 2002. pp. 231–248. CEEL, CEPTL, CSSL, EDIL, GIDRL, HML, IIML, IRMAL, UML.

Desai, I.P. Anti-reservation agitation and structure of Gujarat society. In *Caste, caste conflict and reservations*. Ed. by I.P. Desai, et al. Delhi: Ajanta, 1985. pp. 124–136. CSSL, HML, SETUL.

Desai, I.P. Should 'Caste' be the basis for recognising the backwardness?. In *Caste, caste-conflict and reservation*. By Centre for Social Studies. New Delhi: Ajanta, 1985. pp. 61–101. CSSL, HML, SETUL.

Desai, I.P. *Some aspects of family in Mahuva: a sociological study of jointness in a small town*. Bombay: Asia, 1964. p. 239. CSSL, IIML, SGUL.

Desai, I.P. Tribal autonomy movement in South Gujarat. In *Tribal movements in India*. Vol 2. Ed. by K.S. Singh. New Delhi: Manohar, 1982. pp. 243–259. CSSL, GVL, HML, SETUL, SPIESRL, SPUL.

Desai, I.P. *Untouchability in rural Gujarat*. Bombay: Popular, 1973. p. 265. HML, IIML, SGUL.

Desai, I.P. *Untouchability in rural Gujarat*. Bombay: Popular, 1976. p. 265. CSSL, GIDRL, SPIESRL, SPUL, TRTIL.

Desai, I.P. and Choudhary, Banwarilal. *History of rural development in modern India*. Vol. II. New Delhi: Impex India, 1977. p. 219. CSSL, SGUL, SPIESRL.

Desai, Kiran. Kaleidoscopic panorama of agrarian struggles in Gujarat. In *Sectarianism, politics and development*. Ed. by Uday Mehta and Ram Puniyani. Jaipur: Rawat, 2012. pp. 113–142. CSSL.

Desai, M.B. Baroda city potentialities and pitfalls. In *Profiles of a growing city: socio-economic studies of Baroda city*. Baroda: M.S. University, 1971. pp. 99–98. M.S. University Economics Series No. 1. SPIESRL.

Desai, M.B. Impact of land-reforms in Gujarat. In *Rural sociology in India*. [Ed] by A.R. Desai. Bombay: Popular, 1969. pp. 439–440. AAUL, CSSL, GVL, HML, IIML, SGUL, SPIESRL, TRTIL.

Desai, M.B. and Mehta, R.S. Change and its agencies in community development reflections from the study of a community development block in Gujarat. In *Community development & change in India*. Baroda: M.S. University of Baroda, 1965. pp. 29–53. SGUL.

Desai, M.B. and Mehta, R.S. *Community development and change: case study of a block in Gujarat*. Hyderabad: National Institute of Community Development, 1967. p. 133. AAUL, AERCL, UML.

Desai, M.B. and Vakil, C.N. *Rural economy of Gujarat*. Bombay: Oxford, 1948. p. 352. AAUL.

Desai, Mahadev. *Gandhiji in Indian villages*. Madras: S. Ganeshan, 1927. p. 349. ASL.

Desai, Mahadev. *Story of Bardoli: being a history of the Bardoli satyagraha of 1928 and its sequel*. Ahmedabad: Navajivan, 1957. p. 249. CSSL, GVL.

Desai, Neera. *Social change in Gujarat: a study of nineteenth century Gujarati society*. Bombay: Vora, 1978. p. 479. CSSL, GUL, IRMAL.

Desai, Neera and Gogate, Sudha. Teaching of sociology through the regional language. In *Themes in sociology of education*. Ed. by R. Indira. New Delhi: Sage, 2011. pp. 179–188. Studies in Indian Sociology, Vol. 5. SGUL.

Desai, Renu. Entrepreneurial urbanism in the time of Hindutva city imagineering, place marketing and citizenship in Ahmedabad. In *Urbanizing citizenship contested spaces in Indian cities*. Ed. by Renu Desai and Ramola Sanyal. New Delhi: Sage, 2012. pp. 31–57. IIML.

Deshpande, C.D. Trends in cities & towns of Western India (1961–1971). In *Urbanization in developing countries*. Ed. by S. Manzoor Alam and V.V. Rokshishevsky. Hyderabad: Osmania University, 1976. pp. 321–347. Indo-Soviet Collaborative Volume. CSSL, SGUL.

Deshpande, Uma S. Narasimha Mehta: saint-poet from Gujarat. In *Medieval bhakti movements in India: Sri Caitanya quincentenary commemoration volume*. Ed. by N.N. Bhattacharyya. Delhi: Munshiram Manoharlal, 1989. pp. 106–112: CSSL.

Dhanagare, D.N. Bardoli satyagraha: myth and reality. In *Peasant movements in India 1920–1950*. B D.N. Dhanagare. Delhi: Oxford, 1983. pp. 88–110. CSSL, GUL, SPUL.

Dikshit, N.G. Temporal variations in residents perceptions of a planned city: Gandhinagar. In *Environment, population and development*. Ed. by Prithvish Nag, Chandra Shekhar Kumar and Smita Sengupta. New Delhi: Concept, 2001. pp. 309–319. HML.

Doshi, Harish. *Traditional neighbourhood in a modern city*. New Delhi: Abhinav, 1974. p. 154. CSSL, IIML, SGUL.

Doshi, Harish. Traditional neighbourhood in modern Ahmedabad: the Pol. In *Reader in urban sociology*. Ed. by M.S.A. Rao, Chandrashekar Bhat and Laxmi Narayan Kadekar. New Delhi: Orient Longman, 1991. pp. 179–208. CSSL, GVL.

Dreze, Jean. Palanpur, 1957–93: occupational change, landownership and social inequality. In *Social change in post-independence India*. Ed. by A.K. Lal and S. Sami Ahmad. Jaipur: Rawat, 2001. pp. 29–77. CSSL.

D'Souza, Paul. Dalit identity in Gujarat. In *Pain and awakening: the dynamics of dalit identity in Bihar, Gujarat and Uttar Pradesh*. Ed. by Fernando Franco. New Delhi: Indian Social Institute, 2002. pp. 156–267. CSSL, GIDRL.

D'Souza, Paul. Scavengers towards freedom: dynamic of power paradox among Bhangis of Gujarat. In *Restoration of human rights and dignity to dalits: with special reference to scavengers in India*. Ed. by Ram Gopal Singh and Ravindra D. Gadkar. Delhi: Manak, 2004. pp. 178–193. CSSL, GVL.

Dubey, S.L. Gujarat. In *Land alienation and restoration in tribal communities in India*. Ed. by S.N. Dubey and Ratna Murdia. Bombay: Himalaya, 1977. pp. 76–84. CSSL, HML, TRTIL.

Durkal, Darshini and Pandya, Rameshwari. Training women to start day care centres in Baroda city. In *Women & entrepreneurship issues & challenges*. Ed. by Asha Patil and Anuradha Mathu. Delhi: Kalpaz, 2007. pp. 101–125. CSSL, SGUL.

Ekka, William and Danda, A.K. Halpati movement among the Dublas of South Gujarat. In *Tribal movements in India*. Vol. 2. Ed. by K.S. Singh. New Delhi: Manohar, 1982. pp. 273–283. CSSL, GVL, SETUL, SPIESRL, SPUL.

Elson, Vickie C. *Dowries from Kutch*. California: Museum of Cultural History, 1979. p. 119. TRTIL.

Elson, Vickie C. Dowry as a perpetuator of culture in Kutch. In *Cultural heritage of the Indian village*. Ed. by Brian Durrans and Richard T. Blurton. London: British Museum, 1991. pp. 63–74. GVL.

Engineer, Asghar Ali. *Religion, state & civil society*. Mumbai: Vikas, 2005. p. 252. CSSL.

Gaekwad, Fatesinghrao P. *Analysis of food riots in Gujarat*. Baroda: Imprint, 1974. p. 50. HML, IIML.

Gatade, Subhash. Inverting dalit consciousness: hindutvaising the dalits, communalizing the movement. In *Fascism in India: faces, fangs and facts*. Ed. by Chaitanya Krishna. New Delhi: Manak, 2003. pp. 336–354. CSSL, UML.

Ghurye, G.S. *Anthropo-sociological papers*. Bombay: Popular, 1963. p. 381. CSSL.

Gillion, Kenneth L. *Ahmedabad: a study in Indian urban history*. Los Angels: University of California, 1968. p. 195. CSSL, IIML, SPIESRL.

Giri, Ananta Kumar. *Self-development and social transformations?: the vision and practice of the self-study ymobilization of Swadhyaya*. Jaipur: Rawat, 2008. p. 314. CSSL.

Gujarat Mineral Development Corporation. *Ecological restoration strategies for mining areas of Gujarat*. Vadodara: Gujarat Ecological Society, 1997. p. 128. CEEL.

Gumber, Anil. Rural development and seasonal migration in Gujarat: pattern, determinants and consequence. In *Other Gujarat: social transformations among weaker sections.* Ed. by Takashi Shinoda. Mumbai: Popular, 2002. pp. 159–203. ASL, CEEL, CSSL, EDIL, GIDRL, SETUL, SPIESRL.

Gupta, Ishwar Parkash. Urbanization in Gujarat during the seventeenth century. In *Studies in urban history.* Ed. by J.S. Grewal and Indu Banga. Amritsar: Guru Nanak Dev University, 1978. pp. 43–60. CSSL, HML.

Hardiman, David. Adivasi assertion in South Gujarat: the Devi movement of 1922–33. In *Subaltern studies III: writing on south Asian history and society.* Ed. by Ranajit Guha. Delhi: Oxford, 1984. pp. 196–230. CSSL, GVL, SETUL, UML.

Hardiman, David. Assertion, conversion, and Indian nationalism: Govind's movement amongst the Bhils. In *Religious conversion in India: modes, motivations, and meanings.* Ed. by Rowena Robinson and Sathianathan Clarke. New Delhi: Oxford, 2007. pp. 255–284. CEEL, CSSL.

Hardiman, David. Christianity and the adivasis of Gujarat. In *Development and deprivation in Gujarat: in honour of Jan Breman.* Ed. by Ghanshyam Shah, Mario Rutten and Hein Streefkerk. New Delhi: Sage, 2002. pp. 175–195. CEEL, CEPTL, CSSL, EDIL, GIDRL, IIML, UML.

Hardiman, David. *Coming of the Devi: adivasi assertion in Western India*. Delhi: Oxford, 1987. p. 248. AAL, CSSL, SGUL, UML.

Hardiman, David. Farming in the forest: the Dangs 1830–1992. In *Village voices, forest choices: joint forest management in India.* Ed. by Mark Poffenberger and Betsy McGean. Delhi: Oxford, 1996. pp. 101–130. CSSL.

Hardiman, David. From custom to crime: the politics of drinking in colonial South Gujarat. In *Subaltern studies IV: writing on South Asian history and society.* Ed. by Ranjit Guha. Delhi: Oxford, 1985. pp. 165–228. CSSL, GVL, SETUL, UML.

Hardiman, David. Origins and transformations of the Devi. In *Subaltern studies reader, 1986–1995*. Ed. by Ranjit Guha. New Delhi: Oxford, 2013. pp. 100–139. CSSL, GVL, SETUL, UML.

Hardiman, David. *Peasant nationalists of Gujarat: Kheda district 1917–1934.* Delhi: Oxford, 1981. p. 309. CSSL, IIML, SUL, TRTIL, UML.

Hardiman, David. Power in the forests: the Dangs, 1820–1940. In *Subaltern studies VIII: essays in honour of Ranajit Guha.* Ed. by David Arnold and David Hardiman. New Delhi: Oxford, 2003. pp. 89–147. CSSL, GVL, SETUL, UML.

Hardiman, David. Usury in Western India: state policy and peasant resistance, 1876–1947. In *Social transformation in India: essays in honour of professor I.P. Desai.* Vol. 1. Ed. by Ghanshyam Shah. Jaipur: Rawat, 1997. pp. 157–198. CSSL, GVL, HML, SGUL, SPUL.

Heredero, J.M. *Rural development and social change: an experiment in non-formal education*. New Delhi: Manohar, 1977. p. 181. CSSL.

Hesselberg, Jan, ed. *Issues in Urbanisation: Study of Ahmedabad city.* Jaipur: Rawat, 2002. p. 224. SPIESRL.

Ibrahim, Farhana. *Settlers, saints and sovereigns: an ethnography of state formation in Western India*. New Delhi: Routledge, 2008. p. 215. CSSL.

Indian Institute of Agricultural Economics. Changes in social life in a Gujarat village: a comparative study (1915–1955). In *Rural sociology in India.* [Ed.] by A.R. Desai. Bombay: Popular, 1969. pp. 364–371. AAUL, CSSL, GUL, GVL, HML, IIML, SGUL, SPIESRL, TRTIL.

Iyengar, Sudarshan. Voluntary initiatives for tribal development in Gujarat. In *Tribal situation in India: issues in development: with special reference to western India*. Ed. by Vidyut Joshi. Jaipur: Rawat, 1998. pp. 175–214. CSSL, GVL, SGUL, UML.

Jagani, N.A. Muharram scroll-a living moment from the past. In *Art, culture and natural history of Kutch.* Ed. by S.K. Bhowmik. Vadodara: Government Press, 1976–77. pp. 74–77. CSSL, TRTIL.

Jain, K.C. Ahmedabad: expanding metropolis. In *Million cities of India.* Ed. by R.P. Misra. New Delhi: Vikas, 1978. pp. 213–241. CSSL, SPIESRL.

Jani, S.V. Social reforms in Saurashtra in nineteenth century. In *Dr. H.G. Shastri Felicitation volume (Essay on Sanskrit Literature Indian History, Culture and Archaeology).* Ed. by P.C. Parikh, Bharati Shelat and Thomas Parmar. Ahmedabad: Dr. H.G. Shastri Felicitation volume committee, 1994. pp. 176–178. SPUL.

Jasani, Rubina. Potted history of neighbours and neighbourliness in Ahmedabad. In *Idea of Gujarat: history, ethnography and text.* Ed. by Edward Simpson and Aparna Kapadia. Hyderabad: Orient Blackswan, 2010. pp. 153–167. AAL, ASL, BUL, CEPTL, CSSL, GIDRL, IRMAL, MICAL, SETUL.

Jhala, V.B. and Sompura, Rashmin. Developing workers: Baroda Productivity Council experience. In *HRD in the new economic environment.* Ed. by T.V. Rao, et al. New Delhi: Tata McGraw Hill, 1994. pp. 327–332. HML.

Joshi, Rajendra. Integrated slum development: case of Pravinnagar-Guptanagar. In *Poverty and vulnerability in a globalising metropolis Ahmedabad.* Ed. by Amitabh Kundu and Darshini Mahadevia. New Delhi: Manak, 2002. pp. 268–308. CEPTL, CSSL.

Joshi, Satyakam. Social security schemes in tribal areas of Gujarat: a study in the Dangs district. In *Long road to social security: assessing the implementation of national social security initiatives for the working poor in India.* Ed. by K.P. Kannan and Jan Breman. New Delhi: Oxford, 2013. pp. 371–403. CSSL.

Joshi, V.H. Politico-economic change and social transformation in Saurashtra. In *Rural social transformation.* Ed. by Sheo Kumar Lal and Umed Raj Nahar. Jaipur: Rawat, 1992. pp. 210–217. CSSL, SGUL, TRTIL.

Joshi, V.H. Some observation on changing agrarian relation in two villages of Gujarat. In *Changing agrarian relations in India.* Hyderabad: National Institute of Community Development, 1974. pp. 102–110. AAUL, TRTIL.

Joshi, Vidyut. *Submerging villages: problems and prospects.* New Delhi: Ajanta, 1987. p. 144. CSSL, SGUL.

Judge, Paramjit S. Gujarat: discrepancy in government claims and actual situation. In *Social changes through land reforms.* By Paramjit S. Judge. Jaipur: Rawat, 1999. pp. 103–136. HML.

Jyyal, B.N. Grambharti: case study of a Gandhian programme of rural development. In *Population poverty and hope.* Ed. by Center for Policy Research. New Delhi: Uppal, 1983. pp. 337-[ ]. SPIESRL

Kanhere, Usha. Differential socialisation of boys and girls: a study of lower socio-economic households among Gujarati caste/communities in Ahmedabad. In *Gender and the households domain: social and cultural dimensions.* Ed. by Maithreyi Krishnaraj and Karuna Chanana. New Delhi: Sage, 1981. pp. 31–53. CSSL.

Kanhere, Usha S. *Women and socialisation: a study of their status & role in lower castes of Ahmedabad.* Delhi: Mittal, 1987. p. 171. CSSL.

Kansara, N.M. Early Bhakti movement in Gujarat. In *New dimensions of indology (Dr. Praveen Chandra Parikh felicitation volume).* Ed. by Dinesh Chandra, Mahendra R. Trivedi and Balaji Ganorkar. Delhi: Bhartiya Vidya Prakashan, 1997. pp. 48-[ ]. GVL.

Khan, Dominique-Sila. Liminality and legality: a contemporary debate among the Imamshahis of Gujarat. In *Lived Islam in South Asia: adaptation, accommodation and conflict*. Ed. by Imtiaz Ahmad and Helmut Reifeld. Delhi: Social Science Press, 2004. pp. 209–232. CSSL, SETUL.

Kim, Hanna H. Swaminarayan movement and religious subjectivity. In *Idea of Gujarat: history, ethnography and text.* Ed. by Edward Simpson and Aparna Kapadia. Hyderabad: Orient Blackswan, 2010. pp. 207–228. AAL, ASL, BUL, CEPTL, CSSL, GIDRL, IRMAL, MICAL, SETUL.

Kochhar, Sameer and Dhanjal, Gursharan. E-village, global village: Gujarat shows the way. In *Building from the bottom: infrastructure and poverty alleviation.* Ed. by Sameer Kochhar and M. Ramachandran. New Delhi: Academic Foundation, 2010. pp. 177-[ ]. SPIESRL.

Kolhatkar, V.V. and Mahabal, S.B. Impact of land reforms in Baroda district. In *Rural sociology in India*. [Ed.] by A.R. Desai. Bombay: Popular, 1969. pp. 427–429. AAUL, CSSL, GUL, GVL, HML, IIML, SGUL, SPIESRL, TRTIL.

Krishnamachari, V.T. Community development in Baroda state. In *Evolution of community development programme in India*. Ed. by B.S. Murthy. [ ]: Community Development Cooperation, 1952. pp. 36–44. AAUL.

Kulkarni, K.M. *Geographical patterns of social well-being: with special reference to Gujarat*. New Delhi: Concept, 1990. p. 104. CSSL, GIDRL, GVL, HML.

Kulkarni, K.M. *Geography of crowding and human response: a study of Ahmedabad city*. New Delhi: Concept, 1983. p. 155. CSSL.

Kulkarni, K.M. Outgrowths beyond municipal limits in Gujarat: a study on some of the demographic characteristics and related changes. In *Urban fringe of Indian cities*. Ed. by Jutta K. Dikshit. Jaipur: Rawat, 2011. pp. 201–209. CSSL, IIML.

Kulkarni, K.M. Social infrastructure: a study of housing in Ahmedabad city. In *Urbanisation, development and environment: C.D. Deshpande memorial volume.* Ed. by V.S. Phadke and S. Banerjee-Guha. Jaipur: Rawat, 2007. pp. 196–208. CSSL, HML.

Kumar, Sharawan and Parikh, Sonal. Slum networking in Ahmedabad: an alternate paradigm. In *Poverty and vulnerability in a globalising metropolis Ahmedabad.* Ed. by Amitabh Kundu and Darshini Mahadevia. New Delhi: Manak, 2002. pp. 309–348. CEPTL, CSSL.

Kundu, Debolina. Provision of infrastructure and basic amenities: analysing institutional vulnerability. In *Poverty and vulnerability in a globalising metropolis Ahmedabad.* Ed. by Amitabh Kundu and Darshini Mahadevia. New Delhi: Manak, 2002. pp. 133–178. CEPTL, CSSL.

Kuruvachira, J. *Politicisation of Hindu religion in postmodern India*. Jaipur: Rawat, 2008. p. 360. CSSL.

Lakha, Salim. *Capitalism and class in colonial India: the case of Ahmedabad.* New Delhi: Sterling, 1988. p. 199. CSSL, GVL, HML.

Lakhani, Aruna, Schensul, Stephen L. and Mahale, Pramodini. Married women in extra-marital relationships in a rural area of Gujarat. In *Sexuality in the time of AIDS: contemporary perspectives from communities in India.* Ed. by Ravi K. Verma, et al. New Delhi: Sage, 2004. pp. 217–239. CSSL.

Lal, R.B. Centuries of changing tribals in South Gujarat. In *Seminar on-tribals of Western India issues of development and marginalisation.* Surat: Centre for Social Studies and Ahmedabad: Tribal Research & Training Institute, 1997. pp. [ ]. TRTIL.

Lal, R.B. Problems of tribal development in Gujarat. In *Tribes of India ongoing challenges.* Ed. by R.S. Mann. New Delhi: MD, 1996. pp. 143–150. GVL.

Lal, R.B. Socio-religious movements among the tribals of South Gujarat. In *Tribal movements in India.* Vol. 2. Ed. by K.S. Singh. New Delhi: Manohar, 1982. pp. 285–308. CSSL, GVL, SETUL, SPIESRL, SPUL.

Lal, R.B. and Solanki, S.S. Problems of tribals in the hilly tracts of Gujarat. In *Planning for tribal development.* Ed. by Ranjit Gupta. New Delhi: Ankur, 1976. pp. 54–69. CSSL, GVL, HML, SPIESRL.

Lal, Shyam. Studies in social protest. In *Balai uplift movement in Delhi and Gujarat.* Jaipur: Rawat, 2010. pp. 288–302. HML.

Lambat, I.A. Change among Muslims in an urban area. In *Winners and losers: styles of development and change in an Indian region.* Ed. by S. Devadas Pillai and Chris Baks. Bombay: Popular, 1979. pp. 202–224. CSSL, HML, SPIESRL.

Lobo, Lancy. Christianization, Hinduization and indigenous revivalism among the tribals of Gujarat. In *Margins of faith: dalit and tribal Christianity in India.* Ed. by Rowena Robinson and Joseph Marianus Kujur. New Delhi: Sage, 2010. pp. 211–233. CSSL.

Lobo, Lancy. Land acquisition and displacement in Gujarat, 1947–2004. In *Sectarianism, politics and development.* Ed. by Uday Mehta and Ram Puniyani. Jaipur: Rawat, 2012. pp. 95–112. CSSL.

Lobo, Lancy. Land acquisition and displacement among tribals, 1947–2004. In *Tribal development in western India.* Ed. by Amita Shah and Jharna Pathak. New Delhi: Routledge, 2014. pp. 285–309. CSSL.

Lobo, Lancy. Tribal and Christianity in Gujarat. In *Scheduled tribes and development.* Ed. by H.S. Saksena, Vinay Kumar Srivastava and Sukant K. Chaudhary. New Delhi: Serials, 2006. pp. 268–291. CSSL, HML.

Lobo, Lancy and Kumar, Shashikant. *Land acquisition, displacement and resettlement in Gujarat 1947–2004.* New Delhi: Sage, 2009. p. 303. CSSL, GIDRL.

Madani, Z.H. *Literary and cultural activities in Gujarat.* Bombay: Bazm-Ishaat, Ismail Yusuf College, 1960. p. 62. HML.

Mahadevia, Darshini. Changing economic scenario: informalisation and increased vulnerability. In *Poverty and vulnerability in a globalising metropolis Ahmedabad.* Ed. by Amitabh Kundu and Darshini Mahadevia. New Delhi: Manak, 2002. pp. 30–79. CEPTL, CSSL.

Mahadevia, Darshini. Interventions in development: a shift towards a model of exclusion. In *Poverty and vulnerability in a globalising metropolis Ahmedabad.* Ed. by Amitabh Kundu and Darshini Mahadevia. New Delhi: Manak, 2002. pp. 80–132. CEPTL, CSSL.

Mahadevia, Darshini. Social security for the urban poor: a study in Gujarat. In *Long road to social security: assessing the implementation of national social security initiatives for the working poor in India.* Ed. by K.P. Kannan and Jan Breman. New Delhi: Oxford, 2013. pp. 335–370. CSSL.

Mahadevia, Darshini. Urban reforms in three cities: Bangalore, Ahmedabad and Patana. In *Public service delivery in India: understanding the reform process.* Ed. by Vikram K. Chand. New Delhi: Oxford, 2010. pp. 226–295. GVL, HML.

Mahadevia, Darshini and Bhatt, Vatsal. Economic liberalization and the urban land market: trends from Ahmedabad. In *Issues in urbanisation: study of Ahmedabad city.* Ed. by Jan Hesselberg. Jaipur: Rawat, 2002. pp. 128–164. SPIESRL.

Mahadevia, Darshini and Brar, Harpreet Singh. Basic infrastructure, public finance and slum dwellers: Ahmedabad. In *Inside the transforming urban Asia: processes, policies and public actions.* Ed. by Darshini Mahadevia. New Delhi: Concept, 2008. pp. 361–390. CSSL.

Mahadevia, Darshini and Brar, Harpreet Singh. Changes and continuities in development priorities: Ahmedabad. In *Inside the transforming urban Asia: processes, policies and public actions.* Ed. by Darshini Mahadevia. New Delhi: Concept, 2008. pp. 132–169. CSSL.

Majumdar, D.N. *Race realities in cultural Gujarat: report on the anthropometric, serological and health survey of Maha Gujarat.* Bombay: Gujarat Research Society, 1950. p. 87. BVL, CSSL, SPUL.

Majmudar, M.R. Iconography of Vayu and Vayu-worshippers in Gujarat. In *Professor Ghurye felicitation volume.* Ed by K.M. Kapadia. Bombay: Popular, 1954. pp. 277–283. CSSL, GUL.

Makwana, Manubhai. Socio-economic development of dalits in Gujarat. In *Contemporary Indian society issues and perspectives.* Ed. by Raja Reddy Kalluri. Delhi: Shipra, 2011. pp. 265–277. HML.

Mandal, S.K. and Malhotra, R. Agrarian situation in hill tribal village: a case of the Warlis in Gujarat. In *Studies in tribal development.* Vol. 2. Ed. by G.P. Gupta. Jaipur: Arihant, [ ]. pp. 59–73. TRTIL.

Mankodi, Kashyap. Resettlement and rehabilitation of dam outstees: a case study of Ukai dam. In *Big dams, displaced people: rivers of sorrow rivers of change.* Ed. by Enakshi Ganguly Thukral. New Delhi: Sage, 1992. pp. 77–100. CSSL.

Mann, R.S. and Singh, Bageshwar. Tribals polity in Western India. In *Tribal development in India: problems and prospects.* Ed. by Buddhadeb Chaudhari. Delhi: Inter-India, 1982. pp. 117–128. CSSL, SGUL.

Masavi, Mustali I. Role of the weekly markets in the economic and social development of the tribal of Gujarat. In *Perspective of tribal economy.* Ed. by Basant Mehta and Prakash Chandra Mehta. New Delhi: Intellectual, 1997. pp. 121–126. CSSL.

Mathur, Shubh. *Everyday life of Hindu nationalism: a ethnographic account.* New Delhi: Three Essays, 2008. p. 222. CSSL.

Mavalankar, Dileep and Sharma, Bharti. Quality of care in sterilization camps: evidence from Gujarat. In *Improving quality of care in India's family welfare programme: the challenge.* Ed. by Michael A. Koenig and M.E. Khan. New York: Population Council, 1952. pp. 293–313. IIML.

Mazgaonkar, Anand. Gujarat: screaming fiction and mute facts. In *Sectarianism, politics and development.* Ed. by Uday Mehta and Ram Puniyani. Jaipur: Rawat, 2012. pp. 75–94. CSSL.

Mehta, Anupa, Schensul, Stephen L. and Fall, Suzanne. Public social reputation vs. private sexual risk for young women in a rural area in Gujarat. In *Sexuality in the time of AIDS: contemporary perspectives from communities in India.* Ed. by Ravi K. Verma, et al. New Delhi: Sage, 2004. pp. 90–108. CSSL.

Mehta, M.J. From Sahajanand to Gandhi: role perception and method. In *Social and religious reform movement in the nineteenth and twentieth centuries.* Ed. by S.P. Sen. Calcutta: Institute of Historical Studies, 1979. pp. 229–247. IIML.

Mehta, Makrand. Dalit temple entry movements in Maharashtra and Gujarat, 1930–1948. In *Other Gujarat: social transformations among weaker sections.* Ed. by Takashi Shinoda. Mumbai: Popular, 2002. pp. 1–20. ASL, CEEL, CSSL, EDIL, GIDRL, SETUL, SPIESRL.

Mehta, Meera and Mehta, Dinesh. *Metropolitan housing market: a study of Ahmedabad.* New Delhi: Sage, 1989. p. 208. CSSL.

Mehta, Mona G. River of no dissent: Narmada movement and coercive Gujarati nativism. In *Gujarat beyond Gandhi: identity, conflict and society.* Ed. by Nalin Mehta and Mona G.Mehta. New Delhi: Routledge, 2010. pp. 60–87. BVL, CSSL, GIDRL, IRMAL, UML.

Mehta, Sanat. Pardi grass land satyagraha. In *Non-violent struggles of the twentieth century: retrospect and prospect*. Ed. by Siby K. Joseph, John Moolakkattu and Bharat Mahodaya. New Delhi: Gandhi Peace Foundation, 2009. pp. 116–151. CSSL.

Mehta, Shirin. Role of women in the peasant movements of Gujarat: a study in Gandhian phase 1915–1928. In *Regional roots of Indian nationalism*. Ed. by Makrand J. Mehta. New Delhi: Criterion, 1990. pp. 65–79. GVL.

Mehta, Sushila. Student movement in Gujarat. In *Student power in India*. Ed. by G.S. Mansukhani. New Delhi: Oxford and IBH, 1975. pp. 18–44. SPUL.

Mehta, Uday. Gujarat-Hindu rashtra laboratory. In *Religion, power & violence: expression of politics in contemporary times*. Ed. by Ram Puniyani. New Delhi: Sage, 2005. pp. 290–305. CSSL.

Mehta, Uday. Gujarat: historical backdrop and a brief appraisal of the recent trends in Gujarat polity and society. In *Sectarianism, politics and development*. Ed. by Uday Mehta and Ram Puniyani. Jaipur: Rawat, 2012. pp. 11–52. CSSL.

Mehta, Uday and Puniyani, Ram, ed. *Sectarianism, politics and development*. Jaipur: Rawat, 2012. p. 294. CSSL.

Mishra, R.R. *Effects on land reforms in Saurashtra*. Bombay: Vora, 1961. p. 240. GUL, SUL.

Misra, S.C. Dissent & reform in medieval India: a case study of the Ismaili Nizari Mission in Gujarat. In *Dissent protest and reform in Indian civilization*. Ed. by S.C. Malik. Simla: Indian Institute of Advanced Study, 1977. pp. 145–158. CSSL, GVL, HML, SPUL.

Mukherjee, Aditi and Padmanabhan, B.S.V. Impact of Maldhari resettlement programme on the Maldhari of Gir forest. In *Relevance of anthropology: the Indian scenario*. Ed. by B.G. Halbar and C.G. Hussain Khan. Jaipur: Rawat, 1991. pp. 199–204. CSSL.

Mukherjee, Ramakrishna, I.P. Desai and the sociology of India. In *Social transformation in India: essays in honour of professor I.P. Desai*. Vol. 1. Ed. by Ghanshyam Shah. Jaipur: Rawat, 1997. pp. 17–36. CSSL, GVL, HML, SGUL, SPUL.

Mukherjee, Ramkrishna. Indian sociology of sociology of India: post-1947 writings of I.P. Desai & his Indian contemporaries. In *Emerging Trends in Indian Sociology*, Vol. I. Ed. by Ishwar Modi. Jaipur: Rawat, 1986. pp. 17–35. SGUL.

Mukhtayar, G.C. and Vakil, C.N. *Life and labour in a South Gujarat village*. Bombay: Longmans Green, 1930. p. 303. CSSL, GVL.

Nag, N.G. Some demographic characteristics of scheduled tribes with special reference to Gujarat, Madhya Pradesh, Rajasthan and Maharashtra. In *Demography of tribal development*. Ed. by Ashish Bose, U.P. Sinha and R.P. Tyagi. Delhi: B.R., 1990. pp. 105–124. CSSL, GVL.

Naik, K.N. Trends in co-operative democracy. In *Community development & change in India*. Baroda: M.S. University of Baroda, 1965. pp. 54–62. SGUL.

Naik, T.B. Social status in Gujarat. In *Tribe caste and peasantry*. Ed. by K.S. Mathur and B.C. Agrawal. Lucknow: Ethnographic and Folk Culture Society, 1974. pp. 230–236. CSSL, GVL.

Naik, T.B. Socio-economic profile of the tribals of Gujarat. In *Indian tribes*. Ed. by R.C. Swarankar. Jaipur: Rupa, 1995. pp. 165-[ ]. TRTIL.

Nanavati, Arti. Performance evaluation of non-government development organizations: a study in Vadodara, Gujarat. In *NGOs and social welfare: new research approaches*. Ed. by David Lewis and N. Ravichandran. Jaipur: Rawat, 2008. pp. 276–305. CSSL, SPUL.

Nanavati, J.M. Evidence of early man in Kutch. In *Art, culture and natural history of Kutch*. Ed. by S.K. Bhowmik. Vadodara: Government Press, 1976–77. pp. 78–79. CSSL, TRTIL.

Nanavati, Manilal B. *Rural life problems*. Bombay: Indian Society of Agricultural Economics, 1966. p. 141. SGUL, SPIESRL.

Narayan, Jayaprakash. Crime in Gujarat. In *Nation building in India*. Ed. by Brahmanand. Varanasi: Navachetna, 1975. pp. 179–184. CSSL, SPUL.

Nayak, Lona. Tadvis of Gujarat under displacement by Narmada valley project. In *Narmada basin-land and people: an anthropological pilot study of Madhya Pradesh and Gujarat*. Ed. by D. Tyagi. Calcutta: Anthropological Survey of India, 1998. pp. 93–98. CSSL.

Naz, Farhat. *Socio-cultural context of water: study of a Gujarat village*. Hyderabad: Orient Blackswan, 2014. p. 255. CSSL.

Oommen, T.K. Coming crisis of India: portent from Gujarat. In *Crisis and contention in Indian society*. New Delhi: Sage, 2005. pp. 105–126. CSSL, IIML.

Panchanadikar, K.C. and Panchanadikar, J. *Determinants of social structure and social change in India and others papers*. Bombay: Popular, 1970. p. 241. AAUL, CSSL, GUL, GVL, HML, SPIESRL.

Panda, Damodar. States of deployment: Gujarat. *In Exploitation and deprivation*. Ed. by Damodar Panda. Calcutta: Sujan, 1997. pp. 149–154. SPIESRL.

Pandya, D.G. Ahmedabad: urban renewal in the walled city. In *Urban renewal the Indian experience*. Ed. by D. Ravindra Prasad. New Delhi: Sterling, 1989. pp. 107–124. CSSL.

Pandya, D.G. *Pattern of urban settlements in Gujarat*. Ahmedabad: Karnavati, 1999. p. 202. GVL, HML, TRTIL.

Pandya, Rameshwari. Old age homes of Baroda. In *Ageing: an interdisciplinary approach*. Ed. by Sarjoo Patel and Veena Gandotra. Jaipur: Rawat, 2011. pp. 187–206. CSSL.

Pandya, Rameshwari and Sidhpura, Megha. Development role played by NGOs in Baroda: a survey project. In *WTO and Indian Economic Reforms*. Ed. by Sabana Talwar. New Delhi: Serials, 2008. pp. 289-[ ]. HML.

Parasuraman, S. Anti-dam movement and rehabilitation policy. In *Dam and the nation: displacement and resettlement in the Narmada valley*. Ed. by Jean Dreze, Meera Samson and Satyajit Singh. Delhi: Oxford, 1997. pp. 26–65. CSSL.

Parasuraman, S. and Rajan, Irudaya S. On the estimation of vital rates among the scheduled tribes in Western India. In *Demography of tribal development*. Ed. by Ashish Bose, U.P. Sinha and R.P. Tyagi. New Delhi: D.K, 1990. pp. 131–140. CSSL, GVL.

Parikh, C.D. *Welfare of other backward classes in Gujarat state*. Ahmedabad: Navbharat, 1998. p. 187. GVL, SETUL.

Parikh, Gokul O. *Fact-finding and needs assessment survey of tribal people in Gujarat state*. [ ]: International Labour Organization, 1992. p. 105. SPIESRL.

Parikh, R.D. *Press and society: a sociological study*. Bombay: Popular, 1965. p. 154. CSSL.

Patel, Anil. Resettlement politics and tribal interests. In *Dam and the nation: displacement and resettlement in the Narmada valley*. Ed. by Jean Dreze, Meera Samson and Satyajit Singh. Delhi: Oxford, 1997. pp. 66–92. CSSL.

Patel, Anil. What do the Narmada valley tribals want? In *Toward sustainable development: struggling over India's Narmada river*. Ed. by William F. Fisher. Jaipur: Rawat, 1997. pp. 179–200. CSSL.

Patel, Anil and Mehta, Ambrish. Independent review: was it a search for truth? In *Toward sustainable development: struggling over India's Narmada river*. Ed. by William F. Fisher. Jaipur: Rawat, 1997. pp. 381–417. CSSL.

Patel, Arjun. Dalit movements in Gujarat: from 'Imitation' to 'Transformation'. In *Sectarianism, politics and development*. Ed. by Uday Mehta and Ram Puniyani. Jaipur: Rawat, 2012. pp. 145–178. CSSL.

Patel, Arjun. Hinduisation of adivasis: a case study from South Gujarat. In *Dalits in modern India vision and values*. Ed. by S.M. Michael. New Delhi: Sage, 1999. pp. 186–212. CSSL, GVL, HML.

Patel, B.B. *Slums in Ahmedabad: a study in migration, poverty and housing*. Ahmedabad: SPIESR, 1977. p. 250. SPIESRL.

Patel, B.B. Social justice through Sardar Sarovar Narmada project in Gujarat. In *Sardar Sarovar Project: a promise for plenty*. Ed. by Mahesh T. Pathak. New Delhi: Oxford, 1991. pp. 81–100. CSSL.

Patel, B.B. Voluntary schemes of life insurance for agricultural labourers, handloom weavers and forest labourers in Gujarat. In *Social security for unorganized labour*. Ed. by B.B. Patel. New Delhi: Oxford, 1993. pp. 123–138. CSSL.

Patel, C.N. *Moral and social thinking in modern Gujarat*. Gandhinagar: Gujarat Sahitya Akademi, 1988. p. 93. SPUL.

Patel, Dhanji B. and Chandragupt, Sanon. Understanding the issue of child rights abuse arising due to physical and psychological punishment in Rapar taluka, Kutch district (Gujarat). In *Medical for health*. Ed. by Binod C. Agrawal. New Delhi: Concept, 2009. pp. 168–180. HML.

Patel, M.S. and Patel, N.T. Ecology and human development in tribal Gujarat. In *Ecology and human development*. Ed. by K.L. Bhowmik. Delhi: Inter-India, 1988. pp. 61–73. TRTIL.

Patel, Narsi. Hinduism outside India: selective retention in Gujarati families. In *Family and social change in modern India*. Ed. by Giri Raj Gupta. New Delhi: Vikas, 1976. pp. 233–256. CSSL, SPIESRL.

Patel, Priyavadan. Assessing the impact and constraint of tribal development in Gujarat. In *Tribal development: past efforts and new challenges*. Ed. by J.P. Singh and N.N Vyas. Udaipur: Himanshu, 1989. pp. 109–128. CEEL, CSSL, HML.

Patel, Priyavadan. Status of tribal development in Gujarat case of ITDP, Dahod. In *Socio-economic and ecological development*. Ed. by Buddhadeb Chaudhuri. New Delhi: Inter-India, 1992. pp. 70–80. GVL.

Patel, Priyavadan. Status of tribal development in Gujarat: case of ITDP, Dahod. In *Tribal Transformation in India*. Vol. 2. Ed. by Buddhadeb Chaudhuri. New Delhi: Inter-India, 1992. pp. 70–80. TRTIL.

Patel, Shivani A. Status of adivasis/indigenous peoples land series-1: Gujarat. Delhi: Aakar, 2011. p. 126. AAL, EDIL, GIDRL, TRTIL.

Patel, Sujata. Urbanization, development and communalization of society in Gujarat. In *Other Gujarat: social transformations among weaker sections*. Ed. by Takashi Shinoda. Mumbai: Popular, 2002. pp. 204–220. ASL, CEEL, CSSL, EDIL, GIDRL, SETUL, SPIESRL.

Pathy, Jaganath. *Tribal peasantry dynamics of development*. New Delhi: Inter-India, 1984. p. 233. CSSL, SGUL, UML.

Patkar, Medha. Struggle for participation and justice: a historical narrative. In *Toward sustainable development: struggling over India's Narmada river*. Ed. by William F. Fisher. Jaipur: Rawat, 1997. pp. 157–178. CSSL.

Pereira, Winin. Sustainable lifestyle of Warlis. In *Indigenous vision: peoples of India attitudes of the environment*. Ed. by Geeti Sen. New Delhi: Sage, 1992. pp. 189–204. CSSL, HML.

Pillai, S. Devadas and Baks, Chris, ed. Winners and losers: styles of development and change in an Indian region. Bombay: Popular, 1979. p. 407. CSSL, HML, IIML, SPIESRL.

Pinto, Stany. Land alienation and adivasi assertion in Bharuch district. In *Development and deprivation in Gujarat: in honour of Jan Breman*. Ed. by Ghanshyam Shah, Mario Rutten and Hein Streefkerk. New Delhi: Sage, 2002. pp. 214–230. CEEL, CEPTL, CSSL, EDIL, GIDRL, IIML, IRMAL, UML.

Prakash, Anjal. Groundwater vending and appropriation of women's labour: gender, water scarcity and agrarian change in a Gujarat village, India. In *Diverting the flow: gender equity and water in south Asia*. Ed. by Margreet Zwarteveen, Sara Ahmed and Sumanrimal Gautam. New Delhi: Zubaan, 2012. pp. 312–336. IIML.

Prakash, Cedric. Justice for peace: challenges from Gujarat. In *Other India: realities of an emerging Power*. Ed. by Rajesh Chakrabarti. New Delhi: Sage, 2009. pp. 110–119. CSSL.

Pruthi, Surinder L.S. *Reflection events, people, policies and practices*. New Delhi: Pitambar, 2008. p. 260. IIML.

Punalekar, S.P. Decoding tribal development: a narrative on South Gujarat. In *Contemporary society: tribal studies*. Vol. 3. Ed. by Deepak Kumar Behera and George Pfeffer. New Delhi: Concept, 1999. pp. 63–84. CSSL, GVL.

Punalekar, S.P. Growth with contradictions: tribal situation in South Gujarat. In *Tribal situation in India: issues in development: with special reference to Western India*. Ed. by Vidyut Joshi. Jaipur: Rawat, 1998. pp. 285–304. CSSL, GVL, SGUL, UML.

Punalekar, S.P. New economic policy and tribal reality: a case of Gujarat. In *New economic policy and dalits*. Ed. by P.G. Jogdand. Jaipur: Rawat, 2000. pp. 287–303. CSSL, GVL.

Puniyani, Ram. Hindutva and human rights: a case of Gujarat. In *Sectarianism, politics and development*. Ed. by Uday Mehta and Ram Puniyani. Jaipur: Rawat, 2012. pp. 53–72. CSSL.

Raghavaiah, V. *Tribal Revolts*. Nellore: Andhra Rashtra Adimajati Sevak Sangh, 1971. p. 269. CSSL, GVL, TRTIL.

Raju, K.V. and Sarkar, Sabyasachi. *Growing rural-urban disparity in Gujarat*. New Delhi: Serials, 2009. p. 114. GIDRL.

Ramchandani, G. Tribal development in Gujarat: problems and perspectives. In *Tribal development: past efforts and new challenges*. Ed. by J.P. Singh and N.N. Vyas. Udaipur: Himanshu, 1989. pp. 109–128. CEEL, CSSL, HML.

Rana, Malchand S. Anti reservation agitations in Gujarat. In *Reservations in India: myths and realities*. New Delhi: Concept, 2008. pp. 121–136. GUL.

Rangaswami, Vimala. Urban fringe of Vadodara: development and transformation. In *Urban fringe of Indian cities*. Ed. by Jutta K. Dikshit. Jaipur: Rawat, 2011. pp. 191–200. CSSL.

Rangaswami, Vimala and Vyas, Jyoten. Trend of urbanization in the tribal region of Central Gujarat. In *Behavioral dimensions of tribal landscapes*. Ed. by G.P. Gupta. Jaipur: Arihant, 1992. pp. 62–78. Studies in Tribal Development IV. CEEL, GVL, TRTIL.

Rao, V.K.R.V. *Gandhian alternative to Western socialism*. Bombay: Bharatiya Vidya Bhavan, 1970. p. 83. SUL.

Rathod, C.S. Role of 'Co-Operation' in rural development of Gujarat. In *Geography and rural development*. Ed. by R.N.P. Sinha. New Delhi: Concept, 1992. pp. 135–138. GVL.

Rathod, P.V. and Kumar, Vijay. Working of the scheduled castes and scheduled tribes (Prevention of Atrocities) act 1989 in Gujarat. In *Dalits and the state*. Ed. by Ghanshyam Shah. Mussoorie: Centre for Rural Studies, 2002. pp. 290–309. CSSL, GUL, SPUL, TRTIL.

Ratnagar, Shereen. *Being Tribal*. New Delhi: Primus, 2010. p. 111. AAL.

Raval, R.L. *Socio-religious reform movements in Gujarat during the nineteenth century*. New Delhi: Ess Ess, 1987. p. 274. CSSL, GIDRL, GUL, GVL, HML, SGUL, SPIESRL, SPUL, TRTIL.

Ray, Arup and Soni, Lok Nath. Collection of ethnographic specimens from Gujarat. In *Narmada basin-land and people: an anthropological pilot study of Madhya Pradesh and Gujarat*. Ed. by D. Tyagi. Calcutta: Anthropological Survey of India, 1998. pp. 99–121. CSSL.

Ray, C.N. *Politics of rural development*. Jaipur: Rawat, 1994. p. 171. CSSL.

Rice, A.K. *Productivity and social organization: the Ahmedabad experiment*. London: Tavistock, 1958. p. 298. GVL, SPUL.

Risley, Herbert. *People of India*. New Delhi: Munshiram Manoharlal, 1991. p. 472. CSSL.

Sah, D.C. State, civil society and community: tribal displacement in Gujarat. In *Tribal issues in India*. Ed. by D.C. Sah and Yatindra Singh Sisodia. Jaipur: Rawat, 2004. pp. 269–292. CEEL, CSSL, GVL, HML, TRTIL.

Sah, D.C. and Sisodia, Yatindra Singh, ed. *Tribal issues in India*. Jaipur: Rawat, 2004. p. 344. CEEL, CSSL, GVL, HML, TRTIL.

Sahoo, Narottam and Vinu, T.J. Policy for creating science literacy for sustainable development: a case of Gujarat. In *Sustainable development and earth care: searching for policy initiatives*. Ed. by K.V. Sundaram, M. Mrityunjay and P.S. Tiwari. New Delhi: Concept, 2009. pp. 106–118. SPIESRL.

Sankaran, Unni K. *Ecology of river Narmada*. New Delhi: A.P.H., 1996. p. 371. CSSL.

Sanon, Chandragupt S. *Working children: a sociological analysis*. New Delhi: A.P.H, 1998. p. 338. SPUL.

Saraswathi, T.S. and Dutta, Ranjana. *Invisible boundaries: grooming for adult roles: a descriptive study of socialization in a poor rural and urban slum setting in Gujarat*. New Delhi: Northern, 1988. p. 246. GIDRL.

Savara, M. Dairy development amongst the tribals in the Surat district. In *Resources, institutions and strategies*. Ed. by Doornbos Martin and K.N. Nair. New Delhi: Sage, 1990. pp. 274–299. HML.

Schenk-Sandbergen, Loes Ch. and Schenk, Hans. Setting of polarity: introduction to the research area. In *Winners and losers: styles of development and change in an Indian region*. Ed. by S. Devadas Pillai and Chris Baks. Bombay: Popular, 1979. pp. 18–35. CSSL, HML, SPIESRL.

Shah, A.M. Division and hierarchy: an overview of caste in Gujarat. In *Social inequality in India: profiles of caste class, power and social mobility*. Ed. by K.L. Sharma. Jaipur: Rawat, 1995. pp. 192–227. CSSL, GUL, GVL, HML, SPIESRL.

Shah, A.M. *Exploring India's rural past: a Gujarat village in the early nineteenth century*. New Delhi: Oxford, 2002. p. 245. CSSL, GIDRL, GVL.

Shah, A.M. *Family in India: critical essays*. Hyderabad: Orient, 1998. p. 173. CSSL.

Shah, A.M. *Household dimension of the family in India: a field study in a Gujarat village and a review of other studies*. New Delhi: Orient Longman, 1973. p. 281. CSSL, GIDRL, IIML.

Shah, A.M. Lineage structure and change in a Gujarat village. In *Dimensions of social change in India*. Ed. by M.N. Srinivas, S. Seshaiah and V.S. Parthasarathy. Bombay: Allied, 1977. pp. 339–367. AAUL, GUL, GVL, SGUL, SPIESRL, SPUL.

Shah, A.M. Lineage structure and change in a Gujarat village. In *Family, kinship and marriage in India.* Ed. by Patricia Uberoi. Bombay: Oxford, 1993. pp. 119–146. CSSL, GVL, HML.

Shah, A.M. M.N. Srinivas in Baroda. In *M.N. Srinivas: the man and his work.* Ed. by P.K. Misra., K.K. Basa and H.K. Bhat. Jaipur: Rawat, 2007. pp. 41–61. CEPTL, CSSL, IIML.

Shah, A.M. Studying the present and the past: a village in Gujarat. In *Fieldworker and the field: problems and challenges in sociological investigation*. Ed. by M.N. Srinivas, A.M. Shah and E.A. Ramaswamy. Delhi: Oxford, 1979. pp. 29–37. CEEL, CSSL, SPIESRL, SPUL.

Shah, A.M. and Desai, I.P. *Division and hierarchy: an overview of caste in Gujarat.* Delhi: Hindustan, 1988. p. 150. CEPTL, CSSL, IRMAL, SGUL, SPUL.

Shah, A.M. and Shroff, R.G. Vahivancā Bārots of Gujarat: a caste of genealogists and mythographers. In *Traditional India: structure and change*. Ed. by Milton Singer. Jaipur: Rawat, 1975. pp. 40–70. CSSL.

Shah, A.M. and Shroff, R.G. Vahivanca Barots of Gujarat: a caste of genealogists and mythographers. In *Traditional India structure and change*. Ed. by Milton Singer. United State: United State of America, 1970. pp. 40–72. SPUL.

Shah, Amita and Pathak, Jharna, ed. *Tribal development in Western India.* New Delhi: Routledge, 2014. p. 344. CSSL.

Shah, Anil C. and Iyengar, Sudarshan. Contribution of NGOs to development: some issues and a case study. In *Social change through voluntary action*. Ed. by M.L. Dantwala, Harsh Sethi and Pravin Visaria. New Delhi: Sage, 1998. pp. 92–112. CSSL.

Shah, Dilip. *Random and reflections on rural development.* Jaipur: ABD, 2012. p. 292. CEPTL, GVL.

Shah, Dilip. *Sustainable tribal development model case of Vadi*. Mumbai: National Bank for Agriculture and Rural Development, [ ]. p. 270. UML.

Shah, Ghanshyam. Anti-untouchability movements. In *Caste, caste-conflict and reservation*. By Centre for Social Studies. New Delhi: Ajanta, 1985. pp 102–123. CSSL, SETUL.

Shah, Ghanshyam. Caste in contemporary India. In *Caste, caste-conflict and reservation*. By Centre for Social Studies. New Delhi: Ajanta, 1985. pp 1–12. CSSL, SETUL.

Shah, Ghanshyam. Direct action in India: a study of Gujarat and Bihar agitations. In *Social movements and the state*. Ed. by Ghanshyam Shah. New Delhi: Sage, 2002. pp. 335–360. CSSL, GUL, UML.

Shah, Ghanshyam. Introduction: I.P. Desai and social transformation. In *Social transformation in India: essays in honour of Professor I.P. Desai.* Vol. 1. Ed. by Ghanshyam Shah. Jaipur: Rawat, 1997. pp. 1–16. CSSL, GVL, HML, SGUL, SPUL.

Shah, Ghanshyam. Caste sentiments, class formation and dominance in Gujarat. In *Caste and class in India*. Ed. by K.L. Sharma. Jaipur: Rawat, 1994. pp. 225–270. CSSL, GVL, HML, SGUL, SPUL.

Shah, Ghanshyam. Caste sentiments, class formation and dominance in Gujarat. In *Dominance and state power in modern India*. Vol. II. Ed. by Francine R. Frankel and M.S.A. Rao. Delhi: Oxford, 1990. pp. 59–114. CSSL, TRTIL.

Shah, Ghanshyam. Civil society and poor. In *Footprints of development and change: essays in memory of professor V.K.R.V. Rao commemorating his birth centenary*. New Delhi: Academic Foundation, 2008. pp. 257–283. CSSL.

Shah, Ghanshyam. *Economic differentiations and tribal identity*. Delhi: Ajanta, 1984. p. 148. CSSL, SGUL, TRTIL.

Shah, Ghanshyam. Economy and civic authority in Surat. In *Urban studies*. Ed. by Sujata Patel and Kushal Deb. New Delhi: Oxford, 2006. pp. 274–293. HML.

Shah, Ghanshyam. Office without de facto power: a study of social justice committee in Gujarat. In *Social transformation in India: essays in honour of professor I.P. Desai*. Vol. 2. Ed. by Ghanshyam Shah. Jaipur: Rawat, 1997. pp. 397–419. CSSL, GUL, GVL, HML, SGUL, SPUL.

Shah, Ghanshyam. *Protest movements in two Indian states: a study of the Gujarat and Bihar movements*. Delhi: Ajanta, 1977. p. 171. CSSL, GIDRL, HML.

Shah, Ghanshyam. Strategies of social engineering: reservation and mobility of backward communities of Gujarat. In *Diversity and dominance in Indian politics. Vol. 2: division, deprivation and the congress*. Ed. by Ramashray Roy and Richard Sisson. New Delhi: Sage, 1990. pp. 111–145. CSSL.

Shah, Ghanshyam. Stratification among the scheduled tribes in the Bharuch and Panch Mahals districts of Gujarat. In *Determinants of social status in India*. Ed. by S.C. Malik. Shimla: Indian Institute of Advanced Study, 1986. pp. 149–184. CSSL, HML, IIML, SPIESRL.

Shah, Ghanshyam. Unrest among the adivasis and their struggles. In *Other Gujarat: social transformations among weaker sections*. Ed. by Takashi Shinoda. Mumbai: Popular, 2002. pp. 96–118. ASL, CEEL, CSSL, EDIL, GIDRL, SETUL, SPIESRL.

Shah, Ghanshyam. Untouchability in rural Gujarat: revisited. In *Dalits and the state*. Ed. by Ghanshyam Shah. Mussoorie: Centre for Rural Studies, 2002. pp. 129–146. CSSL, GUL, SPUL, TRTIL.

Shah, Ghanshyam, ed. *Social transformation in India: essays in honour of professor I.P. Desai*. 2 Vol. Jaipur: Rawat, 1997. p. 711. CSSL, GVL, HML, SGUL, SPUL.

Shah, Ghanshyam and Chaturvedi, H.R. *Gandhian approach to rural development: the Valod experiment*. Delhi: Ajanta, 1983. p. 140. CSSL, HML, IIML.

Shah, Haku and Sen, Geeti. Maati: born from the earth. In *Indigenous vision: peoples of India attitudes of the environment*. Ed. by Geeti Sen. New Delhi: Sage, 1992. pp. 129–144. CSSL, HML.

Shah, M.H. and Khatri, T.D. Demographic impact of family welfare programme in Gujarat. In *Population policy in India*. Ed. by M.M. Gandotra and Narayan Das. Bombay: Blackle, 1984. pp. 136–155. SGUL, SPIESRL.

Shah, P.G. *Tribal life in Gujarat: an analytical study of the cultural changes with special reference to the Dhanka tribe*. Bombay: Gujarat Research Society, 1964. p. 344. AERCL, ASL, BVL, CSSL, GVL, SPIESRL, SPUL, TRTIL.

Shah, P.G. *Vimukta jatis denotified communities in Western India*. Bombay: Gujarat Research Society, 1967. p. 164. SPIESRL.

Shah, S.M. Rural class structure in Gujarat. In *Rural sociology in India*. [Ed.] by A.R. Desai. Bombay: Popular, 1969. pp. 287–290. AAUL, CSSL, GUL, GVL, HML, IIML, SGUL, SPIESRL, TRTIL.

Shah, Tushaar. *Catalysing co-operation: design of self-governing organizations*. New Delhi: Sage, 1996. p. 315. CSSL.

Shah, Vimal P., Sheth, N.R. and Visaria, Pravin. Swadhyaya: social change through spirituality. In *Social change through voluntary action*. Ed. by M.L. Dantwala, Harsh Sethi and Pravin Visaria. New Delhi: Sage, 1998. pp. 57–73. CSSL.

Shahi, U.P. *Urbanisation in Gujarat: a geographical analysis*. Gorakhpur: Institute for Rural Eco-Development, 1989. p. 195. GVL.

Sharma, S.S., Raju, K.V. and Sarkar, Sabyasachi. *Growing rural-urban disparity in Gujarat*. New Delhi: Serials, 2009. p. 114. CEPTL, GVL.

Sharma, Shankar Dayal. Gujarat looks ahead. In *Aspects of Indian thought*. New Delhi: Sterling, 1993. pp. 63–66. GUL.

Shashidharan, E.M. Civil society organisation and irrigation management in Gujarat, India. In *Water for food and rural development: approaches and initiatives in South Asia*. Ed. by Peter P. Mollinga. New Delhi: Sage, 2000. pp. 247–265. SPUL.

Sheikh, Samira. Lives of Bahuchara Mata. In *Idea of Gujarat: history, ethnography and text*. Ed. by Edward Simpson and Aparna Kapadia. Hyderabad: Orient Blackswan, 2010. pp. 84–99. AAL, ASL, BUL, CEPTL, CSSL, GIDRL, IRMAL, MICAL, SETUL.

Shelat, Kirit N. *Evolution of rural development*. Ahmedabad: Kathan Education Communication Unit, 1988. p. 287. CSSL, HML.

Sheth, Chimanlal Bhailal. *Jainism in Gujarat, A.D. 1100 to 1600*. Bombay: Shree Vijaydevsur Sangh Gnan Samity, 1953. p. 282. BVL.

Sheth, N.R. Children of the same God: a spiritual approach to social transformation. In *Social transformation in India: essays in honour of professor I.P. Desai*. Vol. 2. Ed. by Ghanshyam Shah. Jaipur: Rawat, 1997. pp. 666–697. CSSL, GVL, HML, SGUL, SPUL.

Sheth, N.R. Spiriual approach to social transformation. In *Other Gujarat: social transformations among weaker sections*. Ed. by Takashi Shinoda. Mumbai: Popular, 2002. pp. 38–65. ASL, CEEL, CSSL, EDIL, GIDRL, SETUL, SPISERL.

Sheth, N.R. Trial and error in a new field: a factory in Gujarat. In *Fieldworker and the field: problems and challenges in sociological investigation*. Ed. by M.N. Srinivas, A.M. Shah and E.A. Ramaswamy. Delhi: Oxford, 1979. pp. 163–172. CEEL, CSSL, SPIESRL, SPUL.

Shinoda, Takashi. Structure of stagnancy: sweepers in Ahmedabad district. In *Dalit and the state*. Ed. by Ghanshyam Shah. New Delhi: Concept, 2002. pp. 241–271. CSSL, GUL, SPUL, TRTIL.

Shokoohy, Mehrdad. Sidi Sayyid-or Sidi Said-mosque in Ahmedabad. In *African elites in India: Habshi Amarat*. Ed. by Kenneth X. Robbins and John Macleod. Ahmedabad: Mapin, 2006. pp. 144–161. BUL, TRTIL.

Shroff, Beheroze. Spiritual journeys: Parsis and Sidi Saints. In *Journeys and dwellings: Indian Ocean themes in South Asia*. Ed. by Helene Basu. Hyderabad: Orient Longman, 2008. pp. 256–275. CSSL.

Shukla, B.M. *Law and social justice: a critical review of justice D.A. Desai's important*. Jaipur: Rawat, 1998. p. 344. CSSL.

Shukla, Rohit et al. *Forest and tribal life (Study of a Micro-Region): socio-cultural traits sustaining tribal ecology, a case study of Danta taluka - Banaskantha district, North Gujarat*. New Delhi: Concept, 1990. p. 141. GIDRL.

Shukla, R.N. Rural development in Gujarat. In *Strategies for rural development*. Ed. by J.K. Gehlawat and K. Kant. Bombay: Arnold, 1987. pp. 287–294. HML, SPIESRL, TRTIL.

Sidhpura, Megha and Pandya, Rameshwari. Development role played by NGOs in Baroda: a study. In *Networking with NGOs for development: Indian perspective.* By Rameshwari Pandya. New Delhi: Serials, 2006. pp. 117–136. CSSL.

Simhadri, V.C., *Ex-criminal tribes of India*. Delhi: K.L. Malik, 1979. p. 185. TRTIL.

Singh, K.S., ed. *People of India: Gujarat.* 3 Vol. Calcutta: Anthropological Survey of India, 2002. p. 1597. CSSL, EDIL, GIDRL, HML, IIML, IRMAL, SETUL, UML.

Singh, K.S., ed. *Tribal movements in India*. Vol. 2. New Delhi: Manohar, 1982. p. 414. CSSL, SPIESRL.

Singh, K.S., Lal, R.B. and Krishan, Gopal. *People of India-Gujarat (Part-One) Volume XXII.* Mumbai: Popular, 2003. p. 486. CEEL, SPUL.

Singh, L.R. et al. Regional development strategies for special problems areas: a case study of tribal areas of Dediapada taluka. In *Regional planning and rural development*. Allahabad: Technical, 1986. pp. 234–244. HML.

Singhji, Virbhadra. *Rajputs of Saurashtra*. Bombay: Popular, 1994. p. 342. AAL, CSSL, SETUL, SPUL.

Sinha, Aseema. Reforming public services in a high growth state: the case of Gujarat. In *Public service delivery in India: understanding the reform process.* Ed. by Vikarm K. Chand. New Delhi: Oxford, 2010. pp. 126–176. GVL, HML.

Sinha, B.R.K. Participation of human resources in a tribal district of Gujarat. In *Dimensions of scheduled tribes development in India*. Ed. by P.D. Tiwari and R.S. Tripathi. New Delhi: Uppal, 1992. pp. 20–35. TRTIL.

Soni, Lok Nath. Ethnographic collection from Narmada valley. In *Narmada basin-land and people: an anthropological pilot study of Madhya Pradesh and Gujarat*. Ed. by D. Tyagi. Calcutta: Anthropological Survey of India, 1998. pp. 123–135. CSSL.

Srinivas, M.N., Rao, M.S.A. and Shah, A.M. *Survey of research in sociology and social anthropology.* Bombay: Popular, 1972. p. 336. TRTIL.

Standing, Guy, et al. *Social income and insecurity: a study in Gujarat*. New Delhi: Routledge, 2010. p. 232. GIDRL, GVL, HML, IRMAL.

Steed, Gitel P. Notes on an approach to a study of personality formation in a Hindu village in Gujarat. In *Village India: studies in the little community*. Ed. by Mckim Marriott. Chicago: University of Chicago Press, 1955. pp. 102–144. AERCL, CSSL, GUL, SGUL, SPUL.

Streefkerk, Hein. Town, a caste, and two decades of capitalist transformation in South Gujarat. In *Social transformation in India: essays in honour of professor I.P. Desai.* Vol. 1. Ed. by Ghanshyam Shah. Jaipur: Rawat, 1997. pp. 276–323. CSSL, GUL, GVL, HML, SGUL, SPUL.

Sud, Nikita. *Liberalization, Hindu nationalism and the state: a biography of Gujarat.* New Delhi: Oxford, 2012. p. 249. CEPTL, CSSL, EDIL, GIDRL, HML, MICAL, SPUL.

Tambs-Lyche, Harald. *Good country: individual, situation and society in Saurashtra*. New Delhi: Manohar, 2004. p. 354. CSSL, UML.

Tambs-Lyche, Harald. *Power, profit and poetry: traditional society in Kathiawar, Western India*. New Delhi: Manohar, 1997. p. 337. BUL, CSSL, UML.

Tambs-Lyche, Harald. Reflections on caste in Gujarat. In *Idea of Gujarat: history, ethnography and text.* Ed. by Edward Simpson and Aparna Kapadia. Hyderabad: Orient Blackswan, 2010. pp. 100–119. AAL, ASL, BUL, CEPTL, CSSL, GIDRL, MICAL, SETUL.

Thakore, G.D. Jagirdars, then and now, in a North Gujarat area. In *Aspects of changing India.* Ed. by S. Devadas Pillai. Bombay: Popular, 1976. pp. 136–145. HML, SPIESRL.

Trivedi, Harshad R. *Scheduled castes quest for land and social equality.* New Delhi: Concept, 1996. p. 227. CSSL.

Trivedi, Harshad R. Tribal land in Gujarat. In *Tribal situation in India: issues in development: with special reference to Western India.* Ed. by Vidyut Joshi. Jaipur: Rawat, 1998. pp. 151–174. CSSL, GVL, SGUL, UML.

Trivedi, Harshad R. *Tribal land systems: land reform measures and development of tribals.* New Delhi: Concept, 1993. p. 383. CSSL.

Trivedi, Harshad R. and Bhakta, Satish K. Implementation of social legislation pertaining to scheduled castes in Gujarat. In *Social administration: development and change: essays in hounour of professor V. Jagannadham.* New Delhi: Indian Institute of Public Administration, 1980. pp. 112–123. CSSL.

Trivedi, R.K. Slum areas of Ahmedabad city. In *Slums and urbanization.* Ed. by A.R. Desai and S. Devadas Pillai. Bombay: Popular, 1970. pp. 215–217. CSSL, SPIESRL, TRTIL.

Trivedi, R.K. Slum clearance in Ahmedabad. In *Slum and urbanization.* Ed. by A.R. Desai and S. Devadas Pillai. Bombay: Popular, 1970. pp. 382–383. CSSL, SPIESRL, TRTIL.

Tully, Mark. Typhoon in Ahmedabad. In *No full Stops in India.* New Delhi: Viking Penguin, 1991. pp. 237–267. CEPTL.

Tyagi, D., ed. *Narmada basin-land and people: an anthropological pilot study of Madhya Pradesh and Gujarat.* Calcutta: Anthropological Survey of India, 1998. p. 135. CSSL.

Upadhyay, Chandrakant. Land alienation problem among tribals of Gujarat. In *Tribal development.* Ed. by Mahesh Gamit and J.C. Patel. Jaipur: Vista, 2013. pp. 40–52. TRTIL

Van der Veen, Klaas W. Introduction: management and the socio-cultural context. In *Managing rural development: health and energy programmes in India.* Ed. by Hein Streefkerk and T.K. Moulik. New Delhi: Sage, 1991. pp. 11–26. CSSL, HML, IIML, SETUL.

Van Der Veen, Klass W. Social change and the marriage system of the Anavil brahmans of South Gujarat. In *Social transformation in India: essays in honour of professor I.P. Desai.* Vol. 2. Ed. by Ghanshyam Shah. Jaipur: Rawat, 1997. pp. 339–369. CSSL, GUL, GVL, HML, SGUL, SPUL.

Van der Veen, Klaas W. Urbanization, migration and primordial attachments. In *Winners and losers: styles of development and change in an Indian region.* Ed. by S. Devadas Pillai and Chris Baks. Bombay: Popular, 1979. pp. 43–80. CSSL, HML, SPIESRL.

Veena, D.R. *Low income rural housing: a model for government policy and action.* New Delhi: Ashish, 1985. p. 141. IIML.

Visaria, Pravin, Visaria, Leela and Jain, Anrudh. *Contraceptive use and fertility in India: a case study of Gujarat.* New Delhi: Sage, 1995. p. 264. GIDRL, IIML.

Weinstein, Joy A. and Pillai, Vijayan Kumara. Ahmedabad: an ecological perspective. In *Reading in urban structure.* Ed. by G. Vishwanadham. Delhi: Ajanta, 1986. pp. 99–142. SGUL, SPIESRL.

Williams, Raymond B. *New face of Hinduism: Swaminarayan religion.* Landon: Cambridge University press, 1984. p. 217. CSSL.

Williams, Raymond Brady. *Introduction to Swaminarayan Hinduism.* Cambridge: Cambridge University press, 2001. p. 253. CSSL, SETUL.

Wilson, John. *Parsi religion: Zand-Avasta, and propounded and defended by the Zoroastrians of India and Persia.* Bombay: American Mission Press, 1843. p. 610. CSSL.

Wood, John R. Reservations in doubt: backlash against affirmative action in Gujarat. In *Diversity and dominance in Indian politics.* Vol. 2: *division, deprivation and the congress.* Ed. by Ramashray Roy and Richard Sisson. New Delhi: Sage, 1990. pp. 146–169. CSSL.

Yagnik, Achyut. Search for dalit self-identity in Gujarat. In *Other Gujarat: social transformations among weaker sections.* Ed. by Takashi Shinoda. Mumbai: Popular, 2002. pp. 22–37. ASL, CEEL, CSSL, EDIL, GIDRL, SETUL, SPIESRL.

Journal Articles

Advani, L.K. Somanath sager. *Bhavan's Journal.* 47, 1, 2000. pp. 43–48. GVL.

Aiyanger, Rangaswami K.V., Hindu law in Gujarat. *Journal of the Gujarat Research Society.* 8, 2 and 3, 1946. pp. 63–73. GUL.

Aloria, G.R. Urbanisation and urban development. (Gujarat-2010: Challenges and Opportunities). *Anvesak.* 31, 1–2, 2001. pp. 140–152. CSSL.

Antani, P.A. Population problem of Kutch. *Journal of the Gujarat Research Society.* 19, 2/74, 1957. pp. 105–111. GVL.

Ashok, Kumar. Survival mechanisms of Surat city. *Nagarlok.* 33, 3, 2001. pp. 56–76. SPIESRL.

Athavale, V.B. Authenticity of the movements of Krishna in Gujarat and Kathiawad (Anarta Country). *Journal of the Gujarat Research Society.* 10, 4, 1947. pp. 207–214. GUL.

Bates, Crispin N. Nature of social change in rural Gujarat: the Kheda district, 1818–1918. *Modern Asian Studies.* 15, 4, 1981. pp. 771–821. CSSL, HML.

Bhakta, Satish. Uplift of the poor tribals. *Adivasi Gujarat.* 1, 1, 1978. pp. 38–46. CSSL, GVL, SPIESRL, TRTIL.

Bhan, Kuldeep K. Late Harappan Gujarat. *Eastern Anthropologist.* 45, 1–2, 1992. pp. 173–192. CSSL.

Bharti, Madhu. Impact of poor urban services on health and asset creation: a case study of Ahmedabad. *Social Action.* 56, 2, 2006. pp. 155–171. GVL, HML.

Bhatt, B.B. and Joshi, V.N. Diet survey-intersee students hostel, medical college, Baroda. *Journal of the Gujarat Research Society.* 23, 3/91, 1961. pp. 233–236. GVL.

Bhatt, Mahesh. Housing problem of a growing metropolis. *Economic and Political Weekly.* 7, 17, 1972. pp. 849–851. CSSL, IRMAL, SGUL, SPIESRL, UML.

Bhatt, Mahesh and Chawda, V.K. Housing the poor in Ahmedabad. *Economic and Political Weekly.* 11, 19, 1976. pp. 706–711. CEPTL, CSSL, GUL, IIML, IRMAL, SGUL, SPIESRL, TRTIL, UML.

Bhatt, Sonal. Impact of Jyoti Gram scheme on rural life and economy in Gujarat: a case study of four villages in Anand district. *Journal of Rural Development.* 27, 3, 2008. pp. 501–522. CSSL, IIML.

Bhatt, Sonal. Irony of falling sex ratio and rising prosperity: a study of Gujarat state in India. *Anvesak.* 40, 1 and 2, 2010. pp. 20–43. GIDRL.

Bose, Pradip Kumar. Production organization and market relations of potters of Gujarat. *Man in India*. 62, 3, 1982. pp. 246–270. CSSL, SGUL, TRTIL, UML.

Bose, Pradip Kumar. Stratification among tribals in Gujarat. *Economic and Political Weekly*. 16, 6, 1981. pp. 191–196. CEPTL, CSSL, GUL, IIML, IRMAL, SGUL, SPIESRL, TRTIL, UML.

Chakravarty, Sujoy and Dand, Sejal A. Food insecurity in Gujarat: a study of two rural populations. *Economic and Political Weekly*. 41, 22, 2006. pp. 2248–2258. BUL, CEPTL, CSSL, EDIL, GIDRL, IIML, IRMAL, MICAL, SGUL, SPIESRL, SUL, UML.

Chandra, Sudhir. Hindu's protest. *Seminar*. 513, 2002. pp. 49–52. CSSL, MICAL, SPUL, UML.

Chaudhary, B.S. Demographic aspects of the Chaudhary tribe of Gujarat state. *Adivasi Gujarat*. 1, 2, 1978. pp. 3–11. CSSL, GVL, SPIESRL, TRTIL.

Chitharanjan, K.V. Functional specialization of cities and urban growth in Gujarat. *Indian Journal of Regional Science*. 15, 2, 1983. pp. 27–35. GIDRL, SGUL.

Chitharanjan, K.V. Size, Growth and structure of cities in Gujarat. *Nagarlok*. 15, 3, 1983. pp. 62–71. CEPTL.

Chitharanjan, K.V. Urban and regional growth patterns in Gujarat: a cross section analysis. *Urban India*. 4, 4, 1984. pp. 32–46. CEPTL.

Choondawat, Pradeep Singh and Sharma, Anant. Major socio-economic and demographic attributes among the tribes of Gujarat and Rajasthan: a comparative analysis. *Tribal Health Bulletin*. 16, 1 and 2, 2010. pp. 47–51. CSSL.

Choudhary, Amarsinh. Not a single incident of Muslim retaliation in Ahmedabad. *Muslim India*. 4, 44, 1986. pp. 347–348. GVL.

Choudhary, Kameshwar. Development dilemma: resettlement of Gir Maldharis. *Economic and Political Weekly*. 35, 30, 2000. pp. 2662–268. BUL, CEPTL, CSSL, IIML, IRMAL, MICAL, SGUL, SPIESRL, UML.

Dalton, Dennis. Dandi march. *Seminar*. 193, 1975. pp. 17–28. CSSL, GVL, UML.

Das, Biswaroop. Growth trends, physical profile and dwelling character of slums in an industrial city-the case of Surat. *Nagarlok*. 33, 2, 1996. pp. 63–81. CEPTL, SPIESRL.

Das, Biswaroop. Slum dwellers in Indian cities-Surat. *Man & Development*. 21, 3, 1999. pp. 92–124. CSSL, GVL, UML.

Das, Biswaroop. Slum dwellers in Surat city: a socio-demographic profile. *Indian Journal of Social Work*. 58, 1, 1997. pp. 35–56. CSSL.

Das, Biswaroop. Slums, migrants and the urban informal sector in Surat city. *Indian Journal of Labour Economics*. 37, 3, 1994. pp. 391–405. CSSL, IIML.

Das, Biswaroop. Socio-economic differentials among major social and religious groups in city slums. *Indian Journal of Social Work*. 65, 3, 2004. pp. 392–422. CSSL, MICAL.

Das, Biswaroop. Some aspects of urbanization and city planning in Gujarat. *Man & Development*. 18, 1, 1996. pp. 71–86. CSSL, GIDRL, GVL, IRMAL, UML.

Das, Keshab and Visaria, Leela. Issues in rural sanitation: lessons from Gujarat. *Journal of Rural Development*. 21, 1, 2002. pp. 1–26. CSSL, GIDRL, IIML, IRMAL.

Dave, Manjula. Geographical patterns of crimes in Gujarat. *Gujarat Police Journal*. 7, 4, 1989. pp. 3–11. GVL.

Desai, I.P. Anti-reservation agitation and structure of Gujarat society. *Economic and Political Weekly*. 16, 18, 1981. pp. 819–823. CEPTL, CSSL, GUL, IIML, IRMAL, SPIESRL, UML.

Desai, Renu. Governing the urban poor: riverfront development, slum resettlement and the politics of inclusion in Ahmedabad. *Economic and Political Weekly.* 47, 2, 2012. pp. 49–56. BUL, CSSL, IRMAL, SPIESRL, SUL, UML.

Devy, Ganesh. Tribal voice and violence. *Seminar.* 513, 2002. pp. 39–48. CSSL, MICAL, UML.

Devy, Ganesh. Adivasi mahashweta. *Seminar.* 540, 2004. pp. 21–24. CSSL, MICAL, UML.

Dholakia, Ravindra H. and Patel, P.M. Relative growth of tribal population in Gujarat. *Journal of the Gujarat Research Society.* 40, 3/148, 1978. pp. 30–38. GVL.

Dikshit, Moreshwar G. History of Buddhism in Gujarat. *Journal of the Gujarat Research Society.* 8, 2 and 3, 1946. pp. 95–112. GUL.

Dixit, Anita K. Dilution of the public distribution system fallout on tribal communities in Gujarat. *Social Action.* 57,1, 2007. pp. 65–73. CSSL, IRMAL.

Dutta, Indira. Sustainable development in Gujarat-a far cry. *Indian Journal of Public Administration.* 57, 4, 2011. pp. 897–912. CSSL.

Gangrade, K.D. Salt satyagraha: Gandhi's approach to mass awakening. *IASSI Quarterly.* 23, 1, 2004. pp. 5–24. AAUL, CSSL.

Ganguly, Varsha. Displacement, rehabilitation and resettlement: the case of Maldhari families of Gir forest. *Sociological Bulletin.* 54, 1, 2005. pp. 3–17. CSSL.

Gaurha, R.S. Technologies in M.P.A.P. Gujarat and Maharashtra. *Rural India.* 42, 4, 1979. pp. 112–117. IIML.

Haque, M. Anthropometry of the Padar of Ranagadh, Gujarat. *Man in India.* 64, 3, 1984. pp. 294–303. CSSL, UML.

Hardiman, David. Class base of Swaminarayan sect. *Economic and Political Weekly.* 23, 37, 1988. pp. 1907–1912. CEPTL, CSSL, IIML, IRMAL, SGUL, SPIESRL, UML.

Hardiman, David. Purifying the nation: the Arya Samaj in Gujarat 1895–1930. *Indian Economic and Social History Review.* 44, 1, 2007. pp. 41–67. CSSL, GVL, HML, IIML, IRMAL, UML.

Hathi, Tushar. Social exclusion and social protection in Gujarat. *Vishleshan.* 39, 1, 2013. pp. 49–74. CSSL.

Ibrahim, Farhana. Islamic 'Reform', the nation-state and the liberal subject: the cultural politics of identity in Kachchh, Gujarat. *Contributions to Indian Sociology.* 42, 2, 2008. pp. 191–217. AAUL, CSSL, GIDRL, HML, IRMAL, MICAL, UML.

Ibrahim, Farhana. Region and its margins: re-appropriations of the border from 'Mahagujarat' to 'Swarnim Gujarat'. *Economic and Political Weekly.* 47, 32, 2012. pp. 66–72. BUL, CSSL, IRMAL, SPIESRL, SUL, UML.

Irani, Atusha Bharucha. Urbanization in early historic Gujarat. *Indica.* 41, 2, 2004. pp. 103–116. BUL, HML.

Iyengar, Sudarshan. Role of non-governmental organisations in development of Gujarat. *Economic and Political Weekly.* 35, 35 and 36, 2000. pp. 3229–3236. BUL, CEPTL, CSSL, GIDRL, IIML, IRMAL, MICAL, SGUL, SPIESRL, UML.

Iyengar, Sudarshan. Voluntary initiatives for tribal development in Gujarat. *Journal of Entrepreneurship.* 7, 2, 1998. pp. 211–235. EDIL, IRMAL.

Jaitley, Arun. Gujarat revolt. *Seminar.* 176, 1974. pp. 30–32. On Navnirman Andolan. CSSL, GIDRL, UML.

Jayaraman, T.K. Quantitative analysis of fire protection as an urban service: a case study of Baroda. *Nagarlok.* 10, 1, 1978. pp. 51–65. CEPTL.

Jhala, C.I. and Mankad, B.D. Dietary survey of 100 Gujarati families in Ahmedabad. *Journal of the Gujarat Research Society*. 24, 3/95, 1962. pp. 199–205. GVL.

Jhala, P.J. Population of Gujarat: an overview and perspective. (Gujarat 2010: Challenges and opportunities). *Anvesak*. 31, 1–2, 2001. pp. 1–15. CSSL, GIDRL, SPIESRL.

Jones, Dawn E. and Jones, Rodney W. Urban upheaval in India: the 1974 Nav Nirman riots in Gujarat. *Asian Survey*. 16, 11, 1976. pp. 1012–1033. CSSL.

Joshi, Sanat. Power structure and social change in a town in Gujarat. *South Gujarat University Journal*. 2–3, 1973–1974. pp. 119–120. GVL.

Joshi, Vidyut. Impact of ship breaking industry on a coastal village in Gujarat. *Eastern Anthropologist*. 58, 3–4, 2005. pp. 509–518. CSSL, SGUL.

Kajarekar, R.G. Urban housing in Gujarat. *Nirbhay*. 4, 1, 1978. pp. 32–43. TRTIL.

Kanakalath, Mukund. Urbanization and the regional economy of Gujarat in the seventeenth century. *India Past and Present*. 4, 1, 1987. pp. 79–104. HML.

Kapadia, K.M. Changing patterns of Hindu marriage and family. *Sociological Bulletin*. 3, 1, 1954. pp. 61–87. CSSL.

Kapadia, K.M. Changing patterns of Hindu marriage and family-II. *Sociological Bulletin*. 3, 2, 1954. pp. 131–157. CSSL.

Kapadia, K.M. Growth of townships in South Gujarat: Maroli bazar. *Sociological Bulletin*. 10, 2, 1961. pp. 69–87. CSSL, TRTIL.

Kashyap, S.P. Perspective on Gujarat's development with emphasis on human resources. *(Gujarat-2010: Challenges and Opportunities)*. *Anvesak*. 31, 1–2, 2001. pp. 190–213. CSSL, GIDRL, SPIESRL.

Khan, M.E. and Ghosh, B. Determinants of family planning performance at PHC level: some observations from a mass vasectomy campaign in Gujarat. *Journal of Family Welfare*. 25, 3, 1979. pp. 3–19. GVL.

Khare, Harish. Quality men of Ahmedabad. *Muslim India*. 8, 94, 1990. pp. 462–463. GVL.

Koppar, D.H. Economic development and culture change among Dangis. *Adivasi Gujarat*. 1, 1, 1978. pp. 47–53. CSSL, GVL, SPIESRL, TRTIL.

Kotak, Rekha, Dave, Alka and Murty, Sukumar. Population growth and literacy rate in Gujarat: an analysis based on 1991 census data. *Anvesak*. 26, 2, 1996. pp. 25–37. CSSL, GIDRL, IRMAL, SPIESRL.

Kulkarni, K.M. Patterns of social well-being in micro regions of Gujarat: a regional analysis. *Indian Journal of Social Work*. 47, 4, 1987. pp. 389–398. GVL.

Kumar, A. and Joshi, K.M. Family planning methods among the tribal population in South Gujarat: a case study of access and usage. *Development in Practice*. 18, 2, 2008. pp. 258–266. CSSL, IRMAL.

Kundu, Amitabh. Globalising Gujarat: urbanisation, employment and poverty. *Economic and Political Weekly*. 35, 35 and 36, 2000. pp. 3172–3182. BUL, CEPTL, CSSL, IIML, IRMAL, MICAL, SGUL, SPIESRL, UML.

Lal, R.B. Impact of industrialisation on tribals in South Gujarat. *Journal of the Gujarat Research Society*. 37, 3/145, 1975. pp. 26–38. GVL.

Lal, R.B. Social and cultural life in the Dangs a note on some aspects of the tribal. *Adivasi Gujarat*. 1, 1, 1978. pp. 9–27. CSSL, GVL, SPIESRL, TRTIL.

Lal, R.B. Socio-cultural aspects of the people: Vasava Bhils. *Adivasi Gujarat*. 7, 1, 1997. pp. 4–18. CSSL, GVL, TRTIL.

Lal, R.B. Tribals of Gujarat. *Tribals Research Bulletin*. 3, 2, 1981. pp. 25–35. TRTIL.

Lobo, Lancy. Conversion, emigration and social mobility of an ex-scheduled caste from Central Gujarat. *Social Action*. 39, 4, 1989. pp. 423–437. CSSL, IRMAL.

Lobo, Lancy. Koli Kshatriyas of North Gujarat: a shift from sanskritised mobility to politicized mobility. *Eastern Anthropologist*. 42, 2, 1989. pp. 171–192. CSSL.

Lobo, Lancy. Tribals and Christianity in Gujarat. *Eastern Anthropologist*. 56, 2–4, 2003. pp. 311–326. CSSL.

Majumdar, D.N. and Bahadur, S. Study of height and weight of the castes and tribes of Gujarat. *Man in India*. 29, 2, 1949. pp. 110–123. TRTIL, UML.

Majumdar, D.N. and Bahadur, S.N. Comparative study of height and weight of the castes and tribes of Gujarat. *Journal of the Gujarat Research Society*. 11, 3, 1949. pp. 161–171. GUL.

Majumdar, D.N. and Sen, A.R. Anthropometric status of the castes and tribes of Maha-Gujarat. *Journal of the Gujarat Research Society*. 11, 3, 1949. pp. 118–160. GUL.

Majmudar, M.R. Dwarka image of Ranachhodji and the temple at Dakore. *Journal of the University of Bombay*. 16, 4, 1948. pp. 57–91. GVL.

Mann, R.S. Stratification in tribal Gujarat and development perspective. *Indian Anthropologist*. 12, 1, 1982. pp. 37–47. CSSL.

Masavi, M.I. Income and levels of living in tribal areas of Gujarat. *Khadi Gramodyog*. 22, 4, 1976. pp. 195–200. GVL, SGUL, TRTIL.

Masavi, M.I. Problem of land alienation among tribals of Gujarat. *Journal of the Gujarat Research Society*. 37, 3/145, 1975. pp. 39–63. GVL, TRTIL.

Masavi, Mustali I. Dynamics of socio economic life of Gujarat. *Khadi Gramodyog*. 30, 8, 1984. pp. 348–352. GVL, TRTIL.

Masavi, Mustali I. Indebtedness and exploitation in tribal areas of Gujarat. *Khadi Gramodyog*. 27, 1, 1980. pp. 71–77. GVL.

Masavi, Mustali I. and Naik, K.S. Economy of small towns in Gujarat. *Khadi Gramodyog*. 18, 2, 1971. pp. 151–154. TRTIL.

Masavi, Mustali I. and Shah, Kokila J. Socio-economic issues of weaker sections: a study of scheduled castes in Gujarat. *Khadi Gramodyog*. 41, 9, 1990. pp. 374–381. GVL.

Mathur, Navdeep. On the Sabarmati riverfront: urban planning as totalitarian governance in Ahmedabad. *Economic and Political Weekly*. 47, 47 and 48, 2012. pp. 64–75. BUL, CSSL, IRMAL, SPIESRL, SUL, UML.

Mazumdar, Kumkum. Distribution of tribal population in Eastern Gujarat. *National Geographical Journal of India*. 19, 3–4, 1973. pp. 177–192. HML.

Mehta, Dinesh B. Urban development strategy for Gujarat-an over view. *Vishleshan*. 20, 1, 1995. pp. 25–38. IIML.

Mehta, Meera. Metropolitan housing market: a study of Ahmedabad. *Artha Vijnana*. 33, 2, 1991. pp. 155–56. GIDRL, UML.

Mehta, Meera. Urban housing processes and the poor: a case study of Ahmedabad. *Nagarlok*. 14, 2, 1982. pp. 106–128. CEPTL.

Mehta, Meera, Mehta, Dinesh and Shivanand Swamy, H.M. Metropolitan housing analysis: a case of Ahmedabad. *Nagarlok*. 20, 1, 1988. pp. 69–86. CEPTL, SPIESRL.

Mehta, Niti. Food security aspects and diversification of demand in the context of Gujarat. *Anvesak*. 42, 1 and 2, 2012. pp. 31–74. CSSL, SPIESRL, TRTIL.

Modi, D.M. Philosophical ideas of the Gita subsidiary to its teaching of disinterested action, Yoga with special reference to San Karu's, interpretation. *Journal of the Gujarat Research Society*. 2, 3, 1950. pp. 123–139. GUL.

Momin, K.N. Chalcolithic settlement in Kaira District, Gujarat. *Journal of the M.S. University of Baroda.* 22–23, 1, 1973–74. pp. 53–56. GVL.

Momin, K.N. Explorations in Kaira District, Gujarat. *Journal of the M.S. University of Baroda.* 24, 1, 1975. pp. 83–92. GVL.

Moses, S.T. Problem of task management in Gujarat. *Journal of the Gujarat Research Society.* 14, 2, 1952. pp. 85–90. GVL.

Mukherjee, Dhurjati. Khadi programme in Tamil Nadu and Gujarat. *Khadi Gramodyog.* 21, 10, 1975. pp. 460–466. TRTIL.

Mukherjee, Ramkrishna. I.P. Desai and sociology of India. *Economic and Political Weekly.* 21, 4, 1986. pp. 164–168. CEPTL, CSSL, GUL, IIML, IRMAL, SGUL, SPIESRL, UML.

Nagar, G.P. Somnath: the shrine eternal. *Bhavan's Journal.* 29, 13, 1983. pp. 45–47. GVL.

Naik, T.B. Recreation among the primitives of Gujarat. *Journal of the Gujarat Research Society.* 14, 1, 1952. pp. 22–29. GUL, GVL.

Naik, T.B. Anthropology, history and micro planning: an essays into interdisciplinary approach to three social sciences. *Adivasi Gujarat.* 4, 2, 1982. pp. 15–23. CSSL, GVL, SPIESRL, TRTIL.

Nanavati, Arti. Performance evaluation of non-government development organisations: a study in Vadodara, Gujarat. *Journal of Health Management.* 9, 2, 2007. pp. 275–299. CSSL.

Nanavati, Manilal B. Village in Gujarat: a study. *Indian Journal of Agricultural Economics.* 16, 2, 1961. pp. 1–11. HML, IIML, UML.

Nath, Viswa. Female infanticide and the Lewa Kanbis of Gujarat in the nineteenth century. *Indian Economic and Social History Review.* 10, 4, 1973. pp. 386–404. CSSL, UML.

Naz, Farhat. Swaminarayan movement and Gujarati diasporic identity. *Man In India.* 87, 1 and 2, 2007. pp. 129–136. CSSL, UML.

Neveling, Patrick. Structural contingencies and untimely coincidences in the making of neoliberal India: the Kandla free trade zone, 1965–91. *Contributions to Indian Sociology.* 48, 1, 2014. pp. 17–43. CSSL, UML.

Pakvasa, Purnima. Twinkling star in the dark nook: literacy among tribal and the village folk among the Dangs. *IASSI Quarterly.* 16, 2, 1997. pp. 140–147. IIML.

Panchanadikar, K.C. and Panchanadikar, J. Social stratification and institutional change in a Gujarat village. *Sociological Bulletin.* 25, 2, 1976. pp. 225–240. CSSL, HML.

Pandya, Arun N. Impact of recent dynamics of the communicative patterns on a prinstly caste of Central Gujarat: some observations. *VNSGU Journal of Humanities & Social Sciences.* 3, 1, 2011. pp. 110–118. CSSL.

Pandya, B.V. Economic conditions of scheduled castes in Ahmedabad district. *Journal of the University of Bombay.* 26, 4, 1958. pp. 110–113. GVL.

Pandya, B.V. Occupation pattern of scheduled castes in Ahmedabad district. *Journal of the Gujarat Research Society.* 19, 2/74, 1957. pp. 112–124. GVL.

Pandya, D.G. Development of India's secondary cities: a study of Gujarat. *Nagarlok.* 18, 4, 1986. pp. 57–65. CEPTL.

Pandya, Dhaval J. Demographic profile of Surat city. *Vishleshan.* 36, 2, 2011. pp. 32–40. CSSL, IIML.

Pantham, Thomas. On total revolution: learning from the protest movement in Gujarat and Bihar, review article. *Journal of the M.S. University of Baroda.* 27–28, 2, 1978–79. pp. 106–116. GVL.

Parekh, V.S. Image of double-faced Ganesha from Junagadh. *Journal of the Oriental Institute*. 27, 1–2, 1977. pp. 40–42. GVL.

Parikh, Gokul O. Total literacy campaign: Gujarat experience. *Anvesak*. 27, 1 and 2, 1997. pp. 139–158. GIDRL, IRMAL, SPIESRL.

Parikh, Ramlal. Literacy in Gujarat. *Indian Journal of Adult Education*. 58, 2, 1997. pp. 28–32. IRMAL, SGUL.

Parmar, M.N. and Solanki, Jagdish. United way of Vadodara. *Social Welfare*. 42, 12, 1996. pp. 15–18. GVL.

Patel, Arjun. Hinduisation of adivasis: a case of South Gujarat. *Indian Journal of Secularism*. 1, 1, 1997. pp. 30–55. CSSL.

Patel, Chandrakant S. Halpati-Talavia: an evaluation study of housing scheme. *Adivasi Gujarat*. 15, 1, 2005. pp. 1–28. CSSL, GVL, TRTIL.

Patel, Chhaya. Indigenising social work education: a case study from Baroda. *Indian Journal of Social Work*. 62, 2, 2001. pp. 197–218. BUL, CSSL.

Patel, I.C. and Kher, A.O. Integrated rural development in Kutch (Gujarat). *Rural India*. 42, 9, 1979. pp. 222–225. IIML.

Patel, J.C. Sociological study of migrant tribal farm labourers in villages of Anand district of Gujarat. *Man & Development*. 27, 1, 2005. pp. 125–136. BUL, CSSL, GIDRL, GVL, IRMAL, UML.

Patel, Kalhans. Enduring form of dwellings in Gujarat. (Field Work Report). *Man in India*. 67, 3, 1987. pp. 276–286. CSSL, HML, UML.

Patel, Madhukant. Housing problem in urban Gujarat. *Vishleshan*. 12, 3–4, 1986. pp. 86–103. CSSL, GIDRL.

Patel, Madhukant. Note on urbanization pattern in Gujarat. *Nagarlok*. 17, 3, 1985. pp. 33–46. CEPTL.

Patel, Tara. Some reflections on the attitude of married couples towards family planning. *Sociological Bulletin*. 12, 2, 1963. pp. 1–13. CSSL, HML.

Pichholiya, K.R. Urbanisation in Gujarat. *Nagarlok*. 15, 3, 1983. pp. 51–61. CEPTL.

Pool, Robert. Beliefs concerning the avoidance of food during pregnancy and the immediate post-partum period in a tribal area of rural Gujarat, India. *Eastern Anthropologist*. 39, 3, 1986. pp. 251–259. CSSL, HML, TRTIL.

Poonacha, Veena and Pandey, Divya. Responses to domestic violence: government and non-government action in Karnataka and Gujarat. *Economic and Political Weekly*. 35, 7, 2000. pp. 566–574. BUL, CEPTL, CSSL, IIML, IRMAL, MICAL, SGUL, SPIESRL, UML.

Possehl, Gregory L. Harappan civilization in Gujarat: the Sorath and Sindhi Harappans. *Eastern Anthropologist*. 45, 1–2, 1992. pp. 117–154. CSSL.

Pramar, V.S. Sociology of the North Gujarat urban house. *Contributions to Indian Sociology*. 21, 2, 1987. pp. 331–345. CSSL, IRMAL, UML.

Punalekar, S.P. Rehabilitation of institutionalized children: a case study. *Indian Journal of Social Work*. 46, 2, 1985. pp. 231–242. CSSL.

Punalekar, S.P. Voluntary action and rehabilitation: a case of Narmada dam oustees in Gujarat state. *Indian Journal of Social Work*. 44, 4, 1984. pp. 353–364. CSSL.

Purohit, M.L. et al. Imbalances in food consumption and nutrition in Kutch district of Gujarat. *Agricultural Economics Research Review*. 10, 1, 1997. pp. 127–131. IRMAL.

Purohit, Y.S. Ageing in Gujarat: trend analysis of population census. *Vishleshan*. 32, 4, 2007. pp. 28–35. BUL, CSSL.

Rajyalakshmi, C. Population education component in total literacy campaign in a district of Gujarat. *Social Change*. 22, 3, 1992. pp. 19–30. CSSL, HML, IRMAL, UML.

Rami, Gaurang. Social exclusion and social protection: meaning, genesis and policy reflections in Gujarat. *Vishleshan*. 39, 1, 2013. pp. 19–48. CSSL.

Rao, Bahadur and Kavi, C.D. Is the garden of Gujarat becoming a desert? *Journal of the Gujarat Research Society*. 3, 4, 1941. pp. 229–235. GVL.

Rathord, P.V. and Kumar, Vijay. Working of the scheduled castes and scheduled tribes (Prevention of Atrocities) act 1989 in Gujarat. *Administrator*. 42, 1, 1997. pp. 185–201. CSSL, IRMAL.

Ratnawali. Supplementary nutrition to women and children a situational analysis of Anganwadis in tribal areas of Gujarat. *Social Change*. 40, 3, 2010. pp. 319–343. CSSL, IRMAL, UML.

Rawal, R.L. Tradition and modernity in the context of social reform movement in Gujarat during the nineteenth century. *Vidya: The Journal of Gujarat University*. 19, 2, 1976. pp. 88–102. SGUL.

Ray, C.N. Implementation of IRDP: a comparative study of West Bengal and Gujarat. *Journal of Rural Development*. 11, 1, 1992. pp. 69–100. CSSL, IIML.

Ray, C.N. Rural water quality problem and role of NGO in Gujarat. *Indian Journal of Public Administration*. 48, 2, 2002. pp. 236–246. CSSL, GIDRL.

Ray, C.N. Traditional neighbourhoods in a walled city: Pols in Ahmedabad. *Sociological Bulletin*. 57, 3, 2008. pp. 337–352. BUL, CSSL, IIML.

Raychaudhuri, Siddhartha. Colonialism, indigenous elites and the transformation of cities in the non-western world: Ahmedabad(Western India), 1890–1947. *Modern Asian Studies*. 35, 3, 2001. pp. 677–726. HML.

Roy, Nilima. Ahmedabad temple cloth. *Vanyajati*. 19, 4, 1971. pp. 155–161. CSSL, TRTIL.

Sachidananda. Crime and punishment in a Mundra village. *Man in India*. 37, 2, 1957. pp. 124–132. TRTIL, UML.

Saha, Shovan K. Spatital approch to urban renewal: Surat. *Nagarlok*. 31, 4, 1999. pp. 16–23. CEPTL, SPIESRL.

Sahu, S.N. Understanding the enduring significance of Dandi march. *Gandhian Perspectives*. 12,2, 2004 and 13, 1, 2005. pp. 104–115. CSSL.

Sajitha, Og and Parthasarathy, R. Whose child out of school to do work socio-economic and demographic determinants of child workers out of school, Gujarat. *Man in India*. 89, 1–2, 2009. pp. 205–213. CSSL, IRMAL, UML.

Sankalia, H.D. In search of early man along the Sabarmati. *Journal of the Gujarat Research Society*. 5, 2, 1943. pp. 75–86. GVL.

Saraswati, Baidyanath. Note on Rabbari caste panchayat. *Man in India*. 42, 3, 1962. pp. 195–205. SPUL, UML.

Sen, Arup Kumar. Gandhian experiment in Ahmedabad: towards a Gramscian reading. *Economic and Political Weekly*. 27, 37, 1992. pp. 1987–1989. On capital-labour conflict. CEPTL, CSSL, IIML, IRMAL, SGUL, SPIESRL, UML.

Sengupta, Smitha. Residential typology of Ahmedabad, India. *Indian Geographical Journal*. 63, 1, 1988. pp. 22–28. HML.

Sethna, Suresh M. Need for a nutritional survey of Gujarat. *Journal of the Gujarat Research Society*. 2, 4, 1940. pp. 213–219. GUL.

SEWA Relief Team. Re-building our lives. *Seminar*. 513, 2002. pp. 64–67. CSSL, GVL, MICAL, SPUL, UML.

Shah, A.M. Changes in the Indian family: an examination of some assumptions. *Economic and Political Weekly*. 3, 1 and 2, 1968. pp. 127–134. CSSL, IRMAL, SPIESRL, UML.

Shah, A.M. Division and hierarchy: an overview of caste in Gujarat. *Contributions to Indian Sociology*. 16, 1, 1982. pp. 1–33. AAUL, CSSL, HML, IRMAL, UML.

Shah, A.M. For a more humane society. *Seminar*. 513, 2002. pp. 58–60. CSSL, MICAL, SPUL, UML.

Shah, A.M. Government programme to train scheduled caste priests. *Eastern Anthropologist*. 62, 3, 2009. pp. 399–401. CSSL.

Shah, A.M. History and sociology of Central Gujarat: ideology and reality. *Contributions to Indian Sociology*. 44, 3, 2010. pp. 407–424. CSSL, HML, UML.

Shah, A.M. Note on the Hijadas of Gujarat. *American Anthropologist*. 63, 6, 1961. pp. 1325–1330. HML.

Shah, A.M. Sociology in a regional context. *Seminar*. 495, 2000. pp. 45–49. CSSL, MICAL, UML.

Shah, Ghanshyam. Agitations in Gujarat. *Seminar*. 375, 1990. pp. 54–57. CSSL, GIDRL, UML.

Shah, Ghanshyam. Caste, class and the state. *Seminar*. 367, 1990. pp. 31–35. CSSL, GIDRL, UML.

Shah, Ghanshyam. Ethnicity and politics: a study of scheduled tribes in Gujarat. *Indian Journal of Social Science*. 2, 1, 1989. pp. 61–76. CEPTL, IIML.

Shah, Ghanshyam. Gap between representatives and constituents: an aspect of tribal society in Gujarat. *Economic and Political Weekly*. 8, 31–33, 1973. pp. 1441–1444. CSSL, IRMAL, SPIESRL, TRTIL, UML.

Shah, Ghanshyam. Hope and despair: a study of untouchability and atrocities in Gujarat. *Journal of Indian School of Political Economy*. 12, 3 and 4, 2000. pp. 459–472. CSSL, GIDRL, IRMAL.

Shah, Ghanshyam. Polarised communities. *Seminar*. 470, 1998. pp. 30–35. CEPTL, CSSL, IRMAL, MICAL, UML.

Shah, Ghanshyam. Traditional society and political mobilization: the experience of Bardoli satyagraha (1920–1928). *Contributions to Indian Sociology*. 8, 1974. pp. 89–107. CSSL, SPUL, UML.

Shah, Ghanshyam and Desai, Kiran. Globalization and the poor a study of Gujarat. *IASSI Quarterly*. 29, 2, 2010. pp. 43–67. CSSL, IRMAL.

Shah, Haku. Tribals live life. *Adivasi Gujarat*. 1, 1, 1978. pp. 3–8. CSSL, GVL, SPIESRL, TRTIL.

Shah, Kirtee. Housing for the urban poor in Ahmedabad: an integrated urban development approach. *Social Action*. 27, 3, 1977. pp. 335–352. CSSL.

Shah, Maya. Variations in literacy rates and underlying socio-economic factors: a case study of Chorasi taluka in Surat district for 1971. *Journal of the M.S. University of Baroda*. 24, 2, 1980. pp. 153–160. GVL.

Shah, P.G. Anthropology in Gujarat. *Journal of the Gujarat Research Society*. 1, 3, 1939. pp. 5–15. GUL.

Shah, P.G. Anthropometric survey of Maha Gujarat. *Journal of the Gujarat Research Society*. 11, 3, 1949. pp. 115–117. GUL.

Shah, P.G. Literacy in Gujarat. *Journal of the Gujarat Research Society*. 1, 2, 1939. pp. 1–13. GUL.

Sharma, Abha. Opinions of married couples regarding the selection of the marriage partner: a study of couples residing in Baroda. *Sociological Bulletin*. 28, 1–2, 1979. 71–82. CSSL, IIML.

Sharma, Hina. Success story of reconstructing livelihoods in Gujarat through micro credit helpage activity. *Research and Development Journal*, 10, 2, 2004. pp. 32–34. IRMAL.

Shenoy, G.V. and Raju, K.V. Effectiveness of cattle insurance under IRDP: analysis of evidence from Pune and Surat district. *Journal of Rural Development*. 8, 4, 1989. pp. 341–358. CSSL.

Shenoy, Lalitha. Gujarat: of Lord Krishna and Mahatma Gandhi. *Bhavans's Journal*. 52, 1, 2005. pp. 125–132. GVL.

Shepherd, Andrew. Planning and government intervention in the unregulated urban economy: the Rabaris of Ahmedabad. *Nagarlok*. 12, 1, 1980. pp. 73–83. CEPTL.

Shroff, Ramesh. Habitat economy and society in the tribal area of Gujarat. *Tribal Research Bulletin*. 14, 1, 1992. pp. 15–19. TRTIL.

Shull, E.M. Worship of the Tiger-God and religious rituals associated with Tigers among the Dangi hill tribes of the Dangs district, Gujarat state Western India. *Eastern Anthropologist*. 21, 2, 1968. pp. 203–204. SGUL, TRTIL.

Shylendra, H.S. Environmental rehabilitation and livelihood impact: emerging trends from Ethiopia and Gujarat. *Economic and Political Weekly*. 37, 31, 2002. pp. 3286–3292. BUL, CEPTL, CSSL, EDIL, GIDRL, IIML, IRMAL, MICAL, SGUL, SPIESRL, UML.

Shylendra, H.S., Guha, Sampati and Veerashekharappa. Role of SHGs as micro-financial intermediaries: a study in Sabarkantha district of Gujarat. *Journal of Rural Development*. 29, 4, 2010. pp. 399–423. CSSL.

Siddhinathananda, Swami. Somanath, the shrine eternal. *Bhavan's Journal*. 39, 14, 1993. pp. 39–41. GVL.

Sikligar, P.C. Women's empowerment under the Wavli system a study on tribal women in South Gujarat in India. *Asia Pacific Journal of Rural Development*. 14, 2, 2004. pp. 14–23. IRMAL.

Simpson, Edward. Changing perspectives of three Muslim men on the question of saint worship over a 10-year period in Gujarat, Western India. *Modern Asian Studies*. 42, 2/3, 2008. pp. 377–403. CSSL.

Simpson, Edward. 'Gujarat' earthquake and the political economy of nostalgia. *Contributions to Indian Sociology*. 39, 2, 2005. pp. 219–249. AAUL, CSSL, GIDRL, HML, IRMAL, UML.

Simpson, Edward. Migration and Islamic reform in a port town of Western India. *Contributions to Indian Sociology*. 37, 1 and 2, 2003. pp. 83–108. CSSL, MICAL, UML.

Singh, M.M. Gujarat police: two years of achievements. *Gujarat Police Journal*. 7, 1, 1988. pp. 3–7. GVL.

Singh, Surjit. Total literacy campaign: Gujarat experience. *Anvesak*. 27, 1–2, 1997. pp. 139–158. CEPTL, SPIESRL.

Skaria, Ajay. Homeless in Gujarat and India: on the curious love of Indulal Yagnik. *Indian Economic and Social History Review*. 38, 3, 2001. pp. 271–297. CSSL, GIDRL, IIML, IRMAL, UML.

Skaria, Ajay. Some aporias of history: time, truth and play in Dangs, Gujarat. *Economic and Political Weekly*. 34, 15, 1999. pp. 897–904. CEPTL, CSSL, GIDRL, IIML, IRMAL, MICAL, SGUL, SPIESRL, UML.

Solanki, Siddharaj Soorjibhai. Tribal research in Gujarat during 1967–77. *Adivasi Gujarat*. 1, 2, 1978. pp. 20–44. CSSL, GVL, SPIESRL, TRTIL.

Somani, V.J. Socio-economic development of tribals through crossbred Cows in Surat district of Gujarat state in India. *Vishleshan*. 32, 4, 2007. pp. 5–27. BUL, CSSL.

Sonawane, V.H. Fresh light on the specialized crafts of the Harappans in Gujarat. *Eastern Anthropologist*. 45, 1–2, 1992. pp. 155–172. CSSL.

Sopher, David V. Pilgrim circulation in Gujarat. *(Reprinted From) Geographical Review*. 58, 3, 1968. pp. 392–425. CSSL.

Spodek, Howard. Crises and response: Ahmedabad 2000. *Economic and Political Weekly*. 36, 19, 2001. pp. 1627–1638. BUL, CEPTL, CSSL, EDIL, IIML, IRMAL, MICAL, SGUL, SPIESRL, UML.

Sud, Nikita. Secularism and the Gujarat state: 1960–2005. *Modern Asian Studies*. 42, 6, 2008. pp. 1251–1281. IRMAL.

Swayam, S. Sites of ritual construction of identities: a fresh look at the memorial stones of Gujarat. *Man in India*. 84, 3 and 4, 2004. pp. 303–339. CSSL, GVL, UML.

Thaker, Hrima H. and Shiyani, R.L. Socio-economic development in Gujarat: rosy picture with concerns. *Journal of Rural Development*. 28, 4, 2009. pp. 515–528. CSSL, EDIL, IIML.

Thakkar, Usha. Puppets on the periphery: women and social reform in 19th century Gujarati society. *Economic and Political Weekly*. 32, 1 and 2, 1997. pp. 46–52. CEPTL, CSSL, GIDRL, IIML, IRMAL, MICAL, SGUL, SPIESRL, UML.

Thakor, V.M. Gujarat first backward class. *Farmer*. 6, 1955. pp. 49-[ ]. GVL.

Tikekar, S.R. Maharashta and Gujarat. *Bhavan's Journal*. 17, 20, 1971. pp. 43–50. GVL.

Tiwary, Akhileshwar. Little herdsmen of Kutch. *Social Welfare*. 35, 2, 1988. pp. 13–14. GVL.

Trivedi, Harshad R. and Solanki, Siddharaj S. Some aspect of tribal land systems and their development in Gujarat. *Adivasi Gujarat*. 4, 1, 1981. pp. 94–103. GVL, SPIESRL, TRTIL.

Trivedi, J.H. and Vaidya, M.P. Report on intelligence testing of Gujarati speaking children. *Journal of the Gujarat Research Society*. 12, 2, 1950. pp. 51–76. GUL.

Trivedi, Jayprakash M. Globalization and changing caste and gender relations among the educated youth in Central Gujarat. *Prajna*. 14, 2012. pp. 55–59. SPUL.

Trivedi, Jigna, Girach, Arshad and Patel, Samip. Self help groups: an instrument for women empowerment. *Anvesak*. 41, 1, 2011. pp. 97–108. CSSL, SPIESRL.

Trivedi, P.M. Mainland of Gujarat: a study in regional setting and regional ecology. *Journal of the Gujarat Research Society*. 3, 2, 1941. pp. 81–93. GVL.

Upadhyay, Chandrakant and Pancholi, Ravindra. Census study of primitive tribal groups of Gujarat state. *Adivasi Gujarat*. 13, 2, 2003. pp. 41–49. CSSL, GVL, SPIESRL, TRTIL.

Vakil, C.N. and Patel, M.H. Social and economic structure of greater Gujarat. *Journal of the Gujarat Research Society*. 1, 1, 1939. pp. 39–54. GUL.

Vakil, C.N. and Patel, M.H. Social and economic structure of greater Gujarat-II: Occupations. *Journal of the Gujarat Research Society*. 1, 2, 1939. pp. 38–47. GUL.

Vakil, C.N. and Patel, M.H. Social and economic structure of greater Gujarat-III: Agriculture. *Journal of the Gujarat Research Society*. 1, 3, 1939. pp. 22–36. GUL.

Vakil, C.N. and Patel, M.H. Social and economic structure of greater Gujarat-IV: Industrial development of Gujarat. *Journal of the Gujarat Research Society*. 2, 3, 1940. pp. 139–148. GUL, GVL.

Van der Veen, Klaas W. Marriage and hierarchy among the Anavil brahmans of South Gujarat. *Contributions to Indian Sociology*. 7, 1973. pp. 36–52. CSSL, IRMAL, UML.

Van der Veer, Peter. Playing or praying: a Sufi saint's day in Surat. *Journal of Asian Studies*. 51, 3, 1992. pp. 545–564. CSSL.

Visaria, Pravin M. Priorities for the 1971 census. *Economic and Political Weekly*. 2, 42, 1967. pp. 1909–1916. CSSL, SPIESRL, UML.

Vishwanath, L.S. Pilgrimage centre in a tribal Area: the Surpaneshwar Shiva temple in Gujarat. *Man in India*. 65, 3, 1985. pp. 261–268. CSSL, UML.

Vyas, K.C. 'Avidha': a narration of changing life in a Gujarat village. *Sociological Bulletin*. 2, 1, 1953. pp. 18–34. HML.

Wadhva, Kiran. Evaluation of the urban land ceiling legislation: a case study of Ahmedabad. *Nagarlok*. 15, 2, 1983. pp. 76–86. CEPTL.

Wadhva, Kiran. Private sector and urban housing markets: a case study of Ahmedabad. *Nagarlok*. 18, 3, 1986. pp. 61–83. CEPTL.

Whitehead, Judith. Monitoring of Sardar Sarovar resettlers: a further critique. *Economic and Political Weekly*. 35, 45, 2000. pp. 3969–3976. BUL, CEPTL, CSSL, IIML, IRMAL, MICAL, SGUL, SPIESRL, UML.

Yajnik, Javerilal Umiashankar. Notices of Hindu tribes and castes in Gujarat. *Journal of the Bombay Branch of the Royal Asiatic Society*. 10, 28, 1871–74. pp. 93–119. GVL.

Zankharia, Kirti S. Urbanization in Gujarat: problems and prospects. *VNSGU Journal of Humanities & Social Sciences*. 3, 2, 2011. pp. 50–70. CSSL.

Working Papers, Reports and Other Materials

Acharya, Sanghmitra S. *Access to health care and patterns of discrimination: a study of dalit children in selected villages of Gujarat and Rajasthan*. New Delhi: Indian Institute of Dalit Studies and UNICEF, 2010. p. 38. Working Paper Series, Vol. 1, No. 02. CSSL.

Agrawal, Binod and Malek, M.R. *Television in Kheda: a social evaluation of site. (site/ssg/REG/64)*. Ahmedabad: Indian Space Research Organization, 1981. p. 163. SPIESRL.

Agro-Economic Research Centre. *Jambua (Panchmahals district, Gujarat) change in socio-economic life of a tribal village*. Vallabh Vidyanagar: Sardar Patel University, 1980. p. 208. Resurveys of Indian villages, No. 3. GIDRL, SPUL.

Ahmeda, Sara. *Who participates? the Case of rural women, an NGO and joint forest management in Gujarat*. Anand: Institute of Rural Management, 1995. p. 23. Working Paper No. 83. CSSL.

Aloria, G.R. Urbanisation and urban development. In *Gujarat-2010: challenges and opportunities*. By Government of Gujarat. Ahmedabad: Sardar Patel Institute of Economic & Social Research, 2001. pp. 64–72. Seminar volume. CSSL, EDIL, IRMAL, SGUL, SPIESRL.

Amin, R.K. *Valasan: socio-economic study of a Charotar village*. Vallabh Vidyanagar: Sardar Vallabhbhai Vidhyapeeth, p. 72. Studies in Rural Problems: one. GUL, IIML.

Bajpai, Gita and Hasan Mahmud S., ed. *Studies in social and economic change in Western India: Thirteenth to Twentieth centuries*. Baroda: M.S. University, [ ]. p. 78. CSSL.

Baks, Chris, et al. *Modernization, stagnation and steady decline: sociological contributions on social change in South Gujarat, India*. Holland: Centre for Comparative Social-Economic Studies, University of Utrecht, 1976. p. 313. Publication No. 1. CSSL.

Baranda, Babubhai S. *Lending policy for tribals*. Ahmedabad: Tribal Research & Training Institute, Gujarat Vidyapith, 2003. p. 98. Series-391. TRTIL.

Bhakta, Satish K. and Gandhi, R.D. *Evaluation study of the Antyodaya programme in Valod taluka of Surat district: a case study*. Ahmedabad: Gujarat Institute of Area Planning, 1978. p. 23. GIDRL, IIML.

Bhargava, Ashok. Immunization campaign in a rural area in Kachchh Gujarat, 1986–87. Ahmedabad: GIAP, 1988. p. 24. IRMAL.

Bharwada, Charul and Mahajan, Vinay. *Let it be Banni: understanding and sustaining pastoral livelihoods of Banni*. Hyderabad: Centre for Economic and Social Studies, 2012. p. 151. CESS Monograph, RULNR Monograph-13. CSSL.

Bharwada, Charul and Mahajan, Vinay. *Yet to be freed: agariyas' lives and struggle for survival in the little rann of Kutch*. Ahmedabad: Sandarbh Studies and National Consultation for Salt Workers, 2008. p. 76. CSSL.

Bhatt, Anil. *Micro action for development and social justice: a study of small action groups of weaker sections*. Ahmedabad: SETU: Centre for Social Knowledge and Action, 1985. p. 263. CSSL.

Bhatt, Mahesh. Housing problem of growing metropolis. In *Gujarat Economic Association conference papers, Baroda*. Ed. by V.S. Vyas, Pravin Visaria and A.R. Desai. Ahmedabad: Balgovind, 1971. pp. 210–218. GIDRL, IIML.

Bhatt, Mahesh and Chandra, V.K. *Some aspects of co-operative housing societies in Ahmedabad city*. Ahmedabad: Gujarat University, 1970. p. 67. Gujarat University Publication. GUL.

Bhende, Asha A., Rama Rao, G. and Jain, M.K. *Evaluation of the family planning: month in the context of family welfare programme in Bihar, Gujarat and Greater Bombay*. Bombay: International Institute for Population Studies, 1979. p. 354. GIDRL, IIML.

Bhim, Sarala. *Bhakti tradition in Gujarat*. Mumbai: University of Bombay, 1988. p. [ ]. BVL.

Bombay Presidency. *Gazetteer of the Bombay Presidency. Gujarat population: Hindus*. Vol. IX, part-I and II. Ed. by James M. Campbell. Bombay: Government Central Press, 1901. p. 594. Hindu castes and tribes of Gujarat. 2v. Compiled by Bhimbhai Kirparam. Gurgaon: Vintage, 1988. BUL, CSSL, SETUL, TRTIL.

Bose, Pradip Kumar. *Stratification among the scheduled tribes in the Vadodara, Sabarkantha and the Dangs districts of Gujarat*. Surat: Centre for Social Studies, 1978. p. 38. Research Report. CSSL, SPIESRL.

Bose, Pradip Kumar. *Traditional craft in a changing society potters & their craft in Gujarat*. Surat: Centre for Social Studies, 1980. p. 122. CSSL, GIDRL.

Centre for Social Studies. *Gujarat state urban slum policy development: a slum study in Ankleshwar town*. Surat: Centre for Social Studies, 2003. p. 61. CSSL.

Centre for Social Studies. *Gujarat state urban slum policy development: a slum study in Halol town*. Surat: Centre for Social Studies, 2003. p. 28. CSSL.

Centre for Social Studies. *Gujarat-tribal development vision-2010*. Surat: Centre for Social Studies, 2001. p. 178. CSSL.

Choudhary, K.M. and Bapat, M.T. *Study of impact of famine and relief measures in Gujarat and Rajasthan: with special reference to Banaskantha and Barmer district*.

Vallabh Vidyanagar: Agro-Economic Research Centre, 1975. p. 507. Research Study No. 44. AERCL, CSSL.

Christi, Anamika K. *Impact of education on socio-economic condition of tribal women of Chhota Udaipur taluka*. Anand (Vallabh Vidyanagar): Anand Institute of Social Work, Sardar Patel University, 2009. p. 133. AAL.

Citizen's Inquire Committee. *Untold story of Hindukaran (Proselytisation) of adivasis (tribals) in Dang, Gujarat*. New Delhi: Anhad, 2006. p. 30. CSSL.

Commerce Research Bureau. *Fifteen Adivasi villages of Gujarat*. Bombay: CRB, 1975. p. 109. GIDRL, UML.

Commerce Research Bureau. *Report on an integrated programme for eradication of extreme poverty in the village: Vani (Ahmedabad district, Gujarat)*. Bombay: Shri Sadguru Seva Sangh Trust, 1972. p. 48. CSSL, IIML.

Dalsania, Shanti M. Social and cultural aspects of Baroda city. In *Profiles of a growing city: the city of Baroda*. Ed. by K.N. Reddy, et al. Baroda: M.S. University, 1971. pp. 135–143. Souvenir: The 2nd Gujarat Economic conference, 2–3 January 1971. CSSL.

Das, B.R. *Identification of service centres in the tribal region of Panchmahals district, Gujarat*. Ahmedabad: Gujarat Institute Area Planning, 1978. p. 130. IIML.

Das, Biswaroop. *Dwelling environment and housing needs of rural poor in Northern and Central Gujarat*. Surat: Centre for Social Studies, 1998. p. 91. CSSL.

Das, Biswaroop. *Identification of service centre in the tribal region of Bharuch district*. Ahmedabad: Gujarat Institute of Area Planning, 1978. p. 101. IIML.

Das, Biswaroop. *Public utilities in an urban area: the case of Surat city*. Surat: Centre for Social Studies, 1987. p. 258. CSSL.

Das, Biswaroop. *Socio-economic profile of major social and religious groups in the slums of Surat city*. Surat: Centre for Social Studies, 1998. p. 125. Monograph. CSSL.

Das, Biswaroop. *Socio-economic study of slums in Surat city*. Surat: Centre for Social Studies, 1994. p. 211. CSSL.

Das, Biswaroop. *Some aspects of urbanization and city planning in Gujarat*. Centre for Social Studies, 1995. p. 19. Occasional Paper No. 20. CSSL, GIDRL, IRMAL.

Das, Biswaroop and Sinha, Ratnawali. *Socio-economic study of the Lodhva-Singsar region*. Surat: Centre for Social Studies, 2004. p. 95. CSSL.

Das, N.P. Growth and development of scheduled caste and scheduled tribe population in Gujarat and future prospects. In *Gujarat-2010: challenges and opportunities*. By Government of Gujarat. Ahmedabad: Sardar Patel Institute of Economic & Social Research, 2001. pp. 29–63. Seminar volume. CSSL, EDIL, IRMAL, SGUL, SPIESRL.

Das, N.P. and Dey, Devmoni. *Demographic transition in Gujarat*. Ahmedabad: D.T. Lakdawala Memorial trust, 2000. p. 39. Occasional Paper Series 2. CSSL, GIDRL.

Department of Sociology, Gujarat University. *Urbanisation in India and Gujarat: processes and problems: seminar January 25 and 26, 1975*. Ahmedabad: Department of Sociology, Gujarat University, 1975. p. 162. IIML, SGUL.

Desai, Anuradha. *Urban housing in Ahmedabad-India*. Ahmedabad: Foreign Students Department, 1991. p. 211. Series A, No. 15. SPIESRL.

Desai, I.P. *Glimpses of Surat*. Census of India 1971. New Delhi: Ministry of Home Affairs, 1972. p. 99. CSSL.

Desai, I.P. *Preliminary enquiry into the slogan of adivasi swayat (Autonomous) raj*. Surat: Centre for Regional Development Studies, 1970. p. 47. Study No. 6. CSSL.

Desai, I.P. *Some aspects of family in Mahuva: a sociological study of jointness in a small town*. New Delhi: Asia, 1964. p. 239. CSSL.

Desai, I.P. *Vedchhi movement*. Surat: Centre for Regional Development Studies, 1969. p. 158. CSSL.

Desai, I.P. *Water facilities for the untouchables in rural Gujarat*. New Delhi: Indian Council of Social Science Research (ICSSR), 1973. p. 101. ICSSR Occasional Monographs no-8. CSSL, GIDRL, IIML, UML.

Desai, Kiran. *Gujarat state urban slum policy development: a slum study in Porbandar town*. Surat: Centre for Social Studies, 2002. p. 72. CSSL.

Desai, M.B. Baroda city potentialities and pitfalls. In *Profiles of a growing city: the city of Baroda*. Ed. by K.N. Reddy, et al. Baroda: M.S. University, 1971. pp. 99–106. Souvenir: The 2nd Gujarat Economic Conference, 2–3 January 1971. CSSL.

Desai, M.D. *Dhanfulia: Junagadh district, Gujarat: economic life in a Saurashtra village*. Vallabh Vidyanagar: S.P. University, 1967. p. 223. Indian Village Studies No. 11. CSSL.

Dholakia, B.H. Demographic aspects of the growth of Baroda city. In *Profiles of a growing city: the city of Baroda*. Ed. by K.N. Reddy, et al. Baroda: M.S. University, 1971. pp. 52–59. Souvenir: The 2nd Gujarat Economic Conference, 2–3 January 1971. CSSL.

Doshi, Harish. Occupational diversification and removal of untouchability. In *Removal of Untouchability*. Ed. by Vimal P. Shah. Ahmedabad: Department of Sociology, Gujarat University, 1980. pp. 1–6. Seminar proceedings. CSSL, GIDRL.

Doshi, Harish and Joshi, Vidyut. *Benefits of prohibition: a study of the drinkers and the non-drinkers-rural*. Ahmedabad: Government of Gujarat, 1976. p. 151. CSSL.

Eldridge, Philip. *Some reflections on voluntary agencies and action group in Gujarat*. In International Seminar on "Gujarat Society", 17–20 December 1986. Surat: Centre for Social Studies, 1986. pp. 1–31. CSSL.

Fafale, A.B. *On conditions and some aspects of street children in Surat city*. Surat: Centre for Social Studies, 1993. p. [ ]. Seminar on Urban Poor in India, 10–11 February 1993. Unpublished Paper. CSSL.

Fischer, Eberhard and Shah, Haku. *Mogra Dev-tribal Crocodile Gods: wooden Crocodile images of Chodhri, Gamit and Vasava tribes, South Gujarat (India)*. Ahmedabad: Gujarat Vidyapith, 1971. p. 43. Monograph. CSSL.

Fischer, Eberhard. and Shah, Haku. *Vertra ne khambha-memorials for the dead: wooden figures and memorial slabs of Chodhri, Gamit and Vasava tribes, South Gujarat, India*. Ahmedabad: Gujarat Vidyapith, 1973. p. 60. SPUL.

Gandhi, R.D. *Disparities in the availability of basic amenities in the rural areas of Gujarat*. Ahmedabad: Gujarat Institute of Area Planning, 1978. p. 26. CSSL, SPIESRL.

Gandotra, M.M. Population. In *Gujarat Economy in 2001 A.D.: a study in perspective*. Ahmedabad: Sardar Patel Institute of Economic & Social Research, 1980. p. 40. Monograph Series No. 8. GUL.

Gandotra, M.M. Population projection for Gujarat state, 1991–2021. In *Gujarat-2010: challenges and opportunities*. By Government of Gujarat. Ahmedabad: Sardar Patel Institute of Economic & Social Research, 2001. pp. 1–17. Seminar volume. CSSL, EDIL, IRMAL, SGUL, SPIESRL.

Gandotra, M.M. and Dey, A.S. Some correlates of rural development in Gujarat. In *Gujarat economy: problems and prospects*. Ed. by D.T. Lakdawala. Ahmedabad: S.P. Institute of Economic and Social Research, 1982. pp. 351–368. GIDRL.

Gandotra, M.M. and Dey, A.S. Some correlates of rural development in Gujarat. In *Seminar on Development of Gujarat Problems & Prospects, 24–26 August, 1981*. Ahmedabad: Sardar Patel Institute of Economic & Social Research, 1981. pp. 1–27. CSSL.

Gandotra, M.M., et al. *Quality of family welfare services in India: a case study of Gujarat*. New Delhi: Population Council, Population Research Centre, Baroda, 1997. p. 62. GIDRL.

Ganguly, Varsha, Jowher, Zakia and Dabhi, Jimmy. *Changing contours of Gujarati society-identity formation and communal violence*. New Delhi: Indian Social Institute, 2006. p. 119. CSSL.

Glatter, Augusta. *Contributions to the ethnography of the Chodhris: Surat district, Gujarat*. Wien: University of Wien, 1969. p. 199. CSSL.

Gohil, Shankar. *Rural artisans in Gujarat-part I: a study of their status and the role of support agencies*. Ahmedabad: Gujarat Institute of Area Planning, 1982. p. 198. CSSL.

Gujarat University. *Removal of untouchability in Gujarat*. Ahmedabad: Author, 1973. p. 111. Seminar proceeding. CSSL.

Gumber, Anil. *Rehabilitation and resettlement of the oustees of Panam dam in Gujarat*. Ahmedabad: Gujarat Institute of Area Planning, 1992. p. 72. Working Paper No. 40. CSSL.

Hashim, S.R. City in a system of cities. In *Profiles of a growing city: the city of Baroda*. Ed. by K.N. Reddy, et al. Baroda: M.S. University, 1971. pp. 25–34. Souvenir: The 2nd Gujarat Economic Conference, 2–3 January 1971. CSSL.

Hashim, S.R. Report of group discussion on problems of urbanization in Gujarat. In *Gujarat Economic Association Conference Papers, Baroda*. Ed. by V.S. Vyas, Pravin Visaria and A.R. Desai. Ahmedabad: Balgovind, 1971. pp. 227–233. GIDRL.

Idiakunnel, Joseph. *Marching with the marginalized: an anthology of writings*. Rajpipla: Rajpipla Social Service Society, 2000. p. 96. CSSL.

Indian Council of Social Science Research. *Survey of research in sociology and social anthropology*. Vol. III. Bombay: Popular, 1972. p. 335. CSSL.

Isaac, Akkanad M. *Management of public housing: a study of the working of the Gujarat Housing Board*. Ahmedabad: Indian Institute of Management, 1978. p. 145. IIML.

Iyengar, Sudarshan. *Voluntary initiatives for tribal development in Gujarat: a review*.Ahmedabad: Gujarat Institute of Development Research, 1997. p. 50. Working Paper No. 91. CSSL, GIDRL, IRMAL.

Jadeja, Jayraj. *Approaches to social responsibility in industrial houses of Gujarat*. Vallabh Vidyanagar: Sardar Patel University, 1992. p. 270. HML.

Jagawat, Harnath. Tribals in Gujarat: the present conditions and opportunities. In *Gujarat-2010: challenges and opportunities*. By Government of Gujarat. Ahmedabad: Sardar Patel Institute of Economic & Social Research, 2001. pp. 635–637. Seminar volume. CSSL, EDIL, IRMAL, SGUL, SPIESRL.

Jairamdas, Jiwanlal. Socio-economic aspects of achievement of the scheduled castes. In *Removal of untouchability*. Ed. by Vimal P. Shah. Ahmedabad: Department of Sociology, Gujarat University, 1980. pp. 1–10. Seminar Proceedings. CSSL, GIDRL.

Janki, V.A. and Rajan, V.S. *Geography: the impact of transport on the population and land use in Waghodia-taluka*. Baroda: M.S. University, 1965. p. 55. IIML.

Jha, Sadan. *Experiences of city life: contemporary Surat and the question of belongingness*. Surat: Centre for Social Studies, 2013. p. 128. CSSL.

Jhala, P.J. Population of Gujarat: an overview and perspective. In *Gujarat-2010: challenges and opportunities*. By Government of Gujarat. Ahmedabad: Sardar Patel Institute of Economic & Social Research, 2001. pp. 18–28. Seminar Volume. CSSL, EDIL, IRMAL, SGUL, SPIESRL.

Joshi, Rajendra, et al. *From basic services delivery to policy advocacy: community mobilization in Pravinnagar-Guptanagar, Ahmedabad*. Ahmedabad: CEPT University, 2010. p. 35. Working Paper No. 6. CSSL.

Joshi, Rutul and Sanga, Prashant. *Land reservations for the urban poor: the case of town planning schemes in Ahmedabad*. Ahmedabad: CEPT University, 2009. p. 13. Working Paper 4. CSSL.

Joshi, Satyakam. *Development, deprivation and discontent: a case of Dangs tribals*. Surat: Centre for Social Studies, 1997. p. 12. Occasional Paper No. 21. CSSL.

Joshi, Satyakam. *Monitoring the implementation of social security schemes in tribal areas of Gujarat: with reference to Dangs district*. Surat: Centre for Social Studies, 2012. p. 40. CSSL.

Joshi, V.H. *Economic development and social change in a South Gujarat village: social consequences of industrialisation and urbanisation in a village in South Gujarat with special reference to tensions between groups and classes*. Vadodara: M.S. University, 1966. p. 124. CSSL, GUL, SGUL, SPUL, SUL.

Joshi, V.H. *Tribal village in transition: a socio-economic study of a tribal village*. Ahmedabad: Sardar Patel Institute of Economic & Social Research, 1999. p. 59. CSSL.

Joshi, Vidyut. *Genesis of tribal backwardness*. Ahmedabad: Gandhi Labour Institute, [ ]. p. 21. Working Paper. CSSL.

Joshi, Vidyut. *Socio-cultural & ecological impact of Alang & Sosiya ship breaking yard*. Surat: Centre for Social Studies and Bhavnagar: Bhavnagar University, 2003. p. 78. Third Phase Report on Stake Holders' Convergence ASSBY. CSSL.

Kadri, M.I. Ahmedabad municipality. In *Ahmedabad*. Ahmedabad: Rotary Club of Ahmedabad, 1940. pp. 23–30. CSSL.

Kanabar, S.G. *Study of population in Surat district*. Surat: Sarvajanik Education Society, 1955. p. 22. Chunilal Gandhi Vidyabhavan Studies No. 8. SGUL.

Kanhere, Usha. How urban are the towns and cities of Gujarat? In *Urbanisation in India and Gujarat: processes and problems*. Ahmedabad: Gujarat University, 1975. pp. 10–21. Seminar January 25 and 26, 1975. CSSL, SGUL.

Kanhere, Usha. *Research report of the girl child and the family research cum action project in Gujarat*. New Delhi: Department of Women and Child Development, Ministry of Human Resource Development, 1992. p. 849. CSSL.

Kashyap, S.P. Perspective on Gujarat's development with emphasis on human resources. In *Gujarat-2010: challenges and opportunities*. By Government of Gujarat. Ahmedabad: Sardar Patel Institute of Economic & Social Research, 2001. pp. 252–270. Seminar volume. CSSL, EDIL, IRMAL, SGUL, SPIESRL.

Kazi, Babasaheb. *Slums of towns and cities of Gujarat: a case of Surat*. Surat: Centre for Social Studies, 2002. p. 53. CSSL.

Kazi, Babasaheb and Purendra Prasad N. *Benchmark study of Surat city*. Surat: Centre for Social Studies, 2001. p. 219. CSSL.

Khan, Ayesha. *Gujarat development: dissenting rural voices*. Vadodara: Gujarat Foundation for Development Alternatives, [ ]. p. 40. CSSL.

Kothari, V.N. *Study of economic profiles of the scheduled castes in Gujarat.* Baroda: Department of Economics, M.S. University, 1976. p. 43. SPIESRL.

Kumar, B.L. *Target free approach for family welfare in Gujarat: a review of policy and its implementation.* Ahmedabad: Gujarat Institute of Development Research, 2003. p. 42. Working Paper No. 143. CSSL, IRMAL.

Lal, Rash Bihari. *Evaluation of Halpati housing scheme.* Ahmedabad: Tribal Research & Training Institute, Gujarat Vidyapith, 1977. p. 41. Serise-47. TRTIL.

Lal, Rash Bihari. *Socio-religious movements among tribals of South Gujarat.* Ahmedabad: Tribal Research & Training Institute, Gujarat Vidyapith, 1977. p. 52. Serise-48. TRTIL.

Lobo, Lancy. *Assessment of integrated tribal development programme in Songadh, 1980–1990.* Surat: Centre for Social Studies, 1993. p. 109. CSSL.

Lobo, Lancy. *Becoming a marginal native.* Surat: Centre for Social Studies, 1988. p. 50. Occasional Paper No. 3. CSSL.

Lobo, Lancy. Development induced displacement in Gujarat 1947–2004. In *Special Economic Zones (SEZs): issues and challenges ahead.* Ed. by Sunita Nambiyar, Jagdish Solanki and M.N. Parmar. Vadodara: Faculty of Social Work, M.S. University, 2008. pp. 94–110. Seminar Proceeding. CSSL.

Lobo, Lancy. *Encounter with urbanism: coping mechanisms in a slum.* Surat: Centre for Social Studies, 1995. p. 160. CSSL.

Lobo, Lancy. *Religious conversion and social mobility: a case study of the Vankars in Central Gujarat.* Surat: Centre for Social Studies, 1991. p. 195. CSSL, IRMAL.

Lobo, Lancy. *Religious sects among the tribals of South Gujarat.* Surat: Centre for Social Studies, 1992. p. 56. CSSL.

Magrabi, Frances M. and Verma, Amita. *Household resources and their changing relationships: case studies in Gujarat, India.* Illinois: College of Agriculture, University of Illinois, 1987. p. 121. International Agriculture Publications General Series No. 3. GIDRL.

Mahadevia, Darshini. *Moving towards food insecurity? the case of Gujarat.* Mumbai: Vikas Adhyayan Kendra, 2000. p. 48. Monograph. CSSL.

Mahadevia, Darshini. *Report of public hearing on habitat and livelihood displacements.* Ahmedabad: CEPT University, 2010. p. 50. CSSL.

Mahadevia, Darshini, Gogoi, Trishna and Panchal, Purvish. *Transaction processes in urbanizing Lands.* Ahmedabad: CEPT University, 2010. p. 35. Working Paper No. 49. CSSL.

Majumdar, D.N. *Race elements in cultural Gujarat.* Lucknow: Gujarat Research Society, 1940. p. 24. Tenth Anniversary Celebration Lecture. CSSL.

Masavi, Mustaali. *Problem of land alienation among tribals of Gujarat.* Ahmedabad: Gujarat Vidyapith, [ ]. p. 26. CSSL, TRTIL.

Masavi, Mustali and Shah, Kokila. *Working of lamps in tribal areas of Gujarat.* Ahmedabad: Gujarat Vidyapith, 1982. p. 23. Series-114. TRTIL.

Masihi, E.J. and Desai, D.B. *Assessment of drug abuse, drug users and drug prevention service in the city of Ahmedabad.* Ahmedabad: Gujarat University, 1989. p. 180. CSSL, GIDRL.

Masihi, Edwin. *Social engagements of intellectuals in civil society: with special reference to professionals of Gujarat.* Ahmedabad: AWAG, 2006. p. 171. CSSL.

Masihi, Edwin J. and Desai, Dhiru B. Dalit Panther movement in Gujarat. In *Removal of untouchability.* Ed. by Vimal P. Shah. Ahmedabad: Gujarat University, 1980. pp. 1–6. Seminar Proceedings. CSSL, GIDRL, SPIESRL.

Masihi, Edwin, Pathak, Ila and Trivedi, Nalini. *Life snuffed out?: a study of suicides in Gujarat*. Ahmedabad: AWAG, 2010. p. 140. CSSL.

Mehta, J.M. *Study of rural economy of Gujarat: containing possibilities of reconstruction.* Baroda: Baroda State Press, 1930. p. 231. CSSL.

Mehta, Leena. *Prostitution in Surat.* Baroda: Faculty of Social Work, M.S. University, 1991. p. 68. CSSL.

Mehta, S.S. Trends of urbanization in Gujarat. In *Gujarat Economic Association, Conference papers, Vallabh Vidyanagar.* Ed. by D.T. Lakadawala and B.B. Patel. 1985. pp. 35–45. GIDRL.

Mooken, Vincent. *Role of voluntary organizations in Surat slums*. Surat: Centre for Social Studies, 1993. pp. [ ]. Seminar on Urban Poor in India, 10–11 February 1993. Unpublished Paper. CSSL.

Murthy, Nirmala. *Demography of tribal population in Gujarat.* Ahmedabad: Gujarat Institute of Area Planning, 1978. p. 29. IIML.

Navsarjan. *Understanding untouchability: a comprehensive study of practices and conditions in 1589 villages*. Ahmedabad: Navsarjan, 2010. p. 58. CSSL.

Oza, Digant et al. *Untold story of Hindukaran (Proselytisation) of adivasis (Tribals) in Dang, Gujarat*. New Delhi: Anhad, 2006. p. 30. CSSL.

Pancholi, Ravindra and Upadhyaya, Chandrakant. *Primitive tribal groups of Gujarat: a base line survey.* Ahmedabad: Tribal Research & Training Institute, Gujarat Vidyapith, 2006. p. 266. Serise-424. TRTIL.

Panchpinde, Pradip. Atrocities on tribals of South Gujarat. In *Tribal of Western India: issues of development and marginalisation.* Surat: Centre for Social Studies, Ahmedabad: Tribal Research & Training Institute, Gujarat Vidyapith, 1997. pp. [ ]. TRTIL.

Panda, Smita, Mishra and Lund, Ragnhild. *Environmental hazards, women's work and health in rural Kutch, Gujarat (INDIA)*. Anand: IRMA, 2003. p. 26. WP-177. IRMAL.

Pandit, D.P. *Change and the challenge: Mahuva reconsidered.* Surat: Centre for Social Studies, 1989. p. 281. CSSL.

Pandit, D.P. *Earning one's livelihood in Mahuva.* Bombay: Asia, 1965. p. 96. Department of Sociology Publication no-5, M.S. University of Baroda. IIML.

Pandya, D.G. Planning approach for an urban centre and its hinterland. In *Urbanisation in India & Gujarat: processes*. Ed. by Department of Sociology, Gujarat University. Ahmedabad: Department of Sociology, Gujarat University. 1975. pp. 144–151. Seminar 25 and 26, January, 1975. SGUL.

Pandya, N.M. Baroda city as shown in "Socio-economic survey of Baroda city". In *Profiles of a growing city: city of Baroda.* Ed. by K.N. Reddy, et al. Baroda: M.S. University, 1971. pp. 35–39. Souvenir: The 2nd Gujarat Economic Conference, 2–3 January 1971. CSSL, SPIESRL.

Pandya, N.M. Impact of urbanization on fertility ratio in Gujarat. In *Gujarat Economic Association Conference Papers, Baroda*. Ed. by V.S. Vyas, Pravin Visaria and A.R. Desai. Ahmedabad: Balgovind, 1971. pp. 219–226. GIDRL, IIML.

Parikh, Gokul O. *Jambua (Panchmahals District Gujarat) a tribal village on the threshold of modernisation.* Vallabh Vidyanagar: AERC. 1967. p. 190. Indian Village Studies No. 8. AERCL, SPUL.

Parikh, Gokul O. *Study on evaluation of literacy campaign: in Bhavnagar district.* Ahmedabad: Sardar Patel Institute of Economic & Social Research, 1992. p. 92. SPIESRL.

Parmar, B.G. Overview of programmes in Gujarat. In *Removal of untouchability*. Ed. by Vimal P. Shah. Ahmedabad: Depart. of Sociology, Gujarat University, 1980. pp. 1–15. Seminar Proceeding. CSSL, GIDRL, SPIESRL.

Patel, A.S. Profile of urban employees residing in a Charotar village. In *Urbanisation in India and Gujarat: processes and problems*. Ahmedabad: Gujarat University, 1975. pp. 64–76. Semminar January 25 and 26, 1975. CSSL, SGUL.

Patel, Arjun. *Caste in changing society: a study of Kolis of South Gujarat*. International Seminar on Gujarat society, development and deprivation, 6–9 December 1994. Surat: Centre for Social Studies, 1994. pp. 1–35. CSSL.

Patel, Arjun and Trivedi, Vimal. *Solid waste management-midterm evaluation of door to door garbage collection programme in three municipal zones of Surat*. Surat: Centre for Social Studies, 2005. p. 124. CSSL.

Patel, B.B. *Area plan with social inputs for Muli and Sayla talukas, district Surendranagar*. Ahmedabad: Sardar Patel Institute of Economic & Social Research, 1980. Various Pages. Interim Report. CSSL.

Patel, B.B. Forces behind urbanization: an inter district and interstate analysis. In *Gujarat Economic Association Conference Papers, Baroda*. Ed. by V.S. Vyas, Pravin Visaria and A.R. Desai. Ahmedabad: Balgovind, 1971. pp. 143–152. GIDRL, IIML.

Patel, B.B. *Housing and socio-economic issues of slum-dwellers in a metropolitan area: a case study of Ahmedabad*. Ahmedabad: Sardar Patel Institute of Economic & Social Research, 1977. p. 486. CSSL.

Patel, Harbanas. *Tribal Gujarat: a study on ten villages in Poshina region*. Anand: Sardar Patel University, 1989. p. 41. GVL.

Patel, Haribhai. *Development and deprivation in Saurashtra peninsula of Gujarat in Western India*. International seminar on Gujarat society, development and deprivation, 6–9 December 1994. Surat: Centre for Social Studies, 1994. pp. 1–20. CSSL.

Patel, Ila. *Continuity and changes in dominant state ideology in adult literacy primers in Gujarat*. International seminar on Gujarat society, development and deprivation, 6–9 December 1994. Surat: Centre for Social Studies, 1994. pp. 1–40. CSSL.

Patel, Priyavadan. *Tribal development in Gujarat: an evaluative study of Integrated Tribal Development Project, Dahod*. Surat: Centre for Social Studies, 1986. p. 137. CSSL, GIDRL, IRMAL, SGUL.

Patel, R.M. *Abhawa (Surat district, Gujarat) an advanced village in traditional setting*. Vallabh Vidyanagar: Agro-Economic Research Centre, 1966. p. 198. Indian Village Studies No. 7. AERCL, SPUL.

Patel, Rohini. *Voluntary associations as pressure groups: a framework for analysis and an illustrative case study*. Ahmedabad: Gujarat Institute of Development Research, 1996. p. 29. Working Paper No. 74. CSSL, GIDRL.

Pathy, Jaganath. *Agrarian structure in tribal Gujarat and its implications for tribal policies*. Surat: South Gujarat University, 1982. p. 266. CSSL.

Prasad, Purendra. *Rural livelihood strategies: a study on drought in Gujarat*. Surat: Centre for Social Studies, 2000. p. 57. CSSL.

Prathap, K. and Mehta, Madhvi. *Revitalising the public bureaucracy: training as a major intervention strategy in the Vadodara model district project*. Anand: Institute of Rural Management, 2000. p. 30. Working Paper-151. SPIESRL.

Punalekar, S.P. *Child welfare services: constraints and opportunities: a study of girls' remand home, with special emphasis on programmes, support structure and requirements*. Surat: Centre for Social Studies, 1985. p. 52. CSSL.

Punalekar, S.P. *Empowering the urban poor in Surat slums.* Surat: Centre for Social Studies, 1995. p. 206. CSSL.

Punalekar, S.P. *Remand home for boys, Baroda: perspective, programmes, needs.* Surat: Centre for Social Studies, 1985. p. 61. CSSL.

Punalekar, S.P. *Seeds of Marginalisation and instability: a study of street children in Gujarat.* Surat: Centre for Social Studies, 1993. p. 223. CSSL, SETUL.

Punalekar, S.P. *Social mal-adjustment and institutional intervention: problem of destitution and delinquency in Baroda city: an overview.* Surat: Centre for Social Studies, 1986. p. 71. CSSL.

Punalekar, S.P. *Tribal development and its discontents: a narrative.* Surat: Centre for Social Studies, 2000. p. 29. Occasional Paper No. 17. CSSL.

Punalekar, S.P. *Tribal society and socio-legal interventions.* Surat: Centre for Social Studies, 1997. p. 86. CSSL.

Punalekar, S.P. *Weekly market and tribal society: a study of weekly markets in tribal talukas of Surat-Valasad region.* Surat: Centre for Social Studies, 1982. p. 146. CSSL, SPIESRL.

Punalekar, S.P. and Patel, Priyavadan. *Child welfare services in Baroda city: with special emphasis on destitution and delinquence.* Surat: Centre for Social Studies, 1986. p. 51. CSSL.

Punalekar, S.P., et al. *Socio-economic and demographic study of villages affected by proposed Gandhar Gas based power project. Part-I and II.* Surat: Centre for Social Studies, 1992. p. 236. Unpublished Report. CSSL.

Radhakrishna, R., Parikh, Bhanumati and Shah, Naresh C. *Exploratory study on slums: employment, poverty and liquor consumption: a study of Ahmedabad slums.* Ahmedabad: Sardar Patel Institute of Economic & Social Research, 1977. p. 194. CSSL, IIML, TRTIL.

Rajagopal, Arvind. Gujarat as an experiment in Hindu national racism: lessons on secularism. In *Discourse of democracy and difference perspective on community, politics and culture.* Ed. by M.T Ansari and Deeptha Achar. Baroda: National Seminar on Minorits Discourses, 2010. pp. 86–104. GVL.

Raju, K.V., Uma Rani and Patel, Anil. *Non-economic motivation for improving natural resource management: example of Swadhyaya from a village in Gujarat, (INDIA).* Anand: IRMA, 1999. p. 29. WP-135. IRMAL.

Ray, C.N. *Changing pattern of traditional neighbourhood in walled city of Ahmedabad: case of Vad Vali Pol.* Ahmedabad: Faculty of Planning and Public Policy, CEPT University, 2008. p. 25. Working Paper no-44. CEPTL.

Ray, C.N. *Development control, building regulation and judicial activism in Gujarat.* Ahmedabad: School of Planning, CEPT University, 2001. p. 20. Working Paper-18. CEPTL.

Saramma, A.D. and Kantawala, B.S. Urbanisation and its effects on urban services in Baroda. In *Gujarat Economic Association, Conference Papers, Vallabh Vidyanagar.* Ed. by D.T. Lakadawala and B.B. Patel. [ ], 1985. pp. 46–57. GIDRL.

Satya, D.A., ed. *Gujarat tribal landscapes: heralding the change.* Gandhinagar: Development Support Agency of Gujarat, 2009. p. 102. IRMAL.

Self Employed Women's Association. Ahmedabad: SEWA, 1988. p. 139. CSSL.

Sen, Prabal K., et al. *Impact assessment of rural development programmes in Rajkot district of Gujarat.* Anand: IRMA, 2004. p. 351. IRMAL.

Shah, A.K. Rural-urban network in Gujarat. In *International Seminar on "Gujarat Society", 17–20 December 1986.* Surat: Centre for Social Studies, 1986. pp. 1–43. CSSL.

Shah, Amita and Yagnik, Jignasu. *Estimates of BPL-households in rural Gujarat: measurement, spatial pattern and policy imperatives*. Ahmedabad: Gujarat Institute of Development Research, 2007. p. 30. Working Paper No. 176. CSSL, GIDRL.

Shah, B.V. *Social change and college students of Gujarat*. Baroda: M.S. University, 1964. p. 231. CSSL, SPUL.

Shah, B.V. Urbanisation: an independent variable in modernization in India. In *Urbanisation in India and Gujarat: processes and problems*. Ahmedabad: Gujarat University, 1975. pp. 22–44. Seminar January 25 and 26, 1975. CSSL, SGUL.

Shah, B.V. and Thaker, J.D. Occupational status of the scheduled castes in Gujarat. In *Removal of untouchability*. Ed. by Vimal P. Shah. Ahmedabad: Department of Sociology, Gujarat University, 1980. pp. 1–8. Seminar Proceedings. CSSL, GIDRL.

Shah, B.V. and Thaker, J.D. Profile of the scheduled castes in Gujarat. Vallabh Vidyanagar: Department of Sociology, Sardar Patel University, 1974. p. 132. Report. CSSL.

Shah, B.V. and Thaker, J.D. *Scheduled caste and scheduled tribe college Students in Gujarat: a sociological study*. Vallabh Vidyanagar: Sardar Patel University, 1978. p. 357. CSSL.

Shah, G. *Adivasi's of Gujarat*. Surat: Centre for Regional Development Studies, 1980. p. 30. CSSL, IRMAL.

Shah, Ghanshyam. *Caste sentiments, class formation and dominance in Gujarat*. Surat: Centre for Social Studies, 1984. p. 54. CSSL, IRMAL.

Shah, Ghanshyam. City and slums. In *Urbanisation in India and Gujarat: processes and problems*. Ahmedabad: Gujarat University, 1975. pp. 83–93. Seminar January 25 and 26, 1975. CSSL, SGUL.

Shah, Ghanshyam. *Mid-day meals scheme in Gujarat: an evaluation*. Surat: Centre for Social Studies, 1988. p. 166. CSSL, GIDRL.

Shah, Ghanshyam. Middle class politics: a case of anti-reservation agitations in Gujarat. In *International Seminar on Gujarat Society, 17–20 December 1986*. Surat: Centre for Social Studies, 1986. pp. 1–63. CSSL.

Shah, Ghanshyam. Socio-economic stratification and politics in rural Gujarat. In *Gujarat economy: problems and prospects*. Ed. by D.T. Lakdawala. Ahmedabad: Sardar Patel Institute of Economic & Social Research, 1982. pp. 169–192. GIDRL.

Shah, Ghanshyam. *Stratification among the scheduled tribes in the Bharuch and Panch Mahals districts of Gujarat*. Surat: Centre for Social Studies, 1976. p. 49. Project Report. CSSL, GIDRL.

Shah, Ghanshyam. *Stratification among the scheduled tribes in the Surat and Valsad districts of Gujarat*. Surat: Centre for Social Studies, 1977. p. 43. Project Report. CSSL.

Shah, Ghanshyam. *Urban tensions: a case study of Surat*. Surat: Centre for Social Studies, [ ]. p. 134. CSSL.

Shah, Ghanshyam and Das, Biswaroop. *Voluntary organizations in Gujarat: an exploratory study*. Surat: Centre for Social Studies, 1988. p. 95. CSSL.

Shah, Madhuri., Desai, Neera and Deshmukh, Laj. *Report of the survey of the needs and future action programmes for integrated rural development in the nine villages of Pardi taluka-South Gujarat*. Bombay: S.N.D.T. Women's University, 1983. p. 40. CSSL.

Shah, Maya. *Economic factors explaining variations in literacy rates in rural areas: a case study of Gujarat*. Baroda: Department of Economics, M.S. University of Baroda, 1987. p. [ ]. M.S. University Economics Series No. 7. GIDRL.

Shah, S, M. Evaluation of the Integrated Child Development Services project in Chhota Udepur (Gujarat): a case study. In *Seminar on development of Gujarat: problems & prospects, 24–26 August, 1981*. Ahmedabad: Sardar Patel Institute of Economic & Social Research, 1981. pp. 1–20. CSSL.

Shah, S.M. Evaluation of the integrated child development services project in Chhota Udepur (Gujarat)-a case study. In *Gujarat economy: problems and prospects*. Ed. by D.T. Lakdawala. Ahmedabad: S.P. Institute of Economic & Social Research, 1982. pp. 627–640. GIDRL, GUL.

Shah, Vimal. Tribal areas & their problems. In *Seminar on Development of Gujarat problems & prospects, 24–26 August, 1981*. Ahmedabad: Sardar Patel Institute of Economic & Social Research, 1981. pp. 1–8. CSSL.

Shah, Vimal P. Assessment of education among the scheduled castes in Gujarat. In *Removal of untouchability*. Ed. by Vimal P. Shah. Ahmedabad: Department of Sociology, Gujarat University, 1980. pp. 1–12. Seminar Proceedings. CSSL, GIDRL.

Shah, Vimal P. *Elderly residing in homes for the aged in Gujarat*. Ahmedabad: Gujarat Institute of Development Research, 1998. p. 72. Working Paper No. 99. CSSL, GIDRL, IRMAL.

Shah, Vimal P., ed. *Removal of untouchability: proceedings of a Seminar*. Ahmedabad: Department of Sociology, Gujarat University, 1980. p. 322. CSSL, GIDRL.

Shah, Vimal P., Sheth, N.R. and Visaria, Pravin. *Role of the Swadhyaya Parivar in socio-economic changes among the tribals in Khedasan*. Ahmedabad: Gujarat Institute of Development Research, 1998. p. [ ]. GIDR Working Paper No. 95. GIDRL.

Shah, Vimal and Shah, C.H. *Resurvey of Matar taluka*. Bombay: Vora, 1974. p. 336. GUL, IIML.

Shariff, Abusaleh and Visaria, Pravin. *Family planning programme in Gujarat: a qualitative assessment of inputs and impact*. Ahmedabad: Gujarat Institute of Area Planning, 1991. p. 120. CSSL, GIDRL, IIML, IRMAL.

Sharma, B.B.L., Sharma, Sushma and Nair, K.S. *Report on cost variation of family welfare programme in the states of Gujarat and Himachal Pradesh*. New Delhi: National Institute of Health & Family Welfare, 1993. p. 94. CSSL.

Sheth, N.R. *Children of the same God: a spiritual approach to social transformations*. In *International seminar on Gujarat society, development and deprivation, 6–9 December 1994*. Surat: Centre for Social Studies, 1994. pp. 1–38. CSSL.

Sheth, N.R. *Children of the same God: a spiritual approach to social transformations*. Ahmedabad: Gujarat Institute of Development Research, 1994. p. 27. Working Paper No. 59. CSSL.

Sheth, Pravin and Desai, Mahendra T. Profile of problems of urban Gujarat. In *Urbanisation in India and Gujarat: processes and problems*. Ahmedabad: Gujarat University, 1975. pp. 94–114. Seminar January 25 and 26, 1975. CSSL, SGUL.

Shetty, M.C. *Patadia (Sabarkantha District): a tribal village economy in transition*. Anand: S.P. University, 1963. p. 206. SPIESRL.

Shukla, Rohit. Production and consumption aspects of tribals of Vadodara district. In *Seminar on development of Gujarat problems & prospects*, 24–26 August, 1981. Ahmedabad: Sardar Patel Institute of Economic & Social Research, 1981. pp. 1–23. CSSL.

Shylendra, H.S. *Environmental rehabilitation and livelihood impact: Some emerging trends and concerns from Tigray (Ethiopia) and Gujarat (India)*. Anand: IRMA, 2001. p. 22. Working Paper No. 161. IRMAL.

Shylendra, H.S. *Micro-finance and self-help groups (SHGs): a study of the experience of two leading NGOs, SEWA and AKRSP in Gujarat, India*. Anand: IRMA, 1999. p. 41. IRMAL.

Shylendra, H.S. *Promoting women's self-help groups: lessons from an action research project of IRMA*. Anand: Institute of Rural Management, 1998. p. 25. Working Paper 121. CSSL.

Singh, Pramod K. and Hiremath, B.N. *Sustainable livelihood security index in Gujarat: a district-level illustration*. Anand: Institute of Rural Management, 2008. p. 46. Working Paper 205. IRMAL, SPIESRL.

Sinha, S.P. *Tribal Gujarat: some impressions*. Gandhinagar: Government of Gujarat, 1976. p. 100. CSSL.

Solanki, S.S. *Area study of Dangs*. Ahmedabad: Tribal Research & Training Institute, Gujarat Vidyapith, 1981. p. 85. TRTIL.

Solanki, S.S. *Tribes of Kutch*. Ahmedabad: Tribal Research & Training Institute, Gujarat Vidyapith,[ ]. p. 157. Series-107. TRTIL.

Streefkerk, Hein. *Transformation in a small Gujarat town: Bulsar, Suthars and the relevance of caste twenty years later*. New Delhi: Indian Council of Social Science Research, 1990. p. 45. Occasional Papers and Reprints, IDPAD 1990–97. CSSL, GIDRL.

Tirmizi, A.I. Mahdwai movement in Gujarat. In *India & contemporary Islam: proceedings of a Seminar*. Ed. by S.T. Lokhandwala. Shimla: Indian Institute of Advanced Study, 1971, pp. 116–124. SETUL, SGUL.

Tribal Research & Training Institute, Gujarat Vidyapith. *Survey report on basic amenities in scheduled caste: settlement (Falia) of Gujarat State*. Ahmedabad: Tribal Research & Training Institute, Gujarat Vidyapith, 1986. p. 92. GIDRL, TRTIL.

Trivedi, Harshad R. *Report of land systems of tribal areas of India with special reference to tribal areas of Gujarat*. Ahmedabad: I.I.P.A Gujarat State Regional Branch, 1980. p. 58. TRTIL.

Trivedi, Jayprakash M. *Anganwadis in the tribal region of Gujarat*. Vallabh Vidyanagar: Sardar Patel University, 1993. p. 71. GVL.

Trivedi, Vimal. *Socio-economic condition of rag pickers: a case study of Surat city*. Surat: Centre for Social Studies, 2012. p. 79. Mimeograph. CSSL.

Uma Rani and Unni, Jeemol. *Women, work and insecurities in India*. Ahmedabad: Gujarat Institute of Development Research, 2003. p. 30. Working Paper No. 135. CSSL, GIDRL.

Upadhyaya, Chandrakant and Pancholi, Ravindra. *Primitive tribal groups of Gujarat: a base line survey*. Ahmedabad: Gujarat Vidyapith, 2010. p. 241. TRTIL.

Upadhyay, Chandrakant and Pancholi, Ravindra. *Primitive tribal groups of Gujarat*. Ahmedabad: Tribal Research & Training Institute, Gujarat Vidyapith, 2003–2004. p. 129. Series-393. TRTIL.

Upadhyay, Chandrakant and Pancholi, Ravindra. *Primitive tribal groups of Gujarat: a base survey*. Ahmedabad: Tribal Research & Training Institute, Gujarat Vidyapith, 2006. p. 266. Series-419. TRTIL.

Vaidya, Chetan V. *Study of small urban centres in tribal talukas of Surat district: case study Bardoli*. Ahmedabad: Gujarat Institute of Area Planning (GIAP), 1978. p. [ ]. GIDRL.

Visaria, Leela. Literacy in the Dangs: an exploratory analysis. In *Gujarat economy: problems and prospects*. Ed. by D.T. Lakdawala. Ahmedabad: Sardar Patel Institute of Economic & Social Research, 1983. pp. 547–562. Monograph Series-10. GIDRL, GUL, IIML.

Visaria, Leela. Literacy in the Dangs: an exploratory analysis. In *Seminar on Development of Gujarat problems & prospects,* 24–26 August, 1981. Ahmedabad: Sardar Patel Institute of Economic & Social Research, 1981. pp. 1–18. CSSL.

Visaria, Leela. Sex differentials in nutritional status in a rural area of Gujarat state: an interim Report. Ahmedabad: Gujarat Institute of Area Planning March 1987. p. 36. GIDR Working Paper No. 7. GIDRL.

Visaria, Leela. *Two immunization campaigns in a rural area of Kachchh, Gujarat: an assessment*. Ahmedabad: Gujarat Institute of Area Planning, 1988, p. 23. IRMAL.

Visaria, Leela. *Total literacy campaign in Gandhinagar district, 1991: an evaluation* Ahmedabad: Gujarat Institute of Development Research, 1993. p. 79. GIDRL.

Visaria, Leela. *Unmet need for family planning: an analysis of panel data from rural Gujarat.* Ahmedabad: Gujarat Institute of Development Research, 1997. p. 28. Working Paper No. 85. CSSL, GIDRL, IRMAL.

Visaria, Leela and Anandjiwala, Jyoti. *Growth of the children in a drought affected rural area in Gujarat: some results of a longitudinal study*. Ahmedabad: Gujarat Institute of Area Planning, 1988. p. 47. GIAP Working Paper 17. GIDRL, IRMAL.

Visaria, Leela, Kumar, B.L. and Gumber, Anil. *Total literacy campaign in Gandhinagar district, 1991: an evaluation.* Ahmedabad: Gujarat Institute of Development Research, 1993. p. 45. Working Paper No. 51. CSSL.

Visaria, Leela and Visaria, Pravin. *Quality of services and family planning in Gujarat state, India: an exploratory analysis*. Ahmedabad: Gujarat Institute of Area Planning, 1991. p. 42. Working Paper No. 34. CSSL, GIDRL, IRMAL.

Visaria, Pravin, Visaria, Leela and Jain, Anrudh. *Contraceptive use and fertility in Gujarat.* Ahmedabad: Gujarat Institute of Development Research, 1992. p. 286. CSSL, GIDRL, IIML.

Visaria, Pravin and Hashim, S.R. Report of group discussion on problems of urbanization in Gujarat. In *Gujarat Economic Association Conference Papers, Baroda*. Ed. by V.S. Vyas, Pravin Visaria and A.R. Desai. Ahmedabad: Balgovind, 1971. pp. 227–233. GIDRL, IIML.

Vyas, C.P. Problems of urban planning: with special reference to Gujarat. In *Urbanisation in India and Gujarat: processes and problems*. Ahmedabad: Gujarat University, 1975. pp. 129–143. Seminar January 25 and 26, 1975. CSSL, SGUL.

Wood, John R. Reservations in doubt: the backlash against affirmative action in Gujarat, 1985. In *International Seminar on "Gujarat Society", 17–20 December 1986.* Surat: Centre for Social Studies, 1986. pp. 1–23. CSSL.

3

Communalism, Conflict, Violence

Books/Chapter in Books

Ahmad, Aijaz. *On communalism and globalization: offensives of the far right*. New Delhi: Three Essays, 2004. p. 117. CSSL, UML.

Ahmed, Imtiaz. Takeover of state power. In *Fascism in India: faces, fangs and facts*. Ed. by Chaitanya Krishna. New Delhi: Manak, 2003. pp. 288–294. CSSL, UML.

Ahmed, Riaz. Gujarat violence: meaning and implications. In *Fascism in India: faces, fangs and facts*. Ed. by Chaitanya Krishna. New Delhi: Manak, 2003. pp. 416–427. CSSL, UML.

Amin, R.K. Real crisis in Gujarat. In *Black book of Gujarat*. Ed. by M.L. Sondhi and Apratim Mukarji. New Delhi: Manak, 2002. pp. 87–89. AAL, BVL, HML.

Argade, Ranjana. Dialogue of Vali Gujarati and Hanumanji. In *Gujarat: the making of tragedy*. Ed. by Siddharth Varadarajan. New Delhi: Penguin, 2002. pp. 401–403. CSSL, EDIL, HML, SETUL.

Asha Rani. *Gandhian non-violence and India's freedom struggle*. Delhi: Shree, 1981. p. 348. CSSL.

Balagopal, K. Reflections on 'Gujarat Pradesh' of 'Hindu Rashtra'. In *Fascism in India: faces, fangs and facts*. Ed. by Chaitanya Krishna. New Delhi: Manak, 2003. pp. 502–510. CSSL, UML.

Bandukwala, J.S. Muslims and Hindutva in Gujarat. In *Communal violence and minorities: Gujarat society in ferment*. Ed. by Lancy Lobo and Biswaroop Das. Jaipur: Rawat, 2006. pp. 63–76. CEPTL, CSSL, GIDRL, HML, UML.

Banu, Zainab. Two sides of a coin: a comparative study of riots at Godhra and Udaipur. In *Communal riots in post-independence India*. Ed. by Asghar Ali Engineer. Hyderabad: Sangam, 1984. pp. 228–237. CSSL, IIML.

Banu, Zenab. *Politics of communalism: a politico-historical analysis of communal riots in post-independence India with special reference to the Gujarat and Rajasthan riots*. Bombay: Popular, 1989. p. 226. ASL, CSSL.

Baxi, Upendra. Reflections on the reservations crisis in Gujarat. In *Mirrors of violence: communities, riots and survivors in South Asia*. Ed. by Veena Das. New York: Oxford, 1990. pp. 215–239. CSSL, SPUL.

Baxi, Upendra. Second Gujarat catastrophe. In *Fascism in India: faces, fangs and facts*. Ed. by Chaitanya Krishna. New Delhi: Manak, 2003. pp. 58–96. CSSL, UML.

Berenschot, Ward. *Riot politics: Hindu-Muslim violence and the Indian state*. New Delhi: Rupa, 2011. p. 236. CSSL.

Bhagat, Varsha. Unnatural death of women in Gujarat. In *Violence against women: women against violence*. Ed. by Shirin Kudchedker and Sabina Al-Issa. Delhi: Pencraft International, 1998. pp. 129–139. CSSL, SETUL.

Bhambhri, C.P. Society brutalized: is there a way to change people's mindset. In *Fascism in India: faces, fangs and facts.* Ed. by Chaitanya Krishna. New Delhi: Manak, 2003. pp. 563–576. CSSL, UML.

Bhatia, Bela. Step back in Sabarkantha. In *Fascism in India: faces, fangs and facts.* Ed. by Chaitanya Krishna. New Delhi: Manak, 2003. pp. 193–200. CSSL, UML.

Bhatt, Sheela. VHP 'Proud' of targeted violence. In *Fascism in India: faces, fangs and facts.* Ed. by Chaitanya Krishna. New Delhi: Manak, 2003. pp. 620–622. CSSL, UML.

Bose, Pradip Kumar. Social mobility and caste violence: a study of the Gujarat riots. In *Caste, caste-conflict and reservation.* By Centre for Social Studies. New Delhi: Ajanta, 1985. pp. 137–147. CSSL, SETUL.

Breman, Jan. Communal upheaval as resurgence. In *Fascism in India: faces, fangs and facts.* Ed. by Chaitanya Krishna. New Delhi: Manak, 2003. pp. 367–376. CSSL, UML.

Cedric, Prakash. Justice for peace: challenges from Gujarat. In *Other India: realities of an emerging India.* Ed. by Rajesh Chakrabarti. New Delhi: Sage, 2009. pp. 110–122. HML, IIML.

Chakraborty, Anand. Gujarat's doubly alienated Muslims. In *Fascism in India: faces, fangs and facts.* Ed. by Chaitanya Krishna. New Delhi: Manak, 2003. pp. 524–531. CSSL, UML.

Chandra, Sudhir. *Continuing dilemmas: understanding social consciousness.* New Delhi: Tulika, 2002. p. 321. CSSL.

CHARKHA. *Path of humanity: citizens' efforts to promote communal harmony in Gujarat.* Ahmedabad: Charkha, 2004. p. 106. CSSL.

Chenoy, Kamal Mitra, et al. Ethnic cleansing not communal riot. In *Fascism in India: faces, fangs and facts.* Ed. by Chaitanya Krishna. New Delhi: Manak, 2003. pp. 201–216. CSSL, UML.

Choudhary, Kushanava. Hindutva's foreign hand and the middle class. In *Fascism in India: faces, fangs and facts.* Ed. by Chaitanya Krishna. New Delhi: Manak, 2003. pp. 359–364. CSSL, UML.

Das, Bhabani, Agarwal, Manu and Joshi, Rutul. *Impact of communal violence on livelihood of the informal sector: case study of the 2002 riots in Ahmedabad and Vadodara.* Ahmedabad: Samerth Coordination Office, 2003. p. 80. CEPTL.

Datta, Nonica. Gujarat and majority women. In *Fascism in India: faces, fangs and facts.* Ed. by Chaitanya Krishna. New Delhi: Manak, 2003. pp. 355–358. CSSL, UML.

Dayal, John. Gandhi's Gujarat? In *Gujarat 2002: untold and re-told stories of the Hindutva lab.* Ed. by John Dayal. Delhi: Media House, 2002. pp. 62–83. CSSL, UML.

Dayal, John. *Matter of equity: freedom of faith in secular India.* New Delhi: Anamika, 2007. p. 487. CSSL.

Dayal, John, ed. *Gujarat 2002: untold and re-told stories of the Hindutva lab.* Delhi: Media House, 2002. p. 1157. CSSL, UML.

Desai, Kiran. On determinants of communal relations: some observations from case study of Surat. In *Communal violence and minorities: Gujarat society in ferment.* Ed. by Lancy Lobo and Biswaroop Das. Jaipur: Rawat, 2006. pp. 181–205. CEPTL, CSSL, GIDRL, HML, UML.

Devid, Robin. *City of fear.* Delhi: Penguin, 2007. p. 256. CSSL, SETUL, UML.

Devy, G.N. Tribal voice and violence. In *Gujarat: the making of tragedy.* Ed. by Siddharth Varadarajan. New Delhi: Penguin, 2002. pp. 246–266. CSSL, EDIL, HML, SETUL.

Devy, Mahasweta. Where will it end? In *Gujarat: the making of tragedy*. Ed. by Siddharth Varadarajan. New Delhi: Penguin, 2002. pp. 431–433. CSSL, EDIL, HML, SETUL.

Dube, Mukul. *Path of the parivar: articles on Gujarat and Hindutva*. New Delhi: Three Essays, 2004. p. 134. CSSL.

Dutt, Barkha. Women's panel, PUCL-Vadodara and Shanti abhiyan. 'Nothing new?: women as victims. In *Gujarat: the making of tragedy*. Ed. by Siddharth Varadarajan. New Delhi: Penguin, 2002. pp. 214–245. CSSL, EDIL, HML, SETUL.

Engineer, Asghar Ali, ed. *Gujarat carnage*. Hyderabad: Orient Longman, 2003. p. 467. AAL, CSSL, GIDRL, GVL, HML.

Engineer, Asghar Ali. *Communal riots in post-independence India*. Hyderabad: Sangam, 1984. p. 366. CSSL, IIML.

Engineer, Asghar Ali. Gujarat carnage: causes and consequences. In *Communal violence and minorities: Gujarat society in ferment*. Ed. by Lancy Lobo and Biswaroop Das. Jaipur: Rawat, 2006. pp. 124–138. CEPTL, CSSL, GIDRL, HML, UML.

Engineer, Asghar Ali. Now Vadodara goes up in communal-flames. In *Communal riots in post-independence India*. Ed. by Asghar Ali Engineer. Hyderabad: Sangam, 1984. pp. 281–287. CSSL, IIML.

Ganesh, S. and Mody, Mrudul. Ahmedabadi youth: what causes moral amnesia? In *Fascism in India: faces, fangs and facts*. Ed. by Chaitanya Krishna. New Delhi: Manak, 2003. pp. 405–415. CSSL, UML.

Ghassem-Fachandi, Parvis. *Pogrom in Gujarat: Hindu nationalism and anti-Muslim violence in India*. Princeton: Princeton University Press, 2012. p. 335. CSSL, IIML.

Ghosh, Anjan. Will to hate: Gujarat and the violence of identity. In *Democracy, pluralism and conflict*. Ed. by M.N. Karna. Jaipur: Rawat, 2006. pp. 197–211. CSSL, HML.

Ghosh, S.K. Anti reservation agitation and communal riots in Ahmedabad (Gujarat) 1985. In *Communal riots in India: meet the challenge unitedly*. New Delhi: Ashish, 1987. pp. 161–170. GUL, SGUL.

Ghosh, S.K. *Communal riots in India*. New Delhi: Ashish, 1987. p. 230. GUL, SGUL.

Ghosh, S.K. Communal disturbances in Ahmedabad (Gujarat), 1969. In *Communal riots in India: meet the challenge unitedly*. New Delhi: Ashish, 1987. pp. 151–160. GUL, SGUL.

Ghosh, S.K. Communal disturbances in Baroda (Gujarat) 1982. In *Communal riots in India: meet the challenge unitedly*. New Delhi: Ashish, 1987. pp. 171–174. GUL, SGUL.

Goyal, D.R. Communal tension, communal integration: a case study of Ahmedabad riots. In *Regionalism and national integration*. Ed. by Satish Chandra, K.C. Pande and P.C. Mathur. Jaipur: Aalekh, 1976. pp. 65–71. HML.

Grover, Vrinda. Elusive quest for justice: Delhi 1984 to Gujarat 2002. In *Gujarat: the making of tragedy*. Ed. by Siddharth Varadarajan. New Delhi: Penguin, 2002. pp. 356–388. CSSL, EDIL, HML, SETUL.

Guha, Ramchandra. VHP needs to hear the condemnation of the Hindu middle ground. In *Gujarat: the making of tragedy*. Ed. by Siddharth Varadarajan. New Delhi: Penguin, 2002. pp. 426–430. CSSL, EDIL, HML, SETUL.

Gupta, Dipankar. Gujarat riot and beyond. In *Fascism in India: faces, fangs and facts*. Ed. by Chaitanya Krishna. New Delhi: Manak, 2003. pp. 431–440. CSSL, UML.

Gupta, Dipankar. *Justice before reconciliation: negotiating a' new normal in post-riot Mumbai and Ahmedabad*. New Delhi: Routledge, 2011. p. 186. GVL, SPUL.

Haider, Najaf. 'Holi riot' of 1714: versions from Ahmedabad and Delhi. In *Living together separately: cultural Indian in history and politics*. Ed. by Mushirul Hasan and Asim Roy. New Delhi: Oxford, 2005. pp. 127–144. CSSL.

Hameed, Syeda, et al. Testimonies of sexual violence: the survivors speak. In *Fascism in India: faces, fangs and facts.* Ed. by Chaitanya Krishna. New Delhi: Manak, 2003. pp. 174–185. CSSL, UML.

Hardiman, David. Passing blame on Godhra Muslims. In *Fascism in India: faces, fangs and facts.* Ed. by Chaitanya Krishna. New Delhi: Manak, 2003. pp. 627–629. CSSL, UML.

International Initiative for Justice in Gujarat. *Threatened existence: a feminist analysis of the genocide in Gujarat*. [ ]: Author, 2003. p. 317. UML.

Irani, C.R. Gujarat holocaust and editorials. In *Black book of Gujarat*. Ed. by M.L. Sondhi and Apratim Mukarji. New Delhi: Manak, 2002. pp. 359–419. AAL, BVL, HML.

Islam, Shamsul. RSS: marketing fascism as Hindutva. In *Gujarat 2002: untold and re-told stories of the Hindutva lab*. Ed. by John Dayal. Delhi: Media House, 2002. pp. 122–150. CSSL, UML.

Jha, Raj Kamal. *Fireproof.* Great Britain: Picador, [ ]. p. 144. UML.

Kakodkar, Priyanka. Gujarat's children of terror. In *Fascism in India: faces, fangs and facts.* Ed. by Chaitanya Krishna. New Delhi: Manak, 2003. pp. 166–173. CSSL, UML.

Kannabiran, Kalpana. Adivasi and the genocide. In *Fascism in India: faces, fangs and facts.* Ed. by Chaitanya Krishna. New Delhi: Manak, 2003. pp. 332–335. CSSL, UML.

Kannupillai, V. *Communal violence: a sociological study of Gujarat.* Dehli: Shipra, 2006. p. 208. SETUL.

Kooiman, Dick. *Communalism and Indian princely states: Travancore, Baroda and Hyderabad in the 1930s*. New Delhi: Manohar, 2002. p. 249. CSSL.

Kothari, Rajni. Beginning of the end. In *Fascism in India: faces, fangs and facts.* Ed. by Chaitanya Krishna. New Delhi: Manak, 2003. pp. 577–579. CSSL, UML.

Kothari, Rajni. Reversal of ideology and rise of fascism. In *Fascism in India: faces, fangs and facts.* Ed. by Chaitanya Krishna. New Delhi: Manak, 2003. pp. 45–57. CSSL, UML.

Krishna, Chaitanya, ed. *Fascism in India: faces, fangs and facts*. New Delhi: Manak, 2003. p. 661. CSSL, UML.

Krishna, Chaitanya. Fascism in India: faces, fangs and facts. In *Fascism in India: faces, fangs and facts.* Ed. by Chaitanya Krishna. New Delhi: Manak, 2003. pp. 3–19. CSSL, UML.

Krishna, Chaitanya. Left's myopia. In *Fascism in India: faces, fangs and facts.* Ed. by Chaitanya Krishna. New Delhi: Manak, 2003. pp. 580–597. CSSL, UML.

Krishna Iyer, V.R., et al. State complicity. In *Fascism in India: faces, fangs and facts.* Ed. by Chaitanya Krishna. New Delhi: Manak, 2003. pp. 242–277. CSSL, UML.

Lobo, Lancy. Adivasis, Hindutva and post-Godhra riots in Gujarat. In *Communal violence and minorities: Gujarat society in ferment*. Ed. by Lancy Lobo and Biswaroop Das. Jaipur: Rawat, 2006. pp. 88–111. CEPTL, CSSL, GIDRL, HML, UML.

Lobo, Lancy. Adivasis, Hindutva and post-Godhra riots in Gujarat. In *Fascism in India: faces, fangs and facts.* Ed. by Chaitanya Krishna. New Delhi: Manak, 2003. pp. 313–331. CSSL, UML.

Lobo, Lancy and Das, Biswaroop. Gujarat 2002 riots: spatial spread patterns of related aspects. In *Communal violence and minorities: Gujarat society in ferment*. Ed. by Lancy Lobo and Biswaroop Das. Jaipur: Rawat, 2006. pp. 15–40. CEPTL, CSSL, GIDRL, HML, UML.

Lobo, Lancy and Das, Biswaroop. Hindus and Muslims after the 2002 Gujarat riots: 'Imaging' as binary opposites. In *Communal violence and minorities: Gujarat society in ferment*. Ed. by Lancy Lobo and Biswaroop Das. Jaipur: Rawat, 2006. pp. 41–62. CEPTL, CSSL, GIDRL, HML, UML.

Lobo, Lancy and Das, Biswaroop. Religious cover for political power: narratives of people and select extracts from vernacular press on the Gujarat 2002 riots. In *Communal violence and minorities: Gujarat society in ferment*. Ed. by Lancy Lobo and Biswaroop Das. Jaipur: Rawat, 2006. pp. 139–163. Also in *Understanding Indian society*. Ed. by B.S. Baviskar and Tulsi Patel. Hyderabad: Orient BlackSwan, 2010. pp. 146–171. CEPTL, CSSL, GIDRL, GVL, HML, IIML, UML.

Lobo, Lancy and Das, Biswaroop, ed. *Communal violence and minorities: Gujarat society in ferment*. Jaipur: Rawat, 2006. p. 228. CEPTL, CSSL, GIDRL, HML, UML.

Louis, Prakash. Gujarat genocide: the power of the people. In *Fascism in India: faces, fangs and facts*. Ed. by Chaitanya Krishna. New Delhi: Manak, 2003. pp. 539–555. CSSL, UML.

Mahadevia, Darshini. Communal space over life space: saga of increasing vulnerability in Ahmedabad. In *Fascism in India: faces, fangs and facts*. Ed. by Chaitanya Krishna. New Delhi: Manak, 2003. pp. 377–404. CSSL, UML.

Mahadevia, Darshini. From stealth to aggression: economic reforms and communal politics in Gujarat. In *Politics of economic reforms in India*. Ed. by Jos Mooij. New Delhi: Sage, 2005. pp. 291–321. CSSL, HML.

Mander, Harsh. *Cry, my beloved country: reflections on the Gujarat carnage 2002 and its aftermath*. Delhi: Rainbow, 2004. p. 142. CSSL, GIDRL, GVL.

Mander, Harsh. *Towards healing? seeking paths for justice and reconciliation in Gujarat*. New Delhi: Wiscomp, 2008. p. 150. IIML.

Manshardt, Clifford. *Hindu-Muslim problem in India*. London: George Allen & Unwin, 1936. p. 128. CSSL.

Mayaram, Shail. Genocide of the idea of Gujarat. In *Gujarat: the making of tragedy*. Ed. by Siddharth Varadarajan. New Delhi: Penguin, 2002. pp. 404–407. CSSL, EDIL, HML, SETUL.

Mehta, Nalin. Modi and the camera: the politics of television in the 2002 Gujarat riots. In *India on television: how satellite news channels have changed the way we think and act*. New Delhi: Harper Collins, 2008. pp. 274–298. IIML.

Mehta, Pratap Bhanu. Dilemmas of Muslim politics. In *Fascism in India: faces, fangs and facts*. Ed. by Chaitanya Krishna. New Delhi: Manak, 2003. pp. 532–538. CSSL, UML.

Miller, Webb. Account of "Salt March". In *Gandhi: ahimsa and non violence in practice*. Ed. by S.R. Sharma. New Delhi: Cosmo, 2001. pp. 19–27. CSSL.

Mishra, Satish. Gujarat: a case study of the tyranny of power. In *Black book of Gujarat*. Ed. by M.L. Sondhi and Apratim Mukarji. New Delhi: Manak, 2002. pp. 79–88. AAL, BVL, HML.

Mitta, Manoj. *Fiction of fact-finding: Modi and Godhra: a study of the Gujarat 2002 investigations*. Noida: HarperCollins, 2014. p. 261. CSSL.

Mukarji, Apratim. Gujarat riots: when diplomacy floundered. In *Black book of Gujarat*. Ed. by M.L. Sondhi and Apratim Mukarji. New Delhi: Manak, 2002. pp. 12–36. AAL, BVL, HML.

Mustafa, Seema. Witness to a pogrom. In *Gujarat 2002: untold and re-told stories of the Hindutva lab*. Ed. by John Dayal. Delhi: Media House, 2002. pp. 48–61. CSSL, UML.

Muthyalayya Naidu, C.H. Dandi March. In *Facets of Mahatma Gandhi*. Vol. 1: *non-violence and satyagraha*. Ed. by Subrata Mukherjee and Sushila Ramaswamy. New Delhi: Deep & Deep, 1996. pp. 183–191. CSSL.

Namishray, Mohandas. Violence in Gujarat and the dalits. In *Gujarat: the making of tragedy*. Ed. by Siddharth Varadarajan. New Delhi: Penguin, 2002. pp. 267–270. CSSL, EDIL, HML, SETUL.

Nampoothiri, P.G.J. and Sethi, Gagan. *Lest we forget history: tracing the communal violence in Gujarat 2002*. Bangalore: Books for Change, 2012. p. 156. CSSL.

Nandy, Ashish. Obituary of a culture: rise of a fascist to power. In *Fascism in India: faces, fangs and facts*. Ed. by Chaitanya Krishna. New Delhi: Manak, 2003. pp. 235–241. CSSL, UML.

Nariman, Fali S. Gujarat imbroglio. In *Black book of Gujarat*. Ed. by M.L. Sondhi and Aprati M. Mukarji. New Delhi: Manak, 2002. pp. 47–52. AAL, BVL, HML.

Noorani, A.G. India's reaction to international concern. In *Gujarat: the making of tragedy*. Ed. by Siddharth Varadarajan. New Delhi: Penguin, 2002. pp. 389–397. CSSL, EDIL, HML, SETUL.

Noorani, A.G. Practicing fascist trampling on India. In *Fascism in India: faces, fangs and facts*. Ed. by Chaitanya Krishna. New Delhi: Manak, 2003. pp. 278–287. CSSL, UML.

Nussbaum, Martha C. Rape and murder in Gujarat: violence against Muslim women in the struggle for Hindu supremacy. In *Violence and democracy in India*. Ed. by Amita Basu and Stirupa Roy. Culcatta: Seagull, 2007. pp. 101–122. GVL, IIML.

Omvedt, Gail. Reexamining a basic theme. In *Fascism in India: faces, fangs and facts*. Ed. by Chaitanya Krishna. New Delhi: Manak, 2003. pp. 297–303. CSSL, UML.

Oommen, T.K. *Reconciliation in post-Godhra Gujarat: the role of civil society*. New Delhi: Pearson, 2002. p. 288. CSSL, SPIESRL.

Ornit, Shani. Bootlegging politics and corruption: state violence and the routine practices of public power in Gujarat (1985–2002). In *Gujarat beyond Gandhi: identity, conflict and society*. Ed. by Nalin Mehta and Mona G. Mehta. New Delhi: Routledge, 2010. pp. 39–59. BVL, CSSL, GIDRL, IRMAL, UML.

Padgoankar, Dileep, Patel, Aakar and Verghese, B.G. Editor's guild reports on Gujarat riots. In *Black book of Gujarat*. Ed. by M.L. Sondhi and Apratim Mukarji. New Delhi: Manak, 2002. pp. 297–358. AAL, BVL, HML.

Parekh, Bhikhu. Making sense of Gujarat. In *Fascism in India: faces, fangs and facts*. Ed. by Chaitanya Krishna. New Delhi: Manak, 2003. pp. 511–523. CSSL, UML.

Patel, Girish. Narendra Modi's one-day cricket: what and why? In *Fascism in India: faces, fangs and facts*. Ed. by Chaitanya Krishna. New Delhi: Manak, 2003. pp. 441–476. CSSL, UML.

Patel, Priyavadan. Recent history and politics of communalism and communal riots in Gujarat. In *communalism in India*. Ed. by Asghar Ali Engineer and Moin Shakir. Delhi: Ajanta, 1985. pp. 106–146. CSSL.

People's Union for Democratic Rights. Little relief, no rehabilitation. In *Gujarat: the making of tragedy*. Ed. by Siddharth Varadarajan. New Delhi: Penguin, 2002. pp. 307–330. CSSL, EDIL, HML, SETUL.

Poonacha, Veena. Innovative strategies to counter domestic violence: exploring the state and community responses in Karanataka and Gujarat. In *Violence in media and society: literature, film and T.V.* Ed. by Usha Bande and Anshu Kaushal. Jaipur: Rawat, 2011. pp. 50–65. CSSL, GVL.

Prakash, Cedric. Justice for peace-challenges from Gujarat. In *Other India: realities of an emerging power.* Ed. by Rajesh Chakrabarti. New Delhi: Sage, 2009. pp. 110-[ ]. GVL.

Punwani, Jyoti. Carnage at Godhra. In *Gujarat: the making of tragedy.* Ed. by Siddharth Varadarajan. New Delhi: Penguin, 2002. pp. 45–74. CSSL, EDIL, HML, SETUL.

Punwani, Jyoti. Godhra revisited. In *Fascism in India: faces, fangs and facts.* Ed. by Chaitanya Krishna. New Delhi: Manak, 2003. pp. 623–626. CSSL, UML.

Puniyani, Ram. Hindutva's foot soldiers: dalits, adivasis? In *Communal violence and minorities: Gujarat society in ferment.* Ed. by Lancy Lobo and Biswaroop Das. Jaipur: Rawat, 2006. pp. 112–123. CEPTL, CSSL, GIDRL, HML, UML.

Punayani, Ram. Rashtriya Swayamsevak Sangh: politics as 'Culture'. In *Communal violence and minorities: Gujarat society in ferment.* Ed. by Lancy Lobo and Biswaroop Das. Jaipur: Rawat, 2006. pp. 164–180. CEPTL, CSSL, GIDRL, HML, UML.

Rai, Vibhuti Narain. Open letter to my fellow police officers. In *Gujarat: the making of tragedy.* Ed. by Siddharth Varadarajan. New Delhi: Penguin, 2002. pp. 211–213. CSSL, EDIL, HML, SETUL.

Rajagopal, Arvind. Special political zone: urban planning, spatial segregation and the infrastructure of violence in Ahmedabad. In *Gujarat beyond Gandhi: identity, conflict and society.* Ed. by Nalin Mehta and Mona G. Mehta. New Delhi: Routledge, 2010. pp. 88–126. BVL, CSSL, GIDRL, IRMAL, UML.

Rajgopal, P.R. Gujarat: the three agitations of 1974, 1981, and 1985. In *Social change and violence: the Indian experience.* New Delhi: Uppal, 1987. pp. 140–148. CEPTL, SGUL.

Rajgopal, P.R. Land reforms in Gujarat. In *Social change and violence: the Indian experience.* New Delhi: Uppal, 1987. pp. 73–75. CEPTL, SGUL.

Rajgopal, P.R. *Social change & violence: the Indian experience.* New Delhi: Uppal, 1987. p. 227. CEPTL, SGUL.

Rajaram, N. *Social processes and communal tension: a study of Vadodara city.* New Delhi: National Foundation For Communal Harmony, 2006. p. 194. GVL.

Raju, M.P. International law remedies. In *Gujarat 2002: untold and re-told stories of the Hindutva lab.* Ed. by John Dayal. Delhi: Media House, 2002. pp. 84–121. CSSL, UML.

Robinson, Rowena. *Tremors of violence: Muslim survivors of ethnic strife in Western India.* New Delhi: Sage, 2005. p. 148. CSSL, UML.

Robinson, Rowena and Parthasarthy, D. 'After Gujarat…': making sense of reports on the post-Godhra violence and its aftermath. In *Religion, power & violence: expression of politics in contemporary times.* Ed. by Ram Puniyani. New Delhi: Sage, 2005. pp. 306–318. CSSL.

Roy, Arundhati. Gujarat, fascism and democracy. In *Fascism in India: Faces, Fangs and Facts.* Ed. by Chaitanya Krishna. New Delhi: Manak, 2003. pp. 30–44. CSSL, UML.

Roy Burman, J.J. *Gujarat unknown: Hindu-Muslim syncretism and humanistic forays.* New Delhi: Mittal, 2005. p. 212. AAL, CEPTL, GIDRL, IRMAL MICAL, SPUL.

Sambrani, Shreekant. Gujarat's burning train: India's inferno? In *Fascism in India: faces, fangs and facts.* Ed. by Chaitanya Krishna. New Delhi: Manak, 2003. pp. 477–494. CSSL, UML.

Sanghavi, Nagindas. From Navnirman to the anti-Mandal riots: the political trajectory of Gujarat (1974–1985). In *Gujarat beyond Gandhi: identity, conflict and society*. Ed. by Nalin Mehta and Mona G. Mehta. New Delhi: Routledge, 2010. pp. 20–38. BVL, CSSL, GIDRL, IRMAL, UML.

Sarkar, Tanika. Semiotics of terror: Muslim children and women in Hindu rashtra. In *Fascism in India: faces, fangs and facts.* Ed. by Chaitanya Krishna. New Delhi: Manak, 2003. pp. 151–165. CSSL, UML.

Setalvad, Teesta. When guardians betray: the role of the police. In *Gujarat: the making of tragedy*. Ed. by Siddharth Varadarajan. New Delhi: Penguin, 2002. pp. 177–210. CSSL, EDIL, HML, SETUL.

Shah, Ghanshyam. Caste, Hindutva and hideousness. In *Fascism in India: faces, fangs and facts.* Ed. by Chaitanya Krishna. New Delhi: Manak, 2003. pp. 304–312. CSSL, UML.

Shah, Ghanshyam. Caste, Hindutva and the making of mob culture. In *Gujarat: the making of tragedy*. Ed. by Siddharth Varadarajan. New Delhi: Penguin, 2002. pp. 416–425. CSSL, EDIL, HML, SETUL.

Shah, Ghanshyam. 1969 Communal riots in Ahmedabad: a case study. In *Communal riots in post-independence India*. Ed. by Asghar Ali Engineer. Hyderabad: Sangam, 1984. pp. 175–208. CSSL, GVL, IIML.

Shah, Ghanshyam. Communalization and participation of dalits in Gujarat 2002 riots. In *Communal violence and minorities: Gujarat society in ferment*. Ed. by Lancy Lobo and Biswaroop Das. Jaipur: Rawat, 2006. pp. 77–87. CEPTL, CSSL, GIDRL, HML, UML.

Shah, Prakash N. NM and Kalinga? thrice impossible, brother Gill. In *Gujarat: the making of tragedy*. Ed. by Siddharth Varadarajan. New Delhi: Penguin, 2002. pp. 434–439. CSSL, EDIL, HML, SETUL.

Shani, Ornit. *Communalism, caste and Hindu nationalism: the violence in Gujarat.* New Delhi: Cambridge University press, 2008. p. 215. GIDRL, IIML.

Sharma, Ram Nath. *Gujarat holocaust: communalism in the land of Gandhi*. Delhi: Shubhi, 2002. p. 344. GUL, HML, MICAL.

Sharma, Subhash. Dispassionate analysis. In *Fascism in India: faces, fangs and facts.* Ed. by Chaitanya Krishna. New Delhi: Manak, 2003. pp. 556–562. CSSL, UML.

Sheth, Pravin N. *Global terrorism: melting borders, hardened walls*. Jaipur: Rawat, 2005. p. 384. CSSL.

Sheth, Pravin. and Menon, Ramesh. *Caste and communal time bomb*. Ahmedabad: Golewala, 1986. p. 159. GUL.

Singh, Gurpal. Just another day in Ahmedabad. In *Gujarat: the making of tragedy*. Ed. by Siddharth Varadarajan. New Delhi: Penguin, 2002. pp. 440–445. CSSL, EDIL, HML, SETUL.

Sinha, S.P. *Conflict and tension in tribal society.* New Delhi; Concept, 1993. pp. 317–357. GVL.

Sondhi, M.L. BJP's responsibility for the Gujarat tragedy. In *Black book of Gujarat*. Ed. by M.L. Sondhi and Apratim Mukarji. New Delhi: Manak, 2002. pp. 3–11. AAL, BVL, HML.

Sondhi, M.L. and Mukarji, Apratim, ed. *Black book of Gujarat*. New Delhi: Manak, 2002. p. 465. AAL, BVL, HML.

Sondhi, M.L. and Mukarji, Apratim. Reports of human rights watch (New York) on the Gujarat riots. in *Black book of Gujarat*. Ed. by M.L. Sondhi and Apratim Mukarji. New Delhi: Manak, 2002. pp. 183–296. AAL, BVL, HML.

Sundar, Nandini. License to kill: patterns of violence in Gujarat. In *Gujarat: the making of tragedy*. Ed. by Siddharth Varadarajan. New Delhi: Penguin, 2002. pp. 75–134. CSSL, EDIL, HML, SETUL.

Varadarajan, Siddharth. Chronicle of a tragedy foretold. In *Gujarat: the making of tragedy*. Ed. by Siddharth Varadarajan. New Delhi: Penguin, 2002. pp. 1–41. CSSL, EDIL, HML, SETUL.

Varadarajan, Siddharth. I salute you, Geetaben, from the bottom of my heart. In *Gujarat: the making of tragedy*. Ed. by Siddharth Varadarajan. New Delhi: Penguin, 2002. pp. 446–449. CSSL, EDIL, HML, SETUL.

Varadarajan, Siddharth and Sardesai, Rajdeep. PUCL-Vadodara/Shanti Abhiyan and Anil Chamaria. Truth hurts: Gujarat and the role of the media. In *Gujarat: the making of tragedy*. Ed. by Siddharth Varadarajan. New Delhi: Penguin, 2002. pp. 271–304. CSSL, EDIL, HML, SETUL.

Varadarajan, Siddharth, ed. Apart, Yet a Part: Ghettoization, trauma-and some rays of hope. In *Gujarat: the making of tragedy*. Ed. by Siddharth Varadarajan. New Delhi: Penguin, 2002. pp. 331–355. CSSL, EDIL, HML, SETUL.

Varadarajan, Siddharth, ed. *Gujarat: the making of tragedy*. New Delhi: Penguin, 2002. p. 459. CSSL, EDIL, HML, SETUL.

Varadarajan, Siddharth, ed. Narratives from the killing fields. In *Gujarat: the making of tragedy*. Ed. by Siddharth Varadarajan. New Delhi: Penguin, 2002. pp. 135–176. CSSL, EDIL, HML, SETUL.

Varshney, Ashutosh. Ethnic conflict and civil life: Hindus and Muslims in India. New Delhi: Oxford, 2002. p. 382 or pp. 219–278. (Chapter 9–11 on Gujarat). CSSL.

Yagnik, Achyut. Hindutva as a savarna purama. In *Creating a nationality: Ramjanmabhumi movement and fear of the self.* [Ed.] By Ashis Nandy, et al.Delhi: Oxford, 1995. pp. 100–123. CSSL.

Yagnik, Achyut. Pathology of Gujarat. In *Gujarat: the making of tragedy*. Ed. by Siddharth Varadarajan. New Delhi: Penguin, 2002. pp. 408–415. CSSL, EDIL, HML, SETUL.

Yagnik, Achyut. Pathology of Gujarat. In *Fascism in India: faces, fangs and facts.* Ed. by Chaitanya Krishna. New Delhi: Manak, 2003. pp. 495–501. CSSL, UML.

Zakaria, Rafiq. *Communal rage in secular India*. Mumbai: Popular, 2003. p. 248. CSSL.

Zakaria, Rafiq. Economic extermination of Muslims. In *Fascism in India: faces, fangs and facts.* Ed. by Chaitanya Krishna. New Delhi: Manak, 2003. pp. 186–192. CSSL, UML.

Journal Articles

Ahmad, Imtiaz. State of lies and the lies of the state: the Gujarat program and the future of India. *Think India*. 5, 3, 2002. pp. 74–83. CSSL.

Ahmed, Sara. Sustaining peace rebuilding livelihoods the Gujarat harmony project. *Gender and Development.* 12, 3, 2004. pp. 94–102. IRMAL.

Amin, R.K. Real crisis in Gujarat liberalism humanism and democracy go by default. *Vishleshan.* 27, 3, 2002. pp. 13–15. IRMAL.

Amruth, M. Silences and the impossibility of confabulation after Godhra. *Economic and Political Weekly.* 42, 49, 2007. pp. 23–25. BUL, CEPTL, CSSL, EDIL, GIDRL, IIML, IRMAL, MICAL, SGUL, SPIESRL, SUL, UML.

Badigar, Sanjeevini. 'Normal' anomaly: displacement due to communal violence in Gujarat. *Economic and Political Weekly*. 47, 3, 2012. pp. 42–47. BUL, CSSL, IRMAL, SPIESRL, SUL, UML.

Basu RayChaudhury, Anasua. Sabarmati: creating a new divide? *Economic and Political Weekly*. 42, 8, 2007. pp. 697–703. BUL, CEPTL, CSSL, EDIL, IIML, IRMAL, MICAL, SGUL, SPIESRL, SUL, UML.

Bhagat, Rajiv. Origins of unity and communalism in Gujarat, India-I. *Indian Journal of Secularism*. 14, 2, 2010. pp. 102–119. CSSL.

Bhagat, Rajiv. Origins of unity and communalism in Gujarat, India-II. *Indian Journal of Secularism*. 14, 3, 2010. pp. 99–124. CSSL.

Bhatia, Bela. Step backward in Sabarkantha. *Seminar*. 513, 2002. pp. 35–38. CEPTL, CSSL, IIML, MICAL, SPUL, UML.

Bose, Pradip Kumar. Social mobility and caste violence: a study of the Gujarat riots. *Economic and Political Weekly*. 16, 16, 1981. pp. 713–716. CEPTL, CSSL, GUL, IIML, IRMAL, SGUL, SPIESRL, UML.

Breman, Jan. Anti-Muslim pogrom in Surat. *Economic and Political Weekly*. 28, 16, 1993. pp. 737–741. CEPTL, CSSL, IIML, IRMAL, SGUL, SPIESRL, UML.

Chakraborty, Somen. Debate on genocide: Gujarat a case study. *Social Action*. 52, 3, 2002. pp. 273–288. CSSL, IRMAL.

Chandra, Sudhir. Hindu's protest. *Seminar*. 513, 2002. pp. 49–52. CEPTL, CSSL, IIML, IRMAL, MICAL, SPUL, UML.

Chandra, Sudhir. Of communal consciousness and communal violence: impressions from post-riot Surat. *Economic and Political Weekly*. 28, 36, 1993. pp. 1883–1887. CEPTL, CSSL, IIML, IRMAL, SGUL, SPIESRL, UML.

Chopra, Kusum. Peaceful yatra in Ahmedabad. *Muslim India*. 5, 58, 1987. pp. 472–473. GVL.

Chronology of Gujarat events-2002. (Mainstream, Vol. 12–25, 2002). *Social Action*. 52, 3, 2002. pp. 301–326. CSSL, IRMAL.

Copland, Ian. Cambay 'disturbances' of 1890: popular protest in princely India. *Indian Economic and Social History Review*. 20, 4, 1983. pp. 415–437. CEPTL, CSSL, HML, IIML, UML.

Dalwai, Shama and Mhatre, Sandhya. Godhra & after: report of violence in Gujarat. Special Report. *Indian Journal of Secularism*. 6, 2, 2002. pp. 68–119. CSSL.

Dave, Antara Sen. Psycho social care through community level helpers Gujarat and governance. *Voices for Change: Journal on Communications for Development*. 7, 1, 2003. pp. 12–14. IRMAL.

Desai, Kiran. Communal relations and communal consciousness in the wake of communal violence: a case study of Surat city. *VNSGU Journal of Humanities & Social Sciences*. 2, 1, 2010. pp. 126–152. CSSL, SGUL.

Desai, Meghnad. Gujarat and its bhasmita. *Seminar*. 513, 2002. pp. 56–57. CEPTL, CSSL, GVL, IIML, IRMAL, MICAL, SPUL, UML.

Devy, Ganesh. Tribal voice and violence. *Seminar*. 513, 2002. pp. 39–48. CEPTL, CSSL, IIML, IRMAL, MICAL, SPUL, UML.

Dwivedi, H.S. Aftermath of train attack in Godhara. *Rural India*. 65, 2–3. 2002. pp. 25–26. GVL.

Engineer, Asghar Ali. Gujarat riots in the light of the history of communal violence. *Economic and Political Weekly*. 37, 50, 2002. pp. 5047–5054. BUL, CEPTL, CSSL, EDIL, GIDRL, IIML, IRMAL, MICAL, SGUL, SPIESRL, UML.

Engineer, Irfan. Backward communities and migrant workers in Surat riots. *Economic and Political Weekly*. 29, 22, 1994. pp. 1348–1360. CEPTL, CSSL, IIML, IRMAL, SPIESRL, UML.

Gadhavi, Sanat H. Causes and consequences of conflicts in a Saurashtra village. *Journal of the Gujarat Research Society*. 37, 3/145, 1975. pp. 96–101. GVL, TRTIL.

Goyal, D.R. National integration and communal violence. *Economic and Political Weekly*. 5, 8, 1970. pp. 379–381. CSSL, IRMAL, SPIESRL, UML.

Gupta, Dipankar. Citizens or victims? *Seminar*. 602, 2009. pp. 48–53. CSSL, MICAL, UML.

Gupta, Dipankar. Limits of tolerance: prospects of secularism in India after Gujarat. *Economic and Political Weekly*. 37, 46, 2002. pp. 4615–4620. BUL, CEPTL, CSSL, EDIL, GIDRL, IIML, IRMAL, MICAL, SGUL, SPIESRL, UML.

Guzder, Cyrus. Is secularism good for business? *Seminar*. 513, 2002. pp. 68–72. CEPTL, CSSL, IIML, IRMAL, MICAL, SPUL, UML.

Heitmeyer, Carolyn. There is peace here: managing communal relations in a town in Central Gujarat. *Journal of South Asian Development*. 4, 1, 2009. pp. 103–120. IRMAL.

Jaffrelot, Christophe. Gujarat 2002: what justice for the victims? the Supreme Court, the SIT, the police and the state judiciary. *Economic and Political Weekly*. 47, 8, 2012. pp. 77–89. BUL, CSSL, IRMAL, SPIESRL, SUL, UML.

Joshi, Satykam. Tribals, missionaries and Sadhus: understanding violence in the Dangs. *Economic and Political Weekly*. 34, 37, 1999. pp. 2667–2675. CEPTL, CSSL, IIML, IRMAL, MICAL, SGUL, SPIESRL, UML.

Jowher, Zakia. Four years after the Gujarat carnage. *Social Action*. 56, 2, 2006. pp. 128–134. BUL, CEPTL, CSSL, EDIL, GVL, HML, IIML, IRMAL.

Khan, Arshi. Situating riots, communal consciousness and the culture of exclusion in India's liberal democracy. *Social Action*. 52, 3, 2002. pp. 258–272. CSSL.

Khare, Harish. After Gujarat. *Seminar*. 521, 2003. pp. 30–33. CEPTL, CSSL, GIDRL, GVL, IIML, IRMAL, MICAL, SPUL, UML.

Khare, Harish. Gujarat in flames again. *Muslim India*. 4, 44, 1986. pp. 355-[ ]. GVL.

Kothari, Rajni. Culture of communalism in Gujarat. *Economic and Political Weekly*. 37, 48, 2002. pp. 4823–4825. BUL, CEPTL, CSSL, EDIL, IIML, IRMAL, MICAL, SGUL, SPIESRL, UML.

Kumar, Mansi. Journey into the bleeding city: following the footprints of the rubble of riot and violence. *Psychology and Developing Societies*. 19, 1, 2007. pp. 1–36. EDIL.

Lobo, Lancy. Adivasis, Hindutva and post-Godhra riots in Gujarat. *Economic and Political Weekly*. 37, 48, 2002. pp. 4844–4849. BUL, CEPTL, CSSL, EDIL, GIDRL, IIML, IRMAL, MICAL, SGUL, SPIESRL, UML.

Lobo, Lancy. Communal violence in Surat city. *Social Action*. 43, 2, 1993. pp. 144–152. CSSL.

Louis, Prakash. Gujarat carnage: protectors have become predators. *Social Action*. 52, 3, 2002. pp. 241–257. CSSL, IRMAL.

Macwan, Joseph. This 'Unique' land. *Seminar*. 513, 2002. pp. 32–34. CEPTL, CSSL, IIML, IRMAL, MICAL, SPUL, UML.

Mahadevia, Darshini. Communal space over life space: saga of increasing vulnerability in Ahmedabad. *Economic and Political Weekly*. 37, 48, 2002. pp. 4850–4858. BUL, CEPTL, CSSL, EDIL, IIML, IRMAL, MICAL, SGUL, SPIESRL, UML.

Mander, Harsh. Before it is too late Gujarat and governance. *Voices for Change: Journal on Communications for Development*. 7, 1, 2003. pp. 3–11. IRMAL.

Mander, Harsh. Broken lives and compromise: shadow play in Gujarat. *Economic and Political Weekly*. 47, 8, 2012. pp. 90–97. BUL, CSSL, IRMAL, SPIESRL, SUL, UML.

Mander, Harsh. Inside Gujarat's relief colonies: surviving state hospitality and denial. *Economic and Political Weekly*. 41, 51, 2006. pp. 5235–5239. (Insight). BUL, CEPTL, CSSL, EDIL, GIDRL, IIML, IRMAL, MICAL, SGUL, SPIESRL, SUL, UML.

Mander, Harsh. Living in times of fear and hate: failures of reconciliation in Gujarat. *Economic and Political Weekly*. 42, 10, 2007. pp. 847–852. BUL, CEPTL, CSSL, EDIL, HML, IIML, IRMAL, SGUL, SPIESRL, SUL, UML.

Mehta, Uday. Gujarat genocide: a sociological appraisal. *Indian Journal of Secularism*. 6, 3, 2002. pp. 35–45. CSSL, MICAL.

Menon, Meena.That was once my home victims of the genocide in Gujarat have nowhere to go. *Humanscape*. 9, 7, 2002. pp. 6–14. IRMAL.

Menon, Ramesh. Wall of suspicion in Gujarat. *Muslim India*. 4, 44, 1986. pp. 354–355. GVL.

Ohm, Britta. Narratives of the underbelly of democracy. *Economic and Political Weekly*. 42, 49, 2007. pp. 26–31. BUL, CEPTL, CSSL, EDIL, GIDRL, IIML, IRMAL, MICAL, SGUL, SPIESRL, SUL, UML.

Parekh, Bhikhu. Making sense of Gujarat. *Seminar*. 513, 2002. pp. 26–31. CEPTL, CSSL, GVL, IIML, IRMAL, MICAL, SPUL, UML.

Patel, Anil. Crimes of communalism. *Vishleshan*. 27, 3, 2002. pp. 4–12. CSSL.

Patel, Arjun. Issues of dalit conflicts in Gujarat. *VNSGU Journal of Humanities & Social Sciences*. 1, 2, 2009. pp. 51–63. CSSL, SGUL.

Patel, Girish. Narendra Modi's one-day cricket: what and why? *Economic and Political Weekly*. 37, 48, 2002. pp. 4826–4837. BUL, CEPTL, CSSL, EDIL, IIML, IRMAL, MICAL, SGUL, SPIESRL, UML.

Poonacha, Veena and Pandey, Divya. Responses to domestic violence: government and non-government action in Karnataka and Gujarat. *Economic and Political Weekly*. 35, 7, 2000. pp. 566–574. BUL, CEPTL, CSSL, GIDRL, IIML, IRMAL, MICAL, SGUL, SPIESRL, UML.

Raju, M.P. 'Impunity, thy name is Gujarat 2002': a case for international tribunals. *Social Action*. 56, 2, 2006. pp. 109–127. BUL, CEPTL, CSSL, EDIL, GVL, HML, IRMAL.

Ramakrishnan, Nitya. Godhra: the verdict analysed. *Economic and Political Weekly*. 46, 15, 2011. pp. 39–44. BUL, CEPTL, CSSL, EDIL, IRMAL, SPIESRL, SUL, UML.

Ramanathan, Suguna. Ordeal by fire. *Seminar*. 513, 2002. pp. 23–25. CEPTL, CSSL, IIML, IRMAL, MICAL, SPUL, UML.

Rajan, Y.S. Dedicated to victims of Gujarat. *Vishleshan*. 27, 3, 2002. pp. 1–3. IRMAL.

Roy Burman, J.J. Hindu-Muslim relations after Gujarat 2002: some positive reflections. *Social Action*. 56, 2, 2006. pp. 141–154. BUL, CEPTL, CSSL, EDIL, GVL, HML, IIML, IRMAL.

Sadhu, Arun. Political agitation and violence has twisted Gujarat social values. *Muslim India*. 4, 44, 1986. pp. 348–349. GVL.

Sayeed, Ashraf. Gujarat riots. *Muslim India*. 9, 97, 1991. pp. 32–33. GVL.

Sethi, Gagan. Communal cauldron: lesson learnt; way forward. *Social Action*. 56, 2, 2006. pp. 135–139. CSSL, EDIL, GVL.

Shah, Ghanshyam. Anatomy of urban riots: Ahmedabad 1973. *Economic and Political Weekly*. 9, 6, 7 and 8, 1974. pp. 233–240. CSSL, GUL, IRMAL, SGUL, SPIESRL, TRTIL, UML.

Shah, Ghanshyam. Communal riots in Gujarat: report of a preliminary investigation. *Economic and Political Weekly*. 5, 3, 4, and 5, 1970. pp. 187–200. CSSL, HML, IRMAL, SGUL, SPIESRL, TRTIL, UML.

Shah, Ghanshyam. Identity, communal consciousness and politics. *Economic and Political Weekly*. 29, 19, 1994. pp. 1133–1140. CEPTL, CSSL, IIML, IRMAL, MICAL, SPIESRL, UML.

Shah, Ghanshyam. Surat 1993. *Seminar*. 411, 1993. pp. 34–37. CSSL, GIDRL, GVL, UML.

Shani, Ornit. Rise of Hindu nationalism in India: case study of Ahmedabad in the 1980s. *Modern Asian Studies*. 39, 4, 2005. pp. 861–896. CSSL.

Sharan, Shree Shankar. Agony in Gujarat: a report on Gujarat riots. *Indian Journal of Secularism*. 6, 4, 2003. pp. 11–20. CSSL.

Sheth, Suchitra. Gujarat's balance Sheet. *Seminar*. 545, 2005. pp. 51–54. CEPTL, CSSL, GIDRL, IIML, MICAL, SPUL, UML.

Shethi, Harsh. Problem. *Seminar*. 513, 2002. pp. 12–14. CEPTL, CSSL, IIML, IRMAL, MICAL, SPUL, UML.

Siwach, Rajkumar. Social tension and communal conflicts: lesson from Gujarat. *Indian Journal of Public Administration*. 48, 3, 2002. pp. 435–447. CSSL, GIDRL, IRMAL.

Spodek, Howard. From Gandhi to violence: Ahmedabad's 1985 riots in historical perspective. *Modern Asian Studies*. 23, 4, 1989. pp. 765–795. CSSL.

Subramanian, Lakshmi. Capital and crowd in a declining Asian port city: the Anglo-Bania order and the Surat riots of 1795. *Modern Asian Studies*. 19, 2, 1985. pp. 205–237. CSSL.

Subramanian, Lakshmi. Eighteenth-century social order in Surat: a reply and an excursus on the riots of 1788 and 1795. *Modern Asian Studies*. 25, 2, 1991. pp. 321–365. CSSL.

Suhrud, Tridip. In search of Gandhi. *Seminar*. 513, 2002. pp. 61–63. CEPTL, CSSL, GVL, IIML, IRMAL, MICAL, SPUL, UML.

Tellis, Olga. On recurrence of riots in Ahmedabad. *Muslim India*. 5, 50, 1987. pp. 83–84. GVL.

Vaux, Tony. Experience of communal violence. *Seminar*. 619, 2011. pp. 24–28. CSSL, UML.

Yagnik, Achyut. Pathology of Gujarat. *Seminar*. 513, 2002. pp. 19–22. CEPTL, CSSL, GVL, IIML, IRMAL, MICAL, SPUL, UML.

Working Papers, Reports and Other Materials

Chenoy, Kamal Mitra. Violence in Gujarat: test case for a larger fundamentalist agenda: report of the citizen's commission on persecution of Christians in Gujarat, an initiative of the national alliance of women. New Delhi: National Alliance of Women, 1999. p. 88. CSSL.

Dave, V.S. *Report of the commission of inquiry: into the incidents of violence and disturbances which took place at various places in the state of Gujarat since February, 1985 to 18th July, 1985*. Vol. I–III. Ahmedabad: [ ], 1990. p. 286, p. 26. and p. 440. CSSL.

Desai, Kiran and De, Aparajita. *Hindu Muslim relations in Gujarat: case studies of Surat and Vadodara.* Surat: Centre for Social Studies, 2003. p. 238. CSSL.

Desai, R.C., Khan, Javed and Soni, Manoj., ed. *In Search of a third space: for national harmony beyond the Godhra carnage and its aftermath.* Vallabh Vidyanagar: Sardar Patel University, 2002. p. 105. Symposium Volume. CSSL.

Independent People's Tribunal. *Rise of fascism in India: voices beneath the ashes: victims of communal violence speak.* New Delhi: Human Rights Law Network, 2008. p. 424. Report of the Independent People's Tribunal on the Rise of Fascist Forces and the Attack on the Secular State, March 20–22, 2007. CSSL.

Lobo, Lancy and Das, Biswaroop. Geography of Gujarat riots, 2002: causatives and spatial spread patterns of related factors. Vadodara: Centre for Culture and Development, 2002. p. 89. CSSL.

Mander, Harsh and Nanavati, Kiran. *Surviving state hostility and denial: a survey of relief colonies for people affected by mass violence in Gujarat 2002: a report.* Ahmedabad: Nyayagrah, 2006. p. 40. CSSL.

Pangotra, Prem. *City monitor 2002.* Ahmedabad: Ahmedabad Management Association, 2003. p. 189. CEEL.

Patel, Arjun. *Communal riots and its aftermath: a report of preliminary investigation of Palanpur road in Surat.* Surat: Centre for Social Studies, 1994. p. [ ]. Occasional Paper No. 19. CSSL.

Spodek, Howard. 1985 riots in historical perspective. In *International Seminar on "Gujarat Society", 17–20 December 1986.* Surat: Centre for Social Studies, 1986. pp. 1–21. CSSL.

4

Ethnicity, Identity, Social Groups

Books/Chapter in Books

Baptiste, Fitzroy Andre, Mcleod, John and Robbins, Kenneth X. Africans in medieval North India, Bengal and Gujarat. In *African elites in India: Habshi Amarat*. Ed. by Kenneth X. Robbins and John Macleod. India: Mapin, 2006. pp. 124–129. BUL, TRTIL.

Basu, Helene. Ritual communication: the case of the Sidi in Gujarat. In *Lived Islam in South Asia: adaptation, accommodation and conflict*. Ed. by Imtiaz Ahmad and Helmut Reifeld. Delhi: Social Science Press, 2004. pp. 233–253. CSSL, SETUL.

Bhowmik, K.L. Study on symbols in a Gujarat community. In *Society and culture.* Ed. by K.L. Bhowmik. New Delhi: Inter-India, 1988. pp. 193–206. CEPTL, CSSL.

Biswas, D.P. Rebari: a semi-nomadic tribe in arid and semi-arid Gujarat. In *Studies in tribal development,* Volume 1. Ed. by G.P. Gupta. Jaipur: Arihant, [ ]. pp. 257–263. TRTIL.

Chakraborty, Jyotirmoy. Marriage and kinship among the Siddis of Saurashtra. In *Contemporary society: tribal studies.* Vol. 2. Ed. by George Pfeffer and Deepak Kumar Behera. New Delhi: Concept, 1997. pp. 198–204. CSSL.

Chattopadhyay, Kamaladevi. Bhils of Gujarat and Rajasthan. In *Tribalism in India*. Ed. by Kamaladevi Chattopadhyay. New Delhi: Vikas, 1978. pp. 55–79. CSSL, GVL.

Cort, John E. Jains, caste and hierarchy in North Gujarat. In *Caste in question: identity or hierarchy?*. Ed. by Dipankar Gupta. New Delhi: Sage, 2004. pp. 73–112. CEPTL, CSSL, SGUL.

Devy, G.N. *Nomad called thief: reflections on adivasi silence*. Hyderabad: Orient Longman, 2006. p. 199. CSSL, SETUL.

Doshi, S.L. *Tribal ethnicity, class, and integration*. Jaipur: Rawat, 1990. p. 259. SETUL.

Dubey, S.L. Gujarat. In *Land alienation and restoration in tribal communities in India*. Ed. by S.N. Dubey and Ratana Murdia. Bombay: Himalaya, 1977. pp. 76–84. AAUL, CSSL, GVL, SPUL, TRTIL.

Eastwick, E.B. *Gujarat and the Gujaratis*. New Delhi: Cosmo, 2000. p. 189. HML, SGUL, SUL.

Eduljee, H.E. *Kisseh-I Sanjan*. Bombay: Oriental Institute, [ ]. p. 197. UML.

Edwards, Eiluned. Textiles and dress among the Rabari of Kutch. In *Idea of Gujarat: history, ethnography and text*. Ed. by Edward Simpson and Aparna Kapadia. Hyderabad: Orient Blackswan, 2010. pp. 184–206. AAL, ASL, BUL, CEPTL, CSSL, GIDRL, IRMAL, MICAL, SETUL.

Ekka, William. Bhamaiya: a village in South Gujarat. In *Anthropology of weaker sections.* Ed. by Surajit Chandra Sinha. New Delhi: Concept, 1993. pp. 419–442. TRTIL.

Engineer, Asghar Ali. *Bohras*. New Delhi: Vikas, 1980. p. 332. CSSL, SETUL.

Engineer, Asghar Ali, compil. *Muslim communities of Gujarat: an exploratory study of Bohras, Khojas and Memons*. Delhi: Ajanta, 1989. p. 275. CSSL, GIDRL, GUL, GVL, SUL, TRTIL.

Engineer, Asghar Ali. *Muslims and India*. New Delhi: Gyan, 2006. pp. 229–265. GVL.

Flavoni, Darzi Francesco. *Rabari: a pastoral community of Kutch*. New Delhi: Indira Gandhi National Centre for Arts, 1990. p. 135. TRTIL.

Ganguly, Varsha. *Conservation, displacement and deprivation: Maldhari of Gir forest of Gujarat*. Delhi: Indian Social Institute, 2004. p. 195. SETUL.

Gauba, K.L. Western states Gujarat. In *Passive voices: a penetrating study of Muslim in India*. by K.L. Gauba. New Delhi: Sterling, 1973. pp. 159–172. GVL.

Gidwani, Vinay. *Capital, interrupted: agrarian development and the politics of work in India*. Delhi: Permanent Black, 2008. p. 337. CSSL.

Guha, Amalendu. More about the Parsi Sheths: their roots, entrepreneurship, and comprador role, 1650–1918. In *Business communities of India: a historical perspective*. Ed. by Dwijendra Tripathi. New Delhi: Manohar, 1984. pp. 109–150. CSSL.

Haque, M. Ear variability in three tribes of Saurashtra. In *Man*. Ed. by K.L. Bhowmik. New Delhi: Inter-India, 1988. pp. 115–120. GVL.

Haque, M. Physique nutrition among the Charan: a forest dweller tribe of Junagadh, Gujarat: an anthropolometric study. In *Status of scheduled tribes in India*. Ed by Harish Chandra Upadhyay. New Delhi: Anmol, 1999. pp. [ ]. AAL

Hardiman, David. Bhils and Shahukars of Eastern Gujarat. In *Subaltern studies*, Vol. V: *writings on South Asian history and society*. Delhi: Oxford, 1987. pp. 1–54. CSSL, GVL.

Hardiman, David. *Feeding the Baniya: peasants and usurers in Western India*. Delhi: Oxford, 1996. p. 368. CSSL, GIDRL, SETUL.

Ibrahim, Farhana. Boarder transgressions and the frontiers of faith in Kachchh, Gujarat. In *Frontiers of embedded Muslim communities in India*. Ed. by Vinod K. Jairath. New Delhi: Routledge, 2011. pp. 29–48. HML, IIML.

Jaffrelot, Christophe and Thomas, Charlotte. Facing ghettoisation in 'Riot-city': old Ahmedabad and Juhapura between victimisation and self-help. In *Muslims in Indian cities: trajectories of marginalization*. Ed. by Laurent Gayer and Christophe Jaffrelot. Noida: Harper Collins, 2012. pp. 43–79. CSSL.

Jain, Jyotindra. Ethnic background of some hero-stones of Gujarat. In *Memorial stones*. Ed. by S. Settar and Gunther D. Sontheimer. Dharwad: Institute of Indian Art History, 1982. pp. 83–86. GVL.

Jhaveri, Krishanlal Mohanlal. *Gujaratis: the people, their history and the culture*. New Delhi: Cosmo, 2003. p. 1625. 5 Vols. SGUL, SPUL, SUL.

Joshi, Satyakam. Development, deprivation and discontent: a case of Dangs tribals. In *Development and deprivation in Gujarat: in hounour of Jan Breman*. Ed. by Ghanshyam Shah, Mario Rutten and Hein Streefkerk. New Delhi: Sage, 2002. pp. 196–213. CEEL, CEPTL, CSSL, EDIL, GIDRL, HML, IIML, IRMAL, UML.

Joshi, Vidyut. Genesis of tribal problem. In *Social transformation in India: essays in honour of Professor I.P. Desai*. Vol. 2. Ed. by Ghanshyam Shah. Jaipur: Rawat, 1997. pp. 451–465. CSSL, GVL, HML, SGUL, SPUL.

Joshi, Vidyut. Genesis of tribal problems. In *Tribal situation in India: issues in development: with special reference to Western India*. Ed. by Vidyut Joshi. Jaipur: Rawat, 1998. pp. 13–27. CSSL, GVL, SGUL, UML.

Kamerkar, Mani and Dhunjisha, Soonu. *From the plateau to the shores of Gujarat: the story of Parsi settlements and absorption in India*. Mumbai: Allied, 2002. p. 220. CSSL.

Kapadia, K.M. Religious creeds among the Patidars of South Gujarat: a panoramic view. In *Towards a sociology of culture in India*. Ed. by T.K.N. Unnithan, Indra Deva and Yogendra Singh. New Delhi: Prentice-Hall, 1965. pp. 242–261. CSSL.

Kapur, Nandini Sinha. Bhils in Guhila Dungarpur and Caulukyan Gujarat. In *Reconstructing identities: tribes, agro-pastoralists and environment in Western India (Seventh-twentieth Centuries)*. By Nandini Sinha Kapur. New Delhi: Manohar, 2008. pp. 55–70. CSSL.

Karaka, Dosabhai Framji. *History of the Parsis*. 2 Vol. London: Macmillan, 1884. p. 350 and [ ]. ASL.

Khan, Dominique-Sila. Liminality and legality: a contemporary debate among the Imamshahis of Gujarat. In *Lived Islam in South Asia: adaptation, accommodation and conflict*. Ed. by Imtiaz Ahmad and Helmut Reifeld. Delhi: Social Science Press, 2004. pp. 209–232. CSSL.

Khullar, Ava. Parsi Zoroastrians of India. In *Minorities of India: problems & prospects*. Ed. by M.A. Jawaid, K.N. Jehangir and Shankar Bose. New Delhi: Indian Council of Social Science Research, 2007. pp. 71–84. CSSL.

Kothari, Rajni and Maru, Rushikesh. Federating for political interests: the Kshatriyas of Gujarat. In *Caste and democratic politics in India*. Ed. by Ghanshyam Shah. Delhi: Permanent Black, 2002. pp. 234–266. CSSL, HML.

Kothari, Rajni and Maru, Rushikesh. Federating for political interests: the Kshatriyas of Gujarat. In *Writings of Rajni Kothari*. Ed. by Ashis Nandy. New Delhi: Orient Blackswan, 2009. pp. 66–96. GVL.

Kothari, Rita. *Burden of Refuge: the Sindhi Hindus of Gujarat*. Hyderabad: Orient Longman, 2007. p. 206. CSSL, MICAL, SETUL.

Kothari, Rita. Voices from Sindh in Gujarat. In *Idea of Gujarat: history, ethnography and text*. Ed. by Edward Simpson and Aparna Kapadia. Hyderabad: Orient Blackswan, 2010. pp. 168–183. AAL, ASL, BUL, CEPTL, CSSL, GIDRL, IRMAL, MICAL, SETUL.

Krishan, Gopal, Haque, M. and Mukherjee, A. *Morphogenetic variation: a comparative profile of three tribes of Gujarat*. Culcutta: Anthropological Survey of India, 1994. p. 88. GVL.

Lal, R.B. Tribal situation in Gujarat. In *Tribal situation in India: issues in development: with special reference to Western India*. Ed. by Vidyut Joshi. Jaipur: Rawat, 1998. pp. 57–82. CSSL, GVL, SGUL, UML.

Lambat, Ismail A. Marriage among the Sunni Surati Vohras of South Gujarat. In *Family, kinship and marriage among Muslims in India*. Ed. by Ahmad Imtiaz. New Delhi: Manohar, 1976. pp. 49–82. SPIESRL.

Lobo, Lancy. Household and family among Thakors in a North Gujarat village. In *Family in India: structure and practice*. Ed. by Tulsi Patel. New Delhi: Sage, 2005. pp. 267–286. HML.

Lobo, Lancy. Kolis of Gujarat: a conspectus. In *Stagnation, retrograde change or positive progress?: vignettes from the journey of the OBC communities in the process of change in India*. Ed. by H.S. Verma and Nadeem Hasnain. New Delhi: Serials, 2006. pp. 45–69. CSSL.

Lobo, Lancy. *Thakors of North Gujarat: a caste in the village and the region*. New Delhi: Hindustan, 1995. p. 205. CSSL, GVL, TRTIL.

Luhrmann, T.N. *Good Parsi: the fate of a colonial elite in a postcolonial society*. Delhi: Oxford, 1996. p. 317. CSSL.

Makwana, M.H. Cooperatives, dalits and social change. In *Backward classes and social justice*. Ed. by M.H. Makwana and Richard Pais. Jaipur: Rawat, 2011. pp. 153–169. CSSL.

Malabari, Behramji M. *Gujarat & the Gujaratis*. Delhi: Mittal, 1983. p. 358. CSSL, GUL, HML, SGUL, SPIESRL, SUL.

Malabari, Behramji M. *Gujarat & the Gujaratis: pictures of man and manners taken from life*. Bombay: Port Printing Press, 1889. p. 456. ASL, BVL, SETUL.

Malabari, Behramji M. *Gujarat & the Gujaratis: pictures of man and manners taken from life*. Delhi: Asian Educational, 1997. p. 296. GVL, HML.

Masavi, Mustali. *Study of health services in Kathla tribal development block*. Ahmedabad: Gujarat Vidyapith, 1977. p. 39. CSSL, IIML.

Masavi, Mustali and Pandya, Gaurish. *Kathodis of Gujarat*. Ahmedabad: Gujarat Vidyapith, 1987. p. 93. GVL, TRTIL.

Mehta, Prakash Chandra. *Changing face of Bhils*. Udaipur: Shiva, 1998. p. 143. CSSL, GVL.

Mehta, S.S. Tribal development in Gujarat. In *Tribal situation in India: issues in development: with special reference to Western India*. Ed. by Vidyut Joshi. Jaipur: Rawat, 1998. pp. 215–223. CSSL, GVL, SGUL, UML.

Misra, Satish C. *Muslim communities in Gujarat: preliminary studies in their history and social organization*. London: Asia, 1964. p. 207. CSSL, GUL, GVL, HML, SGUL, SUL.

Misra, S.C. *Muslim communities in Gujarat*. Bombay: Munshiram Manoharlal, 1963. [ ]. BVL.

Modi, Nawaz B. ed. *Parsis in Western India: 1818 to 1920*. Bombay: Allied, 1999. p. 288. CSSL.

Mohamed, Jamal T. *Gujaratis: study of socio-economic interactions, 1850–1950*. Delhi: Deputy, 1990. p. 303. GVL, IIML, SPIESRL.

Naik, T.B. *Impact of education on the Bhils*. New delhi: Research Programme Committee Planning Commission, 1969. p. 337. TRTIL.

Naik, T.B. Religion of the Anavils of Surat. In *Traditional India: structure and change*. Ed. by Milton Singer. Jaipur: Rawat, 1975. pp. 183–190. CSSL.

Naik, T.B., Masavi, M.I. and Pandya, G.P. *Kolghas of Gujarat*. Ahmedbad: Gujarat Vidyapith, 1979. p. 122. SPIESRL.

Nancy and Singh, Ram., ed. *Sugar in the milk: Parsis of India*. Ed. by Nancy and Ram Singh. Madras: Institute for Development Education, 1986. p. 149. CSSL.

Narayanan, Leila. *Ethnicity in urban context: the Gujaratis in Madras city*. Jaipur: Rawat, 1989. p. 204. CSSL.

Palkhivala, Nani A. Role of Parsis in India. In *Sugar in the milk: Parsis of India*. Ed. by Nancy and Ram Singh. Madras: Institute for Development Education, 1986. pp. 125–128. CSSL.

Patel, Arjun. Caste in changing society: a study of Kolis of South Gujarat. In *Social transformation in India: essays in honour of Professor I.P. Desai*. Vol. 1. Ed. by Ghanshyam Shah. Jaipur: Rawat, 1997. pp. 324–338. CSSL, GUL, GVL, HML, SGUL, SPUL.

Patel, Arjun. Hinduisation of adivasis: a case study from South Gujarat. In *Dalits in modern India: vision and values*. Ed. by S.M. Michael. New Delhi: Vistaar, 1999. pp. 186–213. GVL.

Patel, Haribhai and Gandhi, Raj S. Changing portrait of the Lewa Patidar caste of North Gujarat: the case of sanskritization and contra-sanskritization. In *Tribes, castes and Harijans: structured inequalities and mobility.* Ed. by Bam Dev Sharda. Delhi: Ajanta, 1991. pp. 131–140. CSSL, TRTIL.

Patel, Jayanti. Sidis of Gujarat and the quest for human dignity: a concluding note. In *Sidis and scholars: essays on African Indians.* Ed. by Amy Catlin-Jairazbhoy and Edward A. Alpers. Noida: Rainbow, 2004. pp. 212–215. CSSL.

Pocock, David F. *Kanbi and Patidar: a study of Patidar community of Gujarat.* London: Oxford, 1972. p. 190. CSSL, GIDRL, GUL, SGUL.

Pocock, D.F. Hypergamy of the Patidars. In *Professors Ghurye felicitation volume*. Ed. by K.M. Kapadia. Bombay: Popular, 1954. pp. 195–204. CSSL, GUL.

Puri, Balraj. Gujarat: threat to Muslim body and Hindu soul. In *Muslims of India since partition*. New Delhi: Gyan, 2007. pp. 187–191. GUL.

Rangarajan, Haripriya. *Spread of Vaisnavism in Gujarat up to 1600 a.d.: a study with special reference to the iconic forms of Vishnu*. Bombay: Somaiya, 1990. p. 201. ASL.

Ray, C.N. Rural artisans in Bhavnagar, Gujarat: a study of their socio-economic conditions. In *Stagnation, retrograde change or positive progress?: vignettes from the journey of the OBC communities in the process of change in India.* Ed. by H.S. Verma and Nadeem Hasnain. New Delhi: Serials, 2006. pp. 255–278. CSSL.

Roy, Shibani and Rizvi, S.H.M. *Dhodia identity: anthropological approach*. Delhi: B.R., 1985. p. 212. CSSL, SGUL.

Rutten, Marrio. Caste and religion in a transnational context: the Patidars of Central Gujarat. In *India's development: social and economic disparities.* Ed. by S. Mahendra Dev and K.S. Babu. New Delhi: Manohar, 2008. pp. 347–364. CSSL, GVL, HML.

Rutten, Marrio. Elite attitudes towards the poor: Patidar entrepreneurs in rural Central Gujarat. In *Other Gujarat: social transformations among weaker Sections*. Ed. by Takashi Shinoda. Mumbai: Popular, 2002. pp. 260–283. ASL, CEEL, CSSL, EDIL, GIDRL, SETUL, SPIESRL.

Sangave, Vilas Adinath. *Jaina community: a social survey*. Bombay: Popular, 1980. p. 455. CSSL.

Sankalia, Hasmukh D. *Studies in the historical and cultural geography and ethnography of Gujarat.* Poona: Deccan College, 1949. p. 245. GUL, TRTIL.

Sarkar Amitabha. *Dhodia: industrialisation and change in a primitive community*. Dehli: Gyan, 1994. p. 185. AAL, CSSL, SETUL.

Sarkar, R. Persistence and change: a study among the Varlis of South Gujarat. In *Transition, change and transformation: impacting the tribes in India.* Ed. by Jayanta Sarkar and Jyotirmoy Chakraborty. Kolkata: Anthropological Survey of India, 2003. pp. 422–444. CSSL, GVL.

Save, K.J. *Warlis*. Bombay: Padma, 1945. p. 280. CSSL, GVL.

Seervai, Kharsedji Nasarvanji and Patel, Bamanji Behraniji. *Gujarat Parsis: from their earliest settlement to the present time (A.D. 1898)*. Bombay: Government Central Press, 1900. p. 84. ASL.

Shah, A.M. and Shroff, R.G. Vahivanca Barots of Gujarat: a caste of genealogist and mythographers. In *Traditional India: structure and change*. Ed. by Milton Singer. Jaipur: Rawat, 1975. pp. 40–70. CSSL.

Shah, Buddhischandra V. *Godavara Parsis: a socio-economic study of a rural community in South Gujarat (1954).* Surat: Godavara Parsi Anjuman Trust, 1955. p. 144. GIDRL.

Shah, Ghanshyam. *Economic differentiations and tribal identity: a re-study of Chaudhris*. Delhi: Ajanta, 1984. p. 148. CSSL, SPUL.

Shah, Ghanshyam. Tribal identity and class differentiations: a case study of the Chaudhri tribe. In *Caste, caste-conflict and reservation*. By Centre for Social Studies. New Delhi: Ajanta, 1985. pp. 44–60. CSSL, SETUL.

Shah, Haku. Tribal memorials in Gujarat. In *Memorial stones*. Ed. by S. Settar and Gunther D. Sontheimer. Dharwad: Institute of Indian Art History, 1982. pp. 101–116. GVL.

Shah, P.G. *Dublas of Gujarat*. Delhi: Bharatiya Adimjati Sevak Sangh, 1958. p. 333. AERCL, CSSL, GUL, GVL, HML, TRTIL.

Shah, P.G. *Ethnic history of Gujarat*. Bombay: Gujarat Research Society, 1968. p. 122. ASL, BVL, GVL, IRMAL, SUL, TRTIL.

Shah, P.G. *Naikas-Naikdas: a Gujarat tribe*. Bombay: Gujarat Research Society, 1959. p. 87. SPUL, TRTIL.

Shah, P.G. Non-Hindu elements in the culture of the Bhils of Gujarat. In *Essays in anthropology*. Ed. by J.P. Mills., et al. Lucknow: Maxwell, 1955. pp. 169–186. GVL.

Shah, P.G. Racial surveys in Gujarat. In *Indian anthropology: essays in memory of D.N. Majumdar*. Ed. by T.N. Madan and Gopal Saran. Bombay: Asia, 1962. pp. 150–162. GVL, TRTIL.

Shinoda, Takashi. Structure of stagnancy: sweepers in Ahmedabad district. In *Dalits and the state*. Ed. by Ghanshyam Shah. Mussoorie: Centre for Rural Studies, 2002. pp. 241–271. CSSL, SPUL.

Shroff, Beheroze. Sidis of Gujarat: a building community: their role in Indian history into contemporary times. In *Frontiers of embedded Muslim communities in India*. Ed. by Vinod K. Jairath. New Delhi: Routledge, 2011. pp. 65–92. HML.

Singh, B.N. and Chatterjee, Manas. Rabaris' of Kutch. In *Tribes in India*. Ed. by B.N. Singh and Manas Chatterjee. Jaipur: RBSA, 2005. pp. 191-[ ]. TRTIL.

Singh, L.R., et al. Geographical study of poverty on space tribal communities of Dangs district in South Gujarat. In *Regional planning and rural development*. Ed. by L.R. Singh. Allahabad: Technical, 1986. pp. 261–273. HML.

Shodhan, Amrita. Caste in the judicial courts of Gujarat, 1800–60. In *Idea of Gujarat: history, ethnography and text*. Ed. by Edward Simpson and Aparna Kapadia. Hyderabad: Orient Blackswan, 2010. pp. 32–49. ASL, BUL, CEPTL, CSSL, GIDRL, IRMAL, MICAL, SETUL.

Shodhan, Amrita. *Question of community: religious groups and colonial law*. Calcutta: Samay, 2001. p. 222. SETUL.

Shodhan, Amrita and Shukla, Sonal. Sidi community in Saurashtra. In *Woman, law and customary practies*. Mumbai: Women's Research & Action Group, 1997. pp. 56–[ ]. SPIESRL.

Soni, Loknath. *Kolcha of Gujarat: extent of social justice and tribal development*. New Delhi: Sarup, 2005. p. 371. AAL.

Tarlo, Emma. Genesis and growth of a business community: a case study of Vaghri street traders in Ahmedabad. In *Webs of trade: dynamics of business communities in Western India. Ed. by Philippe Cadene and Denis Vidal*. New Delhi: Manohar, 1997. pp. 53–84. CSSL.

Thakore, G.D. Jagirdars, then the now, in a North Gujarat area. In *Aspects of changing India: studies in honour of Prof. G.S. Ghurye*. Ed. by S. Devadas Pillai. Bombay: Popular, 1976. pp. 136–145. SGUL.

Thekaekara, Mari Marcel. *Endless filth: the saga of the Bhangis*. Bangalore: Books for Change, 2005. p. 125. CSSL, GVL.

Thoothi, N.A. *Vaishnavas of Gujarat*. Calcutta: Longmans, Green, 1935. p. 489. ASL, BVL, CSSL, GUL, GVL.

Trivedi, Harshad R. *Mers of Saurashtra: exposition of their social structure and organization*. Baroda: M.S. University of Baroda, 1961. p. 114. CSSL, GUL, IIML SPIESRL, TRTIL.

Trivedi, Harshad R. *Mers of Saurashtra revisited and studied in the light of socio-cultural change and cross-cousin marriage*. New Delhi: Concept, 1986. p. 120. CSSL, IIML, TRTIL.

Trivedi, Jayprakash M. *Social structure of Patidar caste in India*. Delhi: Kanishka, 1992. p. 270. CSSL, GUL, SGUL, SPUL.

Varshney, Ashutosh. *Ethnic conflict and civic life: Hindus and Muslims in India*. New Delhi: Oxford, 2002. p. 382. CSSL.

Yagnik, Achyut. Search for dalit self-identity in Gujarat. In *Other Gujarat: social transformations among weaker sections*. Ed. by Takashi Shinoda. Mumbai: Popular, 2002. pp. 22–37. ASL, CEEL, CSSL, EDIL, IRMAL, SETUL, SPIESRL.

Journal Articles

Bhatt, B.J. Baj-Khedaval brahmins of Gujarat. *Journal of the University of Bombay*. 18, 4, 1950. pp. 108–111. GVL.

Cort, John E. Jains, caste and hierarchy in North Gujarat. *Contributions to Indian Sociology*. 38, 1 and 2, 2004. pp. 73–112. AAUL, CEPTL, CSSL, GIDRL, HML, IRMAL, MICAL, SGUL, UML.

Desai, Meghnad. Not a nice Gujarat I to know. *Seminar*. 470, 1998. pp. 14–16. CEPTL, CSSL, IIML, IRMAL, MICAL, UML.

Gould, Ketayun. Sex inequalities in the dual system of education: the Parsis of Gujarat. *Economic and Political Weekly*. 18, 39, 1983. pp. 1668–1676. CEPTL, CSSL, GUL, IIML, IRMAL, SGUL, SPIESRL, UML.

Guha, Amalendu. More about the Parsi Seths: their roots, entrepreneurship and comprador role, 1650–1918. *Economic and Political Weekly*. 19, 3, 1984. pp. 117–132. CSSL, GUL, IIML, IRMAL, SGUL, SPIESRL, UML.

Hakim, Roxanne. Changing religion and ritual in a Vasava Bhil community impacted by involuntary resettlement. *Eastern Anthropologist*. 56, 2–4, 2003. pp. 271–309. CEPTL, CSSL.

Hakim, Roxanne. Vasava identity in transition: some theoretical issues. *Economic and Political Weekly*. 31, 24, 1996. pp. 1492–1499. CEPTL, CSSL, IIML, IRMAL, MICAL, SGUL, SPIESRL, UML.

Haque, M. Anthropometry of the Padar of Ranagadh, Gujarat. *Man in India*. 64, 3, 1984. pp. 294–303. CSSL, SGUL, UML.

Haque, M. Earlobe attachment and Eye brows in three tribes of Saurashtra region. *Vanyajati*. 32, 1, 1984. pp. 9–11. CSSL.

Haque, M. Earlobe attachment among: the Padars of Surendranagar. *Adivasi Gujarat*. 4, 1, 1981. p. 190. SPIESRL, TRTIL.

Ilaiah, Kancha. Development of Muslims: comparing Gujarat and Andhra Pradesh in the early 2000s. *Economic and Political Weekly*. 48, 36, 2013. pp. 74–76. CSSL, SPIESRL, SUL, UML.

Jairamdas, Jiwanlal. Scheduled tribes in Gujarat. *Vanyajati*. 21, 4, 1973. pp. 124–136. CSSL.

Kazi, Babasaheb. Muslims and Gujarat: some observations. *Indian Journal of Secularism*. 6, 4, 2003. pp. 25–31. CSSL.

Kishori, Kalasinh F. Bhils of Gujarat. *Vanyajati*. 10, 2, 1962. pp. 67–69. CSSL.

Kishori, Kalasinh F. Dangs natives at a glance. *Vanyajati*. 10, 3, 1962. pp. 120–123. CSSL.

Krishan, Gopal. Finger dermatoglyphics of the three tribes. *Vanyajati*. 35, 1, 1987. pp. 1–6. CSSL.

Lateef, Shahida. From Shahbano to Sachar. *Seminar*. 583, 2008. pp. 46–50. CSSL, MICAL, UML.

Lobo, Lancy. Household and family among Thakors in a North Gujarat village. *Sociological Bulletin*. 41, 1 and 2, 1992. pp. 49–66. CSSL, IIML.

Lobo, Lancy. Koli Kshatriyas of North Gujarat. *Eastern Anthropologist*. 42, 2, 1989. pp. 171–192. HML, TRTIL.

Lokhandwalla, S.T. Islamic law and Ismaili communities: Khojas and Bohras. *Indian Economic and Social History Review*. 4, 2, 1967. pp. 155–176. CSSL.

Majumdar, D.N. Bhils of Gujarat. *Journal of the Gujarat Research Society*. 4, 4, 1942. pp. 220–237. GVL.

Mankad, B.L. Waghers of Saurashtra. *Journal of the University of Bombay*. 26, 1, 1957. pp. 14–32. GVL.

Masvi, M.I. and Pandya, Gaurish. Kathodis of Gujarat. *Adivasi Gujarat*. 4, 1, 1981. pp. 1–93. CSSL, GVL, SPIESRL, TRTIL.

Masavi, Mustaali I. Padhars of Gujarat socio-economic profile of a primitive tribe. *Madhya Pradesh Journal of Social Sciences*. 2, 1, 1997. pp. 85–100. IRMAL.

Moses, S.T. Machis of Navsari. *Journal of the Gujarat Research Society*. 3, 2, 1941. pp. 61–72. GVL.

Naik, T.B. Aboriginals of Gujarat. *Eastern Anthropologist*. 4, 1, 1950. pp. 42–51. SGUL.

Naik, T.B. Gamits: an aboriginal tribe of Gujarat. *Journal of the Gujarat Research Society*. 9, 2, 1947. pp. 104–121. GUL.

Naik, T.B., Masavi, M.I. and Pandya, G.P. Kolghas of Gujarat. *Adivasi Gujarat*. 3, 2, 1980. pp. 76–170. CSSL, GVL, SPIESRL, TRTIL.

Nath, Viswa. Female infanticide and the Lewa Kanbis of Gujarat in the Nineteenth century. *Indian Economic and Social History Review*. 10, 4, 1973. pp. 386–404. HML, UML.

Panda, Premananda and Panigrahi, Nilkantha. Structure and function of ethnic associations among the migrant Gujaratis in Orissa: an empirical study. *Indian Anthropologist*. 28, 2, 1998. pp. 35–48. CSSL.

Pandya, Gaurish. Dungri Warlis. *Adivasi Gujarat*. 4, 1, 1981. pp. 104–189. CSSL, GVL, SPIESRL, TRTIL.

Patel, Chandrakant S. One district scheduled tribe of Gujarat: Halpati-Talavia. *Adivasi Gujarat*. 15, 1, 2005. pp. 105–131. CSSL, GVL, TRTIL.

Pithawala, M.B. Gujarat region and the Parsees: a historico-geographical survey. *Journal of the Gujarat Research Society*. 7, 2/3, 1945. pp. 88–110. GUL.

Pocock, D.F. Vocation and the avocations of the Guggali brahmans of Dvaraka. *Contributions to Indian Sociology*. 15, 1 and 2, 1981. pp. 321–336. CSSL, SPIESRL, UML.

Punalekar, S.P. Migrants in a city: a case of Dhodia tribals. *Social Scientist*. 11, 7, 1983. pp. 58–66. CSSL, UML.

Raychaudhuri, Bikash. Study of the surnames and physical character of Bengal Kayasthas and Nagar brahmans of Gujarat. *Bulletin of the Anthropological Survey of India.* 17, 4, 1968. pp. 428–438. GVL.

Salzman, Philip Carl. From nomads to dairymen: two Gujarati cases. *Economic and Political Weekly*. 23, 31, 1988. pp. 1582–1586. CEPTL, CSSL, IIML, IRMAL, SGUL, SPIESRL, UML.

Sankalia, H.D. On the origin of Gujarat. *Journal of the Gujarat Research Society.* 8, 2 and 3, 1946. pp. 82–87. GUL.

Sankaran, Vasumathi. Resource management by the Bhils of Gujarat and Rajasthan. *Indian Journal of Social Science.* 4, 4, 1991. pp. 547–566. IIML.

Shah, Ghanshyam. Tribal identity and class differentiations: a case study of the Chaudhri tribe. *Economic and Political Weekly*. 14, 7 and 8, 1979. pp. 459–465. CEPTL, CSSL, GUL, IIML, IRMAL, SGUL, SPIESRL, UML.

Shah, P.G. Moherakapura and Modhas in Gujarat. *Journal of the Gujarat Research Society*. 8, 2 and 3, 1946. pp. 120–122. GUL.

Shah, P.G. Dublas of Gujarat. *Eastern Anthropologist*. 12, 2, 1959. pp. 138-. SGUL.

Shah, P.G. Second note on the physical fitness of Gujarati speaking people. *Journal of the Gujarat Research Society.* 2, 2, 1940. pp. 79–91. GUL.

Shukla, Tara. Community project in Saurashtra. *Journal of the Gujarat Research Society.* 19, 2/74, 1957. pp. 93–104. GVL.

Singh, R.D. and Bhale, R.B. Study of stature and weight-1: the Dubla, the Gamit and the Naika of Gujarat. *Eastern Anthropologist*. 17, 1, 1964. pp. 10–18. HML, SGUL, TRTIL.

Solanki, A.N. Dhodias of South Gujarat. *Journal of the University of Bombay.* 24, 4, 1956. pp. 23–26. GVL.

Streefkerk, Hein. Transformation in Bulsar: Suthars and relevance of caste. *Economic and Political Weekly*. 26, 21, 1991. pp. 1340–1350. CEPTL, CSSL, IIML, IRMAL, SPIESRL, UML.

Working Papers, Reports and Other Materials

Bhatt, Anil., Giridhar, G. and Monappa, Arun. *Urban community development programme of Ahmedabad: a community based evaluation.* Ahmedabad: Indian Institute of Management, 1985. pp. 32–90. PSG Monograph-56. IIML.

Bombay Presidency. Gazetteer of the Bombay Presidency. Gujarat population: *Muslim and Parsi castes and tribes of Gujarat*. Haryana: Vintage, 1899. p. 287. SETUL, TRTIL.

Das, Biswaroop. Comparative socio-economic profile of Hindu and Muslim slum dwellers in Surat. In *Seminar on Muslim community in Western India, 14–16 December 1995.* Surat: Centre for Social Studies, 1995. pp. 1–47. CSSL.

Joshi, Satyakam. *Identity construction among adivasis of Gujarat after independence*. Surat: Centre for Social Studies, 1998. p. 38. CSSL.

Kanungo, Musarrat. Superstitions and beliefs among the Muslims of Gujarat. In *Seminar on Muslim community in Western India, 14–16 December 1995.* Surat: Centre for Social Studies, 1995. pp. 1–7. CSSL.

Lal, R.B. *Sons of the Aravalis: the Garasias.* Ahmedabad: Tribal Research & Training Institute, Gujarat Vidyapith, 1979. p. 233. CSSL, TRTIL.

Lobo, Lancy. *Becoming a marginal native.* Surat: Centre for Social Studies, 1988. p. 50. Occasional Paper III. CSSL, UML.

Lobo, Lancy. *Community, identity and crises: ethnography of Majiranas of North Gujarat.* Surat: Centre for Social Studies, 1998. p. 58. CSSL.

Maheshwari, Usha. Status of Muslim women in the family (In Surat Slums). In *Seminar on Muslim community in Western India, 14–16 December 1995.* Surat: Centre for Social Studies, 1995. pp. 1–12. CSSL.

Masavi, Mustaali L. *Development of Dungri Warlis: a plan of action.* Ahmedabad: Tribal Research & Training Institute, Gujarat Vidyapith 1989. p. 33. Series 268. TRTIL.

Masavi, Mustali. *Kathodis of Gujarat.* Ahmedabad: Gujarat Vidyapith, 1987. p. 146. CSSL, TRTIL.

Masavi, Mustali. *Padhars of Gujarat.* Ahmedabad: Gujarat Vidyapith, 1985. p. 41. Serise-159. TRTIL.

Masavi, Mustali. *Padhars of Gujarat: a house-to-house socio-economic survey and development plan.* Ahmedabad: Gujarat Vidyapith, 1985. p. 118. GVL.

Masavi, Mustali. *Problem of land alienation among tribals of Gujarat.* Ahmedabad: Tribal Research & Training Institute, Gujarat Vidyapith, [ ], p. 26. GIDRL.

Masavi, Mustali and Pandya, Gaurishanker. *Kathodis of Gujarat.* Ahmedabad: Tribal Research & Training Institute, Gujarat Vidyapith, 1977. p. 146. CSSL, GIDRL, IIML, TRTIL.

Naik, T.B. *Kolghas of Gujarat: a socio-economic study and a development plan.* Ahmedabad: Tribal Research & Training Institute, Gujarat Vidyapith, 1979. p. 122. IIML, TRTIL.

Naik, T.B. and Pandya, G.P. *Sidis of Gujarat: a socio-economic study and a development plan.* Ahmedabad: Gujarat Vidyapith, 1993. p. 139. Tribal Research & Training Institute Publication No. 32. CSSL, TRTIL.

Naik, T.B., Masavi, M.I. and Pandya, G.P. *Kolghas of Gujarat: socio-economic study and development plan no. 53.* Ahmedabad: Tribal Research & Training Institute, Gujarat Vidyapith, 1979. p. 122. GIDRL, IIML, TRTIL.

Pandore, G.A. History activities and role of charitable organizations run by the Surati Sunni Vohara Muslim community of South Gujarat. In *Seminar on Muslim community in Western India, 14–16 December 1995.* Surat: Centre for Social Studies, 1995. pp. 1–15. CSSL.

Pandya, Gaurish. *Dungri Warlis: a study of a hill tribe of district Valsad, Gujarat state.* Ahmedabad: Tribal Research & Training Institute, Gujarat Vidyapith, 1986. p. 73. Series-171. TRTIL.

Pandya, Gaurish and Rathod, Jaswantsinh. *Ethnographic study of Rabaris and Bharwads of Gujarat.* Ahmedabad: Tribal Research & Training Institute, Gujarat Vidyapith, 1988. p. 90. TRTIL.

Pandya, Gaurishankar. *Dungri Warlis.* Ahmedabad: Gujarat Vidyapith, 1987. p. 87. TRTIL.

Pandya, Gaurishankar and Patel, Bhikhabahi. *Report of the research on the Halba community.* Ahmedabad: Gujarat Vidhyapith, 1996. p. [ ]. TRTIL.

Patel, Chhotubhai D. *Dilapidated dwellings and rich temples: the Padhars of Gujarat.* Ahmedabad: Gujarat Vidyapith, 1982. p. 89. Serise 116. TRTIL.

Punalekar, S.P. *Migration and social stratification: a case of Dhodias of Surat city.* Surat: Centre for Social Studies, 1980. p. 200. CSSL.

Rathod, Jashwantsinh and Pancholi, Ravindra. *Paradhi: an inquiry into Paradhi community habitated in Kutch district.* Ahmedabad: Gujarat Vidyapith, 2004. p. 51. Serise-400. TRTIL.

Shah, Ghanshyam. *Socio-economic condition of Chodhras: a restudy*. Surat: Centre for Social Studies, 1977. p. 207. CSSL.

Shah, Vimal and Lal, Rash Bihari. *Enquiry into political consciousness among tribals of Gujarat*. Ahmedabad: Tribal Research & Training Institute, Tribal Research & Training Institute, Gujarat Vidyapith, [ ]. p. 27. GIDRL.

Shodhan, Amrita. Colonial construction of caste as the self-governing community (1819–1827) in Bombay presidency. In *International seminar on Gujarat society, development and deprivation, 6–9 December 1994*. Surat: Centre for Social Studies, 1994. pp. 1–4. CSSL.

Shodhan, Amrita and Shukla, Sonal. Sidi community in *Saurashtra*. In *Women, law and customary practices*. By Women's Research and Action Group. Mumbai: Author, 1997. pp. 56–67. CSSL.

Solanki, S.S. *Dhodia tribal customary laws*. Ahmedabad: Gujarat Vidyapith, 1985. p. 8. TRTIL.

Tribal Research & Training Institute. *Dubala/Halpati/Talaviya: an extremely backward scheduled tribe of Gujarat*. Ahmedabad: Gujarat Vidyapith, [ ]. p. 14. TRTIL.

Upadhyay, Chandrakant and Pancholi, Ravindra. *Primitive tribals groups of Gujarat: a base line survey*. Ahmedabad: Tribal Research & Training Institute, Gujarat Vidyapeeth, 2010. p. 241. GVL.

Visaria, Pravin and Gumber, Anil. *Economic activities by social group in Western India: some data on levels and differentials during the 1980s*. Ahmedabad: Gujarat Institute of Development Research, 1993. p. 58. Working Paper No. 48. CSSL, GIDRL.

Vora, Raghuvir and Chowdhury, Mukundbhai. *Kotwalias of South Gujarat: an ethnographic account*. Ahmedabad: Gujarat Tribal Development Corporation,[ ]. p. 77. CSSL.

5

Gender, Women

Books/Chapter in Books

Ahmed, Sara. Negotiating gender equity through decentralized water management in coastal Gujarat: the case of UTTHAN. In *Flowing upstream: empowering women through water management initiatives in India*. Ed. by Sara Ahmed. Ahmedabad: Centre for Environment Education, 2005. pp. 51–92. CEEL, CSSL.

Ahmed, Sara. SEWA: campaigning for water, women and work. In *Flowing upstream: empowering women through water management initiatives in India*. Ed. by Sara Ahmed. Ahmedabad: Centre for Environment Education, 2005. pp. 93–122. CEEL, CSSL.

Basu, Helene. Gendered Indian ocean site: Mai Mishra, African spirit possession and Sidi women in Gujarat. In *Journeys and dwellings: Indian ocean themes in South Asia*. Ed. by Helene Basu. Hyderabad: Orient Longman, 2008. pp. 227–255. CSSL.

Bhagat-Ganguly, Varsha. Social security of widows in Gujarat. In *Widows in India: social neglect and public action*. Ed. by Martha Alter Chen. New Delhi: Sage, 1998. pp. 296–311. CSSL, IIML, SETUL.

Bhagat-Ganguly, Varsha and Shodhan, Amrita. Shifting perspectives on widows' issues in Gujarat. In *Other Gujarat: social transformations among weaker sections*. Ed. by Takashi Shinoda. Mumbai: Popular, 2002. pp. 400–418. ASL, CEEL, CSSL, EDIL, GIDRL, SETUL, SPIESRL.

Bhatia, Bela. Social action with rural widows in Gujarat. In *Widows in India: social neglect and public action*. Ed. by Martha Alter Chen. New Delhi: Sage, 1998. pp. 409–433. CSSL, IIML, SETUL.

Bhatia, Bela. Widows, land right and resettlement in the Narmada valley. In *Widows in India: social neglect and public action*. Ed. by Martha Alter Chen. New Delhi: Sage, 1998. pp. 257–260. CSSL, IIML, SETUL.

Bhatt, Ela R. Empowering women: the SEWA experience. In *Other India: realities of an emerging power*. Ed. by Rajesh Chakrabarti. New Delhi: Sage, 2009. pp. 260–267. CSSL.

Bhatt, Ila R. *We are poor but so many: the story of self-employed women in India*. New Delhi: Oxford, 2006. p. 233. CSSL, SETUL.

Billington, Mary Frances. *Women in India*. New Delhi: Amarko, 1973. p. 269. SGUL.

Brintha Lakshmi, S. Women and habitat. In *Profile of women in Gujarat*. Ed. by Parul Dave. Baroda: M.S. University, 2005. pp. 179–194. GVL.

Chaudhuri, Sutapa. Shifting positionalities of gender in contemporary Gujarati women's writings. In *Indian family in transition*. Ed. by Sanjukta Dasgupta and Lal Malashri. New Delhi: Sage, 2007. pp. 174–187. CSSL, HML.

Chen, Martha Alter, ed. *Widows in India: social neglect and public action.* New Delhi: Sage, 1998. p. 455. CSSL, IIML, SETUL.

Clark, Alice. Limitation on female life chances in rural Central Gujarat. In *Women in colonial India: essays on survival, work and the state.* Ed. by J. Krishnamurty. Delhi: Oxford, 1989. pp. 27–51. CSSL, SETUL.

Das, Narayan P. and Shah, Urvi. Women in Gujarat: a demographic profile. In *Profile of women in Gujarat.* Ed. by Parul Dave. Baroda: M.S. University, 2005. pp. 7–51. GVL.

Datar, Chhaya and Prakash, Aseem. Engendering community rights: women's access to water and wasteland in Gujarat, Maharashtra, Madhya Pradesh, Andhra Pradesh and Karnataka. In *Livelihood and gender: equity in community resource management.* Ed. by Sumi Krishna. New Delhi: Sage, 2004. pp. 137–168. CSSL.

Desai, Hina and Mehta, Bhavana. Rights and justice for women in Gujarat. In *Profile of women in Gujarat.* Ed. by Parul Dave. Baroda: M.S. University, 2005. pp. 299–324. GVL.

Desai, Madhavi. Women and architecture: the colonial bunglow in Gujarat: 1920 to 1970. In *Women and the built environment.* Ed. by Madhavi Desai. New Delhi: Zubaan, 2007. pp. 146–168. CSSL.

Desai, Mira Kapil. Communication strategies and empowerment of women: experiences from Gujarat. In *Communication and empowerment of women: strategies and policy insights from India,* Vol. 2. Ed. by Kiran Prasad. Delhi: Women Press, 2004. pp. 642–661. GVL, TRTIL.

Desai, Padma. Breaking out: an Indian women's American journey. New Delhi: Viking, 2012. p. 222. CSSL.

Ghanchi, Samiullah M. *Status of women among Muslims in India: a case study of Surat.* New Delhi: Serial, 2012. p. 298. CSSL.

Gorhe, Neelam, Bhandari, Chandra and Bhatia, Bela. Widows, family support and land rights: case studies from Maharashtra, Rajasthan, Bihar and Gujarat. In *Widows in India: social neglect and public action.* Ed. by Martha Alter Chen. New Delhi: Sage, 1998. pp. 261–282. CSSL, IIML, SETUL.

Hirway, Indira and Mahadevia, Darshini. Measuring women's development in Gujarat: some conceptual issues and empirical results. In *Other Gujarat: social transformations among weaker sections.* Ed. by Takashi Shinoda. Mumbai: Popular, 2002. pp. 347–373. ASL, CEEL, CSSL, EDIL, GIDRL, SETUL, SPIESRL.

Jhabvala, Renana. Self employed widows: some experiences from Gujarat. In *Widows in India: social neglect and public action.* Ed. by Martha Alter Chen. New Delhi: Sage, 1998. pp. 388–396. CSSL, IIML, SETUL.

Joshi, Uma, Pahad, Anjali and Maniar, Avani. Women and the media. In *Profile of women in Gujarat.* Ed. by Parul Dave. Baroda: M.S. University, 2005. pp. 237–268. GVL.

Kanoja, K.H. Addressing basic issues in women's empowerment: the approach of Gujarat. In *Empowering the poor in the era of knowledge economy.* Ed. by Srinivas Mudrakartha. Ahmedabad: CNRI, Gujarat Chapter, 2007. pp. 56–60. CEEL.

Kothari, Rita, tr. *Speech and silence: literary journeys by Gujarati women.* New Delhi: Kali for Women, 2006. p. 151. AAL, CSSL.

Kothari, V.N., et al. Women in Gujarat: a socio-economic profile. In *Profile of women in Gujarat.* Ed. by Parul Dave. Baroda: M.S. University, 2005. pp. 53–120. GVL.

Kumar, Radha. Family and factory: women in the Bombay cotton textile industry, 1919–1939. In *Women in colonial India: essays on survival, work and the state.* Ed. by J. Krishnamurty. Delhi: Oxford, 1989. pp. 133–162. SETUL.

Lyle, Mary, Pattison, Mattie and Patel, Haribhai. *Problems of adolescent girls in Gujarat state India.* Baroda: Jastina Singh, 1967. p. 60. GVL.

Maniar, Avani. Tribal women of Gujarat: HIV/AIDS awareness and education. In *Women welfare and empowerment in India*. Ed. by Rameshwari Pandya. New Delhi: New Century, 2008. pp. 1–20. SPUL.

Mehta, Shirin. *Women and social change*. Jaipur: Rawat, 2009. p. 337. CSSL, GUL.

Nanavutty, Piloo. Parsi women: their contribution to Indian public life. In *Sugar in the milk: Parsis of India*. Ed. by Nancy and Ram Singh. Madras: Institute for Development Education, 1986. pp. 68–87. CSSL.

Panda, Smita Mishra. Engendering cooperative governance: case of women dairy cooperative societies in Gujarat. In *Engendering governance institutions: state, market and civil society*. Ed. by Smita Mishra Panda. New Delhi: Sage, 2008. pp. 265–292. CSSL.

Parikh, Shailaja Kalelkar. *And still my river flows: story of tribal woman from the hinterlands of Gujarat*. Ahmedabad: Navbharat, 2010. p. 187. GUL.

Parikh, Varsha. Treatment seeking behaviour of women in the urban slums of Vadodara. In *Women in India: issues, perspectives and solutions*. Ed. by Rameshwari Pandya. New Delhi: New Century, 2007. pp. 178–187. CSSL.

Patel, J.C. Tribal widows of Gujarat: problems and their solution. In *Widowhood in modern India*. Ed. by P.K.B. Nayar. Delhi: Women Press, 2006. pp. 255–263. HML.

Pathak, Ila. Need to re-define women's activities in Gujarat: a case study of AWAG. In *Re-defining feminisms*. Ed. by Ranjana Harish and V. Bharathi Harishankar. Jaipur: Rawat, 2008. pp. 32–43. CSSL, GUL, HML.

Pathak, Ila and Joshi, Ila. Women's organisations in Gujarat. In *Decade of women's movement in India*. Ed. by Neera Desai. Bombay: Himalaya, 1988. pp. 13–34. CSSL, GVL, TRTIL.

Punalekar, S.P. Gender, market segmentation and marginalization in urban Gujarat. In *Social work practice: religio-philosophical foundations*. Ed. by Chhaya Patel. Jaipur: Rawat, 1999. pp. 276–310. CSSL.

Punalekar, S.P. Tribal women & development milieu: social context & emerging contradictions. In *Tribal women & development*. Ed. by V.P. Singh, N.N. Vyas and R.S. Mann. Jaipur: Rawat, 1988. pp. 91–108. SGUL.

Rose, Kalima. *Where women are leaders: SEWA movement in India*. New Delhi: Vistaar, 1992. p. 286. CSSL.

Self Employed Women's Association. Linking the informal sector with mainstream markets: case of SEWA. In *Engendering governance institutions: state, market and civil society*. Ed. by Smita Mishra Panda. New Delhi: Sage, 2008. pp. 203–219. CSSL.

Shah, Kalpana. Role of established organisation: a case study of all India women's conference: Akhil Hind Mahila Parished-Surat. In *Decade of women's movement in India*. Ed. by Neera Desai. Bombay: Himalaya, 1988. pp. 1–12. CSSL, GVL, TRTIL.

Shah, Kalpana. *Women's liberation and voluntary action*. Delhi: Ajanta, 1984. p. 155. SETUL.

Shah, Meera Kaul. 'Salt spices': gender issues in participatory programme implementation in AKRSP, India. In *Myth of community: gender issues in participatory development*. Ed. by Irene Gujit and Meera Kaul Shah. New Delhi: Vistaar, 1998. pp. 243–253. CSSL.

Shah, Trupti. Violence against women in Gujarat. In *Profile of women in Gujarat*. Ed. by Parul Dave. Baroda: M.S. University, 2005. pp. 219–235. GVL.

Sheth, Pravin N. Profiles of women in Gujarat. In *Symbols of power: studies on the political status of women in India*. Ed. by Vina Mazumdar. Bombay: Allied, 1979. pp. 200–220. SGUL.

Shukla, Dinesh M. Politicization of women in Gujarat. In *Symbols of power: studies on the political status of women in India*. Ed. by Vina Mazumdar. Bombay: Allied, 1979. pp. 85–118. SGUL.

Sriram, Rajalakshmi, et al. Women in families and households. In *Profile of women in Gujarat*. Ed. by Parul Dave. Baroda: M.S. University, 2005. pp. 195–217. GVL.

Unni, Jeemol. Employment status of women in Gujarat in a drought vs normal year. In *Other Gujarat: social transformations among weaker sections*. Ed. by Takashi Shinoda. Mumbai: Popular, 2002. pp. 374–399. ASL, CEEL, CSSL, EDIL, GIDRL, SETUL, SPIESRL.

Upadhyay, Bhawana. *Gender roles and multiple uses of water in North Gujarat.* Colombo: IWMI, 2004. p. 15. IRMAL.

Warrier, Shrikala. Marriage, maternity, and female economic activity: Gujarati mothers in Britain. In *Enterprising women: ethnicity, economy, and gender relations*. Ed. by Sallie Westwood and Parminder Bhachu. London: Routledge, 1988. pp. 132–152. CSSL.

Westwood, Sallie. Workers and wives: continuities and discontinuities in the lives of Gujarati women. In *Enterprising women: ethnicity, economy, and gender relations*. Ed. by Sallie Westwood and Parminder Bhachu. London: Routledge, 1988. pp. 103–131. CSSL.

Women's Studies Research Centre. *Profile of women in Gujarat*. Vadodara: Author, 2005. p. 366. GVL.

Wood, M.R. Employment and family change: a study of middle-class women in India. In *Women in contemporary India: traditional images and changing roles.* Ed. by Alfred de Souza. New Delhi: Manohar, 1975. pp. 37–53. CSSL, IIML, SGUL, SPUL, TRTIL.

Journal Articles

Bhatia, Bela. We are not alone! a case study of widows' action in North Gujarat. *Social Action*. 45, 4, 1995. pp. 385–404. CSSL, IIML.

Bhatt, Ela R. 'Doosri Azadi': SEWA's perspectives on early years of independence. *Economic and Political Weekly*. 33, 17, 1998. pp. WS-25-WS-27. CEPTL, CSSL, EDIL, IIML, IRMAL, MICAL, SGUL, SPIESRL, UML.

Clark, Alice. Limitations on female life chances in rural Central Gujarat. *Indian Economic and Social History Review*. 20, 1, 1983. pp. 1–25. CEPTL, CSSL, HML, IIML, UML.

Ghorpade, Ashwini. Tribal women: the Vansda model. *Social Change*. 25, 1, 1995. pp. 80–82. CSSL, SPUL, UML.

Jhabvala, Renana. Liberalization and women. *Seminar.* 531, 2003. pp. 34–40. CSSL, MICAL, UML.

Kothari, Uma. Women's paid domestic work and rural transformation: a study in South Gujarat. *Economic and Political Weekly*. 32, 17, 1997. pp. WS-5-WS-12. CEPTL, CSSL, GIDRL, IIML, IRMAL, MICAL, SGUL, SPIESRL, UML.

Kumar, Radha. Family and factory: women in the Bombay cotton textile industry, 1919–1939. *Indian Economic and Social History Review*. 20, 1, 1983. pp. 81–96. CEPTL, CSSL, HML, IIML, UML.

Mehta, Vatsala. Hindu widow with special reference to Gujarat. *Journal of the University of Bombay*. 26, 1, 1957. pp. 50-[ ]. GVL.

Nagbrahmam, D. and Sambrani, Shreekant. Women's drudgery in firewood collection. *Economic and Political Weekly*. 18, 1 and 2, 1983. pp. 33–38. CEPTL, CSSL, GUL, IIML, IRMAL, SGUL, SPIESRL, UML.

Patel, Ila. Gender ideology in adult literacy primers in Gujarat. *Trends in Social Science Research*. 3, 2, 1996. pp. 87–96. IRMAL.

Pathak, Illaben. Social sector of development: women's development and empowerment. (*Gujarat-2010: Challenges and Opportunities*). *Anvesak*. 31, 1–2, 2001. pp. 160–178. CSSL.

Shah, Anil C. Women, water, irrigation: respecting women's priorities. *Economic and Political Weekly*. 37, 43, 2002. pp. 4413–4420. BUL, CEPTL, CSSL, EDIL, IIML, IRMAL, MICAL, SGUL, SPIESRL, UML.

Shah, Hina. Violence against women in Gujarat, trends pattern and responses in Gujarat on gender based violence. *Social Welfare*. 53, 5, 2006. pp. 21–25. GVL.

Sharma, Kalindi, Joshi, P.C. and Sinha, Anil K. Gender and governance in context of post-earthquake Gujarat. *Eastern Anthropologist*. 66, 1, 2013. pp. 61–74. CSSL.

Shodhan, Amrita. Women in the Maharaj Libel case: a re-examination. *Indian Journal of Gender Studies*. 4, 2, 1997. pp. 123–139. CSSL.

Shukla, Sonal. Images of Gujarati women. *Seminar*. 470, 1998. pp. 41–46. CEPTL, CSSL, IRMAL, MICAL, UML.

Velayudhan, Meera. Contextualising women's rights and entitlements to land: insights from Gujarat. *Social Change*. 42, 4, 2012. pp. 505–526. CSSL, IRMAL, UML.

Visaria, Leela. Violence against women: a field study. *Economic and Political Weekly*. 35, 20, 2000. pp. 1742–1751. BUL, CEPTL, CSSL, EDIL, IIML, IRMAL, MICAL, SGUL, SPIESRL, UML.

Wood, M.R. Employment and family change: a study of middle-class women in urban Gujarat. *Social Action*. 25, 3, 1975. pp. 221–234. CSSL.

Working Papers, Reports and Other Materials

Ahmed, Sara. *Search of a drop: women and drinking water management in rural Gujarat (India): the case of SEWA*. Anand: Institute of Rural Management, 2000. p. [ ]. IRMA Working Paper No. 137. GIDRL.

Ahmed, Sara. *Changing gender relations amongst the Bhils in Panchmahals, Gujarat*. Anand: Institute of Rural Management, 2000. p. 29. IRMAL.

Amin, Avni, Fatula, Emily and Khanna, Renu. *Attitudes and behaviours of men in relation to gender and sexuality: evidence from qualitative studies conducted in the Santrampur taluka of Panchmahals district, Gujarat*. Godhara: Sarthi, 1997. p. 23. Working Paper No. 4. CSSL.

Bhaskaran, Seema. *Astitva combats violence against women*. Surat: Centre for Social Studies, 1997. p. 40. CSSL.

Bhaskaran, Seema. *Organisations working with women in Gujarat*. Surat: Centre for Social Studies, 1997. p. 109. CSSL.

Bhatt, Bijal and Shah, Pooja. *Mobilizing women for change: case study of Sanjaynagar, Ahmedabad*. Ahmedabad: CEPT University, 2010. p. 56. Working Paper 7. CEPTL, CSSL.

Chen, Martha Alter. *Self-employed women: a profile of SEWA's membership*. Ahmedabad: SEWA, 2006. p. 108. CSSL.

Gujarat, Government of. *Socio-economic and demographic status of women in Gujarat*. Gandhinagar: Directorate of Economics and Statistics, Government of Gujarat, 2003. p. 69. CSSL.

Gulati, Preeti and Sinha, Shalini, compil. *Gender sensitive regional development strategies: district Banaskantha, Gujarat*. Ahmedabad: School of Planning, Centre of Environmental Planning and Technology, 1999. p. 157. GIDRL.

Hirway, Indira. *Towards empowering women: constraints and possibilities evaluation of Mahila Samakhya programme in Gujarat*. New Delhi: Mahila Samakhya, Ministry of Human Resource Development, [ ]. p. 72. IRMAL.

Jhabvala, Renana, Dhawan, Reva and Mahajan, Krishnan. *Women who role Bidis: two studies of Gujarat*. Ahmedabad: Self Employed Women's Association (SEWA), 1985. p. [ ]. GIDRL.

Mahadevia, Darshini and Khawas, Vimal. *Gender budgeting-impact of policies and programmes on women of agricultural households in Gujarat*. New Delhi: UNDP, 2005. p. 76. Discussion Paper Series 9. CSSL.

Mehta, Leena. *Prostitution in Surat: a study of women in the profession of prostitution in Surat city, 1990*. Baroda: M.S. University, 1991. p. 68. CSSL.

Mehta, Makrand. Emergence of women leaders in Gujarat: the early phase, 1850–1900. In *International seminar on Gujarat society, development and deprivation, 6–9 December 1994*. Surat: Centre for Social Studies, 1994. pp. 1–34. CSSL.

Merchant, Amrapali M. Empowerment of women. In *Gujarat-2010: challenges and opportunities*. By Government of Gujarat. Ahmedabad: Sardar Patel Institute of Economic and Social Research, 2001. pp. 536–558. Seminar Volume. CSSL, EDIL, IRMAL, SGUL, SPIESRL.

Nilkanth, Vidyagauri. Progress of women in Ahmedabad. In *Ahmedabad*. Ahmedabad: Rotary Club, 1940. pp. 59–62. CSSL.

Pathak, Illaben. Social sector of development: women's development and empowerment. In *Gujarat-2010: challenges and opportunities*. By Government of Gujarat. Ahmedabad: Sardar Patel Institute of Economic and Social Research, 2001. pp. 522–535. Seminar Volume. CSSL, EDIL, IRMAL, SGUL, SPIESRL.

Pathak, Ila and Joshi, Ila. Women's organisation in Gujarat. In *Decade of women's movement in India*. Ed. by S.N.D.T. University. Bombay: Himalaya, 1988. pp. 13–34. Collection of papers presented at a Seminar. SGUL.

Seetharam, Mukkavilli. *Gender profile: Gujarat*. New Delhi: Royal Netherlands Embassy, [ ]. p. 63. GIDRL.

Shah, Kalpana. Role of established organisations: a case study of all India women's conference (Akhil Hindu Mahila Parished). In *Decade of women's movement in India*. Ed. by S.N.D.T. University. Bombay: Himalaya, 1988. pp. 1–12. Collection of papers presented at a seminar. SGUL.

Srinivasan, Bina. *Restless boundaries: a study on the impact of urban displacement on women in Baroda*. Mumbai: Vikas Adhyan Kendra, 1997. p. 58. CSSL.

Srinivasan, Bina. *Women & law in the Muslim world, the India project: a report on Muslim personal laws and their implications for women in Baroda, March-July 1994*. Bombay: Women's Research & Action Group, 1994. p. 46. CSSL.

Srinivasan, Bina and Desai, Hina. *Trespassers will be prosecuted!: a study of socially displaced women in Gujarat*. Mumbai: Vikas, 1999. p. 50. CSSL.

Thakkar, Usha. Puppets on the periphery: women and social reform in the nineteenth century Gujarat. In *International seminar on Gujarat society, development and deprivation, 6–9 December 1994*. Surat: Centre for Social Studies, 1994. pp. 1–28. CSSL.

6

Culture, Customs, Diaspora

Books/Chapter in Books

Bagchi, Tilak. Nature, man and crafts of Kachchh. In *Portrait of anthropological research*. Ed. by Debabrata Mandal, Tilak Bagchi and Asok Mukhopadhyay. New Delhi: Sarup, 2008. pp. 427–435. GVL, HML, TRTIL.

Bagchi, Tilak and Soni, Loknath. Crafts of Gujarat: an overview. In *Portrait of anthropological research*. Ed. by Debabrat Mandal, Tilak Bagchi and Ashok Mukhopadhyay. New Delhi: Sarup, 2008. pp. 337–362. GVL, HML, TRTIL.

Bagchi, Tilak and Soni, Loknath. Crafts of Gujarat: an overview. In *Approaches of tribal Development*. [Ed.] By Chaturbhuj. New Delhi: Adhyayan, 2009. pp. 172–193. TRTIL.

Bahadur, K.P. *Caste, tribes and culture of India*. Vol. VII: *Western Maharashtra and Gujarat*. New Delhi: Ess Ess, 1981. p. 201. CSSL, GVL, SPIESRL.

Banks, Marcus. Jain ways of being. In *Desh Pardesh: the South Asian presence in Britain*. Ed. by Roger Ballard. Delhi: B.R., 1996. pp. 231–250. CSSL.

Bhakta, Govind B. *Patels: a Gujarati community history in the United States*. California: Ucla Asian American Studies Centre, 2002. p. 167. SGUL.

Bhatnagar, R.R. and Patel, H.T. *Fairs and festival of Gujarat: socio-cultural and economic impact on communities of Gujarat*. Ahmedabad: Sardar Patel Institute of Economic & Social Research, 2007. p. 157. SPIESRL.

Bhatt, Arvind. Administrator and the poet: language and globalisation in nineteenth century Gujarat. In *Globalisation, diaspora and belonging: exploring transnationalism and Gujarati identity*. Ed. by Sharmina Mawani and Anjoom A. Mukadam. Jaipur: Rawat, 2014. pp. 103–117. CSSL.

Bobbio, Tommaso. From Ahmedabad to Karnavati: cultural roots and socio-spatial aspects of intolerance. In *Globalisation, diaspora and belonging: exploring transnationalism and Gujarati identity*. Ed. by Sharmina Mawani and Anjoom A. Mukadam. Jaipur: Rawat, 2014. pp. 255–276. CSSL.

Bose, Tara. *Folk tales of Gujarat*. New Delhi: Sterling, 1971. p. 119. GVL, TRTIL.

Bose, Tara. *Folk tales of Gujarat*. New Delhi: Sterling, 1986. p. 120. BVL, SGUL, SPUL.

Bose, Tara. Heroes of Gujarat. In *Best loved folk tales of India*. Ed. by P.C. Roy Chaudhary. New Delhi: Sterling, 1994. pp. 79–82. GVL.

Bugg, Laura Beth. Space, representation and belonging: a Swaminarayan temple in Sydney, Australia. In *Globalisation, diaspora and belonging: exploring transnationalism and Gujarati identity*. Ed. by Sharmina Mawani and Anjoom A. Mukadam. Jaipur: Rawat, 2014. pp. 236–254. CSSL.

Chakraborty, Jyotirmoy. Marriage & kinship among the Siddis of Saurashtra. In *Contemporary society: tribal studies,* Vol. II. Ed. by Pfeffer Georg. New Delhi: Concept, 1997. pp. 198–204. Prof. Satya Narayan Ratha felicitation volumes. SGUL.

Chattopadhyaya, Kamaladevi. Bhils of Gujarat and Rajasthan. In *Tribalism in India.* By Kamaladevi Chattopadhyaya. New Delhi: Vikas, 1978. pp. 55–79. CSSL, TRTIL.

Chhanabhai. Potter's craft in South Gujarat. In *Votive terra cottas of Gujarat.* Ed. by Kagal Carmen. New York: Mapin, 1985. pp. 97–122. TRTIL.

Choksi, Nishant. *Tribal literature of Gujarat.* Mysore: Central Institute of Indian Languages, 2009. p. 186. AAL.

Dave, Trimbaklal N. *Study of Gujarati language in the 16th century.* London: Royal Asiatic Society, 1935. p. 197. BVL.

Desai, Anjana. Indian city: a conglomeration of culture: case of Ahmedabad. In *Cultural geography form and process.* Ed. by Neelam Grover. New Delhi: Concept, 2004. pp. 183–191. HML.

Desai, A.R. and D'Costa, Wilfred. *State and repressive culture: a case study of Gujarat.* Bombay: Popular, 1994. p. 144. CSSL.

Desai, Govindbhai H. *Hindu families in Gujarat: being an account of their domestic, social and economic life.* Baroda: State Press, 1932. p. 472. CSSL, TRTIL.

Dewji, Sahir. Being Ismaili in the democratic republic of the Congo: identity maintenance among Gujarati Ismailis in Kinshasa. In *Globalisation, diaspora and belonging: exploring transnationalism and Gujarati identity.* Ed. by Sharmina Mawani and Anjoom A. Mukadam. Jaipur: Rawat, 2014. pp. 58–77. CSSL.

Donley, Linda Wiley. Symbolic meaning within the traditional Hindu and Muslim house of Gujarat (India) and Lamu (Kenya). In *Cultural heritage of the Indian village.* Ed. by Brian Durrans and Richard T. Blurton. London: British Museum, 1991. pp. 75–90. GVL.

Dwyer, Rachel. Caste, religion and sect in Gujarat: followers of Vallabhacharya and Swaminarayan. In *Desh pardesh: the South Asian presence in Britain.* Ed. by Roger Ballard. Delhi: B.R., 1996. pp. 165–190. CSSL.

Enthoven, R.E. *Folklore of Gujarat,* Vol. 1. New Delhi: Asian Educational Service, 1989. p. 159. HML.

Enthoven, R.E. *Folk notes.* Vol. 1. Complied By A.M.T. Jackson. Bombay: British India Press, 1914. p. 159. SETUL.

Fischer, Eberhard and Shah, Haku. *Mogra Dev – tribal Crocodile gods: wooden Crocodile images of Chodhri, Gamit and Vasava tribes, South Gujarat (India).* Ahmedabad: Gujarat Vidyapith, 1971. p. 43. CSSL.

Fischer, Eberhard and Shah, Haku. *Vetra ne Khambha memorials for the dead: wooden figures and memorial slabs of Chodhri, Gamit and Vasava tribes of South Gujarat.* Ahmedabad: Gujarat Vidhyapith, 1973. p. 60. HML.

Ghurye, G.S. *Cultural history of Gujarat.* Bombay: Popular, 1887. p. 364. HML.

Guichard, Sylvie. Gujarat and the dialectics of globalisation. In *Globalisation, diaspora and belonging: exploring transnationalism and Gujarati identity.* Ed. by Sharmina Mawani and Anjoom A. Mukadam. Jaipur: Rawat, 2014. pp. 21–41. CSSL.

Gulati, A.N. *Patolu of Gujarat.* Ahmedabad: Museum of Textiles, 1951. p. 31. TRTIL.

Haynes, Douglas E. *Rhetoric and ritual in colonial India: the shaping of a public culture in Surat city, 1852–1928.* Berkeley: University of California, 1991. p. 363. CSSL, SETUL, SPUL.

Hazra, D. Marine fisher folk of Gujarat: preliminary exploration. In *Research programmes on cultural anthropology and allied disciplines*. Ed. by Surajit Chandra Sinha. Calcutta: Anthropological Survey of India, 1970. pp. 55–73. CSSL.

Hinnells, John R. Parsi Zoroastrians in London. In *Desh pardesh: the South Asian presence in Britain*. Ed. by Roger Ballard. Delhi: B.R., 1996. pp. 251–271. CSSL.

Jackson A.M.T. and Enthoven, R.E. *Falklore of Gujarat. Folk lore notes,* Vol. 1, Gujarat. Haryana: Vintage, 1989. p. 159. BVL, GIDRL, GVL, SPUL, UML,

Jackson, A.M.T. and Enthoven, R.E. *Folklore of Gujarat*. Delhi: K.N. Book House, 1914. p. 159. BVL, HML, TRTIL.

Jadhavbhai. Terra Cotta tradition of Central Gujarat. In *Votive terra cottas of Gujarat*. Ed. by Kagal Carmen. New York: Mapin, 1985. pp. 61–96. TRTIL.

Jain, Jyotindara. *Folk art and culture of Gujarat: guide to the collection of the Shregas folk museum of Gujarat*. Ahmedabad: Shregas, 1980. p. 234. CEPTL.

Jain, Jyotindra. *Painted myths of creation art and ritual of an Indian tribe*. New Delhi: Lalit Kala Academy, 1984. p. 100. AAL.

Jethabhai. Pottery heritage from North Gujarat. In *Votive Terra Cottas of Gujarat*. Ed. by Kagal Carmen. New York: Mapin, 1985. pp. 35–60. TRTIL.

Jhala, Jayasinhji. Tragada Bhavaiya contribution to the making of Hindu identity in Saurastra. In *Popular culture in a globalised India*. Ed. by Gokulsing K. Moti and Vimal Dissanayake. New York: Routledge, 2009. pp. 69–81. GVL, IIML.

Jhaveri, Krishnalal Mohanlal. Folk literature in Gujarat. In *Folk-Culture of India*. Ed. by Suresh K. Sharma. Delhi: Vista, 2010. pp. 37–50. GVL.

Kamat, Nandakumar. Cultural relations of Goa with Gujarat. In *Essays in Goan history*. Ed. by Teotonio R. de-Souza. New Delhi: Concept, 2002. pp. 1–16. CSSL.

Kanji, Shezeleen. Religious education curriculum: addressing the challenges faced by Canadian adolescents of Gujarati ancestry. In *Globalisation, diaspora and belonging: exploring transnationalism and Gujarati identity*. Ed. by Sharmina Mawani and Anjoom A. Mukadam. Jaipur: Rawat, 2014. pp. 210–235. CSSL.

Keshodkar, Akbar. Contesting 'Purity' and zones of inclusion and exclusion among the Gujaratis in contemporary Zanzibar. In *Globalisation, diaspora and belonging: exploring transnationalism and Gujarati identity*. Ed. by Sharmina Mawani and Anjoom A. Mukadam. Jaipur: Rawat, 2014. pp. 169–189. CSSL.

Kincaid, C.A. *Folk Tales of Sind and Guzerat*. New Delhi: Asian Educational Services, 1925. p. 111. MICAL.

Knott, Kim. Gujarati Mochis in Leeds: from leather stockings to surgical boots and beyond. In *Desh pardesh: the South Asian presence in Britain*. Ed. by Roger Ballard. Delhi: B.R., 1996. pp. 213–230. CSSL.

Kothari, Rita. *Translating India: the cultural politics of English*. Delhi: Foundation Books, 2006. p. 137. CSSL.

Kulkarni, Shaunak S. Dance forms of the Siddis. In *Tribal dances of India*. Ed. by Robin D. Tribhuwan. New Delhi: Discovery, 1999. pp. 291–293. TRTIL.

Lambat, Ismail A. Marriage among the Sunni Surati Vohras of South Gujarat. In *Family kinship and marriage among Muslims in India*. Ed. by Imtiaz Ahmad. New Delhi: Manohar, 1976. pp. 49–81. GVL, SETUL, TRTIL.

Leckey, Edward. Principles of Goojuratee grammar. Bombay: Duftur Ashkara Press, 1857. p. 262. CSSL.

Lobo, Lancy. Household and family among Thakors in a North Gujarat Village. In *Family in India: structure and practice*. Ed. by Tulsi Patel. New Delhi: Sage, 2005. pp. 267–286. CSSL, IIML.

Majmudar, M.R. *Cultural history of Gujarat: from early times to pre-British period*. Bombay: Popular, 1965. p. 364. BVL, CEPTL, CSSL, GUL, GVL, HML, IIML, SGUL, SPIESRL.

Majmudar, M.R. *Gujarat: its art-heritage*. Bombay: University of Bombay, 1968. p. 70. ASL, BVL, TRTIL.

Majmudar, M.R. Women in Gujarati folklore. In *Indian folklore: a short survey of their social status and position*. Ed. by Sankar Sen Gupta. Calcutta: Indian, 1969. pp. 138–156. HML.

Mattausch, John. 'Wherever there is one Gujarati, there is Gujarat': the integration of Hindus in the United Kingdom. In *Globalisation, diaspora and belonging: exploring transnationalism and Gujarati identity*. Ed. by Sharmina Mawani and Anjoom A. Mukadam. Jaipur: Rawat, 2014. pp. 190–209. CSSL.

Mawani, Sharmina. Buying and selling an illusion: multinational corporations and young Gujaratis in Mumbai. In *Globalisation, diaspora and belonging: exploring transnationalism and Gujarati identity*. Ed. by Sharmina Mawani and Anjoom A. Mukadam. Jaipur: Rawat, 2014. pp. 78–99. CSSL.

Mawani, Sharmina and Mukadam, Anjoom A., ed. *Globalisation, diaspora and belonging: exploring transnationalism and Gujarati identity*. Jaipur: Rawat, 2014. p. 285. CSSL.

Mehta, Makrand. Patidars of Central Gujarat: historical perspective of their diaspora in East Africa in Twentieth century. In *Indian diaspora in national and regional context*. Ed. by Jayprakash M. Trivedi. Vallabh Vidyanagar: [ ], 2012. pp. 78–86. SPUL.

Mehta, Nanalal C. *Gujarati painting in the Fifteenth century*. London: India Society, 1931. p. 37. BVL.

Mehta, Nivedita. Parsi contribution to the art and cultural life of India. In *Sugar in the milk: Parsis of India*. Ed. by Nancy and Ram Singh. Madras: Institute for Development Education, 1986. pp. 25–51. CSSL.

Mehta, R.C. *Introduction to folk songs of Gujarat: a celebration of a folk culture*. Mumbai: Indian Musicological Society, 2004. p. 78. BVL, GVL.

Mehta, Sandhya Rao. Gendering the Gujarati diaspora: oral narratives and identity. In *Globalisation, diaspora and belonging: exploring transnationalism and Gujarati identity*. Ed. by Sharmina Mawani and Anjoom A. Mukadam. Jaipur: Rawat, 2014. pp. 42–57. CSSL.

Minochehr-Homji, N.D. Ceremonies and rituals of the Parsis. In *Sugar in the milk: Parsis of India*. Ed. by Nancy and Ram Singh. Madras: Institute for Development Education, 1986. pp. 115–124. CSSL.

Mirza, H.K. Fundamentals, customs and traditions of the Zoroastrian faith. In *Sugar in the milk: Parsis of India*. Ed. by Nancy and Ram Singh. Madras: Institute for Development Education, 1986. pp. 88–114. CSSL.

Mukadam, Anjoom A. Indobrits: cultural hybridity as a constantly negotiated lived reality. In *Globalisation, diaspora and belonging: exploring transnationalism and Gujarati identity*. Ed. by Sharmina Mawani and Anjoom A. Mukadam. Jaipur: Rawat, 2014. pp. 118–144. CSSL.

Munshi, K.M. *Linguistic province and the future of Bombay*. Bombay: National Information & Publications, 1948. p. 62. CSSL.

Patel, J.C. Dhodia dances. In *Tribal dances of India*. Ed. by Robin D. Tribhuwan. New Delhi: Discovery, 1999. pp. 67–72. TRTIL.

Patel, Kalahans. *Cultural heritage of Gujarat*. Vadodara: Good Companions, 1996. p. 58. GUL.

Patel, Narsi. *Hinduism outside India: selective retention in Gujarati families*. In *Family and social change in modern India.* Ed. by Giri Raj Gupta. New Delhi: Vikas, 1976. pp. 233–256. Main currents in Indian sociology– II. CSSL, SGUL.

Randeria, Shalini. Mourning, mortuary exchange and memorialisation: creation of local communities among dalits in Gujarat. In *Way of dying: death and its meanings in South Asia.* Ed. by Elisabeth Schombucher and Claus Peter Zoller. New Delhi: Manohar, 1999. pp. 88–111. CSSL.

Ranjan, Aditi and Rajan, M.D. Gujarat. In *Crafts of India handmade in India.* Ed. by Aditi Ranjan and M.D. Rajan. New Delhi: Council of Handicraft Development Corporation, 2007. pp. 408-[ ]. TRTIL.

Ray, Arup. Place names of Saurashtra of Gujarat: a glimpse of culture. In *Portrait of anthropological research*. Ed. by Debabrata Mandal, Tilak Bagchi and Asok Mukhopadhyay. New Delhi: Sarup, 2008. pp. 337–362. GVL, HML, TRTIL.

Sanghvi, Vijay. *Gujaratis of India*. New Delhi: Har-Anand, 2014. p. 239. CSSL.

Sankalia, Hasmukh. *Studies in the historical & cultural geography and ethnography of Gujarat*. Poona: Research Institute, 1949. p. 245. ASL, HML.

Sarkar, Jadunath. Marriage and family: viceroyalthy of Gujarat. In *History of Aurangzib*. New Delhi: Orient Longman, 1973. pp. 31–45. SPUL.

Shah, A.M. Phase of dispersal in the Indian family process. In *Family in India: structure and practice*. Ed. by Tulsi Patel. New Delhi: Sage, 2005. pp. 214–228. CSSL, IIML.

Shah, Dilip and Rahim, Syed. *Cultural factors in rural development*. Jaipur: Rawat, 2000. p. 212. CSSL, HML, TRTIL.

Shah, Sheena. Identity and belonging: the case of the Gujarati diaspora community in the United Kingdom, Singapore and South Africa. In *Globalisation, diaspora and belonging: exploring transnationalism and Gujarati identity*. Ed. by Sharmina Mawani and Anjoom A. Mukadam. Jaipur: Rawat, 2014. pp. 145–165. CSSL.

Shastree, Keshabram Kashiram. Recorded folk literature of Gujarat. In *Studies in Indian folk culture*. Ed. by Sanker Sen Gupta. Culcutta: Indian, 1964. pp. 168-[ ]. TRTIL.

Skaria, Ajay. Development nationalism and the time of the primitive: the Dangs darbar. In *Regional modernities the culture politics of development in India.* Ed. by K. Sivaramakrishnan and Arun Agrawal. New Delhi: Oxford, 2003. pp. 215–236. IIML.

Soni, Loknath and Bagchi, Tilak. Leather work: a vanishing craft of the Marvada Meghwal of Kachh in Gujarat. In *Approaches of tribal development.* [Ed.] By Chaturbhuj. New Delhi: Adhyayan, 2009. pp. 134–171. TRTIL.

Streefkerk-Hubbeling, Arni. Transformation and accommodation: the differential meaning of inter (caste) marriage. In *Winners and losers: styles of development and change in an Indian region*. Ed. by S. Devadas Pillai and Chris Baks. Bombay: Popular, 1979. pp. 241–282. CSSL, SPIESRL.

Tambs-Lyche, Harald. *London Patidars: case study in urban ethnicity*. London: Routledge, 1980. p. 147. CSSL, GVL, TRTIL.

Thakar, Minakshi. *Tribal and folkart of Gujarat.* Ahmedabad: Author, 2005. p. 111. TRTIL.

Tribhuwan, Robin D. Mahalaxmi fair of tribals in South Gujarat and Western Maharashtra. In *Fair and festivals of Indian tribes*. [Ed.] By Robin David Tribhuwan. New Delhi: Discovery, 2003. pp. 225–229. TRTIL.

Tribhuwan, Robin D. and Tribhuwan, Preeti R. Dublas and their dances. In *Tribal dances of India*. Ed. by Robin D. Tribhuwan. New Delhi: Discovery, 1999. pp 64–66. TRTIL.

Tribhuwan, Robin D. and Tribhuwan, Preeti R. Festival dances of the Kotwalia tribe of Gujarat. In *Tribal dances of India*. Ed. by Robin D. Tribhuwan. New Delhi: Discovery, 1999. pp. 158–160. TRTIL.

Trivedi, J.M. Indian diaspora at cross road of change and continuity: a case of non-residents Gujaratis of Charotar region. In *Indian diaspora in national and regional context*. Ed. by Jayprakash M. Trivedi. Vallabh Vidyanagar: [ ], 2012. pp. 87–91. SPUL.

Trivedi, Nivedita. Marriage arrangement and the status of women. In *Winners and losers: styles of development and change in an Indian region*. Ed. by S. Devadas Pillai and Chris Baks. Bombay: Popular, 1979. pp. 229–240. CSSL, SPIESRL.

Unnithan, T.K.N. Some possible variations in family types in Gujarat. In *Family in India: a regional view*. Ed. by George Kurian. Paris: Moution, 1974. pp. 179–190. IIML.

Vahed, Goolam. 'Imagined community' in diaspora: Gujaratis in South Africa. In *Gujarat beyond Gandhi: identity, conflict and society*. Ed. by Nalin Mehta and Mona G. Mehta. London: Routledge, 2010. pp. 210–231. CSSL, GIDRL, IRMAL, UML.

Van Der veen, Klaas W. *I Give the my daughter: a study of marriage and hierarchy among the Anavil Brahmans of South Gujarat*. Assen: Van Gorcum, 1972. p. 297. CSSL, GUL, SGUL.

Vidyarthi, L.P. and Rai, B.K. *Tribal culture of India*. Delhi: Concept, 1977. p. 487. CSSL.

Warrier, Shrikala. Gujarati Prajapatis in London: family roles and sociability networks. In *Desh pardesh: the South Asian presence in Britain*. Ed. by Roger Ballard. Delhi: B.R., 1996. pp. 191–212. CSSL.

Wessel, Margit Van. Cultural contractions and intergenerational relation: the construction of selfhood among middle-class youth in Baroda. In *Being middle-class in India: a way of life*. Ed. by Henrike Ponner. New York: Routledge, 2011. pp. 100–116. IIML.

Yagnik, Hasu. *Study in tribal literature of Gujarat*. [Ed.] by Bhagavandas Patel. Mumbai: Nayan Suryanand Lok-Pratisthan, 2004. p. 232. GVL.

Yagnik, Hasu. Sargu songs: a living tradition within the Devi-worship ritual of the Vaisya Suthar and Sarathia and Bhopa Rabari of Saurashtra. In *Banyan tree: essay on early literature in new Indo-Aryan languages. Proceedings of the Seventh International Conference on Early Literature in New Indo-Aryan Languages, Venice, 1997*. Vol. I. Ed. by Mariola Offredi. New Delhi: Manohar, 2000. pp. 223–234. CSSL.

Yagnik, Hasu and Kansara, N.M. *Folklore of Gujarat*. New Delhi: National Book Trust, 2002. pp. 1–209. GVL, HML.

Journal Articals

Chandervaker, P. Birth of a drink. *Folklore*. 20, 3–4, 1979. pp. 74–75. SPUL.

Chandervaker, Pushker. Khagiyo: a Parrot-god of Bhopas: the cattle breeders of the Okha Mandal in Gujarat. *Folklore*. 18, 9, 1977. pp. 285–287. SPUL.

Chandervaker, Pushker. Rain-making rituals of Gujarat. *Folklore*. 3, 11, 1962. pp. 513–518. SPUL.

Chandervaker, Pushker. Tree cult in Saurashtra. *Folklore*. 5, 6, 1964. pp. 207–212. SPUL.

Charu, Smita. Wall paintings in a Gujarat village: an appraisal of folk traditions. *Folklore*. 18, 11, 1977. pp. 352–358. SPUL.

Dar, M.I. Cultural and literary activities under the Sultans of Gujarat. *Journal of the Gujarat Research Society*. 10, 4, 1948. pp. 240–258. GUL.

Dave, T.N. Language of Maha-Gujarat. *Journal of the Gujarat Research Society*. 10, 2, 1948. pp. 80–134. GUL.

Dave, T.N. Linguistic survey of the borderlands of Gujarat. *Journal of the Gujarat Research Society.* 4, 4, 1942. pp. 262–272. GVL.

Dave, T.N. Linguistic survey of the borderlands of Gujarat (Field work no-40). *Journal of the Gujarat Research Society.* 10, 1, 1948. pp. 23–34. GUL.

Desai, B.L. Folk-songs of Southern Gujarat-rain songs. *Journal of the Gujarat Research Society.* 6, 1, 1944. pp. 22–27. GVL.

Desai, B.L. Tree-worship in Gujarat. *Folklore.* 5, 5, 1964. pp. 183–186. SPUL.

Ghoshal, Subhas C. Brief survey on the festivals of Nalkantha area of Gujarat. *Vanyajati.* 31, 1, 1983. pp. 21–26. CSSL.

Gopalan, G.V. Uniqueness of outlawry and outlaw ballads and tales of Saurashatra, Gujarat. *Folklore*. 22, 2, 1981. pp25-[ ]. TRTIL.

Jhaveri, B.J. Dialect of Gujarat. *Journal of the Gujarat Research Society.* 32, 4/128, 1970. pp. 216–220. GVL.

Joshi, Devdatta. Contemporary Ramayana tradition in Gujarat. *Journal of the Oriental Institute*. 37, 1–2, 1987. pp. 127–142. GVL.

Joshi, Vidyut. Cultural context of development. *Economic and Political Weekly*. 35, 35 and 36, 2000. pp. 3165–3169. CEPTL, CSSL, IIML, IRMAL, MICAL, SGUL, SPIESRL, UML.

Levitt, Hillyer Stephan. Some paintings of Rahu and Ketu from Gujarat. *Journal of the Oriental Institute*. 40, 3–4, 1991. pp. 255–574. GVL.

Majumdar, D.N. and Kisen, K. Serological status of castes and tribes of cultural Gujarat. *Eastern Anthropologist*. 2, 2, 1948. pp. 92–97. TRTIL.

Majumdar, D.N. and Kisen, K. Serological status of castes and tribes of cultural Gujarat. *Journal of the Gujarat Research Society*. 10, 1, 1948. pp. 3–22. GUL.

Meghani, J.K. Marriage songs of Kathiawar. *Journal of the Gujarat Research Society*. 6, 3, 1944. pp. 127–137. GVL.

Meghani, J.K. Marriage songs of Kathiawar-III. *Journal of the Gujarat Research Society*. 7, 1, 1945. pp. 12–15. GUL.

Mehta, B.H. Religious thought and worship among the Chodhras of Gujarat. *Journal of the Anthropological Society of Bombay*. 15, 4, 1933. pp. 285–358. TRTIL.

Naik, C.R. Cultivation of the Persian language and literature by the Nagaras of Gujarat. *Journal of the Oriental Institute*. 14, 2, 1964. pp. 125–133. GVL.

Naik, T.B. Aboriginal festivals in Gujarat. *Eastern Anthropologist*. 2, 1, 1948. pp. 16–21. TRTIL.

Naik, T.B. Anthropology, history and microplanning. *Adivasi Gujarat*. 4, 2, 1982. pp. 15–23. SPUL.

Naik, T.B. Some folk elements in Gujarat culture. *Eastern Anthropologist.* 1, 1, 1947. pp. 16–26. TRTIL.

Naik, T.B. Songs of the Anavils of Gujarat. *Man in India*. 30, 2 and 3, 1950. pp. 29–55. TRTIL, UML.

Nandy, Ashis. Obituary of a culture. *Seminar*. 513, 2002. pp. 15–18. CEPTL, CSSL, MICAL, SPUL, UML.

Pancholi, Ravindra. Modernized tribals keeping their traditions alive. *Adivasi Gujarat.* 19, 1 and 2, 2009. pp. 72–77. CSSL, GVL, TRTIL.

Pandit, P.B. Linguistic survey of the borderlands of Gujarat (Fieldwork no-5). *Journal of the Gujarat Research Society.* 14, 2, 1952. pp. 57–67. GUL, GVL.

Pandya, Suman. Historical relevance of the tribal culture. *Adivasi Gujarat.* 1, 2, 1978. pp. 12–15. CSSL, GVL, SPIESRL, TRTIL.

Patel, Haribhai. Change in structural unit and attitudes towards marriage by exchange. *Sociological Bulletin*. 15, 2, 1966. pp. 63–67. CSSL.

Patel, Madhubhai. Note on folk of Gujarat. *Folklore*. 12, 2, 1971. pp. 47–48. SPUL.

Rafiqasultana, Afrozasultana. Musical instrument of Warli woman. *Adivasi Gujarat*. 14, 2, 2004. pp. 1–3. CSSL, GVL, SPIESRL, TRTIL.

Sebastian, V. Cultural elites and the disciplining of Bhavai. *Economic and Political Weekly*. 49, 7, 2014. pp. 59–66. CSSL.

Shah, Mangaldas. Some problems of Gujarati vegetarian food. *Journal of the Gujarat Research Society*. 2, 4, 1940. pp. 256–263. GUL.

Shah, P.G. Mesolithic culture in Gujarat. *Journal of the Gujarat Research Society*. 23, 4/92, 1961. pp. 277–279. GVL.

Shah, P.G. Studies in the historical and cultural geography and ethnography of Gujarat. *Journal of Gujarat Research Society*. 12, 2, 1951. pp. 83–84. SPUL.

Solanki, Siddharaj. Bhil customary laws. *Adivasi Gujarat*. 8, 2, 1998. p. 93. SPIESRL.

Solanki, Siddharaj. Dhodia tribal customary laws. *Adivasi Gujarat*. 9, 1, 1999. pp. 95–102. GVL, TRTIL.

Solanki, Siddharaj. Traditional laws of Patelias of Gujarat. *Adivasi Gujarat*. 7, 2, 1997. pp. 47–71. GVL, TRTIL.

Solanki, Siddharaj. Traditional laws of the Vasavas. *Adivasi Gujarat*. 7, 2, 1997. pp. 72–86. GVL, TRTIL.

Solanki, Siddharaj. Dhodia tribal customary laws. *Adivasi Gujarat*. 9, 1, 1999. p. 95. SPIESRL.

Solanki, Siddharaj. Dhodia tribal customary Laws: Dhankas. *Adivasi Gujarat*. 10, 1, 2000. pp. 92–105. GVL, SPIESRL, TRTIL.

Solanki, Siddharaj. Tribal customary laws among the Koknas of Gujarat. *Adivasi Gujarat*. 8, 1, 1998. pp. 92–100. GVL, SPIESRL, TRTIL.

Solanki, Siddharaj. Tribal customary laws of Chaudhary tribe. *Adivasi Gujarat*. 10, 2, 2000. pp. 87–101. GVL, SPIESRL, TRTIL.

Solanki, Siddharaj. Tribal customary laws: the Garasias. *Adivasi Gujarat*. 8, 1, 1998. pp. 101–118. GVL, SPIESRL, TRTIL.

Sonawane, V.H. Rock paintings at Tarsang, Gujarat. *Journal of the Oriental Institute*. 31, 3, 1982. pp. 293–299. GVL.

Soundara Rajan, K.V. Teyracotta cult plaque of Kanad (Gujarat). *Journal of the Gujarat Research Society*. 24, 4/96, 1962. pp. 267–270. GVL.

Sultana, Sayed Atroz and Sultana, Sayed Rafiqua. Mask culture of Gujarat tribes. *Adivasi Gujarat*. 18, 1–2, 2008. pp. 97–100. CSSL.

Swayam, S. Sites of ritual construction of identities a fresh look at the memorial stones of Gujarat. *Man in India*. 84, 3–4, 2004. pp. 303–339. CSSL, IRMAL, UML.

Trivedi, H.V. Cultural affinity of Gujarat and Malwa. *Journal of the Oriental Institute*. 5, 1, 1955. pp. 99–102. GVL.

Trivedi, Jayprakash M. Plurality in Indian diaspora: a case of Patidars (Gujarati) diaspora in USA. *VNSGU Journal of Humanities & Social Sciences*. 4, 1, 2013. pp. 48–56. CSSL.

Van Der Veen, Klaas W. Marriage and hierarchy among the Anavil Brahmans of South Gujarat. *Contributions to Indian Sociology*. 7, 1973. pp. 36–52. GUL, SPUL, UML.

Vasavada, R.J. Building on heritage. *Seminar*. 657, 2014. pp. 46–49. CSSL, UML.

Waetjen, Thembisa. Fahmida's World: gender, home and the Gujarati Muslim diaspora in mid-20th century South Africa. *Man in India*. 93, 4, 2013. pp. 627–643. CSSL, UML.

Working Papers, Reports and Other Materials

Bhatt, R.M. *Folk tales of Gujarat*. New Delhi: Publications Division, 1987. p. 37. GVL.

David, Esther. Gujarat 2010-challenges and opportunities. In *Gujarat-2010: challenges and opportunities*. By Government of Gujarat. Ahmedabad: Sardar Patel Institute of Economic & Social Research, 2001. pp. 630–631. Seminar Volume. CSSL, EDIL, IRMAL, SGUL, SPIESRL.

Dekkers, Natascha and Rutten, Mario. *Diaspora philanthropy from a homeland perspective: reciprocity and contestation over donations in Central Gujarat, India*. Bangalore: National Institute of Advanced Studies and Amsterdam Institute for Social Science Research, 2011. p. 24. Provincial Globalisation Working Paper No. 2. CEPTL, CSSL.

Gujarat, Government of. Our archaeological heritage: how to preserve it. In *Gujarat-2010: challenges and opportunities*. By Government of Gujarat. Ahmedabad: Sardar Patel Institute of Economic & Social Research, 2001. pp. 632–634. Seminar Volume. CSSL, EDIL, IRMAL, SGUL, SPIESRL.

Hazra, D. Marine fisherfolk of Gujarat: preliminary exploration. In *Seminar on research programmes in cultural Anthropology and related disciplines*. Ed. by Surajit Chandra Sinha. Calcutta: Anthropological Survey of India, 1967. pp. 47–64. CSSL.

Joshi, O.P. *Art and aesthetics in tribes of South Gujarat*. Surat: Centre for Social Studies, 2003. p. 164. CSSL.

Koppar, D.H. *Tribal art of Dangs*. Baroda: Department of Museums, 1971. p. 166. Monograph. CSSL.

Patel, Pravin J. and Rutten, Mario. *Long-distance familism social linkages between Patidars in India and Britain: a view from Central Gujarat*. New Delhi: ICSSR and IMWOO, 1999. p. [ ]. IDPAD occasional papers and reprints 1999–92. GIDRL.

Patel, Pravin, J. and Rutten, Mario. *Translational linkages between India and Britain: an exploration of socio-economic linkages between Patel's of Central Gujarat and Greater London*. Vallabh Vidyanagar: Sardar Patel University, 2004. p. [ ]. SPU Working Paper Series on Indian Diaspora 1. GIDRL.

Shastri, K.K. Culture and heritage. In *Gujarat-2010: challenges and opportunities*. By Government of Gujarat. Ahmedabad: Sardar Patel Institute of Economic & Social Research, 2001. pp. 622–629. Seminar Volume. CSSL, EDIL, IRMAL, SGUL, SPIESRL.

Solanki, S.S. *Tribal customary laws of Bhils*. Ahmedabad: Gujarat Vidyapith, [ ]. p. 8. TRTIL.

Solanki, S.S. *Traditional laws of the Patelias of Gujarat*. Ahmedabad: Gujarat Vidyapith, 1985. p. 24. Series-120. TRTIL.

Solanki, Sidharaj. *Tribal customary laws among the Koknas of Gujarat*. Ahmedabad: Gujarat Vidyapith, 1985. p. 9. Serise-192. TRTIL.

Solanki, S.S. and TRTI. *Tribal customary laws of Choudhary tribe*. Ahmedabad: Gujarat Vidyapith, [ ]. p. 16. TRTIL.

Veen, Van Der. Dowry and social change in the Indian social setting. In *International seminar on "Gujarat society", 17–20 December 1986*. Surat: Centre for Social Studies, 1986. pp. 1–44. CSSL.

7

Politics, Governance, Democracy, Human Rights

Books/Chapter in Books

Ashraf, Ali. *Government and politics of big cities: an Indian case study*. Delhi: Concept, 1977. p. 201. CSSL.

Baxi, M.J. and Shah, B.C. Role of taluka development officer in the Panchayat raj. In *Revival of Panchayati raj: trends and problems.* Ed. by B.C. Shah and J.N. Pandya. Vallabh Vidyanagar: Sardar Patel University, 1989. pp. 170–194. SPUL.

Bhatt, Anil. Caste and political mobilisation in a Gujarat district. In *Caste in Indian politics.* Ed. by Rajni Kothari. New Delhi: Sangam, 1970. pp. 299–339. CSSL, TRTIL.

Bhatt, Anil. Caste and political mobilisation in a Gujarat district. In *Writings of Rajni Kothari.* Ed. by Ashish Nandy. New Delhi: Orient Blackswan, 2009. pp. 283–323. CSSL, GVL, HML.

Bhatt, Anil. Municipal commissioner in Gujarat: structure, process and style. In *Municipal and urban India: selection from nagarlok*. Ed. by Abhijit Datta. New Delhi: Indian Institute of Public Administration, 1980. pp. 35–44. CSSL, SPUL.

Bhatt, Anil. Power pattern in Gujarat. In *Context of electoral change in India: general elections, 1967*. Ed. by Rajni Kothari, et al. Bombay: Academic, 1969. pp. 148–156. Centre for the Study of Developing Societies. CSSL, GUL.

Bhattacharjea, Ajit. Report on Ahmedabad. In *Expanding governmental lawlessness and organized struggles: violation of democratic rights of the minorities, women, slum dwellers, press and some other violations*. Ed. by A.R. Desai. Bombay: Popular, 1991. pp. 13–22. CSSL.

Boman-Behram, B.K. *Rise of municipal government in the city of Ahmedabad*. Bombay: D.B. Taraporevala, 1937. p. 438. GVL.

Chakraborty, Jyotirmoy. Election power and politics in a multi-ethnic situation of Gujarat. In *Ethnicity, politics and political systems in tribal India.* Ed. by B.B. Goswami and Jayanta Sarkar. Calcutta: Anthropological Survey of India, 1997. pp. 163–190. GIDRL.

Chavada, V.K. Gujarat. In *Historical writings on the nationalist movement in India*. Ed. by S.P. Sen. Calcutta: Institute of Historical Studies, 1977. pp. 108–128. SPUL.

Choudhary, Kameshwar. Governance reforms and development in Gujarat. In *Globalisation governance reforms and development in India*. Ed. by Kameshwar Choudhary. New Delhi: Sage, 2007. pp. 115–160. GUL.

Chowdhry, N.K. *Assembly elections 1994–95: an analysis and results*. Delhi: Shipra, 1995. p. 266. CSSL.

Christophe, Jaffrelot. Gujarat: the meaning of Modi's victory in 2007. In *Religion caste and politics in India*. Ed. by Jaffrelot Christophe. New Delhi: Primus, 2011. pp. 397–410. HML.

Christophe, Jaffrelot. 2002 Program in Gujarat: the post 9/11 face of Hindu nationalist anti-Muslim violence. In *Religion caste and politics in India*. Ed. by Jaffrelot Christophe. New Delhi: Primus, 2011. pp. 376–396. HML.

Coe, J. Congress and the tribals in Surat district in the 1920s. In *Struggling and ruling: the Indian national congress 1885–1985*. Ed. by Jim Masselos. New Delhi: Sterling, 1987. pp. 59–70. CSSL, HML.

Cowlagi, V.R.S. and Mehta, S.S. Lessons from Panchayati raj in Gujarat. In *Decentralisation panchayats in the nineties*. Ed. by Amitava Mukherjee. New Delhi: Vikas, 1994. pp. 211–214. CSSL.

Debroy, Bibek. *Gujarat: governance for growth and development*. New Delhi: Academic Foundation, 2012. p. 165. CSSL, GIDRL, IIML, SPIESRL.

Devadas Pillai, S. District level politics. In *Winners and losers: styles of development and change in an Indian region*. Ed. by S. Devadas Pillai and Chris Baks. Bombay: Popular, 1979. pp. 320–355. CSSL, SPIESRL.

Dobbin, Christine. *Urban leadership in Western India: politics and communities in Bombay city 1840–1885*. London: Oxford, 1972. p. 305. CSSL.

D'Souza, Paul. Scavengers towards freedom: dynamic of power paradox among Bhangis of Gujarat. In *Restoration of human rights and dignity to dalits: with special reference to scavengers in India*. Ed. by Ram Gopal Singh and Ravindra D. Gadkar. New Delhi: Manak, 2004. pp. 178–207. CSSL.

Dube, Mukul and Khusro, A.M. *Path of the Parivar: articles on Gujarat and Hindutva*. New Delhi: Three Essays, 2004. p. 134. CSSL, HML.

Gambhir, Ram and Wattilia, Imtti. Panchayat raj in tribal village of Gujarat. In *Overview of tribal research studies*. Ed. by Navinchandra Jain and Tribhuwan D. Robin. Pune: Tribal Research & Training Institute, 1995. pp. 114–121. TRTIL.

Gatade, Subhash, ed. State and human right: people as trophies in Gujarat. In *Saffron condition: politics of repression and exclusion in neoliberal India*. Ed. by Subhash Gatade. New Delhi: Three Essays, 2011. pp. 369–376. IIML.

Ghassem-Fachandi, Parvis. On the political uses of disgust in Gujarat. In *Gujarat beyond Gandhi: identity, conflict and society*. Ed. by Nalin Mehta and Mona G. Mehta. London: Routledge, 2010. pp. 127–155. BVL, CSSL, GIDRL, IRMAL, UML.

Ghosh, Archana and Sami Ahmad S. *Plague in Surat: crisis in urban governance*. New Delhi: Concept, 1996. p. 124. CSSL.

Ghosh, Buddhadeb and Kumar, Girish. *State politics and Panchayats in India*. New Delhi: Manohar, 2003. pp. 89–146. CSSL.

Ghosh, Pansya Chaya. Surat congress, 1907. In *Development of the Indian national congress*. Calcutta: Firma Ksm, 1985. pp. 163–182. SUL.

Gupta, S.K. *Statewise comprehensive information on human right violation*. New Delhi: ALP, 2009. p. 251. GVL.

Heredero, J.M. Training rural leaders: an experiment with scheduled castes in Gujarat. In *Politics of change and leadership development: the new leaders in India and Africa*. Ed. by Alfred De Souza. New Delhi: Manohar, 1978. pp. 257–276. CSSL, SPUL.

Institute of Rural Management Anand. Gujarat. In *State of Panchayats 2007–08: an independent assessment*. Anand: Institute of Rural Management (IRMA) Anand, [ ]. pp. 117–130. IIML.

Iyengar, Sudarshan. Governance. In *Tribal development in Western India.* Ed. by Amita Shah and Jharna Pathak. New Delhi: Routledge, 2014. pp. 310–328. CSSL.

Jan, Breman. I am the government officer: state protection for the rural proletariat of South Gujarat. In *Politics and the state in India*. Ed. by Zoya Hasan. New Delhi: Sage, 2000. pp. 293–330. HML.

Joshi, Mahipatram H. and Trivedi, Hariprasad M., ed. *Important state of India. Part I.* Vadali, Idar: Mahipatram H. Joshi, 1946. p. 203. CSSL.

Joshi, Satyakam. Functioning of Panchayati raj in scheduled areas of Gujarat. In *Panchayati raj institutions and rural development*. Ed. by Bishnu C. Barik and Umesh C. Sahoo. Jaipur: Rawat, 2008. pp. 158–174. CSSL, SPUL.

Joshi, Satyakam. Local governance and social change in Gujarat. In *Inclusion and exclusion in local governance: field studies from rural India*. Ed. by B.S. Baviskar and George Mathew. New Delhi: Sage, 2009. pp. 407–432. CSSL, IIML.

Kalia, Ravi. *Gandhinagar: building national identity in postcolonial India*. New Delhi: Oxford, 2005. p. 165. CSSL, IIML, SETUL, SGUL.

Khan, Farzana. Rann of Kutch award. In *50 years of Indo-Pak relations*. Ed. by Verinder Grover. New Delhi: Deep & Deep, 1998. pp. 80–90. HML.

Khanna, B.S. *Panchayati raj in India: rural local self-government: national perspective and state studies*. New Delhi: Deep & Deep, 1994. p. 431. CSSL.

Kohli, Atul. *Democracy and development in India: from socialism to pro-business.* New Delhi: Oxford, 2009. p. 431. CSSL.

Kohli, Atul. *Democracy and discontent: India's growing crisis of governability*. Cambridge: Cambridge University press, 1991. p. 420. CSSL.

Kothari, Rajni and Maru, Rushikesh. Federating for political interests: the Kshatriyas of Gujarat. In *Caste in Indian politics.* Ed. by Rajni Kothari. New Delhi: Sangam, 1970. pp. 70–101. CSSL, TRTIL.

Kothari, Rajni and Maru, Rushikesh. Federating for political interests: the Kshatriyas of Gujarat. In *Caste in Indian politics.* Ed. by Rajni Kothari. New Delhi: Orient Longman, 2010. pp. 66–95. HML.

Kothari, Rajni and Maru, Rushikesh. Federating for political interests: the Kshatriyas of Gujarat. In *Politics in India caste in Indian politics rethinking democracy*. Ed. by Rajni Kothari. New Delhi: Orient Blackswan, 2005. pp. 66–95. HML, IIML.

Kothari, Rajni and Shah, Ghanshyam. Caste orientation of political factions: Modasa constituency. In *Indian voting behaviour: studies of the 1962 general elections*. Ed. by Myron Weiner and Rajni Kothari. Calcutta: Firma, 1965. pp. 141–161. CSSL.

Lal, Shiv. *Indian elections since independence Gujarat.* New Delhi: Election Archives, 1972. pp. 54–61. SPIESRL.

Mahadevia, Darshini. From stealth to aggression: economic reforms and communal politics in Gujarat. In *Politics of economic reforms in India.* Ed. by Jos Mooij. New Delhi: Sage, 2005. pp. 291–321. CSSL, IIML.

Maha Gujarat Parishad. *Formation of Maha Gujarat.* Bombay: Asia, 1954. p. 123. BVL.

Malaviya, H.D. Saurashtra. In *Village Panchayats in India*. New Delhi: All India Congress Committee, 1956. pp. 593–608. CSSL, GUL.

Mathur, Navdeep and Bazar, Amir Bashir. Democratic governance through collaborative design: a case study of urban community based partnership in Ahmedabad. In *Urban infrastructure and governance.* Ed. by Ramesh G. and Vishnuprasad Nagadevara. New York: Routledge, 2010. pp. 114–140. IIML.

Mehta, Makrand. Leader and his miliuen: Gandhi and Ahmedabad 1915–1920. In *Regional roots of Indian nationalism*. Ed. by Makrand Mehta. New Delhi: Criterion, 1990. pp. 121–146. GVL.

Mehta, Mona G. River of no dissent: Narmada movement and coercive Gujarati nativism. In *Gujarat beyond Gandhi: identity, conflict and society.* Ed. by Nalin Mehta and Mona G. Mehta. London: Routledge, 2010. pp. 60–87. BVL, CSSL, GIDRL, IRMAL, UML.

Mehta, Nalin. Ashis Nandy vs the state of Gujarat: authoritarian developmentalism, democracy and the politics of Narendra Modi. In *Gujarat beyond Gandhi: identity, conflict and society.* Ed. by Nalin Mehta and Mona G. Mehta. London: Routledge, 2010. pp. 156–183. BVL, CSSL, GIDRL, IRMAL, UML.

Mehta, Nalin and Mehta, Mona G., ed. *Gujarat beyond Gandhi: identity, conflict and society*. London: Routledge, 2010. p. 242. BVL, CSSL, GIDRL, IRMAL, UML.

Mehta, S.S. and Ahuja, Pratul. Panchayati raj in Gujarat. In *Dynamics of development in Gujarat*. Ed. by Indira Hirway, S.P. Kashyap and Amita Shah. New Delhi: Concept, 2002. pp. 408–438. CSSL, EDIL, GIDRL, GVL, HML, IRMAL, SPUL, UML.

Mehta, Uday. Gujarat: Hindu rashtra laboratory. In *Religion, power & violence: expression of politics in contemporary times*. Ed. by Ram Puniyani. New Delhi: Sage, 2005. pp. 290–305. CSSL.

Misra, S.C. *Rise of Muslim power in Gujarat*. New Delhi: Munshiram Manoharlal, 1982. p. 252. CSSL, SGUL, SUL.

Misra, S.C. *Rise of Muslim power in Gujarat: a history of Gujarat from 1298–1442*. Bombay: Asia, 1963. p. 252. BVL.

Mukta, Parita. On the political culture of authoritarianism. In *Development and deprivation in Gujarat: in honour of Jan Breman*. Ed. by Ghanshyam Shah, Mario Rutten and Hein Streefkerk. New Delhi: Sage, 2002. pp. 59–73. CEEL, CEPTL, CSSL, EDIL, GIDRL, HML, IIML, IRMAL, UML.

Munshi, Aziz A. Background and basis of the Rann of Kutch award. In *50 years of Indo-Pak relations*. Ed. by Verinder Grover. New Delhi: Deep & Deep, 1998. pp. 69–79. HML

Nussbaum, Martha C. *Clash within: democracy, religious violence, and India's future*. Delhi: Permament Black, 2007. p. 403. CSSL.

Panchanadikar, J.M. and Panchanadikar, K.C. Determinants structure and adjustment progress in Panchayati raj bodies: a case study of Mindhola village Panchayat in Gujarat. In *Readings on Panchayati raj*. Ed. by George Jacob. Hyderabad: National Institute of Community, 1967. pp. 1–34. AAUL, HML, SPUL.

Panchanadikar, K.C. and Panchanadikar, J. Constituted structure and adjustment process in Panchayati democracy in a rural community in South Gujarat with references to leadership roles. In *Determinants of social structure and social change in India and others papers*. Bombay: Popular, 1970. pp. 200–223. AAUL, CSSL.

Panchanadikar, K.C. and Panchanadikar, J. *Democratic structure and socialization in rural India: analysis of participation, alienation and consensus*. Bombay: popular, 1980. p. 332. CSSL, HML.

Pandya, J.N. Some aspects of Panchayati raj in Gujarat. In *Revival of Panchayati raj: trends and problems.* Ed. by B.C. Shah and J.N. Pandya. Vallabh Vidyanagar: Sardar Patel University, 1989. pp. 154–169. SPUL.

Pantham, Thomas. Formation of the politically active stratum: evidence from the career origins of party activists in an Indian city. In *Making of politicians: studies from Africa and Asia.* Ed. by W.H. Morris-Jones. London: Athlone press, 1976. pp. 207–226. CSSL.

Pantham, Thomas. *Political parties and democratic consensus: a study of party organisations in an Indian city*. Delhi: Macmillan, 1976. p. 215. CSSL.

Pantham, Thomas. *Voting behaviour in Baroda city: a 1967 general election study*. Baroda: M.S. University, 1968. p. 92. Political Science Series No. 4. HML.

Parikh, R.G. Vadodara rajaya prajamandal and the demand for responsible government in Baroda state. In *Regional roots of Indian nationalism*. Ed. by Makrand Mehta. New Delhi: Criterion, 1990. pp. 158–164. GVL.

Patel, C.N. *Mahatma Gandhi in his Gujarati writings*. New Delhi: Sahitya Academic, 1981. p. 97. BVL.

Patel, Chhaya. Empowering women through Panchayat raj institutions in Gujarat: some field experiences. In *Functioning of Panchayat raj system*. Ed. by Yatindra Singh Sisodia. Jaipur: Rawat, 2005. pp. 164–175. HML.

Patel, H.B. Village level political leadership. In *Revival of Panchayati raj: trends and problems*. Ed. by B.C. Shah and J.N. Pandya. Vallabh Vidyanagar: Sardar Patel University, 1989. pp. 206–211. SPUL.

Patel, Priyavadan M. Gujarat: signs of anti-incumbency. In *Electoral politics in Indian states*. Ed. by Sandeep Shastri, K.C. Suri and Yogendra Yadav. New Delhi: Oxford, 2009. pp. 148–175. CSSL.

Patel, Sujata. City conflicts and communal politics: Ahmedabad 1985–86. In *Urban studies*. Ed. by Sujata Patel and Kushal Deb. Delhi: Oxford, 2006. pp. 318–339. CSSL, HML.

Patel, Sujata. Regional politics, city conflicts and communal riots: Ahmedabad 1985–1986. In *Region, culture, and politics in India*. Ed. by Rajendra Vora and Anne Feldhaus. New Delhi: Manohar, 2006. pp. 353–376. CSSL.

Pathak, D.N. Political behaviour in Gujarat with reference to the fourth general elections. In *Studies in the fourth general elections*. By Aloo J. Dastur, et al. Bombay: Allied, 1972. pp. 43–71. CSSL, SPIESRL.

Pathak, D.N. Some aspects of the Panchayati raj in Gujarat: a critique. In *Community development & democratic growth*. Ed. by N.R. Inamdar. Bombay: Popular, 1974. pp. 110–112. IIML, SGUL.

Pathak, D.N. State politics in Gujarat: some determinates. In *State politics in India*. Meerut: Meenakshi, [ ]. pp. 122–133. SUL.

Pathak, D.N., Parekh, M.G. and Desai, K.D. *Three general elections in Gujarat: development of a decade 1952–1962*. Ahmedabad: Gujarat University, 1966. p. 267. CSSL, GUL, GVL, HML, IIML.

Rajagopal, Arvind. Gujarat experiment and Hindu national realism: lessons for secularism. In *Crisis of secularism in India*. Ed. by Anuradha Dingwaney Needham and Rajeswari Sunder Rajan. Delhi: Permanent Black, 2007. pp. 208–224. CSSL.

Rajagopal, Arvind. Special political zone: urban planning, spatial segregation and the infrastructure of violence in Ahmedabad. In *Gujarat beyond Gandhi: identity, conflict and society*. Ed. by Nalin Mehta and Mona G. Mehta. London: Routledge, 2010. pp. 88–126. BVL, CSSL, GIDRL, IRMAL, UML.

Rajput, R.S. Gujarat. In *Dynamics of democratic politics in India*. Ed. by R.S. Rajput. New Delhi: Deep and Deep, 1986. pp. 142–149. HML.

Ramesh, Asha and Ali, Bharti. *$33^1/_3$%: Reservation towards political empowerment*. Bangalore: Books for Change, 2001. p. 88. CSSL.

Roop, Arjun and Yadappanavar, A.V. Interventions for women empowerment in India: a study in Gujarat state. In *Grassroots planning and local governance in India*. Ed. by Sundar Ram. New Delhi: Kanishka, 2010. pp. 298–307. SPUL.

Samant, S.V. *Village Panchayats: with special reference to Bombay state.* Bombay: Local Self-Government Institute, 1957. p. 192. CSSL.

Sanghavi, Nagindas. From Navnirman to the anti-Mandal riots: the political trajectory of Gujarat (1974–1985). In *Gujarat beyond Gandhi: identity, conflict and society.* Ed. by Nalin Mehta and Mona G. Mehta. London: Routledge, 2010. pp. 20–38. BVL, CSSL, GIDRL, IRMAL, UML.

Sanghavi, Nagindas. *Gujarat at cross-roads*. Mumbai: Bharatiya Vidya Bhavan, 2010. p. 223. BVL, CSSL, HML.

Sanghavi, Nagindas. *Gujarat: a political analysis.* Surat: Centre for Social Studies, 1996. p. 333. BUL, CSSL, HML, IIML, SGUL, UML.

Shah, B.C. Dynamics of factional politics in a village Panchayat. In *Revival of Panchayatri raj: trends and problems.* Ed. by B.C. Shah and J.N. Pandya. Vallabh Vidyanagar: Sardar Patel University, 1989. pp. 195–205. SPUL.

Shah, B.C. Panchayat poll of 1987 in Gujarat. In *Revival of Panchayati raj: trends and problems*. Ed. by B.C. Shah and J.N. Pandya. Vallabh Vidyanagar: Sardar Patel University, 1989. pp. 212–228. SPUL.

Shah, B.C. Political profile of a village Panchayat in Gujarat. In *Revival of Panchayat raj: trends & problems.* Ed. by B.C. Shah and J.N. Pandya. Vallabh Vidyanagar: Sardar Patel University, 1986. pp. 143–153. SPUL.

Shah, Dilip. Panchayati raj institutions and decentralised rural development in Gujarat: a post new Panchayati act period analysis. In *Emerging institutions for decentralised rural development*. Ed. by S.P. Jain. Hyderabad: National Institute of Rural Development, 2001. pp. 314–327. HML.

Shah, Ghanshyam. BJP and backward castes in Gujarat. In *Caste and democratic politics in India*. Ed. by Ghanshyam Shah. Delhi: Permanent Black, 2002. pp. 295–314. also In *Religion, religiosity and communalism*. Ed. by Praful Bidwai, Harbans Mukhia and Achin Vanaik. New Delhi: Manohar, 1996. pp. 217–235. CSSL, HML.

Shah, Ghanshyam. BJP's riddle in Gujarat: caste, factionalism and Hindutva. In *BJP and the compulsions of politics in India.* Ed. by Thomas Blom Hansen and Jaffrelot Christophe. New Delhi: Oxford, 1998. pp. 243–266. CSSL, HML, IIML.

Shah, Ghanshyam. BJP's rise to power in Gujarat. In *Fascism in India: faces, fangs and facts.* Ed. by Chaitanya Krishna. New Delhi: Manak, 2003. pp. 219–234. CSSL, UML.

Shah, Ghanshyam. *Caste association and political process in Gujarat: a study of Gujarat Kshatriya sabha.* Bombay: Popular, 1975. p. 218. CSSL, GUL, GVL, HML, IIML, IRMAL, SPIESRL, SPUL, TRTIL, UML.

Shah, Ghanshyam. Caste sentiments, class formation and dominance in Gujarat. In *Dominance and state power in modern India*. Vol. II. Ed. by Francine R. Frankel and M.S.A. Rao. Delhi: Oxford, 1990. pp. 59–114. ASL, CSSL, TRTIL.

Shah, Ghanshyam. Contestation and negotiation: Hindutva sentiments and temporal interests in Gujarat elections. In *Religious politics and communal violence.* Ed. by Steven I. Wilkinson. New Delhi: Oxford, 2005. pp. 377–390. Critical issues in India. CSSL, HML, IIML.

Shah, Ghanshyam. Economy and civic authority in Surat. In *Urban studies.* Ed. by Sujata Patel and Kushal Deb. Delhi: Oxford, 2006. pp. 274–293. CSSL.

Shah, Ghanshyam. Goebbel's propaganda and governance: the 2009 Lok Sabha elections in Gujarat. In *India's 2009 elections: coalition politics, party competition and congress continuity.* Ed. by Paul Wallace and Ramashray Roy. New Delhi: Sage, 2011. pp. 167–191. GVL, HML, IIML, SPUL.

Shah, Ghanshyam. Governance of Gujarat: good governance for whom and for what? In *Growth or development: which way is Gujarat going?* Ed. by Indira Hirway, Amita Shah and Ghanshyam Shah. New Delhi: Oxford, 2014. pp. 517–556. CSSL.

Shah, Ghanshyam. Gujarat after Godhra. In *India's 2004 elections: grass-roots and national perspectives*. Ed. by Ramashray Roy and Paul Wallace. New Delhi: Sage, 2007. pp. 151–179. CSSL.

Shah, Ghanshyam. *Politics of scheduled castes and tribes: adivasi and Harijan leaders of Gujarat*. Bombay: Vora, 1975. p. 164. CSSL, GIDRL, SPIESRL.

Shah, Ghanshyam. Rural politics in Gujarat. In *Land caste and politics in Indian states.* Ed. by Omvedt Gail. Delhi: Authors Guild, 1982. pp. 134–155. GUL, TRTIL.

Shah, Ghanshyam. Strategies of social engineering reservation and mobility of backward communities of Gujarat. In *Diversity and dominance in Indian politics.* Vol. 2. Ed. by Ramashray Roy and Richard Sisson. New Delhi: Sage, 1990. pp. 111–145. SPUL.

Shani, Ornit. Bootlegging, Politics and corruption: state violence and the routine practices of public power in Gujarat (1985–2002). In *Gujarat beyond Gandhi: identity, conflict and society.* Ed. by Nalin Mehta and Mona G. Mehta. London: Routledge, 2010. pp. 39–59. BVL, CSSL, GIDRL, IRMAL, UML.

Sharma, Mukul. Human rights in a globalised world. New Delhi: Sage, 2010. (Corporate complicity and Gujarat – one chapter in book, pp. 112–117) CSSL.

Sharma, S.R., Nagori, K. and Tadi, Vertika. *India needs Narendra Modi.* Jaipur: Sublime, 2005. p. 412. GVL.

Sheth, Pravin. *Happening state Gujarat: a live case of can-doism.* Mumbai: R.R. Sheth, 2012. p. 175. IRMAL.

Sheth, Pravin. *Political development in Gujarat*. Ahmedabad: Karnavati, 1998. p. 193. CSSL, GIDRL, HML.

Sheth, Pravin. *Political development in Gujarat*. Ahmedabad: Sahitya Mudranalay, 1976. p. 323. SUL.

Sheth, Pravin N. Elections in Gujarat: the emerging pattern. In *Fourth general election in India.* Ed. by S.P. Varma and Iqbal Narain. Bombay: Orient Longmans, 1968. pp. 169–200. CSSL, SPIESRL.

Sheth, Pravin N. Gujarat: the case of small majority politics. In *State politics in India*. Ed. by Iqbal Narain. New Delhi: Meenakshi, 1976. pp. 68–87. CSSL, HML.

Sheth, Pravin N. Gujarat. In *Symbols of power: studies on the political status of women in India*. Ed. by Vina Mazumdar. Bombay: Allied, 1979. pp. 200–220. CSSL, GVL, SETUL.

Sheth, Pravin N. *Images of transformation: Gujarat and Narendra Modi*. Ahmedabad: Team Spirit, 2007. p. 258. CSSL, EDIL, GVL.

Sheth, P.N. *Nav Nirman & political change in India: from Gujarat 1974 to New Delhi 1977*. Bombay: Vora, 1977. p. 192. CSSL, SPIESRL.

Sheth, P.N. *Patterns of political behaviour in Gujarat*. Ahmedabad: Sahitya Mudranalaya, 1976. p. 323. CSSL, GIDRL, HML, SPIESRL.

Shri Prakash. Reservation system in Gujarat. In *Politics of backwardness: reservation policy in India.* Ed. by V.A. Pai Panandiker. New Delhi: Konark, 1997. pp. 198–220. CSSL, IIML.

Shukla, Dinesh M. Gujarat. In *Symbols of power: studies on the political status of women in India*. Ed. by Vina Mazumdar. Bombay: Allied, 1979. pp. 85–118. CSSL, GVL, SETUL.

Singh, Biswanath. Kutch-award: a study in Indo-Pakistan relations. In *50 years of Indo-Pak relations*. Ed. by Verinder Grover. New Delhi: Deep & Deep, 1998. pp. 61–68. HML.

Singh, Iqbal. Surat in reverse. In *National congress: a reconstruction*. Vol. I: 1885–1918. New Delhi: Manohor, 1987. pp. 243–264. CSSL, GVL, SUL.

Sinha, Aseema. Gujarat: bureaucratic developmentalism in Gujarat. In *Regional roots of development politics in India*. New Delhi: Oxford, 2005. pp. 92–98. HML.

Sinha, Aseema. Gujarat: the roots of classic competitive capitalism. In *Regional roots of development politics in India*. New Delhi: Oxford, 2005. pp. 161–183. HML.

Sinha, Assema. Ideas, interests, and institutions in policy change: a comparison of West Bengal and Gujarat. In *Regional reflections: comparing politics across India's states*. Ed. by Rob Jenkins. New Delhi: Oxford, 2004. pp. 66–108. HML.

Sinha, Aseema. Sticky: institutions in West Bengal, Gujarat and Tamil Nadu after 1991: a comparative institutional analysis. In *Regional roots of development politics in India*. Ed. by Rob Jenkins. New Delhi: Oxford, 2005. pp. 153–157. HML.

Sisodia, Yatindra Singh. Grassroots governance and people's of participation at work after implementation of PESA evidences from tribal regions of Madhya Pradesh, Rajasthan and Gujarat states. In *Grassroots planning and local governance in India: policy initiatives and people's participation*. Ed. by Sundar Ram. New Delhi: Kanishka, 2010. pp. 112–127. SPUL.

Spodek, Howard. From Gandhi to Modi: Ahmedabad, 1915–2007. In *Idea of Gujarat: history, ethnography and text*. Ed. by Edward Simpson and Aparna Kapadia. Hyderabad: Orient Blackswan, 2010. pp. 136–152. AAL, ASL, BUL, CEPTL, CSSL, GIDRL, IRMAL, MICAL, SETUL.

Spodek, Howard. From "Parasitic" to "Generative" cities: the transformation of post-colonial Saurashtra. In *City in Indian politics*. Ed. by Donald B. Rosenthal. Faridabad: Thomson, 1976. pp. 27–43. CSSL, IIML.

Shriman, Narayan. *Those ten months: President's rule in Gujarat*. Delhi: Vikas, 1973. p. 204. BVL, CSSL, GUL, GVL, HML, SPIESRL, SPUL, SUL.

Subramanian, K.S. *Political violence and the police in India*. New Delhi: Sage, 2007. p. 257. CSSL.

Sud, Nikita. Politics of land in post-colonial Gujarat. In *Idea of Gujarat: history, ethnography and text*. Ed. by Edward Simpson and Aparna Kapadia. Hyderabad: Orient Blackswan, 2010. pp. 120–135. AAL, ASL, BUL, CEPTL, CSSL, GIDRL, IRMAL, MICAL, SETUL.

Thakore, G.D. Portrait of municipal councilors. In *Winners and losers: styles of development and change in an Indian region*. Ed. by S. Devadas Pillai and Chris Baks. Bombay: Popular, 1979. pp. 289–301. CSSL, SPIESRL.

Thakore, J.M. *Development of local self-government in Bombay and Saurashtra*. Bombay: Local Self Government Institute, 1957. p. 158. CSSL, SPUL.

Vakil, F.D. Gujarat. In *Patterns of Panchayati raj in India*. Ed. by Ram G. Reddy. Delhi: Macmillan, 1977. pp. 91–109. GVL, HML.

Valiani, Arafaat A. *Militant publics in India: physical culture and violence in the making of a modern city*. New York: Palgrave Macmillan, 2011. p. 266. SETUL, UML.

Vishwanath, L.S. Village in Anand parliamentary constituency in Gujarat. In *Grassroots of democracy: field studies of Indian elections*. Ed. by A.M. Shah. Ranikhet: Permanent Black, 2007. pp. 267–278. CSSL.

Vithal, C.P. Devolution of powers and function to PRIs in Daman. In *Panchayati raj, participation and decentralization*. Ed. by Ramesh K. Arora and Meenakshi Hooja. Jaipur: Rawat, 2009. pp. 237–241. HML.

Wallace, Paul and Roy, Ramashray, ed. *India's 2009 elections: coalition politics, party competition and Congress continuity.* New Delhi: Sage, 2011. p. 419. GVL.

Wilkinson, Steven I. Commentary: putting Gujarat in perspective. In *Religious politics and communal violence.* Ed. by Steven I. Wilkinson. New Delhi: Oxford, 2005. pp. 391–404. Critical issues in India politics series. CSSL, HML, IIML.

Wood, John R. Reservations in doubt: the backlash against affirmative action in Gujarat. In *Diversity and dominance in Indian politics.* Vol. 2. Ed by Ramashray Roy and Richard Sisson. New Delhi: Sage, 1990. pp. 146–169. CSSL, SPUL.

Yashaschandra, Sitanshu. Social and political thought in Gujarat: some pathways from the past to present. In *Political ideas in modern India: thematic explorations.* Ed. by V.R. Mehta and Thomas Pantham. New Delhi: Sage, 2006. History of Science, Philosophy and Culture in Indian Civilization. Vol. X part 7. pp. 121–137. CSSL.

Journal Articles

Alagh, Yoginder K. Powerhouse and its nemesis. *Seminar.* 513, 2002. pp. 73–76. CSSL, MICAL, SPUL, UML.

Amin, R.K. Real crisis in Gujarat. *Vishleshan.* 27, 3, 2002. pp. 13–15. CSSL, IIML.

Ashraf, Ali. Politics of development and decay: a study of politics and city government in Ahmedabad and Kanpur. *ICSSR Research Abstracts Quarterly*. 6, 384, 1977. pp. 41–51. HML.

Baxi, Upendra. Notes on holocaustian politics. *Seminar*. 513, 2002. pp. 77–83. CSSL, MICAL, SPUL, UML.

Baxi, Upendra. Second Gujarat catastrophe. *Economic and Political Weekly*. 37, 34, 2002. pp. 3519–3531. BUL, CEPTL, CSSL, EDIL, GIDRL, IIML, IRMAL, MICAL, SGUL, SPIESRL, UML.

Bhatt, Anil. Gujarat. *Seminar*. 95, 1967. pp. 25–29. CSSL, GIDRL, GVL, UML.

Bhatt, Anil. Man in middle. *Seminar*. 230, 1978. pp. 18–22. (on Administrator) CSSL, UML.

Bhatt, Anil. Two-party system emerging in Gujarat. *Economic and Political Weekly.* 1, 17, 1966. pp. 711–712. CSSL, SGUL, SPIESRL, UML.

Cedric, Prakash. Gujarat: rule of the majority. *Social Action.* 59, 2, 2009. pp. 135–142. CSSL, IRMAL.

Chatterjee, Ipsita. Governance as 'performed', governance as 'inscribed' new urban politics in Ahmedabad. *Urban Studies*. 48, 12, 2011. pp. 2571–2590. CEPTL.

Choudhary, Kameshwar. Violation of human rights: the case of dalits in Gujarat. *IASSI Quarterly*. 18, 3, 2000. pp. 83–97. CSSL, GIDRL, IIML.

Dasgupta, Swapan. Modi phenomenon. *Seminar*. 581, 2008. pp. 36–39. CSSL, MICAL, SPUL, UML.

Desai, I.P. Caste and politics. *Economic and Political Weekly*. 2, 17, 1967. pp. 797–799. CSSL, SPIESRL, UML.

Dholakia, Ravindra H. Liberalisation in Gujarat: review of recent experience. (*Gujarat-2010: Challenges and Opportunities*). *Anvesak*. 31, 1–2, 2001. pp. 179–189. CSSL, GIDRL.

Engineer, Asghar Ali. BJP sweep in Gujarat: a moment of reflection for India. *Indian Journal of Secularism*. 6, 4, 2003. pp. 21–24. CSSL.

Gupta, Dipankar. Limits of tolerance: prospects of secularism in India after Gujarat. *Economic and Political Weekly*. 37, 46, 2002. pp. 4615–4620. BUL, CEPTL, CSSL, EDIL, IIML, IRMAL, MICAL, SGUL, SPIESRL, UML.

Gupta, Dipankar. New trends versus old truths. *Seminar*. 656, 2014. pp. 23–26. CSSL, UML.

Haynes, Douglas. Imperial ritual in a local setting: the ceremonial order in Surat, 1890–1939. *Modern Asian Studies*. 24, 3, 1990. pp. 493–527. CSSL.

Jaitley, Arun. Gujarat revolt. *Seminar*. 176, 1974. pp. 30–32. GVL, IIML, UML.

Jena, A.C. Panchayati raj and development administration: a comparative analysis of structural features of different models: Gujarat, West Bengal, Karnataka and Andhra Pradesh. *Journal of Rural Development*. 10, 5, 1991. pp. 647–664. CSSL, IIML, IRMAL.

Jones, Dawn E. and Jones, Rodney W. Urban upheaval in India: 1974 Nav-Nirman riots in Gujarat. *Asian Survey*. 16, 11, 1976. pp. 1012–1033. IRMAL.

Joshi, Satyakam. Panchayati raj leadership in Gujarat. *IASSI Quarterly*. 21, 3 and 4, 2003. pp. 79–91. CSSL, GIDRL, HML, IIML, SGUL, SPUL.

Khare, Harish. After Gujarat. *Seminar*. 521, 2003. pp. 30–33. CEPTL, CSSL, MICAL, UML.

Khare, Harish. Unending struggle for Gujarat's political soul. *Seminar*. 470, 1998. pp. 17–23. CEPTL, CSSL, GVL, IIML, IRMAL, MICAL, UML.

Mehta, Uday. Gujarat: post-script. *Indian Journal of Secularism*. 7, 1, 2003. pp. 74–81. CSSL.

Mishra, Srijit. Gujarat elections 2002: vote shares across regions. *Economic and Political Weekly*. 38, 18, 2003. pp. 1804–1809. BUL, CEPTL, CSSL, EDIL, GIDRL, IIML, IRMAL, MICAL, SGUL, SPIESRL, UML.

Ohm, Britta. Narratives of the underbelly of democracy. *Economic and Political Weekly*. 42, 49, 2007. pp. 26–31. BUL, CEPTL, CSSL, EDIL, GIDRL, IIML, IRMAL, MICAL, SGUL, SPIESRL, SUL, UML.

Pandya, Hiren and Pandey, Gajanand. Rural leadership in Gujarat: a profile. *South Gujarat University Journal*. 6, 1977. pp. 29–39. GVL.

Parekh, Bhikhu. Making sense of Gujarat. *Seminar*. 513, 2002. pp. 26–31. CSSL, MICAL, UML.

Patel, Priyavadan. Gujarat: anti-incumbency begins. *Economic and Political Weekly*. 39, 51, 2004. pp. 5473–5476. CEPTL, CSSL, EDIL, IIML, IRMAL, MICAL, SGUL, SPIESRL, UML.

Patel, Priyavadan. Gujarat: hindutwa mobilization and electoral dominance of the BJP. *Journal of Indian School of Political Economy*. 15, 1 and 2, 2003. pp. 123–142. CEPTL, CSSL, GIDRL, IIML, IRMAL.

Patel, Priyavadan. Sectarian mobilization, factionalism and voting in Gujarat. *Economic and Political Weekly*. 34, 34 and 35, 1999. pp. 2423–2433. CEPTL, CSSL, GIDRL, IIML, IRMAL, MICAL, SGUL, SPIESRL, UML.

Patel, Satish L. Democratic governance and administrative initiatives for women welfares with reference to human rights in Gujarat. *Indian Journal of Political Science*. 73, 1, 2012. pp. 101–110. CSSL.

Prakash, Aseem. Re-imagination of the state and Gujarat's electoral verdict. *Economic and Political Weekly*. 38, 16, 2003. pp. 1601–1610. BUL, CEPTL, CSSL, EDIL, GIDRL, IIML, IRMAL, MICAL, SGUL, SPIESRL, UML.

Prakash, Cedric. Gujarat: rule of the majority. *Social Action*. 59, 2, 2009. pp. 135–142. CSSL.

Rangarajan, Mahesh. Congress in crisis. *Seminar*. 521, 2003. pp. 34–37. CEPTL, CSSL, MICAL, UML.

Roy, Indrajit. Representation and development in urban peripheries: reflections on governance in Ahmedabad suburbs. *Economic and Political Weekly*. 41, 41, 2006. pp. 4363–4368. BUL, CEPTL, CSSL, EDIL, IIML, IRMAL, MICAL, SGUL, SPIESRL, SUL, UML.

Sen, Aveek. Gujarat bricolage. *Seminar*. 641, 2013. pp. 105–112. CSSL, UML.

Shah, Ghanshyam. Bureaucracy and urban improvement-can it made to last?: post-plague scenario in Surat. *Economic and Political Weekly*. 32, 12, 1997. pp. 607–613. CEPTL, CSSL, IIML, IRMAL, MICAL, SGUL, SPIESRL, UML.

Shah, Ghanshyam. Contestation and negotiations: Hindutva sentiments and temporal interests in Gujarat elections. *Economic and Political Weekly*. 37, 48, 2002. pp. 4838–4843. BUL, CSSL, EDIL, GIDRL, IIML, IRMAL, MICAL, SGUL, SPIESRL, UML.

Shah, Ghanshyam. Gujarat: BJP's rise to power. *Economic and Political Weekly*. 31, 2 and 3, 1996. pp. 165–170. CEPTL, CSSL, GIDRL, IIML, IRMAL, MICAL, SGUL, SPIESRL, UML.

Shah, Ghanshyam. Panchayati raj and the dalits: a study of social justice committee in Gujarat. *Administrator*. 42, 1, 1997. pp. 153–171. CSSL, IRMAL.

Shah, Ghanshyam. Tenth Lok sabha elections and the BJP's victory in Gujarat. *Islamic Perspective*. 8, 1, 1998. pp. 195–211. CSSL.

Shah, Ghanshyam. Upsurge in Gujarat. *Economic and Political Weekly*. 9, 32, 33 and 34, 1974. pp. 1429–1454. CSSL, GUL, HML, IRMAL, SGUL, SPIESRL, TRTIL, UML.

Shah, Ghanshyam. Voting behaviour of adivasi and Harijan leaders: a study of the 1971 elections. *Indian Journal of Political Science*. 33, 1–4, 1972. pp. 431–442. CSSL.

Sheth, P.N. Bipolarization in the Lok sabha election in Gujarat in 1977. *Political Science Review*. 18, 3, 1979. pp. 76–93. CSSL.

Sheth, Pravin. Gujarat: dynamics of development. *Seminar*. 234, 1979. pp. 12–16. CSSL, GIDRL, IIML, UML.

Sheth, Pravin N. Mass upsurge in Gujarat. *Political Science Review*. 13, 1–4, 1974. pp. 241–253. CSSL.

Somjee, A.H. Political dynamics of a Gujarat village. *Asian Survey*. 12, 7, 1972. pp. 602–608. CSSL, HML, IRMAL.

Somjee, A.H. Social cohesion and political clientilism among the Kshatriyas of Gujarat. *Asian Survey*. 21, 9, 1981. pp. 1000–1010. CSSL, HML.

Spodek, Howard. "Injustice to Saurashtra": a case study of regional tensions and harmonies in India. *Asian Survey*. 12, 5, 1972. pp. 416–428. CSSL.

Spodek, Howard. On the origins of Gandhi's political methodology: the heritage of Kathiawad and Gujarat. *Journal of Asian Studies*. 30, 2, 1971. pp. 361–372. CSSL.

Sud, Nikita. From land to the tiller to land liberalization: the political economy of Gujarat's shifting land policy. *Modern Asian Studies*. 41, 3, 2007. pp. 603–637. CSSL.

Thakkar, Usha. Gujarat assembly elections 2002: results and ramifications. *Indian Journal of Secularism*. 8, 1, 2004. pp. 65–82. CSSL.

Varadarajan, Siddharth. Cult of cronyism. *Seminar*. 656, 2014. pp. 60–63. CSSL, UML.

Vishvanathan, Shiv. Remaking of Narendra Modi. *Seminar*. 641, 2013. pp. 52–58. CSSL, UML.

Vishwanath, L.S. Gujarat kisan sabha, 1936–56. *Economic and Political Weekly*. 20, 28, 1985. pp. 1197–1200. CEPTL, CSSL, GUL, IIML, IRMAL, SGUL, SPIESRL, UML.

Wilkinson, Steven I. Putting Gujarat in perspective. *Economic and Political Weekly*. 37, 17, 2002. pp. 1579–1583. BUL, CEPTL, CSSL, EDIL, IIML, IRMAL, MICAL, SGUL, SPIESRL, UML.

Working Papers, Reports and Other Materials

Ashraf, Ali. *Politics of development and decay: a study of politics and city government in Ahmedabad & Kanpur*. New Delhi: Indian Council of Social Science Research, 1975. p. 212. CSSL.

Bhatt, Anil and Pathak, H.N. *Training needs of Mamlatdars: report submitted to government of Gujarat*. Ahmedabad: Indian Institute of Management, 1979. p. 47. IIML.

Chokshi, H.P. *Study of mobilization of resource for village Panchayat in Baroda district, 1951–1965*. Baroda: Government of India, 1971. p. [ ]. SPUL.

Desai, K.S. *Problems of administration in two Indian villages*. Baroda: M.S. University, 1961. p. [ ]. SPUL.

Desai, N.B. *Report on the administrative survey of the Surat district*. Bombay: Indian Society of Agricultural Economics, 1958. p. [ ]. SPUL.

Dholakia, Ravindra H. *Liberalization in Gujarat: review of experience*. Ahmedabad: Institute of Management, 1999. p. [ ]. IIM Working Paper No. 99–07–02. GIDRL.

Dholakia, Ravindra H. Liberalisation in Gujarat: review of recent experience. In *Gujarat-2010: challenges and opportunities*. By Government of Gujarat. Ahmedabad: Sardar Patel Institute of Economic & Social Research, 2001. pp. 638–645. Seminar volume. CSSL, EDIL, IRMAL, SGUL, SPIESRL.

General Administration Department, Government of Gujarat. People oriented administration. In *Gujarat-2010: challenges and opportunities*. By Government of Gujarat. Ahmedabad: Sardar Patel Institute of Economic & Social Research, 2001. pp. 571–576. Seminar volume. CSSL, EDIL, IRMAL, SGUL, SPIESRL.

Ginwalla, Persis. *Samras scheme and democratization process: an analytical study*. Ahmedabad: MARAG, 2008. p. 180. CSSL.

Gujarat Election Watch Committee. *Gujarat election watch (2002): candidates with criminal background contesting the 2002 assembly elections in Gujarat*. Ahmedabad: Author, 2002. p. 50. CSSL.

Gujarat, Government of. *Report of the high level committee on Panchayati raj*. 2 Vols. Baroda: Government Press, 1973. p. [ ], [ ]. CSSL.

Inamdar, N.R. Panchayati raj in Maharashtra and Gujarat: comparative profiles. In *Western regional workshop on Panchayats, 23–25 February, 1994*. Surat: Centre for Social Studies, 1994. pp. 1–20. CSSL.

Joshi, Satyakam. *Functioning of Panchayati raj in scheduled area of Gujarat: with reference to implementation of Panchayats Extension to Scheduled area Act (PESA)*. Surat: Centre for Social Studies, 2007. p. 173. CSSL.

Joshi, Satyakam. *Study on inclusion of excluded communities for social cohesion through Panchayati raj in Gujarat: a case study of Surat District*. Surat: Centre for Social Studies, 2002. p. 43. CSSL.

Kothari, Rajni and Sheth, Tarun. Extent and limit of community voting: the case of Baroda East. In *Party system and election studies*. By Rajni Kothari et al. Bombay: Allied, 1967. pp. 114–136. Centre for the Study of Developing Societies Occasional Papers No. 1. IIML.

Lal, Rash Bihari. *Comparative study of traditional panch and statutory panchayat.* Ahmedabad: Tribal Research & Training Institute, Gujarat Vidyapith, p. [ ], [ ]. CSSL.

Mehta, Makrand. Gandhi and Ahmedabad 1915–1920: a study of leadership style. In *International seminar on "Gujarat society", 17–20 December 1986*. Surat: Centre for Social Studies, 1986. pp. 1–33. CSSL.

Mehta, Rekhaben. *Survey report on powers, rights and duties of Gramsabha under the Gujarat Panchayat act, 1993 and significance of Gramsabha under the Gujarat panchayat act*. Ahmedabad: Tribal Research & Training Institute, Gujarat Vidyapith, 2000–01. p. 259. Series-358. TRTIL.

Panchanadikar, K.C. and Panchanadikar, J. *Democratic socialization and participant alienation in Mahi village Panchayat, Kaira district, Central Gujarat.* Vol. I. Baroda: M.S. University, 1968. p. 178. Project report. CSSL.

Panchanadikar, K.C. and Panchanadikar, J. *Democratic structure and allegiant adjustment in Mindola village Panchayat, Bulsar district, South Gujarat.* Vol. II. Baroda: M.S. University, 1968. p. 181. Project report. CSSL.

Pandya, H.J. *Leadership in Panchayati raj: its composition and changing pattern*. Surat: South Gujarat University, 1974. p. 424. CSSL.

Patel, Harbans. *Village-level political leadership: a case study of Kaira district, Gujarat.* Surat: Centre for Social Studies, 1986. p. 34. CSSL.

Pathak, Devavrat N. Political culture in Gujarat: the shifting scenes. In *International seminar on "Gujarat society", 17–20 December 1986.* Surat: Centre for Social Studies, 1986. pp. 1–20. CSSL.

Pathak, Devavrat N. and Desai, Kirtidev D. *Study of political behavior in Gujarat: with special reference to the fourth general elections, 1967*. Ahmedabad: Gujarat University, 1970. p. 135. CSSL.

Ratnawali. *Decentralisation and issues in self governance in tribal areas of South Gujarat.* Surat: Centre for Social Studies, 2006. p. 33. Working Paper No. 4. CSSL, GIDRL.

Shah, B.S. *Democratic decentralisation and political development: a case study of Mogri village Panchayat in Gujarat*. Vallabh Vidyanagar: Sardar Patel University, 1993. p. 156. AAUL.

Shah, D.C. and Joshi, Satyakam. *Peoples' initiative in development: Khuntali experiment*. Surat: Centre for Social Studies, 1996. p. 16. CSSL.

Shah, Dilip. Panchayati raj institutions and decentralized rural development in Gujarat state. In *NIRD foundation day seminar on emerging institutions for decentralized rural development (January 7 2001)*. Hyderabad: National Institute of Rural Development, 2001. pp. 1–12. SPIESRL.

Shah, Ghanshyam. Current social situation of scheduled castes in Gujarat state: some reflections on the role of 'Panchayati raj' institutions. In *Report of the orientation seminar on involvement of Panchayati raj institutions in the welfare of scheduled castes.* New Delhi: National Institute of Public Cooperation and Child Development, 1981. pp. 98–108. CSSL.

Shah, Ghanshyam. Decentralisation and weaker sections. In *Western regional workshop on Panchayats, 23–25 February, 1994*. Surat: Centre for Social Studies, 1994. pp. 1–18. CSSL.

Shah, Ghanshyam. *Integration through political participation: a study of adivasi and Harijan leaders in Gujarat*. Delhi: Centre for the Study of Developing Societies and Surat: Centre for Regional Development Studies, 1972. p. 204. CSSL.

Shah, Ghanshyam. *Office without de facto power: a study of social justice committee in Gujarat*. International seminar on Gujarat society, development and deprivation, 6–9 December 1994. Surat: Centre for Social Studies, 1994. pp. 1–27. CSSL.

Shah, Ghanshyam. Socio-economic stratification and politics in rural Gujarat. In *Gujarat economy problems and prospects.* Ed. by D.T. Lakdawala. Ahmedabad: Sardar Patel Institute of Economic & Social Research, 1983. pp. 169–192. Monograph-10. GUL, IIML.

Shah, Ghanshyam, et al. *Panchayati raj in Gujarat: a study.* Surat: Centre for Social Studies, 1997. p. 203. CSSL.

Shah, Manubhai. *Impact of the changes in the district administration since independence on Kheda District.* Vallabh Vidyanagar: Sardar Patel University, 1969. p. 200. SPUL.

Shah, Ramesh M. Gujarat Panchayat act, 1993: x-rayed. In *Western regional workshop on Panchayats, 23–25 February, 1994.* Surat: Centre for Social Studies, 1994. pp. 1–6. CSSL.

Shah, Ramesh M. and Shah, Ambubhai. Gujarat Panchayati raj vikas sangathan. In *Western regional workshop on Panchayats, 23–25 February, 1994.* Surat: Centre for Social Studies, 1994. pp. 1–4. CSSL.

Shah, Vimal and Lal, Rash Bihari. *Enquiry into political consciousness among tribals of Gujarat.* Ed. Vimal Shah. Ahmedabad: Tribal Research & Training Institute, 1976. p. 27. Series-33. TRTIL.

Sheth, P.N. Gujarat: "Panchayati development and decay". In *Western regional workshop on Panchayats, 23–25 February, 1994.* Surat: Centre for Social Studies, 1994. pp. 1–28. CSSL.

Sheth, Pravin. Ahmedabad: a perspective of change. In *International seminar on "Gujarat society", 17–20 December 1986.* Surat: Centre for Social Studies, 1986. pp. 1–14. CSSL.

Sheth, Pravin. Caste, class and political development: an overview. In *Gujarat economy problems and prospects.* Ed. by D.T. Lakdawala. Ahmedabad: Sardar Patel Institute of Economic & Social Research, 1983. pp. 193–210. Monograph-10. GUL, IIML.

Sheth, Pravin. Caste, class and political development: an overview. In *Seminar on development of Gujarat problems & prospects,* 24–26 August, 1981. Ahmedabad: Sardar Patel Institute of Economic & Social Research, 1981. pp. 1–19. CSSL.

Sheth, Pravin. Political culture in Gujarat: patterns of change. In *International seminar on "Gujarat society", 17–20 December 1986.* Surat: Centre for Social Studies, 1986. pp. 1–12. CSSL.

Shylendra, H.S. *Strengthening Panchayati raj institutions: issues before the Gujarat third state finance commission.* Anand: Institute of rural Management, 2013. pp. 1–61. Workshop report-25. SPIESRL.

Soni, Jayshree. *Case study on psycho-social aspects of leadership.* Surat: Centre for Social Studies, 2007. p. 60. Monitoring & Evaluation of R&R of SSP Series. CSSL.

Trivedi, Vimal. *Municipal service delivery and urban local governance: a performance appraisal by the citizen of Surat, India.* Surat: Centre for Social Studies, 2010. p. 114. CSSL.

Wagle, Dileep and Rao, N.V. *Power sector in India.* Bombay: Popular, 1978. p. 133. Tata Economic Consultancy Services. CSSL.

Wood, John R. On the periphery but in the thick of it: some current Indian political crises viewed from Gujarat. In *International seminar on Gujarat society, development and deprivation, 6–9 December 1994.* Surat: Centre for Social Studies, 1994. pp. 1–22. CSSL.

8

Economics, Economic Growth, Development

Books/Chapter in Books

Acharya, Shrawan Kumar. Managing waste in a peri-urban locality: Vejalpur, Ahmedabad. In *Solid waste management in Indian cities: status and emerging practices.* Ed. by Darshini Mahadevia and Jeanne M. Wolfe. New Delhi: Concept, 2008. pp. 312–328. CSSL.

Agrawal, S.N. *Gandhian plan.* Bombay: Padma, 1944. p. 115. SPIESRL.

Alagh, Y.K. and Buch, D.T. Sardar Sarovar Project and sustainable development. In *Toward sustainable development: struggling over India's Narmada river*. Ed. by William F. Fisher. Jaipur: Rawat, 1997. pp. 291–317. CSSL.

Alagh, Y.K., Bhalla, G.S. and Kashyap, S.P. *Structural analysis of Gujarat, Punjab and Haryana economies: an input-output study.* New Delhi: Allied, 1980. p. 239. CSSL, GIDRL, GVL, IRMAL, SPIESRL, SPUL.

Alagh, Y.K., Pathak, Mahesh and Buch, D.T. *Narmada and environment: an assessment.* New Delhi: Har-Anand, 1995. p. 356. AERCL, IIML, SETUL, SPUL, TRTIL.

Alagh, Y.K., Shah, Jayshree and Shah, Vinod K. *Power economics in Gujarat.* Ahmedabad: Sardar Patel Institute of Economic & Social Research, 1998. p. 176. CSSL.

Alagh, Y.K., et al. *Economic dimensions of the Sardar Sarovar Project.* New Delhi: Har-Anand, 1995. p. 214. CSSL.

Alagh, Yoginder K. *Land and man: essays in sustainable development.* New Delhi: Har-Anand, 1996. p. 354. CSSL, GIDRL, GVL.

Alagh, Yogindar K. Sardar Sarovar Project: task ahead. In *Development imperatives and environment concerns Sardar Sarovar Project plan.* Ed. by Mahesh Pathak. Vallabh Vidyanagar: Agro Economic Research Centre, 1995. pp. 206–210. IIML.

Alvares, Claude and Billorey, Ramesh. *Damming the Narmada.* Dehradun: Natraj, 1988. p. 196. SETUL, TRTIL.

Asopa, V.N., Shingi, P.M. and Iyer, Mala. *Development and management of irrigation: a bench-mark survey of the Ukai-Kakrapar project.* New Delhi: Oxford, 1987. p. 413. CSSL, IIML, SETUL.

Athavale, R.N. Discovering science behind local innovations and practices: community based water conservation practices in Alwar and Saurashtra. In *Farmer led participatory research: cases from Western India.* Ed. by Astad Pastakia, Brij Kothari and Vijaya Sherry Chand. Bangalore: Books for Change, 2002. pp. 36–61. CSSL.

Awasthi, Dinesh N. Recent changes in industrial economy in Gujarat: issues and evidences. In *Dynamics of development in Gujarat*. Ed. by Indira Hirway, S.P. Kashyap and Amita Shah. New Delhi: Concept, 2002. pp. 166–196. CSSL, EDIL, GIDRL, GVL, HML, IRMAL, SPUL, UML.

Bagchi, Amiya Kumar, Das, Panchanan and Chattopadhyay, Sudhan Kumar. Growth and structural change in the economy of Gujarat, 1970–2000. In *Gujarat economy: the way ahead*. Ed. by Sudha V. Menon. Hyderabad: ICFAI University, 2009. pp. 12–39. EDIL, HML, SPIESRL.

Barot, Nafisa. People's initiatives for sustainable solutions: water harvesting and management in Gujarat. In *Water and sanitation: institutional challenges in India*. Ed. by Christine Sijbesma and Meine Pieter Van Dijk. New Delhi: Manohar, 2006. pp. 121–134. CSSL.

Baviskar, Amita. Displacement and the Bhilala tribals of the Narmada valley. In *Dam and the nation: displacement and resettlement in the Narmada valley*. Ed. by Jean Dreze, Meera Samson and Satyajit Singh. Delhi: Oxford, 1997. pp. 103–135. CSSL, SPUL.

Bhatia, Bela. Forced evictions in the Narmada valley. In *Dam and the nation: displacement and resettlement in the Narmada valley*. Ed by Jean Dreze, Meera Samson and Satyajit Singh. Delhi: Oxford, 1997. pp. 267–321. CSSL, SPUL.

Bhatt, Anil and Dholakia, R.H. *Training plan for municipal personnel in Gujarat*. Ahmedabad: Indian Institute of Management, 1988. p. 340. IIML, SPIESRL.

Bhatt, Atul. *Santalpur block after seven years: evaluation of implementation of block level plan: a case study of Santalpur block of Banaskantha district, Gujarat state*. Pune: National Institute of Bank Management, 1991. p. 122. IIML.

Bhatt, B.K. *Gujarat economy*. Delhi: Vrinda, 2003. p. 227. CSSL, HML.

Bhattacharya, S.N. Economic development in Gujarat. In *Strategy for economic development in agricultural, industrial and tertiary sectors in different Indian states*. New Delhi: Metropolitan, 1985. pp. 137–147. CSSL, IIML.

Bkinkhorn, Thomas A. and Smith, William T. India's Narmada: river of hope. In *Toward sustainable development: struggling over India's Narmada river*. Ed. by William F. Fisher. Jaipur: Rawat, 1997. pp. 89–112. CSSL.

Blankenberg, Floris. Strategic management of the national biogas development project in Gujarat and Tamil Nadu. In *Managing rural development: health and energy programmes in India*. Ed. by Hein Streefkers and T.K. Moulik. New Delhi: Sage, 1991. pp. 136–152. CSSL, HML, IIML, SETUL, SPIESRL, UML.

Bliss, C.J. and Stem, N.H. Markets in Palanpur. In *Palanpur: the economy of an Indian village*. Delhi: Oxford, 1982. p. 340. HML.

Buch, D.T. Farmer participation for Sardar Sarovar (Narmada) Project-issues and broad framework. In *Development imperatives and environment concerns Sardar Sarovar Project plan*. Ed. by Mahesh Pathak. Vallabh Vidyanagar: Agro-Economic Research Centre, 1995. pp. 163–183. IIML.

Bulsari, Smruti. National telecom policy (NTP) 1994 and structural change in telecommunication sector of Gujarat. In *Gujarat economy: the way ahead*. Ed. by Sudha V. Menon. Hyderabad: ICFAI University, 2009. pp. 133–141. EDIL, HML, SPIESRL.

Centre for Social Studies, Surat. Resettlement and rehabilitation in Gujarat. In *Dam and the nation: displacement and resettlement in the Narmada valley*. Ed. by Jean Dreze, Meera Samson and Satyajit Singh. Delhi: Oxford, 1997. pp. 215–235. CSSL, SPUL.

Chambers, Robert. *Managing canal irrigation: practical analysis from South Asia.* Cambridge: Cambridge University press, 1988. p. 279. CSSL.

Chatterjee, Ipsita. From red tape to red carpet? Violent narratives of neoliberalizing Ahmedabad. In *India's new economic policy: a critical analysis.* Ed. by Waquar Ahmed, Amitabh Kundu and Richard Peet. Jaipur: Rawat, 2010. pp. 154–178. CSSL, GVL.

Chavan, Sanat A. Environmental up gradation through Sardar Sarovar Project. In *Sardar Sarovar project on the river Narmada*. Vol. 1. Ed. by R. Parthasarathy and Ravindra H. Dholakia. New Delhi: Concept, 2011. pp. 187–195. CEPTL, CSSL, EDIL, HML, IIML, SETUL, SPUL, TRTIL, UML.

Choksey, R.D. *Economic life in the Bombay Gujarat: 1800–1939*. Bombay: Asia, 1968. p. 288. AERCL, CSSL, GIDRL, GUL, IIML, SPIESRL.

Dabholkar, Dattaprasad. *Oh mother Narmada...: on the hot trial of a controversy.* New Delhi: Wiley Eastern, 1993. p. 127. CSSL.

Das, Amritananda. *Foundations of Gandhian economics.* Bombay: Allied, 1979. p. 146. SPIESRL.

Das, Biswaroop. Status of agriculture and animal husbandry among Narmada oustees: narratives from some re-settled sites. In *Sardar Sarovar Project on the river Narmada*. Vol. 2. Ed. by R. Parthasarathy and Ravindra H. Dholakia. New Delhi: Concept, 2011. pp. 444–472. CEPTL, CSSL, EDIL, HML, IIML, SETUL, SPUL, TRTIL, UML.

Das, Keshab. Managing finance for drinking water: pointers from Gujarat villages. In *Elixir of life: the socio-ecological governance of drinking water.* Ed. by K.V. Raju. Bangalore: Books for Change, 2006. pp. 235–245. CSSL.

Das, Keshab and Gupta, Ruchi. Management by participation? Village institutions and drinking water supply in Gujarat. In *Elixir of life: the socio-ecological governance of drinking water.* Ed. by K.V. Raju. Bangalore: Books for Change, 2006. pp. 246–256. CSSL.

Datta, Samar K. Exploring institutional alternatives to tap fishing potentials of Sardar Sarovar reservoir. In *Sardar Sarovar project on the river Narmada*. Vol. 3. Ed. by R. Parthasarathy and Ravindra H. Dholakia. New Delhi: Concept, 2011. pp. 819–866. CEPTL, CSSL, EDIL, HML, IIML, SETUL, SPUL, TRTIL, UML.

Dave, K.M. Farmers' involvement in water management for the Sardar Sarovar Project, Gujarat. In *India: irrigation management partnerships*. Ed. by M.V.K. Sivamohan. Hyderabad: Booklinks, 1994. pp. 227–236. CSSL.

Dave, K.M. Some aspects of water management in the command area of Sardar Sarovar Project. In *Development imperatives and environment concerns Sardar Sarovar Project plan.* Ed. by Mahesh Pathak. Vallabh Vidyanagar: Agro Economic Research Centre, 1995. pp. 135–162. IIML.

Dave, Pooja. Gujarat initiatives for development. In *Gujarat economy: the way ahead.* Ed. by Sudha V.Menon. Hyderabad: ICFAI University, 2009. pp. 206–227. EDIL, HML, SPIESRL.

Dawson, W.G. Union response to technological change: the Ahmedabad experience. In *Technological change and industry.* Ed. by C.P. Thakur and G.S. Aurora. New Delhi: Shri Ram Centre for Industrial Relations, 1971. pp. 265–279. SPIESRL.

De, Jayashree and Rotee, Kanchan. Identifying the factors of economic growth for micro-level planning: the case of Gujarat. In *Essays on regional science regional development and planning.* Ed. by C.R. Pathak. Calcutta: Regional Science Association, 1998. pp. 164–169. IIML.

Debroy, Bibek. *Gujarat: governance for growth and development.* New Delhi: Academic, 2012. p. 165. CEPTL, CSSL, IIML, SPUL.

Deegan, Chris. Narmada in myth and history. In *Toward sustainable development: struggling over India's Narmada river.* Ed. by William F. Fisher. Jaipur: Rawat, 1997. pp. 47–68. CSSL.

Desai, Anjana P. *Spatial aspects of settlement patterns: a study of the Narmada command area of Mahesana district, Gujarat.* New Delhi: Concept, 1985. p. 134. CEPTL, IRMAL.

Desai, Anjana P. *Study of settlement pattern: six talukas in the Narmada command area of Mahesana district of Gujarat.* Ahmedabad: Sardar Patel Institute of Economic & Social Research, 1982. p. 184. SPIESRL.

Desai, H.P. and Gandhi, Pankaj., ed. *Glimpses of Gujarat: geography, demography and government policies. 2v.* Jaipur: ABD, 2007. p. 243 and p. 253. CEPTL.

Desai, Morarjibhai. Baroda watans. In *Indian land problems and legislation.* Bombay: N.M. Tripathi, 1954. pp. 114–128. HML.

Desai, M.B. *Rural economy of Gujarat.* Bombay: Oxford, 1948. p. 352. ASL, BVL, GIDRL, GVL, SPIESRL, SPUL.

Desai, M.B. Rural economy of Gujarat, 1946. In *Dissertation in economics 1921–1971.* Ed. by C.H. Shah. Bombay: University of Bombay, 1974. pp. 5–7. SPIESRL.

Desai, N.B. Evolution and implementation of Sardar Sarovar dam. In *Sardar Sarovar Project on the river Narmada.* Vol. 2. Ed. by R. Parthasarathy and Ravindra H. Dholakia. New Delhi: Concept, 2011. pp. 295–309. CEPTL, CSSL, EDIL, HML, IIML, SETUL, SPUL, TRTIL, UML.

Desai, N.B. Irrigated agriculture through Sardar Sarovar. In *Sardar Sarovar Project on the river Narmada.* Vol. 3. Ed. by R. Parthasarathy and Ravindra H. Dholakia. New Delhi: Concept, 2011. pp. 637–650. CEPTL, CSSL, EDIL, HML, IIML, SETUL, SPUL, TRTIL, UML.

Desai, R.M. Economics survey of Baroda state (1935). In *Dissertation in economics 1921–1971.* Ed. by C.H. Shah. Bombay: University of Bombay, 1974. pp. 647–650. SPIESRL.

Desai, Vaidya Prerana. Irrigation impacts of Sardar Sarovar Project: a field evaluation. In *Sardar Sarovar Project on the river Narmada.* Vol. 3. Ed. by R. Parthasarathy and Ravindra H. Dholakia. New Delhi: Concept, 2011. pp. 665–692. CEPTL, CSSL, EDIL, HML, IIML, SETUL, SPUL, TRTIL, UML.

Dhagamwar, Vasudha. NGO movements in the Narmada valley: some reflections. In *Dam and the nation: displacement and resettlement in the Narmada valley.* Ed. by Jean Dreze, Meera Samson and Satyajit Singh. Delhi: Oxford, 1997. pp. 93–102. CSSL, SPUL.

Dhagamwar, Vasudha, Ganguly Thukral, Enakshi and Singh, Mridula. Sardar Sarovar Project: a study in sustainable development? In *Toward sustainable development: struggling over India's Narmada river.* Ed. by William F. Fisher. Jaipur: Rawat, 1997. pp. 265–288. CSSL.

Dharmadhikary, Shripad. Hydropower at Sardar Sarovar: is it necessary, justified, and affordable? In *Toward sustainable development: struggling over India's Narmada river.* Ed. by William F. Fisher. Jaipur: Rawat, 1997. pp. 135–153. CSSL.

Dholakia, Ravindra H. Economic growth and fluctuations in Gujarat. In *Gujarat economy: problems and prospects.* Ed. by D.T. Lakdawala. Ahmedabad: Sardar Patel Institute of Economic & Social Research, 1982. pp. 3–18. GIDRL.

Dholakia, Ravindra H. Economic reforms and development strategy in Gujarat. In *New development paradigms & challenges for Western & Central India*. Vol. 1. Ed. by R. Parthasarthy and Sudarshan Iyengar. New Delhi: Concept, 2006. pp. 30–54. CSSL, EDIL, GIDRL, SPIESRL.

Dholakia, Ravindra H. Liberalization in Gujarat: review of recent experience. In *Dynamics of development in Gujarat*. Ed. by Indira Hirway, S.P. Kashyap and Amita Shah. New Delhi: Concept, 2002. pp. 48–60. CSSL, EDIL, GIDRL, GVL. HML, IRMAL, SPUL, UML.

Dholakia, Ravindra H. Macroeconomic framework for development in Gujarat. In *Gujarat: perspectives of the future*. Ed. by R. Swaminathan. New Delhi: Academic, 2008. pp. 105–150. CSSL, EDIL, GIDRL, GVL, IIML, IRMAL, SETUL, SPIESRL.

Dholakia, Ravindra H. Review of social cost-benefit analyses for the Sardar Sarovar Project. In *Sardar Sarovar Project on the river Narmada*. Vol. 1. Ed. by R. Parthasarathy and Ravindra H. Dholakia. New Delhi: Concept, 2011. pp. 199–225. CEPTL, CSSL, EDIL, HML, IIML, SETUL, SPUL, TRTIL, UML.

Dholakia, Ravindra H. Role of the state government in promoting private sector growth: the case of Gujarat. In *State-level reforms in India: towards more effective government*. Ed. by Stephen Howes, Ashok K. Lahiri and Stem Nicholas. Delhi: Macmillan, 2003. pp. 302–320. IIML.

Dholakia, Ravindra H. and Hirway, Indira H. *Block level planning for full employments Jambughoda*. Ahmedabad: Sardar Patel Institute of Economic & Social Research, 1979. p. 235. SPIESRL.

Dholakia, Ravindra H. and Iyengar, Sudarshan. *Planning for rural development: issues and case studies*. Bombay: Himalaya, 1988. p. 133. CEPTL, IIML, SPUL.

Dinesh Kumar, M. and Bassi, Nitin. Maximising the social and economic returns from Sardar Sarovar Project: thinking beyond the convention. In *Sardar Sarovar Project on the river Narmada*. Vol. 3. Ed. by R. Parthasarathy and Ravindra H. Dholakia. New Delhi: Concept, 2011. pp. 800–818. CEPTL, CSSL, EDIL, HML, IIML, SETUL, SPUL, TRTIL, UML.

Dinesh, Kumar, Chopde, Shashikant and Anjal, Prakash. Dug well recharging in Saurashtra, Gujarat: a local response to water scarcity. In *Rethinking the mosaic investigation into local water management*. Ed. by Marcus Moench, Elisabeth Caspari and Ajaya Dixit. Kathmandu: Nepal Water Conservation, 1999. pp. 247–260. SPIESRL.

Dinesh, Kumar, et al. Addressing water scarcity local strategies for water supply and conservation management in the Sabarmati basin, Gujarat. In *Rethinking the mosaic investigation into local water management*. Ed. by Marcus Moench, Elisabeth Caspari and Ajaya Dixit. Kathmandu: Nepal Water Conservation, 1999. pp. 191–246. SPIESRL.

Divekar, V.D. Western India. In *Cambridge economic history of India*, Vol. 2. Ed. by Dharma Kumar. Delhi: Orient Longman, 1982. pp. 332–352. CSSL, SUL.

Dubash, Navroz. Local politics of groundwater in North Gujarat. In *Waterscapes: the cultural politics of a natural resource*. Ed. by Amita Baviskar. Ranikhet: Permanent Black, 2007. pp. 88–114. CSSL.

Dubash, Navroz. Local politics of groundwater in North Gujarat. In *Sociology and anthropology of economic life-I: the moral embedding of economic action*. Ed. by Veena Das and Ranedra K. Das. New Delhi: Oxford, 2010. pp. 136–161. HML, IIML.

Dudhat, Bharat L. and Shiyani, R.L. Equity, comparative feasibility and economic viability of groundwater investment in Saurashtra India. In *Managing water in the face of growing scarcity inequity and declining returns: exploring fresh approaches* (Vol. 1). Ed. by Dinesh Kumar and International Water Management Institute. Hyderabad: International Water Management Institute (IWMI), 2008. pp. 378–390. SPIESRL.

Faldu, D.G. Water resources, potential, development utilization and water management. In *Economy of Saurashtra: problems and prospects*. Ed. by D.T. Lakdawala, et al. Bhavnagar: Bhavnagar University, 1990. pp. 98–106. GUL.

Fisher, William F. Development and resistance in the Narmada valley. In *Toward sustainable development: struggling over India's Narmada river*. Ed. by William F. Fisher. Jaipur: Rawat, 1997. pp. 3–46. CSSL.

Fisher, William F. Full of sound and fury? Struggling toward sustainable development in India's Narmada valley. In *Toward sustainable development: struggling over India's Narmada river*. Ed. by William F. Fisher. Jaipur: Rawat, 1997. pp. 445–461. CSSL.

Fisher, William F., ed. *Toward sustainable development: struggling over India's Narmada river*. Jaipur: Rawat, 1997. p. 481. CSSL.

Fukazawa, H. Western India. In *Cambridge economic history of India*, Vol. 2. Ed. by Dharma Kumar. Delhi: Orient Longman, 1982. pp. 177–206. CSSL, SUL.

Gaikwad, V.R. and Parmar, D.S. *Rural development administration under democratic decentralization: expenditure pattern and organizational realities*. New Delhi: Wiley, 1979. p. 155. SPIESRL.

Gandhi, Vasant P. and Namboodiri, N.V. *Improving irrigation management in India: a study of participatory irrigation management in the states of Andhra Pradesh, Gujarat and Maharashtra*. New Delhi: Allied, 2011. p. 128. IIML.

Gandotra, M.M. and Shah, N.C. *Gujarat economy in 2001 A.D.: a study in perspective*. New Delhi: Allied, 1980. p. 374. SGUL.

Garg, Amit, et al. Impacts of Narmada water on agriculture in Gujarat. In *Sardar Sarovar Project on the river Narmada*. Vol. 3. Ed. by R. Parthasarathy and Ravindra H. Dholakia. New Delhi: Concept, 2011. pp. 651–664. CEPTL, CSSL, EDIL, HML, IIML, SETUL, SPUL, TRTIL, UML.

Gautam, Manu. Rehabilitation and status of human rights: tribal displacement in Gujarat. In *Tribal issues in India*. Ed. by D.C. Sah and Yatindra Singh Sisodia. Jaipur: Rawat, 2004. pp. 293–304. CSSL, GVL, TRTIL.

Gohil, B.K. Provision of infrastructure in Gujarat. In *Economic development of backward regions problems and prospects*. Ed. by H.M. Patel, V.S. Vyas and M.T. Pathak. Vallabh Vidyanagar: Sardar Patel University, 1974. pp. 69–99. GUL, GVL.

Gosh, R., Goel, R.K. and Lole, B.S. District level planning: a case study for Panchmahals district using remote sensing and GIS techniques. In *ICORG-92 remote sensing applications and geographic information systems: recent trends*. Ed. by I.V. Muralikrishna. New Delhi: Tata McGraw-Hill, 1992. pp. 376-[ ]. CEEL.

Goswami, Subhrangsu. Revisiting Sardar Sarovar canal based drinking water project in Gujarat. In *Sardar Sarovar Project on the river Narmada*. Vol. 3. Ed. by R. Parthasarathy and Ravindra H. Dholakia. New Delhi: Concept, 2011. pp. 693–726. CEPTL, CSSL, EDIL, HML, IIML, SETUL, SPUL, TRTIL, UML.

Hakim, Roxanne P. Resettlement and rehabilitation in the context of 'Vasava' culture. In *Dam and the nation: displacement and resettlement in the Narmada valley*. Ed. by Jean Dreze, Meera Samson and Satyajit Singh. Delhi: Oxford, 1997. pp. 136–167. CSSL, SPUL.

Hein, Streefkerk. Centralised and decentralised rural drinking water supply systems and the public-private nexus. In *Managing rural development: health and energy programmes in India.* Ed. by Hein Streefkerk and T.K. Moulik. New Delhi: Sage, 1991. pp. 95–113. CSSL, SETUL, SPIESRL, UML.

Hirway, Indira. Assessing the inclusiveness of growth in Gujarat. In *Growth or development: which way is Gujarat going?* Ed. by Indira Hirway, Amita Shah and Ghanshyam Shah. New Delhi: Oxford, 2014. pp. 83–138. CSSL.

Hirway, Indira. Challenges to sustainable development: some issues in the context of Gujarat. In *New development paradigms & challenges for Western & Central India.* Vol. 1. Ed. by R. Parthasarthy and Sudarshan Iyengar. New Delhi: Concept, 2006. pp. 55–81. CSSL, EDIL, GIDRL, SPIESRL.

Hirway, Indira. Critical evaluation of the first phase of the block level planning experiment in Gujarat. In *Employment, poverty and public policy.* Ahmedabad: Y.K. Alagh, 1981. pp. 220-[ ]. TRTIL.

Hirway, Indira. Dynamics of development in Gujarat: some issues. In *Dynamics of development in Gujarat.* Ed. by Indira Hirway, S.P. Kashyap and Amita Shah. New Delhi: Concept, 2002. pp. 1–47. CSSL, EDIL, GIDRL, GVL, HML, IRMAL, SPUL, UML.

Hirway, Indira. *Dynamics of drinking water in rural Gujarat.* Ahmedabad: Centre for Water Resources, 1994. p. 119. CEPTL.

Hirway, Indira. Ensuring drinking water to all: a study in Gujarat. In *Elixir of life: the socio-ecological governance of drinking water.* Ed. by K.V. Raju. Bangalore: Books for Change, 2006. pp. 74–116. CSSL.

Hirway, Indira and Terhal, Piet. Contradiction of growth. In *Development and deprivation in Gujarat: in honour of Jan Breman.* Ed. by Ghanshyam Shah, Mario Rutten and Hein Streefkerk. New Delhi: Sage, 2002. pp. 37–58. CEPTL, CSSL, EDIL, GIDRL, HML, IIML, IRMAL, UML.

Hirway, Indira, Kashyap, S.P. and Shah, Amita. ed. *Dynamics of development in Gujarat.* New Delhi: Concept, 2002. p. 468. CSSL, EDIL, GIDRL, GVL, HML, IRMAL, SGUL, SPUL, UML.

Hirway, Indira, Shah, Amita and Shah, Ghanshyam. Growth and development in Gujarat: an introduction. In *Growth or development: which way is Gujarat going?* Ed. by Indira Hirway, Amita Shah and Ghanshyam Shah. New Delhi: Oxford, 2014. pp. 1–19. CSSL.

Ibrahim, Farhana. Capitalism, multiculturalism and tolerance: a perspective on 'Vibrant Gujarat'. In *Gujarat economy: the way ahead.* Ed. by Sudha V. Menon. Hyderabad: ICFAI University, 2009. pp. 197–205. EDIL, HML, SPIESRL.

Indu, Rajnarayan, Borkar, Ajinkya and Dave, Alpa. Turning point? Water saving technologies in North Gujarat's groundwater socio-ecology. In *Managing water in the face of growing scarcity, inequity and declining returns: exploring fresh approaches* (Vol. 1). Ed. by Dinesh Kumar and International Water Management Institute. Hyderabad: International Water Management Institute, 2008. pp. 83–97. SPIESRL.

Iyengar, Sudarshan. Resettlement and rehabilitation in Sardar Sarovar Project: policy evolution and implementation. In *Sardar Sarovar Project on the river Narmada.* Vol. 2. Ed. by R. Parthasarathy and Ravindra H. Dholakia. New Delhi: Concept, 2011. pp. 475–511. CEPTL, CSSL, EDIL, HML, IIML, SETUL, SPUL, TRTIL, UML.

Iyengar, Sudarshan. Resettlement and rehabilitation in the Sardar Sarovar Project: a review of policy reforms and implementation. In *Other Gujarat: social transformation among weaker sections*. Ed. by Takashi Shinoda. Mumbai: Popular, 2002. pp. 119–158. ASL, CEEL, CSSL, EDIL, GIDRL, SETUL, SPIESRL.

Iyengar, Sudarshan. Role of non-governmental organisations in the development of Gujarat: a review on the eve of the new millennium. In *Dynamics of development in Gujarat*. Ed. by Indira Hirway, S.P. Kashyap and Amita Shah. New Delhi: Concept, 2002. pp. 387–407. CSSL, EDIL, GIDRL, GVL, HML, IRMAL, SPUL, UML.

Jagadeesan, S. Connecting the last mile. In *Sardar Sarovar Project on the river Narmada*. Vol. 3. Ed. by R. Parthasarathy and Ravindra H. Dholakia. New Delhi: Concept, 2011. pp. 892–913. CEPTL, CSSL, EDIL, HML, IIML, SETUL, SPUL, TRTIL, UML.

Jain, S.C. *Area skill survey: Bharuch district*. Jaipur: Rawat, 1975. p. 311. HML.

Jani, B.M. Water resource utilization and disposal of waste water in class-I cities and class-II towns in Gujarat. In *Water resources, sustainable livelihoods and eco-system services*. Ed. by Kanchan Chopra, C.H. Hanumatha Rao and Ramprasad Sengupta. New Delhi: Concept, 2003. pp. 204–219. AAUL, CSSL, HML, SPIESRL.

Java, G.L. Sardar Sarovar Project: features of the main dam. In *Sardar Sarovar Project on the river Narmada*. Vol. 1. Ed. by R. Parthasarathy and Ravindra H. Dholakia. New Delhi: Concept, 2011. pp. 32–71. CEPTL, CSSL, EDIL, HML, IIML, SETUL, SPUL, TRTIL, UML.

Java, G.L. Seismicity and safety of the Sardar Sarovar dam. In *Sardar Sarovar Project on the river Narmada*. Vol. 1. Ed. by R. Parthasarathy and Ravindra H. Dholakia. New Delhi: Concept, 2011. pp. 72–113. CEPTL, CSSL, EDIL, HML, IIML, SETUL, SPUL, TRTIL, UML.

Jhala, B.K. Sardar Sarovar Project vis-a-vis the environment. In *Development imperatives and environment concerns Sardar Sarovar Project plan*. Ed. by Mahesh Pathak. Vallabh Vidyanagar: Agro Economic Research Centre, 1995. pp. 102–112. IIML.

Johri, Taapsi and Chadha, Amrita. Anti-dam protests: Narmada Bachao Andolan. In *Social auditing of environmental laws in India*. Ed. by Nomita Aggarwal. Delhi: New Century, 2003. pp. 155–171. HML.

Joshi, M.B. and Acharya, K.D. Challenges involved in operation of SSP canal conveyance system and use of state-of-the-art technology. In *Sardar Sarovar Project on the river Narmada*. Vol. 3. Ed. by R. Parthasarathy and Ravindra H. Dholakia. New Delhi: Concept, 2011. pp. 869–891. CEPTL, CSSL, EDIL, HML, IIML, SETUL, SPUL, TRTIL, UML.

Joshi, V.H. Pattern of sectoral change and growth potentiality: a regional dimension. In *Economy of Saurashtra: problems and prospects*. Ed. byD.T. Lakdawala, etal.Bhavnagar: Bhavnagar University, 1990. pp. 27–30. GUL.

Joshi, V.H. Strategy for the development of backward areas: with special reference to Gujarat. In *Backward area development*. Ed. by D.M. Nanjundappa and R.K. Sinha. New Delhi: Sterling, 1982. pp. 299–316. HML.

Joshi, V.H., Parmar, B.D. and Joshi, B.H. *Changing pattern of sectorial behaviour*. Delhi: B.R., 1988. p. 576. HML, IIML, SPUL, UML.

Joshi, Vidyut. Cultural context of development in Gujarat. In *Dynamics of development in Gujarat*. Ed. by Indira Hirway, S.P. Kashyap and Amita Shah. New Delhi: Concept, 2002. pp. 372–386. CSSL, EDIL, GIDRL, GVL, HML, IRMAL, SPUL, UML.

Joshi, Vidyut. *Rehabilitation: a promise to keep: a case of SSP*. Ahmedabad: Tax, 1991. p. 76. CSSL.

Joshi, Vidyut. Rehabilitation at Sardar Sarovar Narmada project. In *Sardar Sarovar Project: a promise for plenty*. Ed. by Mahesh T. Pathak. New Delhi: Oxford, 1991. pp. 49–79. CSSL, SPUL.

Joshi, Vidyut. Rehabilitation in the Narmada valley: human rights and national policy issues. In *Dam and the nation: displacement and resettlement in the Narmada valley*. Ed. by Jean Dreze, Meera Samson and Satyajit Singh. Delhi: Oxford, 1997. pp. 168–183. CSSL, SPUL.

Joshi, Vidyut. *Rehabilitation is possible: the Sardar Sarovar Narmada-project*. Ahmedabad: Tax, 2000. p. 136. CSSL.

Judge, Paramjit S. Development, displacement and rehabilitation: a case of oustees of Sardar Sarovar Project on the Narmada. In *Sustainable development: ecological and sociological dimensions*. Ed. by K. Gopal Iyer. New Delhi: Vikas, 1996. pp. 320–329. CSSL, SPUL.

Kapasi, C.B. Economic development of the Baroda state, 1946. In *Dissertation in economics 1921–1971*. Ed. by C.H. Shah. Bombay: University of Bombay, 1974. pp. 223–224. SPIESRL.

Kashyap, S.P. Irrigation induced agricultural growth, occupational diversification and poverty alleviation: experience of a prosperous district in Gujarat. In *Growth, employment and poverty: change and continuity in rural India*. Ed. by G.K. Chadha and Alakh N. Sharma. New Delhi: Vikas, 1997. pp. 243–262. CSSL.

Kashyap, S.P. Level of living, inequalities and consumption pattern: a comparative analysis of Ahmedabad. In *Development policy and administration in India*. Ed. by Ramesh K. Arora and P.C. Mathur. New Delhi: Associated, 1986. pp. 241–271. IIML.

Kashyap, S.P. *Regional planning in a consistency framework: a study of Gujarat*. New Delhi: Sardar Patel Institute, 1979. p. [ ]. CEPTL.

Kashyap, S.P., Tiwari, R.S. and Veena, D.R. *Facets an urban economy: economic base study of Ahmedabad*. Ahmedabad: Sardar Patel Institute of Social Science Research, 1980. p. 312. SPIESRL.

Khagram, Sanjeev. *Dams and development: transnational struggles for water and power*. New Delhi: Oxford, 2004. p. 270. CSSL.

Kolavali, Shashi, et al. Joint management in medium irrigation systems in Gujarat: two cases. In *Strategic change in Indian irrigation*. Ed. by Mark Svensen and Ashok Gulati. New Delhi: Macmillan India, 1995. pp. 291–336. CSSL.

Koppa, G.G. Institutional change and water productivity: a scenario testing of canal irrigation cooperatives in Northern Gujarat for financial viability. In *Managing water in the face of growing scarcity inequity and declining returns: exploring fresh approaches* (Vol. 1). Ed. by Dinesh Kumar and International Water Management Institute. Hyderabad: International Water Management Institute (IWMI), 2008. pp. 646–664. SPIESRL.

Kothari, Smitu. Damming the Narmada and the politics of development. In *Toward sustainable development: struggling over India's Narmada river*. Ed. by William F. Fisher. Jaipur: Rawat, 1997. pp. 421–444. CSSL.

Krishnan, Sunderrajan. Duel among duala? Popular science of basaltic hydrogeology in a village of Saurashtra. In *Managing water in the face of growing scarcity inequity and declining returns: exploring fresh approaches* (Vol. 1). Ed. by Dinesh Kumar and International Water Management Institute. Hyderabad: International Water Management Institute (IWMI), 2008. pp. 391–411. SPIESRL.

Kulkarni, K.M. and Bayanwala, Vishakha. Electricity supply in Ahmedabad: an indicator of development. In *Urban and regional development in India.* Vol. 1. Ed. by B. Thakur, et al. New Delhi: Concept, 2005. pp. 335–350. HML.

Kumarappa, J.C. *Economic survey of Matar taluka (Kheda district).* Ahmedabad: Gujarat Vidyapith, 1952. p. 155. CSSL, GUL, IIML, SPUL, UML.

Kumarappa, J.C. *Survey of Matar taluka: Kaira district.* Ahmedabad: Gujatat Vidyapith, 1931. p. 179. CSSL.

Kundu, Amitabh. Urbanisation, employment generation and poverty under the shadow of globalization: the case of Gujarat, India. In *Dynamics of development in Gujarat.* Ed. by Indira Hirway, S.P. Kashyap and Amita Shah. New Delhi: Concept, 2002. pp. 99–130. CSSL, EDIL, GIDRL, GVL, HML, IRMAL, SPUL, UML.

Kundu, Debolina. Provision of infrastructure and basic amenities: analysing institutional vulnerability. In *Poverty and vulnerability in a globalising metropolis Ahmedabad.* Ed. by Amitabh Kundu and Darshini Mahadevia. New Delhi: Manak, 2002. pp. 133–178. CEPTL, CSSL.

Lal, P.N. and Pandey, D.N. Impact of Sardar Sarovar dam: a human ecological study of the two villages of Gujarat. In *Narmada basin-land and people: an anthropological pilot study of Madhya Pradesh and Gujarat.* Ed. by D. Tyagi. Calcutta: Anthropological Survey of India, 1998. pp. 69–91. CSSL.

Lalitha, N. and Oza, Arti. Employment trends in the manufacturing sector of Gujarat. In *Dynamics of development in Gujarat.* Ed. by Indira Hirway, S.P. Kashyap and Amita Shah. New Delhi: Concept, 2002. pp. 322–339. CSSL, EDIL, GIDRL, GVL, HML, IRMAL, SPUL, UML.

Lanjouw, Peter and Stern, Nicholas. *Economic development in Palanpur: over five decades.* Delhi: Oxford, 1998. p. 640. IIML.

Lobo, Lancy and Kumar, Shashikant. *Land acquisition displacement and resettlement in Gujarat 1947–2004.* New Delhi: Sage, 2009. p. 303. AAL, CEPTL, CSSL, EDIL, HML, IIML, TRTIL.

Mahadevia, Darshini. Changing economic scenario: informalisation and increased vulnerability. In *Poverty and vulnerability in a globalising metropolis Ahmedabad.* Ed. by Amitabh Kundu and Darshini Mahadevia. New Delhi: Manak, 2002. pp. 30–79. CEPTL, CSSL.

Mahadevia, Darshini. Dynamics of urbanization in Gujarat. In *Growth or development: which way is Gujarat going?* Ed. by Indira Hirway, Amita Shah and Ghanshyam Shah. New Delhi: Oxford, 2014. pp. 340–379. CSSL.

Mahadevia, Darshini. *Economic growth and environmental degradation: case of Gujarat.* New Delhi: [ ], 1999. p. 79. CEPTL.

Mahadevia, Darshini. From stealth to aggression: economic reforms and communal politics in Gujarat. In *Politics of economic reforms in India.* Ed. by Jos Mooji. New Delhi: Sage, 2005. pp. 291–321. CSSL, SPUL.

Mahadevia, Darshini. Interventions in development: a shift towards a model of exclusion. In *Poverty and vulnerability in a globalising metropolis Ahmedabad.* Ed. by Amitabh Kundu and Darshini Mahadevia. New Delhi: Manak, 2002. pp. 80–132. CEPTL, CSSL.

Mahadevia, Darshini. Municipal finances and development in small and medium towns: Gujarat. In *New development paradigms & challenges for Western & Central India.* Vol. 1. Ed. by R. Parthasarthy and Sudarshan Iyengar. New Delhi: Concept, 2006. pp. 217–260. CSSL, EDIL, GIDRL, SPIESRL.

Mahadevia, Darshini and Bhatt, Vatsal. Economic liberalisation and the urban land market: trends from Ahmedabad. In *Issues in urbanisation: study of Ahmedabad city*. Ed. by Jan Hesselberg. Jaipur: Rawat, 2002. pp. 128–164. SPIESRL.

Mahadevia, Darshini and Brar, Harpreet Singh. Basic infrastructure public finance and slum dwellers: Ahmedabad. In *Inside the transforming urban Asia: processes, policies and public actions*. Ed. by Darshini Mahadevia. New Delhi: Concept, 2008. pp. 361–390. GVL.

Mahadevia, Darshini and Brar, Harpreet Singh. Changes and continuities in development priorities: Ahmedabad. In *Inside the transforming urban Asia: processes, policies and public actions*. Ed. by Darshini Mahadevia. New Delhi: Concept, 2008. pp. 132–169. GVL.

Mallison, Francoise. Bombay as the intellectual capital of the Gujaratis. In *Bombay mosaic of modern culture*. Ed. by Sujata Patel and Alice Thorner. Bombay: Oxford, 1995. pp. 76–87. CSSL.

Mankodi, Kashyap. Resettlement and rehabilitation of dam oustees: a case study of Ukai dam. In *Big dams, displaced people: divers of sorrow rivers of change*. Ed. by Enakshi Ganguly Thakaral. New Delhi: Sage, 1992. pp. 77–100. CSSL, HML, IIML, SETUL.

Marvania, P.G. Salinity ingress and technological and institutional solution-some results: a case of coastal Saurashtra. In *Water resources, sustainable livelihoods and eco-system services*. Ed. by Kanchan Chopra, C.H. Hanumantha Rao and Ramprasad Sengupta. Delhi: Indian Society for Ecological Economics, 2003. pp. 159–168. CSSL, HML, SPIESRL.

McKay, Jennifer and Diwakara, H. Groundwater irrigation in Northern Gujarat: digging deep for answers. In *Water conflicts in India: a million revolts in the making*. Ed. by K.J. Joy, et al. London: Routledge, 2008. pp. 122–126. CSSL.

Mehta, J.M. *Study of rural economy of Gujarat*. Baroda: State Press, 1930. p. 230. BVL, CSSL, TRTIL.

Mehta, Meera and Mehta, Dinesh. Planning for metropolitan water supply and sewerage: a case study of Ahmedabad. In *Urbanization in developing countries*. Ed. by Bidyut Mohanty. New Delhi: Concept, 1993. pp. 260–280. HML, SGUL.

Mehta, Meera and Mehta, Dinesh. Urban drinking water security and sustainability in Gujarat. In *Sardar Sarovar Project on the river Narmada*. Vol. 3. Ed. by R. Parthasarathy and Ravindra H. Dholakia. New Delhi: Concept, 2011. pp. 727–743. CEPTL, CSSL, EDIL, HML, IIML, SETUL, SPUL, TRTIL, UML.

Mehta, Niti. Imbalance in development between regions and social group: evidences from Gujarat. In *Gujarat economy: the way ahead*. Ed. by Sudha V. Menon. Hyderabad: ICFAI University, 2009. pp. 40–75. EDIL, HML, SGUL, SPIESRL.

Mehta, S.S. Sardar Sarovar Project: planning and data base. In *Sardar Sarovar Project: a promise for plenty*. Ed. by Mahesh T. Pathak. New Delhi: Oxford, 1991. pp. 1–21. CSSL, SPUL.

Mehta, Sanat, Laheri, P.K. and Kale, S.G. Economics of Gujarat and Maharashtra. In *Economics of the states of the Indian union*. Ed. by Malcolm S. Adiseshiah. New Delhi: Lancer International, 1989. pp. 219–270. GUL.

Menon, Sudha V. Driver's of economic growth in Gujarat. In *Gujarat economy: the way ahead*. Ed. by Sudha V. Menon. Hyderabad: ICFAI University, 2009. pp. 79–88. EDIL, HML, SGUL, SPIESRL.

Menon, Sudha V. Energy sector in Gujarat: performance and prospects. In *Gujarat economy: the way ahead*. Ed. by Sudha V. Menon. Hyderabad: ICFAI University, 2009. pp. 161–169. EDIL, HML, SGUL, SPIESRL.

Menon, Sudha V. Gujarat economy: an overview. In *Gujarat economy: the way ahead*. Ed. by Sudha V. Menon. Hyderabad: ICFAI University, 2009. pp. 3–11. EDIL, HML, SGUL, SPIESRL.

Menon, Sudha V. Gujarat economy: the way ahead. In *Gujarat economy: the way ahead*. Ed. by Sudha V.Menon. Hyderabad: ICFAI University, 2009. pp. 228–236. EDIL, HML, SGUL, SPIESRL.

Menon, Sudha V., ed. *Gujarat economy: the way ahead.* Hyderabad: ICFAI University, 2009. p. 240. EDIL, HML, SGUL, SPIESRL.

Mishra, Deepti, et al. Drinking water problem in rural areas of Gujarat. In New *technologies for rural development having potential of commercial section.* Ed. by Jai Prakash Shukla. New Delhi: Allied, 2009. pp. 1–7. CEPTL, HML.

Modi, Renu. Sardar Sarovar oustees: coping with displacement. In *Adivasi question: issues of land, forest and livelihood.* Ed. by Indra Munshi. Hyderabad: Orient Blackswan, 2012. pp. 264–271. CSSL.

Mookherjee, Surya. *Joint management councils: a study of practices and performance in Gujarat.* Ahmedabad: Gandhi Labour Institute, 1984. p. 110. IRMAL.

Morris, Sebastian. Comparative analysis of Gujarat's economic growth. In *Growth or development: which way is Gujarat going?* Ed. by Indira Hirway, Amita Shah and Ghanshyam Shah. New Delhi: Oxford, 2014. pp. 20–82. CSSL.

Morris, Sebastian. Energy and infrastructure strategy for Gujarat. In *Gujarat: perspectives of the future*. Ed. by R. Swaminathan. New Delhi: Academic, 2008. pp. 271–297. CSSL, EDIL, IIML, GIDRL, GVL, IRMAL, SETUL, SPIESRL.

Morse, Bradford and Berger, Thomas. Findings and recommendations of the independent review. In *Toward sustainable development: struggling over India's Narmada river*. Ed. by William F. Fisher. Jaipur: Rawat, 1997. pp. 371–380. CSSL, UML.

Moulik, T.K. Introduction of community biogas plant in a Gujarat village: a case study of technological and organization inventions. In *Action research for development*. Ed. by Kuldeep Mathur and Harsh Sethi. New Delhi: Indian Institute of Public Administration, 1983. pp. 36–59. GVL, SPIESRL.

Moulik, T.K. and Srivastava, V.K. *Bio-gas plants at the village level: problems and prospects in Gujarat.* Ahmedabad: Centre for Management in Agriculture, 1975. p. 148. SPIESRL.

Moulik, T.K., et al. *Regional energy demand model and analysis for Gujarat, Kerala and Rajasthan*. New Delhi: Oxford and IBH, 1991. p. 80. Monograph No. 140. HML, IIML.

Mudrakartha, Srinivas, Sheth, Jatin and Srinath, J. Unclogging the Khari river in Ahmedabad: stakeholders come together to halt pollution. In *Water conflicts in India: a million revolts in the making*. Ed. by K.J. Joy, et al. London: Routledge, 2008. pp. 198–206. CSSL.

Nagabrahmam, D. Farmers' organization for irrigation management: some experiences from the Mahi Kadana project. In *India: irrigation management partnerships*. Ed. by M.V.K. Sivamohan. Hyderabad: Booklinks, 1994. pp. 107–121. CSSL.

Naik, D.G. Economics of milk marketing in Gujarat. In *Milk pricing and marketing practices of cooperative dairy industry in Gujarat*. Ed. by Dilip Shah. Pune: Maricheemalee, 1987. pp. 253–261. CSSL, GIDRL, SPIESRL.

Narain, A., Beena Kumari and Raman, Mini. Observation of a persistent coastal up welling off Gujarat by NOAA-AVHRR and its implication on fisheries. In *ICORG-92 remote sensing applications and geographic information systems: recent trends.* Ed. by I.V. Muralikrishna. New Delhi: Tata McGraw-Hill, 1992. pp. 337-[ ]. CEEL.

Oza, Nila. Decentralised planning: a study of Bhavnagar district. In *Decentralised planning*. Ed. by Ramayan Prasad. New Delhi: Deep & Deep, 1980. pp. 185–193. CEEL.

Panchanadikar, K.C. and Panchanadikar, J. *Rural modernization in India: a study in developmental infrastructure*. Bombay: Popular, 1978. p. 398. CSSL, SPIESRL.

Pandit, Virendra. Gujarat making strides in infrastructure. In *Gujarat economy: the way ahead*. Ed. by Sudha V. Menon. Hyderabad: ICFAI University, 2009. pp. 123–130. EDIL, HML, SGUL, SPIESRL.

Pandya, B.V. Economic conditions of scheduled castes Ahmedabad district (1957). In *Dissertation in economics 1921–1971*. Ed. by C.H. Shah. Bombay: University of Bombay, 1974. pp. 630–632. SPIESRL.

Pandya, Hinal. *Sardar Sarovar: hope and reality*. New Delhi: Mohit, 2004. p. 154. CSSL.

Paranjape, Suhas and Joy, K.J. Alternative restructuring of the Sardar Sarovar Project: breaking the deadlock. In *Water conflicts in India: a million revolts in the making*. Ed. by K.J. Joy, et al. London: Routledge, 2008. pp. 338–343. CSSL.

Parasuraman, S. Anti-dam movement and rehabilitation policy. In *Dam and the nation: displacement and resettlement in the Narmada valley*. Ed. by Jean Dreze, Meera Samson and Satyajit Singh. Delhi: Oxford, 1997. pp. 26–65. CSSL, SPUL.

Parekh, K.M. Resource mobilization by Indian states: a structural analysis with special reference to Gujarat. In *Stability and development*. Ed. by Yogindar K. Alagh, Raghuvir J. Mody and Rohit D.Desai. New Delhi: Har-Anand, 1993. pp. 142–153. CSSL, HML, SPIESRL.

Parikh, Nayan and Raghuram, G. Bot project planning experience: Bharuch road over bridge in Gujarat: a case study. In *Infrastructure development and financing: towards a public-private partnership*. Ed. by G.Raghuram, et al. New Delhi: Macmillan, 1999. pp. 504–517. CSSL, HML.

Parmar, B.D. *Regional development and agricultural wages*. Bombay: Himalaya, 1986. p. 243. CSSL, UML.

Parmar, B.J. and Gupta, R.L. Final stage diversion of Narmada river fair weather flows during construction of Sardar Sarovar dam. In *Sardar Sarovar Project on the river Narmada*. Vol. 1. Ed. by R. Parthasarathy and Ravindra H. Dholakia. New Delhi: Concept, 2011. pp. 126–138. CEPTL, CSSL, EDIL, HML, IIML, SETUL, SPUL, TRTIL, UML.

Parmar, B.J. and Rathod, K.G. Siltation study of Sardar Sarovar Project with present status. In *Sardar Sarovar Project on the river Narmada*. Vol. 1. Ed. by R. Parthasarathy and Ravindra H. Dholakia. New Delhi: Concept, 2011. pp. 114–125. CEPTL, CSSL, EDIL, HML, IIML, SETUL, SPUL, TRTIL, UML.

Parthasarathy, R. Participatory irrigation management programme in Gujarat: institutional and financial issues. In *Dynamics of development in Gujarat*. Ed. by Indira Hirway, S.P. Kashyap and Amita Shah. New Delhi: Concept, 2002. pp. 268–289. CSSL, EDIL, GIDRL, GVL, HML, IRMAL, SPUL, UML.

Parthasarathy, R. Social limits and economic partnership potentials in the SSP command. In *Sardar Sarovar Project on the river Narmada*. Vol. 3. Ed. by R. Parthasarathy and Ravindra H. Dholakia. New Delhi: Concept, 2011. pp. 747–776. CEPTL, CSSL, EDIL, HML, IIML, SETUL, SPUL, TRTIL, UML.

Parthasarathy, R. and Dholakia, Ravindra H. Implementation of Sardar Sarovar Project: overview and impact. In *Sardar Sarovar project on the river Narmada*. Vol. 2. Ed. by R. Parthasarathy and Ravindra H. Dholakia. New Delhi: Concept, 2011. pp. 257–291. CEPTL, CSSL, EDIL, HML, IIML, SETUL, SPUL, TRTIL, UML.

Parthasarathy, R. and Dholakia, Ravindra H. Sardar Sarovar Project: background and overview. In *Sardar Sarovar Project on the river Narmada*. Vol. 1. Ed. by R. Parthasarathy and Ravindra H. Dholakia. New Delhi: Concept, 2011. pp. 1–12. CEPTL, CSSL, EDIL, HML, IIML. SETUL, SPUL, TRTIL, UML.

Parthasarathy, R. and Dholakia, Ravindra H. Sardar Sarovar Project: performance so far, plans and opportunities. In *Sardar Sarovar Project on the river Narmada*. Vol. 3. Ed. by R. Parthasarathy and Ravindra H. Dholakia. New Delhi: Concept, 2011. pp. 617–634. CEPTL, CSSL, EDIL, HML, IIML, SETUL, SPUL, TRTIL, UML.

Parthasarathy, R. and Dholakia, Ravindra H., ed. *Sardar Sarovar Project on river Narmada*. 3 Vols. New Delhi: Concept, 2011. pp. 1–960. CEPTL, CSSL, EDIL, HML, IIML, SETUL, SPUL, TRTIL, UML.

Parthasarathy, R. and Iyengar, Sudarshan. Economic reforms and development strategy in Gujarat. Vol. I. In *New development paradigms & challenges for Western & Central India*. Ed. by R. Parthasarathy and Sudarshan Iyengar. New Delhi: Concept, 2006. pp. 30–54. CSSL, EDIL, GIDRL, SPIESRL.

Parthasarathy, R. and Iyengar, Sudarshan, ed. *New development paradigms & challenges for Western & Central India*. 2 Vol. New Delhi: Concept, 2006. p. 684. CSSL, EDIL, GIDRL, SPIESRL.

Patel, Anil. Resettlement politics and tribal interests. In *Dam and the nation: displacement and resettlement in the Narmada valley*. Ed. by Jean Dreze, Meera Samson, and Satyajit Singh. Delhi: Oxford, 1997. pp. 66–92. CSSL, SPUL.

Patel, Anil. What do the Narmada valley tribals want? In *Sardar Sarovar Project on the river Narmada*. Vol. 2. Ed. by R. Parthasarathy and Ravindra H. Dholakia. New Delhi: Concept, 2011. pp. 318–340. CEPTL, CSSL, EDIL, HML, IIML, SETUL, SPUL, TRTIL, UML.

Patel, Anil and Mehta, Ambrish. Independent review: was it a search for the truth? In *Sardar Sarovar Project on the river Narmada*. Vol. 2. Ed. by R. Parthasarathy and Ravindra H. Dholakia. New Delhi: Concept, 2011. pp. 341–379. CEPTL, CSSL, EDIL, HML, IIML, SETUL, SPUL, TRTIL, UML.

Patel, Bimal, et al. Reforming urban land management in Gujarat. In *India infrastructure report 2009*. New Delhi: Oxford, 2009. pp. 176–189. CSSL.

Patel, C.C. Sardar Sarovar Project: a victim of time. In *Toward sustainable development: struggling over India's Narmada river*. Ed. by William F. Fisher. Jaipur: Rawat, 1997. pp. 71–88. CSSL.

Patel, Jasavant M. and Pathole, B.P. Geological mapping of the Kachh area, Gujarat state, India using satellite remote sensing. In *ICORG-92 remote sensing applications and geographic information systems: recent trends*. Ed. by I.V. Muralikrishna. New Delhi: Tata McGraw-Hill, 1992. p. 39. CEEL.

Patel, Ramnik. Pipavav port. In *Economy of Saurashtra: problems and prospects*. Ed. by D.T. Lakdawala, et al.Bhavnagar: Bhavnagar University, 1990. pp. 152–156. GUL.

Patel, Ramu. *Western times Gujarat and its infrastructure*. Ahmedabad: Western Times Press, 1979. p. 339. IIML, SPIESRL.

Patel, S. Anand pattern: a socio-historical analysis of its origin and growth. In *Resource, institutions and strategies*. Ed. by Martin Doornbos and K.N. Nair. New Delhi: Sage, 1990. pp. 27-[ ]. TRTIL.

Patel, S.M. and Patel, K.V. *Studies on economics of rural electrification and lift irrigation (Gujarat state)*. Ahmedabad: Indian Institute of Management, 1969. p. 172. IIML, SPIESRL.

Patel, V.M. Sardar Sarovar Project: benefit-cost analysis. In *Sardar Sarovar Project: a promise for plenty*. Ed. by Mahesh T. Pathak. New Delhi: Oxford, 1991. pp. 101–113. CSSL.

Pathak, Mahesh. Environment, World Bank and Sardar Sarovar Project. In *Development imperatives and environment concerns Sardar Sarovar project plan.* Ed. by Mahesh Pathak. Vallabh Vidyanagar: Agro Economic Research Centre, 1995. pp. 79–94. IIML.

Pathak, Mahesh. Memoirs of a Narmada planner. In *Sardar Sarovar Project on the river Narmada*. Vol. 1. Ed. by R. Parthasarathy and Ravindra H. Dholakia. New Delhi: Concept, 2011. pp. 141–172. CEPTL, CSSL, EDIL, HML, IIML, SPUL, TRTIL, UML.

Phillips, W.S.K. Perspectives in the development of the tribal affected by the Sardar Sarovar (Narmada) Project. In *Tribal situation in India: issues in development: with special reference to Western India*. Ed. by Vidyut Joshi. Jaipur: Rawat, 1998. pp. 239–251. CSSL, GVL, UML.

Pillai, Pheba Anandan. Successful performance and prospects of SEZs in Gujarat. In *Gujarat economy: the way ahead*. Ed. by Sudha V. Menon. Hyderabad: ICFAI University, 2009. pp. 153–160. EDIL, HML, SGUL, SPIESRL.

Pinto, Stany. Land alienation and adivasi assertion in Bharuch district. In *Development and deprivation in Gujarat: in hounour of Jan Breman*. Ed. by Ghanshyam Shah, Mario Rutten and Hein Streefkerk. New Delhi: Sage, 2002. pp. 214–230. CEEL, CEPTL, CSSL, EDIL, GIDRL, HML, IIML, IRMAL, UML.

Pitroda, Sam and Mody, R.J. *Development of Gujarat-people's perceptions.* Ahmedabad: Sardar Patel Institute of Economic & Social Research, 1997. p. 415. IIML, SPUL.

Pocock, David. Social anthropology: its contribution to planning. In *Crisis of Indian planning: economic policy in the 1960s*. Ed. by Paul Streeten and Michael Lipton. London: Oxford, 1972. pp. 271–289. CSSL.

Prakash, Anjal. *Dark zone: groundwater irrigation, politics and social power in North Gujarat.* New Delhi: Orient Longman, 2005. p. 239. IRMAL.

Prakash, Anjal. Political economy of groundwater governance in Gujarat: a micro-level analysis. In *Governance of water: institutional alternatives and political economy.* Ed. by Vishwa Ballabh. New Delhi: Sage, 2008. pp. 215–236. GVL, IIML, SPIESRL.

Prakash, Anjal. Social differentiation and the politics of access to ground water in North Gujarat. In *Controlling the water matching technology and institutions in irrigation management in India and Nepal.* Ed. by D.K. Roth and Linden Vincent. New Delhi: Oxford, 2013. pp. 200–228. IIML.

Prakash, Anjal and Sama, R.K. Social undercurrents in a Gujarat village: irrigation for the rich versus drinking water for the poor. In *Water conflicts in India: a million revolts in the making*. Ed. by K.J. Joy, et al. London: Routledge, 2008. pp. 38–43. CSSL.

Prathap, Reddy K. Water sector reform policy and operationalization experiences in Gujarat. In *Water and sanitation: institutional challenges in India*. Ed. by Christine Sijbesma and Meine Pieter Van Dijk. New Delhi: Manohar, 2006. pp. 97–120. CSSL.

Prem, Pangotra and Jaryal, Sunil. Public private partnership in infrastructure: C.G. road redevelopment in Ahmedabad: a case study. In *Infrastructure development and financing*. Ed. by G.Raghuram, Rekha Jain and Sidharth Sinha. New Delhi: Macmillan, 1999. pp. 575–586. HML.

Pulparampil, John K. *Nation building from below: a historical study of the municipal government system of an Indian state*. New Delhi: Amarko Book, 1977. p. 143. CSSL.

Punalekar, S.P. Growth, poverty and perception: village level studies in Gujarat and Maharashtra. In *Agrarian structure land reforms and agricultural growth in India.* Ed. by Nasim Ansari. New Delhi: Tata-McGraw Hill, 1991. pp. 286–309. IIML, SPUL.

Raghuram, G. Privatisation of ports and framework for governmental action: Gujarat maritime board: a case study. In *Infrastructure development and financing*. Ed. by G.Raghuram, Rekha Jain and Sidharth Sinha. New Delhi: Macmillan, 1999. pp. 518–547. HML.

Raj, P.A. Sardar Sarovar Project some technical issues. In *Development imperatives and environment concerns Sardar Sarovar Project plan.* Ed. by Mahesh Pathak. Vallabh Vidyanagar: Agro Economic Research Centre, 1995. pp. 40–47. IIML.

Raju, K.V., ed. *Elixir of life: the socio-ecological governance of drinking water.* Bangalore: Books for Change, 2006. p. 408. CSSL.

Raju, K.V., Das, Keshab and Manasi, S. Emerging trends in rural water supply: a comparative analysis of Karnataka and Gujarat. In *Elixir of life: the socio-ecological governance of drinking water.* Ed. by K.V. Raju. Bangalore: Books for Change, 2006. pp. 1–73. CSSL.

Ramachandran, Smitha. Service sector economy of Gujarat. In *Gujarat economy: the way ahead*. Ed. by Sudha V.Menon. Hyderabad: ICFAI University, 2009. pp. 170–183. EDIL, HML, SGUL, SPIESRL.

Ramachandran, Smitha. Ports privatization in Gujrat. In *Gujarat economy: the way ahead*. Ed. by Sudha V.Menon. Hyderabad: ICFAI University, 2009. pp. 142–152. EDIL, HML, SGUL, SPIESRL.

Ramaiah, T.G. Performance of Indira Awaas Yojana: a study in Gujarat state. In *Rural resources and development initiatives*. Ed. by B.S. Vasudeva Rao and G. Rajanikanth. India: Associated, 2007. pp. 22–33. HML.

Ram, Rahul N. Benefits of the Sardar Sarovar Project: are the claims reliable? In *Toward sustainable development: struggling over India's Narmada river*. Ed. by William F. Fisher. Jaipur: Rawat, 1997. pp. 113–134. CSSL.

Rao, K.S. Renewable energy development in Gujarat: potential and constraints. In *Renewable energy for rural development.* Ed. by V.V.N. Kishore and N.K. Bansal. New Delhi: Tata McGraw-Hill, 1989. pp. 543–549. SPUL.

Rathore, N.S. Application of remote sensing for forest cover mapping of South Aravali ranges, Rajasthan and Gujarat, India. In *ICORG-92 remote sensing applications and geographic information systems: recent trends.* Ed. by I.V. Muralikrishna. New Delhi: Tata McGraw-Hill, 1992. p. 280. CEEL.

Ray, C.N. Gujarat. In *Socio-economic profile of rural India,* Vol. 3. Ed. by Rajendra Vora. New Delhi: Centre for Rural Studies, 2005. pp. 341–374. IIML.

Reddy, K.N. *Trend of government activity in India since independence.* Baroda: M.S. University, 1976. p. 85. SPIESRL.

Ruchika Rani. Dynamics of growth in Gujarat. In *Poverty amidst prosperity: essays on the trajectory of development in Gujarat*. Ed. by Atul Sood. Delhi: Aakar, 2012. pp. 39–44. CSSL, IRMAL, MICAL.

Sah, D.C. State, civil society and community: tribal displacement in Gujarat. In *Tribal issues in India.* Ed. by D.C. Sah and Yatindra Sisodia. Jaipur: Rawat, 2004. pp. 269–292. CSSL, GVL.

Sah, D.C. and Tomar, Shubhra S. Sardar Sarovar Project: some contentious issues. In *Sardar Sarovar Project on the river Narmada*. Vol. 2. Ed. by R. Parthasarathy and Ravindra H. Dholakia. New Delhi: Concept, 2011. pp. 380–442. CEPTL, CSSL, EDIL, HML, IIML, SETUL, SPUL, TRTIL, UML.

Sanghvi, P.S. Land problems and reforms in Saurashtra (1955). In *Dissertation in economics 1921–1971*. Ed. by C.H. Shah. Bombay: University of Bombay, 1974. pp. 155–158. SPIESRL.

Sangvai, Sanjay. People's struggle in the Narmada valley: quest for just and sustainable development. In *Water conflicts in India: a million revolts in the making*. Ed. by K.J. Joy, et al. London: Routledge, 2008. pp. 331–337. CSSL.

Sarkar, S.K. Recent initiatives in developing regulatory framework in Gujarat's water sector. In *Regulation in infrastructure services: progress and the way forward*. Ed. by S.K. Sarkar and Kaushik Deb. New Delhi: Tata Energy Research Institute, 2001. pp. 59–67. CEEL.

Sathyapalan, Jyothis and Iyengar, S. Economic valuation of ecosystem changes: salinity ingress and ground water depletion in costal Gujarat. In *Ecology and human well-being*. Ed. by Pushpam Kumar and Sudhakara Reddy B. New Delhi: Sage, 2007. pp. 404-[ ]. SPIESRL.

Satish, S. and Sundar, A. Voluntary agency and cooperative lift irrigation societies: a case study of Panchmahal district in Gujarat. In *People's participation and irrigation management*. New Delhi: Commonwealth, 1990. pp. 9–42. IIML.

Schenk, Hans. Patterns of regional planning in Bulsar district. In *Winners and losers: styles of development and change in an Indian region*. Ed. by S. Devadas Pillai and Chris Baks. Bombay: Popular, 1979. pp. 361–379. CSSL, SPIESRL.

Schenk-Sandbergen, Loes. Women and cooking technology: the vicissitudes of improved stove projects in rural Gujarat. In *Managing rural development: health and energy programmes in India*. Ed. by Hein Streefkerk and T.K. Moulik. New Delhi: Sage, 1991. pp. 161–190. CSSL, HML, IIML, SETUL, SPIESRL, UML.

Shah, Amita. Watershed programmes in Gujarat: a long way to go! In *Dynamics of development in Gujarat*. Ed. by Indira Hirway, S.P. Kashyap and Amita Shah. New Delhi: Concept, 2002. pp. 290–321. CSSL, EDIL, GIDRL, GVL, HML, IRMAL, SPUL, UML.

Shah, Ashvin A. Technical overview of the flawed Sardar Sarovar Project and a proposal for a sustainable alternative. In *Toward sustainable development: struggling over India's Narmada river*. Ed. by William F. Fisher. Jaipur: Rawat, 1997. pp. 319–367. CSSL.

Shah, B.M. Propagation of solar cookers and smokeless chulhas: a case study for Gujarat state. In *Renewable energy for rural development*. Ed. by V.V.N. Kishore and N.K. Bansal. New Delhi: Tata McGraw-Hill, 1989. pp. 295–299. SPUL.

Shah, Ghanshyam and Shah, D.C. Development and resettlement of tribals: Sardar Sarovar in Gujarat. In *Antiquity to modernity in tribal India*. Ed. by S.C. Dube. New Delhi: Inter-India, 1998. pp. 301–333. GVL.

Shah, K.R. *Essays on economics of human resources*. Rohtak: Spellbound, 1997. p. 330. CSSL.

Shah, Maya. Human resource development in Saurashtra. In *Economy of Saurashtra: problems and prospects*. Ed. by D.T. Lakdawala, et al. Bhavnagar: Bhavnagar University, 1990. pp. 51–59. GUL.

Shah, Parmesh. Economics of wasteland development projects undertaken by Gujarat state rural development corporation. In *Wastelands diagnosis and treatment*. Ed. by Hridai R. Yadav. New Delhi: Concept, 1987. pp. 189–216. IIML.

Shah, S.A. Liabilities and assets of Kutch. In *Art, culture and natural history of Kutch*. Ed. by S.K. Bhowmik. Vadodara: Government Press, 1976–77. pp. 64–66. CSSL, TRTIL.

Shah, Tushaar and Bhattacharya, Saumindra. Farmer organization for lift irrigation: irrigation companies and tubewell cooperatives of Gujarat. In *Cooperative management of natural resources*. Ed. by Katar Singh and Vishwa Ballabh. New Delhi: Sage, 1996. pp. 156–175. CSSL.

Shah, Tushaar, et al. Case for pipelining water distribution in the Narmada irrigation system in Gujarat, India. In *Sardar Sarovar Project on the river Narmada*. Vol. 3. Ed. by R. Parthasarathy and Ravindra H. Dholakia. New Delhi: Concept, 2011. pp. 777–799. CEPTL, CSSL, EDIL, HML, IIML, SETUL, SPUL, TRTIL, UML.

Sharan, Girja. *Energy use in rural Gujarat*. New Delhi: Oxford and IBH, 1987. p. 186. IIML, IRMAL, SPUL, TRTIL.

Sharan, Girja and Gopinath, C. *Energy use in rural North Gujarat*. Ahmedabad: Indian Institute of Management, 1983. p. 221. CEEL.

Shelat, Kirit. *Mapping development: based on the experience of Gujarat, India*. Ahmedabad: Deep & Deep, 2003. p. 273. IIML, GIDRL, SPIESRL.

Shelat, Kirit N. *Evolution of rural development*. Ahmedabad: Kathan Education Communication Unit, 1988. p. 287. CSSL, IIML, SPIESRL.

Sheth, Pravin. *Narmada project: politics of eco development*. New Delhi: Har-Anand, 1994. p. 198. CSSL, HML, IIML, SPIESRL, SPUL, TRTIL.

Sheth, Pravin. Narmada project: some critical issues. In *Development* imperatives *and environment concerns Sardar Sarovar Project plan*. Ed. by Mahesh Pathak. Vallabh Vidyanagar: Agro Economic Research Centre, 1995. pp. 184–205. IIML.

Sheth, Pravin. Story of the Sardar Sarovar Project: a development model with a difference. In *Sardar Sarovar Project on the river Narmada*. Vol. 2. Ed. by R. Parthasarathy and Ravindra H. Dholakia. New Delhi: Concept, 2011. pp. 559–585. CEPTL, CSSL, EDIL, HML, IIML, SETUL, SPUL, TRTIL, UML.

Shinoda, Takashi. Institutional change and entrepreneurial development in the SSI sector of Gujarat. In *Dynamics of development in Gujarat*. Ed. by Indira Hirway, S.P. Kashyap and Amita Shah. New Delhi: Concept, 2002. pp. 197–237. CSSL, EDIL, GIDRL, GVL, HML, IRMAL, SPUL, UML.

Shivananda, H.M. and Mukundan, K. Gujarat: urban development dynamics. In *New development paradigms and challenges for Western and Central India*. (Vol. 2). Ed. by R. Parthsarathy and Sudarshan Iyenger. Ahmedabad: Gujarat Institute of Development Recearch, 2006. pp. 181–216. CSSL, EDIL, GIDRL, SPIESRL.

Shivanand Swamy, H.M. and Mukundan, K. Gujarat urban development dynamics. In *Gujarat: perspectives of the future*. Ed. by R. Swaminathan. New Delhi: Academic, 2008. pp. 195–212. CSSL, EDIL, GIDRL, GVL, IIML, SETUL, SPIESRL.

Shroff, Manu. Economic viability of the SSP. In *Development imperatives and environment concerns Sardar Sarovar Project plan*. Ed. by Mahesh Pathak. Vallabh Vidyanagar: Agro Economic Research Centre, 1995. pp. 113–117. IIML.

Shylendra, H.S. and Uma Rani. Rural-urban linkages, occupational diversification, and sustainable rural livelihood systems. In *In search of sustainable livelihood systems: managing resources and change*. Ed. by Ruedi Baumgartner and Ruedi Hogger. New Delhi: Sage, 2004. pp. 126–149. CSSL, SPUL.

Singh, Baldev. *Regional planning: explorations in agriculture and industry*. New Delhi: Oxford, 1981. p. 247. CSSL.

Singh, Mridula, et al. *Displacement by Sardar Sarovar and Tehri: a comparative study of two dams.* New Dehli: Multiple Action Research Group, 1992. p. 175. CSSL.

Skutsch, Margaret M. Success of mixed motives: stove and forestry programmes in Gujarat. In *Managing rural development: health and energy programmes in India.* Ed. by Hein Streefkerk and T.K. Moulik. New Delhi: Sage, 1991. pp. 191–207. CSSL, HML, IIML, SETUL, SPIESRL, UML.

Sood, Atul. Rousing growth amidst raging disparities. In *Poverty amidst prosperity: essays on the trajectory of development in Gujarat*. Ed. by Atul Sood. Delhi: Aakar, 2012. pp. 1–38. CSSL, IRMAL, MICAL.

Spodek, Howarch. *Urban-rural integration in regional development: a case study of Saurashtra, India, 1800–1960.* Chicago: University of Chicago, 1976. p. 144. SPUL.

Srinivas, K. Quiet flows the Narmada: a recapitulation of events surrounding the efforts to harness the Narmada waters for the public weal. In *Sardar Sarovar Project on the river Narmada*. Vol. 2. Ed. by R. Parthasarathy and Ravindra H. Dholakia. New Delhi: Concept, 2011. pp. 512–531. CEPTL, CSSL, EDIL, HML, IIML, SETUL, SPUL, TRTIL, UML.

Srivastava, V.K. and Sharan, Girja. *Wind energy for water pumping from policy to action(An evaluation of progress in Gujarat.* New Delhi: Oxford and IBH, 1986. p. 105. CEEL, IIML.

Subnis, S.B. Eco-environmental and wildlife management studies of Narmada basin in Gujarat an update. In *Development imperatives and environment concerns Sardar Sarovar Project plan.* Ed. by Mahesh Pathak. Vallabh Vidyanagar: Agro Economic Research Centre, 1995. pp. 95–101. IIML.

Sulaiman, Naushad A. *Sardar Sarovar: a boon or a disaster*? New Delhi: Mohit, 2007. p. 158. CSSL.

Swaminathan, R., ed. *Gujarat: perspectives of the future*. New Delhi: Academic, 2008. p. 357. CSSL, EDIL, GIDRL, GVL, IIML, SETUL, SPIESRL, IRMAL.

Tiwari, S.P., Pande, V.C. and Virendra Kumar. Antisar watershed development plan through people empowerment-Antisar. In *Participatory rural appraisal for watershed management(Case studies).*Ed. by J.S. Samra and A.S. Mishra. Dehradun: Central Soil & Water Conservation Research & Training Institute, 1998. pp. 87–114. SPIESRL.

Trivedi, A.B. and Mehta, Gaganvihari L. *Post-war Gujarat: an economic survey after world war-II*. Bombay: Bhagirathi Press, 1949. p. 289. AAUL, ASL, CSSL, IRMAL, SPUL.

Udall, Lori. International Narmada campaign: a case study of sustained advocacy. In *Toward sustainable development: struggling over India's Narmada river*. Ed. by William F. Fisher. Jaipur: Rawat, 1997. pp. 201–227. CSSL.

Uma Rani. Core issues in the economy and society of Gujarat. In *In Search of sustainable livelihood systems: managing resources and change*. Ed. by Ruedi Baumgartner and Ruedi Hogger. New Delhi: Sage, 2004. pp. 81–93. CEEL, CSSL, SPUL, SPIESRL.

Unni, Jeemol. *Sustainable development and social security: role of the non-farm Sector.* New Delhi: Vikas, 2000. p. 275. CSSL.

Vaidya, R.D. Prototype developed by Gujarat matikam kalakari and rural technology institute. In *Technology and rural India*. Ed. by S.V. Prabhath and P. Sita Devi. New Delhi: Global Research, 2012. pp. 231–244. AAUL.

Vakil, C.N. History of economic research in India, its importance and the need for its encouragement: with particular reference to Gujarat. In *Poverty, planning and inflation*. by C.N. Vakil. New Delhi: Allied, 1978. pp. 198–210. CSSL, HML.

Vakil, C.N. Role of the economist in the economic development of Gujarat. In *Poverty, planning and inflation*. by C.N. Vakil. New Delhi: Allied, 1978. pp. 184–197. CSSL, HML.

Vakil, C.N., Lakdawala, D.T. and Desai, M.B. *Economic survey of Saurashtra*. Bombay: University of Bombay, 1953. p. 664. CSSL, UML.

Van Dorsten, F. Impact of Amul on the milk economy of the Kheda district. In *Resource, institutions and strategies*. Ed. by Martin Doornbos and K.N. Nair. New Delhi: Sage, 1990. pp. 67–76. TRTIL.

Vasavada, Shilpa. Mainstreaming gender concerns in participatory irrigation management: the role of AKRSP(I) in South Gujarat. In *Flowing upstream: empowering women through water management initiatives in India*. Ed. by Sara Ahmed. Ahmedabad: Centre for Environment Education, 2005. pp. 123–152. CEEL, CSSL.

Vashisht, Pankaj and Arya, Gaurav. Public-private partnership: insights from infrastructure development. *In Poverty amidst prosperity: essays on the trajectory of development in Gujarat*. Ed. by Atul Sood. Delhi: Aakar, 2012. pp. 61–87. CSSL, IRMAL, MICAL.

Veerashekharappa, Raju, K.V. and Manasi, S. Financing rural drinking water supply: a case study of Karnataka and Gujarat. In *Elixir of life: the socio-ecological governance of drinking water*. Ed. by K.V. Raju. Bangalore: Books for Change, 2006. pp. 212–234. CSSL.

Vishwanath, B.N. Environmental perceptions in irrigation projects: overview. In *Sardar Sarovar Project: a promise for plenty*. Ed. by Mahesh T. Pathak. New Delhi: Oxford, 1991. pp. 23–47. CSSL, SPUL.

Vishwanath, B.N. and Nair, E. Narayanan. *Socio-economic study of Karjan command area Bharuch Gujarat*. Ahmedabad: Centre for Environmental Planning and Technology, 1979. p. 114. CEPTL, IIML.

Vittal, N. Organisational challenges in police-Gujarat experiment. In *Red tape guerrilla: a game of tactics*. New Delhi: Vikas, 1996. pp. 245–247. CSSL, IIML.

Vyas, Jay Narayan. Saradar Sarovar Project: the engineering marvel. In *Sardar Sarovar Project on the river Narmada*. Vol. 1. Ed. by R. Parthasarathy and Ravindra H. Dholakia. New Delhi: Concept, 2011. pp. 15–31. CSSL, SETUL, SPUL, UML.

Vyas, V.S., Bhatt, Anil and Shah, S.M. *Decentralised planning in India*. Delhi: Oxford, [ ]. p. 87. CEEL, GVL.

Whitby, Caroline. Community participation in lift irrigation management in Panchmahals district, Gujarat. In *India: irrigation management partnerships*. Ed. by M.V.K. Sivamohan. Hyderabad: Booklinks, 1994. pp. 351–368. CSSL.

Whitehead, Judy. Submerged voice and transnational environmentalism: the movement against the Sardar Sarovar dam. In *Water first: issues and challenges for nations and communities in South Asia*. Ed. by Kuntalal Lahiri Dutt and Robert J. Wasson. New Delhi: Sage, 2008. pp. 295–315. IIML.

Wood, John R. *Politics of water resource development in India: the Narmada dams controversy*. New Delhi: Sage, 2007. p. 285. AERCL, CEEL, CSSL, IIML, SPUL.

World Bank. India – Sardar Sarovar (Narmada) Project. In *Development imperatives and environment concerns Sardar Sarovar Project plan*. Ed. by Mahesh Pathak. Vallabh Vidyanagar: Agro Economic Research Centre, 1995. pp. 118–127. IIML.

Journal Articles

Acharya, Akash. Land acquisitions loss of employment and women's participation in income generation: a case study of coastal belt of South Gujarat. *Man and Development*. 24, 3, 2002. pp. 79–86. CSSL, IRMAL, UML.

Aditya Srinivas, V. and Pandya, Ashish N. Infrastructure development: a reference to port policy of Gujarat and Surat's position. *Vishleshan*. 31, 2, 2006. pp. 30–36. IIML.

Advani, P.B. Electricity supply in Gujarat. *Journal of the Gujarat Research Society*. 11, 1, 1949. pp. 2–5. GUL.

Alagh, Y.K. Gujarat: the decisive phase. *Anvesak*. 25, 1, 1995. pp. 116–123. GIDRL, IRMAL, SPIESRL.

Alagh, Y.K., Shah, Jayshree and Shah, Vinod K. Infrastructure planning. *Anvesak*. 27, 1 and 2, 1997. pp. 47–64. GIDRL, SPIESRL.

Alagh, Yoginder K. Education, technology and growth in Gujarat. *Artha-Vikas*. 34, 1, 1998. pp. 1–10. CSSL, GIDRL, IRMAL.

Alagh, Yoginder K., Kashyap, S.P. and Desai, Rohit D. Consistent forecasting model of Gujarat's economy. *Anvesak*. 2, 2, 1972. pp. 123–137. CSSL, IRMAL, SGUL, SPIESRL.

Anand, P.B. and Vyas, Anjana. Some issues in management of urban water supply systems: a case study of Ahmedabad. *Nagarlok*. 20, 2, 1988. pp. 66–79. SPIESRL.

Baba Amte. Narmada project: the case against and an alternative perspective. *Economic and Political Weekly*. 25, 16, 1990. pp. 811–818. CEPTL, CSSL, IIML, IRMAL, SGUL, SPIESRL, UML.

Bagchi, Amiya Kumar, Das, Panchanan and Chattopadhyay, Sadhan Kumar. Growth and structural change in the economy of Gujarat, 1970–2000. *Economic and Political Weekly*. 40, 28, 2005. pp. 3039–3047. BUL, CEPTL, CSSL, EDIL, GIDRL, IIML, IRMAL, MICAL, SGUL, SPIESRL, UML.

Bagdi, G.L., Samra, J.S. and Kumar, V. Adoption of soil and water conservation technologies by the farmers of Sardar Sarovar Project catchment in Gujarat state. *Indian Journal of Soil Conservation*. 29,1,2001. pp. 65–68. GIDRL.

Bajpai, Gita. Some aspects of urban growth in colonial India: a case study of Surat city in the second half of the nineteenth century. *Anvesak*. 16, 1, 1986. pp. 33–47. CSSL, GIDRL, SPIESRL.

Basant, Rakesh. Diversification of economic activities in rural Gujarat: key results of a primary survey. *Indian Journal of Labour Economics*. 36, 3, 1993. pp. 361–386. CEPTL, CSSL, IRMAL.

Bayanwala, Vishakha and Kulkarni, K.M. Communication network crucial infrastructure for growth and modernity: a study of Ahmedabad city. *Indian Journal of Regional Science*. 32, 2, 2000. pp. 32–41. CSSL.

Berenschot, Ward. Everyday mediation: the politics of public service delivery in Gujarat, India. *Development and Change*. 41, 5, 2010. pp. 883–905. CSSL, EDIL, GIDRL.

Bhat, V.G. Tribal economy of Gujarat. *Khadi Gramodyog*. 14, 3, 1967. pp. 286–287. TRTIL.

Bhatt, Madhubhai P. Role of district planning boards in the rural water supply in Gujarat: a case study (1980–1990). *Vishleshan*. 17, 3, 1992. pp. 117–125. CSSL, IRMAL.

Bhatt, Mahesh and Chawda, V.K. Economic growth of Gujarat deceleration in the third plan: some reasons. *Economic Weekly*. 17, 39, 1965. pp. 1481–1486. HML, SPIESRL, UML.

Bhatt, Mahesh P. Grim picture of basic infrastructure in Gujarat. *Vishleshan*. 23, 2, 1998. pp. 70–75. IIML, IRMAL.

Bhatt, Sonal. Impact of Jyoti Gram Scheme on rural life and economy in Gujarat: a case study of four villages in Anand district. *Journal of Rural Development*. 27, 3, 2008. pp. 501–522. CSSL, IRMAL.

Bhatt, Sonal. Users' perceptions on pricing of canal irrigation and service delivery: an empirical study in Fatewadi canal command area in Gujarat. *Artha Vijnana*. 48, 4, 2006. pp. 341–360. CSSL, GIDRL, UML.

Bhattacharya, B. and Loganathan, M. Social forces pervading Narmada valley development project. *Journal of Rural Development*. 8, 5, 1989. pp. 485–496. CSSL.

Bidwai, Praful. Sardar Sarovar and the Morse report: a damning indictment. *Social Action*. 42, 3, 1992. pp. 316–327. CSSL.

Capoor, H.K.L. Gujarat: the collector in different states. *Indian Journal of Public Administration*. 11, 3, 1965. pp. 441–452. SGUL.

Chinchmalatpure, Anil R., Nayak, A.K. and Rao, Gururaja G. Land use planning of the Bara tract area under Sardar Sarovar canal command of Gujarat. *Indian Farming*. 60, 1, 2010. pp. 15–19. GVL.

Chitharanjan, K.V., Vyas, Anjana and Gupta, Pankaj Kumar. Pricing urban services: case of water supply and sewerage in Baroda city. *Nagarlok*. 25, 2, 1993. pp. 48–55. SPIESRL.

Chudasama, K.M. Port-based development in Gujarat: analysis and opportunities ahead. *Vishleshan*. 35, 2, 2010. pp. 1–14. CSSL, IIML.

Dadi, M.M., Shah, M.N. and Parikh, Y.O. Survey of research on Gujarat economy. *Anvesak*. 12, 2, 1982. pp. 1–32. CEPTL, CSSL, GIDRL, IRMAL, SPIESRL.

Das, Biswaroop. Submerging tribal belt in Gujarat: spatial variations, and stratification. *Vishleshan*. 6, 1, 1986. pp. 24–52. CSSL.

Das, Keshab. Village water tanks in Gujarat's desert region potential and relevance. *International Journal of Rural Management*. 5, 2, 2009. pp. 129–144. IRMAL.

Das, Panchanan. Deregulations, output growth and structural change: a comparative study of West Bengal and Gujarat. *Social Change and Development*. 4, 2006. pp. 83–102. CSSL.

Dave, J.B. Rural water supply programme in Gujarat. *Vishleshan*. 6, 1, 1980. pp. 13–20. CSSL, GIDRL, IIML.

Desai, Anjana and Subramanian, Chandra. Sustainable development for backward rural areas: Nalkantha region of Gujarat, India. *Journal of Human Ecology*. 6, 3, 1995. pp. 177–180. CSSL.

Desai, Anjana, Khanna, Sulbha and Subramanian, Chandra. Economic sustainability in a backward region of Gujarat: Nalkantha region. *Journal of Rural Development*. 14, 3, 1995. pp. 287–299. CSSL, GVL, IIML, IRMAL.

Desai, Hasmukh G. Economic study of milk business in South Gujarat: problems and remedies: with context of Valsad and Dangs district. *Vishleshan*. 35, 3, 2010. pp. 1–16. CSSL, IIML.

Desai, M.B. and Shah, C.H. Rural economy of reconstituted Gujarat. *Journal of the Gujarat Research Society*. 14, 3, 1952. pp. 111–148. GUL.

Dhagamwar, Vasudha. Reflections on the Narmada movement. *Seminar*. 413, 1994. pp. 91–94. CSSL, MICAL, UML.

Dharmadhikary, Shripad. Hydropower from Sardar Sarovar: need, justification and viability. *Economic and Political Weekly*. 27, 48, 1993. pp. 2584–2588. CEPTL, CSSL, IIML, IRMAL, SGUL, SPIESRL, UML.

Dholakia, Archana R. Provision of municipal fire services with special reference to Baroda. *Nagarlok*. 16, 2, 1984. pp. 61–69. CEPTL, SPIESRL.

Dholakia, Ravindra and Shah, Vinod K. Changing ranks of talukas over a short period of time: a study of Gujarat. *Artha-Vikas*. 15, 1, 1979. pp. 74–88. AAUL, CEPTL, GIDRL, GVL, HML, SGUL.

Dholakia, Ravindra H. Liberalisation in Gujarat: review of recent experience. *Economic and Political Weekly*. 35, 35 and 36, 2000. pp. 3121–3124. BUL, CEPTL, CSSL, EDIL, GIDRL, IIML, IRMAL, MICAL, SGUL, SPIESRL, UML.

Dholakia, Ravindra H. Sources of economic growth and acceleration in Gujarat. *Economic and Political Weekly*. 42, 9, 2007. pp. 770–778. BUL, CEPTL, CSSL, EDIL, GIDRL, IIML, IRMAL, MICAL, SGUL, SPIESRL, SUL, UML.

Diwakara, H. Determinants of trust and cooperation case study of self managed tube well organization in North Gujarat, India. *International Journal of Rural Management*. 2, 2, 2006. pp. 163–189. IRMAL.

Dixit, Anita K. Dilution of the public distribution system fallout on tribal communities in Gujarat. *Social Action*. 57, 1, 2007. pp. 65–73. CEPTL, CSSL, EDIL, GVL, IIML.

D'Souza, Rohan, Mukhopadhyay, Pranab and Kothari, Ashish. Re-evaluating multi-purpose river valley projects: a case study of Hirakund, Ukai and IGNP. *Economic and Political Weekly*. 33, 6, 1998. pp. 297–302. CEPTL, CSSL, IIML, IRMAL, MICAL, SGUL, SPIESRL, UML.

Dubash, Navroz K. Ecologically and socially embedded exchange. *Economic and Political Weekly*. 35, 16, 2000. pp. 1376–1385. BUL, CEPTL, CSSL, GIDRL, IIML, IRMAL, MICAL, SGUL, SPIESRL, UML.

Durgaprasad, P. and Srinivasan, S. Partnerships and networking in drinking water projects: user group, NGO and training institute initiatives in Gujarat. *Journal of Rural Development*. 20, 4, 2001. pp. 721–742. CSSL, GIDRL, GVL, IIML, IRMAL.

Dutta, Indira. Sustainable development in Gujarat: a far cry. *Indian Journal of Public Administration*. 57, 4, 2011. pp. 897–912. CSSL, EDIL.

Dwivedi, Ranjit. Displacement, risks and resistance: local perceptions and actions in the Sardar Sarovar. *Development and Change*. 30, 1, 1999. pp. 43–78. GVL, IIML.

Garg, Priti and Garg, Renuka. In pursuit of making water everybody's concern: experiences from Gujarat. *Nagarlok*. 36, 3, 2004. pp. 1–9. GIDRL, SPIESRL.

Garg, Priti and Garg, Renuka. Reinventing the city: the Surat municipal corporation way... *Nagarlok*. 36, 4, 2004. pp. 24–27. GIDRL, SPIESRL.

Garikipati, Supriya. Resettlement sites of Narmada valley project: some revealing insights. *Economic and Political Weekly*. 37, 23, 2002. pp. 2257–2266. BUL, CEPTL, CSSL, EDIL, IIML, IRMAL, MICAL, SGUL, SPIESRL, UML.

George, P.V. Gibrat's law and growth of corporations in Gujarat: a regional study. *Anvesak*. 2, 1, 1972. pp. 1–10. CSSL, GIDRL, IRMAL, SGUL, SPIESRL.

Gidwani, Vinay. Cultural logic of work: explaining labour deployment and piece-rate contracts in Matar Taluka, Gujarat parts I and II. *Journal of Development Studies*. 38, 2, 2001. pp. 57–108. GIDRL.

Gohil, B.K. Provision of infrastructure in Gujarat. *Artha-Vikas*. 9, 1–2, 1973. pp. 69–99. GVL, HML, SGUL.

Gohil, D.C. Growth and development of SSI in Gujarat: a study. *Southern Economist*. 44, 17, 2006. pp. 10–12. SGUL.

Gontia, N.K. and Sikarwar, R.S. Rainwater harvesting and groundwater recharge in Saurashtra region of Gujarat: a success story. *Indian Journal of Soil Conservation*. 33, 3, 2005. pp. 256–258. GIDRL.

Guha, G.S. Planning for difficult land and water regimes: a case of the Panchal region of Gujarat. *Anvesak*. 21, 2, 1991. pp. 145–150. CSSL, SPIESRL.

Gupta, D.B. and Acharya, B.V. Investigation into urban growth: a case study of Surat city. *Artha-Vikas*. 10, 2, 1974. pp. 86–91. AAUL, SGUL.

Gupta, Shibshankar P. Reforms of urban property: a case study of municipal corporation in Gujarat. Anvesak. 1,1,1971. pp. 35–55. CSSL, IRMAL, SPIESRL.

Gururaja Rao, G. and Nayak, A.K. Land use planning of the bara tract area under Sardar Sarovar canal command of Gujarat. *Indian Farming*. 60, 1, 2010. pp. 15–17. IRMAL.

Hashim, S.R. Block level planning in Gujarat. *Journal of the M.S. University of Baroda*. 29, 2, 1980. pp. 1–8. GVL.

Hirway, Indira. Cricital evaluation of the first phase of the block level planning experiment in Gujarat. *Anvesak*. 11, 2, 1981. pp. 220–246. CSSL, IRMAL, SPIESRL.

Hirway, Indira. Dynamics of development: some issues. *Economic and Political Weekly*. 35, 35 and 36, 2000. pp. 3106–3120. BUL, CEPTL, CSSL, GIDRL, IIML, IRMAL, MICAL, SGUL, SPIESRL, UML.

Hirway, Indira. Economic growth, rural labour markets and rural poverty: understanding the linkages. *Indian Journal of Labour Economics*. 38, 1, 1995. pp. 63-[ ]. SPIESRL.

Hirway, Indira. Selective development and widening disparities in Gujarat. *Economic and Political Weekly*. 30, 41 and 42, 1995. pp. 2603–2618. CEPTL, CSSL, IIML, IRMAL, MICAL, SGUL, SPIESRL, TRTIL, UML.

Hirway, Indira. Some aspects of the pattern of economic development in Gujarat. *Vishleshan*. 18, 3, 1993. pp. 85–112. CSSL, IIML, IRMAL.

Hirway, Indira and Goswami, Subhrangsu. Functioning of the drinking water component of the Narmada pipeline project in Gujarat. *Economic and Political Weekly*. 43, 9, 2008. pp. 51–59. BUL, CEPTL, CSSL, EDIL, IIML, IRMAL, MICAL, SGUL, SPIESRL, SUL, UML.

Jain, Sunder Singh. Sardar Sarovar and Narmada sagar projects. *Agricultural Situation in India*. 42, 3, 1987. pp. 177-[ ]. SPIESRL.

Jain-Govil, Pallavi. Watershed development in village Kavadia Kheda. *Administrator*. 41, 2, 1996. pp. 81–99. CSSL, TRTIL.

Javadekar, P.A. Survey of research on Gujarat economy. *Anvesak*. 20, 1–2, 1990. pp. 163–178. CEPTL, CSSL, IRMAL, SPIESRL.

Jayaraman, T.K. Watershed projects in Gujarat: an evaluation through production function analysis. *Vishleshan*. 4, 4, 1978. pp. 284–292. CSSL, GIDRL, IIML.

Jayaraman, T.K. and Savdasia, V.B. Development of backward areas in Gujarat state. *Indian Journal of Public Administration*. 23, 3, 1977. pp. 668–687. GVL, SGUL.

John, Mathew. Interpreting Narmada judgment. *Economic and Political Weekly*. 36, 32, 2001. pp. 3030–3034. BUL, CEPTL, CSSL, EDIL, IIML, IRMAL, MICAL, SGUL, SPIESRL, UML.

Joshi, G.N. Agricultural and economic development in Gujarat. *Anvesak*. 16, 2, 1986. pp. 57–84. CSSL, IRMAL, SPIESRL.

Joshi, G.N. Dynamics of sectoral development in Gujarat. *Vishleshan*. 26, 1, 2001. pp. 51–55. IIML, IRMAL.

Joshi, Rakesh Mohan. Gujarat electricity board's turn around. *Administrator*. 50, 1, 2007.99–120. CSSL, IRMAL.

Judge, Paramjit S. Response to dams and displacement in two Indian states. *Asian Survey*. 37, 9, 1997. pp. 840–851. CSSL.

Kala, Pablo. In the spaces of erasure: globalisation, resistance and Narmada river. *Economic and Political Weekly*. 36, 22, 2001. pp. 1991–2002. BUL, CEPTL, CSSL, EDIL, IIML, IRMAL, MICAL, SGUL, SPIESRL, UML.

Kalaiyarasan, A. Comparison of developmental outcomes in Gujarat and Tamil Nadu. *Economic and Political Weekly*. 49, 15, 2014. pp. 55–63. CSSL, UML.

Kamdar, K.H. Some observations on marketing in Northern Gujarat and Kathiawad and at Bombay. *Indian Journal of Economics*. 9, 1929. pp. 548–562. HML.

Kashyap, Manjari. Spread of infrastructure facilities in rural Gujarat: a preliminary exercise. *Anvesak*. 25, 2, 1995. pp. 31–45. CSSL, GIDRL, IRMAL, SPIESRL.

Kashyap, Majari. Spread of infrastructure facilities in rural Gujarat: a preliminary exercise. *Anvesak*. 27, 1 and 2, 1997. pp. 181–193. GIDRL, SPIESRL.

Kashyap, S.P. Nature of growth process in Gujarat: a survey of research. *Anvesak*. 12, 1, 1982. pp. 1–56. CEPTL, CSSL, GIDRL, IRMAL, SPIESRL.

Kashyap, S.P. and Desai, Rohit D. Hirschman's linkage hypothesis: a regional test. *Indian Journal of Labour Economics*. 17, 3–4, 1974–75. pp. 143–154. SPIESRL.

Khatri, M.R. and Suryanarayana, T.M.V. Estimation of water requirement of cotton and tur grown in the command area of Waghodia branch of Deo irrigation project, Gujarat. *Journal of Agrometeorology*. 10, 2, 2008. pp. 333–335. IRMAL.

Kothari, Ashish and Bhartari, Rajiv. Narmada valley project: development or destruction? *Economic and Political Weekly*. 19, 22 and 23, 1984. pp. 907–920. CEPTL, CSSL, GUL, IIML, IRMAL, SGUL, SPIESRL, UML.

Kulkarni, K.M. and Bayanwala, V. Geographical analysis of intraurban transport infrastructure in Ahmedabad city. *Deccan Geographer*. 37, 1, 1999, pp. 32–48. HML.

Kumar, Dinesh M. Institutions for efficient and equitable use of groundwater irrigation management institutions and water markets Gujarat. *Asia-Pacific Journal of Rural Development*. 10, 1, 2000. pp. 52–65. IRMAL.

Kundu, Amitabh. Globalising Gujarat: urbanisation, employment and poverty. *Economic and Political Weekly*. 35, 35 and 36, 2000. pp. 3172–3182. BUL, CEPTL, CSSL, GIDRL, IIML, IRMAL, MICAL, SGUL, SPIESRL, UML.

Kurien, Verghese. Amul saga. *Seminar*. 498, 2001. pp. 41–44. CSSL, MICAL, UML.

Lahiri, Ashok K., et al. Economic consequences of Gujarat earthquake. *Economic and Political Weekly*. 36, 21, 2001. pp. 1319–1332. BUL, CEPTL, CSSL, EDIL, GIDRL, IIML, IRMAL, MICAL, SGUL, SPIESRL, UML.

Mehta, Dinesh B. Urban development strategy for Gujarat: an over view. *Vishleshan*. 20, 1, 1995. pp. 25–38. CSSL, IRMAL.

Mehta, L. Manufacture of popular perceptions of scarcity: dams and water-related narratives in Gujarat, India. *World Development*. 29, 12, 2001. pp. 2025–2041. GIDRL, IRMAL.

Mehta, Lyla. Contexts and constructions of water scarcity. *Economic and Political Weekly*. 38, 48, 2003. pp. 5066–5072. BUL, CEPTL, CSSL, EDIL, IIML, IRMAL, MICAL, SGUL, SPIESRL, UML.

Mehta, Niti. Imbalances in development between religions and social groups: evidences from Gujarat. *Anvesak*. 36, 1, 2006. pp. 1–31. CSSL, SPIESRL.

Mehta, R.S. and Desai, M.B. Changes and its agencies in community development: reflections from the study of a community development block in Gujarat. *Indian Journal of Agricultural Economics*. 19, 3/4, 1964. pp. 147–166. TRTIL, UML.

Mehta, S.S. Deceleration of Gujarat economy since 1960. *Vishleshan*. 14, 1, 1989. pp. 29–32. GIDRL.

Mehta, Sanat. Changing economic profile of Gujarat. *Vishleshan*. 34, 2, 2009. pp. 25–51. CSSL, IIML, IRMAL.

Misra, V.N. Acreage response in Gujarat: an inter district analysis. *Anvesak*. 3, 1–2, 1973. pp. 103–136. CSSL, SPIESRL.

Mohidden, Md. Azeez. Some observations on the impact of development programmes in Kutch district of Gujarat state. *Vanyajati*. 36, 1, 1988. pp. 5–9. CSSL.

Morris, Sebastian. Regulatory strategy and restructuring: model for Gujarat power sector. *Economic and Political Weekly*. 35, 23, 2000. pp. 1915–1929. BUL, CEPTL, CSSL, GIDRL, IIML, IRMAL, MICAL, SGUL, SPIESRL, UML.

Mote, V.L. and Shah, B.G. Concept of planning: a case study. *Economic and Political Weekly*. 7, 9, 1972. pp. M-7-M-14. CSSL, IRMAL, SPIESRL, UML.

Moulik, T.K. Introduction of community biogas plant in a Gujarat village: case study of technological and organizational interventions. *Changing Villages*. 4, 4, 1982. pp. 1–14. CSSL, GVL.

Nagaraj, R. and Pandey, Shruti. Have Gujarat and Bihar outperformed the rest of India? a statistical note. *Economic and Political Weekly*. 48, 39, 2013. pp. 39–41. CSSL, SPIESRL, SUL, UML.

Naik, K.S. and Masavi, Mustali I. Economy of small town in Gujarat. *Khadi Gramodyog*. 18, 2, 1971. pp. 151–154. TRTIL.

Nambiar, R.G. Future water demands: the impact of growth on the water use patterns in selected sectors of the Gujarat's economy: 1969–2000. *Arth-Vikas*. 13, 1, 1977. pp. 1–13. GIDRL, GVL, HML, SGUL.

Nambiar, R.G. Impact of growth on the water use patterns in selected sectors of the Gujarat. *Journal of Economic Development*. 12, 1, 1977. pp. 1–13. CEPTL.

Narala, Anuraddha and Zala, Y.C. Technical efficiency of Rice farms under irrigated conditions in Central Gujarat. *Agricultural Economic Research Review*. 23, 2, 2010. pp. 375–382. IIML.

Narayanan, E. Regionalisation analysis: a case study of the Surendranagar district economy. *Artha-Vikas*. 16, 1, 1980. pp. 41–50. CEPTL, CSSL, GIDRL, HML.

Narayanan Nair, E. Ahmedabad urban economy and its planning perspectives. *Nagarlok*. 14, 1, 1982. pp. 28–32. CEPTL.

Painuly, J.P., Parikh, Jyoti K. and Shah, D.R. Rural energy system and agriculture: alternative scenarios for Gujarat. *Economic and Political Weekly*. 27, 34, 1992. pp. 1801–1809. CEPTL, CSSL, IIML, IRMAL, SPIESRL, UML.

Pandya, Hinal. Resettlement and rehabilitation programme of Sardar Sarovar Project in Gujarat. *Third Concept*. 23, 274, 2009. pp. 19–30. CSSL, SPUL.

Pandya, N.M. Growth characteristics of South Gujarat towns. *Journal of the Maharaja Sayajirao University of Baroda*. 19, 2, 1970. pp. 79–86. GVL.

Parekh, K.M. Determinants of urban services in Gujarat: a preliminary analysis. *Nagarlok*. 21, 1, 1989. pp. 68–75. CEPTL.

Parekh, K.M. Growth of Gujarat economy: 1960–61 to 1978–79: a preliminary analysis. *Anvesak*. 10, 2, 1980. pp. 195–201. CEPTL, CSSL, SPIESRL.

Parekh, K.M. Some aspects of growth performance of Gujarat state: a structural analysis. *Artha-Vikas*. 20, 1 and 2, 1984. pp. 94–104. CSSL, GIDRL, GVL, HML.

Parikh, Kirit S. Equitable sustainable development of Gujarat. *Economic and Political Weekly*. 31, 19, 1996. pp. 1151–1164. Also in *Vishleshan*. 20, 1, 1995. pp. 1–24. CSSL, GIDRL, IIML, IRMAL, SGUL.

Parmar, B.D. Intra-regional imbalances in development of Saurashtra: a quantitative. *Indian Journal of Regional Science*. 17, 2, 1985. pp. 87–94. GIDRL.

Parthasarathy, R. Economic status, poverty and diversification of activities among rural artisan households in Gujarat. *Indian Journal of Labour Economics*. 37, 4, 1994. pp. 685–694. CSSL.

Patel, A.S. Canal water rates: a critical review: a case study of Gujarat in India. *Anvesak*. 20, 1–2, 1990. pp. 59–74. CEPTL, CSSL, IRMAL, SPIESRL.

Patel, Anil, et al. Rehabilitation and resettlement in Sardar Sarovar Project: are the critics right? *Social Action*. 41, 3, 1991. pp. 327–344. CSSL.

Patel, D.A. and Singh, P.K. Management of cooking energy needs by the rural households of Gujarat. *Arth-Vikas*. 28–30, 1992–1994. pp. 23–28. GIDRL, IRMAL.

Patel, D.A., Singh, P.K. and Desai, M.M. Economic evaluation of gobar gas plants in Mehsana districts of Gujarat state. *Agricultural Situation in India*. 48, 1, 1993. pp. 17–22. IIML.

Patel, Jashbhai. Is national interest being served by Narmada project? *Economic and Political Weekly*. 29, 30, 1994. pp. 1957–1964. CEPTL, CSSL, IIML, MICAL, SPIESRL, UML.

Patel, Madhukant. Study on prosperity of economic development in Gujarat: through SEZ. *Artha-Vikas*. 45, 2, 2009. pp. 37–44. CSSL.

Patel, Nilesh B. Consumption pattern of food and non-food in India and in Gujarat: a comparative analysis. *VNSGU Journal of Humanities & Social Sciences*. 3, 1, 2011. pp. 98–109. CSSL.

Patel, R.J., Vaishnav, M.R. and Desai, D.R. Economic analysis of surface and sprinkler methods of irrigation in Gujarat. *Agriculture and Agro-Industries Journal*. 13, 3, 1980. pp. 9–14. IIML.

Patel, S.M. Performance of bio-gas plants in Gujarat. *Khadi Gramodyog*. 21, 11, 1975. pp. 493–502. GVL, SGUL.

Patel, Surendra J. Growing regional inequalities in Gujarat. *Economic and Political Weekly*. 26, 26, 1991. pp. 1618–1623. CEPTL, CSSL, IIML, IRMAL, SPIESRL, UML.

Pathak, B.S. Energy crisis and biogas technology: an experience in Gujarat state. *Khadi Gramodyog*. 31, 3, 1984. pp. 154–161. GVL.

Pathak, B.S. Energy crisis and biogas technology: an experience in Gujarat state. *Khadi Gramodyog*. 31, 4, 1985. pp. 182–189. GVL, TRTIL.

Pathak, Mahesh. Environmental planning for Sardar Sarovar Project. *Artha-Vikas*. 24, 1 and 2, 1988. pp. 1–20. CSSL.

Pathak, Pravin G. Regional development in the perspective of allied agricultural activities: a case study of Gujarat. *Anvesak*. 26, 1, 1996. pp. 1–50. GIDRL, SPIESRL.

Paul, Samuel. Pricing Gujarat natural gas: an alternative approach. *Economic and Political Weekly*. 3, 37, 1968. pp. 1405–1408. CSSL, SPIESRL, UML.

Pramod, Kumar., et al. Socio economic condition with special reference to common access resources: a case study from Gujarat and Rajasthan. *Indian Forester*. 130, 9, 2004. pp. 981–990. IIML.

Punalekar, S.P. Voluntary action and rehabilitation: a case of Narmada dam oustees in Gujarat state. *Indian Journal of Social Work*. 44, 4, 1984. pp. 353–364. GVL.

Puri, Mukesh. Report of the twelfth finance commission: implications for Gujarat. *Anvesak*. 37, 1, 2007. pp. 1–16. CSSL, GIDRL, SPIESRL.

Raj, P.A. and Mistry, J.F. Quest for hydro power in Gujarat. *Bhagirath*. 31, 3, 1984. pp. 115–119. AAUL.

Rana, V.M. and Kapadia, Vivek P. Auto controller for interconnected canal pools of canal system of the Sardar Sarovar Project, Gujarat. *Water and Energy International Quarterly*. 68, 3, 2011. pp. 44–47. IRMAL.

Rangacharyulu, S.V. Monitoring of IRDP: a mailed questionnaire study in Gujarat, Karnataka, Kerala, Maharashtra, Punjab, Tripura. *Journal of Rural Development*. 5, 2, 1986. pp. 241–256. CSSL, GVL, IRMAL.

Ray, C.N. Municipal solid waste management in Ahmedabad. *Nagarlok*. 32, 2, 2003. pp. 51–64. SPIESRL.

Ray, C.N. Rural water quality problem and role of NGO in Gujarat. *Indian Journal of Public Administration*. 48, 2, 2002. pp. 236–246. IRMAL.

Ray, C.N. and Sanghvi, Ajaykumar S. Partnership for development and maintenance of public gardens: the case of Ahmedabad. *Nagarlok*. 37, 1, 2005. pp. 21–29. SPIESRL.

Ruitenbeek, H. Jack and Cartier, Cynthia M. Evaluation of Narmada projects: an ecological economics perspective. *Economic and Political Weekly*. 30, 34, 1995. pp. 2138–2145. CEPTL, CSSL, IIML, IRMAL, MICAL, SGUL, SPIESRL, UML.

Sah, D.C. Avoiding impoverishment risk: towards a policy frame for rehabilitation and resettlement of dam affected people. *Review of Development and Change*. 3, 1, 1998. pp. 59–89. CSSL.

Sah, D.C. Community biogas plants: economic evaluation. *Artha Vijnana*. 27, 2, 1985. pp. 168–182. CSSL, UML.

Sah, D.C. Pressure on land, employment and migration: evidences from Sardar Sarovar Project. *Review of Development and Change*. 4, 2, 1999. pp. 237–269. CSSL.

Sah, D.C. Second generation problems of involuntary migration: evidences from Sardar Sarovar Project. *Indian Journal of Agricultural Economics*. 52, 4, 1997. pp. 707–727. CSSL, UML.

Sah, D.C. Variations in food and calorie-intake: some evidence from Sardar Sarovar Project. *Administrator*. 43, 2, 1998. pp. 93–124. CSSL.

Sandhu, H.S. Patterns of consumption in Punjab and Gujarat: a comparative study. *Indian Journal of Regional Science*. 17, 2, 1985. pp. 23–29. CSSL, GIDRL.

Sangvai, Sanjay. Movements, media and mediations. *Seminar*. 455, 1997. pp. 19–22. (On Narmada). CSSL, MICAL, UML.

Sarma, Atul and Parekh, K.M. Methodology of estimation of government purchases with illustrations of Maharashtra, Gujarat, Rajasthan and Madhya Pradesh. *Anvesak*. 10, 2, 1980. pp. 169–194. CEPTL, CSSL, IRMAL, SPIESRL.

Sena, D.R. and Kurothe, R.S. Application of rainfall analysis for planning soil and water conservation structures in semi-arid Gujarat: case study. *Indian Journal of Soil Conservation*. 32, 2, 2004. pp. 156–161. GIDRL.

Shah, Amita. Watershed programmes: a long way to go. *Economic and Political Weekly*. 35, 35 and 36, 2000. pp. 3155–3164. BUL, CEPTL, CSSL, IIML, IRMAL, MICAL, SGUL, SPIESRL, UML.

Shah, Amita and Sah, D.C. Inefficiency and efficacy of soil testing services: a case study of Gujarat. *Artha Vijnana*. 37, 1, 1995. pp. 77–100. CSSL, UML.

Shah, C.H. Co-operation, development and socio-economic force: a case study of Kodinar taluka. *Sociological Bulletin*. 15, 2, 1966. pp. 36–43. CSSL.

Shah, H.C. "Bio gas development in Gujarat state". *Changing Villages*. 6, 4, 1984. pp. 310–317. CSSL, GVL.

Shah, N.R. Evaluation of catchment area development programme: a case study of Dantiwada catchment in Gujarat. *Arth-Vikas*. 26, 1 and 2, 1990. pp. 1–29. GIDRL, HML.

Shah, Tushaar. Ground water grids in the villages of Gujarat: evolution, structure, working and impacts. *Wamana*. 4, 1, 1989. pp. 14–29. IRMAL.

Shah, Tushaar and Verma, Shilp. Co-management of electricity and groundwater: an assessment of Gujarat's Jyotigram scheme. *Economic and Political Weekly*. 43, 7, 2008. pp. 59–66. BUL, CEPTL, CSSL, EDIL, HML, IIML, IRMAL, MICAL, SGUL, SPIESRL, SUL, UML.

Shah, Vimal. Problems of economic development in tribal areas of Gujarat. *Khadi Gramodyog*. 15, 9, 1969. pp. 670–672. TRTIL.

Shah, Vinod K. Infrastructure in Gujarat a cross section study. *Madhya Pradesh Journal of Social Sciences*. 3, 1, 1998. pp. 45–58. IRMAL.

Shaheen, F.A. and Shiyani, R.L. Equity redistribution: groundwater bore-well in North Gujarat. *Economic and Political Weekly*. 40, 4, 2005. pp. 307–312. BUL, CEPTL, CSSL, EDIL, GIDRL, IIML, IRMAL, MICAL, SGUL, SPIESRL, UML.

Shaikh, A.S. and Zala, Y.C. Production performance and economic appraisal of broiler farmsin Anand district of Gujarat. *Agricultural Economics Research Review*. 24, 2, 2011. pp. 317–323. IIML.

Shanmukham, P.S. and Santhanam, K.V. Technological change in the Indian economy: 1953–54 to 1964–65. *Anvesak*. 5, 1–2, 1975. pp. 99–114. SPIESRL.

Sharma, U.S. Some aspects of drinking water supply in rural Gujarat: adequacy and operation-maintenance. *Anvesak*. 28, 1, 1998. pp. 1–11. CSSL, GIDRL, IRMAL, SPIESRL.

Sharma, Usha S. Taluka-level development in 1980–81 and 1990–95 in Sabarkantha district. *Anvesak*. 30, 2, 2000. pp. 1–17. CSSL, SPIESRL.

Shivanand Swamy, H.M., Bhardwaj, V.P. and Chandra, Turush. Development management in metropolitan periphery: a case of Western Ahmedabad. *Anvesak*. 27, 1 and 2, 1997. pp. 165–180. GIDRL, SPIESRL.

Shiyani, R.L., Kakadia, B.H. and Tarpara, V.D. Socio-economic impact of watershed development in South Saurashtra region of Gujarat. *Journal of Rural Development*. 21, 3, 2002. pp. 411–431. BUL, CSSL, GIDRL, IIML.

Shukla, Shital. Data gaps in measuring the status of human development at micro level. *Anvesak*. 41, 2, 2011. pp. 93–105. CSSL, SPIESRL.

Sidhu, Hina. Industrialisation for sustainable development in Gujarat. *Indian Journal of Regional Science*. 41, 2, 2009. pp. 60–72. CSSL.

Sidhu, Hina. Privatisation of state level undertakings in Gujarat. *Decision*. 22, 1–2, 1995. pp. 99–127. IRMAL.

Sikligar, P.C. Gokul gaon yojana: a new approach of development in Gujarat. *Anvesak*. 30, 1, 2000. pp. 1–6. CSSL, GIDRL, SPIESRL.

Singh, P.K. and Patel, H.F. Growth performance and prospects of seafood exports from Gujarat: an econometric study. *Artha-Vikas*. 31, 1, 1994. pp. 10–18. CSSL, GIDRL.

Singh, S.B. SFDA and MFAL programmes in Gujarat. *Agriculture and Agro-Industries Journal*. 11, 2, 1978. pp. 17–18. IIML.

Sisodia, O.P. Sardar Sarovar Project and fundamental rights. *Administrator*. 43, 2, 1998. pp. 81–92. CSSL.

Sivasubramanian, M.N. Biogas plants in Gujarat. *Changing Villages*. 4, 5, 1982. pp. 38–48. CSSL.

Srinivas, Aditya V. and Pandya, Ashish N. Infrastructure development: a reference to port policy of Gujarat and Surat's position. *Vishleshan*. 31, 2, 2006. pp. 30–36. BUL, IRMAL.

Srivastava, D.C. Regional linkages in a backward economy: a case study of Gujarat. *Vishleshan*. 7, 3 and 4, 1981. pp. 190–195. CSSL, GIDRL, IIML.

Subramaniam, K. Science and ethics in public decision-making: case of big dams. *Economic and Political Weekly*. 29, 14, 1994. pp. 813–818. CEPTL, CSSL, IIML, IRMAL, MICAL, SPIESRL, UML.

Thaker, Hrima and Shiyani, R.L. Socio-Economic development in Gujarat: rosy picture with concerns. *Journal of Rural Development*. 28, 4, 2009. pp. 515–528. CSSL, EDIL.

Thakar, V.J. Development of basic infrastructure facilities at fish landing centres in Gujarat. *Fishing Chimes*. 16, 5, 1996. pp. 45–46. IRMAL.

Thakkar, Usha and Kulkarni, Mangesh. Environment and development: the case of the Sardar Sarovar Project. *South Asia Bulletin*. 12, 2, 1992. pp. 96–103. CSSL.

Timbadiya, P.V., Patel, P.L. and Porey, P.D. Application of innovative trend analysis methodology and distribution fitting: study on annual peak inflow into Ukai dam, Gujarat, India. *Water and Energy International Quarterly*. 69, 9, 2012. pp. 40–44. IRMAL.

Tiwari, T.D. Conceptual framework of manpower planning: a case study of ABAD Bank, Ahmedabad. *Manpower Journal*. 36, 3, 2000. pp. 61–66. CSSL, UML.

Trivedi, Harshad R. Towards a policy of differentiated method of reservation in the light of Gujarat State. *Indian Journal of Public Administration*. 36, 4, 1990. pp. 869–875. GVL.

Vakil, C.N. Economic research for planning and development in Gujarat. *Journal of the Gujarat Research Society*. 23, 2/90, 1961. pp. 119–121. GVL.

Veena, D.R. Input-output model for manpower projection by occupations and educational levels in Gujarat's economy. *Anvesak*. 4, 2, 1974. pp. 119–143. CEPTL, SPIESRL.

Veena, D.R. Pattern of education for economic development: an experience of developing Gujarat region-Gujarat. *Journal of Gujarat Research Society*. 38, 3/146, 1976. pp. 29–62. GVL.

Visaria, Pravin and Iyengar, Sudarshan. Economic prospects. *Seminar*. 470, 1998. pp. 24–30. CEPTL, CSSL, IRMAL, MICAL, UML.

Vishakha, B. Growth of urban infrastructure in Ahmedabad and its influence on level of living. *Nagarlok*. 31, 3, 1999. pp. 34–48. CEPTL.

Vyas, V.S. Macro-economic policies and rural sector in Gujarat. *Vishleshan*. 3, 1, 1977. pp. 1–14. CSSL, GIDRL, IIML.

Vyas, V.S. Planning for the micro-regions Dharampur approach. *Arth-Vikas*. 14, 2, 1978. pp. 1–12. GIDRL.

Wade, Robert H. Muddy waters: inside the World Bank as it struggled with the Narmada projects. *Economic and Political Weekly*. 46, 40, 2011. pp. 44–65. BUL, CEPTL, CSSL, EDIL, IRMAL, SPIESRL, SUL, UML.

Wadhva, Kiran. Land-use pattern in urban fringe areas: case study of Ahmedabad. *Economic and Political Weekly*. 18, 14, 1983. pp. 541–545. CEPTL, CSSL, GUL, IIML, IRMAL, SGUL, SPIESRL, UML.

Whitehead, J. Statistical concoctions and everyday lives: queries from Gujarat resettlement sites. *Economic and Political Weekly*. 34, 28, 1999. pp. 1940–1947. CEPTL, CSSL, GIDRL, IIML, IRMAL, MICAL, SGUL, SPIESRL, UML.

Yogananda Shastry, C., Naidu, K.K. and Sridhor, M.J. Case studies of beneficiaries of IRDP in Gujarat, Karnataka and Rajasthan. *Journal of Rural Development*. 6, 2, 1987. pp. 171–179. IIML, IRMAL.

Working Papers, Reports and Other Materials

Aandahl, Guro. *Technocratic dreams and troublesome beneficiaries: the Sardar Sarovar (Narmada) Project in Gujarat*. Oslo: University of Oslo, 2010. p. 388. IRMAL.

Adhvaryu, J.H. and Patel, A.S. *Socio-economic surveys of medium irrigation project areas in Gujarat: a consolidated view*. Vallabh Vidyanagar: Sardar Patel University, 1984. p. 162. IRMAL.

Adhvaryu, J.H., Patel, A.S. and Bagchi, D. *Jhuj irrigation project: a socio-economic survey of command area, districts Valsad & Surat, Gujarat state*. Vallabh Vidyanagar: Sardar Patel University, 1980. p. 62. CSSL.

Agricultural Finance Consultants. *Monitoring and evaluation of Gujarat watershed management project (With financial assistance from European economic community)*. Bombay: Agricultural Finance Consultants, 1989. p. 145. Third year report (1989–90). SPIESRL.

Agro-Climatic Regional Planning Unit. *Application of geology in water resources management water harvesting and basin analysis in parts of North Gujarat India. Final report*. Ahmedabad: Agro-Climatic Regional Planning Unit, 1999. p. 157. SPIESRL.

Agro-Economic Research Centre. *Baseline survey of Ahmedabad district under command of Narmada irrigation project*. Gujarat: Agro-Economic Research Centre, 1982. p. 52. CSSL, SPIESRL.

Agro-Economic Research Centre. *Economic survey of Borsad taluka (Gujarat state) with special reference to the impact of community development programme*. Vallabh Vidyanagar: Agro Economic Research Centre, 1966. p. 178. Indian Village Studies No. 11. GUL, UML.

Agro-Economic Research Centre. *Rampura (Mehsana district, Gujarat) economic survey of a North Gujarat village*. Vallabh Vidyanagar: Agro-Economic Research Centre, 1970. p. 154. Indian Village Studies No. 15. GUL, IRMAL, SPUL.

Agro-Economic Research Centre. *Samaldevi: Panchmahals district, Gujarat: an economic survey in a backward district*. Vallabh Vidyanagar: Agro-Economic Research Centre, 1966. p. 125. Indian Village Studies No. 21. GUL, UML.

Agro-Economic Research Centre. *Socio-economic profile Narmada command area, Ahmedabad district*. Vallabh Vidyanagar: Agro-Economic Research Centre, 1982. p. 66. CSSL.

Ahmad, Sara. *In search of a drop: women and drinking water management in rural Gujarat(India): the case of SEWA*. Anand: Indian Institute of Rural Management, 2000. p. 24. Working Paper 137. IRMAL, SPIESRL.

Aithal, Rajesh K. *Structure of distribution in rural areas: empirical evidence from villages in Karnataka and Gujarat*. Anand: Institute of Rural Management, 2008. p. [ ]. IRMAL.

Ahmed, Sara. *En-gendering policy discourse an water management: negotiating gender relations and changing water worlds-insights from rural Gujarat.* Anand: Institute of Rural Management, 2001. p. 39. Working Paper 162. IRMAL, SPIESRL.

Ahmed, Sara and Hari Krishna, N. *Changing gender roles in irrigation management: the case of Sadguru's lift-irrigation co-operatives*. Anand: Institute of Rural Management, 1998. p. 39. Working Paper 120. CSSL.

Alagh, Y.K., Mody, R.J. and Thakar, B.C. Macro-economic framework. In *Gujarat economy in 2001 A.D.: a study in perspective*. Ahmedabad: Sardar Patel Institute of Economic & Social Research, 1980. pp. 41–64. Monograph Series No. 8. GUL.

Alagh, Yoginder K. *Sardar Sarovar revisited.* Ahmedabad: Sardar Patel Institute of Economic & Social Research, 2013. p. 33. Working Paper 15. CSSL, SPIESRL.

Alagh, Yoginder K. *Morse mission: a mission of omissions*. Baroda: Gujarat Foundation for Development Alternatives, [ ]. p. 27. CSSL.

Anjal, Prakash and Vishwa, Ballabh. *Win-some lose-all game! Social differentiation and politics of groundwater markets in North Gujarat.* Anand: Institute of Rural Management, 2004. p. 39. Working Paper 183. SPIESRL.

ARCH-Vahini. *Morse-berger review: a search for truth?.* Mangrol: Author, 1992. p. 24. CSSL.

Arya, Anita and Mehta, Niti. *Performance of Gujarat economy: an analysis of growth and instability.* Ahmedabad: Sardar Patel Institute of Economic & Social Research, 2011. p. 30. Working Paper 7. SPIESRL.

Asopa, V.N. and Tripathi, B.L. *Command area development in Mahi-Kadana*. Ahmedabad: Centre for Management in Agriculture, Indian Institute of Management, 1978. p. 112. CMA Monograph No. 76. CSSL, IIML.

Bajpai, Gita. Urban growth in Central Gujarat: case study of Baroda city in the second half of the 19th century. In *Studies in trade and urbanisation in Western India.* Ed. by V.K. Chavda. Baroda: M.S. University, 1985. pp. 111–124. CSSL.

Baroda Municipal Corporation. *Basic plan for Baroda: a perspective for growth and structure,* Vol. 1. Baroda: Baroda Municipal Corporation, 1975. p. 144. SPIESRL.

Barua, Samir K. and Patel, Nitin R. *Computer stimulation model for reservoir operations at Sardar Sarovar, Gujarat.* Ahmedabad: Indian Institute of Management, 1983. p. 26. SPIESRL.

Basant, Rakesh. *Agro-mechanical technology in Gujarat before independence: a survey of literature*. Ahmedabad: Gujarat Institute of Area Planning, 1987. p. 114. IRMAL.

Basant, Rakesh. *Diversification of economic activities in rural Gujarat: key results of a field survey.* Ahmedabad: Gujarat Institute of Development Research, 1993. p. 43. Working Paper No. 53. CSSL, GIDRL, IRMAL.

Basnat, Rakesh. *Economic diversification in rural areas: a review of processes with special reference to Gujarat*. Ahmedabad: Gujarat Institute of Development Research, 1994. p. 31. Working Paper No. 57. CSSL, GIDRL, IRMAL.

Basant, Rakesh. *Trends in agro mechanical technology in Gujarat: a district level analysis*. Ahmedabad: Gujarat Institute of Area Planning, 1987. p. 169. IRMAL.

Batley, Richard. *Generating economic development in smaller towns of Gujarat, India.* Delhi: Development Administration Group, 1990. p. 165. IIML.

Bharaara, L.P. *Preliminary report on socio economic survey of Banni area, Kutch district, Gujarat*. New Delhi: ICAR, 1987. p. 44. IRMAL.

Bhat, Anil and Pathak, H.N. *Baroda's experiment in urban decentralization: a study of some administrative aspects.* Ahmedabad: Indian Institute of Management, 1977. p. 44. Working Paper No. 1977/179. IIML.

Bhat, Anil, et al. *No tags management information system for decentralized delivery of urban service in Ahmedabad municipal corporation*. Ahmedabad: Indian Institute of Management, 1983. p. 89. IIML.

Bhat, M.L. *Economic survey of Borsad taluka (Gujarat state) with special reference to the impact of community development programme*. Vallabh Vidyanagar: Agro-Economic Research Centre, 1966. p. 178. Research Study No. 11. AERCL, SPUL.

Bhatt, Atul. *Santalpur block after seven years: evaluation of implementation of block level plan: a case study of Santalpur block of Banaskantha district, Gujarat state*. Pune: National Institute of Bank Management, 1991. p. 124. GIDRL.

Bhatt, Atul. *Santalpur block after seven years: evaluation of implementation of block level plan: a case study of Santalpur block of Banaskantha district, Gujarat state.* Pune: National Institute of Bank Management, 1988. p. 178. IIML.

Bhushan, Chandra and Hazra, Monali Zeya. *Rich lands poor people: is 'Sustainable' mining possible?* New Delhi: Centre for Science and Environment, 2008. pp. 263–275. CEEL.

Blankenberg, Floris. *Implementation of biogas plants in Gujarat, India.* Enschede: Twente University of Technology, 1983. p. 102. CSSL, IRMAL.

Brahmbhatt, D.M. *Samaldevi (Panchmahals district, Gujarat): an economic survey in a backward district.* Vallabh Vidyanagar: Agro-Economic Research Centre, 1977. p. 125. Indian Village Studies No. 21. AERCL, IIML, IRMAL, SPUL.

Centre for Environmental Planning and Technology. *Area development plan for social inputs: interim plan for Panchmahal district, Gujarat.* Ahmedabad: Centre for Environmental Planning and Technology, 1980. p. 99. CSSL.

Centre for Environmental Planning and Technology. *Socio-economic benchmark: Narmada command area*. Phase II, Vol. I. Ahmedabad: Centre for Environment Planning and Technology, 1982. p. 194. CSSL.

Centre for Environmental Planning and Technology. *Socio-economic benchmark: Narmada command area*. Phase 1, Vol. 1. Ahmedabad: Centre for Environment Planning and Technology, 1981. p. 356. CSSL.

Centre for Social Studies. *Block level planning papers: Olpad taluka.* Surat: Centre for Social Studies, 1979. p. [ ]. CSSL, IIML.

Centre for Social Studies. *Monitoring and evaluation of resettlement and rehabilitation programme for Sardar Sarovar Project, Report No. 13*. Surat: Centre for Social Studies, 1992. p. 89. CSSL.

Centre for Social Studies. *Monitoring and evaluation of resettlement and rehabilitation programme for Sardar Sarovar Project, Report No. 14*. Surat: Centre for Social Studies, 1992. p. 79. CSSL.

Centre for Social Studies. *Monitoring and evaluation of resettlement and rehabilitation programme for Sardar Sarovar Project, Report No. 15*. Surat: Centre for Social Studies, 1992. p. 109. CSSL.

Centre for Social Studies. *Monitoring and evaluation of resettlement and rehabilitation programme for Sardar Sarovar Project, Report No. 16*. Surat: Centre for Social Studies, 1993. p. 118. CSSL.

Centre for Social Studies. *Monitoring and evaluation of resettlement and rehabilitation programme for Sardar Sarovar Project, Report No. 17*. Surat: Centre for Social Studies, 1993. p. 72. CSSL.

Centre for Social Studies. *Monitoring and evaluation of resettlement and rehabilitation programme for Sardar Sarovar Project, Report No. 18*. Surat: Centre for Social Studies, 1994. p. 75. CSSL.

Centre for Social Studies. *Monitoring and evaluation of resettlement and rehabilitation programme for Sardar Sarovar Project, Report No. 19*. Surat: Centre for Social Studies, 1994. p. 123. CSSL.

Centre for Social Studies. *Monitoring and evaluation of resettlement and rehabilitation programme for Sardar Sarovar Project, Report No. 20*. Surat: Centre for Social Studies, 1995. p. 98. CSSL.

Centre for Social Studies. *Monitoring and evaluation of resettlement and rehabilitation programme for Sardar Sarovar Project, Report No. 22*. Surat: Centre for Social Studies, 1996. p. 133. CSSL.

Centre for Social Studies. *Monitoring and evaluation of resettlement and rehabilitation programme for Sardar Sarovar Project, Report No. 23*. Surat: Centre for Social Studies, 1996. p. 82. CSSL.

Centre for Social Studies. *Monitoring and evaluation of resettlement and rehabilitation programme for Sardar Sarovar Project, Report No. 24*. Surat: Centre for Social Studies, 1997. p. 76. CSSL.

Centre for Social Studies. *Monitoring and evaluation of resettlement and rehabilitation programme for Sardar Sarovar Project, October'96-March'97.* Composite report. Surat: Centre for Social Studies. 2000. p. 136. CSSL.

Centre for Social Studies. *Resettlement and rehabilitation: Sardar Sarovar Project on the Narmada. Reports No. 2 and 3*. Surat: Centre for Social Studies, 1987. p. 70. CSSL.

Centre for Social Studies. *Resettlement and rehabilitation: Sardar Sarovar Project on the Narmada. Reports No. 4*. Surat: Centre for Social Studies, 1987. p. 25. CSSL.

Centre for Social Studies. *Resettlement and rehabilitation: Sardar Sarovar Project on the Narmada. Reports No. 5*. Surat: Centre for Social Studies, 1987. p. 61. CSSL.

Centre for Social Studies. *Resettlement and rehabilitation: Sardar Sarovar Project on the Narmada. Reports No. 6*. Surat: Centre for Social Studies, 1988. p. 99. CSSL.

Centre for Social Studies. *Resettlement and rehabilitation: Sardar Sarovar Project on the Narmada. Reports No. 7*. Surat: Centre for Social Studies, 1988. p. 78. CSSL.

Centre for Social Studies. *Resettlement and rehabilitation: Sardar Sarovar Project on the Narmada. Reports No. 8*. Surat: Centre for Social Studies, 1989. p. 113. CSSL.

Centre for Social Studies. *Resettlement and rehabilitation: Sardar Sarovar Project on the Narmada. Reports No. 9*. Surat: Centre for Social Studies, 1989. p. 171. CSSL.

Centre for Social Studies. *Resettlement and rehabilitation: Sardar Sarovar Project on the Narmada. Reports No. 10*. Surat: Centre for Social Studies, 1990. p. 122. CSSL.

Centre for Social Studies. *Resettlement and rehabilitation: Sardar Sarovar Project on the Narmada. Reports No. 11*. Surat: Centre for Social Studies, 1991. p. 98. CSSL.

Centre for Social Studies. *Resettlement and rehabilitation: Sardar Sarovar Project on the Narmada. Reports No. 12*. Surat: Centre for Social Studies, 1991. p. 118. CSSL.

Charan, A.S. *Narmada command talukas in Vadodara district: a socio-economic bench-mark survey phase II*. Vol. II. Surat: Centre for Social Studies, 1983. p. 198 and p. 656. CSSL.

Charan, A.S., Radhakrishnan, P. and Shah, Ghanshyam. *Narmada command talukas in Vadodara district: socio-economic profile.* Surat: Centre for Social Studies, 1982. p. 57. CSSL, SPIESRL.

Chauhan, Devraj. Saurashtra: a regional dimension. In *Economy of Saurashtra: problems and prospects.* Ed. by D.T. Lakdawala, et al. Bhavnagar: Bhavnagar University, 1990. pp. 31–42. GUL.

Commerce Research Bureau. *Village development programme Pandatirath. (Surendranagar district Gujarat).* Bombay: Shri Sad Guru Seva Sangh Trust, 1972. p. 35. SPIESRL.

Dadi, M.M. Planning for minimum needs in Gujarat: some issues. In *Gujarat economic association.* Ed. by D.T. Lakdawala and B.B. Patel. Ahmedabad: Gujarat Economic Association, 1981. pp. 49–62. SGUL.

Das, Biswaroop. *Studies on rehabilitation of submerging villages: Mokhdi.* Surat: Centre for Social Studies, 1983. p. 84. CSSL.

Das, Biswaroop. *Studies on rehabilitation of submerging villages: Vadgam.* Surat: Centre for Social Studies, 1982. p. 84. CSSL.

Das, Biswaroop and Charan, A.S. *Cost of submergence: a study of Sardar Sarovar Project.* Surat: Centre for Social Studies, 1983. p. 92. CSSL.

Das, Biswaroop and Nakoom, Pravin. *Studies on rehabilitation of submerging villages: Lamdi.* Surat: Centre for Social Studies, 1981. p. 49. CSSL.

Das, Biswaroop and Vishwanath, L.S. *Studies on rehabilitation of submerging villages: Ferakada.* Surat: Centre for Social Studies, 1983. p. 65. CSSL.

Das, Keshab. *Traditional water harvesting for domestic use: potential and relevance of village tanks in Gujarat's desert region.* Ahmedabad: Gujarat Institute of Development Research, 2006. p. 18. Working Paper No. 173. CSSL, SPIESRL.

Das, Keshab and Gupta, Ruchi. *Management by participation? Village institutions and drinking water supply in Gujarat.* Ahmedabad: Gujarat Institute of Development Research, 2005. pp. 1–77. Working Paper No. 158. CSSL, GIDRL, SPIESRL.

Das, Keshab and Visaria, Leela. *Issues in rural sanitation: lessons from Gujarat.* Ahmedabad: Gujarat Institute of Development Research, 1998. p. 36. Working Paper No. 98. CSSL, GIDRL, IRMAL.

Das, Keshabananda and Kumar, B.L. *Managing drinking water supply in rural Gujarat: issues and evidence.* Ahmedabad: Gujarat Institute of Development Research, 1996. p. 52. Working Paper No. 71. CSSL, GIDRL, IRMAL.

Dasgupta, Swapan and Malik, Ashok. *Spirit of Gujarat: turning adversity into opportunity.* Ahmedabad: Government of Gujarat, 2009. p. 119. SPIESRL.

Dave, A.S. and Gandotra, M.M. Some correlates of rural development in Gujarat. In *Gujarat economy problems and prospects.* Ed. by D.T. Lakdawala. Ahmedabad: Sardar Patel Institute of Economic & Social Research, 1983. pp. 351–368. Monograph 10. IIML.

Desai, A.R. and Raval, M.N. Rapporteur's report on "Teaching of economics in Gujarat". In *Gujarat economic association conference papers, Baroda.* Ed. by V.S. Vyas, Pravin Visaria and A.R. Desai. Ahmedabad: Balgovind, 1971. pp. 278–281. GIDRL, IIML.

Desai, Babubhai D. *Socio-economic study of the milk producers of South Gujarat.* Surat: Centre for Social Studies, 1979. p. 25. CSSL.

Desai, B.M. *Moti Khadal (Kaira district, Gujarat) an economic survey of a Charotar village.* Vallabh Vidyanagar: Agro-Economic Research Centre, 1967. p. 210. Indian Village Studies No. 10. AERCL.

Desai, D.B. *Matar Taluka benchmark survey (Narmada planning group) phase 1 report.* Ahmedabad: Gujarat University, 1981. p. 52. CSSL, GIDRL.

Desai, K.G. Development of psychological test in Gujarat. In *Bunch of current Indian studies*. Ed. by M.R. Sinha. Bombay: Indian Institute of Asian Studies, 1969. pp. 83–87. SPUL.

Desai, M.D. *Dhanfulia (Junagadh district, Gujarat): economic life in a Saurashtra village.* Vallabh Vidyanagar: Agro-Economic Research Centre, 1967. p. 223. IIML, IRMAL.

Desai, M.D. *Rampura (Mahessana district, Gujarat) economic survey of a North Gujarat village*. Vallabh Vidyanagar: Agro-Economic Research Centre, 1970. p. 155. Indian Village Studies No. 15. IIML.

Desai, N.B. *Report on the administrative survey of the Surat district.* Bombay: Indian Society of Agricultural Economics, 1958. p. 336. GUL, GVL, HML, SGUL, SPIESRL, TRTIL.

Development Support Centre. *Participatory irrigation management compilation of orders of government of Gujarat (2nd edition-June 1999).* Ahmedabad: Development Support Centre, 1999. p. 93. SPIESRL.

Dholakia, B.H. Inter-district urban growth differentials in Gujarat. In *Gujarat economic association. conference papers.* Ed. by V.S. Vyas, Pravin Visaria and A.R. Desai. Ahmedabad: Balgovind, 1971. pp. 178–184. GIDRL, IIML.

Dholakia, Ravindra H. Analysis of economic growth in Gujarat. In *Seminar on development of Gujarat: problems & prospects, 24–26 August, 1981.* Ahmedabad: Sardar Patel Institute of Economic & Social Research, 1981. pp. 1–31. CSSL.

Dholakia, Ravindra H. Economic growth and fluctuations in Gujarat. In *Gujarat economy problems and prospects.* Ed. by D.T. Lakdawala. Ahmedabad: Sardar Patel Institute of Economic & Social Research, 1983. pp. 3–18. Monograph 10. GUL, IIML.

Dholakia, Ravindra H. Some reflection on modern theories consumer demand. In *Gujarat economic association*. Ed. by D.T. Lakdawala and B.B. Patel. Ahmedabad: Gujarat Economic Association, 1981. pp. 1–34. SGUL.

Dholakia, Ravindra H. and Datta, Samar K. *High growth trajectory and structural changes in Gujarat agriculture.* Delhi: Macmillan, 2010. p. 174. GIDRL.

Dhot, Jaspal Kaur. *Economy and society of Northern Gujarat circa 1750–1850.* New Delhi: [ ], 1995. p. [ ]. GIDRL.

D.P.A.P Agency. *Fifty Five year plan (1974–75 to 1978–79) drought prone area programme (Viramgam and Dhandhuka) (district. Ahmedabad).* Ahmedabad: D.P.A.P Agency, [ ]. p. 355. IIML.

Durga Prasad, M.V. and Singh, Pramod K. *Applying AHP and GIS techniques for locating milk-chilling facilities in a backward tribal district of Gujarat.* Anand: Institute of Rural Management, 2009. p. 29. Working Paper 209. IRMAL, SPIESRL.

Dutta, Rajeshree. *Some aspects of land use planning in Gujarat.* Trivandrum: Nabaard, 1992. p. 113. IRMAL.

Foundation for Public Interest. *Appraisal of 22 World Bank support projects in Gujarat state: economic rehabilitation of resettled households.* Ahmedabad: Foundation for Public Interest, 1991. p. 48. SPIESRL.

Gaekwad, Fatesinghrao. *Gujarat and 'Bombay high' gas.* Baroda: [ ], 1979. p. 43. IRMAL.

Gandotra, M.M. and Dey, A.S. Some correlates of rural development in Gujarat. In *Gujarat economy: problems and prospects*. Ed. by D.T. Lakdawala. Ahmedabad: Sardar Patel Institute of Economic & Social Research, 1983. pp. 351–368. Monograph Series No. 10. GUL.

Gangopadhyay, Tanushree. *Studies on rehabilitation of submerging villages: Katkhadi.* Surat: Centre for Social Studies, 1983. p. 72. CSSL.

Ghatak, Ram Narayan and Singh, Katar. *Contingent valuation method of pricing canal irrigation water: an exploratory study in Kheda district of Gujarat*. Anand: Institute of Rural Management, 1994. p. 22. Working Paper 64. GIDRL, IRMAL.

Ghatak, Ram Narayan and Singh, Katar. *Economics of tube-well irrigation: a case study in Hardoi district of Uttar Pradesh and Kheda district of Gujarat*. Anand: Insitute of Rural Management, 1994. p. 13. Working Paper 67. CSSL, GIDRL.

Gohil, B.K. Provision of infrastructure in Gujarat. In *Economic development of backward regions problems & prospects (Proceedings of an all-India seminar on the development of backward regions with special reference to Gujarat)*. Ed. by H.M. Patel, et al. Vallabh Vidyanagar: Sardar Patel University, 1974. pp. 69–99. GIDRL, HML.

Gopaldas, Tara, Verma, Amita and Saraswathi, T.S. *Social inputs plans for Waghodia & Sankheda taluka Baroda district*. Baroda: M.S. University, 1981. p. 169. CSSL.

Gopinath, C., Kalro, A.H. and Singh, Ramadhar. Need, role and job analysis and training and manpower requirements for irrigation water management in Gujarat state. Ahmedabad: Indian Institute of Management, 1988. p. 203. IIML.

Gujarat, Government of. *Block development plan for Chhotaudepur taluka Vadodara district. (Report)*. Baroda: M.S. University, 1980. p. 91, CSSL.

Gujarat, Government of. *Block development plan for Jabugam Vadodara district. (Report)*. Baroda: M.S. University, 1979. p. 47. CSSL, SPIESRL.

Gujarat, Government of. *Sardar Sarovar Project: on the river Narmada*. Gandhinagar: Sardar Sarovar Narmada Nigam, 1992. p. 15. CSSL.

Gujarat, Government of. *Development indicators: Gujarat*. Gandhinagar: Government of Gujarat, 1999. p. 60. CSSL.

Gujarat, Government of. Gujarat economy: present status and challenges infrastructural facilities (Energy). In *Gujarat-2010: challenges and opportunities*. By Government of Gujarat. Ahmedabad: Sardar Patel Institute of Economic & Social Research, 2001. pp. 514–521. Seminar volume. CSSL, EDIL, IRMAL, SGUL, SPIESRL.

Gujarat, Government of. People oriented administration. In *Gujarat-2010: challenges and opportunities*. By Government of Gujarat. Ahmedabad: Sardar Patel Institute of Economic & Social Research, 2001. pp. 571–576. Seminar volume. CSSL, EDIL, IRMAL, SGUL, SPIESRL.

Gujarat, Government of. *Perspective plan of Gujarat, 1974–1984*. 3 Vols. Ahmedabad: General Administration Department, 1972. p. 433, 539, and 311. CSSL.

Gujarat, Government of. *Study of settlement pattern: Six talukas in the Narmada command area of Mahesana district of Gujarat*. Ahmedabad: Narmada Planning Group, Government of Gujarat, 1982. p. 184. CSSL, GIDRL.

Gujarat, Government of. *Tribal sub-plan: annual development programme 1993–94*. Gandhinagar: Social Welfare and Tribal Development Department, Government of Gujarat, 1993. p. 316. CSSL.

Gujarat Institute of Area Planning. *Baseline survey of Mehmadabad taluka of Kheda district under command of Narmada irrigation project, First phase report*. Vol. 1–2. Ahmedabad: Author, 1982. Various. CSSL.

Gujarat Institute of Area Planning. *Baseline survey of six taluka of Mehsana under command of Narmada irrigation project.* Ahmedabad: Author, [ ]. Various. CSSL.

Gujarat Institute of Area Planning. *Planning for Sanand taluka: Ahmedabad district.* Ahmedabad: Gujarat Institute of Area Planning, 1979. p. 315. CSSL.

Gujarat Institute of Area Planning. *Planning For Kalyanpur taluka: Jamnagar district.* Ahmedabad: Gujarat Institute of Area Planning, 1980. p. 260. CSSL.

Gujarat Institute of Area Planning. *Planning For Sanand taluka (Ahmedabad district).* Ahmedabad: Gujarat Institute of Area Planning, 1980. p. 296. IIML.

Gujarat Institute of Area Planning. *Planning for social inputs in Junagadh district: an interim report.* Ahmedabad: Gujarat Institute of Area Planning, [ ]. p. 37. CSSL.

Gujarat Maritime Board. *Ecological restoration and planning for Alang-Sosiya ship-breaking yard, Gujarat.* Vadodara: Gujarat Ecology Society, 1998. p. 262. CEEL.

Gujarat University. *Nadiad taluka bench-mark survey: Narmada planning group phase 1 tables.* Ahmedabad: Department of Sociology, Gujarat University, 1981. p. 64. GIDRL.

Gumber, Anil. *Rehabilitation and resettlement of the oustees of Panam dam in Gujarat: key results of a survey in 1984–85.* Ahmedabad: Gujarat Institute of Area Planning, 1992. p. 72. Working Paper No. 40. CSSL, IRMAL.

Gumber, Anil and Visaria, Pravin. *Inter-village differences in social overheads and their correlates in Matar taluka.* New Delhi: Indian Institute of Social Science Research, 1994. p. 54. CSSL.

Gupta, Anand P. and Rao, T.V. *Disadvantaged groups in Valsad district: a plan for their uplift.* Ahmedabad: Indian Institute of Management, 1980. p. 81. CSSL, IIML.

Gupta, D.B. and Acharya, B.V. Teaching of economics in Gujarat. In *Gujarat economic association conference papers, Baroda.* Ed. by V.S. Vyas, Pravin Visaria and A.R. Desai. Ahmedabad: Balgovind, 1971. pp. 234–266. GIDRL, IIML.

Gupta, Ranjit. *Prelude to block level planning in Gujarat.* Ahmedabad: Centre for Management in Agriculture, 1980. p. 215. CMA Monograph No. 85. IIML.

Hakim, Roxanne. Vasava economy in transition: implications of resettlement on the economy of a village affected by the Sardar Sarovar (Narmada dam) Project, India. In *Seminar on development, displacement and rehabilitation at Centre for Social Studies, Surat, 11–13 May, 1994.* Surat: Centre for Social Studies, 1994. pp. 1–37. CSSL.

Hashim, S.R. Proximity to urban influence for the districts of Gujarat. In *Gujarat economic association conference papers, Baroda.* Ed. by V.S. Vyas, Pravin Visaria and A.R. Desai. Ahmedabad: Balgovind, 1971. pp. 165–177. GIDRL, IIML.

Hashim, S.R. and Dadi, M.M. Population pressure, size distribution of land holdings and land productivity: an analysis of interregional variations in Gujarat. In *Gujarat economic association conference papers, Baroda.* Ed. by V.S. Vyas, Pravin Visaria and A.R. Desai. Ahmedabad: Balgovind, 1971. pp. 65–78. GIDRL, IIML.

Hirway, Indira. *Cost of action and cost of inaction: estimating alternative costs of depletion and degradation of drinking and domestic water supply in Gujarat.* Ahmedabad: Centre for Development Alternatives, 2003. p. 40. Working Paper No. 3. CSSL, IRMAL.

Hirway, Indira and Goswami, Subhrangsu. *Performance based Narmada-based drinking water supply in Gujarat: second round results from ITP-PRAVAH-CFDA citizens'monitoring system (Highlight).* Vallabh Vidyanagar, IWMI-Tata Water Policy Program, 2005. p. [ ]. IWMI-TATA water policy program No. 10. GIDRL.

Hirway, Indira and Lodhia, Shital. *Status of drinking water in Gujarat: towards a sustainable approach.* Ahmedabad: Centre for Development Alternatives (CFDA), 2004. p. [ ]. GIDRL.

Hirway, Indira and Mahadevia, Darshini. *Human development report 1999: Gujarat.* Ahmedabad: Gandhi Labour Institute (GLI), 1999. p. 332. CSSL, GIDRL, IIML.

Hirway, Indira and Patel, P.P. *Dynamics of drinking water in rural Gujarat.* Ahmedabad: Utthan, Centre for Water Resources, 1994. p. [ ]. GIDRL.

Indian Agricultural Research Institute. *Resource analysis and plan for efficient water management: a case study of Mahi right bank canal command area Gujarat.* New Delhi: Water Technology Centre, 1983. p. [ ]. IARI research bulletin 42. SPIESRL.

Indian Society of Agricultural Economics. *Bhadkad: social and economic survey of a village, a comparative study(1915–1955).* Bombay: Author, 1957. p. 71. CSSL, IIML.

Indian Society of Agricultural Economics. *Economic and social survey of Mehsana district.* Bombay: Indian Society of Agricultural Economics, 1954. p. 213. IIML, UML.

Iyengar, Sudarshan. *Level and pattern of economic growth in Gujarat: 1980–94.* Ahmedabad: Gujarat Institute of Development Research, 1996. p. 52. Working Paper No. 72. CSSL, GIDRL, IRMAL.

Iyengar, Sudarshan. *Level and pattern of economic growth in Gujarat: 1980–94.* Ahmedabad: D.T. Lakdawala Memorial Trust, Gujarat Institute of Development Research, 2000. p. 31. D.T. Lakdawala Memorial Trust Occasional Paper Series No. 1. IRMAL.

Iyengar, Sudarshan. *Level and pattern of economic growth in Gujarat: 1980–94.* Ahmedabad: D.T. Lakdawala Memorial Trust, Gujarat Institute of Development Research, 2000. p. 31. Occasional Paper Series 1. CSSL.

Iyengar, Sudarshan. *Public distribution system in Gujarat: a synoptic overview.* Ahmedabad: Gujarat Institute of Development Research, 2003. p. 43. Working Paper No. 138. CSSL, GIDRL, IRMAL.

Iyengar, Sudarshan. *Resettlement and rehabilitation in Sardar Sarovar Project: a review of policy reforms and implementation.* Ahmedabad: Gujarat Institute of Development Research, 1997. p. [ ]. Working Paper No. 84. CSSL, GIDRL.

Iyengar, Sudarshan. Sardar Sarovar Project: issues in potential and prospects. In *Gujarat economic association conference papers (Key papers), Vadodara.* Ed. by D.T. Lakadawala and B.B. Patel. Ahmedabad: Gujarat Economic Association, 1982. pp. 51–88. GIDRL.

Iyengar, Sudarshan and Dholakia, Ravindra H. *Planning for special programmes at district level: an exercise in DPAP planning Panchmahals.* Godhra: District Level Planning Cell Panchmahals, 1979. p. 87. CSSL.

Iyengar, S. and Shukla, N. Common property resources (CPLRs) in India: some issues in regeneration and management. In *National seminar on common property resources and planned development in Western India: challenges and prospects, January 19–21, 1999.* Seminar volume. Nanded: School of Social Sciences and School of Earth Sciences, S.R.T.M. University, 1999. pp. 31–66. CSSL.

Jain, S.C. *Block level planning: Uchchhal taluka.* II Vol. Surat: South Gujarat University, 1980. Verious. CSSL.

Jain, S.C. *Block level planning: Valsad taluka.* 3 Vols. Surat: South Gujarat University, 1979. Various. CSSL.

Jain, S.C. *Project on social inputs in the area development plan: Surat district. First phase report: Songadh & Uchchhal talukas*. Surat: South Gujarat University, 1980. p. 156. CSSL, IRMAL.

Janki, Y.A. *Kandla: the gateway of North West India*. Baroda: M.S. University, 1973. p. 140. Research Paper Series No. 6. SPIESRL.

Jarman, Heather and Scrivener, Brain. *Sardar Sarovar: report of the independent review*. Ottawa(Canada): Research Futures International, 1992. p. 363. CEEL.

Joshi, Nandini. Imported chalk: teaching of economics in underdeveloped countries. In *Gujarat economic association conference papers, Baroda*. Ed. by V.S. Vyas, Pravin Visaria and A.R. Desai. Ahmedabad: Balgovind, 1971. pp. 267–273. GIDRL, IIML.

Joshi, Vidyut. In search of a national rehabilitation policy. In *Seminar on development, displacement and rehabilitation at Centre for Social Studies, Surat, 11–13 May, 1994*. Surat: Centre for Social Studies, 1994. pp. 1–17. CSSL.

Joshi, Vidyut. Issue of canal affected persons at Sardar Sarovar Project. In *International seminar on Gujarat society, development and deprivation, 6–9 December 1994*. Surat: Centre for Social Studies, 1994. pp. 1–12. CSSL.

Joshi, Vidyut. *Socio-cultural & ecological impact of Alang & Sosiya ship breaking yard: third phase report on stake holders' Convergence at ASSBY*. Surat: Centre for Social Studies & Bhavnagar University, Bhavnagar, 2003. p. 78. CSSL.

Joshi, Vidyut. *Studies on rehabilitation of submerging villages: there was a village Navagam*. Surat: Centre for Social Studies, 1982. p. 103. CSSL.

Joshi, Vidyut. *Studies on rehabilitation of submerging villages: Dhumna, Chharbara and Antras*. Surat: Centre for Social Studies, 1983. p. 109. CSSL.

Joshi, Vidyut. *Studies on rehabilitation of submerging villages: general report (Sardar Sarovar-Narmada Project)*. Surat: Centre for Social Studies, 1983. p. 270. CSSL.

Joshi, Vidyut. *Studies on rehabilitation of submerging villages: interim report on Navagam, Limdi, Khalvani, Panchmuli and Zer*. Surat: Centre for Social Studies, 1982. p. 94. CSSL.

Joshi, Vidyut. *Sustainable development of Along and Sosiya ship breaking yard*. Bhavnagar: Bhavnagar University, 2001. p. 138. CSSL.

Joshi, Vidyut and Gangopadhyay, Tanushree. *Studies on rehabilitation of submerging villages: Gadher*. Surat: Centre for Social Studies, 1983. p. 105. CSSL.

Joshi, Vidyut and Nakoom, Pravin. *Studies on rehabilitation of submerging villages: Panchmuli*. Surat: Centre for Social Studies, 1982. p. 79. CSSL.

Joshi, Vidyut and Soni, Jayshree. *Water scarcity and people: with special reference to women's emancipation, implications for SSNNL for sustainable water management*. Surat: Centre for Social Studies, 2007. p. 182. CSSL.

Kalathil, Mathew. *Studies on rehabilitation of submerging villages: Makadkhada*. Surat: Centre for Social Studies, 1983. p. 75. CSSL.

Kashyap, S.P. Nature of growth process in Gujarat: a survey of research. In *Seminar on development of Gujarat: problems & prospects, 24th-26th August, 1981*. Ahmedabad: Sardar Patel Institute of Economic & Social Research, 1981. pp. 1–72. CSSL.

Kashyap, S.P. Perspective in a consistency frame. In *Gujarat economy in 2001 A.D.: a study in perspective*. Ahmedabad: Sardar Patel Institute of Economic & Social Research, 1980. pp. 65–108. GUL.

Kashyap, S.P. *Regional planning in a consistency frame-work: study of Gujarat*. Ahmedabad: Sardar Patel Institute of Economic & Social Research (SPIESR), 1979. p. 158. Monograph Series 6. GIDRL, GVL, IIML, UML.

Kashyap, S.P. and Vyas, V.S. Report on the discussion group on concept of regional balance within a region and development of backward areas of Gujarat. In *Gujarat economic association conference papers, Baroda.* Ed. by V.S. Vyas, Pravin Visaria and A.R. Desai. Ahmedabad: Balgovind, 1971. pp. 110–113. GIDRL, IIML.

Khadi and Village Industries Commission. *Borkhadi village plan at work: an assessment.* Bombay: Khadi and Village Industries Commission, 1958. p. 44. UML.

Khan, Ayesha. *Gujarat development: dissenting rural voices.* Vadodara: Gujarat Foundation for Development Alternatives, [ ]. p. 40. CSSL.

Khandelwal, M.K., et al. *Rescheduling canal irrigation in MRBC command using the cropwat model: a proposal.* Anand: Institute of Rural Management, 1996. p. 16. Working Paper 96. CSSL.

Kolavalli, Shashi, Kalro, Amar H. and Naik, Gopal. *Management of irrigation system: the cases of Meshwo and Phophal in Gujarat, India.* Ahmedabad: Centre for Management in Agriculture, 1995. p. 69. CMA Monograph Series No. 171. IIML.

Korah, Mathen. Power that paralyses: a survey of electricity consumers in the rural area of Gujarat. Ahmedabad: Consumer Education & Research Centre, [ ]. p. [ ]. GIDRL.

Kothari, V.N. *Study of economic profiles of the scheduled castes in Gujarat.* Baroda: M.S. University, 1976. p. 43. M.S. University Economics Series No. 3. GIDRL.

Kothari, V.N. Process of urban expansion. In *Gujarat economic association conference papers, Baroda.* Ed. by V.S. Vyas, Pravin Visaria and A.R. Desai. Ahmedabad: Balgovind, 1971. pp. 114–122. GIDRL, IIML.

Kothari, V.N. and Dadi, M.N. *Economic benefits of rural electrification in Gujarat.* Baroda: M.S. University, 1977. p. 232. M.S. University Economic Series No. 5. CSSL, GIDRL, IRMAL, SPIESRL.

Kumar, B.L. *Post-independence changes in land, labour and credit markets: evidence from a village resurvey in Gujarat*. Ahmedabad: Gujarat Institute of Development Research, 1997. p. 34. GIDR Working Paper No. 81. CSSL, GIDRL, IRMAL.

Kumar, Dinesh, et al. *Study of water - saving and energy - saving micro irrigation technologies in Gujarat.* Anand: INREMF, 2004. p. 53. IRMAL.

Kumar, Seelhan S. *Planning for development of Surat district.* Part-III: Water resources. Ahmedabad: Gujarat Institute of Area Planning, 1977. p. 17. CSSL.

Kumar, T.E. *Governance and decentralization: study in rural Gujarat*. Anand: Indian Institute of Rural Management, 2012. p. [ ]. IRMAL.

Kumarappa, J.C. *Study of Matar taluka Kaira district.* Ahmedabad: Gujarat Vidyapith, 1931. p. 179. CSSL, GIDRL.

Lakdawala, D.T. *Economics of Gujarat & Maharashtra 1960–1988.* Bombay: Center for Monitoring Indian Economy, 1988. p. 27. SPIESRL.

Lakdawala, D.T. *Economy of Saurashtra: problems and prospects.* Bhavnagar: Bhavnagar University, 1990. p. 177. IIML.

Lakdawala, D.T. and Patel, B.B. *Gujarat Economic Association*. Ahmedabad: Gujarat Economic Association, 1981. p. 128. SGUL

Lakdawala, D.T., ed. *Gujarat economy: problems and prospects.* Ahmedabad: Sardar Patel Institute of Economic & Social Research, 1982. p. 643. GIDRL.

Lakdawala, D.T., ed. *Gujarat economy: problems and prospects.* Ahmedabad: Sardar Patel Institute of Economic & Social Research, 1983. p. 648. GIDRL, IRMAL, UML.

Lal, R.B. *Evaluation study of integrated tribal development project in Dangs.* Ahmedabad: Tribal Research & Training Institute, Gujarat Vidyapith, [ ]. p. 47. Series 126. TRTIL.

Lal, R.B. *Evaluation study of Palanpur integrated tribal development project.*Ahmedabad: Tribal Research & Training Institute, Gujarat Vidyapith, 1989. p. 159. TRTIL.

Lal, R.B. *Evaluation study of Rajpipla integrated tribal development project.* Ahmedabad: Tribal Research & Training Institute, Gujarat Vidyapith, [ ]. p. 226. Series 231. TRTIL.

Lal, R.B. *Land alienation among the tribes of Gujarat.* Ahmedabad: Tribal Research & Training Institute, Gujarat Vidyapith, 1988. p. 94. Series 235. TRTIL.

Lal, R.B. and Naik, T.B. *Block level planning for full employment: Danta.* Amdavad: Tribal Research & Training Institute, Gujarat Vidyapith, 1979. p. 215. CSSL.

Lobo, Lancy. Development induced displacement in Gujarat 1947–2004. In *Special economic zones (SEZs): issues and challenges ahead.* Ed. by Sunita Nambiyar, Jagadish Solanki and M.N. Parmar. Vadodara: Faculty of Social Work, M.S. University, 2008. pp. 94–110. Seminar proceeding. CSSL.

Madan, P.J. *Block development plan for Chhotaudepur taluka, Vadodara district.* Baroda: M.S. University, 1980. p. 91. CSSL, SPUL.

Madan, P.J. *Block development plan for Jabugam, Vadodara district.* Baroda: M.S. University, 1979. Various. CSSL.

Mahadevia, Darshini. *Development dichotomy in Gujarat.* New Delhi: Research Foundation for Science, Technology and Ecology, 1998. p. 71. CSSL, GIDRL.

Mahadevia, Darshini. *Economic growth and environmental degradation: case of Gujarat.* New Delhi: Research Foundation for Science, Technology and Ecology, 1999. p. 79. CSSL, GIDRL.

Mahadevia, Darshini, Jain, Trupti and Acharya, Binoy. *Impact of Structural Adjustment Programme (SAP) on the household economy of poor in Gujarat: first round results of a longitudinal study 1994.* Ahmedabad: Unnati Organisation for Development Education, 1994. p. 35. GIDRL.

Mahajan, Vinay and Bharwada, Charul. *Virdas to waterpipes: past & present of drinking water scarcity in rural Kutch.* Ahmedabad: Author, 1997. p. 110. CSSL.

Malkani, H.C. *Socio-economic survey of Baroda city.* Baroda: M.S. University,1957. p. 179. SGUL.

Mankodi, Kashyap and Gangopadhyay, Tanushree. *Rehabilitation: ecological and economic costs.* Surat: Centre for Social Studies, 1983. p. 133. CSSL.

Mehat, B.V. and Bhatt, P.K. Analysis of factors affecting growth of entrepreneurship. In *Gujarat economy problems and prospects.* Ed. by D.T. Lakdawala. Ahmedabad: Sardar Patel Institute of Economic & Social Research, 1983. pp. 433–440. Monograph 10. IIML.

Mehta, Lyla. *Water, difference and power Kutch and the Sardar Sarovar (Narmada) Project.* UK: IDS, 1997. Working Paper 54. IIML.

Mehta, S.S. Planning problems and prospects of Gujarat. In *Gujarat economy problems and prospects.* Ed. by D.T. Lakdawala. Ahmedabad: Sardar Patel Institute of Economic & Social Research, 1983. pp. 19–44. Monograph 10. GIDRL, GUL, IIML.

Mehta, S.S. Planning problems and prospects of Gujarat. In *Seminar on development of Gujarat: problems & prospects, 24th-26th August, 1981.* Ahmedabad: Sardar Patel Institute of Economic & Social Research, 1981. pp. 1–34. CSSL.

Mehta, Sanatbhai. Challenge of balanced development of Gujarat. In *Economy of Saurashtra problems and prospects.* Ed. by D.T. Lakdawala, et al. Bhavnagar: Bhavnagar University, 1990. pp. 15–17. GUL.

Mehta, Sukhdev. Saurashtra: development and gas. In *Economy of Saurashtra: problems and prospects*. Ed. by D.T. Lakdawala, et al. Bhavnagar: Bhavnagar University, 1990. pp. 135–146. GUL.

Mishra, Harekrishna. *Understanding ICT enabled development interventions with MDG perspectives in Indian context: a study in Panchmahal district.* Anand: Institute of Rural Management, 2012. pp. 1–36. Working Paper 230. SPIESRL.

Mishra, Pradeep Kumar. *Management and impact of watershed development project in Gujarat: a study of implementation processes and outcomes*. Anand: Indian Institute of Rural Management, 2010. pp. [ ]. IRMAL.

Mody, R.J. *Development of Gujarat: people's perceptions.* Ahmedabad: Sardar Patel Institute of Economic & Social Research, p. [ ]. 416. GIDRL.

Morse, Bradford. *Sardar Sarovar: report of the independent review.* Bombay: Narmada Bachao Andolan, et al., 1992. p. 363. CSSL, SETUL, SPIESRL.

Moulik, T.K. *Dharampur block level plan.* Ahmedbad: Indian Institute of Management, [ ]. p. 127. IIML.

Moulik, T.K. and Srivastava, V.K. *Bio-gas plants at the village level problems and prospects in Gujarat.* Ahmedbad: Indian Institute of Management, 1975. p. 147. CMA Monograph No. 59. CEEL, GIDRL, IIML, IRMAL.

Moulik, T.K., et al.*Regional energy demand model and analysis for Gujarat, Kerala and Rajasthan.* [ ]: [ ], [ ]. p. 80. IRMAL.

Mukherji, Aditi and Kishore, Avinash. *Tubewell transfer in Gujarat: a study of the GWRDC.approach.* Colombo: IWMI, 2003. p. 34. IRMAL.

Mukherjee, Aditi and Kishore, Avinash. *Public tubewell transfer in Gujarat: marketing approach to IMT (Highlight).* Vallabh Vidyanagar: IWMI-tata water policy program, 2005. p. [ ]. IWMI-TATA Water Policy Program No. 2. GIDRL.

Murlidaran, V. and Krishna, K.V.S.M. *Dynamics of irrigation system performance: a comparative study of two secondary canal reaches in Mahi-Kadana, Gujarat.* Colombo: Indian Institute of Management, 1993. p. 68. IRMAL.

Murthy, Nirmala. *Evaluation of TRYSEM in Gujarat.* Ahmedabad: Indian Institute of Management, 1981. p. 54. IRMAL.

Murty, G.V.S.N. and Shah, N.C. Household consumption. In *Gujarat economy in 2001 A.D.: a study in perspective*. Ahmedabad: Sardar Patel Institute of Economic & Social Research, 1980. pp. 109–158. GUL.

Namar, Regassa E. et al. *Adoption and impacts of micro-irrigation technologies: empirical results from selected localities of Maharashtra and Gujarat states of India.* Colombo: IWMI, 2005. p. 42. IRMAL.

Nanavati, Arti. Infrastructural facilities in Gujarat. In *Gujarat-2010: challenges and opportunities*. By Government of Gujarat. Ahmedabad: Sardar Patel Institute of Economic & Social Research, 2001. pp. 478–494. Seminar volume. CSSL, EDIL, SGUL, SPIESRL.

Nanavati, Manilal B. *Economic and social survey of Mehsana district*. Bombay: Indian Society of Agricultural Economics, 1954. p. 213. GUL.

Narmada Control Authority. *Sardar Sarovar Project: land acquisition and rehabilitation of oustees.* 1984. p. 45. CSSL.

Narmada Planning Group. *Area development in Gujarat-Narmada region.* Baroda: Operations Research Group, 1992. p. 52. SPIESRL.

Narmada Planning Group. *Economic appraisal of Sardar Sarovar Project.* Bombay, Tata Economic Consultancy Services, 1983. p. 92. CSSL.

Narmada Planning Group. *Planning for prosperity: Sardar Sarovar development plan*. Gandhinagar: Sardar Sarovar Narmada Nigam, 1989. p. 565. CSSL, SETUL.

Narmada Planning Group. *Sardar Sarover Narmada project studies on ecology and environment*. Baroda: M.S. University, 1983. p. 104. SETUL, SPIESRL.

Narmada Planning Group. *Socio-economic benchmark: Narmada command area: taluka Wadhan Limbdi, Dasada, Dhrangadhra, Lakhtar, Halvad*. Vol. 1 and 2. Ahmedabad: Study Cell, Centre for Environmental Planning and Technology, 1982. p. 194 and [ ]. CSSL.

National Council of Applied Economic Research. *Techno-economic survey of Gujarat*. New Delhi: National Council of Applied Economic Research, 1963. p. 260. IIML, UML.

Operations Research Group. *Area development plan for social inputs: Dediapada and Sagbara, Bharuch district*. Baroda: Operations Research Group, 1980. p. 80. CSSL.

Operations Research Group. *Study on the main canal system for the Narmada irrigation project in Gujarat*. Baroda: Operations Research Group, 1980. p. 68. CSSL.

Pahwa, Arun K. *Planning for development of Surat district, first phase study. Part V: industry*. Ahmedabad: Gujarat Institute of Area Planning, 1977. p. 86. CSSL.

Panchanadikar, K.C. and Panchanadikar, J. *Rural civic structure and economic resources, planned development of Anand and Navsari talukas*. Vol. III. Baroda: M.S. University, 1975. p. 236. CSSL.

Panda, Haribandhu, et al. *Techno-economic feasibility study of micro distribution units for electricity in the five regions of Gujarat*. Anand: Institute of Rural Management, 2003. Various. IRMAL.

Parekh, K.M. Structural analysis of the growth of Gujarat economy. In *Seminar on development of Gujarat: problems & prospects, 24th-26th August, 1981*. Ahmedabad: Sardar Patel Institute of Economic & Social Research, 1981. pp. 1–17. p. 29. CSSL.

Parthasarthy, R. *Coordinating participation to transfer irrigation management: a game theoretic paradigm*. Ahmedabad: Gujarat Institute of Development Research, 1998. Working Paper No. 105. CSSL, GIDRL.

Parthasarthy, R. *Reforms in irrigation management: bottoms-up versus top-down models*. Ahmedabad: Gujarat Institute of Development Research, 1998. p. 30. Working Paper No. 104. CSSL, GIDRL.

Patel, Anil. What do the tribals want in the valley of Narmada? In *Seminar on development, displacement and rehabilitation at Centre for Social Studies, Surat, 11–13 May, 1994*. Surat: Centre for Social Studies, 1994. pp. 1–17. CSSL.

Patel, Arjun. Social and culture implications of displacement: a case of SSP. In *Seminar on development, displacement and rehabilitation at Centre for Social Studies, Surat, 11–13 May, 1994*. Surat: Centre for Social Studies, 1994. pp. 1–16. CSSL.

Patel, Arjun. *Socio-economic and demographic survey of PAFs of the NTPC project at Kawas*. Surat: Centre for Social Studies, 1994. p. 190. CSSL.

Patel, Arjun. *Studies on rehabilitation of submerging villages: Kadana*. Surat: Centre for Social Studies, 1983. p. 99. CSSL.

Patel, Arjun. *Studies on rehabilitation of submerging villages: Turkheda*. Surat: Centre for Social Studies, 1983. p. 95. CSSL.

Patel, Arjun. *Studies on rehabilitation of submerging villages: Zer*. Surat: Centre for Social Studies, 1983. p. 121. CSSL.

Patel, Arjun and Soni, Jayshree. *Post resettlement and rehabilitation (R&R) study of Sardar Sarovar Project (SSP), affected families (PAF) of Madhya Pradesh (MP) and Maharashtra (MH) resettled in Gujarat.* Surat: Centre for Social Studies, 2008. p. 90. CSSL.

Patel, Arun S. Water resource management: some issues. In *Development imperatives and environment concerns Sardar Sarovar Project plan.* Ed. by Mahesh Pathak. Vallabh Vidyanagar: Agro Economic Research Centre, 1995. pp. 128–134. IIML.

Patel, Arunbhai B. *Effectiveness of excise policy in tribal areas(With reference to prohibition).* Ahmedabad: Tribal Research & Training Institute, Gujarat Vidyapith, 2003. p. 67. TRTIL.

Patel, B.B. *Area plan with social inputs for Muli and Sayla talukas, district Surendranagar.* Ahmedabad: Sardar Patel Institute of Economic & Social Research, 1980. Various. CSSL, SPIESRL.

Patel, B.B. Urban expansion in Gujarat dimensions and implications. In *Gujarat economic association, conference papers.* Ed. by D.T. Lakadawala and B.B. Patel. Vallabh Vidyanagar: [ ],1985. pp. 7–18. GIDRL.

Patel, C.C. *Sardar Sarovar Project (SSP): on the river Narmada, India.* Gandhinagar: Sardar Sarovar Narmada Nigam, 1990. p. 44. CSSL.

Patel, C.C. *Sardar Sarovar Project with special reference to controversies raised by activists.* Gandhinagar: Sardar Sarovar Narmada Nigam, 1991. p. 25. CSSL.

Patel, C.C. Sardar Sarovar Project with special reference to controversies raised by the activists. In *Development imperatives and environment concerns Sardar Sarovar Project plan.* Ed. by Mahesh Pathak. Vallabh Vidyanagar: Agro Economic Research Centre, 1995. pp. 12–39. IIML.

Patel, H.M., Adhvaryu, J.H. and Vyas, V.S. *Economic development of backward regions problems and prospects (Proceeding of an all-India seminar on the development of backward regions with special reference to Gujarat).* Vallabh Vidyanagar: K.A. Amin, 1974. p. 260. HML, IIML.

Patel, Himmat. *Financial working of irrigation projects: a case study of our projects in Gujarat: a study.* Vallabh Vidyanagar: Sardar Patel University, 1990. p. [ ]. GIDRL.

Patel, Ila, Modi, Pradyut J. and Mehta, Madhavi. *Assessment-cum-evaluation of Mahiti Shakti project in Panchamahals district of Gujarat.* Anand: Institute of Rural Management, 2003. p. 85. IRMAL.

Patel, N.M. *Planning for development of Surat district, first phase study, part VI: animal husbandry.* Ahmedabad: Gujarat Institute of Area Planning, 1977. p. 89. CSSL.

Patel, R.M. *Glimpses of change and development in Borsad taluka (Kheda district Gujarat).* Vallabh Vidyanagar: Agro Economic Research Centre, 1982. p. 174. Resurvey Indian Village Studies No. 4. AERCL, GIDRL, IRMAL.

Patel, S.M. *Wells and pump-sets in Panchmahals district: a report on sources and equipment used for lift irrigation in Panchmahals district.* Ahmedabad: Institute of Co-Operative Management, 1980. p. 166. SPIESRL.

Patel, S.M. and Patel, K.V. *Studies on economics of rural electrification & lift irrigation (Gujarat state).* Ahmedabad: Indian Institute of Management (IIM), 1969. [ ] p. Monograph No. 17. GIDRL.

Patel, S.M., Madappa, P.P. and Desai, B.M. *Management of lift irrigation: report on a pilot research project in Gujarat.* Ahmedabad: Indian Institute of Management (IIM), 1969. p. 153. Monograph No. 15. GIDRL, IIML.

Patel, Sujata. 'Anand pattern': a socio-historical analysis of its origin and growth. In *International seminar on "Gujarat society", 17–20 December 1986.* Surat: Centre for Social Studies, 1986. pp. 1–49. CSSL.

Patel, V.P. and Mansuri, J.S. Development of backward areas in Gujarat state: a method of identification. In *Gujarat economic association conference papers, Baroda.* Ed. by V.S. Vyas, Pravin Visaria and A.R. Desai. Ahmedabad: Balgovind, 1971. pp. 1–15. GIDRL, IIML.

Pathak, Mahesh. Development of backward regions in Gujarat: some basic issues. In *Gujarat economic association conference papers, Baroda.* Ed. by V.S. Vyas, Pravin Visaria and A.R. Desai. Ahmedabad: Balgovind, 1971. pp. 102–109. GIDRL, IIML.

Pathak, Mahesh T. *Impact of a public sector project on a backward region.* Vallabh Vidyanagar: Department of Economics, Sardar Patel University, 1971. p. 183. TRTIL.

Pathak, Mahesh. T. and Shah, Navin R. *Block level plan: Thasra taluka Kheda district Gujarat.* Vallabh Vidyanagar: Agro-Economic Research Centre, 1981. p. 253. Research Study No. 56. SPIESRL, SPUL.

Pathak, Mahesh, et al. *Economics of tubewell irrigation in Gujarat.* Vallabh Vidyanagar: Agro-Economic Research Centre, 1985. p. 205. IRMAL.

Pisupati, Rupa. *Human resource management practices in Anand taluka Panchayat, Kheda district, Gujarat.* Anand: Institute of Rural Management, 1996. IRMA Working Paper No. 106. GIDRL.

Pitroda, Sam and Mody, R.J. *Development of Gujarat: people's perceptions.* Ahmedabad: Sardar Patel Institute of Economic & Social Research, 1997. p. 416. IRMAL.

Prakash, Anjal and Ballabh, Vishwa. *Win-some lose-all game social differentiation and politics of groundwater markets in North Gujarat.* Anand: Institute of Rural Management, 2004. IRMA Working Paper No. 183. p. 39. GIDRL, IRMAL.

Punalekar, S.P. *Action plan framework for Baroda city-level project.* Surat: Centre for Social Studies, 1986. p. 53. CSSL.

Punalekar, S.P. Interface between development and environment: a micro narrative on tribal society in Gujarat. In *National seminar on common property resources and planned development in Western India: challenges and prospects, January 19–21, 1999.* Seminar volume. Nanded: School of Social Sciences and School of Earth Sciences, S.R.T.M. University, 1999. pp. 94–111. CSSL.

Punalekar, S.P. and Gupta, Dipankar. *Block level planning papers: Olpad taluka.* III Vol. Surat: Centre for Social Studies, 1979. p. 105. CSSL.

Punalekar, S.P. and Patel, Priyavadan. *Development plan with social inputs: Sabarkantha district, 1980–81 to 1984–85.* Surat: Centre for Social Studies, 1981. p. 56. CSSL.

Punalekar, S.P. and Patel, Priyavadan. *Social input plan for Bayad & Malpur talukas of Sabarkantha district. interim report.* Surat: Centre for Social Studies, 1980. p. 42. CSSL.

Punalekar, S.P. and Patel, Priyavadan. *Social input plan for Bayad and Malpur talukas of Sabarkantha district: with special reference to the requirements of women and children.* Surat: Centre for Social Studies, 1980. p. 45. CSSL.

Pundir, R.S. and Singh, Katar. *Rural-urban linkages and socio-economic development: a case study of two villages in Gujarat.* Anand: Institute of Rural Management, 2001. p. 36. Research Paper 18. IRMAL, SPIESRL.

Rana, J.S. Infrastructure facilities (IT) and people oriented administration. In *Gujarat-2010: challenges and opportunities.* By Government of Gujarat. Ahmedabad: Sardar Patel Institute of Economic & Social Research, 2001. pp. 510–513. Seminar volume. CSSL, EDIL, IRMAL, SGUL, SPIESRL.

Rao, V.N. Themes in rural economics: I-nature of underdevelopment – a field view. In *Seminar on development of Gujarat problems & prospects, 24th-26 August, 1981*. Ahmedabad: Sardar Patel Institute of Economic & Social Research, 1981. pp. 1–36. CSSL.

Ray, C, N. *Development control, building regulation and judicial activism in Gujarat*. Ahmedabad: Centre for Environment Planning & Technology, 2001. p. [ ]. CEPT Working Paper No. 18. CEPTL, GIDRL.

Ray, C.N. and Sanghvi, Ajaykumar S. *Development and maintenance of public gardens in Ahmedabad*. Ahmedabad: Centre for Environment Planning & Technology, 2005. p. 30. Working Paper No. 28. CSSL.

Ray, C.N., Panneervel, P. and Patel, Paresh. *Recent change in urban management: e-governance initiative by the Ahmedabad municipal corporation*. Ahmedabad: CEPT University, 2005. p. 26. Working Paper No. 31. CSSL.

Roy Chowdhury, P.N. Note on Gujarat-2010 challenges & opportunities-port sector. In *Gujarat-2010: challenges and opportunities*. By Government of Gujarat. Ahmedabad: Sardar Patel Institute of Economic & Social Research, 2001. pp. 497–509. Seminar volume. CSSL, EDIL, IRMAL, SGUL, SPIESRL.

Roy, Raghu. *Planning for development of Surat district, first phase study. Part II: population*. Ahmedabad: Gujarat Institute of Area Planning, 1977. p. 73. CSSL.

Sah, D.C. Avoiding impoverishment risk: towards a policy frame for R&R of dam affected people. In *Seminar on development, displacement and rehabilitation at Centre for Social Studies, Surat, 11–13 May, 1994*. Surat: Centre for Social Studies, 1994. pp. 1–35. CSSL.

Sahai, Baldev and Shelat, K.N. *Desert development plan for Sami-Harij area, Gujarat*. Ahmedabad: ISRO, 1982. p. 105. SPIESRL.

Sahni, B.M. Sustainable development of ground water as a common property resources: lesson from Maharashtra and Gujarat. In *National seminar on common property resources and planned development in Western India: challenges and prospects, January 19–21, 1999*. Seminar volume. Nanded: School of Social Sciences and School of Earth Sciences, S.R.T.M. University, 1999. pp. 193–201. CSSL.

Samanta, B.B. *Planning for development of Surat district, first phase study. Part I: an approach paper on district frame*. Ahmedabad: Gujarat Institute of Area Planning, 1977. p. 17. CSSL.

Samanta, B.B. *Planning for development of Surat district, first phase study. Part IV: agriculture*. Ahmedabad: Gujarat Institute of Area Planning, 1977. p. 59. CSSL.

Samanta, B.B., et al. *Planning for development of Surat district*. Ahmedabad: Gujarat Institute of Area Planning, 1977. p. 109. CSSL.

Sardar Patel Institute of Economic & Social Research. *Gujarat economy in 2001 A.D.: a study in perspective*. Ahmedabad: Author, 1980. p. 376. Monograph Series 8. CSSL, SPUL, SUL, UML.

Sarder Patel Institute of Economic and Social Research. *Study on performance evaluation of Ursts and Ugcds (Surendranagar district)*. Ahmedabad: Sardar Patel Institute of Economic & Social Research, 2002. p. 83. SPIESRL.

Sardar Patel Institute of Economic & Social Research. *Study on some aspects of rural drinking water supply in Gujarat*. Ahmedabad: Sardar Patel Institute of Economic & Social Research, 1995. p. 134. SPIESRL.

Sardar Patel Institute of Economic & Social Research. *Planning atlas of Panchmahals district: Gujarat*. Ahmedabad: Sardar Patel Institute of Economic & Social Research, 1990. p. 239. GIDRL.

Savdasia, V.B., Jhala, P.J. and Thakar, P.H. *Impact of economic reforms on economic growth, labour and employment in Gujarat 2004*. Ahmedabad: Mahatma Gandhi Labour Institute (GLI), 2004. p. 144. GIDRL.

Saxena, Ravi. Infrastructure development in Gujarat. In *Gujarat-2010: challenges and opportunities*. By Government of Gujarat. Ahmedabad: Sardar Patel Institute of Economic & Social Research, 2001. pp. 472–477. Seminar Volume. CSSL, EDIL, IRMAL, SGUL, SPIESRL.

Sen, Jai. *Study of rivers movements around the Narmada dams project in India: some thoughts on history and dynamics: a discussion paper*. [ ], [ ]. 1995. p. 73. CSSL.

Sen, Prabal K. et al. *Impact assessment study of rural development programmes in Sabarkantha district of Gujarat*. Anand: Institute of Rural Management, 2004. p. [ ]. IRMAL.

Shah, Amita. *Who benefits from watershed development?: evidences from Gujarat*. Ahmedabad: Gujarat Institute of Development Research, 2000. p. 27. Working Paper No. 118. GIDRL.

Shah, Amita and Yagnik, Jignasu. *Estimates of BPL-households in rural of Gujarat: measurement, spatial pattern and policy imperatives*. Ahmedabad: Gujarat Institute of Development Research, 2007. pp. 1–27. Working Paper No. 176. SPIESRL.

Shah, Amita, Nandani, Dipak and Joshi Hasmukh. *Marginalisation or mainstreaming? evidence from special economic zones in Gujarat*. Ahmedabad: Gujarat Institute of Development Research, 2012. p. 47. Working Paper No. 210. CSSL, GIDRL.

Shah, Ashvin. *Water for Gujarat: an alternative*. Vishakhapatnam: Jan Vikas Andolan, 1993. p. 72. A technical overview of the flawed Sardar Sarovar Project and a proposal for a sustainable alternative. CSSL.

Shah, Dilip. 'Development of rural poor' through IRDP and NREP in Gujarat (1980–84).In *Rural development and rural poor, 26–28 February 1987*. Surat: Centre for Social Studies, 1987. Seminar Paper. pp. 79–98. CSSL.

Shah, K, R. *Economic growth and human development in Gujarat-lessons forlong-term sustainable growth*. Ahmedabad: D.T. Lakdawala Memorial Trust, 2000. p. [ ]. D.T.L. Occasional Paper Series No. 4. GIDRL.

Shah, K.R., Alagh, Raksha and Patel, B.B. Planning for minimum needs in Gujarat. In *Gujarat economic association*. Ed. by D.T. Lakdawala and B.B. Patel. Ahmedabad: Gujarat Economic Association, 1981. pp. 35–48. SGUL.

Shah, Manubhai M. *Impact of the changes in the district administration since independence on Kheda district*. Gujarat: Sardar Patel University, 1969. p. 200. GVL.

Shah, M.H. *Rural economics of Central Gujarat, part I*. Baroda: Author, 1939. p. 37. CSSL.

Shah, N.M. *Teaching of economics in Gujarat. In Gujarat economic association conference papers, Baroda*. Ed. by V.S. Vyas, Pravin Visaria and A.R. Desai. Ahmedabad: Balgovind, 1971. pp. 274–277. GIDRL, IIML.

Shah, Navin R. *Evaluation of catchment area development programme: a case study of Dantiwada catchment in Gujarat*. Vallabh Vidyanagar: Agro-Economic Research Centre, 1987. p. 58. Research Study No. 76. AERCL, IRMAL, SPIESRL, SPUL.

Shah, Tushaar. *Managing conjunctive water use in canal commands: lessons from the analysis of the Mahi right bank canal, Gujarat*. Anand: Institute of Rural Management, 1988. p. 24. IRMAL.

Shah, V.D. *Impact of national watershed development project for rainfed areas (NWDPRA) in Gujarat: a rapid assessment*. Vallabh Vidyanagar: Sardar Patel University, 1999. p. 68. SPIESRL.

Shah, V.D. and Patel, V.G. *Impact of national watershed development project for rainfed area. (NWDPRA) in Gujarat.* Vallabh Vidyanagar: Agro-Economic Research Centre, 1996. p. 176. Research Study No. 102. IIML, SPUL.

Shah, Vimal. *Planning for Malpur taluka: Sabarkantha district.* Ahmedabad: Gujarat Institute of Area Planning, 1979. p. 384. CSSL.

Shah, Vimal. *Planning for Talala block: a study in micro-level planning.* Ahmedabad: Gujarat Institute of Area Planning, 1974. p. 182. CSSL, SGUL.

Shah, Vimal and Kumbhar, B.L. *Area development plan for social inputs for Junagadh district final report.* Ahmedabad: Gujarat Institute of Area Planning (GIAP), 1987. p. [ ]. GIDRL.

Shah, Vimal and Shah, C.H. *Resurvey of Matar taluka.* Bombay: Vora, 1974. p. 336. CSSL, SGUL, UML.

Sharan, Girja. *Dew harvest: to supplement drinking water sources in arid coastal belt of Kutch.* Ahmedabad: Centre for Environment Education, 2006. p. 59. CEEL.

Sharma, Atul and Parekh, K.M. Government sector. In *Gujarat economy in 2001 A.D.: a study in perspective.* Ahmedabad: Sardar Patel Institute of Economic & Social Research, 1980. pp. 253–268. GUL.

Sharma, S.D. *Tribal area sub-plan-integrated tribal development project Dahod.* Dahod: Tribal Development Department, 1978. p. 65. SPIESRL.

Sheth, N.R. Some thoughts on administration and people. In *Gujarat-2010: challenges and opportunities.* By Government of Gujarat. Ahmedabad: Sardar Patel Institute of Economic & Social Research, 2001. pp. 568–570. Seminar volume. CSSL, EDIL, IRMAL, SGUL, SPIESRL.

Sheth, Pravin N. and Sisodia, Yatindra Singh. *Politics of the Narmada project: the role of the states and NGOs.* Ujjain: Madhya Pradesh Institute of Social Science Research, 1995. p. 80. CSSL.

Shetty, M.C. *Patadia (Sabarkantha district, Gujarat) a tribal village economy in transition.* Vallabh Vidyanagar: Agro-Economic Research Centre, 1963. p. 206. Indian Village Studies No. 1. AERCL.

Shingi, P.M., Seetharaman, S.P. and Patel, M.S. Peoples participation in wastelands development: an evaluative case study of Padhar Mahila Cooperative Society. Ahmedabad: Centre for Management in Agriculture, 1994. p. [ ]. IIML.

Shingi, Prakash M. *Production route to wood fuel energy: a case study of Gujarat's social forestry programme.* Ahmedabad: Centre for Management in Agriculture, 1989. p. 50. IIML.

Shingi, Prakash M. and Asopa, V.N. *Independent evaluation of checkdams in Gujarat strategies and impacts.* Ahmedabad: Centre for Management in Agriculture, Indian Institute of Management, 2002. p. 96. IIML.

Singh, P.K. *Building up of an efficient marketing system to obviate the need for large scale state intervention in Gujarat.* Vallabh Vidyanagar: Sardar Patel University, 2004. p. 130. Research Study No. 126. SPIESRL.

Soni, Jayshree. *Human aspects of water management: a trend report.* Surat: Centre for Social Sudies, 2001. p. 83. CSSL.

Soni, Jayshree. *Monitoring & evaluation of R&R of SSP series: general report: Gujarat.* Surat: Centre for Social Studies, 2007. p. 440. CSSL.

Soni, Jayshree. *Study on the impact of Jyotigram Yojana: a case study of Navsari district.* Anand: International Water Management Institute, 2007. p. 58. CSSL.

Soni, Jayshree. *Water scarcity and gender dimension.* Surat: Centre for Social Studies, 2001. p. 36. CSSL.

Streefkerk, Hein. Drinking water supply in Gujarat and the Netherlands: a comparison. In *International seminar on "Gujarat society", 17–20 December 1986.* Surat: Centre for Social Studies, 1986. pp. 1–13. CSSL.

Surat Municipal Corporation and Environmental Planning. *Surat inner city revitalization plan*. Surat: Author, 1998. p. 94. CSSL.

Tata Economic Consultancy Services. *Economic appraisal of Sardar Sarovar Project*. Bombay: Author, 1983. p. [ ]. CSSL.

Tata Economic Consultancy Services. *Methodological framework for economic appraisal of Narmada project.* Bombay: Tata Economic Consultancy Services, 1981. p. 78. CSSL.

Tata Institute of Social Science. *Performance and development effectiveness of the Sardar Sarovar Project.* Mumbai: Author, 2008. p. 102. CSSL.

Transportation and Housing, Department of. Challenges and opportunities in the transportation sector. In *Gujarat-2010: challenges and opportunities*. By Government of Gujarat. Ahmedabad: Sardar Patel Institute of Economic & Social Research, 2001. pp. 495–496. Seminar volume. CSSL, EDIL, IRMAL, SGUL, SPIESRL.

Tribal Research & Training Institute. *Mapping in ITDP talukas of Gujarat*. Ahmedabad: Tribal Research & Training Institute, 2010. p. [ ]. TRTIL.

Trivedi, Harshad R. *Some aspects of role of Panchayats and institutional arrangements for canal irrigation in two talukas of Ahmedabad district.* Ahmedabad: Institute of Cultural and Urban Anthropology, 1982. p. 73. SPIESRL.

Trivedi, T.K. and Savdashia, V.B. Identification of backward area. In *Gujarat economic association conference papers, Baroda.* Ed. by V.S. Vyas, Pravin Visaria and A.R. Desai. Ahmedabad: Balgovind, 1971. pp. 16–21. GIDRL, IIML.

Trivedi, Vimal. *Door to door garbage collection program in Surat city*. Surat: Centre for Social Studies, 2009. p. 20. Working Paper No. 7. CSSL, SPIESRL.

Upadhyaya, Chandrakant. *Evaluation study of vocational training centre in tribal areas of Gujarat*. Ahmedabad: Tribal Research & Training Institute, Gujarat Vidyapith, 1998. p. 108. Serise 349. TRTIL.

Vaidya, Chunibhai. Resettlement and rehabilitation Sardar Sarovar Project: role of the people and the NGOs. In *Seminar on development, displacement and rehabilitation at Centre for Social Studies, Surat, 11–13 May, 1994*. Surat: Centre for Social Studies, 1994. pp. 1–12. CSSL.

Vaidya, Jitendra. *Community structuring in Gujarat planning aspects.*Ahmedabad: Centre for Environment Planning & Technology, 1971. p. 199. IRMAL.

Van Dorsten, F. *Impact of Amul on the milk economy of Kheda district (Gujarat).* The Hague: Institute of Social Studies, 1986. p. [ ]. Working paper-series on dairy aid and development No. 21. CSSL.

Viswanathan, L.S. *Studies on rehabilitation of submerging villages: Surpan.* Surat: Centre for Social Studies, 1983. p. 89. CSSL.

Viswanathan, L.S. and Chaudhury, S.K. *Studies on rehabilitation of submerging villages: Gadher.* Surat: Centre for Social Studies, 1982. p. 80. CSSL.

Viswanathan, P.K. *Will neoliberal policies resolve water sector dilemmas?: learning from Maharashtra and Gujarat.* Ahmedabad: Gujarat Institute of Development Research, 2011. pp. 1–40. Working Paper Series No. 202. CSSL, SPIESRL.

Vittal, N. Public administration for Gujarat incorporated. In *Gujarat-2010: challenges and opportunities*. By Government of Gujarat. Ahmedabad: Sardar Patel Institute of Economic & Social Research, 2001. pp. 559–567. Seminar volume. CSSL, EDIL, IRMAL, SGUL, SPIESRL.

Von, Vorgelegt and Mehta, Lyla. *Tribal women facing submergence: the Sardar Sarovar(Narmada) Project in India and the social consequences of involuntary resettlement*. [ ]: [ ], 1992. p. 219. CSSL.

Wadhva, Kiran. Performance of Gujarat's economy: growth and stability. In *Gujarat economy problems and prospects.* Ed. by D.T. Lakdawala. Ahmedabad: Sardar Patel Institute of Economic & Social Research, 1983. pp. 45–88. Monograph 10. GIDRL, IIML.

Wadhva, Kiran. Performance of Gujarat's economy: growth and stability. In *Seminar on development of Gujarat: problems & prospects, 24th-26 August, 1981.* Ahmedabad: Sardar Patel Institute of Economic & Social Research, 1981. pp. 1–24. CSSL.

World Bank. *Gujarat earthquake recovery program: assessment report, March 14, 2001*. Washington, DC: World Bank, 2001. p. 87. GIDRL.

9

Finance, Cooperatives

Books/Chapter in Books

Alagh, Y.K., Bhalla, G.S. and Kashyap, S.P. *Structural analysis of Gujarat, Punjab and Haryana economics*. New Delhi: Allied, 1980. p. 239. CSSL, SPUL.

Amin, T.C. and Kapadia, P.R. Pricing policy in cooperative dairy sector in Gujarat. In *Milk pricing and marketing practices of cooperative dairy industry in Gujarat*. Ed. by Dilip Shah. Pune: Maricheemalee, 1987. pp. 109–114. CSSL, GIDRL, SPIESRL.

Amin, Vithalbhai P. *Gujarat urban co-operative banks federation Ahmedabad.* Ahmedabad: Gujarat Urban Co-Operative Bank Federation, 1984. p. 101. IIML.

Apte, D.P. Role of co-operative dairy schemes in rural development in India. In *Who shares?: co-operatives and rural development*. Ed. by D.W. Attwood and B.S. Baviskar. Delhi: Oxford, 1988. pp. 378–393. AERCL, CSSL, SPUL, TRTIL.

Arya, Anita. Recent development in the farmer market linkages of agri-business in Gujarat. In *Managing rural finances in India.* Ed. by Gursharan Singh Kainth. New Delhi: Concept, 2010. pp. 278–286. HML, IIML, SPIESRL.

Attwood, D.W. and Baviskar, B.S., ed. *Who shares?: co-operatives and rural development*. Delhi: Oxford, 1988. p. 432. AERCL, CSSL, SPUL, TRTIL.

Bapat, M.T. Durgapura Sarvodaya Samudayik Kheti Sahakari Mandali Ltd. (Bhavanagar district). In *Assessment of cooperative farming societies in Gujarat and Rajasthan.* Ed. by K.M. Choudhary, M.T. Bapat and D.P. Gupta. Anand: Sardar Patel University, 1972. pp. 137–159. GVL.

Barua, S.K., Dholakia, R.H. and Seetharaman, S.P. Integrated resource based co-operative development: Panchmahals. Ahmedabad: Indian Institute of Management, 1990. p. 74. IIML.

Baviskar, B.S. Dairy co-operatives and rural development in Gujarat. In *Resource, institutions and strategies*. Ed. by Martin Doornbos and K.N. Nair. New Delhi: Sage, 1990. pp. 256–273. HML, TRTIL.

Baviskar, B.S. Dairy co-operatives and rural development in Gujarat. In *Who shares?: co-operatives and rural development*. Ed. by D.W. Attwood and B.S. Baviskar. Delhi: Oxford, 1988. pp. 345–361. AERCL, CSSL, SPUL, TRTIL.

Bhatt, Mahesh and Trivedi, M.S. *Metropolitan finance in a developing economy: Ahmedabad municipal corporation: a case Study*. Ahmedabad: Balgovind, 1969. p. 52. GUL, SPUL.

Bhatt, R.N. *History of the co-operative movement in Surat district 1944–54.* Surat: Chunilal Gandhi Vidyabhavan, 1956. p. 212. GVL, SGUL, SPUL.

Bhatt, Sonal. Pricing of canal irrigation and service delivering: an empirical study in Fatewadi canal command area in Gujarat. In *Democratisation of water.* Ed. by

B.K. Thapliyal, et al. Hyderabad: National Institute of Rural Development, 2008. pp. 343–364. SPUL.

Buddha, K.D. *Co-operation in Gujarat.* Ahmedabad: Gujarat State Co-Operative Union, 1975. p. 33. GVL.

Chaudhari, Jaydip and Lad, Chetankumar J. Role of microfinance for bridging the gap of energy supply and demand in rural Gujarat. In *Entrepreneurship: innovations and strategy*. Ed. by Sudipta Kishore Nanda and Tapankumar Lenka. Mumbai: Himalaya, 2012. pp. 79–87. GUL.

Chen, Marty and Dholakia, Anila. Sewa's women's dairy cooperatives: a case study from Gujarat. In *Indian women: a study of their role in the dairy movement*. [Ed.] by Marty Chen, et al. Sahidabad: Vikas, 1986. pp. 70–106. CSSL, HML.

Choudhary, K.M. Crop insurance scheme for hybrid-4 cotton in Gujarat: field problems and prospects. In *Crop insurance India.* Ed. by M.L. Dantwala. Anand: Sardar Patel University, 1983. pp. 137-[ ]. SPIESRL.

Das, Biswaroop. *Micro-finance and rural credit markets: a study of clients using micro-credit in Gujarat and Maharashtra*. Ahmedabad: Friends of Women's World Banking, 2005. p. 163. CSSL.

Das, Santosh Kumar. Sources and patterns of private investment in Gujarat. In *Poverty amidst prosperity: essays on the trajectory of development in Gujarat.* Ed. by Atul Sood. Delhi: Aakar, 2012. pp. 45–60. CSSL, IRMAL, MICAL.

Dave, Bharati D. Social sector in the fiscal operations of Gujarat in the post reforms period. In *State level fiscal reforms in the Indian economy*. Ed. by D.K. Srivastava and M. Narasimhulu. New Delhi: Deep & Deep, 2006. pp. 727–735. HML.

Dave, P.K., Patel, R.J. and Bhatt, M.P. Revenue implications of agricultural holding tax in Gujarat state. In *Role of direct and indirect taxes in underdeveloped countries.* Ed. by M.P. Bhatt. Ahmedabad: Gujarat University, 1981. pp. 163–171. SPIESRL.

Desai, B.H. *Financial structure of cotton textile mills of Ahmedabad*. Anand: Sardar Patel University, 1983. p. 371. GVL.

Desai, D.B., et al. Sources and utilization pattern of agricultural credit among the farmers of South Gujarat. In *Agricultural finance-problems and prospects.* Ed. by D.M. Kuchhadiya and R.L. Shiyani. Junagadh: Department of Agricultural Economics, 1997. pp. 83–86. SPIESRL.

Desai, Himanshu. State level fiscal reforms: a case study of Gujarat's budget. In *State level fiscal reforms in the Indian economy*. Ed. by D.K. Srivastava and M. Narasimhulu. New Delhi: Deep & Deep, 2006. pp. 543–554. HML.

Desai, M.B. and Mehta, R.S. Cooperation: a democratic agency of change. In *Community development & democratic growth*. Ed. by N.R. Inamdar. [ ]: [ ], 1974. pp. 140–160. SGUL.

Dholakia, Archana R. Non-tax revenue and subsidies in Gujarat. In *Dynamics of development in Gujarat*. Ed. by Indira Hirway, S.P. Kashyap and Amita Shah. New Delhi: Concept, 2002. pp. 131–165. CSSL, EDIL, GIDRL, GVL, HML, IRMAL, SPUL, UML.

Dholakia, Archana R. and Yadav, Yogesh T. Fiscal financing for tribal development. In *Tribal development in Western India*. Ed. by Amita Shah and Jharna Pathak. New Delhi: Routledge, 2014. pp. 259–284. CSSL.

Dodkey, M.D., Kuchhadiya, D.B. and Visawadia, H.R. Short term credit gap and credit requirements for different categories of farmers of Junagadh district(Gujarat). In *Agricultural finance-problems and prospects.* Ed. by D.B. Kuchhadiya and R.L.

Shiyani. Junagadh: Department of Agricultural Economics, 1997. pp. 130–135. SPIESRL.

Doornbos, Martin, et al. *Dairy and development: India's operation flood*. New Delhi: Sage, 1990. p. 336. CSSL.

Dwivedi, R.C. Growth of Surat district co-operative spinning mills. In *Glimpses of co-operatives through press*. New Delhi: Coop Time, 1987. pp. 61–65. Compendium 25 years clipping co-operatives image series. IIML.

Elavia, B.H. *Innovations in rural refinancing: the Indian experience*. Baroda: Author, 1988. p. 178. HML.

Elavia, B.H. *Study of co-operative land development banking in Gujarat*. Baroda: M.S. University, 1979. p. 151. GVL, HML, IIML.

Franco, F. and Vijaya Sherry Chand, P.G. *Operation flood and the voluntary sector: a study of tribal dairy cooperatives in South Gujarat*. New Delhi: Indian Social Institute, 1991. p. 250. CSSL, IRMAL.

Gadhavi, Archana. Effect of financial crisis on tourism industry in India with special reference to Gujarat. In *Global financial crisis and India*. Ed. by Krishan A. Goyal. Jaipur: Prateeksha, 2012. pp. 203–216. GUL.

Gare, G.M. and Birari, D.T. Forest labour co-operative societies in Maharashtra and Gujarat: their significance in tribal development. In *Tribal life and forests*. Ed. by Devendra Thakur and D.N. Thakur. New Delhi: Deep & Deep, 1994. pp. 240–267. SPUL.

Gautam, I.P. Financing the Sardar Sarovar Project: challenges and solutions. In *Sardar Sarovar Project on the river Narmada*. Vol. 1. Ed. by R. Parthasarathy and Ravindra H. Dholakia. New Delhi: Concept, 2011. pp. 174–186. CEPTL, CSSL, EDIL, HML, IIML, SETUL, SPUL, TRTIL, UML.

George, Shanti. Beyond Anand: comparing the Kheda and Choryasi dairy cooperatives. In *Finding middle path: the political economy of cooperation in rural India*. By B.S. Baviskar and Donald W. Attwood. New Delhi: Vistar, 1995. pp. 237–254. CSSL, HML.

George, Shanti. Co-operatives and Indian dairy policy: more Anand than pattern. In *Who shares?: co-operatives and rural development*. Ed. by D.W. Attwood and B.S. Baviskar. Delhi: Oxford, 1988. pp. 394–426. AERCL, CSSL, SPUL, TRTIL.

George, Shanti. *Matter of people: co-operative dairying in India and Zimbabwe*. Delhi: Oxford, 1994. p. 540. CSSL.

George, Shanti. *Operation flood: an appraisal of current Indian dairy policy*. Delhi: Oxford, 1985. p. 320. CSSL.

Govinda Rao, M. *Entry tax as an alternative to octroi: the base and rate structure of the proposed entry tax in Gujarat*. New Delhi: National Institute of Public Finance and Policy, 1984. p. 113. SPIESRL.

Gujarat Co-Operative Farming Survey Committee, Ahmedabad. *Co-operative farming in Gujarat: a study into the working of the co-operative farming societies in Gujarat*. Bombay: Indian Society of Agricultural Economics, 1959. p. 138. CSSL.

Heredero, J.M. Milk cooperatives and tribal poverty in Gujarat: need of education and management. In *National development and tribal deprivation*. Ed. by Walter Fernandes. New Delhi: Indian Social Institute, 1992. pp. 285–315. CSSL.

Heredia, Ruth. *Amul India story*. New Delhi: Tata McGraw Hill, 1997. p. 297. IIML, SPUL.

Jani, B.M. State government finances in Gujarat. In *Fiscal deficit of states in India*. Ed. by Janak Raj Gupta. New Delhi: Atlantic, 2001. pp. 54–62. GVL, HML.

Jodha, N.S. Study of the co-operative short-term credit movement in selected areas of Gujarat. In *Serving the small farmer: policy choices in Indian agricultural development*. Ed. by Guy Hunter and Anthony Bottrall. London: Croom Helm, 1974. pp. 59–91. AAUL, AERCL, IIML, SPUL.

Joshi, P.C. Tax structure of the Surat municipal corporation. In *Role of direct and indirect taxes in underdeveloped countries.* Ed. by M.P. Bhatt. Ahmedabad: Gujarat University, 1981. pp. 31–39. SPIESRL.

Joshi, Satyakam. Role of forest labour cooperative societies in tribal development. In *Tribal situation in India: issues in development: with special reference to Western India*. Ed. by Vidyut Joshi. Jaipur: Rawat, 1998. pp. 127–150. CSSL, GVL, UML.

Kulkarni, K.M. City size and municipal finance in Gujarat. In *India's urban land policy and development finance*. Ed. by R.C. Sharma. Delhi: Seema, 1988. pp. 263–270. HML.

Kulkarni, Shirish R. Urban cooperative banks: an appraisal. In *Profile of urban co-operative banks in Indian and Gujarat*. New Delhi: Anmol, 1996. pp. 5–26. HML.

Lakdawala, D.T. *Justice in taxation in India: with special reference to British Gujarat.* Bombay: Popular, 1946. p. 312. SPIESRL.

Lalitha, N. *SHGs and microfinance: a research compendium.* Delhi: Dominant, 2008. p. 246. GVL.

Makwana, Ashish. Anand pattern: a model for developing countries for milk production. In *Gujarat economy: the way ahead*. Ed. by Sudha V. Menon. Hyderabad: ICFAI University, 2009. pp. 184–194. EDIL, HML, SPIESRL.

Mandalia, V.K. Study on cost of production of milk. In *Milk pricing and marketing practices of cooperative dairy industry in Gujarat*. Ed. by Dilip Shah. Pune: Maricheemalee, 1987. pp. 101–108. CSSL.

Maniar, Ramniklal. *Co-operation in Gujarat.* Ahmedabad: Gujarat State Co-Operative Union, 1969. p. 112. GVL.

Mehta, C.A. Historical and analytical study of the British land revenue policy in Deccan and Gujarat, 1930. In *Dissertation in economics 1921–1971*. Ed. by C.H. Shah. Bombay: University of Bombay, 1974. pp. 117–119. SPIESRL.

Mulani, J.M. *Co-operative movement in Gujarat*. Ahmedabad: Author, 1998. p. 59. IRMAL, TRTIL.

Munshi, K.G. Productivity of urban co-operative bank in Gujarat. *In Financial management techniques: a study of urban co-operative bank.* New-Delhi: Anmol, 1990. pp. 105–118. IIML.

Naik, Umesh and Nair, Sandhya. Structure and design of horticultural produce co-operatives: two contrasting cases. In *Rediscovering co-operation.* Vol. III: *co-operatives in the emerging context*. Ed. by R. Rajagopalan. Anand: Institute of Rural Management, 1996. pp. 369–384. CSSL.

Nair, Tara S. and Shankar, Bhawani. Livelihoods and financial behaviour of tribal households: linking experience and strategies. In *Tribal development in Western India*. Ed. by Amita Shah and Jharna Pathak. New Delhi: Routledge, 2014. pp. 241–258. CSSL.

National Council of Applied Economic Research. *Incidence of taxation in Gujarat.* New Delhi: National Council of Applied Economic Research, 1970. p. 118. GVL, SPIESRL, SPUL.

Nizar, Jetha. Gujarat state finances. In *State finances in India.* Ed. by Amaresh Bagchi, J.L. Bajaj and A. William Burd. New Delhi: Vikas, 1992. pp. 373–429. HML, SPIESRL, SPUL.

Panda, Smita Mishra. Engendering cooperative governance: case of women dairy co-operative societies in Gujarat. In *Engendering governance institutions*. Ed. by Smita Mishra Panda. New Delhi: Sage, 2008. pp. 249–264. SGUL.

Patani, M.R. and Antani, K.L. Repayment and over dues of agricultural advances by Dena bank in Banaskantha district of Gujarat state. In *Agricultural finance-problems and prospects*. Ed. by D.B. Kuchhadiya and R.L. Shiyani. Junagadh: Department of Agricultural Economics, 1997. pp. 122–126. SPIESRL.

Patel, A.S. Co-operative dairying and rural development: a case study of Amul. In *Who shares?: co-operatives and rural development*. Ed. by D.W. Attwood and B.S. Baviskar. Delhi: Oxford, 1988. pp. 362–377. AERCL, CSSL, SPUL, TRTIL.

Patel, A.S. Oilseeds growers' cooperatives in Gujarat: Patidar factor. In *Finding middle path: the political economy of cooperation in rural India*. By B.S. Baviskar and Donald W. Attwood. New Delhi: Vistar, 1995. pp. 255–272. CSSL, HML.

Patel, B.B. *Bank finance for self employment in a metropolitan labour market: Ahmedabad-utilisation and issues*. Ahmedabad: Gandhi Labour Institute, 1985. p. 105. SPIESRL.

Patel, R.J. Cess on commercial crops: a case for Gujarat. In *Role of direct and indirect taxes in underdeveloped countries*. Ed. by M.P. Bhatt. Ahmedabad: Gujarat University, 1981. pp. 60–62. CSSL, SPIESRL.

Patel, Ramu. *Finances of Gujarat*. Ahmedabad: Western Times, 1982, p. 238. AAUL, SPIESRL.

Patel, S.K. and Vaswani, L.K. Attitude of the farmers towards tobacco co-operatives: pre-and post-establishment comparison. In *Co-operatives and economic development*. Ed. by Tapas R. Dash and K.K. Sen. Jaipur: Rawat, 1998. pp. 114–123. CSSL.

Patel, V.G. *Innovations in banking: Gujarat experiments*. Bombay: Industrial Development Bank, 1981. p. 68. SPIESRL.

Pathak, Mahesh T. *Significance of public investment for backward regions: a case study of the fluorsper project in Gujarat*. Vallabh Vidyanagar: Department of Economics, 1972. p. 156. IIML, UML.

Pathak, Mahesh T. and Patel, Arun S. *Agricultural taxation in Gujarat*. Bombay: Asia, 1968. p. 93. AAUL, GVL, HML, IRMAL, SPIESRL, TRTIL.

Rajaram, N. Impact of liberalisation on village milk co-operatives: a sociological study of Kheda district. In *Rediscovering co-operation*. Vol. III: *co-operatives in the emerging context*. Ed. by R. Rajagopalan. Anand: Institute of Rural Management, 1996. pp. 158–175. CSSL, HML.

Rajaram, N. Sociological analysis of cotton cooperatives in Baroda district. In *Finding middle path: political economy of cooperation in rural India*. By B.S. Baviskar and Donald W. Attwood. New Delhi: Vistar, 1995. pp. 273–289. CSSL, HML, IIML.

Rajgopalan, R., ed. *Rediscovering co-operation*. Vol. 3: *co-operatives in the emerging context*. Anand: Institute of Rural Management, 1996. p. 500. CSSL.

Reddy, K.N. Finances of Baroda municipal corporation. In *Profiles of a growing city: socio-economic studies of Baroda city*. Baroda: M.S. University, 1971. pp. 40–51. Maharaja Sayajirao University Economics Series No. 1. SPIESRL.

Row, S.V.L.N. Financing state plans problems and prospects: with particular reference to Gujarat. In *Financing of state plane problems and prospects*. Ed. by Jagannath Mishra and R.K. Sinha. New Delhi: Sterling, 1984. pp. 33–89. HML, SPUL.

Sachdeva, R.K. and Kajarekar, R.G. Computerised financial information system: a case study of government of Gujarat. In *Financial planning and management*. Ed. by Asit K. Ghosh and Prem Kumar. New Delhi: Anmol, 1991. pp. 131–152. GVL.

Sathe, Arun. Law of defection and present Gujarat crisis. In *Striking the balance: Indian fiscal scene 2000.* Mumbai: English Edition, 1999. pp. 136-[ ]. SPUL.

Shah, D.R. *Cooperative dairy farming in Gujarat.* New Delhi: Somaiya, 1985. p. 169. IIML.

Shah, D.R. *Economic analysis of co-operative dairy farming in Gujarat.* Bombay: Somaiya, 1985. p. 169. CSSL.

Shah, Dilip. *Co-operativization liberalization and dairy industry in India.* Jaipur: ABD, 2000. p. 183. CSSL, HML.

Shah, Dilip. Insurance for the members of the dairy cooperatives in Gujarat: possibility and issues. In *Social security for unorganized labour*. Ed. by B.B. Patel. New Delhi: Oxford, 1993. pp. 239–248. CSSL.

Shah, Dilip. *Milk pricing marketing practices: of cooperative dairy industry in Gujarat.* Pune: Maricheemalee, 1987. p. 286. CSSL, GIDRL, IIML, SPIESRL.

Shah, Dilip. Milk pricing: a case study of urban cooperative dairy of Baroda. In *Milk pricing and marketing practices of cooperative dairy industry in Gujarat.* Ed. by Dilip Shah. Pune: Maricheemalee, 1987. pp. 115–132. CSSL, GIDRL, IIML, SPIESRL.

Shah, Dilip. Performance and problems of Gujarat cooperative milk marketing federation. In *Milk pricing and marketing practices of cooperative dairy industry in Gujarat.* Ed. by Dilip Shah. Pune: Maricheemalee, 1987. pp. 180–212. CSSL, GIDRL.

Shah, Dilip. Private sector dairies in Vadodara: impact and future strategy for the Vadodara district co-operative union. In *Rediscovering co-operation.* Vol. III: *co-operatives in the emerging context*. Ed. by R. Rajagopalan. Anand: Institute of Rural Management, 1996. pp. 176–211. CSSL, HML.

Shah, Dilip. *Random reflection on rural development.* Jaipur: ABD, 2012. p. [ ]. SPUL.

Shah, Dilip R. *Dairy cooperativization: an instrument of social change.* Jaipur: Rawat, 1992. p. 171. CSSL.

Shah, J.M. Mechanism of pricing policies. In *Milk pricing and marketing practices of cooperative dairy industry in Gujarat*. Ed. by Dilip Shah. Pune: Maricheemalee, 1987. pp. 35–45. CSSL.

Shah, Manubhai M. *Industrial co-operatives in Kaira district: a depth study.* Nadiad: Kaira District Co-Operative Union, 1975. p. [ ]. SPUL.

Shah, Manubhai M. *Integration of district dairy cooperatives in Gujarat.* Anand: Sardar Patel University, 1977. p. 276. GVL, HML, SPUL.

Shah, N.R. Paldi Samyukta Krishi Sahakari Mandali Ltd(Surat district). In *Assessment of cooperative farming societies in Gujarat and Rajasthan.* Ed. by K.M. Choudhary, M.T. Bapat and D.P. Gupta. Anand: Sardar Patel University, 1972. pp. 11–59. GVL.

Shah, N.R. Laxmanpura Samyukta Krishi Sahakari Mandali Ltd (Bhavanagar district). In *Assessment of cooperative farming societies in Gujarat and Rajasthan.* Ed. by K.M. Choudhary, M.T. Bapat and D.P. Gupta. Anand: Sardar Patel University, 1972. pp. 83–107. GVL.

Shah, Tushaar. *Catalysing co-operation: design of self-governing organisations.* New Delhi: Sage, 1996. p. 315. CSSL, HML.

Shah, Tushaar. *Making farmers' co-operatives work: design, governance and management*. New Delhi: Sage, 1995. p. 275. CSSL, SPUL.

Shah, V.B. and Maharaja, M. Crop insurance scheme in Gujarat. In *Crop insurance India.* Ed. by M.L. Dantwala. Anand: Sardar Patel University, 1983. pp. 125-[ ]. SPIESRL.

Sharma, Atul. Gujarat finances: reform of budgetary management. In *Dynamics of development in Gujarat*. Ed. by Indira Hirway, S.P. Kashyap and Amita Shah. New Delhi: Concept, 2002. pp. 61–98. CSSL, EDIL, GIDRL, GVL, HML, IRMAL, SPUL, UML.

Shroff, Sangeeta. Cotton marketing through co-operatives: case of the Gujarat state co-operative cotton federation. In *Rediscovering co-operation*. Vol. III: *co-operatives in the emerging context*. Ed. by R. Rajagopalan. Anand: Institute of Rural Management, 1996. pp. 43–60. CSSL, HML.

Singh, Katar and Bhattacharya, Saumindra. Salt miners' cooperatives in the little rann of Kachchh in Gujarat. In *Cooperative management of natural resources*. Ed. by Katar Singh and Vishwa Ballabh. New Delhi: Sage, 1996. pp. 122–140. CSSL.

Singh, P.K. Comparative analysis of performance of rural energy co-operatives. In *Rediscovering co-operation*. Vol. III: *co-operatives in the emerging context*. Ed. by R. Rajagopalan. Anand: Institute of Rural Management, 1996. pp. 276–293. CSSL, HML.

Sridhar, Kala Seetharam and Venugopala Reddy, A. Ahmedabad. In *State of urban services in India's cities: spending and financing*. New Delhi: Oxford, 2010. pp. 16–52. CSSL.

Sriram, M.S., Prathap Reddy, K. and Agrawal, Rajesh. Capital formation strategies of district level dairy co-operative unions in Gujarat. In *Rediscovering co-operation*. Vol. III: *co-operatives in the emerging context*. Ed. by R. Rajagopalan. Anand: Institute of Rural Management, 1996. pp. 237–275. CSSL, HML.

Subrahmanyam, B. and Reddy, Dharma M. *Deposit mobilisation: a case study of Kheda district central co-operative bank*. Bombay: National Federation of State Co-operative Bank, 1985. p. 67. IIML.

Thakar, B.C. *Jamngar Gramin Bank: a study*. Ahmedabad: Sardar Patel Institute of Economic & Social Research, 1989. p. 57. SPIESRL.

Trivedi, A.B. *Wealth of Gujarat*. Jaipur: Author, 1943. p. 447. ASL, CSSL, GVL, HML, SETUL, SPUL.

Trivedi, A.B. Wealth of Gujarat (1944). In *Dissertation in economics 1921–1971*. Ed. by C.H. Shah. Bombay: University of Bombay, 1974. pp. 616–617. SPIESRL.

Trivedi, H.K. and Dholakia, R.V. *Impact of foreign remittances on the economy of Baladia (dist. Bhuj, Kutch): a case study*. Ahmedabad: Gujarat University, 1981. p. 47. IIML, SPIESRL.

Upadhyay, Ghanshyam. Fiscal reforms in Gujarat. In *State level fiscal reforms in the Indian economy*. Ed. by D.K. Srivastava and M. Narasimhulu. New Delhi: Deep & Deep, 2006. pp. 590–595. HML.

Vyas, Jay Narayan, Patel, D.R. and Joshi, Ashish. *Financing an industrial unit*. Ahmedabad: Sapana Industrial & Allied, 1999. pp. 31–49 SPIESRL.

Vyas, M.M. *Diversified and development co-operative banking: a case study of the Gujarat state co-operative bank*. Ahmedabad: Gujarat State Co-Operative Bank, 1991. p. 35. IIML.

Vyas, Sima H. and Shiyani, R.L. Loan performance portfolio of RRBs in Gujarat with special reference to Junagadh Amreli Gramin Bank. In *Agricultural finance-problems and prospects*. Ed. by D.B. Kuchhadiya and R.L. Shiyani. Junagadh: Department of Agricultural Economics, 1997. pp. 39–49. SPIESRL.

Vyas, V.S. *Economics of dairy farming Mehsana district of Gujarat state*. Anand: Sardar Patel University, 1971. p. 143. SPIESRL.

Journal Articles

Angrish, A.C., Kuchhadiya, D.B. and Thumor, B.L. Growth rate of loans recovery outstanding of Gujarat state co-operative land. *Indian Co-operative Review*. 14, 3, 1977. pp. 259–270. SGUL.

Asthana, A.K. Development of consumer cooperatives in Gujarat. *Cooperative Perspective*. 33, 1, 1998. pp. 48–51. IRMAL.

Asthana, A.K. Marketing of banking services: case study of the Mehsana Urban Cooperative Bank Ltd., Mehsana Gujarat. *Cooperative Perspective*. 32, 2, 1997. pp. 28–32. IRMAL.

Attwood, D.M. and Baviskar, B.S. Why do some co-operatives work but not others?: a comparative analysis of sugar co-operatives in India. *Economic and Political Weekly*. 22, 26, 1987. pp. A-38-A-56. CEPTL, CSSL, GUL, IIML, IRMAL, SGUL, SPIESRL, UML.

Bapat, M.T. Working of a farmer's service society in Banaskantha district of Gujarat. *Indian Cooperative Review*. 16, 3, 1979. pp. 262–285. HML.

Baviskar, B.S. and George, Shanti. Development and controversy: National Dairy Development Board. *Economic and Political Weekly*. 23, 13, 1988. pp. A-35-A-43. CEPTL, CSSL, IIML, IRMAL, SGUL, SPIESRL, UML.

Bhatt, Karthik. Study of trends in the expenditure of Gujarat government. *Vishleshan*. 20, 2, 1995. pp. 21–28. CSSL, IIML, IRMAL.

Bhatt, Mahesh P. and Shah, Ramesh M. Financial implications of Gujarat state finance commission's recommendations. *Vishleshan*. 25, 1, 2000. pp. 22–31. IIML, IRMAL.

Bhatt, Mahesh and Thaker, C.H. Finances of the Gujarat government. *Economic and Political Weekly*. 2, 15, 1967. pp. 727–731. CSSL, HML, SPIESRL, TRTIL, UML.

Bhattacharya, B. Wealth of Gujarat in manuscripts. *Journal of the Gujarat Research Society*. 8, 2 and 3, 1946. pp. 125–126. GUL.

Bhushri, Narendra K. and Veena, D.R. District income estimation: a study of Surendranagar. *Vishleshan*. 5, 2–3, 1979. pp. 249–262. CSSL, GIDRL.

Bishnoi, T.R. and Sobita Devi, Ksh. Three decades of banking in Gujarat. *Vishleshan*. 39, 2, 2013. pp. 13–25. CSSL.

Chakrabarty, Gurupada. Level and distribution of income among scheduled castes and tribes in rural Gujarat. *Artha-Vikas*. 35, 1, 1999. pp. 28–37. AAUL, CSSL, GIDRL, IRMAL.

Chari, V.C. and Patel, R.K. Growth of urban co-operative banks in Gujarat. *Southern Economist*. 45, 15–16, 2006. pp. 15–20. SGUL.

Chaturvedi, H.R. and Mitra, Subrata. Rural co-operatives: hope or despair?: a comparative study of Gujarat and Orissa. *Social Change*. 17, 2, 1987. pp. 16–25. CSSL, HML, IRMAL, UML.

Chavda, Kishorsinh N. and Patel, Chetankumar C. Analysis of financial statements: a case study of the Surat District Co-operative Bank Ltd. *VNSGU Journal of Humanities & Social Sciences*. 3, 1, 2011. pp. 1–18. CSSL.

Dave, Dhaval and Dave, Rina. Study on measuring policy holders' perception for the selected insurance companies in Anand city. *Vishleshan*. 36, 3, 2011. pp. 31–42. CSSL, IIML.

Dave, P.K., Patel, R.J. and Bhatt, M.P. Revenue implications of agricultural holding tax in Gujarat state. *Vishleshan*. 4, 2, 1978. pp. 104–121. CSSL, GIDRL, IIML.

Desai, B.M. Formal and informal credit sources in tribal areas: a case of Dharampur taluka. *Artha-Vikas*. 12, 2, 1976. pp. 78–94. GIDRL, SGUL.

Desai, Bhupat M. Financial viability of the PACS in Gujarat. *Vishleshan*. 23, 3, 1998. pp. 140–150. IRMAL.

Desai, M.R. Study of the finance of municipal corporation of Gujarat. *Arth-Vikas*. 12, 1, 1976. pp. 70–78. GIDRL, GVL, HML, SGUL.

Desai, S.V. Survey of the mobilisation of saving among the textile workers of Ahmedabad. *Journal of the Gujarat Research Society*. 23, 2/90, 1961. pp. 164–165. GVL.

Desai, U.T., Desai, H.A. and Desai, M.P. Diagnosis of financial health of sugar mills of Gujarat state. *Vishleshan*. 35, 3, 2010. pp. 38–45. CSSL, IIML.

Dholakia, Archana R. Changes in the trend and structure of fiscal expenditure in Gujarat. *Anvesak*. 28, 1, 1998. pp. 13–27. CSSL, GIDRL, IRMAL, SPIESRL.

Dholakia, Archana R. Fiscal imbalance in Gujarat: non-tax revenue and subsidies. *Economic and Political Weekly*. 35, 35 and 36, 2000. pp. 3217–3227. BUL, CEPTL, CSSL, EDIL, GIDRL, IIML, IRMAL, MICAL, SGUL, SPIESRL, UML.

Dholakia, Archana R. Growth and structure of tax and non-tax revenue of Gujarat. *Indian Journal of Regional Science*. 30, 1, 1998. pp. 91–107. CSSL, GIDRL.

Dholakia, Archana R. Role of the centre in fiscal balance of states: case of Gujarat. *Journal of Indian School of Political Economy*. 11, 2, 1999. pp. 259–275. CSSL, GIDRL, GVL, IRMAL.

Dholakia, Archana and Dholakia, Ravindra H. Macroeconomic performance and tax revenue: case of Gujarat state. *Journal of Indian School of Political Economy*. 12, 1, 2000. pp. 21–34. CSSL, GIDRL, GVL, IRMAL.

Dholakia, Ravindra H. Measurement issues in comparing fiscal performance of states. *Economic and Political Weekly*. 38, 10, 2003. pp. 991–994. BUL, CEPTL, CSSL, EDIL, IIML, IRMAL, MICAL, SGUL, SPIESRL, UML.

Ebrahim, Alnoor. Agricultural cooperatives in Gujarat, India: agents of equity or differentiation. *Development in Practice*. 10, 2, 2000. pp. 178–188. CSSL, IRMAL.

Gadhavi, B.K. and Vekariya, S.B. Financial performance of RRBs in Saurashtra region of Gujarat. *Journal of Rural Development*. 33, 1, 2014. pp. 33–49. CSSL.

Ghate, Prabhu. Serving migrants sustainably: remittance services provided by an MFI in Gujarat. *Economic and Political Weekly*. 40, 17, 2005. pp. 1740–1746. BUL, CEPTL, CSSL, EDIL, GIDRL, IIML, IRMAL, MICAL, SGUL, SPIESRL, UML.

Gumber, Anil and Kulkarni, Veena. Health insurance for informal sector: case study of Gujarat. *Economic and Political Weekly*. 35, 40, 2000. pp. 3607–3613 BUL, CEPTL, CSSL, GIDRL, IIML, IRMAL, MICAL, SGUL, SPIESRL, UML.

Gupta, Shibshankar P. Reforms of urban property taxes: a case study of municipal corporation in Gujarat. *Anvesak*. 1, 1, 1971. pp. 35–55. CSSL, SPIESRL.

Gupta, Shibshankar, Radhakrishna, R. and Sarma, Atul. Revenue potential of agricultural income-tax in Gujarat. *Anvesak*. 1, 2, 1971. pp. 184–192. CSSL, SPIESRL.

Heredeo, J.M. Milk cooperatives and tribal poverty in Gujarat: the need of education and management. *Social Action*. 33, 3, 1983. pp. 285–307. CSSL, GVL, IRMAL.

Hirway, Indira. Safety net of the national renewal fund: some basic issues. *Indian Journal of Labour Economics*. 38, 2, 1995. pp. 185–200. SPIESRL.

Jayaraman, T.K. Analysis of inter-district variations in cooperative credit disbursement in Gujarat. *Artha-Vikas*. 15, 1, 1979. pp. 89–98. AAUL, CEPTL, GIDRL, GVL, HML, SGUL.

Jayaraman, T.K. Quantitative analysis of entertainment tax revenues: a case study of Gujarat. *Margin.* 9, 2, 1977. pp. 16–33. GIDRL, HML, SGUL.

Jayaraman, T.K. Savings behavior in Gujarat. *Margin.* 12, 1, 1979. pp. 83–92. GIDRL, HML.

Jeobhankar, S.G. Working of district co-operative bank in Gujarat: some issues. *Indian Co-operative Review*. 22, 2, 1984. pp. 201–208. SGUL.

Jha, P.N. and Kher, A.O. Towards strengthening the primary agricultural credit societies in Gujarat. *Indian Co-operative Review*. 18, 3, 1981. pp. 274–280. SGUL.

Jodha, N.S. Nature and extent of diversion of long term agricultural loans in Gujarat. *Artha-Vikas*. 7, 1, 1972. pp. 53–68. HML.

Jodha, N.S. and Brahmbhatt, D.M. Note on performance of primary credit institutions in Gujarat: a district analysis. *Artha-Vikas.* 12, 1, 1976. pp. 117–127. GIDRL, GVL, HML, SGUL.

Joshi, G.N. Domestic terms of trade and income distribution: a comparative study of Gujarat and India. *Vishleshan*. 13, 3, 1987. pp. 159–167. CSSL.

Joshi, G.N. Gujarat governments' budgetary operations and resource transfer to agriculture. *Artha-Vikas*. 23, 1 and 2, 1987. pp. 52–71. CSSL, GIDRL.

Joshi, V.A. and Dave, M.B. Determinants of municipal expenditure: an empirical study of the Saurashtra region. *Artha-Vikas*. 34, 1, 1998. pp. 67–76. CSSL.

Kher, A.O. and Jha, P.N. Credit utilisation pattern in respect of primary agricultural credit society in Kodinar taluka of Gujarat. *Indian Co-operative Review*. 16, 4, 1979. pp. 380–385. SGUL.

Kothari, V.N. Agricultural taxation in Gujarat. *Indian Journal of Agricultural Economics.* 26, 2, 1971. pp. 161–162. GVL, UML.

Mehta, L.R. and Bharadwaj, V.P. Municipal finance in a growing port town: a study of Gandhidham municipality. *Nagarlok*. 15, 3, 1983. pp. 72–81. CEPTL.

Mehta, Raghuvir. Some aspects of long term co-operative agricultural finance (a study of two areas in Gujarat). *Artha-Vikas*. 8, 2, 1972. pp. 90–91. SGUL.

Misra, P.N. Optimal government expenditure policy: a case study of expenditure on social services in Gujarat, India. *Vishleshan.* 7, 3 and 4, 1981. pp. 165–175. CSSL, GIDRL.

Misra, P.N. and Jayaraman, T.K. Performance evaluation of sales tax administration: a case study of Gujarat. *Vikalpa.* 6, 2, 1981. pp. 87–92. GVL, IRMAL.

Moradiya, B.V. Capital market modifies and investors' satisfaction. *Vishleshan.* 39, 2, 2013. pp. 1–12. CSSL.

Murthy, G.V.S.N. Pattern of consumer expenditure in Gujarat. *Anvesak.* 1, 2, 1971. pp. 175–183. CSSL, IRMAL, SPIESRL.

Narayana Rao, K.V. Finances of Panchayati raj institutions in Gujarat. *Journal of Rural Development*. 1, 3, 1982. pp. 387–444. CSSL, GVL, IIML, IRMAL.

Oza, K.V. Role of co-operatives in agricultural finance in Gujarat. *Artha-Vikas*. 12, 1, 1976. pp. 109–116. GIDRL, GVL, HML, SGUL.

Panwala, Manisha. Indian retail banking and customer satisfaction: a study of Surat. *Vishleshan.* 34, 3, 2009. pp. 54–60. CSSL, IIML.

Parekh, K.M. Determinants of municipal expenditure in Gujarat. *Artha-Vikas*. 26, 1 and 2, 1990. pp. 37–48. CSSL, GIDRL, HML.

Parekh, K.M. Some aspects of state government expenditure: a case study of Gujarat (1980–81 – 1997–98). *Artha-Vikas.* 36, 2, 2000. pp. 1–10. CSSL, GIDRL, IRMAL, SGUL.

Parekh, K.M. Some aspects of state government expenditure: a case study of Gujarat 1980–81 to 1997–98. *Anvesak.* 32, 1, 2002. pp. 1–12. GIDRL.

Parthasarathy, R. Participatory irrigation management programme in Gujarat: institutional and financial issues. *Economic and Political Weekly.* 35, 35 and 36, 2000. pp. 3147–3154. BUL, CEPTL, CSSL, GIDRL, IIML, IRMAL, MICAL, SGUL, SPIESRL, UML.

Patel, C.P. Planning and progress of cooperatives in Kadana project area. *Indian Cooperative Review.* 10, 4, 1973. pp. 537–547. HML.

Patel, Himmat. Finances of Gujarat state: an enquiry into the federal finance relations. (Gujarat 2010: challenges and opportunities). *Anvesak.* 31, 1–2, 2001. pp. 16–34. CSSL, GIDRL, SPIESRL.

Patel, Jayesh I. Development of co-operatives in Gujarat state. *Rural India.* 42, 10–11, 1979. pp. 253–256. IIML.

Patel, Jayesh I. and Patel, R.D. Acquisition and repayment patterns of agricultural co-operative credit in Anand taluka, Gujarat state. *Indian Co-operative Review.* 17, 3, 1980. pp. 231–240. SGUL.

Patel, Madhukant. Primary agriculture credit co-operative societies in Gujarat. *Vishleshan.* 34, 1, 2009. pp. 21–35. CSSL, IIML, IRMAL.

Patel, R.J., Patil, M. and Bhatt, Mahesh P. Performance of co-operative agricultural credit in North Gujarat. *Indian Co-operative Review.* 15, 3, 1978. pp. 389–404. SGUL.

Phansalkar, S.J. Political process and co-operative laws in Gujarat. *Economic and Political Weekly.* 32, 39, 1997. pp. A-140-A-148. CSSL, CEPTL, GIDRL, IIML, IRMAL, MICAL, SGUL, SPIESRL, UML.

Puri, Mukesh. Gujarat economy in the 1990s. *Anvesak.* 33, 2, 2003. pp. 12–23. CSSL, GIDRL, SPIESRL.

Radhakrishna, R. and Murthy, G.V.S.N. Approach to estimate complete set of demand elasticities based on two stage budgeting: with an application to the patterns of Gujarat demand. *Anvesak.* 3, 1–2, 1973. pp. 165–176. CSSL, SPIESRL.

Rajagopalan, R. and Shah, Tushaar. Role of design informal share markets in success of sugar co-operatives. *Economic and Political Weekly.* 29, 35, 1994. pp. M-129-M-135. CEPTL, CSSL, IIML, IRMAL, MICAL, SPIESRL, UML.

Rajaram, N. Politics and cotton co-operatives in Central Gujarat. *Economic and Political Weekly.* 34, 30, 1999. pp. 2095–2103. CSSL, GIDRL, IIML, IRMAL, MICAL, SGUL, SPIESRL, UML.

Rangarajan, C. and Padia, Veena. Private corporate investment in Gujarat in 1980 and forecast for 1981. *Economic and Political Weekly.* 16, 19, 1981. pp. 871–873. CEPTL, CSSL, GUL, IIML, IRMAL, SGUL, SPIESRL, UML.

Reddy, K.N. Case for the abolition of octroi in Gujarat: some alternatives. *Arth-Vikas.* 12, 1, 1976. pp. 90–99. GIDRL, GVL, HML, SGUL.

Reddy, K.N. Case for the abolition of octroi in Gujarat: some alternatives. *Journal of the M.S. University of Baroda.* 20, 2, 1971. pp. 45–52. GVL.

Sachdeva, R.K. and Kajarekar, R.G. Computerised financial information system in government of Gujarat: a case study. *Indian Journal of Public Administration.* 32, 1, 1986. pp. 169–185. GVL.

Sarma, Atul. Gujarat finances: reform of budgetary management. *Economic and Political Weekly.* 35, 35 and 36, 2000. pp. 3125–3136. CEPTL, CSSL, GIDRL, IIML, IRMAL, MICAL, SGUL, SPIESRL, UML.

Sarma, Atul, Parekh, K.M. and Singh, L. Tombi. Determinants of urban-local expenditures: an exploration in the Gujarat context. *Anvesak.* 4, 2, 1974. pp. 171–178. CEPTL, CSSL, IRMAL, SPIESRL.

Sarma, Atul, Rao, M. Govinda and Radhakrishna, R. Gujarat's state tax revenue: growth, responsiveness, determinants and projections. *Anvesak.* 3, 1–2, 1973. pp. 226–237. CSSL, SPIESRL.

Sarma, J.V.M. and Bhatt, Kartik. Causality between government expenditure and economic growth at sub-national level: a case study of Gujarat state in India. *Vishleshan.* 21, 4, 1996. pp. 10–16. CSSL, IRMAL.

Shah, Dilip. Economic analysis of Baroda dairy milk price problem. *Vishleshan.* 7, 1, 1981. pp. 43–56. CSSL, GIDRL.

Shah, Dilip and Rajput, Himat. Empowerment of tribal women through 'Grameen Vikas Kendra' with micro-finance approach: a case study of Dharampur tribal area of Gujarat. *Adivasi Gujarat.* 20 and 21, 1–2, 2010–11. pp. 9–26. CSSL.

Shah, Jignesh and Meena, P.C. Social transition in dairying: a case study from Anand district of Gujarat. *Journal of Rural Development.* 30, 3, 2011. pp. 307–319. CSSL.

Shah, Manubhai M. and Muranjan, S.W. Integration of district dairy co-operatives in Gujarat. *Indian Journal of Agricultural Economics.* 33, 2, 1972. pp. 94–96. SGUL, UML.

Shah, N.R. and Patel, A.S. Demand for short-term credit in the context of new strategy and the role of credit cooperatives in Gujarat. *Agricultural Situation in India.* 27, 6, 1972. pp. 399–403. GVL, IRMAL.

Shah, Neha. Can micro finance provide a sustainable solution for poverty?: some empirical evidences from Gujarat. *Anvesak.* 38, 2, 2008. pp. 27–42. CSSL, GIDRL, SPIESRL.

Sharma, Atul and Rao, Govind. Structural differences in municipal finance: a cross section analysis of Gujarat. *Artha-Vikas.* 12, 1, 1976. pp. 79–89. GIDRL, GVL, HML, SGUL.

Shiyani, R.L. and Bhatt, B.U. Cost of farm credit: a case study of commercial bank in Junagadh district of Gujarat. *Indian Cooperative Review.* 28, 1, 1990. pp. 1–10. HML, SGUL.

Shylendra, H.S. and Bhirdikar, Kishore. Microfinance based disaster mitigation a study of two donor supported projects in Kutch, Gujarat. *Journal of Social and Economic Development.* 11, 1, 2009. pp. 46–67. IRMAL.

Shylendra, H.S., Guha, Samapti and Veerashekharappa. Role of SHGs as micro-financial intermediaries: a study in Sabarkantha district of Gujarat. *Journal of Rural Development.* 29, 4, 2010. pp. 399–423. CSSL, EDIL, IIML, IRMAL.

Singh, R.B. Performance of Gujarat state cooperative land development bank. *Indian Cooperative Review.* 15, 3, 1978. pp. 333–353. HML.

Sinha, Tara, et al. Barriers to accessing benefits in a community based insurance scheme lessons learnt from SEWA insurance, Gujarat. *Health Policy and Planning.* 21, 2, 2006. pp. 132–142. IRMAL.

Tripathi, B.L. Forest labour co-operatives. *Indian Journal of Labour Economics.* 20, 1–2, 1977. pp. 16–23. SPIESRL.

Trivedi, K.B. Incidence of taxation on sales on households in Gujarat. *Anvesak.* 7, 1, 1977. pp. 95–99. CEPTL, CSSL, IRMAL, SPIESRL.

Trivedi, T.K. and Parikh, P.A. Local finance in Gujarat. *Arth-Vikas.* 12, 1, 1976. pp. 100–108. GIDRL, GVL, HML, SGUL.

Vachha, Homira S. and Iyengar, Sampath S. Financial institutions and backward regions: a case Study of Gujarat. *Artha-Vikas.* 9, 1–2, 1973. pp. 185–202. GVL, HML, SGUL.

Vaidya, Chetan. Role of community savings and loan association, Baroda in meeting credit needs of urban poor. *Nagarlok.* 27, 1, 1995. pp. 33–37. CEPTL.

Vaidya, Chetan and Johnson, Brad. Ahmedabad municipal bond: lessons and pointers. *Economic and Political Weekly.* 36, 30, 2001. pp. 2884–2891. BUL, CEPTL, CSSL, EDIL, IIML, IRMAL, MICAL, SGUL, SPIESRL, UML.

Vyas, C.P. Gujarat municipal finance board: a case study. *Urban India.* 11, 1, 1991. pp. 151–168. CEPTL, CSSL.

Working Papers, Reports and Other Materials

Acharya, Akash. *Women's participation in income generation in Hazira area.* Surat: Centre for Social Studies, 2000. p. 36. CSSL.

Acharya, B.V. and Bhatt, P.K. *Development and finance of a growing university: a case study of South Gujarat university.* Surat: South Gujarat University, 1993. p. 273. CSSL.

Agro Economic Research Centre. *Some aspects of long term co-operative agricultural finance: a case study of two areas in Gujarat.* Vallabh Vidhyanagar: Sardar Patel University, 1971. p. 174. GIDRL, GVL.

ARDC. *Dairy development in Banaskantha: evaluation of a scheme refinanced.* Bombay: Evaluation and Monitoring Cell, 1991. p. 47. IIML.

Baviskar, B.S. *Dairy cooperatives and rural development in Gujarat.* Hague, Netherland: ISS, 1986. p. 30. IRMAL.

Bhatt, Mahesh and Chawda, V.K. *Some aspects of co-operative housing societies in Ahmedabad city.* Ahmedabad: Gujarat University, 1970. p. 68. GIDRL.

Chavda, V.K. Currency in Gujarat. In *Studies in trade and urbanisation in Western India.* Ed. by V.K. Chavda. Baroda: M.S. University, 1985. pp. 155–161. CSSL.

Das, Biswaroop and Sahu, Gagan Bihari. *Understanding financial behavior of urban migrant workers: the case of Surat city.* Surat: Centre for Social Studies, 2013. p. 149. CSSL.

Dave, V.J. and Chauhan, D.J. *Flow of credit to small and marginal farmers in Gujarat(a case study in Panchmahal district).* Gujarat: Agro-Economic Research Centre, 2002. p. 93. Research study no-118. GVL, SPIESRL.

Desai, B.M. and Narayanarao, Y. *Project approach in agricultural financing: a study of the Gujarat state cooperative land development bank.* Ahmedabad: Centre for Management in Agricultural, 1981. p. 64. CMA Monograph No. 91. GIDRL, IIML.

Desai, B.M., Gupta, Ranjit and Tripathi, B.L. *Framework for an integrative role of rural financial institutions: a study of Malpur taluka in Gujarat.* New Delhi: Oxford and IBH, 1989. p. 220. CMA Monograph 134. GIDRL, IIML.

Desai, B.M., Gupta, Ranjit and Tripathi, B.L. *Framework for an integrative role of rural financial institutions: a study of Malpur taluka in Gujarat.* Ahmedabad: Indian Institute of Management, 1988. p. 259. IIML.

Desai, M.B. *Co-operation in Karjan: a report on the working of the co-operative movement in Karjan taluka.* Bombay: Indian Society of Agricultural Economics, 1961. p. 131. IIML, TRTIL.

Desai, M.D. *Saving and investment in an agriculturally prosperous area: a case study of Surat district in Gujarat 1970–71*. Vallabh Vidyanagar: Agro-Economic Research Centre, 1974. p. 92. Research Study No. 35. AERCL, SPUL.

Desai, M.D. *Saving and investment in an agriculturally prosperous area: a study of farmers in Surat district 1969–70*. Vallabh Vidyanagar: Agro-Economic Research Centre, 1973. p. 186. Research Study No. 30. AERCL, SPUL.

Desai, M.D. *Saving and investment in an agriculturally prosperous area: a case study of Surat district in Gujarat: 1971–72*. Vallabh Vidyanagar: Agro-Economic Research Centre, 1975. p. 89. Research Study No. 40. AERCL.

Desai, M.D. and Chauhan, A.D. *Saving and investment in an agriculturally prosperous area: a study in the Surat district Gujarat*. Vallabh Vidyanagar: Agro-Economic Research Centre, 1976. p. 186. Research Study No. 47. AERCL.

Dholakia, Archana. *Problems and prospects of fiscal balance in Gujarat.* Ahmedabad: D.T. Lakdawala Memorial Trust, 2000. p. 51. Occasional Paper Series 3. CSSL, GIDRL.

Dholakia, Archna R. SWOT analysis of taxation in Gujarat. In *Gujarat-2010: challenges and opportunities*. By Government of Gujarat. Ahmedabad: Sardar Patel Institute of Economic & Social Research, 2001. pp. 245–251. Seminar volume. CSSL, EDIL, IRMAL, SGUL, SPIESRL.

Dholakia, Archana R. and Dholakia, Ravindra, H. *Budgetary subsidies in the health sector: a case of Gujarat state.* Ahmedabad: Indian Institute of Management, 1999. p. [ ]. IIM Working Paper No. 99–10–02 GIDRL, IIML.

Franco, F. and Sherrychand, P.G.V. *Operation flood and voluntary sector: a study of tribal dairy cooperatives in South Gujarat*. New Delhi: Indian Social Institute, 1991. p. 238. GIDRL.

India, State Bank of. *Dairy development in Banaskantha: evaluation of a scheme refinanced by ARDC.* Bombay: State Bank of India, 1981. Various. CSSL.

Indian Cooperative Union. *Income generating activities for women: some case studies.* New Delhi: Author, 1980. p. 144. CSSL.

Jain, Trupti. *Micro finance programme (of Vardan: vigorous action for resources development and networking) Dahod, Gujarat.* Ahmedabad: FWWB, 2004. Various. CSSL.

Joshi, V.H. *Operation flood: constraints and potentialities in Saurashtra.* The Hague: Institute of Social Studies, 1986. p. 49. Working paper series on dairy aid and development No. 6. CSSL.

Kapoor, Rajesh. Watershed: unit of co-operation. In *Rediscovering co-operation.* Vol. III: *co-operatives in the emerging context*. Ed. by R. Rajagopalan. Anand: Institute of Rural Management, 1996. pp. 489–500. CSSL.

Kotdawala, M.R. *Report on the working of co-operative farming societies in Gujarat with special reference to Surat district*. Surat: Chunilal Gandhi Vidyabhavan, 1958. p. 267. Chunilal Gandhi Vidyabhavan Studies No. 8. SPUL.

Kulkarni, B.N. Rural credit delivery in Gujarat: retrospect and prospects. Business session 3. *In Seminar on agricultural and rural financing-issues & prospects. May 18–19, 1992 at Ahmedabad.* Ahmedabad: National Productivity Council, 1992. pp. 1–14. SPIESRL.

Kumar, Nalini. *Operation flood: literature review and reconciliation.* Anand: Institute of Rural Management, 1997. p. 47. Occasional Publication 13. CSSL.

Lakdawala, D.T. and Shah, K.R. *Optimum utilization of educational expenditure in Gujarat.* Ahmedabad: Sardar Patel Institute of Economic & Social Research, 1978. p. 269. SPIESRL.

Lalita Krishnaswami. *Status of women's cooperatives in Gujarat.* Ahmedabad: Self Employment Women Association, 1995. p. 36. IRMAL.

Linck, Florien. *Necessity is the mother of invention: an explorative study on Indian mutual savings and credit associations in Surat.* Amsterdam: Amsterdam School for Social Science Research, 1995. p. 151. Unpublished document. CSSL.

Mahadevia, Darshini and Khawas, Vimal. *Gender budgeting-impact of policies and programmes on women of agricultural households in Gujarat.* [ ]: [ ], 2005. p. 76. Discussion Paper Series 9. CEEL, CSSL, SPIESRL.

Mehta, J.M. *Study of rural economy of Gujarat.* Baroda: State Press, 1930. p. 231. GIDRL.

Misra, P.N. *Optional government expenditure policy: a case study of expenditure on social services in Gujarat, India.* Ahmedabad: Indian Institute of Management, 1981. p. 148. IRMAL.

Mitra, Manoshi. *Impact of dairy cooperatives in selected areas of Banaskantha district, Gujarat.* The Hague: Institute of Social Studies, 1986. p. 34. Working paper series on dairy aid and development No. 10. CSSL, IRMAL.

Nanavati, Manilal B. *Fifty years of co-operation in Kodinar taluka: a case study.* Bombay: Indian Society of Agricultural Economics, 1964. p. 37. CSSL.

National Dairy Development Board, Anand. *Gujarat cooperative oilseeds growers' federation in groundnut economy of Gujarat: performance and prospects.* Anand: National Dairy Development Board, 1984. p. 30. Research Report No. 1. CSSL.

National Dairy Development Board, Anand. *Oilseed project for Idar regional oilseeds growers' co-operative union: a project proposal.* Anand: National Dairy Development Board, 1987. p. 49. CSSL.

National Dairy Development Board, Anand. *UROC-Gujarat: some preliminary observations.* Anand: National Dairy Development Board, 1985. p. 14. Oilseeds and vegetable oil project. CSSL.

Oza, K.V. Working of agricultural co-operative credit institutions in Gujarat. In *Agricultural finance: problems and prospects.* Ed. by D.B. Kuchhadiya. and R.L. Shiyani. Junagadh: Department of Agricultural Economics, 1997. pp. 50–53. SPIESRL.

Parikh, P.T. *Brief history of the co-operative movement in the Surat district.* Surat: Surat District Co-Operative Bank, 1934. p. 57. HML.

Patel, A.S. Participation of different groups in the development process: a case study of a milk producer's co-operative in a Kheda village. In *Gujarat economy: problems and prospects.* Ed. by D.T. Lakdawala. Ahmedabad: Sardar Patel Institute of Economic & Social Research, 1982. pp. 335–350. GIDRL, IIML.

Patel, Himmat. Finances of Gujarat state: an inquiry in to the federal finance relations. In *Gujarat-2010: challenges and opportunities.* By Government of Gujarat. Ahmedabad: Sardar Patel Institute of Economic & Social Research, 2001. pp. 225–244. Seminar volume. CSSL, EDIL, IRMAL, SGUL, SPIESRL.

Patel, Himmat. *Financial working of irrigation project: a case study of four projects in Gujarat.* Vallabh Vidyanagar: Agro-Economic Research Centre, 1990. p. 71. IRMAL.

Patel, V.G. *Innovations in banking: the Gujarat experiment.* Bombay: IDBI, 1981. p. 68. GIDRL.

Pathak, Mahesh T. *Significance of public investment for backward regions: a case study of the fluorspar project in Gujarat.* Vallabh Vidyanagar: Department of Economics, Sardar Patel University, 1972. p. 156. SPUL.

Phansalkar, S.J. *Symposium on management of rural cooperatives on co-operatives in the polity of Gujarat state on December 7–11, 1992.* Anand: Institute of Rural Management, 1992. p. 58. IRMAL.

Punalekar, S.P. *Milk cooperative in Sabarkantha: a case study*. Surat: Centre for Social Studies, 1981. p. 75. CSSL.

Rajaram, N. Cooperatives and rural poor: a sociological analysis of milk cooperatives in Kheda district, Gujarat. In *Rural Development and Rural Poor, 26–28 February 1987*. Seminar Paper. Surat: Centre for Social Studies, 1987. pp. 259–273. CSSL.

Rajaram, N. Deprivation and development in cotton cooperatives of Central Gujarat. In *International seminar on Gujarat society, development and deprivation, 6–9 December 1994*. Surat: Centre for Social Studies, 1994. pp. 1–29. CSSL.

Ranade, C.G., et al. *Performance of integrated milk co-operatives: a study of selected co-operative dairies in Gujarat and Maharashtra*. New Delhi: Concept, 1988. p. 143. CMA Monograph Series No. 111. GIDRL, SPUL.

Rathod, C.S. *Enquiry into management of district central co-operative bank in Gujarat*. Baroda: Department of Co-operation, 1981. p. 42. CSSL, HML.

Reddy, K.N. Finances of Baroda municipal corporation. In *Profiles of a growing city: the city of Baroda*. Ed. by K.N. Reddy et al. Baroda: M.S. University, 1971. pp. 40–51. Souvenir: the 2nd Gujarat economic conference, 2–3 January 1971. CSSL.

Reddy, K. Prathap and Nagabrahman, D. *Changing culture of an organization: the case study of Sitapur dairy*. Anand: Institute Rural Management, 1992. p. 36. Working Paper 34. SPIESRL.

Sarma, Atul. Gujarat finances reform of budgetary management. In *Gujarat-2010: challenges and opportunities*. By Government of Gujarat. Ahmedabad: Sardar Patel Institute of Economic & Social Research, 2001. pp. 183–205. Seminar volume. CSSL, EDIL, IRMAL, SGUL, SPIESRL.

Savara, M. *Organized dairying in the tribal areas of Surat district*. The Hague: Institute of Social Studies, 1986. p. 52. Working paper series on dairy aid and development No. 9. CSSL.

Saxena, Rakesh. *Case study of the Vatra Tree Growers' Co-operative Society Ltd*. Anand: Institute of Rural Management, 1992. p. 31, Working Paper 32. CSSL.

Shah, Kalpana. *Role of women in milk producer's cooperative societies for women: a case study of five milk producer's societies for women in Surat district*. Surat: South Gujarat University, [ ]. p. 74. CSSL.

Shah, Manubhai M. *Integration of district dairy cooperatives in Gujarat*. Vallabh Vidyanagar: Sardar Patel University, 1977. p. 276. GIDRL.

Shah, N.R. Chamanpura Cooperative Collective Farming Society Ltd (Surat district). In *Assessment of cooperative farming societies in Gujarat and Rajasthan*. Ed. by K.M. Choudhary, M.T. Bapat and D.P. Gupta. Anand: Sardar Patel University, 1972. pp. 159–193. GVL.

Shah, Tushaar. *Logic of a co-operative company*. Anand: Institute of Rural Management, 1993. p. 14. Working Paper 44. CSSL.

Shah, Tushaar and Modak, Shrikant. *Co-operative organizations in Indian oilseed systems: a study of the role of grofed in groundnut system of Gujarat*. Anand: Institute of Rural Management, 1986. p. 122. Research Report No. 2. CSSL.

Shah, V.D. *Repayment of minor irrigation loans of land development bank in Gujarat: a case study Dhanera taluka of Banaskantha district*. Vallabh Vidyanagar: Agro-Economic Research Centre, 1986. p. 190. AERC Research Study No. 70. AERCL, GIDRL, IRMAL.

Shah, Vimal P. *Role of milk co-operative in articulating rural-urban interactions: experiences in Gujarat, India.* Ahmedabad: Gujarat University, 1981. p. 103. Unpublished report. CSSL.

Shylendra, H.S. *Micro-finance and self-help groups (SHGs): a study of the experience of two leading NGOs, SEWA and AKRSP in Gujarat (India).* Anand: Institute of Rural Management, 1999. p. 41. Working Paper 16. CSSL, GIDRL, IRMAL, SPIESRL.

Shylendra, H.S. and Bhirdikar, Kishore. *Microfinance-based disaster mitigation: a study of the design and implementation of two projects in earthquake-affected Kutch district of Gujarat(India).* Anand: Institute of Rural Management, 2007. p. 27. Working Paper 201. IRMAL, SPIESRL.

Shylendra, H.S., Guha, Sama and Veerashekharappa. *Role of self-help groups (SHGS) as micro financial intermediaries: a study in Sabarkantha district of Gujarat(India).* Anand: Institute of Rural Management, 2009. p. 44. Working Paper 211. IRMAL, SPIESRL.

Spodek, Howard. From project to organization to movement: the Self-Employed Women's Association (SEVA), 1972–1994. In *International seminar on Gujarat society, development and deprivation, 6–9 December 1994.* Surat: Centre for Social Studies, 1994. pp. 1–5. CSSL.

Tejani, K.L. State financial resources. In *Gujarat-2010: challenges and opportunities.* By Government of Gujarat. Ahmedabad: Sardar Patel Institute of Economic & Social Research, 2001. pp. 206–224. Seminar volume. CSSL, EDIL, IRMAL, SGUL, SPIESRL.

Vachha, Homiars and Iyengar, Samath S. Financial institutions and backward regions: a case study of Gujarat. In *Economic development of backward regions problems & prospects. Proceedings of an all-India seminar on the development of backward regions with special reference to Gujarat).* Ed. by H.M. Patel, et al. Vallabh Vidyanagar: Sardar Patel University, 1974. pp. 185–202. GIDRL, GUL, HML.

Veerashekharappa. *Performance of Self-Help Group (SHG)-bank linkage programme in India: a comparative study of Karnataka and Gujarat.* Anand: Institute of Rural Management, 2007. p. 165. IRMAL.

10

Labour, Employment, Migration

Books/Chapter in Books

Baks, Chris. Inevitable decline of the small farmer's social position, Eastern Surat district, India. In *Work and social change in Asia: essays in honour of Jan Breman*. Ed. by Arvind N. Das and Marcel Van Der Linden. New Delhi: Manohar, 2003. pp. 31–52. CSSL.

Barik, Bishnu C. Unorganised migrant labour in the textile industry of Surat: a case study. In *Migrant labour and related issues*. Ed. by Vidyut Joshi. New Delhi: Oxford and IBH, 1987. pp. 165–178. CSSL, HML, SPIESRL, TRTIL.

Basant, Rakesh and Joshi, Harish. Employment diversification in an agriculturally developed region: some evidence from rural Kheda, Gujarat. In *Non-agricultural employment in India: trends and prospects*. Ed. by Pravin Visaria and Rakesh Basant. New Delhi: Sage, 1994. pp. 222–257. CSSL, HML, SETUL, SPUL, TRTIL.

Basant, Rakesh, Kumar, B.L. and Parthasarathy, R. *Non-agricultural employment in rural India: the case of Gujarat*. Jaipur: Rawat, 1998. p. 302. AERCL, CSSL, GIDRL, IIML.

Baxi, Upendra. Struggle for implementation: some marginal notes. In *Migrant labour and related issues*. Ed. by Vidyut Joshi. New Delhi: Oxford, 1987. pp. 257–263. CSSL, HML, SPIESRL, TRTIL.

Brahmbhatt, D.M. Agricultural labour in a North Gujarat village. In *Agricultural labour in four Indian villages*. Ed. by V.S. Vyas. Gujarat: Sardar Vallabhbhai Vidyapeeth, 1967. pp. 46–67. AAUL, GVL, SPUL.

Brahmbhatt, D.M., Patel, V.M. and Dave, V.J. *National rural employment programme in Gujarat: a case study Kheda district*. Vallabh Vidyanagar: Agro-Economic Research Centre, 1987. p. 155. GVL, SPUL.

Breman, Jan. *At work in the informal economy of India: a perspective from the bottom up*. New Delhi: Oxford, 2013. p. 457. CSSL.

Breman, Jan. *Beyond patronage and exploitation: changing agrarian relations in South Gujarat*. New Delhi: Oxford, 1993. p. 399. CEPTL, CSSL, GUL, IRMAL, UML.

Breman, Jan. Extension of scale in fieldwork: from village to region in Southern Gujarat. In *Conversations between economists and anthropologists*. Ed. by Pranab Bardhan. New Delhi: Oxford, 1989. pp. 127–136. CSSL, IIML, SETUL.

Breman, Jan. *Footloose labour: working in India's informal economy*. New York: Cambridge University press, 1996. p. 278. CSSL, GVL, SETUL, SPIESRL, UML.

Breman, Jan. From cane fields to court rooms: legal action for and against rural labour in Gujarat, India. In *Capitalist development: critical essays. felicitation volume in honour of Prof. A.R. Desai*. Ed. by Ghanshyam Shah. Bombay: Popular, 1990. pp. 270–288. CSSL, HML.

Breman, Jan. Hali system in South Gujarat. In *World of the rural labour in colonial India*. Ed. by Gyan Prakash. Delhi: Oxford, 1992. pp. 248–281. CSSL.

Breman, Jan. Labour nomads in South Gujarat: wage hunters and gatherers. In *Social transformation in India: essays in honour of professor I.P. Desai*. Vol. 2. Ed. by Ghanshyam Shah. Jaipur: Rawat, 1997. pp. 532–580. CSSL, GVL, HML, SGUL, SPUL.

Breman, Jan. Labour relations in the 'formal' and 'informal' sectors: the South Gujarat experience. In *Informal sector in India*. Ed. by P.M. Mathew. New Delhi: Khama, 1995. pp. 171–190. GVL.

Breman, Jan. *Labouring poor in India: patterns of exploitation, subordination and exclusion*. New Delhi: Oxford, 2003. p. 351. CSSL, HML, IIML.

Breman, Jan. *Making and unmaking of an industrial working class: sliding down the labour hierarchy in Ahmedabad, India*. New Delhi: Oxford, 2004. p. 315. CSSL, HML, IIML.

Breman, Jan. Market for non-agrarian labour: the formal versus informal sector. In *Winners and losers: styles of development and change in an Indian region*. Ed. by S. Devadas Pillai and Chris Baks. Bombay: Popular, 1979. pp. 122–166. CSSL, SPIESRL.

Breman, Jan. Mobilisation of landless labourers: Halpatis of South Gujarat. In *Agrarian relations in India*. Ed. by Arvind N. Das and V. Nilakant. New Delhi: Manohar, 1979. pp. 147–168. CSSL.

Breman, Jan. Mobilisation of landless labourers: Halpatis of South Gujarat. In *Agrarian struggles in India after independence*. Ed. by A.R. Desai. Delhi: Oxford, 1986. pp. 362–383. CSSL, GUL, SPUL.

Breman, Jan. Mobilisation of landless labourers: the Halpatis of South Gujarat. In *Social stratification*. Ed. by Dipankar Gupta. Bombay: Oxford, 1992. pp. 399–418. CSSL, GVL, TRTIL.

Breman, Jan. *Of peasants, migrants and paupers: rural labour circulation and capitalist production in West India*. Delhi: Oxford, 1985. p. 472. CSSL, SPIESRL, UML.

Breman, Jan. *Patronage and exploitation: changing agrarian relation in South Gujarat India*. California: University of California, 1974. p. 287. CSSL, GIDRL, GVL, TRTIL, UML.

Breman, Jan. *Wage hunters and gatherers: search for work in the urban and rural economy of South Gujarat*. Delhi: Oxford, 1994. p. 422. CSSL, GIDRL, HML, IRMAL, SETUL, UML.

Breman, Jan. *Working in the mill, no more*. New Delhi: Oxford, 2004. p. 208. CSSL, SETUL, UML.

Chatterjee, Merai. Organizing for maternity benefits: the experiences of agricultural labourers in Gujarat. In *Social security for unorganized labour*. Ed. by B.B. Patel. New Delhi: Oxford, 1993. pp. 174–201. CSSL.

Chavda, V.K. Study of homework in Ahmedabad city. In *Problems of home-based workers in India: proceedings of a national workshop held at Ahmedabad, from 29 to 31 March, 1986*. Ed. by B.B. Patel. New Delhi: Oxford, 1989. pp. 107–127. CSSL.

Danda, Ajit K. Surat (Gujarat) village. In *Weaker sections in Indian villages-II*. New Delhi: Inter-India, 1991. pp. 454–475. CSSL, SGUL.

Dantwala, M.L. and Shah, C.H. *Study of rural employment: with reference to sixteen villages in Gujarat.* Bombay: University of Bombay, 1966. p. 282. SPIESRL.

Dass, Asha. Study of female child workers in Baroda city. In *Child labour: malti dimensional problem.* Ed. by Kamla Srinivasan and Veena Gandotra. Delhi: Ajanata, 1993. pp. 113–120. CSSL, TRTIL.

Desai, A.R. Ahmedabad. In *Labour movement in India: documents: 1918–1920.* Ed. by A.R. Desai. Bombay: Popular, 1988. pp. 45–70. CSSL.

Desai, Anjana P. and Gupta, Smita Sen. *Suburban growth through step-wise migration: case of Ahmedabad.* New Delhi: Inter India, 1988. pp. 209–222. SGUL.

Desai, Anjana P. and Sulaiman, Omar Hamid. Seasonal migration of labour and management of resource in tribal areas of Gujarat. In *Perspectives in resource management in developing countries,* Vol. 2, Part 1. Ed. by Baleshwar Thakur. New Delhi: Concept, 2007. pp. 487–495. CSSL, GVL.

Desai, Kiran. Options of survival for marginalized labouring poor in deteriorating employment situation: floating in informal fringe sector. In *Globalization, growth and employment: challenges and opportunities.* Ed. by Lancy Lobo and Jayesh Shah. Jaipur: Rawat, 2012. pp. 163–204. CSSL, EDIL.

Desai, Kiran. Searching for space: workers in the fringe sector of Surat. In *Development and deprivation in Gujarat: in honour of Jan Breman.* Ed. by Ghanshyam Shah, Mario Rutten and Hein Streefkerk. New Delhi: Sage, 2002. pp. 150–172. CEEL, CEPTL, CSSL, EDIL, GIDRL, HML, IIML, IRMAL, UML.

Desai, Kiran. Secondary labour market in India: a case study of workers in small scale industrial units in Gujarat. In *Labour segmentation in India.* Ed. by Maya Shah. Mumbai: Himalaya, 1999. pp. 13–28. HML.

Desai, M.B. and Varma, S.K. *Marginal farmer's and agricultural labourer's development agency, Baroda.* Baroda: M.S. University, 1978. p. 122. HML, SPIESRL.

Dholakia, J.L. *Industrial labour and economic development in India.* Ahmedabad: Anada, 1965. p. 175. GUL, *GVL.

Dholakia, J.L. Worker's participation in management: with special reference to Ahmedabad. In *Industrial labour and economic development in India.* By J.L. Dholakia. Ahmedabad: Anada, 1965. pp. 114–134. GUL.

Dholakia, Jitendra. Employment survey of the alumni of Gujarat University. In *Unemployment and employment policy in India.* By Jitendra Dholakia. New Delhi: Sterling, 1977. pp. 60–69. SPUL.

Dholakia, Jitendra. Job performance of the graduates of the Gujarat University. In *Unemployment and employment policy in India.* By Jitendra Dholakia. New Delhi: Sterling, 1977. pp. 54–59. SPUL.

Dholakia, Jitendra. Pilot study of registrants of the employment exchanges in Gujarat. In *Unemployment and employment policy in India.* By Jitendra Dholakia. New Delhi: Sterling, 1977. pp. 49–53. SPUL.

Engelshoven, Miranda. Rural to urban migration and the significance of caste: the case of the Saurashtra Patels of Surat. In *Development and deprivation in Gujarat: in hounour of Jan Breman.* Ed. by Ghanshyam Shah, Mario Rutten and Hein Streefkerk. New Delhi: Sage, 2002. pp. 294–313. CEEL, CEPTL, CSSL, EDIL, GIDRL, HML, IIML, IRMAL, UML.

Gidwani, Vinay. Labour landscapes: agro-ecological change in Central Gujarat, India. In *Social nature: resources, representations, and rule in India.* Ed. by Arun Agrawal and K. Sivaramakrishnan. New Delhi: Oxford, 2001. pp. 216–247. CEEL, CSSL.

Gumber, Anil. Rural development and seasonal migration in Gujarat: pattern, determinants and consequence. In *Other Gujarat: social transformation among weaker sections.* Ed. by Takashi Shinoda. Mumbai: Popular, 2002. pp. 159–203. ASL, CEEL, CSSL, EDIL, GIDRL, SPIESRL.

Haynes, Douglas E. Artisans and the shaping of labour regimes in urban Gujarat, 1600–1960. In *Development and deprivation in Gujarat: in honour of Jan Breman.* Ed. by Ghanshyam Shah, Mario Rutten and Hein Streefkerk. New Delhi: Sage, 2002. pp. 77–95. CEEL, CEPTL, CSSL, EDIL, GIDRL, HML, IIML, IRMAL, UML.

Hirway, Indira. *Denial of maternity benefits to women workers: a study of the factory sector in Gujarat.* New Delhi: Oxford, Gandhi Labour Institute, Ahmedabad, 1986. p. 151. GIDRL, IIML, SPIESRL.

Hirway, Indira. Dynamics of occupational diversification of female labour force: a study of the factory sector in Gujarat. In *Women as a workforce in the organized sector: empirical perspectives.* Ed. by I.S. Singh. New Delhi: Oxford and IBH, 1995. pp. 170–187. IIML.

Hirway, Indira. Employment and income generation among the tribal population: some critical issues. In *Tribal development in Western India.* Ed. by Amita Shah and Jharna Pathak. New Delhi: Routledge, 2014. pp. 58–83. CSSL.

Hirway, Indira. Female employment in rural Gujarat: some issues. In *Women and work changing scenario in India.* Ed. by Alakh Sharma and Seema Singh. Delhi: B.R., 1993. pp. 170–178. SPIESRL.

Hirway, Indira. Protection to rural seasonal migrants: some issues. In *Migrant labour and related issues.* Ed. by Vidyut Joshi. New Delhi: Oxford, 1987. pp. 121–135. CSSL, HML, SPIESRL, TRTIL.

Hirway, Indira. *Wage employment programmes in rural development:* a *study of NREP in Gujarat.* New Delhi: Oxford, 1986. p. 112. CSSL, GIDRL, GVL, HML, IRMAL.

Hirway, Indira and Abraham, Joseph. *Organising rural workers: the Gujarat.* New Delhi: Oxford, 1990. p. 107. GIDRL, HML, IIML, IRMAL.

Hirway, Indira and Terhal, Piet. *Towards employment guarantee in India: Indian and international experiences in rural public works programmes.* New Delhi: Sage, 1994. p. 283. CSSL, GVL, HML.

Hirway, Indira, Saluja, M.R. and Yadav, Bhupesh. *Employment guarantee programme and pro-poor growth: the study of a village in Gujarat.* New Delhi: Academic, 2010. p. 225. GIDRL.

Hommes, Enno W. and Trivedi, Nivedita. Functioning of the labour-market for local graduates. In *Winners and losers: styles of development and change in an Indian region.* Ed. by S. Devadas Pillai and Chris Baks. Bombay: Popular, 1979. pp. 81–99. CSSL, SPIESRL.

Iyengar, Sudarshan. Fair deal to home workers: some conceptual issues. In *Problems of home-based workers in India: proceedings of a national workshop held at Ahmedabad, from 29 to 31 March, 1986.* Ed. by B.B. Patel. New Delhi: Oxford, 1989. pp. 255–260. CSSL.

Jani, V.K. and Pandya, B.A. *Rural artisan and modernization: a study of artisans of Saurashtra.* Jaipur: Illustrated, 1994. p. 136. CSSL.

Jha, Shankar and Jha, Sangeeta. Globalization and employment: a case study of changing structure of employment in Gujarat. In *Globalization, growth and employment: challenges and opportunities.* Ed. by Lancy Lobo and Jayesh Shah. Jaipur: Rawat, 2012. pp. 151–162. CSSL, EDIL.

Joshi, Vidyut. Casualisation of labour in textile industry. In *Indian textiles: an intersectoral perspective.* Ed. by S.S. Mehta and Vinod Shanbhag. New Delhi: Oxford, 1990. pp. 144–157. CSSL.

Joshi, Vidyut. Experiment in workers' education among migrant workers. In *Migrant labour and related issues.* Ed. by Vidyut Joshi. New Delhi: Oxford and IBH, 1987. pp. 291–299. CSSL, HML, SPIESRL, TRTIL.

Joshi, Vidyut. Labour migration: some socio-economic issues. In *Migrant labour and related issues.* Ed. by Vidyut Joshi. New Delhi: Oxford and IBH, 1987. pp. 9–22. CSSL, HML, SPIESRL, TRTIL.

Joshi, Vidyut, ed. *Migrant labour and related issues*. New Delhi: Oxford and IBH, 1987. p. 334. CSSL, HML, SPIESRL, TRTIL.

Joshi, Vidyut. *Organising unorganized labour: a study of the national labour institute's rural labour camps*. New Delhi: Oxford, 1990. p. 75. CSSL.

Kashyap, S.P. Earning profile and prospects for child labour in diamond processing units: a case study of Surat. In *Towards eradication of child labour*. Ed. by Indira Hirway and Jacqui Cottyn. New Delhi: Oxford and IBH, 1991. pp. 178–187. HML, SPIESRL.

Kiso, Junko. Factory workers and their mobility in Ahmedabad city. In *Other Gujarat: social transformations among weaker sections.* Ed. by Takashi Shinoda. Mumbai: Popular, 2002. pp. 221–259. ASL, CEEL, CSSL, EDIL, GIDRL, SETUL, SPIESRL.

Kiso, Junko. Job loss and job opportunities of factory workers in Ahmedabad: flexible labour rethink. In *Globalization employment and mobility: the South Asian experience.* Ed. by Hiroshi Sato and Mayumi Murayama. Kenkyujo: Institute of Developing Economics (IDE) JETRO, 2008. pp. [ ]. IIML.

Kothari, Uma. Landless labour and agrarian change in South Gujarat: the experiences of Halpati women. In *Development and deprivation in Gujarat: in honour of Jan Breman*. Ed. by Ghanshyam Shah, Mario Rutten and Hein Streefkerk. New Delhi: Sage, 2002. pp. 115–132. CEEL, CEPTL, CSSL, EDIL, GIDRL, HML, IIML, IRMAL, UML.

Krishnaswami, Lalita. Women workers in food processing industries in Ahmedabad. In *Problems of home-based workers in India: proceedings of a national workshop held at Ahmedabad, from 29 to 31 March, 1986.* Ed. by B.B. Patel. New Delhi: Oxford, 1989. pp. 214–254. CSSL.

Lobo, Lancy and Shah, Jayesh. Employment potential in SEZs and SIRs in Gujarat. In *Globalization, growth and employment: challenges and opportunities.* Ed. by Lancy Lobo and Jayesh Shah. Jaipur: Rawat, 2012. pp. 290–297. CSSL, EDIL.

Lobo, Lancy and Shah, Jayesh, ed. *Globalization, growth and employment: challenges and opportunities.* Jaipur: Rawat, 2012. p. 302. CSSL, EDIL.

Mahadevia, Darshini. Informalisation of employment and poverty in Ahmedabad. In *Informal sector in India: perspectives and policies*. Ed. by Amitabh Kundu and Alakh N. Sharma. New Delhi: Institute for Human Development, 2001. pp. 142–159. CSSL, HML.

Mehta, Meera. *Employment, income and the urban poor: a case of lower strata workers in an Indian metropolis*. New Delhi: Harman, 1990. p. 207. CSSL.

Mehta, Meera and Acharya, Shrawan. Structure of 'Chhipa' activity, Ahmedabad: a dynamic perspective of technological innovation and changing role relationships. In *Problems of home-based workers in India: proceedings of a national workshop held at Ahmedabad, from 29 to 31 March, 1986.* Ed. by B.B. Patel. New Delhi: Oxford, 1989. pp. 183–193. CSSL.

Mehta, Niti. Quality and employability aspects of rural labour force in Gujarat. In *Globalization, growth and employment: challenges and opportunities.* Ed. by Lancy Lobo and Jayesh Shah. Jaipur: Rawat, 2012. pp. 122–150. CSSL, EDIL.

Mehta, Sanat. Some issues regarding the future policy for migrant labour with special reference to Gujarat. In *Migrant labour and related issues.* Ed. by Vidyut Joshi. New Delhi: Oxford and IBH, 1987. pp. 301–309. CSSL, HML, SPIESRL, TRTIL.

Mishra, Lakshmidhar. *Child labour in India*. New Delhi: Oxford, 2000. p. 360. CSSL.

Mohite, P.B. Gujarat experience in implementation of social security schemes for rural labour. In *Social security for unorganized labour*. Ed. by B.B. Patel. New Delhi: Oxford, 1993. pp. 202–206. CSSL.

Mukherjee, Arpita and Goyal, Tanu M. Fuelling the retail boom: need for the right employment policy for Gujarat. In *Globalization, growth and employment: challenges and opportunities.* Ed. by Lancy Lobo and Jayesh Shah. Jaipur: Rawat, 2012. pp. 268–289. CSSL, EDIL.

Mukhtyar, G.C.; Vakil, C.N., ed. *Life and labour in a South Gujarat village*. Calcutta: Longmans Green, 1930. p. 302. BVL, CSSL, GIDRL, HML.

Mukhtyar, G.C. Life and labour in a South Gujarat village (1928). In *Dissertation in economics 1921–1971*. Ed. by C.H. Shah. Bombay: University of Bombay, 1974. pp. 114–116. SPIESRL.

Nakasato, Tsuguo. Differentiated diversification of occupations in a multi-caste village. In *Other Gujarat: social transformations among weaker sections.* Ed. by Takashi Shinoda. Mumbai: Popular, 2002. pp. 284–313. ASL, CEEL, CSSL, EDIL, GIDRL, SETUL, SPIESRL.

Nakasato, Tsuguo. Differentiated diversification of occupations in a multi-caste village: a survey report from Kheda district in Central Gujarat. In *Economic changes and social transformation in modern and contemporary South Asia*. Ed. by S. Taniguchi, et al. Tokyo: Hitotsubashi University, 1994. pp. 153–186. CSSL.

Nanda, Sudip Kumar. *Tribal migration: a case study of Dahod district*. Ahmedabad: Rannade, 2005–06. p. 213. SETUL.

Ogale, Nalini. Child labour in the rural area of Baroda district. In *Child labour: multi dimensional problem*. Ed. by Kamla Srinivasan and Veena Gandotra. Delhi: Ajanata, 1993. pp. 154–164. CSSL, TRTIL.

Pandya, Rameshwari and Thakkar, Dhara. *Working women: issues and challenges*. Gurgaon: Madhav Books, 2010. p. 118. IIML.

Patel, Arjun. Pattern of development and tribal migration: a case of tribes from Dangs and Panchmahal in Gujarat. In *Tribal issues in India*. Ed. by D.C. Sah and Yatindra Singh Sisodia. Jaipur: Rawat, 2004. pp. 175–194. CEEL, CSSL, GVL, HML, TRTIL.

Patel, Arjun. Secondary labour market in India: a case study of rural migrant labour in Gujarat. In *Labour segmentation in India*. Ed. by Maya Shah. Mumbai: Himalaya, 1999. pp. 29–36. HML.

Patel, B.B. Growth and pattern of employment in Gujarat. In *Planning employment for educated youth.* New Delhi: Oxford and IBH, 1992. pp. 37–44. HML.

Patel, B.B. Rehabilitating workers of closed mills in Ahmedabad: experience and issues. In *Indian textiles an intersectoral perspective.* Ed. by S.S. Mehta and Vinod Shanbhag. New Delhi: Oxford, 1990. pp. 178–200. CSSL, SPIESRL.

Patel, B.B. Seasonal rural migration pattern and some alternatives for effective protection of legal rights of migrant labour. In *Migrant labour and related issues.* Ed. by Vidyut Joshi. New Delhi: Oxford, 1987. pp. 143–151. CSSL, HML, SPIESRL, TRTIL.

Patel, B.B. *Structure of inter-district inter-sectoral and inter-industry wage differentials in Gujarat.* Baroda: M.S. University, 1985. p. 198. SPIESRL.

Patel, B.B. Technology, employment and occupations of women workers in the manufacturing sector in Gujarat. In *Women as a workforce in the organized sector: empirical perspectives.* Ed. by I.S. Singh. New Delhi: Oxford and IBH, 1995. pp. 153–169. IIML.

Patel, B.B. Work, working conditions and earnings: Agarbatti workers in Ahmedabad. In *Problems of home-based workers in India: proceedings of a national workshop held at Ahmedabad, from 29 to 31 March, 1986.* Ed. by B.B. Patel. New Delhi: Oxford, 1989. pp. 128–154. CSSL.

Patel, B.B., ed. *Problems of home-based workers in India: proceedings of a national workshop held at Ahmedabad, from 29 to 31 March, 1986.* New Delhi: Oxford, 1989. p. 503. CSSL.

Patel, Haribhai G. Keralite migrant female labour in fishing units of Veraval city of Western India. In *Migrant labour and related issues.* Ed. by Vidyut Joshi. New Delhi: Oxford and IBH, 1987. pp. 179–185. CSSL, HML, SPIESRL, TRTIL.

Patel, J.M. Agricultural labour in a South Gujarat village. In *Agricultural labour in four Indian villages.* Ed. by V.S. Vyas. Vallabh Vidyanagar: Sardar Vallabhbhai Vidyapeeth, 1967. pp. 92–119. AAUL, GVL, SPUL.

Pichholiya, K.R. and Tripathi, B.L. Prevention of child labour: an action programme for Gujarat state. In *Children at work problems and policy options.* Ed. by Bhagwan P.D. Singh and Mahanty Shukla. New Delhi: B.R., 1993. p. 265. SPIESRL.

Popat, R.C. Changing scenario of agriculture and rural employment in Gujarat: challenges and opportunities. In *Globalization, growth and employment: challenges and opportunities*. Ed. by Lancy Lobo and Jayesh Shah. Jaipur: Rawat, 2012. pp. 105–121. CSSL, EDIL.

Raj, Mulkh. Employment income and housing. In *Housing assistance for antodya families (HALF) Vedichhi Intensive Area Scheme (VIAS) Valod, district Surat Gujarat.* New Delhi: Ess Ess, 1987. pp. 11–28. IIML.

Rose, Kalima. *Where women are leaders: the SEWA movement in India*. Delhi: Vistaar, 1992. p. 285. CSSL, SETUL.

Ruchika Rani and Kalaiyarasan, A. Galloping growth stagnant employment: mapping regional and social differences. In *Poverty amidst prosperity: essays on the trajectory of development in Gujarat.* Ed. by Atul Sood. Delhi: Aakar, 2012. pp. 163–179. CSSL, IRMAL, MICAL.

Rutten, Mario and Patel, Pravin J. Twice migrants and linkages with Central Gujarat: Patidars in East Africa and Britain. In *Development and deprivation in Gujarat: in hounour of Jan Breman*. Ed. by Ghanshyam Shah, Mario Rutten and Hein Streefkerk. New Delhi: Sage, 2002. pp. 314–328. CEEL, CEPTL, CSSL, EDIL, GIDRL, HML, IIML, IRMAL, UML.

Saramma, A.D. Child labour in diamond cutting and polishing units in Gujarat: a case study of Bhavnagar city. In *Exploited children: a comprehensive blueprint for child labour rehabilitation*. Ed. by M. Koteswara Rao. New Delhi: Kanishka, 2010. pp. 248–260. GUL, HML.

Saxena, S.B. Profile of working children in a village of Gujarat. In *Child labour: multi dimensional problem*. Ed. by Kamla Srinivasan and Veena Gandotra. Delhi: Ajanata, 1993. pp. 137–153. CSSL, TRTIL.

Shah, Amita. Changing pattern of rural artisans in Gujarat: need for a fresh policy? In *Other Gujarat: social transformations among weaker sections*. Ed. by Takashi Shinoda. Mumbai: Popular, 2002. pp. 314–346. ASL, CEEL, CSSL, EDIL, GIDRL, SETUL, SPIESRL.

Shah, Amita. Implementing NREGS in Gujarat: evidence from the initial phase. In *Globalization, growth and employment: challenges and opportunities*. Ed. by Lancy Lobo and Jayesh Shah. Jaipur: Rawat, 2012. pp. 205–238. CSSL, EDIL.

Shah, Amita. Uneven development and migration: insights from micro initiatives. In *Development and deprivation in Gujarat: in honour of Jan Breman*. Ed. by Ghanshyam Shah, Mario Rutten and Hein Streefkerk. New Delhi: Sage, 2002. pp. 273–293. CEEL, CEPTL, CSSL, EDIL, GIDRL, HML, IIML, IRMAL, UML.

Shah, Amita and Dhak, Biplab. Labour migration and welfare in Gujarat: recent evidence and issues. In *Growth or development: which way is Gujarat going?* Ed. by Indira Hirway, Amita Shah and Ghanshyam Shah. New Delhi: Oxford, 2014. pp. 301–339. CSSL.

Shah, C.H. Rural migration: an analytical approach. In *Migrant labour and related issues*. Ed. by Vidyut Joshi. New Delhi: Oxford and IBH, 1987. pp. 37–54. CSSL, HML, SPIESRL, TRTIL.

Shah, Ghanshyam and Rutten, Mario. Capitalist development and Jan Breman's study of the labouring class in Gujarat. In *Development and deprivation in Gujarat: in honour of Jan Breman*. Ed. by Ghanshyam Shah, Mario Rutten and Hein Streefkerk. New Delhi: Sage, 2002. pp. 17–36. CEEL, CEPTL, CSSL, EDIL, GIDRL, HML, IIML, IRMAL, UML.

Shah, Ghanshyam, Rutten, Mario and Streefkerk, Hein, ed. *Development and deprivation in Gujarat: in honour of Jan Breman*. New Delhi: Sage, 2002. p. 345. CEEL, CEPTL, CSSL, EDIL, GIDRL, HML, IIML, IRMAL, UML.

Shah, Maya. Labour market segmentation in Vadodara. In *Labour segmentation in India*. Ed. by Maya Shah. Mumbai: Himalaya, 1999. pp. 151–170. HML.

Sharma, Marla. *Bonded labour in India*. New Delhi: Goel Sita Ram, 1981. p. 227. TRTIL.

Sheth, K.A. Legal and administrative aspects of the implementation of the interstate migrant workmen (RECS) act, 1979 in Gujarat state. In *Migrant labour and related issues*. Ed. by Vidyut Joshi. New Delhi: Oxford and IBH, 1987. pp. 237–255. CSSL, HML, SPIESRL, TRTIL.

Shinoda, Takashi. Legal, institutional development and sweepers in Ahmedabad. In *Other Gujarat: social transformations among weaker sections*. Ed. by Takashi Shinoda. Mumbai: Popular, 2002. pp. 66–95. ASL, CEEL, CSSL, EDIL, GIDRL, SETUL, SPIESRL.

Shinoda, Takashi. *Marginalization in the midst of modernization: sweepers in Western India*. Delhi: Manohar, 2005. p. 280. CSSL, GIDRL, UML.

Shinoda, Takashi. Socio-economic conditions of sweepers employed by local bodies in Ahmedabad district, India. In *Economic changes and social transformation in modern and contemporary South Asia*. Ed. by S. Taniguchi, et al. Tokyo: Hitotsubashi University, 1994. pp. 241–270. CSSL.

Shinoda, Takashi, ed. *Other Gujarat: social transformations among weaker sections*. Mumbai: Popular, 2002. p. 425. ASL, CEEL, CSSL, EDIL, GIDRL, SETUL, SPIESRL.

Shukla, J.B. Life and labour in Gujarat taluka (1933). In *Dissertation in economics 1921–1971*. Ed by C.H. Shah. Bombay: University of Bombay, 1974. pp. 130–133. SPIESRL.

Shukla, J.B. *Life and labour in a Gujarat taluka*. C.N. Vakil, ed. Bombay: Longmans, 1937. p. 291. AAUL, GIDRL, GVL, HML, SUL.

Shylendra, H.S. and Rani Usha. *Diversification and sustainable rural livelihood: a study in the semi-arid villages of Western India*. New Delhi: Concept, 2005. p. 208. CSSL.

Singal, Savita and Shukul, Maneesha. Cost benefit analysis of rearing children as perceived by mothers in low income group families of urban slums of Baroda. In *Child labour: Multi dimensional problem.* Ed. by Kamla Srinivasan and Veena Gandotra. Delhi: Ajanata, 1993. pp. 127–134. CSSL, TRTIL.

Srinivasan, Kamala. Child labour: an alleviation cum eradication model based on a study of child labour in Baroda city. In *Child labour: Multi dimensional problem*. Ed. by Kamla Srinivasan and Veena Gandotra. Delhi: Ajanata, 1993. pp. 67–76. CSSL, TRTIL.

Streefkerk, Hein. Casualisation of the workforce: thirty years of industrial labour in South Gujarat. In *Development and deprivation in Gujarat: in honour of Jan Breman*. Ed. by Ghanshyam Shah, Mario Rutten and Hein Streefkerk. New Delhi: Sage, 2002. pp. 133–149. CEEL, CEPTL, CSSL, EDIL, GIDRL, HML, IIML, IRMAL, UML.

Surti, Kirtida. Stitching garments: not enterprise but labour. In *Problems of home-based workers in India: proceedings of a national workshop held at Ahmedabad, from 29 to 31 March, 1986.* Ed. by B.B. Patel. New Delhi: Oxford, 1989. pp. 404–420. CSSL.

Trebbi, Lisetta M. Marginalisation of textile workers in Ahmedabad. In *Issues in urbanisation: study of Ahmedabad city.* Ed. by Jan Hesselberg. Jaipur: Rawat, 2002. pp. 165–183. SPIESRL.

Unni, Jeemol et al. Social income: community, state and private support mechanisms for inclusive growth in Gujarat. In *Globalization, growth and employment: challenges and opportunities*. Ed. by Lancy Lobo and Jayesh Shah. Jaipur: Rawat, 2012. pp. 239–267. CSSL, EDIL.

Unni, Jemol and Naik, Ravikiran. Gujarat's employment story: growth with informality. In *Growth or development: which way is Gujarat going?* Ed. by Indira Hirway, Amita Shah and Ghanshyam Shah. New Delhi: Oxford, 2014. pp. 270–300. CSSL.

Yagnik, Achyut and Randeria, Shalini. Holiday from labour laws: a case of brick-kiln workers. In *Migrant labour and related issues.* Ed. by Vidyut Joshi. New Delhi: Oxford and IBH, 1987. pp. 283–290. CSSL, HML, SPIESRL, TRTIL.

Yanagisawa, Haruka. Diversification of jobs in rural lower classes: the report of a survey in Ahmedabad district. In *Economic changes and social transformation in modern and contemporary South Asia*. Ed. by S. Taniguchi. et al. Tokyo: Hitotsubashi University, 1994. pp. 187–220. CSSL.

Journal Articles

Acharya, Akash. Land acquisition, loss of employment and women's participation in income generation: a case study of coastal belt of South Gujarat. *Man and Development.* 24, 3, 2002. pp. 79–87. CSSL, GVL, UML.

Amin, Poornima. Labour-induced technology relations in small size factory units of Gujarat: disaggregated level study in sub-regional perspective. *Asian Economic Review*. 38, 1, 1996. pp. 13–43. IRMAL.

Bagchi, Amiya Kumar and Das, Panchanan. Changing pattern of employment under neo-liberal reforms: a comparative study of West Bengal and Gujarat. *Indian Journal of Labour Economics.* 48, 4, 2005. pp. 945–958. CSSL, EDIL, GIDRL, IIML, IRMAL, SGUL.

Barik, Bishnu C. Rural-urban migration and economic development: a case study of Oriya agricultural labourers in Surat. *Man and Development*. 6, 3, 1984. pp. 39–50. GIDRL, SPIESRL, UML.

Bhardwaj, V.P. Model of trade union on Gandhian lines of thinking: a case of textile labour association (TLA) Ahmedabad. *Indian Journal of Labour Economics.* 30, 1 and 2, 1987. pp. [ ]. IIML.

Bharadwaj, V.P. and Dave, P.K. Measurement of rural underemployment in Gujarat: a fixed time-coefficient approach. *Artha-Vikas.* 12, 1, 1976. pp. 21–35. AAUL, GIDRL, GVL, HML.

Bharadwaj, V.P. and Dave, P.K. Measurement of rural underemployment in Gujarat. *Indian Journal of Labour Economics.* 15, 1–2, 1972. pp. 70–86. SPIESRL.

Bhatt, Ela R. Unprotected labour. *Indian Journal of Labour Economics.* 37, 3, 1994. pp. 437–448. CSSL.

Bhatt, Jigar. Study under the national food for work programme (NFFWP) with respect to national rural employment guarantee scheme (NREGS): with special reference to Dahod district of Gujarat. *Artha-Vikas.* 46, 2, 2010. pp. 6–16. CSSL.

Bhatt, M.P. Some economic aspects of Gujarati migrants. *Vishleshan.* 7, 1, 1981. pp. 72–75. CSSL, GIDRL.

Bino Paul, G.D., Krishna, M. and Saritha, C.T. Does change in science and technology explain dynamics in human capital?: an enquiry in to emergent trends in nursing labour market. *Contributions to Indian Social Science.* 30, 3–4, 2011. pp. 33-[ ]. SPIESRL, UML.

Breman, Jan. Dualistic labour system?: a critique of the 'informal sector' concept II: a fragmented labour market. *Economic and Political Weekly.* 11, 49, 1976. pp. 1905–1908. CEPTL, CSSL, GUL, IIML, SPIESRL, UML.

Breman, Jan. 'Even dogs are better off': the ongoing battle between capital and labour in the cane-fields of Gujarat. *Journal of Peasant Studies.* 17, 4, 1990. pp. 546–608. CSSL.

Breman, Jan. 'I am the government labour officer…': state protection for rural proletariat of South Gujarat. *Economic and Political Weekly.* 20, 24, 1985. pp. 1043–1055. CEPTL, CSSL, GUL, IIML, SGUL, SPIESRL, UML.

Breman, Jan. Infomalised labour system: end of labour market dualism. *Economic and Political Weekly.* 36, 52, 2001. pp. 4804–4821. BUL, CEPTL, CSSL, EDIL, IIML, MICAL, SGUL, SPIESRL, UML.

Breman, Jan. Labour relation in the 'formal' and 'informal' sectors: report of a case study in South Gujarat, India. Part-I. *Journal of Peasant Studies.* 4, 3, 1977. pp. 171–205. HML, IRMAL, SGUL.

Breman, Jan. Labour relations in the formal and informal sectors: report of a case study in South Gujarat, India. Pt 2 (RP 220–5). *Journal of Peasant Studies.* 4, 4, 1977. pp. 337–359. HML, IRMAL, SGUL.

Breman, Jan. Mobilisation of landless labourers: Halpatis of South Gujarat. *Economic and Political Weekly.* 9, 12, 1974. pp. 489–496. CSSL, GUL, SGUL, SPIESRL, TRTIL, UML.

Breman, Jan. Seasonal migration and co-operative capitalism: the crushing of cane and labour by the sugar factories of Bardoli. *Economic and Political Weekly.* 12, 31, 32 and 33, 1978. pp. 1317–1360. CEPTL, CSSL, GUL, IIML, SGUL, SPIESRL, UML.

Breman, Jan. Seasonal migration and co-operative capitalism: the crushing of cane and labour by the sugar factories of Bardoli, South Gujarat-part-1. *Journal of Peasant Studies.* 6, 1, 1978. pp. 41–70. CSSL, HML, SGUL.

Breman, Jan. Seasonal migration and co-operative capitalism: the crushing of cane and labour by the sugar factories of Bardoli, South Gujarat-part-2. *Journal of Peasant Studies.* 6, 2, 1979. pp. 168–209. CSSL, HML, SGUL.

Breman, Jan. Silencing the voice of agricultural labourers in South Gujarat. *Modern Asian Studies*. 33, 1, 1999. pp. 1–22. CSSL, IRMAL.

Chakravarty, Sujoy and Somanathan, E. Discrimination in an elite labour market?: job placements at IIM-Ahmedabad. *Economic and Political Weekly*. 43, 44, 2008. pp. 45–51. BUL, CEPTL, CSSL, EDIL, IIML, IRMAL, MICAL, SGUL, SPIESRL, SUL, UML.

Chavda, Kishorsinh N. and Mahida, Indrajitsinh D. Agriculture labour and their wages: a study of Surat district of Gujarat. *Vishleshan*. 36, 2, 2011. pp. 24–31. CSSL, IIML.

Dadi, M.M. and Patel, B.B. Structure of industrial wages in Gujarat. *Journal of the M.S. University of Baroda*. 20, 2, 1971. pp. 53–56. GVL.

Das, Biswaroop. Migrant labour in the construction sector. *Man & Development*. 14, 1, 1992. pp. 119–132. CSSL, UML.

Das, Panchnan. Wage inequality in manufacturing industries 1979–2002: a case of West Bengal and Gujarat. *Indian Journal of Labour Economics*. 50, 2, 2007. pp. 303 316. AAUL, CSSL, EDIL, GIDRL, IIML.

Das, Panchanun and Bagchi, Amiyakumar. Changing pattern of employment under eco-liberal reforms: a comparative study of West Bengal and Gujarat. *Indian Journal of Labour Economics*. 48, 4, 2005. pp. 945–958. AAUL, EDIL.

Dave, Forum. Gujarat: trends and employment pattern of urban regions. *Nagarlok*. 44, 1, 2012. pp. 66–74. GIDRL.

Desai, Bharati S. Migration and social mobility in a South Gujarat village W.SP.r.t. DHED: a land-less agriculturist caste. *Journal of the M.S. University of Baroda*. 29, 2, 1980. pp. 57–88. GVL.

Desai, Bhavesh N. Performance and implementation of NREGA in Gujarat. *Vishleshan*. 35, 2, 2010. pp. 36–45. CSSL, IIML.

Desai, M.B. and Shah, C.H. Problem of form labour in Gujarat. *Indian Journal of Agricultural Economics*. 6, 2, 1951. pp. 47–64. IIML, SGUL.

Dholakia, Bakul H. and Dholakia, Ravindra, H. Interstate variation in female labour force participation rates in India. *Indian Journal of Labour Economics*. 20, 4, 1978. pp. 290-[ ]. SPIESRL.

Dholakia, Jitendra. Manpower imbalances in the economy of Gujarat. *Manpower Journal*. 12, 1, 1976. pp. 39–47. HML, SGUL, UML.

Dholakia, Jitendra. Worker's participation in management: a case study of Gujarat. *Indian Journal of Labour Economics*. 20, 4, 1978. pp. 231–236. SPIESRL.

Dholakia, R.H. District worker rates in Gujarat: a factor analysis. *Journal of the Gujarat Research Society*. 37, 3/145, 1975. pp. 79–88. GVL, TRTIL.

Dholakia, Sudha B. Determinants of the interdistrict disparity in labour participation rates in Gujarat. *Journal of the Gujarat Research Society*. 38, 3/146, 1976. pp. 9–22. GVL.

Dixit, Anita K. Growth and non-farm employment: the case of Gujarat. *Indian Journal of Labour Economics*. 52, 3, 2009. pp. 519–536. AAUL, CSSL, IIML.

Gajj, B.L. Impact of environment degradation on employment under canal command area in Gujarat state: an employment decomposition approach. *Current Agriculture*. 24, 1–2, 2000. pp. 49–55. AAUL.

Gumber, Anil. Rural development and seasonal migration in Gujarat: pattern, determinants and consequence. *Labour & Development*. 1, 2, 1996. pp. 85–120. HML.

Gumber, Anil K. Occupational mobility of displaced families: a study of the Panam irrigation project in Gujarat. *Anvesak*. 19, 1 and 2, 1989. pp. 151–173. GIDRL.

Gumber, Anil K. Sectoral level of development and migration in Gujarat: a district level analysis. *Anvesak*. 13, 1, 1983. pp. 25–46. CEPTL, CSSL, GIDRL, IRMAL.

Hirway, Indira. Female employment in rural Gujarat: some issues. *Indian Journal of Labour Economics*. 22, 3, 1979. pp. 161–170. CSSL.

Hirway, Indira. Integration occupational changes in a green revolution area: a study of Matar taluka. *Indian Journal of Labour Economics*. 21, 4, (I), 1979. pp. 27–36. CSSL.

Hirway, Indira. Trend in agricultural wages in Gujarat. *Indian Journal of Agricultural Economics*. 28, 3, 1973. pp. 65–72. GVL, UML.

Hirway, Indira and Shah, Neha. Labour and employment under globalization: the case of Gujarat. *Economic and Political Weekly*. 46, 22, 2011. pp. 57–65. BUL, CEPTL, CSSL, EDIL, IRMAL, SPIESRL, SUL, UML.

Ibrahim, Farhana. Defining a border: Harijan migrants and the state in Katchchh. *Economic and Political Weekly*. 40, 16, 2005. pp. 1623–1630. CEPTL, CSSL, EDIL, IIML, IRMAL, MICAL, SGUL, SPIESRL, UML.

Jain, Hem Chand. Employment situation in rural areas of Narmada basin district. *Khadi Gramodhyog*. 17, 2, 1970. pp. 155–160. TRTIL.

Jhala, P.J. and Thakar, P.H. Priorities in work opportunities: Perceptions from Gujarat. *IASSI Quarterly*. 9, 1 and 2, 1990. pp. 84–87. CSSL, GIDRL, IIML.

Joshi, Nandini U. Nature and implications of the input output structure of labour force in Gujarat. *Artha Vijnana*. 15, 4, 1973. pp. 397–420. CSSL, GVL, HML, UML.

Kadam, Snehal, Patel, R.H. and Bhatt, B.K. Impact of optimization on income and employment of tobacco growers in Anand district of Middle Gujarat agro-climatic zone. *Artha-Vikas*. 46, 2, 2010. pp. 1–5. CSSL.

Kannan, K.P. and Raman, K. Ravi. Neither here nor there?: informal sector workers in South Gujarat. *Indian Journal of Labour Economics*. 41, 1, 1998. pp. 125–132. AAUL, GIDRL, IIML, IRMAL.

Kantawala, B.S. and Padaria, V.K. Income and poverty of urban unorganized labour: a study in Baroda. *Indian Journal of Labour Economics*. 35, 2, 1992. pp. 166–176. CSSL, GIDRL.

Kantor, Paula, Uma Rani and Unni, Jeemol. Decent work deficits in informal economy: case of Surat. *Economic and Political Weekly*. 41, 21, 2006. pp. 2089–2097. BUL, CEPTL, CSSL, EDIL, IIML, IRMAL, MICAL, SGUL, SPIESRL, SUL, UML.

Kashyap, S.P. Diamond shapers of Surat: characteristics of workforce. *Indian Journal of Industrial Relations*. 19, 4, 1984. pp. 425–442. CSSL, IIML, SPUL.

Kothari, Devendra and Visaria, Pravin. Rural-urban migration and its counter-stream in Gujarat: a study of census data. *Indian Journal of Labour Economics*. 28, 1 and 2, 1985. pp. 43–76. GIDRL, IIML.

Krishan, Shri. Peasant mobilization, political organizations and modes of interaction: the Bombay countryside 1934–1941. *Indian Economic and Social History Review*. 32, 4, 1995. pp. 429–446. CSSL.

Kumar, A. and Joshi, K.M. Family-planning methods among the tribal population in South Gujarat: a case study of access and usage. *Development in Practice*. 18, 2, 2008. pp. 258–266. CSSL.

Mahadevia, Darshini. Informalisation of employment and incidence of poverty in Ahmedabad. *Indian Journal of Labour Economics*. 41, 3, 1998. pp. 514–530. AAUL, IIML,

Majumdar, P. Bonus disputes in the textiles mill industry of Ahmedabad. *Indian Journal of Labour Economics*. 6, 1–2, 1963. pp. 160–163. IIML.

Masavi, Mustaali I. Tribal agricultural labourers in Gujarat. *Khadi Gramodyog*. 37, 11, 1991. pp. 439–450. GVL.

Mehta, Niti. Employability of rural labour in the neo-liberal era: a study of Gujarat. *Indian Journal of Labour Economics*. 56, 2, 2013. pp. 243–267. CSSL.

Mehta, Niti. Some aspects of employment and wellbeing of farm labour households: evidence from Gujarat. *Anvesak*. 39, 2, 2009. pp. 1–22. CSSL, GIDRL, SPIESRL.

Misra, Hrudanand. Determinants of remittances: a case study of migrant labourers in Alang ship-breking yard. *Artha Vijnana*. 50, 2, 2008. pp. 151–168. CSSL, UML.

Misra, Hrudanand. Rights of migrant labour at the Alang ship breaking yard. *Indian Journal of Social Work*. 70, 3, 2009. pp. 487–498. CSSL.

Mistry, M.D. Forest workers of Gujarat. *Social Action*. 40, 2, 1990. pp. 184–195. CSSL.

Naik, T.B. Labour problems of tribal Gujarat. *Eastern Anthropologist*. 3, 1, 1950. pp. 22–27. SGUL.

Nanavaty, Reema. Women agriculture workers. *Seminar*. 531, 2003. pp. 41–46. CSSL, MICAL, UML.

Padaria, V.K. and Kantawala, B.S. Income and poverty of urban unorganized labour: a case study of Baroda. *Indian Journal of Labour Economics*. 35, 2, 1992. pp. 166–176. IIML.

Pandya, B.V. Problems of training and leather working of Chamars in Ahmedabad district. *Journal of the Gujarat Research Society*. 22, 2/86, 1960. pp. 127–132. GVL.

Papola, T.S. Structure of a local labour market: a study in Ahmedabad. *Economic and Political Weekly*. 8, 4–6, 1973. pp. 289–296. CSSL, IRMAL, SGUL, SPIESRL, TRTIL, UML.

Parmar, B.D. Rural labour market: an empirical study of farm wages in Saurashtra region. *Indian Journal of Industrial Relations*. 23, 2, 1987. pp. 229–239. CSSL, IIML.

Parikh, Yatin U. Migration in Baroda-interregional and inter-caste analysis. *Journal of the M.S. University of Baroda*. 24, 2, 1980. pp. 125–136. GVL.

Parthasarathy, R. Economics status, poverty and diversification of activities among rural artisan households in Gujarat. *Indian Journal of Labour Economics*. 37, 4, 1994. pp. 685–694. AAUL, CSSL, IIML, IRMAL.

Parthasarathy, R. Impact of tractor use on agricultural employment in Gujarat. *Indian Journal of Labour Economics*. 35, 2, 1992. pp. 132–44. GIDRL.

Parthasarathy, R. Tradition and change: artisan producers in Gujarat. *Journal of Entrepreneurship*. 8, 1, 1999. pp. 45–65. EDIL, IRMAL.

Patel, A.S. Tribal migrants as farm labourers in a Kheda village. *Adivasi Gujarat*. 3, 2, 1980. pp. 63–75. CSSL, GVL, SPIESRL, TRTIL.

Patel, J.C. Landless tribal agricultural labourers and human rights. *Adivasi Gujarat*. 13, 1, 2003. pp. 36–39. CSSL, GVL, SPIESRL, TRTIL.

Patel, M.S. Labour resource utilization in tribal areas. *Indian Journal of Labour Economics*. 21, 3, 1978. pp. 67–74. CSSL.

Patel, P.N., et al. Employment availability among the tribals of Banaskantha district of Gujarat state. *Adivasi Gujarat*. 13, 1, 2003. pp. 48–53. CSSL, GVL, SPIESRL, TRTIL.

Patel, Sujata. Class conflict and workers' movement in Ahmedabad textile industry, 1918–23. *Economic and Political Weekly*. 19, 20 and 21, 1984. pp. 853–864. CEPTL, CSSL, GUL, IIML, IRMAL, SGUL, SPIESRL, UML.

Patel, Sujata. Contract labour in Ahmedabad textile industry. *Economic and Political Weekly*. 21, 41, 1986. pp. 1813–1820. CEPTL, CSSL, GUL, IIML, IRMAL, SGUL, SPIESRL, UML.

Patel, V.J. Minimum wages of agricultural labourers and capacity to pay of the agricultural farms in Gujarat. *Vishleshan*. 1, 3, 1975. pp. 296–302. GIDRL, IIML.

Pathak, Mahesh T. and Patel, Arun S. Crash scheme for rural employment in Gujarat. *Artha-Vikas*. 10, 1, 1974. pp. 1–11. GVL, HML, SGUL.

Pichholiya, K.R. Women workers in metropolitan city: a study of Ahmedabad. *Indian Journal of Labour Economics*. 20, 4, 1978. pp. 319–328. SPIESRL.

Pradhan, A.K., Pandya, J.G. and Gosai, S.P. Challenges and opportunities: employment and human resource development. (*Gujarat-2010: challenges and opportunities*). *Anvesak*. 31, 1–2, 2001. pp. 124–139. CSSL, SPIESRL.

Purohit, Y.S. and Bharadwaj, V.P. Determinants of labour mobility in a backward area: a study of Bharuch Ankleshwar region. *Anvesak*. 19, 1 and 2, 1989. pp. 65–76. GIDRL, SPIESRL.

Roy Chowdhury, Supriya. Industrial restructuring, unions and the state: textile mill workers in Ahmedabad. *Economic and Political Weekly*. 31, 8, 1996. pp. L-7-L-13. CEPTL, CSSL, IIML, IRMAL, MICAL, SGUL, SPIESRL, UML.

Sahu, Gagan Bihari and Das, Biswaroop. Urban labour markets and the return to migration: destination Surat. *Review of Development & Change*. 15, 2, 2010. pp. 129–152. CSSL, GIDRL.

Sajitha, O.G. and Parthasarthy, R. Whose child out of school to do work? socio-economic and demographic determinants of child workers out of school, Gujarat. *Man in India*. 89, 1–2, 2009. pp. 205–213. CSSL, UML.

Sambrani, Shreekant and Pichholia, K.R. Planning for employment generation: a study of Panchmahals. *Indian Journal of Labour Economics*. 20, 1–2, 1977. pp. 53–71. SPIESRL.

Saxena, Pradeep Kumar. Rural female work participation rate in Gujarat: an inter-district analysis. *Margin*. 22, 1 and 2, 1989–1990. pp. 124–132. GIDRL, HML.

Shah, Amita. Employment linkages of industrial growth in rural economy: evidence from an industrial estate in Gujarat. *Indian Journal of Labour Economics*. 44, 2, 2001. pp. 183–204. AAUL.

Shah, Amita. Water scarcity induced migration: can watershed projects help? *Economic and Political Weekly*. 36, 35, 2001. pp. 3405–3410. BUL, CEPTL, CSSL, EDIL, IIML, IRMAL, MICAL, SGUL, SPIESRL, UML.

Shah, C.H. and Patel, B.V. Rural migration: its nature and implication: an experience of Gujarat (India). *Indian Journal of Regional Science*. 11, 2, 1979. pp. 1–9. SGUL, SPIESRL.

Shah, Dilip. Estimate of employment and benefits generated by Amul dairy. *Anvesak*. 11, 2, 1981. pp. 281–301. SPIESRL.

Shah, Dilip R. Long term movement of rural wage rates in Gujarat. *M.S. University of Baroda*. 23–24, 2, 1974–75. pp. 71–86. GVL.

Shah, J.K. and Srikantiah, S. Incidence of under-employment and unemployment: an analysis with reference to Gujarat state. *Artha-Vikas*. 12, 1, 1976. pp. 59–69. GIDRL, GVL, HML, SGUL.

Shah, J.P. Changing patterns of manpower needs in Gujarat. *Indian Journal of Industrial Relations*. 6, 2, 1970. pp. 187–196. SPUL.

Shah, S.M. Employment patterns in rural Gujarat. *Journal of the Gujarat Research Society*. 14, 3, 1952. pp. 166–174. GUL.

Shah, V.D. and Makwana, Manish. Impact of NREGA on wage rates, food security and rural urban migration in Gujarat state. *Artha-Vikas*. 48, 2, 2012. pp. 19–36. CSSL.

Shukla, Rohit. Employment behaviour in a labour surplus economy in a famine situation: a study of Gujarat. *Anvesak*. 7, 1, 1977. pp. 1–13. CSSL, IRMAL, SPIESRL.

Sidhu, Hina. Employment generation in small scale industries in Gujarat. *Indian Journal of Labour Economics*. 41, 1, 1998. pp. 133–140. AAUL.

Sikligar, P.C. Employment opportunities for tribals under Swarnjayanti Gram Swarozgar Yojana: a case study. *Anvesak*. 34, 2, 2004. pp. 1–8. CSSL.

Singh, B.K. Pattern of rural employment and migration in drought affected areas of Gujarat. *Gujarat Agricultural University Research Journal*. 21, 1, 1995. pp. 80–84. GVL.

Singh, P.K. Pattern of rural employment and migration in drought affected areas of Gujarat. *Gujarat Agricultural University Research Journal*. 21, 2, 1996. pp. 80–84. AAUL, GVL.

Singh, Sukhpal. Gender and child labour in cottonseed production in India: a case study of Gujarat. *Indian Journal of Labour Economics*. 51, 3, 2008. pp. 445–458. AAUL, CSSL, EDIL, GIDRL, IIML.

Solanki, Aruna. Socio-economic condition of migrant workers in Bardoli sugar industry with special reference to cutting and loading workers. *VNSGU Journal of Humanities & Social Sciences*. 3, 2, 2011. pp. 38–49. CSSL.

Streefkerk, Hein. Too little to live on, too much to die on: employment in small scale industries in rural South Gujarat. *Economic and Political Weekly*. 16, 15, 1981. pp. 659–668. CEPTL, CSSL, GUL, IIML, IRMAL, SGUL, SPIESRL, UML.

Swaminathan, Madhura. Do child workers acquire specialized skills?: a case study of teenage workers in Bhavnagar. *Indian Journal of Labour Economics*. 40, 4, 1997. pp. 829–839. AAUL, CSSL.

Uma Rani and Shylendra, H.S. Seasonal migration and rural-urban interface in semi-arid tropics of Gujarat: study of a tribal village. *Journal of Rural Development*. 20, 2, 2001. pp. 187–217. CSSL, GIDRL, GVL, IIML, IRMAL.

Unni, Jeemol. Diversification of economic activities and non-agricultural employment in rural Gujarat. *Economic and Political Weekly*. 31, 33, 1996. pp. 2243–2251. CSSL, GIDRL, IIML, IRMAL, MICAL, SGUL, SPIESRL, UML.

Unni, Jeemol. Occupational choice and multiple job holding in rural Gujarat. *Indian Economic Review*. 31, 2, 1996. pp. 157–183. CSSL, IRMAL.

Veena, D.R. Forecasting frame of demand for manpower by skill in Gujarat's economy. *Artha-Vikas*. 11, 2, 1975. pp. 54–60. GVL.

Veena, D.R. Input-output model for manpower projection by occupations and educational levels in Gujarat's economy. *Anvesak,* 4, 2, 1974. pp. 119–143. CSSL, IRMAL, SPIESRL.

Veena, D.R. Technological change and employment: experience of Gujarat's manufacturing sector. *Vishleshan*. 2, 3, 1976. pp. 269–276. CSSL.

Veena, D.R. and Patel, P.M. Pattern and determinants of net migration in microframe of Gujarat. *Journal of the Gujarat Research Society*. 40, 3/148, 1978. pp. 39–52. GVL.

Verma, Pramod. Wages in India: towards a national wage policy. *Indian Journal of Labour Economics*. 20, 3, 1977. pp. 109-[ ]. SPIESRL.

Vyas, Mohanlal. Labour welfare in Gujarat. *Indian Labour Journal*. 7, 12, 1966. pp. 1135–1146. GVL, SPUL.

Yadav, S.K. and Bhandari, U.S. Quality of life of the workers engaged in minor forest products gathering economy: a case study of five districts of three states. *Manpower Journal*. 42, 1, 2007. pp. 133–158. CSSL, UML.

Zachariah, K.C. Maharashtrian and Gujarati migrants in Greater Bombay. *Sociological Bulletin*. 15, 2, 1966. pp. 68–87. CSSL.

Zankharia, Kirti S. Child labour: problems and remedies. *VNSGU Journal of Humanities and Social Sciences*. 1, 1, 2009. pp. 29–49. CSSL, SGUL.

Working Papers, Reports and Other Materials

Basant, Rakesh and Joshi, Harish. *Diversification of employment in an agriculturally developed region: some evidence from rural Kheda, Gujarat*. Ahmedabad: Gujarat Institute of Development Research, 1991. p. 34. Working Paper No. 33. GIDRL, IRMAL.

Basant, Rakesh and Kumar, B.L. *Non-agricultural employment in rural Gujarat: a review of evidence*. Ahmedabad: Gujarat Institute of Area Planning, 1990. p. 57. Working Paper No. 28. CSSL, EDIL, GIDRL, IRMAL.

Basant, Rakesh and Parthasarathy, R. *Inter-regional variations in rural non-agricultural employment in Gujarat, 1961–81*. Ahmedabad: Gujarat Institute of Area Planning, 1991. p. 37. Working Paper No. 36. CSSL, GIDRL, IRMAL.

Behavioural Science Centre. *Situation of tribal migrant labourers of Sabarkantha and Banaskantha districts of North Gujarat*. Ahmedabad: Behavioural Science Centre, 2009. p. 45. CSSL.

Bhatt, Atul. *Study of working and living environments of seasonal migrants*. Ahmedabad: Gujarat Institute of Area Planning, 1979. p. 59. CSSL, GIDRL.

Bramhmbhatt, D.M. Agricultural labourers in a North Gujarat village. In *Agricultural labourers in four Indian villages*. Ed. by V.S. Vyas. Vallabh Vidyanagar: Agro-Economic Research Centre, 1964. pp. 48–71. Ad-hoc Research Studies No. 4. AERCL, SPUL.

Brahmbhatt, D.M., Patel, V.M. and Dave, V.J. *National rural employment programme in Gujarat; a case study of Kheda district*. Vallabh Vidyanagar: Agro-Economic Research Centre(AERC), 1987. p. 155. AERC Research Study No. 75. GIDRL, IRMAL.

Breman, Jan. *Even dogs are better off': the on-going battle between capital and labour in the cane fields of Gujarat*. New Delhi: ICSSR and IMWOO, 1990. p. [ ]. IDPAD occasional papers and reprints 1990–2. GIDRL.

Breman, Jan. *Labour nomads in South Gujarat*. Surat: Centre for Social Studies, 1996. p. 38. I.P. Desai memorial lecture No. 8. CSSL, TRTIL.

Buch, A.N. Labour management relations: the Ahmedabad-experience. In *Future perspectives for the textile industry*. By Ahmedabad textile industry's research association. Ahmedabad: ATIRA, 1974. pp. 109–114. Series of lectures delivered on the occasion of the silver jubilee of ATIRA. CSSL.

Chokshi, H.P. *Study of mobilization of resources for village panchayats in Baroda district (1951–1965)*. Baroda: Department of Business Economics, Faculty of Commerce, 1971. p. 226. SPIESRL.

Dadi, M.M. Employment structure of Baroda city. In *Profiles of a growing city: the city of Baroda*. Ed. by K.N. Reddy et al. Baroda: M.S. University, 1971. pp. 60–63. Souvenir: the 2nd Gujarat economic conference, 2–3 January 1971. CSSL.

Dalsania, Shanti M. Migration and urbanization in the districts of Gujarat. *In Gujarat Economic Association conference papers, Baroda*. Ed. by V.S. Vyas, Pravin Visaria and A.R. Desai. Ahmedabad: Balgovind, 1971. pp. 200–209. GIDRL, IIML.

Dantwala, M.L. and Shah, C.H. Study of rural employment: with reference to sixteen villages in Gujarat. Bombay: Department of Economics, University of Bombay, 1966. p. [ ]. GIDRL.

Das, Biswaroop. *Migrant labour in urban areas*. Surat: Centre for Social Studies, 1990. p. 109. CSSL.

Dept. of Social Justice and Empowerment. Gujarat's economic condition and challenges. In Gujarat-2010 challenges and opportunities(seminar volume). Ed. by Rohit Shukla. Ahmedabad: Sardar Patel Institute of Economic & Social Research, 2001. pp. 298–303. CSSL, EDIL, IRMAL, SGUL, SPIESRL.

Desai, Gunvant M. and Schluter, Michael G.G. Generations employment in rural areas. In *Rural development for weaker sections*. Ed. by Indian Society of Agricultural Economics (M.L. Dantwala). Mumbai: Indian Society of Agricultural Economics, 1974. pp. 143–152. Seminar Series – XII. SGUL.

Desai, Ishvarlal Pragji. *Patterns of migration and occupation in a South Gujarat village*. Poona: Deccan College, 1964. p. 166. Building centenary and silver jubilee series No. 19. CSSL, GIDRL, GUL, GVL, SGUL, TRTIL.

Desai, Kiran. *Nature and conditions of workers in small scale industrial units in Gujarat*. Surat: Centre for Social Studies, 1995. p. 245. CSSL.

Desai, Kiran. Nature and conditions of workers in small scale industrial units in Gujarat: some observations. In *International Seminar on Gujarat society, development and deprivation, 6–9 December 1994*. Surat: Centre for Social Studies, 1994. pp. 1–38. CSSL.

Desai, Kiran. Surviving in adverse condition: workers of small scale industrial units in Gujarat. In *Small scale industrial development and labour, (26–27 March 1997)*. Surat: Centre for Social Studies, 1997. pp. 1–16. CSSL.

Desai, Kiran and Patel, Arjun. Profile of the rural migrant labour in Gujarat. In *Migrant labour in India*. Surat: Centre for Social Studies, 1989. pp. 20–29. Workshop report. CSSL.

Desai, Kiran and Raj, Nikhil. *Child labour in diamond industry of Surat*. Noida: V.V. Giri National Labour Institute, 2001. p. 173. CSSL.

Desai, M.B. Fixation of minimum wages in unorganized occupations in Gujarat: an empirical analysis. In *Gujarat economic association conference papers, Nadiad*. Ed. by D.T. Lakdawala and R.J. Mody. 1976. pp. 1–23. GIDRL.

Desai, M.B. and Varma, S.K. *Bonded labour system in Gujarat: a study of 3 districts of Gujarat state*. Baroda: M.S. University, 1978. p. 188. CSSL.

Desai, Mahendra D. Problems of low-income sections in rural areas. In *Rural development for weaker sections*. Ed. by Indian Society of Agricultural Economics (M.L. Dantwala). Mumbai: Indian Society of Agricultural Economics, 1974. pp. 58–73. Seminar Series – XII. SGUL.

Desai, M.D. *Employment, income and levels of living of agricultural labourers: a study in the Surat District, Gujarat 1969–70*. Vallabh Vidyanagar: Agro-Economic Research Centre, 1974. p. 17. IRMAL.

Dhak, Biplab and Shah, Amita. *International migration from Gujarat: an exploratory analysis.* Ahmedabad: Gujarat Institute of Development Research, 2011. p. 28. Working Paper 206. CSSL, GIDRL.

Dhawan, Reva and Jhabvala, Renana. *Bidi home-workers of Gujarat*. Ahmedabad: Self Employed Women's Association, [ ]. p. 90. CSSL.

Dholakia, Ravindra H. *Block level planning for full employment Jambughoda.* Ahmedabad: Sardar Patel Institute of Economic & Social Research, 1979. p. 235. IIML.

Dholakia, Ravindra H., Hirway, Indira A. and Patel, Premji M. *Block level planning for full employment*: *Jambughoda.* Ahmedabad: Sardar Patel Institute of Economic & Social Research, 1979. p. 235. CSSL.

Fafale, A.B. Small scale sector: a present relevance. In *Small scale industrial development and labour, (26–27 March 1997).* Surat: Centre for Social Studies, 1997. pp. 1–10. CSSL.

Gandhi, R.D. and Shah, C.H. *Rural seasonal migration.* Ahmedabad: Gujarat Institute of Area Planning, 1978. p. 84. CSSL.

Gujarat Agricultural University, Department of Economic and Angrish, A.C. *Block level planning for full employment Visavadar taluka district Junagadh.* Junagadh: Department of Economics, Gujarat Agricultural University, p. [ ]. 173. GIDRL.

Hirway, Indira. *Block level planning for full employment*. Ahmedabad: Sardar Patel Institute of Economic & Social Research, 1979. p. 235. CSSL.

Hirway, Indira. Note on employment problems of rural women in Gujarat. In *Gujarat economy problems and prospects.* Ed. by D.T. Lakdawala. Ahmedabad: Sardar Patel Institute of Economic & Social Research, 1983. pp. 157–168. Monograph 10. GUL, IIML.

Hirway, Indira. Note on employment problems of rural women in Gujarat. In *Gujarat economy: problems and prospects.* Ed. by D.T. Lakdawala. Ahmedabad: Sardar Patel Institute of Economic & Social Research, 1982. pp. 157–168. GIDRL.

Hirway, Indira. Note on employment problems of rural women in Gujarat. In *Seminar on development of Gujarat: problems & prospects, 24th-26th August, 1981.* Ahmedabad: Sardar Patel Institute of Economic & Social Research, 1981. pp. 1–21. CSSL.

Hirway, Indira and Abraham, Joseph. *Organising rural workers: Gujarat government experiment.* Ahmedabad: Gandhi Labour Institute, 1985. p. 160. IIML.

Hirway, Indira, et al. *Block level plan for full employement: Jambusar taluka Bharuch district.* Ahmedabad: Vikas, 1979. p. 168. CSSL.

Hirway, Indira and Unni, Jeemol. *Employment and occupational mobility among women workers in manufacturing industries in Ahmedabad, India.* New Delhi: International Labour Organization, 1995. p. 171. SAAT working papers. GUL, IIML.

Jain, Devki. *Khet Majoor Mahajan Gujarat: study of a peasant organisation.* New Delhi: Institute of Social Studies, [ ]. p. [ ]. GIDRL.

Jhabvala, Renana. Closing doors: a study on the decline in women workers in the textile mills of Ahmedabad. Ahmedabad: SETU, 1985. p. 63. SETUL.

Jhabvala, Renana and Shaikh, Rahima.*Wage fixation for home-based piece-rate workers: technical study based on a survey of workers in Gujarat, India*. Ahmedabad: Self Employed Women's Association (SEWA), [ ]. p. 25. GIDRL.

Jhabvala, Renana, Dhawan, Reva and Mahajan, Krishan. *Woman who roll Bidis two studies of Gujarat.* Ahmedabad: Self Employed Women's Association, 1985. p. 54. SPIESRL.

Joshi, Rajendra. et al. *From basic services delivery to policy advocacy-community mobilisation in Pravinnagar-Guptanagar Ahmedabad.* Ahmedabad: Centre for Urban Equity, 2010. p. 36. Working Paper 6. CEPTL.

Joshi, Vidyut. *Bonded labour in Gujarat.* Ahmedabad: Gandhi Labour Institute, 1985. p. 77. CSSL.

Joshi, Vidyut. *Social context of bonded labour*. Ahmedabad: Gandhi Labour Institute, [ ]. p. 21. Working Paper. CSSL.

Joshi, Vidyut. *Study of rural labour camps*. Ahmedabad: Gandhi Labour Institute, 1989. p. 111. CSSL.

Kanetkar, S.S. Migration to Baroda city. In *Profiles of a growing city: the city of Baroda.* Ed. by K.N. Reddy et al. Baroda: M.S. University, 1971. pp. 125–134. Souvenir: 2nd Gujarat Economic Conference, 2–3 January 1971. CSSL, SPIESRL.

Kanetkar, S.S. Some estimates of immigration and out migration for the cities of Gujarat. In *Gujarat Economic Association conference papers, Baroda.* Ed. by V.S. Vyas, Pravin Visaria and A.R. Desai. Ahmedabad: Balgovind, 1971. pp. 185–199. GIDRL, IIML.

Khandelwal, Ashok, Katiyar, Sudhir and Vaishnav, Madan Das. *Child labour in cottonseed production: a case study of cottonseed farms in North Gujarat*. Pal Deol: Dakshini Rajasthan Mazdoor Union, 2008. p. 71. CSSL.

Lal, R.B. *Block level planning for full employment [DANTA].* Ahmedabad: [ ], 1979. p. 215. Serise-54. TRTIL.

Lal, R.B. and Desai, Bharati. *Block level planning for full employment: Sagbara district-Bharuch.* Ahmedabad: Gujarat Vidyapith, 1982. p. 278. TRTIL.

Lal, Rash Bihari. *Bonded labour in Gujarat: dose it exist in Gujarat*? Ahmedabad: Gujarat Vidyapith, 1977. p. 25. CSSL, GIDRL, TRTIL.

Lobo, Lancy. Social stratification and mobility among the Kolis of North Gujarat. In *International seminar on "Gujarat Society", 17–20 December 1986.* Surat: Centre for Social Studies, 1986. pp. 1–41. CSSL.

Mangaldas, Madanmohan. Labour management relations: the Ahmedabad experience. In *Future perspectives for the textile industry.* By Ahmedabad textile industry's research association. Ahmedabad: ATIRA, 1974. pp. 115–126. Series of lectures delivered on the occasion of the silver jubilee of ATIRA. CSSL.

Mehta, M.J. Origin and growth of trade union movement in Ahmedabad. In *Proceedings of the seminar on socialism in India 1919–1939.* New Delhi: Nehru Memorial Museum and Library, 1970. pp. 533–560. IIML.

Mehta, Meera and Mehta, Dinesh. Implications of urban policy and regulations for self-employed workers: a case study of hawkers in Ahmedabad. In *Self-employed women population & human resource development.* Ed. by Pravin Visaria and Jeemol Unni. Ahmedabad: Gujarat Institute of Development Research, 1992. pp. 134–150. CSSL, SPIESRL.

Mehta, S.S., Shivanand Swamy, H.M. and Gulati, Preeti. Employment, unemployment and growth in Gujarat. In *Gujarat-2010: challenges and opportunities*. By Government of Gujarat. Ahmedabad: Sardar Patel Institute of Economic & Social Research, 2001. pp. 304–327. Seminar volume. CSSL, EDIL, IRMAL, SGUL, SPIESRL.

Pandya, Kiran. Refelection on planning for employment in Gujarat. In *Gujarat-2010: challenges and opportunities*. By Government of Gujarat. Ahmedabad: Sardar Patel Institute of Economic & Social Research, 2001. pp. 328–337. Seminar volume. CSSL, EDIL, IRMAL, SGUL, SPIESRL.

Papola, T.S. and Subrahmanian, K.K. *Wage structure and labour mobility in a local labour market: a study in Ahmedabad.* Ahmedabad: Sardar Patel Institute of Economic & Social Research, 1975. p. 214. IIML, SPIESRL.

Parikh, Gokul O. *Economic and social survey of agricultural labourers in Gujarat state.* Ahmedabad: Sardar Patel Institute of Economic & Social Research, 1985. p. 267. CSSL, SPIESRL.

Parthasarathy, R. *Economic status and labour allocation strategy of rural artisan households in Gujarat.* Ahmedabad: Gujarat Institute of Development Research, 1993. p. 41. Working Paper No. 54. CSSL, GIDRL, IRMAL.

Patel, Arjun. On arrival of major industries and its impact on rural society: a case of PAFs of KGPP of Surat, Gujarat. In *Small scale industrial development and labour, (26–27 March 1997).* Surat: Centre for Social Studies, 1997. pp. 1–20. CSSL.

Patel, Arjun and Desai, Kiran. *Migrant labour in rural Gujarat*. Surat: Centre for Social Studies, 1991. p. 94. CSSL.

Patel, Arjun. Study of tribal migrations of Dangs and Dahod. Surat: Centre for Social Studies, 2001. p. 94. CSSL.

Patel, B.B. *Blue-collar women workers in Ahmedabad, employment, occupational structure, and earnings.* Ahmedabad: Sardar Patel Institute of Economic & Social Research, 1979. p. 97. CSSL, SPIESRL.

Patel, B.B. Evolution and pattern of factory employment in the district of a Baroda. In *Profiles of a growing city: socio-economic studies of Baroda city.* Baroda: M.S. University, 1971. pp. 83–91. M.S. University Economics Series No. 1. SPIESRL.

Patel, B.B. Evolution and pattern of factory employment in the district of Baroda. In *Profiles of a growing city: the city of Baroda.* Ed. by K.N. Reddy et al. Baroda: M.S. University, 1971. pp. 83–91. Souvenir: the 2nd Gujarat economic conference, 2–3 January 1971. CSSL.

Patel, B.B. *Planning employment for educated youth in Gujarat: a study of post-graduate on live registers of employment exchange*. Ahmedabad: Gandhi Labour Institute (GLI), 1990. p. [ ]. GIDRL.

Patel, B.B. Population pressure and real wage of agricultural labourers in Gujarat. In *Gujarat economy problems and prospects.* Ed. by D.T. Lakdawala. Ahmedabad: Sardar Patel Institute of Economic & Social Research, 1983. pp. 273–312. Monograph 10. GIDRL, GUL, IIML.

Patel, B.B. and Veena, D.R. Manpower. In *Gujarat economy in 2001 A.D.: a study in perspective*. Ahmedabad: Sardar Patel Institute of Economic & Social Research, 1980. pp. 269–290. GUL.

Patel, J.M. Agricultural labourers in a South Gujarat villages. In *Agricultural labourers in four Indian villages*. Ed. by V.S. Vyas. Vallabh Vidyanagar: Agro-Economic Research Centre, 1964. pp. 96–122. Ad-hoc Research Studies No. 4. AERCL, SPUL.

Patel, Jagdish. Scenario of occupational safety and health in small scale units. In *Small scale industrial development and labour, (26–27 March 1997).* Surat: Centre for Social Studies, 1997. pp. 1–12. CSSL.

Patel, Jagdish, ed. *Stoned: plight of agate workers, Gujarat*. Vadodara: Peoples Trainig & Research Centre, 2012. p. 76. CSSL.

Patel, V.C., Indu, R. and Patel, Vilas P. *Employment pattern in rural Gujarat: a study of four villages in Anand taluka 1970–71*. Vallabh Vidyanagar: Agro-Economic Research Centre, 1975. p. 101. Research Study No. 37. AERCL, IRMAL, SPUL.

Patel, Vithalbhai G. *Problems of agricultural labour in Bharuch district.* Vallabh Vidyanagar: Sardar Patel University, 1985. p. 268. SPUL.

Pradhan, A.K., Pandya, J.G. and Gosai, S.P. Challenges and opportunities: employment and human resource development. In *Gujarat-2010: challenges and opportunities*. By Government of Gujarat. Ahmedabad: Sardar Patel Institute of Economic & Social Research, 2001. pp. 286–297. Seminar volume. CSSL, EDIL, IRMAL, SGUL, SPIESRL.

Prakash, Anjal. *Sharecropping, migration and the new face of water markets: a case of Sangpura village in North Gujarat (Highlight)*. Vallabh Vidyanagar, IWMI-TATA Water Policy Program, 2005. p. [ ]. IWMI-TATA Water policy program No. 23. GIDRL.

Punalekar, S.P. *Female casual labourers in urban Gujarat: a case study*. Surat: Centre for Social Studies, 1990. p. 40. Occasional Paper No. 6. CSSL.

Punalekar, S.P. Industry society interface: new questions and contradictions. In *Small scale industrial development and labour, (26–27 March 1997)*. Surat: Centre for Social Studies, 1997. pp. 1–14. CSSL.

Punalekar, S.P. *Informalisation and dependency: a study of Jari and Embroidery workers in South Gujarat*. Surat: Centre for Social Studies, 1988. p. 176. CSSL, GIDRL.

Punalekar, S.P. *Migration and social stratification: a case study of Dhodias of Surat city.* Surat: Centre for Social Studies, 1980. p. 200. CSSL.

Punalekar, S.P. and Desai, Kiran. *Nature and conditions of workers in small scale industrial units of Gujarat.* Surat: Centre for Social Studies, 1994. p. 94. CSSL.

Punalekar, S.P. and Patel, Arjun. *Survival and struggles of female casual labourers in Gujarat: a study of female workers of casual labour markets/chakla bazaars in South and Central Gujarat cities.* Surat: Centre for Social Studies, 1990. p. 19. CSSL.

Rajaram, N. Planned rural development and Jawahar Rozgar Yojna in Central Gujarat: some observation. In *National seminar on common property resources and planned development in Western India: challenges and prospects, January 19–21, 1999.* Seminar volume. Nanded: School of Social Sciences and School of Earth Sciences, S.R.T.M. University, 1999. pp. 81–93. CSSL.

Rajakutty, S., Chatterjee, S. and Reddy, D.P.R. *Study on wage employment programme in Kurnool (Andhra Pradesh) and Surat (Gujarat) districts*. Hyderabad: National Institute of Rural Development, 2001. p. 124. NIRD Research Reports Series No. 25. GIDRL, GVL, HML, IRMAL.

Ray, C.N. and Mishra, Aseem. *Vendors and informal sector: a case study of street vendors of Surat city.* Ahmedabad: CEPT University, 2011. p. 31. Working Paper 15. CSSL.

Sahu, Gagan Bihari and Das, Biswaroop. *Urban labour markets and returns to migration: destination Surat.* Jaipur: Institute of Development Studies, 2010. p. 22. IDSJ Working Paper 153. CSSL.

Samanta, B.B., et al. *Block level planning for full employment: Jafrabad.* Baroda: Operations Research Group, 1979. p. 98. IIML.

Savdasia, V.B., Jhala, P.J. and Thakor, P.H. *Impact of economic reforms on economic growth labour and employment in Gujarat*. Ahmedabad: Mahatma Gandhi Labour Institute, 2004. p. 144. GUL.

Shah, C.H. *Economic profile of marginal farmers and labourers (a study in the Borsad taluka of Gujarat)*. Anand: Sardar Patel University, 1972. p. [ ]. Research Series No. 24. SPIESRL.

Shah, Ghanshyam. *Agricultural labourers: are they bonded?*. Surat: Center for Social Studies, 1978. p. 41. CSSL, SPIESRL.

Shah, Ghanshyam and Bose, Pradip Kumar. *Supply of, and demand for, skilled and unskilled labour for the construction of Sardar Sarovar*. Surat: Centre for Social Studies, 1981. p. 114. CSSL.

Shah, V.D. and Makwana, Manish. *Impact of NREGA on wage rates, food security and rural urban migration in Gujarat*. Vallabh Vidyanagar: Agro-Economic Research Centre, 2011. p. 199. Research Study No. 141. AERCL.

Shah, Vimal P. and Thaker, J.D. Occupational status of the scheduled castes in Gujarat. In *Removal of untouchability(proceeding of a seminar)*. Ed. by Vimal P. Shah. Ahmedabad: Gujarat University, 1980. pp. 1–8. SPIESRL.

Shramjivi Mahila Sewa Trust. *Survey on socio-economic conditions women home workers in Ahmedabad*. Nadiad: Shramjivi Mahila Sewa Trust, 1987. p. 51. IIML.

Social Justice and Employment, Department of. Gujarat's economic condition and challenges. In *Gujarat-2010: challenges and opportunities*. By Government of Gujarat. Ahmedabad: Sardar Patel Institute of Economic & Social Research, 2001. pp. 298–303. Seminar volume. CSSL, EDIL, IRMAL, SGUL, SPIESRL.

South Gujarat University. *Working and living conditions of the Surat textile workers: a survey*. Surat: South Gujarat University, 1984. p. [ ]. CSSL, GIDRL.

Srinivasan, Kamala. *Study of working children in Baroda city*. Ahmedabad: Gandhi Labour Institute, 1989. p. 165. IIML.

Subrahmanian, K.K., Veena, D.R. and Parikh, Bhanumati K. *Construction labour market: a study in Ahmedabad*. Ahmedabad: Sardar Patel Institute of Economic & Social Research, 1980. p. 255. HML, SPIESRL.

Uma Rani and Shylendra, H.S. *Seasonal migration and rural-urban interface in semi arid tropics of Gujarat: a study of a tribal village*. Ahmedabad: Gujarat Institute of Development Research, 1999. p. 31. Working Paper No. 111. GIDRL.

Unni, Jeemol. *Diversification of economic activities and non-agricultural employment among rural households in Gujarat, India*. Ahmedabad: Gujarat Institute of Development Research, 1994. p. 30. Working Paper No. 56. CSSL, GIDRL, IRMAL.

Unni, Jeemol. *Employment and wages of rural labourers: recent trends*. Ahmedabad: Gujarat Institute of Development Research, 1997. p. 37. Working Paper No. 83. CSSL, GIDRL.

Unni, Jeemol and Uma Rani. *Insecurities of informal workers in Gujarat, India*. Geneva: International Labour Organization (ILO), 2002. p. 56. SES Papers 30. GIDRL.

Upadhyay, Shashi Bhushan. *Dissension and unity: the origins of workers solidarity in the cotton mills of Bombay, 1875–1918*. Surat: Centre for Social Studies, 1990. p. 54. CSSL.

Verma, J.B. Agricultural labour in a Central Gujarat village. In *Agricultural labour in four Indian villages*. Ed. by V.S. Vyas. Vallabh Vidyanagar: Sardar Vallabhbhai Vidyapeeth, 1967. pp. 68–91. AAUL, GVL, SPUL.

Verma, J.B. Agricultural labourers in a Central Gujarat village. In *Agricultural labourers in four Indian villages*. Ed. by V.S. Vyas. Vallabh Vidyanagar: Agro-Economic Research Centre, 1964. pp. 72–95. Ad-hoc Resarch Studies No. 4. AERCL, SPUL.

Verma, Pramod. *Labour in a textile city: a study of worker's needs and welfare in Ahmedabad*. Ahmedabad: Indian Institute of Management, 1973. p. 71. SPUL.

Verma, Pramod. *Profile of labour*: socio-economic *studies in Ahmedabad*. Ahmedabad: Mahatma Gandhi Institute of Labour Studies, 1981. p. 139. IIML.

Visaria, Leela and Kothari, Devendra. *Migration in Gujarat: an analysis of census data*. Ahmedabad: Sardar Patel Institute of Economic & Social Research, 1984. p. 598. CSSL, GIDRL.

Visaria, Pravin. Changes in employment structure in Gujarat 1961–1988. *In Essays on economic policy methodology and human resources.* Ed. by Maya Shah. Baroda: M.S. University, 1995. pp. 104–112. HML, IIML.

Visaria, Pravin. Level and structure of employment in Gujarat 1901–81. In *Gujarat economy problems and prospects.* Ed. by D.T. Lakdawala. Ahmedabad: Sardar Patel Institute of Economic & Social Research, 1983. pp. 129–156. Monograph 10. GIDRL, GUL, IIML.

Visaria, Pravin. Level and structure of employment in Gujarat 1901–81. In *Seminar on developments of Gujarat: prospects and prospects, 24–26 August, 1981.* Ahmedabad: Sardar Patel Institute of Economic & Social Research, 1981. pp. 1–28. CSSL.

Visaria, Pravin and Jacob, Paul. *Child labour in India: results of a methodological survey in Surendranagar and Surat districts of Gujarat state.* Ahmedabad: Gujarat Institute of Development Research, 1995. p. 328. SPIESRL.

Visaria, Pravin and Unni, Jeemol. Self-employed workers and households in India and Gujarat: a macro view. In *Self-employed women population & human resource development.* Ed. by Pravin Visaria and Jeemol Unni. Ahmedabad: Gujarat Institute of Development Research, 1992. pp. 14–62. CSSL, SPIESRL.

11

Environment, Natural Resources, Disaster

Books/Chapter in Books

Ahmed, Sara and UTTHAN. Dialogue along the Jholapuri river, coastal Gujarat: addressing water and gender conflicts through multi-stakeholder partnerships. In *Water conflicts in India: a million revolts in the making*. Ed. by K.J. Joy et al. London: Routledge, 2008. pp. 115–121. CSSL.

Anand, Javed and Savara, Mira. Operation flood in Surat district. In *Another revolution fails: an investigation into how and why India's operation flood project, touted as the world's largest dairy development programme, funded by EEC, went off the rails*. Ed. by Claude Alvares. Delhi: Ajanta, 1985. pp. 133–158. CSSL.

Bagchi, Kathakali S. Drought-prone Western India: Gujarat. In *Drought-prone India: problem and perspectives.vol-1*. New Delhi: Agricole, 1991. pp. 3–109. CSSL, IIML, SPIESRL.

Bagchi, Kathakali S. Gujarat. In *Natural resource management: western region*. By Kathakali S. Bagchi. New Delhi: Upalabdhi, 2000. pp. 15–77. CSSL.

Bagchi, Kathakali S. and Phillip, Mini. *Wastelands in India: an untapped potential.* New Delhi: Upalabdhi, 1993. pp. 43–52. CEEL.

Bhatnagar, G.C. and Naik, S.D. Quality of ground water as evaluated from remotely sensed data in a part of coastal plain of Gujarat mainland. In *Remote sensing in development and management of water resources.* Ed. by Baldev Sahai, R.S. Chaturvedi and H.S. Iyre. Dehradun: Indian Society Photo Interpretation & Remote Sensing, 1983. pp. 231–237. SPUL.

Bhavsar, Bharti and Baloch, Femida. Battle for water: a conflict between vested interests and women at Vouva, Gujarat. In *Locked horns: conflicts and their resolution in community based natural resource management*. Ed. by Astad Pastakia. Bangalore: Books for Change, 2008. pp. 175–185. CSSL, GVL.

Bhatt, D.C. Studies on some ethnobotanical plants from Saurashtra. In *Ethno botany*. Ed. by Pravin Chandra Trivedi. Jaipur: Aavishkar, 2002. pp. 119–127. HML.

Bhatt, D.C. et al. Studies on some ethno medicinal plants Talaja taluka of Bhavanagar district, Gujarat. In *Ethno Botany*. Ed. by Pravin Chandra Trivedi. Jaipur: Aavishkar, 2002. pp. 295–310. HML.

Bora, Mamita and Bhalani, Dheeraj. Joint forest management: an experience from Bharuch district, Gujarat. In *Joint forest management and community forestry in India: an ecological and institutional assessment*. Ed. by N.H. Ravindranath, K.S. Murali and K.C. Malhotra. New Delhi: Oxford, 2000. pp. 121–134. CSSL.

Centre for Education and Documentation. *Operation flood: development or dependence?*. Bombay: Cite, 1982. p. 110. CSSL.

Chandurkar, Dharmendra. Change of guard: manifestation of a gender-based latent conflict at Ubhariya, Gujarat. In *Locked horns: conflicts and their resolution in community based natural resource management*. Ed. by Astad Pastakia. Bangalore: Books for Change, 2008. pp. 217–230. CSSL, GVL.

Chaudhari, K.M. and Bapat, M.T. *Study of impact of famine and relief measures in Gujarat and Rajasthan.* Anand: Sardar Patel University, 1975. p. 507. SPIESRL.

Chaudhari, Sachin. One step forward, two step backward: consequences of internal strife in a model JFM village in Bharuch district, Gujarat. In *Locked horns: conflicts and their resolution in community based natural resource management*. Ed. by Astad Pastakia. Bangalore: Books for Change, 2008. pp. 231–244. CSSL, GVL.

Chen, Martha Alter. *Coping with seasonality and drought*. New Delhi: Sage, 1991. p. 254. CSSL.

Chhaya, N.D. *Minding our marine wealth: an appraisal of Gujarat's coastal resources.* Ahmedabad: Centre for Environment Education, 1997. p. 107. CEEL, CSSL.

Dabholkar, Dattaprasad. *Oh mother Narmada…: on the hot trial of a controversy.* New Delhi: Wiley, 1990. p. 127. CEEL, CSSL.

Desai, Anjana. Development problems of rural settlements in difficult ecological environments: cases from Gujarat. In *Urbanisation, development and environment: C.D. Deshpande memorial volume*. Ed. by V.S. Phadke and S. Banerjee-Guha. Jaipur: Rawat, 2007. pp. 147–159. CSSL, HML.

Desai, Anjana. Differential perception of residents to environmental quality of an urban area: the case of Ahmedabad. *In Urbanization and environmental problems.* Ed. by S.D. Maurya. Allahabad: Chugh, 1989. pp. 249–266. CEEL.

Dixit, Anita and Macwan, Jyotsna. For a few vighas of land: struggle for socio-economic emancipation by the dalits of Sunderpura, Gujarat. In *Locked horns: conflicts and their resolution in community based natural resource management*. Ed. by Astad Pastakia. Bangalore: Books for Change, 2008. pp. 117–132. CSSL, GVL.

Geevan, C.P., Dixit Arun M. and Silori, C.S. Dynamics of the resource economics of open access Grasslands-Kutch district (Gujarat). In *Biodiversity and quality of life.* Ed. by Nirmal Sengupta and Jayanta Bandyopadhyay. New Delhi: Indian Society for Ecological Economics(INSEE), 2005. pp. 236–252. SPIESRL.

Goel, S.L. Earthquakes: a case study of Gujarat. In *Management of natural disasters*. New Delhi: Deep & Deep, 2010. pp. 3–96. HML.

Gujarat Ecology Commission. *Threatened biodiversity of Gujarat: baseline information.* Vadodara: Gujarat Ecological Society, 2001. p. 140. CEEL.

Gupta, L.C. and Sharma, Vinod K. *Drought in Gujarat 1999–2000 & 2000–2001.* New Delhi: Indian Institute of Public Administration, 2001. p. 96. GVL, SPIESRL.

Gupta, L.C., et al. *Gujarat earthquake: 26th January 2001.* New Delhi: Indian Institute of Public Administration, 2002. p. 192. EDIL, GVL.

Hardiman, David. Politics of water scarcity in Gujarat. In *Waterscapes: the cultural politics of a natural resource*. Ed. by Amita Baviskar. Ranikhet: Permanent Black, 2007. pp. 40–64. CSSL.

Hathi, Tusar. Water crisis and indigenous approach towards resource utilization: a case study of Saurashtra region. In *Environment and economic development*. Ed. by N. Rajalakshmi. Delhi: Manak, 2000. pp. 315–329. HML.

Hathi, Tushar R. Environment and human development: an analytical case study of Saurashtra region of Gujarat state in India. In *Sustaining development: human resources, gender and environment*. Ed. by G.R.N. Ghosh, R. Gabbay and K.C. Roy. New Delhi: Atlantic, 1999. pp. 172–190. GVL.

Hirway, Indira and Goswami, Subhrangsu. *Valuation of coastal resources: the case of Mangroves in Gujarat*. New Delhi: Academic, 2007. p. 170. CSSL, GIDEL, GIDRL.

Iyengar, Sudarshan and Bandopadhyay, Somnath. Environmental strategies for Gujarat. In *Gujarat: perspectives of the future*. Ed. by R. Swaminathan. New Delhi: Academic, 2008. pp. 221–246. CSSL, EDIL, GIDRL, GVL, IIML, IRMAL, SETUL, SPIESRL.

Jethwa, Ghanshyamsinh. Upstream versus downstream: an inter-village conflict over access to surface water in Surendranagar district, Gujarat. In *Locked horns: conflicts and their resolution in community based natural resource management*. Ed. by Astad Pastakia. Bangalore: Books for Change, 2008. pp. 187–199. CSSL, GVL.

Joshi, Mahesh V. *Green-revolution and its impacts: economic development of Saurashtra: its problems and future prospects*. New Delhi: A.P.H., 1999. pp. 25–38. CEPTL.

Joshi, Mahesh V. *Green-revolution and its impacts: green revolution in Saurashtra*. New Delhi: A.P.H., 1999. pp. 51–60. CEPTL.

Joshi, V.H. Operation flood: constructions and potentialities in Saurastra. In *Resource, institutions and strategies*. Ed. by Martin Doornbos and K.N. Nair. New Delhi: Sage, 1990. pp. 97–115. TRTIL.

Jothimani, P. and Garg, J.K. Mapping and monitoring of Rann ingress in Banni plains Kachchh, Gujarat, using multi temporal satellite data. In *Global environmental change*. Ed. by R.B. Singh. New Delhi: Oxford and IBH, 1995. pp. 133-[ ]. HML.

Kanani, P.R. Everything is written in the sky! participatory meteorological assessment and prediction based on traditional beliefs and indicators in Saurashtra. In *Farmer-led participatory research: cases from Western India*. Ed. by Astad Pastakia, Brij Kothari and Vijaya Sherry Chand. Bangalore: Books for Change, 2002. pp. 76–95. CSSL.

Kapadia, Ajit C. and Bhatt, Vipul R. Natural gas availability and utilization in regions of Saurashtra and Kutch. In *Economy of Saurashtra: problems and prospects*. Ed. by D.T. Lakdawala, et al. Bhavnagar: Bhavnagar University, 1990. pp. 126–134. GUL.

Kulkarni, A.V. One dimensional model of ground water flow in the Kabutary river Basin, Panchmahals district, Gujarat. In *Remote sensing in development and management of water resources*. Ed. by Baldev Sahai, R.S. Chaturvedi and H.S. Iyre. Dehradun: Indian Society Photo Interpretation & Remote Sensing, 1983. pp. 116–124. SPUL.

Mahadevia, Darshini. Impact of structural adjustment programme on land and water resources of Gujarat. In *Sustainable agriculture and food security: the impact of globalisation*. Ed. by Vandana Shiva and Gitanjali Bedi. New Delhi: Sage, 2002. pp. 121–160. HML.

Maruania, P.G. Salinity ingress and technology and institutional solutions some results: a case of Coastal Saurashtra. In *Water resources, sustainable livelihoods and eco-system services*. Ed. by Kanchan Chopra and Hanumantha Rao. New Delhi: Concept, 2003. pp. 159–168. AAUL.

Mehta, Lyla. *Politics and poetics of water: the naturalisation of scarcity in Western India*. New Delhi: Manohar, 2005. p. 396. AERCL, CSSL, GIDRL.

Menon, Ajit. UTTHAN's work in Nathugadh, Gujarat. In *Community-based natural resources management*. New Delhi: Sage, 2007. pp. 72–114. GVL, IIML.

Mitaliya, K.D. Observations on antiseptic value of some ethno botanical plants from Saurashtra. In *Ethno botany*. Ed. by Pravin Chandra Trivedi. Jaipur: Aavishkar, 2002. pp. 289–294. HML.

Modi, Narendra. *Convenient action: Gujarat's response to challenge of climate change.* New Delhi: Macmillan, 2011. p. 226. IRMAL, MICAL.

Mohandas, L.V., Mehdewan, S.S. and Rajalingam, K. Forecasting of occurrence of heavy rainfall over Hyderabad area and Gujarat. In *Advance in tropical meteorology: meteorology and national development.* Ed. by Rattan K. Datta. New Delhi: Concept, 1996. pp. 222–230. SPIESRL.

Mudrakartha, Srinivas, Kaushal, Vijay and Kumar, Sujit G. Poles apart?: conflict over benefit-sharing between people and the forest department in JFM at Abhapur, Gujarat. In *Locked horns: conflicts and their resolution in community based natural resource management*. Ed. by Astad Pastakia. Bangalore: Books for Change, 2008. pp. 277–296. CSSL, GVL.

Murthy, R.S. and Pandey, S. Geomorphology, soil and land use in desert regions of Gujarat. In *Desertification and its control.* New Delhi: Indian Council of Agricultural Research, 1977. pp. 375-[ ]. SPIESRL.

Nambiar, Prithi, Oza, G.M. and Khacher, Lavkumar. Gulf of Kutch marine national park. In *Protecting endangered national parks.* New Delhi: Rajiv Gandhi Institute for Contemporary Studies, 1995. pp. 67–95. SPIESRL.

Nayak, S.R. and Desai, S.D. Bauxite deposit at Kutch. In *Art, culture and natural history of Kutch.* Ed. by S.K. Bhowmik. Vadodara: Government Press, 1976–77. pp. 120–125. CSSL, TRTIL.

Palanithurai, G. *Panchayats in disaster: preparedness and management: Gujarat, Orissa, Andhra Pradesh and Tamil Nadu (with successful case studies)*. New Delhi: Concept, 2009. p. 198. GIDRL.

Parmar, M.N. and Solanki, Jagdish. NGOs and the preservation of environment: a case study of clean Baroda movement. In *Environmental movements in India: strategies and practices.* Ed. by R.B. Pawar, R.B. Patil and S.A. Salunkhe. Jaipur: Rawat, 2005. pp. 114-[ ]. CEEL.

Pastakia, Astad. With a pebble of jaggery: review of traditional conflict resolution mechanisms and institutions in Gujarat and Rajasthan. In *Locked horns: conflicts and their resolution in community based natural resource management*. Ed. by Astad Pastakia. Bangalore: Books for Change, 2008. pp. 53–73. CSSL, GVL.

Pastakia, Astad, ed. *Locked horns: conflicts and their resolution in community based natural resource management*. Bangalore: Books for Change, 2008. p. 332. CSSL, GVL.

Patel, Jyotin D. *Flora, fauna, eid and em of SSP-command: between Narmada and Sabarmati rivers*. Gandhinagar: Narmada Planning Group, 1995. p. 228. SPUL.

Patel, P.K. and Desai, S.D. Bentonite deposits of Kutch. In *Art, culture and natural history of Kutch.* Ed. by S.K. Bhowmik. Vadodara: Government Press, 1976–77. pp. 114–119. CSSL, TRTIL.

Pathak, Bharat J. Management options for Gir protected area: an alternative view. In *People and protected areas: towards participatory conservation in India*. Ed. by Ashish Kothari, Neena Singh and Saloni Suri. New Delhi: Sage, 1996. pp. 226–233. CSSL, SETUL.

Prakash, Anjal. Political economy of groundwater governance in Gujarat: a micro-level analysis. In *Governance of water: institutional alternatives and political economy.* Ed. by Vishwa Ballabh. New Delhi: Sage, 2008. pp. 215–236. CSSL.

Prathap Reddy, K. Water sector reform policy and operationalization: experiences in Gujarat. In *Water and sanitation: institutional challenges in India*. Ed. by Christine Sijbesma and Meine Pieter Van Dijk. New Delhi: Manohar, 2006. pp. 97–119. CSSL.

Raju, K.V., Uma Rani and Patel, Anil. Role of non-economic motivation in natural resource management: the example of Swadhyaya in a Gujarat village. In *In search of sustainable livelihood systems: managing resources and change*. Ed. by Ruedi Baumgartner and Ruedi Hogger. New Delhi: Sage, 2004. pp. 150–165. CEEL, CSSL. SPIESRL. SPUL.

Randeria, Shalini. Globalising Gujarat: environmental action in the legal arena. In *Development and deprivation in Gujarat: in honour of Jan Breman*. Ed. by Ghanshyam Shah, Mario Rutten and Hein Streefkerk. New Delhi: Sage, 2002. pp. 249–269. CEEL, CEPTL, CSSL, EDIL, GIDRL, HML, IIML, IRMAL, UML.

Rathawa, Ratan. Right to confiscated goods: a conflict triggered by lack of procedural consensus in JFM at Chodvani, Gujarat. In *Locked horns: conflicts and their resolution in community based natural resource management*. Ed. by Astad Pastakia. Bangalore: Books for Change, 2008. pp. 263–267. CSSL, GVL.

Rathawa, Ratan. Superior to Supreme: how tribal people rejected a supreme court order and saved their Mahuda forests at Chotaudepur, Gujarat. In *Locked horns: conflicts and their resolution in community based natural resource management*. Ed. by Astad Pastakia. Bangalore: Books for Change, 2008. pp. 269–276. CSSL, GVL.

Raychoudhury, T. and Krishnan, S. Ingress of saline water in coastal aquifers of Junagadh, Gujarat. In *Groundwater quality and environment*. Ed. by K. Palanisami and B. Neupane. Delhi: Macmillan, 2008. pp. 51–59. IIML.

Reddy, L.R. *Pain and horror: Gujarat earthquake*. New Delhi: A.P.H., 2001. p. 297. CSSL, EDIL, GVL, HML, MICAL, TRTIL.

Roshani Devi. Bhuj earthquake rural-urban differentiation. In *Disasters in India: studies of grim reality*. [Ed.] by Anu Kapur, et al. Jaipur: Rawat, 2005. pp. 161–200. CSSL, GUL.

Sagar, Kuldeep and Patel, Rajendra. Strategic encroachment by water-merchants: conflict over formation of primary irrigation cooperative at Thalota, Gujarat. In *Locked horns: conflicts and their resolution in community based natural resource management*. Ed. by Astad Pastakia. Bangalore: Books for Change, 2008. pp. 201–216. CSSL, GVL.

Saha, Hasmukh. *Biological diversity of Gujarat: current knowledge*. Vadodara: Gujarat Ecology Commission, 1996. p. 330. SPIESRL.

Sahoo, Narottam and Vinu, T.J. Policy for creating science literacy for sustainable development: a case of Gujarat. In *Sustainable development and earth care*. Ed. by K.V. Sundaram, Mrityunjay Jha and P.S. Tiwari. New Delhi: Concept, 2009. pp. 106–118. HML.

Sarkar, S.K. Recent initiatives in developing regulatory framework in Gujarat's water sector. In *Regulation in infrastructure services: progress and the way forward*. Ed. by S.K. Sarkar and Kaushik Deb. New Delhi: Tata Energy Research Institute, 2001. pp. 59–64. CSSL.

Satija, Kalpana. *Spread effects of mineral resources in Kutch region*. Ahmedabad: GMDC, 2007. p. 120. SPIESRL.

Sathyapalan, Jyothis and Iyengar, S. Economic valuation of ecosystem changes: salinity ingress and ground water depletion in Coastal Gujarat. In *Ecology and human well-being*. Ed. by Pushpam Kumar and Sudhakar B. Reddy. New Delhi: Sage, 2007. pp. 38–49. GVL, IIML.

Sathyapalan, Jyothis and Johnson, Derek. Livelihood security in the marine fisheries sector of Gujarat state. In *India's development: social and economic disparities*. Ed. by S. Mahendra Dev and K.S. Babu. New Delhi: Manohar, 2008. pp. 277–304. CSSL, GVL, HML.

Sengupta, R. and Deshmukhe, Geetanjali. *Coastal and maritime environments of Gujarat: ecology and economics*. Vadodara: Gujarat Ecological Society, 2000. p. 150. CEEL, CSSL, GIDEL, GIDRL, SGUL, SPIESRL.

Seshagiri Rao, Rolla. *Flora of Goa, Diu, Daman, Dadara and Nagarhaveli*. Vol. 2. Howrah: Botanical Survey of India, 1985. p. 546. GIDEL.

Sevak, R.D. *Drought prone area programme: a case study of the Banaskantha district in Gujarat.* Vallabh Vidyanagar: Sardar Patel University, 1973. p. 97. GVL.

Shah, Ashvin. *Water for Gujarat: an alternative.* Vishakhapatnam: Jan Vikas Andolan(JVA), 1993. p. 72. CEEL, CSSL.

Shah, Tushaar. *Groundwater markets and irrigation development: political economy and practical policy*. Delhi: Oxford, 1993. p. 241. CSSL.

Shome, Porag and Prajapati, Girish. Of the village but not for the village: a conflict related to user-rights of Vidi in Hirawa, Gujarat. In *Locked horns: conflicts and their resolution in community based natural resource management*. Ed. by Astad Pastakia. Bangalore: Books for Change, 2008. pp. 165–174. CSSL, GVL.

Shylendra, H.S. and Uma Rani. *Diversification and sustainable rural livelihood: a study in the semi-arid villages of Western India*. New Delhi: Concept, 2005. p. 208. CSSL.

Simpson, Edward. *Political biography of an earthquake: aftermath and amnesia in Gujarat, India*. New Delhi: Oxford, 2013. p. 302. CSSL.

Singh, H.S. Biological diversity in Gujarat. In *Gujarat: perspectives of the future*. Ed. by R. Swaminathan. New Delhi: Academic, 2008. pp. 247–269. CSSL, EDIL, GIDRL, GVL, IIML, IRMAL, SETUL, SPIESRL.

Singh, Katar and Bhattacharya, Saumindra. Salt miners cooperatives in the little Rann of Kachchh in Gujarat. In *Cooperative management of natural resources.* Ed. by Katar Singh and Vishwa Ballabh. New Delhi: Sage, 1996. pp. 122–140. AAUL, CSSL, GVL, IIML.

Singh, Manmohan. *Environment awareness in Gujarat.* Ahmedabad: Vikram A. Sarabhai Community Science Centre, 1984. p. 113. CEEL.

Sinha Bakshi, D. and Ghosh, Arun K. *Sanitation and environment: evaluation of low cost sanitation in Gujarat*. New Delhi: Arnold, 1994. p. 127. GIDRL.

Sud, Nikita. Politics of land in post-colonial Gujarat. In *Idea of Gujarat: history, ethnography and text.* Ed. by Edward Simpson and Aparna Kapadia. Hyderabad: Orient Blackswan, 2010. pp. 120–135. ASL, CEPTL, CSSL, GIDRL, IRMAL, MICAL.

Sunderraj, S.F., Wesley Joshua, Justus and Kumar, Vijaya. Sea Turtles and their nesting habitats in Gujarat. In *Marine Turtles of the Indian subcontinent*. Ed. by Kartik Shanker and B.C. Choudhury. Chennai: Orient Longman, 2006. pp. 156–173. CEEL.

Vadher, P.G., et al. Seawater intrusion and impact of groundwater recharge in coastal line of Saurashtra region. In *Groundwater resources assessment, recharge and modeling.* Ed. by M.V. Ranghaswami, K. Palanisami and Swami C. Mayil. Delhi: Macmillan, 2008. pp. 222–228. IIML.

Vakil, Arun C. Cost of refuse collection and transportation: the Gujarat experience. In *Economic aspects of environment pollution in India.* Ed. by Arun C. Vakil. Bombay: Arun C. Vakil, 1984. p. 261. SPIESRL.

Vegad, Amritlal. *Narmada: river of beauty*. Delhi: Penguin, 2008. p. 187. SETUL.

Vijayakumar, T. Psycho-social dimension of Gujarat earthquake disaster. In *Psychological perspectives on social issues and human development*. Ed. by Arunkumar Tiwari. New Delhi: Concept, 2009. pp. 179–198. HML.

Viswanathan, P.K. and Pathak, Jharna. Economic growth and the state of natural resources and environment in Gujarat: a critical assessment. In *Growth or development: which way is Gujarat going?* Ed. by Indira Hirway, Amita Shah and Ghanshyam Shah. New Delhi: Oxford, 2014. pp. 380–433. CSSL.

Vyas, Jyoten P. Physical processes and landforms: a study of the Rajpipla hills and the neighbouring coastal plains. In *Environmental management*. Ed. by R.K. Rai, A.C. Mohapatra and N.P. Goel. Jaipur: Rawat, 1992. pp. 51–68. HML.

Wadhawan, S.K. Some aspects of environmental of salt and beach sand mining on the coastal fringe of South Gujarat, India. In *Mining and environment in India*. Ed. by G. Bhattacharya and S.C. Joshi. Nainital: Himalayan Research Group, 1988. pp. 254–259. CEEL.

Wood, John R. *Politics of water resource development in India: the Narmada dams controversy*. New Delhi: Sage, 2007. p. 285. CSSL, UML.

Journal Articles

Adhvaryu, J.H. and Patel, Arun S. Environmental impact of Dantiwada irrigation project in Gujarat. *Artha-Vikas*. 18, 1 and 2, 1982. pp. 30–44. GIDRL.

Ali, Salim. Why an ornithological survey of Gujarat?. *Journal of the Gujarat Research Society*. 6, 3, 1944. pp. 138–143. GVL.

Anand, Yashpal, Tatu, Ketan and Pandey, C.N. First record of feeding trails of dugong in Gulf of Kachchh, Gujarat. *Indian Forester*. 138, 10, 2012. pp. 968–969. GIDEL, IRMAL.

Anbazhagan, S., Biswal, T.K. and Roy, T. Remote sensing study of granulitic terrain in parts of Gujarat and Rajasthan. *Journal of the Indian Society of Remote Sensing*. 34, 4, 2006. pp. 331–341. IRMAL.

Asari, R.S. and Padate, S.N. Flora and vegetation of Jambooghoda, Mahal and surrouding hills, dist. Panchmahal. *Journal of the M.S. University of Baroda*. 27–28, 3, 1978–79. pp. 29–44. GVL.

Bedi, S.J. On the occurrence of Fissendocarpa Linifolia (VAHL) Bennet and the cagonum ovatifolium (CAV) babu prom Gujarat state. *Journal of the M.S. University of Baroda*. 19–20, 3, 1970–71. pp. 53–54. GVL.

Bhagia, Indra G. Floral toponyms of Vadodara district. *Journal of the Oriental Institute*. 34, 3–4, 1985. pp. 241–248. GVL.

Bharwada, Charul and Mahajan, Vinay. Drinking water crisis in Kutch: a natural phenomenon?. *Economic and Political Weekly*. 37, 48, 2002. pp. 4859–4866. BUL, CEPTL, CSSL, EDIL, IIML, IRMAL, MICAL, SGUL, SPIESRL, UML.

Bhat, G.K., et al. Addressing flooding in the city of Surat beyond its boundaries. *Environment & Urbanization*. 25, 2, 2013. pp. 429–441. CSSL.

Bhatt, R.P. and Sabnis, S.D. Aquatic vegetation of Khed-Bhrahma and surrounding region of North Gujarat. *Journal of the M.S. University of Baroda*. 25–26, 3, 1976–77. pp. 27–30. GVL.

Bhatt, R.P. and Sabnis, S.D. Further contribution to the flora and vegetation of Khedbrahma region of North Gujarat. *Journal of the M.S. University of Baroda*. 21, 3, 1972. pp. 7–34. GVL.

Bharwada, Charul and Mahajan, Vinay. Lost and forgotten: grasslands and pastoralists of Gujarat. *Seminar*. 564, 2006. pp. 35–40. CEPTL, CSSL, GIDRL, GVL, IRMAL, MICAL, SPUL, UML.

Bhatia, Bela. Official drought relief measures: a case study of Gujarat. *Social Action*. 38, 2, 1988. pp. 138–161. CSSL, IRMAL, SGUL.

Billore, K.V. Interesting case of epiphytism of Euphoria neriifolia linn from Gujarat. *Indian Forester*. 114, 2, 1988. pp. 89–90. IIML.

Chauhan, Devraj. Gujarat water crisis: caution against complacency. *Vishleshan*. 18, 4, 1993. pp. 150–156. CSSL, IIML.

Choudhary, K.M. and Sevak, R.D. Drought prone area programme in Gujarat. *Artha-Vikas*. 10, 1, 1974. pp. 27–37. GVL, HML, SGUL.

Dabadghao, P.D. Field experiment on natural grassland in the former Baroda state. *Indian Journal of Agricultural Sciences*. 24, 3, 1954. pp. 239–252. GVL.

Das, Biswaroop. Some aspects of disaster mitigation and management in India. *Indian Journal of Public Administration*. 48, 2, 2002. pp. 183–196. CSSL.

Desai, Anjana. Differential perception of residents of environmental quality of an urban area: the case of Ahmedabad. *Geographical Review of India*. 43, 2, 1981. pp. 155-[ ]. HML.

Desai, Anjan P. and Lodhi, S. Application of GIS package in the study of coastal environment of Gujarat. *Deccan Geographer*. 36, 2, 1998. pp. 1–14. HML.

Desai, B.N. Has the climate of Gujarat changed during the last sixty years? No. *Journal of the Gujarat Research Society*. 3, 4, 1941. pp. 236–247. GVL.

Desai, B.N. Mechanism of heavy rainfall during the monsoon season in Gujarat (with special reference to heavy rain in September 1945). *Journal of the Gujarat Research Society*. 8, 1, 1946. pp. 2–10. GUL.

Desai, P.N. and Desai, S.D. Fluorite mineralization at Ambadonagar, Baroda district, Gujarat state. *Journal of the M.S. University of Baroda*. 19–20, 3, 1970–71. pp. 13–18. GVL.

Desai, Rinku J. and Raole, Vinay M. Addition to the grass flora of Gujarat state. *Indian Forester*. 137, 1, 2011. pp. 125–128. GIDEL, IRMAL.

Desai, Rinku J. and Raole, Vinay M. Further contribution to the grass flora of Gujarat. *Indian Forester*. 138, 5, 2012. pp. 449–452. GIDEL, IRMAL.

Desai, S.D. Geology of the deccan trap formation of Saurashtra, Kathiawar. *Journal of the M.S. University of Baroda*. 19–20, 3, 1970–71. pp. 1–12. GVL.

Dixit, A.M., Geevan, C.P. and Silori, C.S. Status of natural terrestrial vegetation in Gujarat: a reassessment. *Indian Forester*. 127, 5, 2001. pp. 533–546. GIDEL, IIML.

Environment Division, NPC. Hazardous waste generation in India-Gujarat. *Productivity*. 36, 1, 1995. pp. 165–168. SPUL.

Gadani, Maulik. Tree diversity of Gandhinagar city, Gujarat, India. *Indian Forester*. 137, 9, 2011. pp. 1103–1108. GIDEL, IRMAL.

Gadekar, D.R. Some aspects of environmental pollution in mineral resource exploration and exploitation with special reference to Gujarat. *Journal of the M.S. University of Baroda*. 22–23, 3, 1973–74. pp. 185–196. GVL.

Guha, G.S. Emerging water scenario in Gujarat. *Anvesak*. 25, 1, 1995. pp. 131–134. GIDRL, IRMAL, SPIESRL.

Jain, R.C. and Sinha, A.K. Sustainable management of the water stressed aquifers in Sabarmati basin Gujarat, India. *Journal of Indian Water Resources Society*. 30, 1, 2010. pp. 21–30. IRMAL.

Java, R.L. Environment and wildlife conservation in Gujarat state: a status paper. *Indian Forester*. 117, 10, 1991. pp. 818–842. IIML.

Joshi, Ekta B., Jain, B.K. and Joshi, P.N. Diversity pattern of habitats and vascular plant species in Tapkeshwari hill ranges in the Kachchh island Gujarat, India. *Indian Forester*. 137, 6, 2011. pp. 757–766. GIDEL, IRMAL.

Joshi, P.N. and Patel, Yatin. Floristic inventory in the Banni region of Bhuj taluka, Kachchh district, Gujarat. *Indian Forester*. 137, 9, 2011. pp. 1114–1121. GIDEL, IRMAL.

Joshi, S.N. Managing rainfed areas in Gujarat. *Anvesak*. 30, 1, 2000. pp. 7–15. CSSL, SPIESRL.

Kalapesi, A.S. Two earthquakes in Gujarat. *Journal of the Gujarat Research Society*. 4, 4, 1942. pp. 240–261. GVL.

Kalapesi, A.S. Useful aspects of the geology of Gujarat. *Journal of the Gujarat Research Society*. 2, 4, 1940. pp. 197–212. GUL, GVL.

Kapadia, G.A. Plant life of Maha Gujarat. *Journal of the Gujarat Research Society*. 11–12, 4–1, 1949–1950. pp. 191–225. GUL, GVL.

Keve, Joseph. Earthquake in Gujarat: global outpouring sympathy & charity: will the poor benefit? *Vikalp: Alternatives*. 8, 3 and 4, 2000. pp. 199–210. CSSL.

Khanna, Pradeep and Mahendra, A.K. Consumption behaviour of fuel wood in Gujarat. *Indian Forester*. 121, 2, 1995. pp. 88–97. IIML.

Kulkarni, A.K., Mandal, B.N. and Sangam, R.B. Analysis of heavy rain spell of 7–8th September, 1994 over Gujarat region. *Deccan Geographer*. 35, 1, 1997. pp. 49–60. HML.

Kumar, Shivesh. Emergence of gall inducing insect leptocybe invasa (Hymenoptera: eolophidae) in eucalyptus plantations in Gujarat, India. *Indian Forester*. 133, 11, 2007. pp. 1566–1568. GIDEL, IIML.

Lodhia, Shital. Application of remote sensing technique for mapping the salt affected areas in coastal areas: a case of Gujarat. *Indian Journal of Regional Science*. 37, 2, 2005. pp. 122–129. CSSL, GIDRL.

Louis, Prakash. Gujarat: earthquake and after. *Economic and Political Weekly*. 36, 11, 2001. pp. 908–910. BUL, CEPTL, CSSL, EDIL, GIDRL, IIML, IRMAL, MICAL, SGUL, SPIESRL, UML.

Lunagaria, M.M., Pandey, Vyas and Patel, H.R. Climate trends in Gujarat and its likely impact on different crops. *Journal of Agrometeorology*. 14, 1, 2012. pp. 41–44. IRMAL.

Maitra, Shubhada, Ramaswamy, Sheila and Sirur, Sulakshana. Use of play and art forms with children in disaster: the Gujarat experience. *Indian Journal of Social Work*. 63, 2, 2002. pp. 263–282. CSSL, GIDRL, IIML, IRMAL.

Majumdar, M.R. Gujarat: its natural environments. *Journal of the Gujarat Research Society*. 2, 3, 1940. pp. 159–179. GUL, GVL.

Mallyel, K.G. Tregedy in the desert: the prosperous Bhuj that was. *Bhavan's Journal*. 47, 14, 2001. pp. 38–42. GVL.

Meena, R.L., Bava, J.G. and Jadeja, R.S. Unique habitat of Great Indian Bustard(GIB) in Kachchh: protection and management. *Indian Forester*. 131, 12, 2005. pp. 1554–1558. GIDEL, IIML.

Meena, R.L., et al. Note on greater Rann of Kachchh, Kachchh, district, Gujarat with special reference to Flamingo city. *Indian Forester*. 134, 10, 2008. pp. 1393–1397. GIDEL, IIML.

Mehta, Lyla. Reflections on the Kutch earthquake. *Economic and Political Weekly*. 36, 31, 2001. pp. 2931–2936. BUL, CEPTL, CSSL, EDIL, IIML, IRMAL, MICAL, SGUL, SPIESRL, UML.

Meshram, D.T., Apparao, V.V. and Bagle, B.G. Frequency analysis for one to five consecutive days annual maximum rainfall for Panchmahals of Central Gujarat. *Journal of Agrometeorlogy*. 8, 2, 2006. pp. pp. 237–242. IRMAL.

Mishra, Pramod K. Beyond reconstruction: some innovative aspects of the Gujarat earthquake reconstruction programme. *Indian Journal of Public Administration*. 51, 2, 2005. pp. 235–248. CSSL, GIDRL, GVL, IRMAL.

Padate, S.N. Vegetation of the ravines of Savli taluka (Baroda), (Gujarat). *Journal of M.S. University of Baroda*. 25–26, 3, 1976–77. pp. 13–16. GVL.

Pandey, R.P., et al. Conversation of a rare and threatened species capparis cartilaginea decne in Gujarat state, India. *Indian Forester*. 138, 7, 2012. pp. 589–592. GIDEL, IRMAL.

Pandey, Vyas and Patel, A.T. Rainfall zonation of North Gujarat. *Gujarat Agricultural University Research Journal*. 14, 2, 1989. pp. 7–14. AAUL.

Pandey, Vyas, Vaidya, V.B. and Varshney, M.C. Forecasting models for seasonal rainfall for different region of Gujarat. *Journal of Agrometeorology*. 12, 2, 2010. pp. 202–207. IRMAL.

Parikh, Alka. Skimming through the socioeconomic losses from an earthquake: a case study from Kachchh. *Indian Journal of Social Work*. 63, 2, 2002. pp. 223–235. CSSL, GVL, IIML.

Parikh, H.B. Flood control in Gujarat. *Journal of the Gujarat Research Society*. 8, 1, 1946. pp. 11–15. GUL.

Patel, A.A. and Sharma, B.M. Impact of drought prone areas programme in Banaskantha district of Gujarat. *Gujarat Agricultural University Research Journal*. 10, 2, 1985. pp. 34–36. GVL.

Patel, A.S. Green revolution: its present position prospects and problems in Gujarat State. *Agriculture and Agro-Industries Journal*. 4, 4, 1971. pp. 25–28. IIML.

Patel, C.C. Water: Scarce and valuable resource. (*Gujarat-2010: Challenges and Opportunities). Anvesak*. 31, 1 and 2, 2001. pp. 91–109. CSSL.

Patel, V.J. Rational approach towards fuel wood crisis in rural India. *Economic and Political Weekly*. 20, 32, 1985. pp. 1366–1368. CEPTL, CSSL, GUL, IIML, IRMAL, SGUL, SPIESRL, UML.

Phansalkar, S.J. Scarce water resources and public policy: the case of Kutch district, Gujarat. *Vishleshan*. 15, 1, 1990. pp. 14–24. CSSL.

Prabhakar, R. and Vani, Vina. Water resource dynamics and the water use pattern in a hard rock area of Gujarat. *Journal of Indian Water Resources Society*. 19, 2, 1999. pp. 27–35. IRMAL.

Pradeepkumar, G. and Prathapasenan. Tree diversity of Shoolpaneshvear wildlife sanctuary in Gujarat. *Indian Forester*. 127, 11, 2001. pp. 1027–1214. GIDEL, IIML.

Pramod, Kumar, et al. Socio-economic conditions with special reference to common access resources: a case study from Gujarat and Rajasthan. *Indian Forester*. 130, 9, 2004. pp. 981–990. GIDEL, SGUL.

Rajput, Kishore S. and Raole, Vinay M. Solanum pesudo-capsicum L.: addition to the flora of Gujarat state. *Indian Forester*. 135, 9, 2009. pp. 1293–1295. GIDEL, IIML.

Rao, M.N. and Modi, V.V. On the atmospheric sulphor dioxide and benzo (a) pyrene pollution in Baroda. *Journal of the M.S. University of Baroda*. 29, 3, 1980. pp. 1–8. GVL.

Ray, C.N. Earthquake relief and rehabilitation in Gujarat: issues in disaster management. *Indian Journal of Public Administration*. 47, 2, 2001. pp. 129–152. GIDRL, GVL, IRMAL.

Ray, C.N. and Rout, P.R. Environmental risk assessment of municipal corporations of Gujarat. *Nagarlok*. 32, 2, 2000. pp. 11–31. CEPTL, GIDRL, SPIESRL.

Reddy, Sudhakar C. and Mehta, B.V. Relationship of Carbon, Nitrogen and Sulphar in Gujarat soils. *Indian Journal of Agricultural Science*. 40, 7, 1970. pp. 630–633. GVL.

Rutten, Mario. Involvement and indifference: Gujarat earthquake in wider perspective. *Economic and Political Weekly*. 36, 35, 2001. pp. 3358–3361. BUL, CEPTL, CSSL, EDIL, GIDRL, IIML, IRMAL, MICAL, SGUL, SPIESRL, UML.

Sah, D.C. and Shah, Amita. Inefficiency and efficacy of soil testing services: a case study of Gujarat. *Artha-Vijnana*. 37, 1, 1995. pp. 77–100. GIDRL, UML.

Sahu, O.O. and Patel, R.R. Probability study of rainfall for Banaskantha district, North Gujarat region. *Gujarat Agricultural University Research Journal*. 10, 2, 1985. pp. 27–33. GVL.

Sanderson, David and Sharma, Anshu. Winners and losers from the 2001 Gujarat earthquake. *Environment and Urbanization*. 20, 1, 2008. pp. 177–186. CSSL, IRMAL.

Sanderson, David, Sharma, Anshu and Anderson, Juliet. NGO permanent housing 10 years after the Gujarat earthquake: revisiting the FICCI-CARE Gujarat rehabilitation programme. *Environment and Urbanization*. 24, 1, 2012. pp. 233–247. CSSL, IRMAL.

Santapau, Rev H. Iter Kathiawarense: being notes on a botanical tour in Nawanagar state. *Journal of the Gujarat Research Society*. 11–12, 4–1, 1949–1950. pp. 226–237. GUL.

Shah, G.L. and Yogi, D.V. Critical notes on some interesting plants of Gujarat. *Vidya: The Journal of Gujarat University*. 16, 1, 1973. pp. 10–20. SGUL.

Shah, Hasmukh. Ecological concerns. *Seminar*. 470, 1998. pp. 36–40. CEPTL, CSSL, IRMAL, MICAL, UML.

Shah, N.R. Evaluation of catchment area development programme: a case study of Dantiwada catchment in Gujarat. *Artha-Vikas*. 26, 1 and 2, 1990. pp. 1–29. CSSL.

Sharma, Rajesh. Status of the urban environment: Delhi, Bombay, Ahmedabad, Vadodara. *Urban India*. 13, 2, 1993. pp. 1–27. CSSL, GIDRL.

Shelat, R.N. and Vashi, N.V. Ground water pollution due to landfilling in Surat: a case study. *South Gujarat University Journal*. 4, [ ], 1975. pp. 125–131. GVL.

Shishodia, Anil. Environmental issues and natural resource management strategies in Gujarat. *Artha-Vikas*. 39, 1, 2003. pp. 22–33. CSSL, IRMAL.

Shiyani, R.L. Growth and instability of inland fish production in Gujarat: spati-temporal analysis. *Artha Vijnan*. 44, 2, 2002. pp. 189–198. CSSL, UML.

Shukla, Rohit. Forestry and environmental concerns of Gujarat. (*Gujarat-2010: Challenges and Opportunities*). *Anvesak*. 31, 1–2, 2001. pp. 69–90. CSSL, GIDRL, SPIESRL.

Silori, C.S., Geevan, C.P. and Dixit, A.M. Livestock population vis-à-vis common property land resources: trends from Gujarat. *Indian Forester*. 132, 10, 2006. pp. 1303–1314. GIDEL, IIML.

Simpson, Edward. State of play six years after Gujarat earthquake. *Economic and Political Weekly*. 42, 11, 2007. pp. 932–937. BUL, CEPTL, CSSL, EDIL, GIDRL, IIML, IRMAL, MICAL, SGUL, SPIESRL, SUL, UML.

Singh, A.P. and Parabia, Minoo. floral diversity of Gujarat state: a review. *Indian Forester.* 129, 12, 2003. pp. 1461–1469. GIDEL, IIML.

Singh, A.P. and Parabia, Minoo. Status of medicinal plants consumption by the pharmaceutical industries in Gujarat state. *Indian Forester.* 129, 2, 2003, pp. 198–212. GIDEL, SGUL.

Singh, Gajendra and Bhogal, T.S. Assessment of food security situation for disaster risk management: an analysis for the Gujarat state. *Anvesak.* 36, 1, 2006. pp. 32–44. CSSL, SPIESRL.

Singh, H.S. Antelopes and gazelles: distribution and population status in Gujarat, India. *Indian Forester.* 127, 10, 2001. pp. 1098–1106. GIDEL, IIML, SGUL.

Singh, H.S. Biodiversity of Ratanmahals wildlife sanctuary: an overview of floral and faunel diversity and their conservation strategy in Malwa region in Gujarat state India. *Indian Forester.* 130, 4, 2004. pp. 359–366. GIDEL, IIML, SGUL.

Singh, H.S. Growing man-leopard conflicts in Gujarat state. *Indian Forester.* 132, 10, 2006. pp. 1243–1253. GIDEL, IIML.

Singh, H.S. Mangroves in Gujarat on path of recovery: a success story. *Indian Forester.* 127, 4, 2001. pp. 379–388. GIDEL, IIML.

Singh, H.S. Successional stages of mangroves in the gulf of Kutch. *Indian Forester.* 122, 3, 1996. pp. 212–219. IIML.

Singh, H.S. and Soni, V.C. Status of wildlife in wild ass sanctuary. (Little ran of Kutch, Gujarat state India). *Indian Forester.* 125, 10, 1999. pp. 1018–1026. IIML.

Smith, J.H. Note on the geology of Cutch. *Journal of the Gujarat Research Society.* 7, 2–3, 1945. pp. 111–114. GUL, GVL.

Srivastava, R.L., et al. Initial performance of tissue culture raised bamboos in Rajasthan and Gujarat. *Indian Forester.* 134, 7, 2008. pp. 916–922. GIDEL, IIML, IRMAL.

Sukheshwala, R.N. Mineral wealth of Gujarat. *Journal of the Gujarat Research Society.* 4, 4, 1942. pp. 287–292. GVL.

Surendran, Sapnaa. Avian influenza syndrome in the eurasian migratory flyway of Central Gujarat. *Environmental Awareness.* 29, 1–2, 2006. pp. 18–28. GVL.

Swayam, S. Variations in pastoral economy three recent case studies from Gujarat. *Man in India.* 81, 1–2, 2001. pp. 49–85. CSSL, IRMAL, UML.

Tatu, Ketan. Population status of Indian Sarus Crane (Grus antigone antigone) in Gujarat state. *Indian Forester.* 126, 10, 2000. pp. 1085–1093. GIDEL, IIML.

Tewari, V.P. Generalised diameter-height equations for even-aged stands of Azadirachta Indica in Gujarat state of India. *Indian Forester.* 132, 1, 2006. pp. 79–90. GIDEL, IIML, IRMAL, SGUL.

Varshneya, M.C., Vaidya, V.B. and Shekh, A.M. Validation of astrometeorological rainfall forecast for Gujarat. *Journal of Agrometeorology.* 10, 2, 2008. pp. 345–348. IRMAL.

Vora, Amrish. Ground water resources management of Gujarat: with special reference to Mehsana district. *Anvesak.* 20, 1–2, 1990. pp. 151–162. CEPTL, CSSL, SPIESRL.

Vora, Amrish and Parikh, Dilip H. Water management to combat droughts. *Anvesak.* 26, 2, 1996. pp. 19–24. CSSL, GIDRL, SPIESRL.

Vyas, A.B., Bhatt, P.L. and Buch, A.U. Contribution to ecological study of aquatic hetero ptera of Ahmedabad. *Vidya: The Journal of Gujrat University.* 16, 1, 1973. pp. 86–91. SGUL.

Vyas, Raju. Present conservation scenario of reptile fauna in Gujarat state, India. *Indian Forester.* 133, 10, 2007. pp. 1381–1394. GIDEL, IIML, IRMAL.

Vyas, Raju. Review of the current diversity and richness of amphibians of Gujarat, India. *Indian Forester.* 134, 10, 2008. pp. 1381–1392. GIDEL, IIML.

Wood, John R. Community natural resource management institutions in Gujarat and Madhya Pradesh. *VNSGU Journal of Humanities & Social Sciences.* 1, 2, 2009. pp. 1–18. CSSL, SGUL.

Yadaiah, G., Joshi, Parul and Oza, Bindiya. Traditional knowledge of wild medicinal plants of Baria forest division, Dahod district, Gujarat state. *Indian Forester.* 137, 7, 2011. pp. 814–821. GIDEL, IRMAL.

Yadaiah, G., Oza, Bindiya and Joshi, Parul. Ethno-medico-botany of Godhra forest division of Panchmahal district, Gujarat state. *Indian Forester.* 137, 8, 2011. pp. 948–961. GIDEL, IRMAL.

Working Papers, Reports and Other Materials

Acharya, R.M., Patnayak, B.C. and Ahuja, L.D. Salt and by-product resources of Gujarat and Rajasthan. In *Desertification and its control.* New Delhi: Indian Council of Agricultural, 1977. pp. 375-[ ]. SPIESRL.

Agro-Climatic Regional Planning Unit Planning Commission. *Impact of green-revolution in Saurastra (part-2).* Rajkot: Center for Economic Rural and Gandhian Studies, [ ]. p. 785. SPIESRL.

Amin, J.V. ed. *Eco environmental studies of Sardar Sarovar environs.* Baroda: M.S. University, 1992. p. 388. M.S. University Environment Series 2. GIDRL.

Bagchi, Kathakali S. *Natural resource management: Western region.* New Delhi: Upalabdhi, 2000. p. 201. India watch Monograph 3. CSSL.

Ballabh, V., Dave, Shibani and Baloomi, Kulbhushan. *Why local resources management institutions decline: a comparative analysis of van Panchayats and forest protection committees.* Anand: Institute of Rural Management, 1998. p. 27. Working Paper 122. CSSL.

Ballabh, Vishwa and Shunmugam, V. *Database needs in decision making for sustainable basin management: illustrations from Sabarmati basin.* Anand: Institute of Rural Management, 1999. p. 20. Working Paper 132. CSSL.

Bhanujan, K.V. DPAP-Gujarat experience. In *All-India seminar on strategies for drought proofing and management Ahmedabad 6–7 February 1987.* Ahmedabad: Bhaikaka Bhavan, 1987. pp. 125–146. IIML.

Centre for Environmental Planning & Technology. *Integrated environmental improvement plan tribal talukas Panchmahals.* Ahmedabad: Centre for Environmental Planning & Technology, 1978. p. 186. CSSL.

Centre for Social Studies and Depart. of Human Resource Development, VNSGU. *Surat 2006 floods: a citizen's report.* Surat: Authors, 2006. p. 24. CSSL.

Chaudhari, K.M. and Sevak, R.D. *Drought prone area programme: a case study of the Banaskantha district in Gujarat (Kharif-1972–1973).* Vallabh Vidyanagar: Agro-Economic Research Centre, 1973. p. 97. Research Study No. 32. IIML.

Chavan, A.R. and Oza, G.M. *Flora of Pavagadh: Gujarat state, India.* Baroda: M.S. University, 1966. p. 296. Botanical memoirs No. 1. CSSL.

Chhaya, N.D. *Minding our marine wealth: an appraisal of Gujarat's coastal resources.* Ahmedabad: Centre for Environment Education, 1997. p. 107. Environment and development series. CSSL.

Choudhary, K.M. and Bapat, M.T. *Study of impact of famine and relief measures in Gujarat and Rajasthan.* Vallabh Vidhyanagar: Sardar Patel University, 1975. p. [ ]. GIDRL.

Deshinglar, Priya. *Markets, natural resource mobility and the rural poor: crop residues in South Gujarat.* Surat: Centre for Social Studies, 1989. p. [ ]. Occasional Paper No. 5. CSSL.

Dixit, A.M. *Kachchh sub-state biodiversity strategy and action plan.* Bhuj: Gujarat Institute of Desert Ecology, 2002. p. 124. GIDEL.

Forest and Environment, Department of, Government of Gujarat. Gujarat 2010 challenges and opportunitites. In *Gujarat-2010: challenges and opportunities*. By Government of Gujarat. Ahmedabad: Sardar Patel Institute of Economic & Social Research, 2001. pp. 617–621. Seminar volume. CSSL, EDIL, IRMAL, SGUL, SPIESRL.

Gujarat Ecological Education and Research Foundation (GEER). *Mangroves in Gujarat: current status and strategy for conservation.* Gandhinagar: Gujarat Ecological Education and Research, 2000. p. 128. GIDRL.

Gujarat Ecological Education and Research Foundation (GEER). *Ecological survey of wild Ass sanctuary: current status (Interim report).* Gandhinagar: Gujarat Ecological Education and Research, 1998. p. 239. GIDRL.

Gujarat Ecology Commission. State environment report on rann of Kachchh, Gujarat state 2013. In *Association with Gujarat institute of desert ecology, Bhuj.* [ ]: [ ], 2013. p. [ ]. GIDEL.

Gujarat Ecology Commission (GEC), Vadodara. *Gujarat state environmental action programme (SEAP): coastal and marine environment, phase-I report*. Nagpur: National Environmental Engineering Research Institute, 2000. Verious. CSSL.

Gujarat Ecology Commission. *REMAG: restoration of mangroves in Gujarat: a community-based approach*. Vadodara: Author, 2006. p. 76. CSSL.

Gujarat Ecology Commission. *State environmental action programme (SEAP): action plan for water resource management in Gujarat*. Anand: INREM, 2001. p. 100. CSSL.

Gujarat Ecology Commission. *State environmental action programme: industrial pollution.* Pune: Tata Consultancy Services, 2000. Verious. Phase I report. CSSL.

Gujarat Ecology Commission. *State of the environment Gujarat.* Vadodara: Gujarat Ecology Commission, 2001. p. 69. GIDRL.

Gujarat Institute of Desert Ecology. *Assessment of the impact of salinity ingression prevention structure along the coastal belt of Kachchh, Gujarat*. Bhuj: Gujarat Institute of Desert Ecology, 2011. p. [ ]. GIDEL.

Gujarat Institute of Desert Ecology. *Ecological study on great Indian Bustard sanctuary, Kachchh: a management perspective*. Bhuj: Gujarat Institute of Desert Ecology, 1998. p. [ ]. GIDEL.

Gujarat Institute of Desert Ecology. *Flora and fauna status, impact on sanctuary and wild life assessment report.* Bhuj: Gujarat Institute of Desert Ecology, 2009. p. [ ]. GIDEL.

Gujarat Institute of Desert Ecology. *Marine environmental monitoring in Gujarat Adani port, Kachchh, Gujarat.* Bhuj: Gujarat Institute of Desert Ecology, 2006. p. [ ]. GIDEL.

Gujarat Institute of Desert Ecology. *Studies on the impact of the salinity prevention structures along the coastal belt of Kachchh, Gujarat*. Bhuj: Gujarat Institute of Desert Ecology, 2010. p. [ ]. GIDEL.

Gujarat Institute of Development Research. *Rapid assessment of earthquake affected areas in Gujarat. Final report,* Vol. I and II. Ahmedabad: Gujarat Institute of Development Research, Tata Institute of Social Sciences, Kachchh Navnirman Abhiyan, 2001. p. [ ] GIDRL.

Gujarat Institute of Development Research. *Socio-economic and ecological benefits of mangrove plantation: a study of community based mangrove restoration activities in Gujarat.* Gandhinagar: Gujarat Ecology Commission, [ ]. p. 128. MICAL.

Hirway, Indira and Goswami, Subhrangsu. *Valuation of mangroves in Gujarat.* Ahmedabad: Centre for Development Alternatives, 2005. p. 46. Working Paper 6. CSSL, IRMAL.

Iyengar, Sudarshan. Conflict over vision: the case of drinking water in Gujarat. In *Conflict resolution in the water sector.* Ed. by Rohit Desai. Ahmedabad: Sardar Patel Institute of Economic & Social Research, 2000. pp. 57–81. Proceeding of the seminar on issues related water resources use in India, role of social scientists in conflict management. CSSL.

Iyengar, Sudarshan. *Land use statistics: implications for environmental database.* Ahmedabad: Gujarat Institute of Development Research, 1998. p. 41. Working Paper No. 97. CSSL.

Joshua, J., et al. *Ecological study on the great Indian Bustard sanctuary, Kachchh: a management perspective.* Bhuj: Gujarat Institute of Desert Ecology, 2001. p. 53. GIDEL.

Joshua, J., et al. *Grassland action plan for Kachchh district, Gujarat state. 2 Vols.* Bhuj: Gujarat Institute of Desert Ecology, 2004. p. 333. and p. 129. GIDEL.

Khera, P.D. *Social class and drought: a case study of Kutch. In Drought and famine 1980s: crises and response - December 12–14, 1988.* (Seminar papers). Surat: Centre for Social Studies, 1988. pp. 1–24. CSSL.

Koshy, C.K. Management of drought in Gujarat. In *All-India seminar on strategies for drought proofing and management Ahmedabad 6–7 February 1987.* Ahmedabad: Bhaikaka Bhavan, 1987. pp. 147–157. IIML.

Lahiri, Ashok, K. et al. *Economic consequences of the Gujarat earthquake.* New Delhi: National Institute of Public Finance and Policy, 2001. p. [ ]. NIPFP Discussion Paper No. 1. GIDRL.

Lobo, Lancy and Kazi, Babasaheb. *Coping with disaster: flash floods in Mehesana district.* Surat: Centre for Social Studies, 1998. p. 59. CSSL.

Lodhia, Shital. *Management of groundwater resources through community participation approach in the coastal saline region of Gujarat.* Ahmedabad: Centre for Development Alternatives, 2006. p. [ ]. Working Paper 12. CSSL.

Mahadevia, Darshini. *Economic growth and environmental degradation: case of Gujarat.* New Delhi: Research Foundation for Science, Technology and Ecology, 1999. p. 79. CSSL.

Mehta, Raghuvir. Drought prone area programme: a review of problems and prospects. In *Gujarat economy problems and prospects.* Ed. by D.T. Lakdawala. Ahmedabad: Sardar Patel Institute of Economic & Social Research, 1983. pp. 313–318. Monograph-10. GUL, IIML.

Mehta, Raghuvir. Drought prone area programme: a review of problems and prospects. In *Seminar on development of Gujarat: problems & prospects, 24th-26th August, 1981.* Ahmedabad: Sardar Patel Institute of Economic & Social Research, 1981. pp. 1–8. CSSL.

Merh, S.S. *Geology of Gujarat.* Bangalore: Geological Society of India, 1995. p. 222. GIDEL.

Mistry, J.F. and Modi, K.J. Drought probability and role of surface water resources in the regions of Saurashtra and Kuchchh. In *All-India seminar on strategies for drought proofing and management Ahmedabad 6–7 February 1987*. Ahmedabad: Bhaikaka Bhavan, 1987. pp. 167–200. IIML.

Murty, C.V.R., et al. *Earthquake rebuilding in Gujarat, India: an EERI recovery reconnaissance report*. Oakland: Earthquake Engineering Research Institute (EERI), 2005. p. 120. GIDRL.

Nambiar, R.G. Water. In *Gujarat economy in 2001 A.D.: a study in perspective*. Ahmedabad: Sardar Patel Institute of Economic & Social Research, 1980. pp. 291–306. GUL.

National Bureau of Soil Survey and Land Use Planning. *Soil series of Gujarat.* Nagpur: National Bureau of Soil Survey and Land Use Planning, 2006. p. 329. GIDEL.

Panda, Smita Mishra and Choudhary, Kameshwar. *Abhiyan's setu approach to partnertship in rehabilitation: case of Gujarat earthquake*. Anand: Institute of Rural Management, 2002. p. 25. IRMA Working Paper No. 167. GIDRL, IRMAL, SPIESRL.

Pandey, C.N. *Gujarat's wild destinations: a passage through the national parks, sanctuaries and other wild destinations of Gujarat*. Gandhinagar: Gujarat Ecological Education and Research, 2010. p. 81. IRMAL.

Pandey, C.N. *Medicinal plants of Gujarat.* Gandhinagar: Gujarat Ecological Education and Research, 2005. p. 410. IRMAL.

Pandey, Vikash N. and Jain, Pankaj S. *Village woodlots in Gujarat: an experiment in social forestry.* Anand: Institute of Rural Management, 1991. p. 32. Working Paper 17. CSSL.

Pandya, D.G. Gujarat: state environmental action programme: land degradation: review of policies, institutions and action. In *Gujarat-2010: challenges and opportunities*. By Government of Gujarat. Ahmedabad: Sardar Patel Institute of Economic & Social Research, 2001. pp. 577–586. Seminar volume. CSSL, EDIL, IRMAL, SGUL, SPIESRL.

Parthasarathy, R. and Iyengar, Sudarshan. *Participatory water resources development in Western India: influencing policy through process documentation research.* Ahmedabad: Gujarat Institute of Development Research, 1998. p. 27. Working Paper No. 93. CSSL.

Patel, V.B. and Shankard Iyer, D.R. Water resources projects and strategies for water management for drought affected areas including drinking water supplies based on Gujarat experience. In *All-India seminar on strategies for drought proofing and management Ahmedabad 6–7 February 1987*. Ahmedabad: Bhaikaka Bhavan, 1987. pp. 1–22. IIML.

People's Committee on Gujarat flood-2006: a report. Ahmedabad: Narmada Abhiyan, 2007. p. 262. CSSL.

Raju, G., Vaghela, Raju and Raju, Manju S. *Development of people's institution for management of forests*. Ahmedabad: Viksat, 1993. p. 172. CSSL.

Raju, K.V, Uma Rani and Patel, Anil. *Non-economic motivation for improving natural resource management: example of Swadhyaya from a village in Gujarat, India.* Anand: Institute of Rural Management, 1999. p. 27. Working Paper 135. CSSL, GIDRL, SPIESRL.

Ray, C.N. *Comparative environmental risk assessment of Ahmedabad city.* Ahmedabad: Centre for Environmental Planning and Technology, 1996. p. 10. Working Paper No. 3. CEPTL, CSSL.

Ray, C.N. *Nature and extent of tenancy in North Gujarat villages.* Ahmedabad: Centre for Rural Studies, CEPT University, 2012. p. 32. Working Paper No. 1. CSSL.

Sathyapalan, Jyothis and Iyengar, Sudarshan. *Evaluation study of terre des hommes response to Gujarat earthquake and communal riots.* Surat: Centre for Social Studies, 2005. p. 84. CSSL.

Saurashtra Coast. *Coastal marine environment of Gujarat.* Vadodra: Gujarat Ecological Society, 1999. p. 181. CEEL.

Saxena, Rakesh, et al. *Soil degradation and salinity in Gujarat.* Anand: Institute of Rural Management, 2000. p. 430. IRMAL.

Sengupta, R. and Deshmukhe, Geetanjali. *Coastal and maritime environments of Gujarat ecology and economics.* Vadodara: Gujarat Ecological Society, 2000. p. 150. CSSL, GIDEL, IRMAL.

Shah, Amita. *Linking conservation with livelihood: lessons from management of Gir-protected area in Western India.* Ahmedabad: Gujarat Institute of Development Research, 2004. p. 42. Working Paper No. 148. CSSL.

Shah, Navin R. Evaluation of catchment area development programme: a case study of Dantiwada catchment in Gujarat. Vallabh Vidyanagar: Agro-Economic Research Centre, 1987. p. 58. AERC research Study No. 76. GIDRL.

Sharan, Girja, Shah, Nitin and Gupta, K.K. *Drought identification and rainfall pattern(Panchmahal).* Ahmedabad: Indian Institute of Management, 1987. p. 90. Centre for Management in Agriculture Monograph Series No. 125. IIML.

Shukla, Rohit. Drought in Saurashtra: regional profile. In *Economy of Saurashtra: problems and prospects.* Ed. by D.T. Lakdawala, et al. Bhavnagar: Bhavnagar University, 1990. pp. 75–85. GUL.

Shukla, Shital Hardik. *Drivers of vulnerability towards climate variability in Gujarat.* Ahmedabad: Sardar Patel Institute of Economic & Social Research, 2012. p. 29. Working Paper 8. CSSL, SPIESRL.

Singh, H.S. *Mangroves in Gujarat (Current status and strategy for conservation).* Gandhinagar: Gujarat Ecological Education and Research, 2000. p. 128. IRMAL.

Singh, H.S. *Natural heritage of Gujarat: forests and wildlife.* Gandhinagar: Gujarat Ecological Education and Research, 2001. p. 262. GIDEL, GIDRL, IRMAL.

Singh, H.S. and Tatu, Ketan. *Biodiversity study on Rampara wildlife sanctuary, Rajkot district: a comprehensive ecological study.* Gandhinagar: Gujarat Ecological Education and Research, 1999. p. 106. GIDEL.

Singh, Y.D., et al. *Process of desertification in Kachchh and Banaskantha districts of Gujarat, India. 1961–1991.* Bhuj: Gujarat Institute of Desert Ecology, 1996. p. 83. GIDEL.

Sinha, Bitapi C. *Impact of land use on the ecodegradation of the wild Ass habitat in little Rann of Kutch, Gujarat.* Garhwal: Hemvati Nandan Bahuguna University, 1993. p. 153. GIDRL.

Soni, Jayshree. *Water scarcity and gender dimension.* Surat: Centre for Social Studies, 2001. p. 36. CSSL.

South Gujarat Coast. *Coastal marine environment of Gujarat.* Vadodra: Gujarat Ecological Society, 1999. p. 93. CEEL.

State Environmental Action Programme (SEAP). *Action plan for water resource management in Gujarat.* Anand: INREM, Gujarat Ecological Commission, Vadodara, 2001. p. 100. GIDRL.

State Environmental Action Programme (SEAP). *Reconciling water use and environment: water resource management in Gujarat: resources, problems, issues, strategies and framework for action.* Vadodara: Gujarat Ecological Commission, 2001. p. 183. GIDRL.

Subrahmanian, K.K. and Veena, D.R. Energy. In *Gujarat economy in 2001 A.D.: a study in perspective*. Ahmedabad: Sardar Patel Institute of Economic & Social Research, 1980. pp. 307–367. GUL.

Surat Citizens' Council Trust. *Surat 2006 floods: an analysis of causes, consequences and management: report of a group of concerned citizens*. Surat: Surat Citizens' Council Trust, 2007. p. 46. CSSL.

Thivakaran, G.A., Sunderraj, S.F.W. and Gajera, N.B. *Study on the effect of desertification and climate change in Kachchh, Banaskantha and Patan districts of Gujarat state.* Bhuj: Gujarat Institute of Desert Ecology, 2011. p. [ ]. GIDEL.

Vadher, P.C. and Raichur, M.G. Geochemical evaluation of ground water in Banaskatha district, Gujarat state. In *Fifty-eighth research and development session Bangalore 19–22, April 1993.* New Delhi: Central Board of Irrigation and Power, 1993. pp. 10–18. Publication No. 223. IIML.

Vathsala, S., Srivastava, U.K. and Behl, Mohan. *Research and development project to determine the commercial viability of guayule as an additional source for natural rubber: under the auspices of biocentre, Ahmedabad.* Ahmedabad: Indian Institute of Management, 1985. p. 161. CSSL.

Vijaykumar, V. *Studies on benthnic and planktonic diversity of Kachchh coast-Gujarat.* Bhuj: Gujarat Institute of Desert Ecology, 2007. p. [ ]. GIDEL.

Vijaykumar, V., et al. *Ecorestoration of Banni grassland.* Bhuj: Gujarat Institute of Desert Ecology, 1999. p. 90. GIDEL.

Vyas, Darshna. Survival strategies in 'Banni' during drought: a case study of four villages. In *Drought and famine 1980s: crises and response - December 12–14, 1988, (Seminar papers)*. Surat, Centre for Social Studies, 1988. pp. 1–24. CSSL.

World Wide Fund for Nature-India. *Focus on some conservation issues of Gujarat.* Baroda: World Wide Fund for Nature-India, [ ]. p. 30. CSSL.

12

Industry

Books/Chapter in Books

Agrawal, M.N. State level public enterprises in Gujarat. In *Management of state level public enterprises in India.* Ed. by R.K. Mishra and S. Ravishankar. New Delhi: National, 1989. pp. 68–78. IIML.

Alagh, Yoginder K. and Pathak, Pravin G. Industrial development in Gujarat: regional structure and policies. In *Economic development of backward regions problems and prospects.* Ed. by H.M. Patel, V.S. Vyas and M.T. Pathak. Vallabh VidyaNagar: Sardar Patel University, 1974. pp. 143–202. GVL.

Alok, Vishwa N. Gujarat. In *Incentives for industrial development by central and state governments.* New Delhi: Northern Region Development Division, 1999. pp. 103–127. IIML.

Amin, T.C. and Kapadia, P.R. Pricing policy in cooperative dairy sector in Gujarat. In *Milk pricing and marketing practices*. Ed. by Dilip Shah. Pune: Maricheemalee, 1987. pp. 109–114. CSSL, HML.

Awasthi, Dinesh N. *Study on impact of incentive schemes on industrialisation of Gujarat. 2v.* Ahmedabad: Entrepreneurship Development, 1998. p. 145 and p. 192. SPIESRL.

Awasthi, Dinesh N. and Kashyap, S.P. Emerging industrialization process in Gujarat: nature and composition. In *Gujarat: perspectives of the future*. Ed. by R. Swaminathan. New Delhi: Academic, 2008. pp. 25–57. CSSL, EDIL, GIDRL, GVL, IIML, IRMAL, SETUL, SPIESRL.

Charles, A. Myers. Union welfare activities: the Ahmedabad example. In *Industrial relations in India*. Bombay: Asia, 1960. pp. 153–165. GUL.

Chauhan, A.B. *Organisation and working of public enterprises in Gujarat.* Vallabh Vidyanagar: Sardar Patel University, 1978. p. 580. GVL, SPUL.

Dahyabhai, Indulal. Industrial development of backward areas in Gujarat. In *Economic development of backward regions problems and prospects.* Ed. by H.M. Patel, V.S. Vyas and M.T. Pathak. Vallabh Vidya Nagar: Sardar Patel University, 1974. pp. 240–244. GUL, GVL.

De, Jayasree. Industrial pattern of Gujarat. In *Perspectives on industrial development in India.* Ed. by N.K.P. Sinha and M.B. Singh. Jaipur: Rawat, 1993. pp. 61–74. SPUL.

Deobhankar, Mukund. *Industrial growth in Gujarat: challenges and opportunities.* Ahmedabad: Vishva Samvad Kendra Gujarat, 2003. p. 216. CEEL, CEPTL.

Desai, B.H. *Financial structure of cotton textile mills of Ahmedabad*. Anand: Sardar Patel University, 1983. p. 359. GVL.

Desai, Rohit D. *Household sector: a study of Jari industry in Surat*. New Delhi: National Council of Applied Economic Research, 1966. p. 178. SPIESRL.

Desai, V.D. *Industrial development of Gujarat*. Baroda: Author, 1965. p. 205. GVL, UML.

Dupont, Vernique. *Decentralized industrialization and urban dynamics: the case of Jetpur in West India*. New Delhi: Sage, 1995. p. 431. BUL, CSSL, EDIL, GVL, IIML, SETUL, UML.

Dupont, Veronique. Industrial clustering and flexibility in the textile-printing industry of Jetpur(Gujarat). In *Decentralized production in India*. Ed. by Philippe Cadene and Mark Holmstom. New Delhi: Sage, 1998. pp. 308–311. GVL.

Engelshoven, Miranda. Diamonds and Patels: a report on the diamond industry of Surat. In *Worlds of Indian industrial labour*. Ed. by Jonathan P. Parry, Jan Breman and Karin Kapadia. New Delhi: Sage, 1999. pp. 353–377. CSSL, GUL.

Erdman, Howard L. *Political attitudes of Indian industry: a case study of the Baroda business elite*. London: University of London, 1971. p. 62. CSSL.

Erdman, Howard L. *Politics and economic development in India: the Gujarat state fertilizers company as a joint sector enterprise*. Delhi: D.K., 1973. p. 148. IIML.

Fawcett, Charles. *English factories in India*. Vol. III (New series), *Bombay, Surat, and Malabar Coast*. Oxford: Clarendon Press, 1954. p. 436. CSSL.

Ghosh, Sangeeta. Selective development in Gujarat: a study of the manufacturing sector. In *Poverty amidst prosperity: essays on the trajectory of development in Gujarat*. Ed. by Atul Sood. Delhi: Aakar, 2012. pp. 128–146. CSSL, IRMAL, MICAL.

Gorter, Pieter. *Small industrialists, big ambitions: economic and political networks on a large industrial estate in West India*. Delhi: Oxford, 1996. p. 204. CSSL.

Gumber, Anil and Kulkarni, Veena. Health insurance for workers in the informal sector: a case study of Gujarat. In *Informal economy centre stage: new structures of employment*. New Delhi: Sage, 2003. pp. 217–257. CSSL, GIDRL, HML.

Haynes, Douglas. Dynamics of continuity in Indian domestic industry: Jari manufacture in Surat, 1900–47. In *Cloth and commerce: textiles in colonial India*. Ed. by Tirthankar Roy. New Delhi: Sage, 1996. pp. 299–325. CSSL, HML.

Haynes, Douglas E. Artisanal origins of Surat's contemporary industrialization, 1870–1950. In *Social transformation in India: essays in honour of professor I.P. Desai*. Vol. 1. Ed. by Ghanshyam Shah. Jaipur: Rawat, 1997. pp. 199–235. CSSL, GUL, HML.

Haynes, Douglas E. Just like a family? recalling the relations of production in the textile industries of Surat and Bhiwandi, 1940–60. In *Worlds of Indian industrial labour*. Ed. by Jonathan P. Parry, Jan Breman and Karin Kapadia. New Delhi: Sage, 1999. pp. 141–170. CSSL, GUL.

Hess, Jeffrey. Indian ocean odyssey: Malagasy raffia ikat textiles in Gujarat. In *Textiles from India: the global trade*. Ed. by Rosemary Crill. Calcutta: Segull, 2006. pp. 195–216. HML.

Hirway, Indira, Shah, Neha and Sharma, Rajeev. Political economy of subsidies and incentives to industries in Gujarat: some issues. In *Growth or development: which way is Gujarat going?* Ed. by Indira Hirway, Amita Shah and Ghanshyam Shah. New Delhi: Oxford, 2014. pp. 139–192. CSSL.

Indian Inventment Centre. *Gujarat: potential for industrial development*. New Delhi: Indian Inventment Centre, 1969. p. 48. IIML.

Jani, B.M. Missing links in technological advances in common effluent treatment plant at industrial estate: a case study of Ankleshwar GIDC estate. In *Population, environment and health: emerging issues*. Ed. by K.N. Bhatt. Jaipur: Rawat, 2008. pp. 218–234. CSSL.

Joshi, V.H. *Economic development and social change in a South Gujarat village: social consequences of industrialization and urbanization in a village in South Gujarat with special reference to tensions between groups and classes*. Baroda: M.S. University, 1966. p. 124. CSSL, UML.

Joshi, V.H. Social consequences of industrialization in a South Gujarat village. In *Industrial sociology in India: a book of readings*. Ed. by N.R. Sheth. Bombay: Allied, 1982. pp. 77–86. CSSL, HML, SPUL.

Joshi, V.H., Parmar, B.D. and Joshi, B.H. Modern industrial development in Saurashtra. In *Changing pattern of sectral behaviour in a regional economy*. Delhi: B.R., 1988. pp. 220–285. SUL.

Kachhara, R.C., compil. *Ceramic industry in Gujarat*. Ahmedabad: Industrial Extension Bureau, 1983. p. 89. SPIESRL.

Kanwar, Kamlendra. *Icons of Gujarat industry: stories of rare grit and enterprise*. Ahmedabad: Harmony, 2000. p. 295. EDIL, GVL, IIML, MICAL.

Kapadia, K.M. and Devadas Pillai, S. *Industrialization and rural society: a study of Atul-Bulsar region*. Bombay: Popular, 1972. p. 269. CSSL.

Kashyap, S.P. and Mehta Niti. Rural non-farm sector in Gujarat: growth and emerging nature. In *Rural transformation in India: the role of non-farm sector*. Ed. by Rohini Nayyar and Alakh N. Sharma. New Delhi: Institute of Human Development, 2005. pp. 221–238. CSSL.

Kashyap, S.P. and Tiwari, R.S. *Shaping of diamonds in Surat some passas (facets)*. Ahmedabad: Sardar Patel Institute of Economic & Social Research, 1986. p. 139. SPIESRL.

Kashyap, S.P. and Tiwari, R.S. *Shaping of diamonds in Surat: an enquiry into some of its passas (facets)*. Ahmedabad: Sardar Patel Institute of Economic & Social Research, 1982. p. 203. SPIESRL.

Kashyap, S.P. and Tiwari, R.S. Small-scale industry or large-scale trade? diamond shaping industry in Surat. In *Informal sector in India*. Ed. by P.M. Mathew. New Delhi: Khama, 1995. pp. 75–93. GVL.

Kurien, Varghese. Amul: agony and ecstasy. In *Corporate success: institutional transformations by the leaders*. Ed. by N.K. Singh. New Delhi: Spantech, 1992. pp. 1–38. SPUL.

Majmudar, Paresh. *Anatomy of peaceful industrial relations*. Bombay: N.M. Tripathi, 1973. p. 291. SETUL.

Mehta, B.V. and Gupte, D.B. *Credit problem of small scale industries in Bombay and Surat*. Surat: South Gujarat University, 1976. p. 119. GVL.

Mehta, M.M. *Structure of Indian industries*. Bombay: Popular, 1955. p. 269. GVL, SPIESRL.

Mehta, Makrand. *Ahmedabad cotton textile industry-genesis and growth*. Ahmedabad: New order book, 1982. p. 207. *GVL, SETUL, SPIESRL.

Misra, R.K. and Navin, B. *Restructuring public enterprises in India: privatisation and disinvestment*. New Delhi: Mittal, 2002. p. 232. GVL.

Misra, Smita. Accounting for costs of water pollution abatement: a case study of the Nandesari industrial area. In *Economics of water pollution: the Indian experience*. By M.N. Murty, A.J. James and Smita Misra. New Delhi: Oxford, 1999. pp. 244–266. CSSL, HML.

Misra, Smita. Valuation of benefits to households from industrial water pollution abatement practices at Nandesari. In *Economics of water pollution: the Indian experience*. By M.N. Murty, A.J. James and Smita Misra. New Delhi: Oxford, 1999. pp. 213–243. CSSL, HML.

Mookherjee, Surya. Gujarat. In *Industrial relations in Indian states.* Ed. by C.S. Venkata Ratnam. Delhi: Global Business, 1996. pp. 146–169. IIML.

Mookherjee, Surya. *Joint management councils: a study of practices and performance in Gujarat*. New Delhi: Oxford and IBH, 1987. p. 155. GVL, HML.

Moulik, T.K. On entrepreneurial achievements in an industrially progressive rural setting: Anand, Gujarat. In *Administration for rural development.* Ed. by D.R. Mehta and Satish K. Batra. Jaipur: Centre for Administrative Change, 1984. pp. 163–179. GVL.

National Council of Applied Economic Research. *Industrial programmes for the fourth plan Gujarat.* New Delhi: National Council of Applied Economic Research, 1966. p. 178. CSSL, GVL, HML, SPIESRL.

Panchal, Nilam. Analysis of post-merer performance of acquiring firms of selected industries in Gujarat. In *Managing in the new world order*. Ed. by Yogeshwary Pathak, Ajit Upadhyaya and Deepak Jarolia. New Delhi: Excel, 2010. pp. 46–53. HML.

Pancholi, D.K. *Salt glazed stoneware pipe industry in Gujarat.* Ahmedabad: Small Industries Service Institute, 1979. p. 57. SPIESRL.

Pandya, Rameshwari and Patel, Sarika. *Women in the unorganised sector in India including a case study of women in the embroidery industry in Surat city*. New Delhi: New Century, 2010. p. 192. GUL.

Papola, T.S. *Informal sector in an urban economy: a study in Ahmedabad.* Lucknow: Giri Institute of Development Studies, 1978. p. 177. SPIESRL.

Papola, T.S. On Introducing technological change: a study of Ahmedabad cotton textile industry. In *Technological change and industry.* Ed. by C.P. Thakur and G.S. Aurora. New Delhi: Shri Ram Centre for Industrial Relations, 1971. pp. 245–264. SPIESRL.

Papola, T.S. *Urban informal sector in a developing economy.* New Delhi: Vikas, 1981. p. 128. IIML.

Parekh, Sunil R. Gujarat's industrial development: a perspective. In *Gujarat: perspectives of the future*. Ed. by R. Swaminathan. New Delhi: Academic, 2008. pp. 59–103. CSSL, EDIL, GIDRL, GVL, IIML, IRMAL, SETUL, SPIESRL.

Parekh, Sunil R. Some facts of industrialization in Gujarat, 1999–2009. In *Growth or development: which way is Gujarat going?* Ed. by Indira Hirway, Amita Shah and Ghanshyam Shah. New Delhi: Oxford, 2014. pp. 193–224. CSSL.

Patel, Arjun. Impact of industries on rural society: a case study. In *Sociology of environment*. Ed. by S.N. Pawar and R.B. Patil. Jaipur: Rawat, 1998. pp. 181–201. CSSL.

Patel, B.B. *Structure of inter-district inter-sectoral and inter-industry wage differentials in Gujarat*. Baroda: M.S. University, 1985. p. 198. HML.

Patel, H.M., Vyas, V.S. and Pathak, M.T. *Economic development of backward regions problems and prospects.* Vallabh Vidyanagar: Sardar Patel University, 1974. p. 260. GVL.

Patel, Sujata. Corporatist patronage in the Ahmedabad textile industry. In *Development and deprivation in Gujarat: in hounour of Jan Breman*. Ed. by Ghanshyam Shah, Mario Rutten and Hein Streefkerk. New Delhi: Sage, 2002. pp. 96–114. CEEL, CEPTL, CSSL, EDIL, GIDRL, IIML, UML.

Patel, Sujata. *Making of industrial relations: the Ahmedabad textile industry 1918–1939*. Delhi: Oxford, 1987. p. 164. CSSL.

Pathak, H.N. Case of the diamond cutting and polishing industry. In *Social security for unorganized labour*. Ed. by B.B. Patel. New Delhi: Oxford, 1993. pp. 249–257. CSSL.

Pathak, H.N. *Diamond cutting and polishing industry of Gujarat: study based on sample survey*. Ahmedabad: Indian Institute of Management, 1984. p. 241. SPIESRL.

Pathak, S.C. Gujarat. In *Industrial development in the states of India*. Ed. by T.N. Kapoor. Delhi: Sterling, 1967. pp. 125–137. SPIESRL, SPUL.

Patil, R.K. *Gold and silver thread industry of Surat: a socio-economic study*. Surat: Chunilal Gandhi Vidyabhavan, 1956. p. 158. CSSL, GVL.

Pillai, Anandan. Gujarat: the industrial hub of India. In *Gujarat economy: the way ahead*. Ed. by Sudha V. Menon. Hyderabad: ICFAI University, 2009. pp. 99–122. EDIL, HML, SPIESRL.

Prakash, Om. *Dutch factories in India 1617–1623: a collection of Dutch East India co. documents pertaining to India*. New Delhi: Munshiram Manoharlal, 1984. p. 332. SETUL.

Purohit, Y.S. *Industrialising economy and labour market in India: a study of Bharuch district*. New Delhi: Mittal, 1989. p. 331. CSSL.

Robert, V. and Makwana, M.H. Impact of industrialisation on rural Gujarat: a case study of impact of KRIBHCO project. In *Agriculture, rural development and Panchayati Raj: regional level strategies and policies*. Ed. by V.S. Mahajan. New Delhi: Deep & Deep, 1996. pp. 529–536. AAUL, SPIESRL.

Rutten, Mario. *Farms and factories: social profile of large farmers and rural industrialists in West India*. Delhi: Oxford, 1995. p. 396. CSSL.

Sahu, Samarendra. *Plastic film and bag industry in Gujarat*. Ahmedabad: Small Industries Service, 1990. p. 125. SPIESRL.

Sanghvi, R.L. Industrial estates in Gujarat and South Gujarat. In *Role of industrial estates in a developing economy*. By R.L. Sanghvi. Bombay: Multi-tech, 1979. pp. 44–67. HML, SPIESRL, SPUL.

Sankar, T.L., Gopal, R. and Mishra, R.K. Gujarat. In *Management of state level public enterprises in India*. Jaipur: Printwell, 1992. pp. 73–86. IIML.

Saramma, A.D. *Petroleum industry: a study of its spread effects*. New Delhi: Deep & Deep, 1984. p. 224. SPIESRL.

Savilani, Hasmukh D. *Industrial relation: a empirical study of the typical contribution of Gujarat*. Vallabh Vidyanagar: Sardar Patel University, 1985. p. 61. GVL.

Savilani, Hasmukh D. *Labour-management relations in selected organised industries of Gujarat*. Vallabh Vidyanagar: Sardar Patel University, 1986. p. 260. GVL, HML, SPUL.

Shah, Dilip R. *Economic analysis of co-operative dairy industry in Gujarat*. New Delhi: Somalya, 1985. p. 169. HML.

Shah, Hina. Developing women's micro enterprises in Dholka, Gujarat. In *Development of micro enterprises by women*. Ed. by Sue Beaumount and Kamal Singh. Ahmedabad: British Council and the Indian Institute of Management, 1992. pp. 163–167. IIML.

Shah, M.N. Organised manufacturing sector of Baroda district. *In Profiles of a growing city: socio-economic studies of Baroda city*. Baroda: M.S. University, 1971. pp. 73–82. M.S. University Economics Series No. 1. SPIESRL.

Shah, R.J. and Ojha, A.K. *Potentialities for industrial development in Saurastra region.* Ahmedabad: Indextb, 1981. p. 314. IIML, TRTIL.

Singh, Gurdev and Asokan, S.R. Biogas technology for rural India. In *Agriculture, rural development and Panchayati raj: regional level strategies and policies.* Ed. by V.S. Mahajan. New Delhi: Deep & Deep, 1996. p. 529. SPIESRL.

Singh, Indira and Singh, Satnam. Ahmedabad – Vadodara industrial region. In *Industrial geography of India.* New Delhi: Srishti, 2006, pp. 56–57. GUL.

Singh, Rajesh Kumar and Dubey, Vijay Nath. Industrial disparity in India: an analysis of up vis-à-vis Maharashtra and Gujarat. In *Dispartites in India.* Ed. by Anil Kumar Thakur and Dilip Kumar. New Delhi: Deep & Deep, 2011. pp. 220–230. GVL.

Singh, Satya Dev and Singh, Rajesh Kumar. Industrial disparities in India.: a case study of Uttar Pradesh vis-a-vis Maharashtra and Gujarat. In *Regional disparities in India's socio-economic development.* Ed. by Kanak Kanti Bagchi. New Delhi: New Century, 2011. pp. 102–110. GVL, IIML.

Solanki, Sandip P. Globalisation international competitiveness of Indian industry: a case study of Jamnagar Brass part industry. In *Globalisation: inclusive growth and Indian economy, issues and policies.* Ed. by Anil Kumar Thakur and Paramanand Singh. New Delhi: Regal, 2010. pp. 132–142. GVL.

Soni, K.C. and Jani, B.B. Comparative study of total factor productivity of the industrial sectors of Gujarat state vis-à-vis all-India. In *Industrial sector development.* Ed. by Devendra Thakur. New Delhi: Deep & Deep, 1992. pp. 347–359. SPUL, TRTIL.

Srivastava, U.K. *Wind energy for water pumping: from policy to action: an evaluation of progress in Gujarat.* New Delhi: Oxford and IBH, 1987. p. [ ]. IRMAL.

Streefkerk, Hein. *Industrial transition in rural India: artisans, traders and tribals in South Gujarat.* Bombay: Popular, 1985. p. 280. CSSL, IIML, IRMAL, SPIESRL.

Streefkerk, Hein. Small entrepreneurs: agents in underdevelopment? In *Winners and losers: styles of development and change in an Indian region.* Ed. by S. Devadas Pillai and Chris Baks. Bombay: Popular, 1979. pp. 100–121. CSSL, SPIESRL.

Streefkerk, Hein. *Tools and ideas: the beginnings of local industrialization in South Gujarat, 1970–2000.* New Delhi: Manohar, 2006. p. 188. CSSL, HML.

Subramanian, Vinkata. *Industrial development potentialities in Junagadh district.* Ahmedabad: Ministry of Industry and Company Affairs, 1985. p. 144. SPIESRL.

Thakker, Girish. *Wage pattern's in the industries in Surat.* New Delhi: S. Chand, 1969. p. 234. GVL, HML, IIML, SPIESRL.

Trivedi, H.K. and Desai, B.H. *Appraisal of socio-economic performance of N.T.C. mills in Gujarat(India).* Ahmedabad: Gujarat University, 1989. p. 126. SPIESRL.

Tully, Mark. Typhoon in Ahmedabad. In *No full stops in India.* New Delhi: Viking Penguin, 1991. pp. 237–267. GUL.

Upadhyaya, D.V. *Thesis on some aspects of household and small industries with reference to Gujarat.* Ahmedabad: B.S. Shah, 1989. p. 259. GUL, GVL, HML, IIML.

Vasava, K.D. *Distribution pattern of cotton textiles in Gujarat.* Anand: Sardar Patel University, 1980. p. 280. GVL.

Journal Articles

Agrawal, Sarita. Division of labour and employment conditions in the Surat art silk industry. *Indian Journal of Labour Economics.* 39, 2, 1996. pp. 259–268. CSSL.

Agrawal, Sarita. Gender discrimination in the labour market: a case study of Surat art silk industry. *Manpower Journal.* 30, 1, 1994. pp. 37–51. CSSL, GIDRL, UML.

Agro-Economic Research Centre. Economic efficiency of Indian sugar industry AERC, Vastrapur Ahmedabad. *Agricultural Situation in India.* 49, 2, 1984. pp. 79–84. IIML.

Alagh, Roginder K., Subrahmanian, K.K. and Desai, Rohit D. Regional cost variations in vanaspati and edible oil industries in India. *Anvesak.* 1, 1, 1971. pp. 78–96. CSSL, SPIESRL.

Alagh, Yoginder. Inert-regional industrial structure in a developing economy: a case study of Gujarat. *Southern Economic Review*, 1, 1, 1971. pp. 40–69. SGUL.

Alagh, Yoginder K. and Pathak, Pravin G. Industrial development in Gujarat: regional structure and policies. *Artha-Vikas.* 9, 1–2, 1973. pp. 143–184. GVL, HML, SGUL.

Amin, Poornima. Infrastructure and regional distribution of small-scale industries in Gujarat. *Asian Economic Review.* 32, 3, 1990. pp. 391–428. EDIL.

Amin, Poornima. Small scale industries in a rapidly developing industrial economy of Gujarat: a study in regional perspective. *Indian Journal of Regional Science.* 23, 1, 1991. pp. 69–88. GIDRL.

Amin, Poornima A. Growth, concentration and efficiency prospects of small scale industries of Gujarat. *Anvesak.* 15, 2, 1985. pp. 67–110. CEPTL, CSSL, GIDRL, IRMAL, SPIESRL.

Amin, Poornima A. Size and efficiency in small scale industry: Gujarat evidence: an aggregate view. *Anvesak.* 17, 1, 1987. pp. 69–86. CSSL, GIDRL, IRMAL, SPIESRL.

Awasthi, Dinesh. Recent changes in Gujarat industry: issues and evidence. *Economic and Political Weekly.* 35, 35 and 36, 2000. pp. 3183–3192. BUL, CEPTL, CSSL, GIDRL, IIML, IRMAL, MICAL, SGUL, SPIESRL, UML.

Bal, Gurpreet. Entrepreneurship among diasporic communities: a comparative examination of Patidars of Gujarat and Jats of Punjab. *Journal of Entrepreneurship.* 15, 2, 2006. pp. 181–203. EDIL.

Bharadwaj, V.P. Industrial growth in Gujarat: acceleration or declaration? *Vishleshan.* 3, 3, 1977. pp. 198–204. CSSL, GIDRL, IIML.

Bhatt, Mahesh and Chavada, V.K. Industrial growth in Gujarat: an appraisal. *Economic and Political Weekly.* 5, 48, 1970. pp. 1929–1932. CSSL, HML, IRMAL, SPIESRL, TRTIL, UML.

Bhatt, Sandip K. History of dairy industry: problems and prospects in Gujarat. *Indian Economic Panorama.* 4, 4, 1995. pp. 30–35. IRMAL.

Chand, Faqir. Lignite based thermal power project for Kutch. *Agricultural Situation in India.* 34, 8, 1979. pp. 541-[ ]. SPIESRL.

Chandel, Himal. Intertemporal interindustry linkage pattern of Gujarat manufacturing industries. *Anvesak.* 21, 1, 1991. pp. 19–39. CEPTL, CSSL, IRMAL, SPIESRL.

Chandel, Himal. Technological change in Gujarat's industrial economy. *Anvesak.* 23, 1 and 2, 1993. pp. 1–25. CSSL, GIDRL, IRMAL, SPIESRL.

Chaudhuri, K.N. Structure of Indian textile industry in the Seventeenth and Eighteenth centuries. *Indian Economic and Social History Review.* 11, 2–3, 1974. pp. 127–182. CSSL.

Chawda, V.K. Appraisal of industrial estate programme of Gujarat. *Vishleshan.* 3, 3, 1977. pp. 221–232. CSSL, IIML.

Chhatrapati, Kusum. Handlooms of Gujarat. *Handloom Journal.* 11, 1, 1958. pp. 16–18. TRTIL.

Chinoy, Sultan. Industrial possibilities of gas oil in Gujarat. *Journal of the Gujarat Research Society*. 7, 2–3, 1945. pp. 46–47. GUL, GVL.

Chittaranjan, K.V. Regional variation in urbanization industrialization and wage rates in Gujarat. *Indian Journal of Regional Science*. 21, 1, 1989. pp. 63–68. CEPTL, GIDRL, SGUL, SPIESRL.

Dadibhavi, R.V. Output variations and labour productivity in small-scale Gujarat industries. *Productivity*. 22, 3, 1981. pp. 85–90. HML, SPUL.

Dahyabhai, Indulal. Industrial development of backward areas in Gujarat. *Artha-Vikas*. 9, 1–2, 1973. pp. 240–244. GVL, HML.

Das, Panchanan. Wage inequality in manufacturing industries 1979–2002: a case of West Bengal and Gujarat. *Indian Journal of Labour Economics*. 50, 2, 2007. pp. 303–316. CSSL, IRMAL.

De, Jayasree. Industrial growth of Baroda: an analysis. *Indian Journal of Regional Science*. 13, 1, 1981. pp. 91–98. GIDRL.

Desai, Ashok V. Origins of Parsi enterprise. *Indian Economic and Social History Review*. 5, 4, 1968. pp. 307–317. CSSL.

Desai, D.K. and Narayanan, A.V.S. Impact of modernization of dairy industry on the economy of Kaira district. *Indian Journal of Agricultural Economics*. 22, 3, 1967. pp. 54–67. GIDRL, IIML, SPUL, UML.

Desai, M.B. Chemical industries in greater Gujarat. *Journal of the Gujarat Research Society*. 3, 4, 1941. pp. 212–228. GVL.

Desai, Rohit and Tewari, R.S. Jari industry of Surat: a study of characteristics of household sector. *Indian Journal of Labour Economics*. 27, 4, 1985. pp. 275–291. GIDRL.

Desai, Rohit D. Jari industry: yesterday and today. *Anvesak*. 25, 2, 1995. pp. 19–29. CSSL, GIDRL, SPIESRL.

Desai, Rohit D. Regional commercialization advantages for cotton textile complex. *Anvesak*. 14, 1, 1984. pp. 69–78. GIDRL, SPIESRL.

Desai, Rohit D. and Dave, Alka K. Electronics industry of Gujarat: some broad traits. *Anvesak*. 21, 2, 1991. pp. 23–35. CEPTL, CSSL, IRMAL, SPIESRL.

Desai, Rohit D. and Kashyap, S.P. Factor-use efficiency in small scale units: a study of industrial estates in Gujarat. *Vishleshan*. 5, 1, 1979. pp. 20–29. CSSL, GIDRL, IIML.

Dholakia, R.H. Estimates of district income and changing industrial structure in Gujarat. *Journal of the Gujarat Research Society*. 38, 3/146, 1976. pp. 1–8. GVL.

Dupont, Veronique. Impact of in-migration on industrial development: case study of Jetpur in Gujarat. *Economic and Political Weekly*. 27, 45, 1992. pp. 2423–2436. CEPTL, CSSL, IIML, IRMAL, SGUL, SPIESRL, UML.

Engelshoven, Miranda. Diamonds and Patels: a report on the diamond industry of Surat. *Contributions to Indian Sociology*. 33, 1 and 2, 1999. pp. 353–377. AAUL, CSSL, HML, MICAL, UML.

George, P.V. Stochastic model for the corporate industrial structure of Gujarat. *Anvesak*. 1, 1, 1971. pp. 155–164. CSSL, IRMAL, SPIESRL.

Gorter, Pieter. Small capitalists or 'agents in under development'?: a case study of a large industrial estate in South Gujarat. *Journal of Entrepreneurship*. 5, 1, 1996. pp. 41–64. EDIL, IRMAL.

Gujar, N.G. Gujarat industrialises. *Indian Export Trade Journal*. 18, 10–11, 1964. pp. 4-[ ]. HML.

Gupta, G.S. Locational factors for industries in Valsad district. *Artha-Vikas*. 16, 1, 1980. pp. 59–70. CEPTL, CSSL, GIDRL, HML.

Gupta, G.S. and Rathi, A.K.A. Small-scale chemical industry in Gujarat: structure, conduct and performance. *Economic and Political Weekly*. 31, 48, 1996. pp. M-79-M-84. CEPTL, CSSL, GIDRL, IIML, IRMAL, MICAL, SGUL, SPIESRL, UML.

Hayne, Douglas E. Just like a family?: recalling the relations of production in the textile industries of Surat and Bhiwandi, 1940–60. *Contributions to Indian Sociology*. 23, 1 and 2, 1999. pp. 141–169. CSSL, HML, UML.

Hirway, Indira. After the global crisis 2008–09: has India learnt lessons? the case of diamond industry. *Indian Journal of Labour Economics*. 56, 2, 2013. pp. 191–214. CSSL.

Jani, B.B. and Soni, K.C. Economies of scale and technical change under cobb-douglas production function for the industrial sector of Gujarat state as compared to all India. *Vishleshan*. 13, 1, 1987. pp. 27–36. CSSL, GIDRL.

Jani, B.B. and Soni, K.C. VES production function with neutral technological sectors of Gujarat state vs. all India. *Anvesak*. 17, 2, 1987. pp. 59–76. GIDRL, SPIESRL.

Jani, B.M. Impact of developmental finance on small scale industries in Saurashtra. *Indian Economic Journal*. 34, 2, 1986. pp. 106–111. CSSL, IIML.

Kamdar, V.P., et al. Survey of crusher plants of Gujarat state. *Indian Highways*. 20, 8, 1992. pp. 23–30. CEPTL.

Kapadia, K.M. Industrial evolution of Navasari. *Sociological Bulletin*. 15, 1, 1966. pp. 1–24. CSSL.

Kashyap, S.P. Industrial scene in Gujarat: a contrast of two patterns. *Anvesak*. 25, 1, 1995. pp. 124–130. CSSL, GIDRL, IRMAL, SPIESRL.

Kashyap, S.P. Updating inter-industry model: a discussion of theoretical issues with illustration of Gujarat's model. *Anvesak*. 6, 2, 1976. pp. 107–125. CSSL, IRMAL, SPIESRL.

Kashyap, S.P. and Shah, Amita. Induced industrial clustering and efficiency: exploratory study of Gujarat's industrial estates. *Journal of Entrepreneurship*. 4, 1, 1995. pp. 71–87. IRMAL.

Kashyap, S.P. and Shah, Jayshree. "Surplus" generation process by micro enterprises in non-farm sector in Gujarat. *Anvesak*. 32, 1, 2002. pp. 13–28. GIDRL, SPIESRL.

Kashyap, S.P. and Singh, Himal. Urban informal sector: issues out of Gujarat's experience. *Indian Journal of Industrial Relations*. 23, 1, 1987. pp. 43–53. CSSL, IRMAL.

Kashyap, S.P. and Tiwari, R.S. Diamond shaping industry in Surat: characteristics of firms by size. *Economic and Political Weekly*. 19, 34, 1984. pp. M-99-M-103. CEPTL, CSSL, GUL, IIML, IRMAL, SGUL, SPIESRL, UML.

Kashyap, S.P., Pathak, Pravin G. and Shah, Jayshree. Industrial estates in Gujarat: a preliminary study of linkage patterns. *Anvesak*. 5, 1–2, 1975. pp. 209–216. CSSL, IRMAL, SPIESRL.

Kashyap, S.P., Tiwari, R.S. and Veena, D.R. Inter-industry transactions in a metropolis: a study of Ahmedabad. *Anvesak*. 13, 2, 1983. pp. 49–86. CEPTL, CSSL, GIDRL, SPIESRL.

Keshari, P.K. and Kota, Ranga. Determinants of the propensity to export: the case of small firms in the diesel engine and chemicals industries in Gujarat. *Journal of Entrepreneurship*. 4, 1, 1995. pp. 35–48. EDIL, IRMAL.

Khakhar, K.K. Role of industrial estates in the regional development of Gujarat. *ICSSR Research Abstracts Quarterly*. 4, 384, 1975 pp. 153-[ ]. HML.

Kochar, Anjini. Constraints on the development of consumer demand based rural household manufacturing units in arid regions-Kutch district Gujarat. *Indian Journal of Agricultural Economics*. 38, 3, 1983. pp. 347–353. AAUL, GVL, HML, UML.

Kulkarni, S.R. Liquidity and profitability analysis: an in-depth study of manufacturing industry in Gujarat. *Journal of Commerce & Management Thought*. 3, 3, 2012. pp. 445–459. EDIL.

Lakdawala, D.T., Shah, C.H. and Dholakia, R.H. Estimates of district income and changing industrial structure in 'Gujarat'. *Journal of the Gujarat Research Society*. 38, 3/146, 1976. pp. 1–8. GVL.

Lal, R.B. From farm to factory. *Adivasi Gujarat*. 4, 2, 1982. pp. 24–28. CSSL, GVL, SPIESRL, TRTIL.

Lal, R.B. Impact of industrialisation on tribals in South Gujarat. *Journal of the Gujarat Research Society*. 37, 3/145, 1975. pp. 26–38. TRTIL.

Lalitha, N. Employment and labour productivity in the unorganized manufacturing sector of Gujarat. *Indian Journal of Regional Science*. 34, 1, 2002. pp. 109–123. CSSL, GIDRL.

Lalitha, N. State level reforms to promote industrialization: a case study of Gujarat. *Indian Journal of Regional Science*. 30, 1, 1998. pp. 1–21. CSSL, GIDRL.

Madalia, V.K. and Patel, A.P. Gur industry in Gujarat: an analysis. *Khadi Gramodyog*. 30, 4, 1984. pp. 178–185. TRTIL.

Mahadevia, Darshini and Bhati, Lalit Kishor. Industrialisation and urbanization pattern in Gujarat: a regional level analysis. *Review of Development and Change*. 6, 1, 2001. pp. 28–50. CSSL, GIDRL, IRMAL.

Malhotra, Gunjan. Structure and performance of industries in Gujarat. *Journal of Scientific and Industry Research*. 67, 9, 2008. pp. 708–716. IRMAL.

Mashihi, Edwin. Profile of outsider and insider trade union leaders in the textile industry of Ahmedabad. *Vishleshan*. 3, 2, 1977. pp. 183–186. IIML.

Mehta, Aman. Gujarat, the industrial paradise. *Economic Scene*. 84, 8, 1984. pp. 39–46. IIML.

Mehta, B.V. Credit problems of small artisans in Bombay and Surat. *South Gujarat University Journal*. 1, 1972. pp. 18–26. GVL.

Mehta, B.V. Industry and employment in India. *Artha-Vikas*. 15, 1, 1979. pp. 1–14. GIDRL.

Mehta, J.D. Changes in the industrial structure of Gujarat. *Journal of the Gujarat Research Society*. 32, 2/126, 1970. pp. 94–97. GVL.

Mehta, J.D. Textile machinery industry in Ahmedabad city: an economic analysis. *Journal of the Gujarat Research Society*. 37, 3/145, 1975. pp. 64–77. GVL, TRTIL.

Mehta, R.N. Excavation at Ahmedabad: Calico mills. *Journal of the M.S. University of Baroda*. 27–28, 1, 1978–1979. pp. 23–52. GVL.

Mehta, S.S. and Harode, Dinesh. Industrial sickness and workers: case of Gujarat textile industry. *Economic and Political Weekly*. 33, 52, 1998. pp. L-71-L-84. CEPTL, CSSL, EDIL, GIDRL, IIML, IRMAL, MICAL, SGUL, SPIESRL, UML.

Mody, R.J. and George, P.V. Analysis of selected industries of Gujarat. *Anvesak*. 4, 1, 1974. pp. 13–22. CEPTL, CSSL, SPIESRL.

Mookherjee, Surya. Joint management councils in Gujarat: a study of current practices and performance. *Indian Journal of Industrial Relations*. 19, 4, 1984. pp. 443–453. CSSL, IIML, IRMAL.

Mookherjee, Surya. Unions in industries in downturn: a study of cotton textile in Gujarat and role of TLA. *Indian Journal of Industrial Relations*. 40, 2, 2004. pp. 213–233. BUL, CSSL, IIML, IRMAL.

Nayak, K.C., Pandya, P.C. and Joshi, A.P. Study of hot mix plants employed in Gujarat state. *Indian Highways*. 14, 2, 1986. pp. 71–76. CEPTL.

Pandya, N.M. Changes in the industrial structure of Gujarat. *Journal of the M.S. University of Baroda*. 20, 2, 1971. pp. 57–66. GVL.

Papola, T.S. Pattern of industrial location in Gujarat: an analysis of new factories. *Vishleshan*. 2, 4, 1976. pp. 296–322. CSSL, GIDRL, IIML.

Paranjape, Jyotsna. Inducing industrial location in backward regions: a study of Maharashtra and Gujarat. *Economic and Political Weekly*. 23, 7, 1988. pp. 321–330. CEPTL, CSSL, IIML, IRMAL, SGUL, SPIESRL, UML.

Patel, Arjun. Cash compensation and rehabilitation: a case of land acquisition for industry. *Administrator*. 43, 1, 1998. pp. 69–86. CSSL.

Patel, B.B. Wage-employment relationship in manufacturing industries in Gujarat. *Indian Journal of Labour Economics*. 17, 3–4, 1974–75. pp. 209–215. SPIESRL.

Patel, J.B. Hazardous power plants of Gujarat. *Occupational and Environmental Health*. 5, 1, 1998. pp. 4–6. IRMAL.

Patel, Pravin J. Trade union movement in a princely state: tradition, industrialization and social change. *Contributions to Indian Sociology*. 45, 1, 2011. pp. 27–54. CSSL.

Patel, V.G. Encouraging entrepreneurs: Gujarat experiment. *Productivity*. 12, 1, 1971. pp. 104–114. HML, IRMAL, SPUL.

Pathak, P.G. Production functions for Gujarat industries. *Anvesak*. 2, 1, 1972. pp. 11–24. CSSL, IRMAL, SGUL, SPIESRL.

Pathak, Pravin G. Constant elasticity of production functions of Gujarat industries: a study of factor-use pattern. *Anvesak*. 24, 1, 1994. pp. 1–43. CSSL, GIDRL, IRMAL, SPIESRL.

Pathak, Pravin G. Decomposition of employment growth in the industries of Gujarat: a regional approach. *Anvesak*. 1, 2, 1971. pp. 193–209. CSSL, SPIESRL.

Pathak, Pravin G. Delineation of industrially homogeneous regions of Gujarat: comparison of regional industrial activity. *Anvesak*. 3, 1–2, 1973. pp. 78–102. CSSL, IRMAL, SPIESRL.

Pathak, Pravin G. Regional cost advantages: a study of Gujarat industries in a comparative spatial dimension. *Anvesak*. 21, 1, 1991. pp. 1–17. CEPTL, CSSL, IRMAL, SPIESRL.

Prajapati, Keerti and Biswas, Saswata Narayan. Effect of entrepreneur network and entrepreneur self-efficacy on subjective performance: a study of handicraft and handloom cluster. *Journal of Entrepreneurship*. 20, 2, 2011. pp. 227–247. EDIL.

Purohit, Y.S. and Bharadwaj, V.P. Role of government in industrialization of a backward region: a study of Bharuch. *Artha-Vikas*. 21, 1–2, 1985. pp. 1–22. AAUL, GIDRL, GVL, HML.

Rajadhyaksha, Ujvala. Marketing potential of handmade paper with special reference to Bombay and Ahmedabad. *Khadi Gramodyog*. 38, 9, 1992. pp. 455–474. GVL.

Rajagopalan, R. and Sekhar, R.C. Distribution and price controls on molasses and industrial alcohol in Gujarat. *Economic and Political Weekly*. 24, 7, 1989. pp. 373–376. CEPTL, CSSL, IIML, IRMAL, SPIESRL, UML.

Rami, Gaurang and Vansiya, Yogesh. Industrial development with special reference to small scale industries in South Gujarat. *VNSGU Journal of Humanities and Social Sciences*. 1, 1, 2009. pp. 7–17. CSSL, SGUL.

Ray, C.N. and Patel, R.M. Backward area industrial development: a case study of Mehsana district, Gujarat. *Indian Journal of Regional Science.* 26, 1, 1994. pp. 1–08. GIDRL.

Shah, Amita. Employment linkages of industrial growth in rural economy: evidence from an industrial estate in Gujarat. *Indian Journal of Labour Economics*. 44, 2, 2001. pp. 183–203. BUL, CSSL, GIDRL, IIML, IRMAL, SGUL.

Shah, Amita. Improving quality of life among informal industrial workers: lessons from an innovative approach. *Indian Journal of Labour Economics*. 44, 4, 2001. pp. 641–650. CSSL.

Shah, Amita. Linkages between small and largescale industries: some evidences from Gujarat. *Artha Vijnan*. 32, 2, 1990. pp. 138–152. AAUL, CSSL, GIDRL, GVL, HML, UML.

Shah, Amita. Mainstreaming the corporate initiatives in social development insights from experiences in Gujarat. *Social Change,* 30, 3–4, 2000. pp. 88–101. IRMAL, UML.

Shah, Amita. Rural industrialization in Gujarat. *Indian Journal of Regional Science*. 18, 1, 1986. pp. 67–80. CEPTL, CSSL, GIDRL.

Shah, Dilip. Production functions in co-operative dairy industry of Gujarat. *Indian Journal of Industrial Relations*. 17, 3, 1982. pp. 395–408. CSSL, IIML, SPUL.

Shah, Dilip, R. Impact of co-operative dairy industry on rural economy of Gujarat. *Indian Co-operative Review*. 17, 3, 1980. pp. 195–204. SGUL.

Shah, Dilip R. Rural poverty, employment and role of dairy industry in Gujarat: a survey. *Vishleshan.* 6, 1, 1980. pp. 35–47. GIDRL, IIML.

Shah, J.K. Growth and behaviour of capital in organized sector of industry Gujarat 1961–65. *Journal of the M.S. University of Baroda.* 23–24, 2, 1974–75. pp. 87–98. GVL.

Shah, J.K. Electricity and employment in industry: Gujarat: a case for rural electrification. *Vishleshan*. 2, 4, 1976. pp. 323–335. CSSL, GIDRL, IIML.

Shah, M.H. Bottling of fruit syrup safety match manufacturing on cottage scale Kosamba health unit: an experiment in rural sanitation. *Rural India*, 4, 6, 1941. pp. 310–316. SGUL

Shah, M.H. Village industries in Baroda. *Rural India*. 4, 10, 1941. pp. 523–525. SGUL.

Shah, M.N. and Kanetkar, S.S. Changes in the location pattern of industries in Gujarat. *Journal of the M.S. University of Baroda.* 20, 2, 1971. pp. 67–74. GVL.

Shinoda, Takashi. Institutional change and entrepreneurial development: SSI sector. *Economic and Political Weekly*. 35, 35 and 36, 2000. pp. 3205–3216. BUL, CEPTL, CSSL, IIML, IRMAL, MICAL, SGUL, SPIESRL, UML.

Shiyani, R.L., Singh, Rajvir and Pandya, H.R. Cost and returns from dairy enterprise in Saurashtra region. *Indian Journal of Dairy Science*. 48, 6, 1995. pp. 399–403. AAUL.

Sidhu, Hina. Employment generation in small scale industries in Gujarat. *Indian Journal of Labour Economics*. 41, 1, 1998. pp. 133–139. AAUL, IIML, IRMAL.

Sidhu, Hina. Factor productivity in the manufacturing sector in Gujarat. *Productivity*. 36, 1, 1995. pp. 86–96. IRMAL, SPUL.

Sidhu, Hina, Growth and structural changes in the manufacturing sector in Gujarat. *Productivity*. 36, 4, 1996. pp. 633–648. HML, IRMAL.

Sidhu, Hina. Growth of micro, small and medium enterprises in Gujarat. *Artha-Vikas*. 48, 2, 2012. pp. 1–18. CSSL.

Sidhu, Hina. Industrial development in Gujarat: inter-district variation. *Indian Journal of Regional Science*. 27, 1 and 2, 1995. pp. 105–126. CSSL, GIDRL.

Sidhu, Hina. Industrial development in the backward region: a case study of Mehsana district in Gujarat. *Journal of Rural Development*. 14, 1, 1995. pp. 1–12. CSSL, GVL, IIML, IRMAL.

Sidhu, Hina. Industrialisation for sustainable development in Gujarat. *Indian Journal of Regional Science*. 41, 2, 2009. pp. 60–72. GIDRL.

Sidhu, Hina. Wage differentials in SSI sector in Gujarat. *Indian Journal of Industrial Relations*. 33, 2, 1997. pp. 211–225. CSSL, GUL, HML, IIML, IRMAL.

Singh, A.P. and Parabia, Minoo. Status of medicinal plants consumption by the pharmaceutical industries in Gujarat state. *Indian Forester*. 129, 2, 2003. pp. 198–212. IIML.

Singh, Baldev. Industrialisation of a backward region: an evaluation of policy instruments: a case study of an Indian district, Surendranagar. *Anvesak*. 7, 2, 1977. pp. 147–162. CSSL, SPIESRL.

Singh, Sukhpal, Narang, Shivani and Annigeri, Gautam V. Agri-business systems study of the Papad industry in Gujarat. *Indian Food Industry*. 20, 6, 2001. pp. 22–25. EDIL, IRMAL.

Sirke, J.M. and Desai, S.D. Origin, occurrence and industrial application of the fireclay deposite, Saurashtra. *Journal of the M.S. University of Baroda*. 25–26, 3, 1976–77. pp. 125–134. GVL.

Soni, K.C. and Jani, B.B. Economies of scale and technical change under cobb-douglas production function for the industrial sectors of Gujarat state as compared to all India. *Vishleshan*. 13, 1, 1987. pp. 27–36. CSSL.

Soni, K.C. and Jani, B.B. VES production function with neutral technological change: a comparative study of the industrial sectors of Gujarat state Vs. all India. *Anvesak*. 17, 2, 1987. pp. 59–75. CEPTL, CSSL, IRMAL, SPIESRL.

Soni, K.C. and Jani, B.B. VES production functions for the industrial sectors of Gujarat state Vs all India. *Decision*. 14, 4, 1987. pp. 199–207. IRMAL.

Spodek, Howard. Traditional culture and entrepreneurship: a case study of Ahmedabad. *Economic and Political Weekly*. 4, 8, 1969. pp. M-27-M-31. CSSL, IRMAL, SPIESRL, UML.

Streefkerk, Hein. Gujarati entrepreneurship: historical continuity against changing perspectives. *Economic and Political Weekly*. 32, 8, 1997. pp. M-2-M-10. CEPTL, CSSL, GIDRL, IIML, IRMAL, MICAL, SGUL, SPIESRL, UML.

Streefkerk, Hein. Industrial entrepreneurship in South Gujarat after two decades: a tentative reappraisal. *Economic and Political Weekly*. 27, 48, 1992. pp. M-130-M-136. CEPTL, CSSL, IIML, IRMAL, SGUL, SPIESRL, UML.

Streefkerk, Hein. Thirty years of industrial labour in South Gujarat: trends and significance. *Economic and Political Weekly*. 36, 26, 2001. pp. 2398–2411. BUL, CEPTL, CSSL, EDIL, GIDRL, IIML, IRMAL, MICAL, SGUL, SPIESRL, UML.

Streefkerk, Hein. Too little to live on, too much to die on: employment in small scale industries in rural South Gujarat. *Economic and Political Weekly*. 16, 15, 1981. pp. 659–668. CSSL, GUL, IRMAL, SGUL, SPIESRL, TRTIL, UML.

Subrahmanian, K.K. and Papola, T.S. Regional differences in profitability and growth: a comparison between Gujarat and Maharashtra firms. *Economic and Political Weekly*. 7, 16, 1972. pp. 811–813. CSSL, IRMAL, SPIESRL, UML.

Thakar, P.H. and Merh, S.C. Wage pattern in major eight industry groups in Gujarat state. *Vishleshan*. 5, 4, 1979. pp. 325–330. CSSL, GIDRL.

Trivedi, A.B. Industrial possibilities in Kathiawar. *Journal of the Gujarat Research Society*. 3, 1, 1941. pp. 31–49. GVL.

Trivedi, A.B. Present industrial growth in Kathiawar with special reference to transport facilities. *Journal of the Gujarat Research Society*. 1, 3, 1939. pp. 37–50. GUL.

Trivedi, A.B. Present industries of Kathiawar. *Journal of the Gujarat Research Society*. 2, 1, 1940. pp. 26–74. GUL, GVL.

Trivedi, A.B. Silk weaving industry of Surat. *Journal of the University of Bombay*. 10, 4, 1942. pp. 105–120. GVL.

Upadhyaya, D.V. Industrial base and specialization in small scale industries with reference to Gujarat state. *Vishleshan*. 13, 1, 1987. pp. 37–44. CSSL, GIDRL.

Vataliya, K.S., Thakkar, Ajay H. and Parmar, Bhavik P. Measuring variances in level of job satisfaction in garment industry by considering key parameters with reference to Bhavnagar city. *International Journal of Development Studies*. 4, 1, 2012. pp. 99–103. BUL.

Veena, D.R. Technological change and employment: experience of Gujarat's manufacturing sector. *Vishleshan*. 2, 3, 1976. pp. 269–276. GIDRL, IIML.

Veena, D.R. and Bhushri, Narendra K. Demographic and social factors affecting the composition of work participation: a study in industrial economy of Gujarat. *Vishleshan*. 7, 1, 1981. pp. 76–81. CSSL, GIDRL.

Vora, A.J. Industrialization in Gujarat: an analysis overtime and space. *Anvesak*. 16, 2, 1986. pp. 85–95. CEPTL, CSSL, GIDRL, IRMAL, SPIESRL.

Vyas, Mohanlal. Industrial peace in Gujarat. *Indian Labour Journal*. 8, 3, 1967. pp. 191–200. GVL, SPUL.

Working Papers, Reports and Other Materials

Alagh, Yoginder K. and Pathak, Pravin G. Industrial development in Gujarat: regional structure and policies. In *Economic development of backward regions problems & prospects. (Proceedings of an all-India seminar on the development of backward regions with special reference to Gujarat)*. Ed. by H.M. Patel, et al. Vallabh Vidyanagar: Sardar Patel University, 1974. pp. 143–184. GIDRL, HML.

Amin, R.B. Industrial development in Gujarat: basic factor. In *Profiles of growing city: socio-economic studies of Baroda city*. Baroda: M.S. University, 1971. pp. 13–20. M.S. University Economics Series No. 1. SPIESRL.

Amin, Raman B. Industrial development in Gujarat: some basic factors. In *Profiles of a growing city: the city of Baroda*. Ed. by K.N. Reddy, et al. Baroda: M.S. University, 1971. pp. 13–19. Souvenir: the 2nd Gujarat economic conference, 2–3 January 1971. CSSL.

Amin, R.K. *Survey of the industrial potential of Kaira district*. Vallabh Vidyanagar: Department of Economics, 1966. p. 135. Studies in economic No. 5. GUL, SPUL.

Arora, Uma. *Some aspects of textile industry in Surat: a note*. Surat: Centre for Social Studies, 1994. p. [ ]. Paper presented at a seminar on 'business, labour and urban growth in Surat city, during 16–17 September 1994. CSSL.

Barik, B.C. *Industrial development and the plight of migrant workers in Surat: a brief reflection on pattern of industrial relations*. Surat: Centre for Social Studies, 1994.

p. [ ]. Paper presented at a seminar on 'business, labour and urban growth in Surat city, during 16–17 September 1994. CSSL.

Bhatt, J.V. *Status report: mineral resources of Gujarat and potentiality of mineral based industries.* Ahmedabad: INDEXTB, 1990. p. 582. IIML.

Bhuva, B.P. *Industrial relations strategies and practices: an in depth study of cement manufacturing units in Gujarat*. Vallabh Vidyanagar: Sardar Patel University, 2007. p. 192. SPUL.

Blankenberg, Floris. *Implementation of windmills in Gujarat, India.* Enschede: Twente Univ of Tech, 1983. p. 70. IRMAL.

Centre for Environmental Planning and Technology. *Impact of new industrial policy of Gujarat government: a forecast for South Gujarat region.* Ahmedabad: Centre for Environmental Planning and Technology, 1978. p. [ ]. SPIESRL.

Cirvante, Suresh R. Prospects of private enterprise industries in Baroda. In *Profiles of a growing city: the city of Baroda.* Ed. by K.N. Reddy, et al. Baroda: M.S. University, 1971. pp. 64–66. Souvenir: the 2nd Gujarat economic conference, 2–3 January 1971. CSSL.

Dahyabhai, Indulal. Industrial development of backward areas in Gujarat. In *Economic development of backward regions problems & prospects. (Proceedings of an all-India seminar on the development of backward regions with special reference to Gujarat).* Ed. by H.M. Patel, et al. Vallabh Vidyanagar: Sardar Patel University, 1974. pp. 240–244. GIDRL, HML.

Das, Biswaroop. *Slums, migrants and the urban informal sector in Surat city.* Surat: Centre for Social Studies, 1994. p. [ ]. Paper presented at a seminar on 'business, labour and urban growth in Surat city, during 16–17 September 1994. Unpublished Paper. CSSL.

Das, Keshab. *Competition and response in small firm clusters: two cases from Western India.* Ahmedabad: Gujarat Institute of Development Research, 2003. p. 22. Working Paper No. 142. CSSL.

Das, Keshab. *Issues in estimating income and employment in informal manufacturing: study of ceramic ware industry in Gujarat*. New Delhi: National Council of Applied Economic Research, 2000. p. 43. CSSL, GIDRL.

Das, Keshab. *Workers and earnings in informal manufacturing: evidence and issues in estimation.* Ahmedabad: Gujarat Institute of Development Research, 2000. p. 32. Working Paper No. 113. CSSL, GIDRL.

Das, Keshabananda. *Collective dynamism and firm strategy: the flooring title cluster in Gujarat, India*. Ahmedabad: Gujarat Institute of Development Research,1996. p. 34. Working Paper No. 76. CSSL, GIDRL, IRMAL.

Das, Keshabananda. *Flexibly together: surviving and growing in a garment cluster, Ahmedabad, India.* Ahmedabad: Gujarat Institute of Development Research, 1996. p. 32. Working Paper No. 79. CSSL, GIDRL.

Desai, Autar S., Ghuman, B.S. and Singh, Surjit. Productivity trends and factor substitutability in manufacturing sector in Gujarat. In *Gujarat economy problems and prospects.* Ed. by D.T. Lakdawala. Ahmedabad: Sardar Patel Institute of Economic & Social Research, 1983. pp. 423–432. Monograph No. 10. GUL, IIML.

Desai, Autar S., Ghuman, B.S. and Singh, Surjit. Productivity trends and factor substitutability in manufacturing sector in Gujarat: implication for planning. In *Seminar on development of Gujarat: problems & prospects, 24th-26th August, 1981.* Ahmedabad: Sardar Patel Institute of Economic & Social Research, 1981. pp. 1–10. CSSL.

Desai, D.K. and Patel, D.A. *Management in seed industry: a case study on hybrid Bajra seed in Gujarat state*. Ahmedabad: Indian Institute of Management, 1968. p. 128. IRMAL.

Desai, Kiran. *Labour union activities in Surat: a case study of Majoor Mahajan Sangh, Surat.* Surat: Centre for Social Studies, 1994. p. [ ]. Paper presented at a seminar on 'business, labour and urban growth in Surat city, during 16–17 September 1994. Unpublished Paper. CSSL.

Desai, Rohit and Dave, Alka K. *Problems of technology oriented industry: study of electronics industry of Gujarat.* Ahmedabad: Sardar Patel Institute of Economic & Social Research, 1992. p. [ ]. GIDRL.

Deseai, Rohit D. *Jari industry: yesterday and today*. Surat: Centre for Social Studies, 1994. p. [ ]. Paper presented at a seminar on 'business, labour and urban growth in Surat city, during 16–17 September 1994. Unpublished Paper. CSSL.

Desai, Rohit D. *Problems of household sector: a study of Jari industry of Surat.* Ahmedabad: Sardar Patel Institute of Economic & Social Research, 1985. p. 142. Unpublished report. CSSL.

Desai, Rohit D. and Shah, Vinod K. Household manufacturing sector in Gujarat. In *Gujarat economy: problem and prospects.* Ed. by D.T. Lakdawala. Ahmedabad: Sardar Patel Institute of Economic & Social Research, 1982. pp. 387–408. GIDRL, GUL.

Desai, Rohit D. and Shah, Vinod K. Household manufacturing sector in Gujarat: a study of its relationship with organised manufacturing sector. In *Seminar on development of Gujarat: problems & prospects, 24th-26th August, 1981.* Ahmedabad: Sardar Patel Institute of Economic & Social Research, 1981. pp. 1–26. CSSL.

Dhesi, Autar S., Ghuman, B.S. and Singh, Surjit. Productivity trends and factor substitutability in manufacturing sector in Gujarat. In *Gujarat economy: problem and prospects.* Ed. by D.T. Lakdawala. Ahmedabad: Sardar Patel Institute of Economic & Social Research, 1982. pp. 423–432. GIDRL.

Dupont, Veronique. *Dyeing and printing industry in Jetpur (Gujarat).* Ahmedabad: Gujarat Institute of Development Research, 1993. p. 57. Working Paper No. 49. CSSL, GIDRL, IRMAL.

Dupont, Veronique. *Impact of in-migration on industrial development in a middle-sized town of Gujarat*. Ahmedabad: Gujarat Institute of Development Research, 1992. p. 33. GIDR Working Paper No. 44. GIDRL, IRMAL.

Elias, Derek. *Impacts and challenges of a large coastal industry: Alang-sosiya ship-breaking yard Gujarat, India*. France: UNESCO, 2004. p. 65. Coastal region and small island papers 17. CSSL.

Erdman, Howard L. Political attitudes of Indian industry: a case study of the Baroda business elite. London: University of London, 1971. p. [ ]. Commonwealth Papers 14. CSSL.

Erdman, Howard L. *Politics and economic development in India: the Gujarat state fertilizers company as a joint sector enterprise*. Delhi: D.K., 1973. p. 148. GIDRL.

Gandhi, R.S., Mehta, Y.C. and Talele, A.B. *Decentralised sector of the Indian textile industry, state-of-the-art report-2*. Ahmedabad: National Information Centre for Textile and Allied Subjects(NICTAS), 1992. p. 152. CSSL.

Gandhi, Vasant P. and Namboodiri, N.V. Cotton revolution in Gujarat: the impact of bt technology. In *Frontiers of agricultural development in Gujarat*. Ed. by Ravindra H. Dholakia. Ahmedabad: Centre for Management in Agriculture, Indian Institute of Management, 2007. pp. 56–76. CMA Publication No. 226. CSSL.

Gokaldas, Premchand. Brief survey of industrial development in Gujarat. In *Small industries conference souvenir special number of Gujarat rajya*. Ahmedabad: Gujarat State Small Industries Federation, [ ]. pp. 70–75. GUL.

Gorter, Pieter. Rise of a new class of industrialists: economic and political network on an industrial estate in West India. In *International seminar on Gujarat society, development and deprivation, 6–9 December 1994*. Surat: Centre for Social Studies, 1994. pp. 1–25. CSSL.

Hashim, S.R. and Singh, Avtar. Perspective on fertiliser industry in Gujarat. In *Gujarat economy: problems and prospects*. Ed. by D.T. Lakdawala. Ahmedabad: Sardar Patel Institute of Economic & Social Research, 1982. pp. 477–492. GIDRL, GUL.

Hashim, S.R., Singh, Avtar and Ramesh, R.A. Perspective on fertiliser and petrochemical industry in Gujarat. In *Seminar on development of Gujarat: problems & prospects, 24th-26th August, 1981*. Ahmedabad: Sardar Patel Institute of Economic & Social Research, 1981. pp. 1–35. CSSL.

Haynes, Douglas E. Artisanal originsof Surat's contemporary industrialization, 1870–1950. In *International seminar on Gujarat society, development and deprivation, 6–9 December 1994*. Surat: Centre for Social Studies, 1994. pp. 1–38. CSSL.

Hirway, Indira and Shah, Amita. *Industrial growth and regional linkages: a study of cement industry in coastal Saurashtra, Gujarat*. Ahmedabad: Centre for Development Alternatives, 2002. p. [ ]. CFDA Working Paper No. 2. GIDRL.

Jaiswal, M.C. Industrial growth of Gujarat state. In *Seminar on development of Gujarat: problems & prospects, 24th-26th August, 1981*. Ahmedabad: Sardar Patel Institute of Economic & Social Research, 1981. pp. 1–35. CSSL.

Jani, V.J. and Pandya, C.G. Status report on working conditions in certain industries. Ahmedabad: Gandhi Labour Institute, 1985. p. 75. CSSL.

Joshi, Vidyut and Dube, H.C. *Sustainable development of Alang and Sosiya ship breaking yard*. Bhavnagar: Bhavnagar University, 2001. p. 138. Unpublished report. CSSL.

Kanwar, Kamlendra. *Icons of Gujarat industry stories of rare grit and enterprise*. Ahmedabad: Harmony, 2000. p. 295. IRMAL.

Kapadia, K.M. and Devadas Pillai, S. *Impact of industrialization on rural social structure: a case study of Atul*. Bombay: University of Bombay, 1969. p. 24. Report. CSSL.

Khurana, Ruchi, Ray, C.N. and Unni, Jeemol. *Change scenario in the garment industry of India: case study of Ahmedabad*. Ahmedabad: CEPT, 2002. p. 26. Working Paper No. 20. CSSL.

Kothari, V.N. Growth potential of Baroda city. In *Profiles of a growing city: the city of Baroda*. Ed. by K.N. Reddy, et al. Baroda: M.S. University, 1971. pp. 115–124. Souvenir: the 2nd Gujarat economic conference, 2–3 January 1971. CSSL.

Lakdawala, D.T., Alagh, Yoginder K. and Sarma, Atul. *Regional variations in industrial development*. Ahmedabad: Sardar Patel Institute of Economic & Social Research, 1974. Various. CSSL.

Lal, R.B. *Impact of industrialization on tribal economy in South Gujarat*. Ahmedabad: Tribal Research & Training Institute, 1976. p. 93. GIDRL.

Lal, R.B. *Modern industry and the tribals: a study of the effects of industrialization on the tribals in South Gujarat*. Ahmedabad: Gujarat Vidyapith, 1982. p. 195. CSSL, TRTIL.

Lalbhai, Kasturbhai. British and growth of the textile industry at Ahmedabad. In *Ahmedabad*. Ahmedabad: Rotary Club, 1940. pp. 31–42. CSSL.

Lalitha, N. *Contribution of the informal sector to the economy*. New Delhi: National Council of Applied Economic Research, 2000. p. 128. CSSL.

Lalitha, N. *Issues in industrial development of Gujarat and policy initiatives by the government of Gujarat*. Ahmedabad: Gujarat Institute of Development Research, 2000. p. 22. Occasional Paper 5. CSSL, GIDRL.

Lalitha, N. *State level reforms to promote industrialisation: a case study of Gujarat*. Ahmedabad: Gujarat Institute of Development Research, 1997. p. 47. Working Paper No. 82. CSSL, GIDRL, IRMAL.

Lalitha, N. and Ramaswami, Bharat. Pesticides use pattern among cotton cultivators in Gujarat. In *Frontiers of agricultural development in Gujarat*. Ed. by Ravindra H. Dholakia. Ahmedabad: Centre for Management in Agriculture, Indian Institute of Management, 2007. pp. 77–98. CMA Publication No. 226. CSSL.

Lalitha, N. and Visalakshi, S. *Status of biopharmaceuticals in India: issues and prospects for growth*. Ahmedabad: Gujarat Institute of Development Research, 2010. p. 114. Report. GIDRL.

Lokanathan, P.S. *Industrial programmes for the fourth plan Gujarat*. New Delhi: National Council of Applied Economic Research, 1996. p. 199. IIML.

Malek, M.A. Note on function and development achieved and envisaged by the Gujarat industrial development corporation. In *Small industries conference souvenir special number of Gujarat rajya*. Ahmedabad: Gujarat State Small Industries Federation, [ ]. pp. 45–49. GUL.

Marvania, P.G. *Ship recycling industry: nature and future: a study based on Alang ship breaking yard*. Rajkot: Foundation for Social Studies, 2004. p. 112. CSSL.

Mehta, B.V. and Bhatt, P.K. Analysis of factors affecting growth of entrepreneurship. In *Gujarat economy: problems and prospects*. Ed. by D.T. Lakdawala. Ahmedabad: Sardar Patel Institute of Economic & Social Research, 1983. pp. 433–440. Monograph Series No. 10. GUL.

Mehta, J.J. Petrochemicals complex near Baroda. In *Profiles of a growing city: the city of Baroda*. Ed. by K.N. Reddy et al. Baroda: M.S. University, 1971. pp. 92–98. Souvenir: the 2nd Gujarat economic conference, 2–3 January 1971. CSSL.

Mehta, P.C. and Gandhi R.S. *Manmade textile industry of Surat*. Surat: Manmade Textile Research Association, 2008. p. 163. CSSL.

Mehta, Shirin. Mhajans and the business communities of Ahmedabad. In *Business communities of India a historical perspective*. Ed. by Dwijendra Tripathi. New Delhi: Manohar, 1984. pp. 173–184. IIMA Monograph in business history 1. IIML.

Misra, Smita. *Measuring benefits from industrial water pollution abatement: use of contingent valuation method in Nandesari industrial area of Gujarat in India*. Delhi: Institute of Economic Growth, 1997. p. 47. Working Paper Series No. E/185/97. CSSL.

Modi, I.A. Industrial scene: challenges and opportunities. In *Gujarat-2010: challenges and opportunities*. By Government of Gujarat. Ahmedabad: Sardar Patel Institute of Economic & Social Research, 2001. pp. 178–182. Seminar volume. CSSL, EDIL, SGUL, SPIESRL.

Modi, S.S. *Development of industries in Saurashtra: a study and the action plan(DISSA)*, Vol. I, II and V. Ahmedabad: Gujarat Industrial and Technical Consultancy Organisation, 1983. p. [ ]. GIDRL.

Moulik, T.K., Basu, S.K. and Patel, M.S. *Rural entrepreneurship: motivations and constraints: a study in Anand taluka, Gujarat*. Ahmedabad: Indian Institute of

Management, 1998. p. 130. CMA Monograph No. 70. CEEL, GIDRL, IIML, IRMAL.

Naik, T.B. and Masavi, Mustali I. *Infrastructural facilities in scheduled castes falias and villages in Gujarat*. Ahmedabad: Tribal Research & Training Institute, Gujarat Vidyapith, 1985. p. 189. TRTIL.

National Council of Applied Economic Research. *Industrial programmes for the fourth plan: Gujarat.* New Delhi: National Council of Applied Economic Research, 1966. p. 199. CSSL, UML.

Odedia, Malderji M. Industrial estates in Gujarat. In *Small industries conference souvenir special number of Gujarat rajya*. Ahmedabad: Gujarat State Small Industries Federation, [ ]. pp. 59–62. GUL.

Ojha, A.K. and Shah, R.J. *Socio-economic effects of industrialization in backward areas: an assessment.* Ahmedabad: INDEXTB, [ ]. p. 332. IIML.

Papola, T.S. and Subrahmanian, K.K. *Wage structure and labour mobility in a local labour market: a study in Ahmedabad*. Ahmedabad: Sardar Patel Institute of Economic & Social Research, 1975. p. 214. Monograph Series 4. CSSL.

Parikh, J.D. Facilities available in Gujarat state for the development of small scale industries. In *Small industries conference souvenir special number of Gujarat rajya*. Ahmedabad: Gujarat State Small Industries Federation, [ ]. pp. 40–44. GUL.

Patel, B.B. *Structure of inter-district inter-sectoral and inter-industry wage differentials in Gujarat.* Baroda: M.S. University, 1985. p. 198. M.S. University Economic Series No. 10. CSSL, IIML.

Patel, Pravin. *Study of class consciousness among the industrial workers of Baroda*. Surat: Centre for Social Studies, 1993. p. [ ]. Seminar on urban poor in India, 10–11 February 1993. unpublished paper. CSSL.

Patel, R.M., et al. *Economics of diary enterprise in Gujarat.* Vallabh Vidyanagar: Agro-Economic Research Centre, 1985. p. 179. GIDRL, IRMAL.

Patel, Sujata. Reexamining some theoretical arguments in "the making of industrial relations". In *International seminar on Gujarat society, development and deprivation, 6–9 December 1994*. Surat: Centre for Social Studies, 1994. pp. 1–21. CSSL.

Patel, Sujata. *Contract labour in textile industry of Ahmedabad.* Ahmedabad: Self Employed Women's Association, 1984. p. 107. CSSL.

Patel, V.G. Industrial health: future of small and medium enterprises in Gujarat. In *Gujarat economy: problems and prospects.* Ed. by D.T. Lakdawala. Ahmedabad: Sardar Patel Institute of Economic & Social Research, 1982. pp. 409–422. GIDRL, GUL, IIML.

Patel, V.G. Industrial health: future of small and medium enterprises in Gujarat. In *Seminar on development of Gujarat: problems & prospects, 24th-26th August, 1981.* Ahmedabad: Sardar Patel Institute of Economic & Social Research, 1981. pp. 1–28. CSSL.

Patel, Veribhai Ambalal. *Agate industry of cambay: a study of the structure and operation of a small industry.* Ahmedabad: Saroj R. Patel, 1992. p. [ ]. SPUL.

Pathak, H.N. Industrial development communications and infrastructure cost of Rajkot Veraval railway line. In *Economy of Saurashtra: problems and prospects*. Ed. by D.T. Lakdawala, et al. Bhavnagar: Bhavnagar University, 1990. pp. 147–151. GUL.

Pathak, H.N. *Problems of smallscale entrepreneurs (Report on a study based on Gujarat).* Bombay: Industrial Development Bank of India, 1975. p. 215. IIML.

Pathak, H.N. and Hermon, Rajender R. Industrialisation in Gujarat: strategic role of smallscale industry. In *Gujarat economy: problems and prospects.* Ed. by D.T. Lakdawala. Ahmedabad: Sardar Patel Institute of Economic & Social Research, 1982. pp. 369–386. GIDRL, GUL, IIML.

Pathak, H.N. and Hermon, Rajender R. Industrialisation in Gujarat: strategic role of small scale industry. In *Seminar on development of Gujarat: problems & prospects, 24th-26th August, 1981.* Ahmedabad: Sardar Patel Institute of Economic & Social Research, 1981. pp. 1–29. CSSL.

Pathak, P.G. Industry. In *Gujarat economy in 2001 A.D.: a study in perspective.* Ahmedabad: Sardar Patel Institute of Economic & Social Research, 1980. pp. 201–252. GUL.

Pathak, Pravin G. Industrial dispersal in Gujarat. In *Gujarat economic association.* Ed. by D.T. Lakdawala and B.B. Patel. Ahmedabad: Gujarat Economic Association, 1981. pp. 63–128. SGUL.

Pathak, Pravin G. Industrial structure in Gujarat: a study in spatial dimension. In *Gujarat economy: problems and prospects.* Ed. by D.T. Lakdawala. Ahmedabad: Sardar Patel Institute of Economic & Social Research, 1982. pp. 441–476. GIDRL, GUL, IIML.

Pathak, Pravin G. and Alagh, Yoginder K. District profiles towards industrial planning in Gujarat. *In Gujarat economic association, conference papers, Baroda.* Ed. by V.S. Vyas, Pravin Visaria and A.R. Deasi. Ahmedabad: Balgovind, 1971. pp. 22–40. GIDRL, IIML.

Pradhan, Debasis. *Understanding promotion mix in rural industries: a study in Gujarat and Rajasthan.* Anand: Indian Institute of Management, 2009. p. [ ]. IRMAL.

Ranade, C.G. and Sah, D.C. *Industrial utilization of cotton stalk: problems and prospets.* Ahmedabad: Indian Institute of Management, 1983. p. 76. CMA Monograph No. 7. CSSL.

Rathod, Jaswantsinh and Vahoniya, Devchandbhai. *Study of industries operated in tribal areas.* Ed. Chandrakant Upadhyaya. Ahmedabad: Tribal Research & Training Institute, Gujarat Vidyapith, 2006. p. 59. Series 416. TRTIL.

Ray, C.N. *Urban informal sector: home based garment workers in Ahmedabad.* Ahmedabad: CEPT University, 2006. p. 26. Working Paper No. 42. CSSL.

Rutton, Mario. Socio-economic profile of rural entrepreneurs and business partnership in Central Gujarat: a case study. In *International seminar on "Gujarat society", 17–20 December 1986.* Surat: Centre for Social Studies, 1986. pp. 1–24. CSSL.

Saurashtra, Government of. *Industries of Saurashtra.* Rajkot: Government of Saurashtra, 1950. p. 104. UML.

Savilani, Hasmukh D. *Industrial relations: an empirical study of the typical construction of Gujarat.* Vallabh Vidyanagar: Sardar Patel University, 1985. p. 61. IRMAL.

Sekhar, R.C. and Rajagopalan, R. *Report on the cost structure of industrial alcohol on Gujarat.* Anand: Institute of Rural Management, 1987. p. 44. IRMAL.

Shah, A. Industrialization and land degradation in Gujarat: evidences and issues. In *National seminar on common property resources and planned development in Western India: challenges and prospects, January 19–21, 1999.* Seminar volume. Nanded: School of Social Sciences and School of Earth Sciences, S.R.T.M. University, 1999. pp. 257–271. CSSL.

Shah, Amita. *Linking industrial growth with rural economy: a case study of Ankleshwar industrial estate in Gujarat.* Ahmedabad: Gujarat Institute of Development Research, 2001. p. 38. Working Paper No. 125. GIDRL, IRMAL.

Shah, Bansilal J. Industrial estates and industrial areas in Gujarat state. In *Small industries conference souvenir special number of Gujarat rajya*. Ahmedabad: Gujarat State Small Industries Federation, [ ]. pp. 63–69. GUL.

Shah, Dilip. Production functions in co-operative dairy industry in Gujarat. In *Seminar on development of Gujarat: problems & prospects, 24th-26th August, 1981*. Ahmedabad: Sardar Patel Institute of Economic & Social Research, 1981. pp. 1–22. CSSL.

Shah, Ghanshyam. *Economy and civic authority in Surat*. Surat: Centre for Social Studies, 1994. p. [ ]. Paper presented at a seminar on 'business, labour and urban growth in Surat city, during 16–17 September 1994. CSSL.

Shah, M.N. Organised manufacturing sector of Baroda district. In *Profiles of a growing city: the city of Baroda*. Ed. by K.N. Reddy et al. Baroda: M.S. University, 1971. pp. 73–82. Souvenir: the 2nd Gujarat economic conference, 2–3 January 1971. CSSL.

Shah, N.R. *Oon: Surat district Gujarat, a village on the periphery of an industrial estate*. Vallabh Vidynagar: Agro-Economic Research Centre, 1968. p. 207. Indian Village Studies No. 13. AERCL, SPUL.

Shah, Narottam. *Some facets of industrial development of Gujarat*. Bombay: Centre for Monitoring Indian Economy, 1979. p. 40. IIML.

Shah, R.J. Problems and prospects of industrial sector in Saurashtra region. In *Economy of Saurashtra: problems and prospects*. Ed. by D.T. Lakdawala, et al. Bhavnagar: Bhavnagar University. 1990. pp. 157–162. GUL.

Shah, R.J. and Ojha, A.K. Gujarat: a decade of industrial development. In *Seminar on development of Gujarat: problems & prospects, 24th-26th August, 1981*. Ahmedabad: Sardar Patel Institute of Economic & Social Research, 1981. pp. 1–24. CSSL.

Shah, Vinod and Desai, Rohit D. Household manufacturing sector in Gujarat. In *Gujarat Economy: problems and prospects*. Ed. by D.T. Lakdawala. Ahmedabad: Sardar Patel Institute of Economic & Social Research, 1983. pp. 387–408. Monograph Series 10. IIML.

Shaw, K.K., Shah, Julie and Desai, Nikhilesh. *SME clusters of Gujarat*. Ahmedabad: Entrepreneurship Development Institute of India (EDI), 2011. p. 124. GIDRL.

Sheth, N.R. Industrial relations in Gujarat. In *Gujarat economy: problems and prospects*. Ed. by D.T. Lakdawala. Ahmedabad: Sardar Patel Institute of Economic & Social Research, 1982. pp. 493–508. GIDRL, GUL, IIML.

Shroff, K.C. Industries in Gujarat: vision 2010. In *Gujarat-2010: challenges and opportunities*. By Government of Gujarat. Ahmedabad: Sardar Patel Institute of Economic & Social Research, 2001. pp. 148–177. Seminar volume. CSSL, EDIL, IRMAL, SGUL, SPIESRL.

Shukla, Ruchira and Dhaduk, B.K. Agro and food processing industry in Gujarat: enablers, constraints and strategic implications. In *Agribusiness potential of Gujarat state(seminar proceeding)2011*. Nagpur: Indian Society of Agricultural Marketing, 2011. pp. 205–217. SPIESRL.

Singh, Avtar and Hashim, S.R. Perspective on fertilizer industry in Gujarat. In *Gujarat economy problems and prospects*. Ed. by D.T. Lakdawala. Ahmedabad: Sardar Patel Institute of Economic & Social Research, 1983. pp. 477–492. Monograph 10. IIML.

Singh, P.N. Entrepreneurial development programme: the Gujarat experience. In *Developing entrepreneurship for economic growth*. New Delhi: Vikas, 1986. pp. 65–69. AIMA-Vikas Management Series. IIML.

Singh, Sukhpal. *Changes in private sector dairy industry after delicensing: a case study of Ahmedabad milk market in Gujarat*. Anand: Institute of Rural Management, 2002. p. 43. IRMAL.

Singh, Sukhpal. Marketing of MIS equipment in India case studies from Gujarat. In *Agricultural machinery industry in India: growth, structure, marketing and buyer behaviour.* New Delhi: Allied, 2010. pp. 151–171. CMA Publication No. 230. IIML.

Srivastava, D.C. *Evaluation of industrial policy for the development of backward regions in India: a case study of Gujarat*. Vallabh Vidyanagar: Sardar Patel University, 1986. p. 230. SPUL.

Tripathi, Dwijendra and Mehta, M.J. Class character of the Gujarati business community. In *Business communities of India a historical perspective.* Ed. by Dwijendra Tripathi. New Delhi: Manohar, 1984. pp. 151–172. IIMA Monograph in business history 1. IIML.

Unni, Jeemol. *Urban informal sector: size and income generation processes in Gujarat part-I.* New Delhi: National Council of Applied Economic Research, 2000. p. 65. CSSL, GIRDL, GVL.

Unni, Jeemol and Bali, Namrata. *Subcontracted women workers in the garment industry in India.* Ahmedabad: Gujarat Institute of Development Research, 2001. p. 44. Working Paper No. 123. CSSL, GIDRL.

Uma Rani and Unni, Jeemol. *Urban informal sector: size and income generation processes in Gujarat part-II.* New Delhi: National Council of Applied Economic Research, 2000. p. 61. CSSL, GIDRL, GVL.

Vadia, B.V. Industrial development of Saurashtra. In *Economy of Saurashtra: problems and prospects*. Ed. by D.T. Lakdawala., et al. Bhavnagar: Bhavnagar University, 1990. pp. 163–174. GUL.

Vyas, Mona and Vyas, Anjana. *"Enquiry in to environmental quality assessment": a case study of Ankleshwar industrial estate.* Ahmedabad: School of Planning, 2000. p. 23. Working Paper 15. CEPTL.

13

Agriculture, Forest and Forestry, Animal Husbandry

Books/Chapter in Books

Acharya, S.S. Production and marketing of pulses in Gujarat with special reference to Panchmahal district. In *Agricultural production, marketing and price policy in India (A case study of pulses)* Delhi: Mittal, 1988. pp. 339–365. GUL, IIML, SPIESRL.

Agarwal, Bina. *Gender and women governance: the political economy of women's presence within and beyond community forestry*. New Delhi: Oxford, 2010. p. 488. CSSL.

Agricultural Finance Corporation. *Integrated watershed development (Plains) project in Gujarat, concurrent evaluation.* Bombay: Agricultural Finance Corporation, 1996. p. 131. SPIESRL.

Agro-Climatic Regional Planning Unit. *Agro-climatic regional planning project: utilisation of waste and marginal lands Kutch region of Gujarat.* Ahmedabad: Agricultural Finance Corporation, 1996. p. 158. SPIESRL.

Alary, Varonique, Degail, Anne-Claire and Riviere, Rachel. Explaining the production of milk in Gujarat and Haryana: a matter of scale. In *Globalization and local development in India: examining the spatial dimension*. Ed. by Frederic Landy and Basudeb Chaudhuri. New Delhi: Manohar, 2004. pp. 199–220. CSSL.

Amin, T.C. and Kapadia, P.R. Pricing policy in cooperative dairy sector in Gujarat. In *Milk pricing and marketing practices of cooperative dairy industry in Gujarat.* Ed. by Dilip Shah. Pune: Maricheenalee, 1987. pp. 109–114. CSSL, HML.

Arya, Anita. *Agricultural marketing in Gujarat*. New Delhi: Concept, 1993. p. 156. AAUL, AERCL, GIDRL, GVL, IRMAL.

Asopa, V.N. and Tripathi, B.L. Water co-operatives for utilization of development and irrigation potential in Gujarat. In *Role of irrigation in the development of India's agriculture.* Bombay: Indian Society of Agricultural Economics, 1976. pp. 59–65. GUL, GVL.

Athavale, R.N. Discovering science behind local innovations and practices: community based water conservation practices in Alwar and Saurashtra. In *Farmer-led participatory research: cases from Western India.* Ed. Astad Pastakia, Brij Kothari and Vijaya Sherry Chand. Bangalore: Books for Change, 2002. pp. 62–75. GIDRL.

Bajpai, Gita. *Agrarian urban economy and social change: the socio-economic profile of select districts of Gujarat*. Delhi: Daya, 1989. p. 198. CSSL, GIDRL, GVL, SPIESRL.

Bapna, S.L. and Rao, K.R. *Supply and price outlook for crops: a study based on preharvest market information in Gujarat.* New Delhi: Oxford, 1987. p. 270. GIDRL, GVL, IIML.

Barmeda, J.N. Agricultural tenancy in Gujarat (1949). In *Dissertation in economics 1921–1971.* Ed. by C.H. Shah. Bombay: University of Bombay, 1974. pp. 8–10. SPIESRL.

Basant, Rakesh and Joshi, Harish. Employment diversification in an agriculturally development region: some evidence from rural Kheda Gujarat. In *Non-agricultural employment in India trends and prospects.* New Delhi: Sage, 1994. pp. 186–221. IIML.

Bhuleshkar, Ashok V. Analysis of production and price trends in pulses with special reference to Gujarat state. In *Indian economic structure and policy.* Ed. by Ashok N. Bhuleskkar and P.G. Mavalankar. Ahmedabad: Dhaval, 1982. pp. 139–145. AAUL, SPIESRL.

Bora, Mamita and Bhalani, Dheeraj. Joint forest management: an experience from Bharuch district, Gujarat. In *Joint forest management and community forestry in India.* Ed. by N.H. Ravindranath, K.S. Murli and K.C. Malhotra. New Delhi: Oxford and IBH, 2000. pp. 121–134. CEEL, CSSL, GIDEL.

Breman, Jan. From Cane fields to court rooms: legal action for and against rural labour in Gujarat, India. In *Capitalist development: critical essays.* Ed. by Ghanshyam Shah. Bombay: Popular, 1990. pp. 270–288. CSSL, IIML.

Charlesworth, Neil. *Peasants and imperial rule: agriculture and agrarian society in the Bombay presidency, 1850–1935.* Cambridge: Cambridge University press, 1985. p. 319. CSSL.

Charlesworth, Neil. Trends in the agricultural performance of an Indian province: Bombay presidency, 1900–1920. In *Economy and society: essays in Indian economic and social history.* Delhi: Oxford, 1979. pp. 113–140. CSSL.

Chauhan, Nikulsingh M. Impact of Krishi Mahotsav 2007 in tot at village level in Gujarat state. In *Extension strategies for agriculture and rural development.* Ed. by Ashok K. Singh. Delhi: Daya, 2010. pp. 204–220. AAUL.

Chauhan, P.M. and Patel, N.C. Sun drying characteristics of groundnut under the drying practices adopted by the farmers of Gujarat. In *Solar drying.* Ed. by A.N. Mathur, Yusuf Ali and R.V. Maheshwari. Udaipur: Himanshu, 1989. pp. 85–91. AAUL.

Chayya, Niranjan C. Recent advances in commercial utilization of Trash fish for edible use in India. In *Fisheries development in India.* U.K. Srivastava and Dharma Reddy. New Delhi: Concept, 1983. pp. 203–210. HML.

Chen, Marty, et al. *Indian women: a study of their role in the dairy movement.* New Delhi: Shakti, 1986. p. 153. CSSL.

Commerce Research Bureau. Profiles of agricultural development in states and Union Territories Gujarat. In *Regional profile of Indian agriculture (Commerce economic studies-XI).* Ed. by Vadilal Dagli. Bombay: Vora, 1974. pp. 61–74. SPIESRL.

Dabadghao, P.M. and Shankarnarayan, K.A. *Grass cover of India. New* Delhi: Indian Council of Agricultural, 1973. p. 713. CEEL.

Dagli, Vadilal. Gujarat. In *Regional profile of Indian agriculture.* Ed. by Vadilal Dagli. Bombay: Vora, 1974. pp. 61–74. CSSL.

Datta, Samar K. Examining Gujarat's success story' in fruits and vegetables. In *High growth trajectory and structural changes in Gujarat agriculture.* Ed. by Ravindra H. Dholakia and Samar K. Datta. New Delhi: Macmillan, 2010. pp. 69–94. AAUL, EDIL, GVL, IIML, IRMAL.

Datta, Samar K. and Desai, Bhupat M. Status and impact of land reforms and new technology on agricultural development. In *Land reforms in India*. Vol. 8. Ed. by Ghanshyam Shah and D.C. Sah. New Delhi: Sage, 2002. pp. 440–463. CSSL, IIML, SETUL, SPUL, UML.

Datta, Samar K. and Kapoor, Sanjeev. *Collective action, leadership and success in agricultural cooperatives: a study of Gujarat and West Bengal*. New Delhi: Oxford, 1986. p. 277. IIML.

Desai, B.M. and Desai, D.K. *Potentialities for mobilizing investible funds in developing agriculture: a study in Baroda district, Gujarat state*. Ahmedabad: Indian Institute of Management, 1971. p. 123. IIML, SPIESRL.

Desai, B.M. and Desai, M.D. *New strategy of agricultural development in operation: a case study of the Kaira district in Gujarat*. Bombay: Thacker, 1969. p. 148. AAUL, IIML, SPIESRL, SPUL.

Desai, D.K. Problems of tribal agriculture in the context of dry farming: a case study of selected villages in the Panchmahal district of Gujarat. In *Management in rural development*. Ed. by D.K. Desai. New Delhi: Oxford, 1983. pp. 1–19. SPIESRL.

Desai, Kiran. Land reforms through people's movements. In *Land reforms in India*. Vol. 8: *performance and challenges in Gujarat and Maharashtra*. Ed. by Ghanshyam Shah and D.C. Sah. New Delhi: Sage, 2002. pp. 319–348. CEEL, CSSL, GIDRL, GVL, HML, IIML, SETUL, SPUL, UML.

Desai, M.B. *Tenancy abolition and the emerging pattern in Gujarat*. Baroda: Author, 1971. p. 194. TRTIL.

Desai, M.B. and Varma, S.K. *Changing farm production and organization in development agriculture: a case study of the developmental effort in agriculture in a district in Gujarat, 1967–72*. Baroda: M.S. University, 1978. p. 501. SPIESRL.

Dholakia, Ravindra H. Has agriculture in Gujarat shifted to high growth path. In *High growth trajectory and structural changes in Gujarat agriculture*. Ed. by Ravindra H. Dholakia and Samar K. Datta. New Delhi: Macmillan, 2010. pp. 1–14. AAUL, EDIL, GVL, IIML, IRMAL.

Dholakia, Ravindra H. and Datta, Samar K., ed. *High growth trajectory and structural changes in Gujarat agriculture*. New Delhi: Macmillan, 2010. p. 174. AAUL, EDIL, GVL, IIML, IRMAL.

Dholakia, Ravindra H., Datta, Samar K. and Sharma, Vijay Paul. Short-term and medium-term prospects of agricultural sector in Gujarat: some policy recommendations. In *High growth trajectory and structural changes in Gujarat agriculture*. Ed. by Ravindra H. Dholakia and Samar K. Datta. New Delhi: Macmillan, 2010. pp. 152–160. AAUL, EDIL, GVL, IIML, IRMAL.

Doornbos, Martin and Nair, K.N. *Resources, institutions and strategies: operation flood and Indian dairying*. New Delhi: Sage, 1990. p. 398. GVL.

Doornbos, Martin, et al. Rural impact studies: methodology and evidence. In *Dairy and development: India's operation flood*. By Martin Doornbos and Frankvan Dorsten. New Delhi: Sage, 1990. pp. 192–287. CSSL, SPUL.

Dubash, Navroz K. *Tubewell capitalism: groundwater development and agrarian change in Gujarat: studies in social ecology and environmental history*. New Delhi: Oxford, 2002. p. 287. CSSL, GIDRL, IIML, IRMAL.

Dudhat, M., et al. Integrated nutrient management for Wheat greengram crop sequence of South Saurashtra region of Gujarat. In *Crop sequence research in Gujarat University*. Ed. by N.M. Patel, et al. Anand: Gujarat Agriculture University, 1997. pp. 12–14. AAUL.

Engineer, Irfan. Struggles of Dangi adivasis for livelihood and land. In *Land reforms in India.* Vol. 8: *performance and challenges in Gujarat and Maharashtra.* Ed. by Ghanshyam Shah and D.C. Sah. New Delhi: Sage, 2002. pp. 295–318. CEEL, CSSL, GIDRL, GVL, HML, IIML, SETUL, SPUL, UML.

Gami, R.C., et al. Zink fertilization for paddy wheat crop sequence in black soil of South Gujarat. In *Crop sequence research in Gujarat agriculture*. Ed. by M.N. Patel, et al. Anand: Gujarat Agriculture University, 1997. pp. 25–27. AAUL.

Gandhi, H.P. *Fresh-water diatoms of Central Gujarat: with a review and some others.* Dehra Dun: Bishen Singh, 1999. p. 324. GIDEL.

Gandhi, Vasant P. and Namboodiri, N.V. Economic and contribution of cotton biotechnology in the agricultural growth of Gujarat. In *High growth trajectory and structural changes in Gujarat agriculture.* Ed. by Ravindra H. Dholakia and Samar K. Datta. New Delhi: Macmillan, 2010. pp. 29–50. AAUL, EDIL, GVL, IIML, IRMAL.

George, Shanti. *Operation flood: an appraisal of current Indian dairy policy.* Delhi: Oxford, 1985. p. 320. CSSL.

Ghosal, S.C. Pardhi of Kutch district: a note on their economy. *In Agrarian situation in India.* Vol. II. Ed. by S.B. Chakrabarti, B.R. Ghosh and Ajit K. Danda. Calcutta: Anthropological Survey of India, 1985. pp. 37–40. CSSL.

Gidwani, Vinay. Labored landscapes: agro-ecological change in Central Gujarat, India. In *Social nature: resources, representations, and rule in India.* Ed. by Arun Agrawal and K. Sivaramakrishnan. New Delhi: Oxford, 2001. pp. 216–247. CSSL.

Gopal Iyer, K. Distribution of government land in Western India. In *Land reforms in India.* Vol. 8. Ed. by Ghanshyam Shah and D.C. Sah. New Delhi: Sage, 2002. pp. 220–244. CEEL, CSSL, GIDRL, GVL, HML, IIML, SETUL, SPUL, UML.

Gopal Iyer, K. Implementation of the land ceiling act in Western India. In *Land reforms in India.* Vol. 8. Ed. by Ghanshyam Shah and D.C. Sah. New Delhi: Sage, 2002. pp. 147–185. CEEL, CSSL, GIDRL, GVL, HML, IIML, SETUL, SPUL, UML.

Gopal Iyer, K. Tenancy reforms in Western India. In *Land reforms in India.* Vol. 8. Ed. by Ghanshyam Shah and D.C. Sah. New Delhi: Sage, 2002. pp. 186–219. CEEL, CSSL, GIDRL, GVL, HML, IIML, SETUL, SPUL, UML.

Gopinath, C., Chary, P.N. and Patel, N.T. *Efficiency of farm irrigation water use in an area irrigation by Wells: a case study in Gujarat state.* Ahmedabad: Indian Institute of Management, 1976. p. 87. CEEL, CSSL, IIML.

Gupta, Dipankar. City connection, Gujarat impact on peasant economy. In *Agrarian structure and peasant revolt in India*. Ed. by Amit Kumar Gupta. New Delhi: Criterion, 1986. pp. 168–184. CSSL, TRTIL.

Hardiman, David. Farming in the forest: the Dangs 1830–1992. In *Village voice, forest choices: joint forest management in India.* Ed. by Mark Poffenberger and Betsy Mcgean. Delhi: Oxford, 1996. pp. 101–131. CEEL, CSSL, SETUL.

Hardiman, David. *Peasant nationalists of Gujarat: Kheda district 1917–1934.* Bombay: Oxford, 1981. p. 309. CSSL, GIDRL.

Heredia, Ruth. *Amul India story*. New Delhi: Tata McGraw-Hill, 1997. p. 297. HML.

Hiremath, B.N., Raju, K.V. and Patel, Anil. Technology adoption and farm management in rural livelihood systems in Gujarat. In *In search of sustainable livelihood systems: managing resources and change*. Ed. by Ruedi Baumgartner and Ruedi Hogger. New Delhi: Sage, 2004. pp. 94–125. CEEL, CSSL, SPUL.

Hogger, Ruedi. Cross-ploughed field. In *In search of sustainable livelihood systems: managing resources and change*. Ed. by Ruedi Baumgartner and Ruedi Hogger. New Delhi: Sage, 2004. pp. 166–182. CEEL, CSSL, SPUL.

Iyengar, S. Common property land resources in Gujarat: some issues in size, status and use. In *Sustainable regeneration of degraded lands.* Ed. by Jyoti Parikh and Sudhakara Reddy. New Delhi: Tata Mcgraw-hill, 1997. pp. 57–80. SPIESRL.

Iyengar, Sudarshan. Common property land resources in Gujarat: some findings about their size, status and use. In *Land reforms in India.* Vol. 8: *performance and challenges in Gujarat and Maharashtra.* Ed. by Ghanshyam Shah and D.C. Sah. New Delhi: Sage, 2002. pp. 464–497. CEEL, CSSL, GIDRL, GVL, HML, IIML, SETUL, SPUL, UML.

Jadav, N.B., Popat, M.N. and Patel, D.V. Entrepreneurial behaviour of mango archard growers in Junagadh district of Gujarat. In *Extension strategies for agriculture and rural development*. Ed. by Ashok K. Singh. Delhi: Daya, 2010. pp. 348–355. AAUL.

Jadav, N.B., et al. Innovative extension strategies for farmer's adoption towards salinity management practices in Coastal area of Western Gujarat. In *Extension strategies for agriculture and rural development*. Ed. by Ashik K. Singh. Delhi: Daya, 2010. pp. 370–381. AAUL.

Jaisani, B.G. Release and popularization of cultivars in Gujarat. In *Seeds of choice: making the most of new varieties for small farmers.* Ed. by John R. Witcombe, Daljit S. Virk and John Farrington. London: Intermediate Technology, 1998. pp. 119–134. IIML.

Jani, Indukumar. Land struggle in the Eastern belt of Gujarat. In *Land reforms in India.* Vol. 8: *performance and challenges in Gujarat and Maharashtra.* Ed. by Ghanshyam Shah and D.C. Sah. New Delhi: Sage, 2002. pp. 349–376. CEEL, CSSL, GIDRL, GVL, HML, IIML, SETUL, SPUL, UML.

Jhala, B.K. Social forestry in tribal areas of Gujarat. In *Social forestry in tribal development*. Ed. by N.N. Vyas. Udaipur: MLV Tribal Research and Training Institute, 1981. pp. 23–29. CSSL.

Joshi, G.N. Gujarat: growth and technological changes in agriculture. In *Agriculture, rural development and Panchayati raj: regional level strategies and policies.* Ed. by V.S. Mahajan. New Delhi: Deep & Deep, 1996. pp. 491–499. AAUL, SPIESRL.

Joshi, G.N. Net resource transfers from agriculture: a study of Gujarat. In *Sectoral growth and change: essays in honour of D.T. Lakadawala.* Ed. by Yoginder K. Alagh, Raghuvir J. Mody and Rohit D. Desai. New Delhi: Har-Anand, 1993. pp. 193–209. CSSL, IIML, SPIESRL.

Joshi, G.N. *Study of resource transfers from agriculture: with special reference to Gujarat.* New Delhi: Commonwealth, 1992. p. 211. CSSL, GIDRL, HML, IIML, SGUL.

Joshi, Himani V. Agricultural sector in Gujarat: performance and prospects. In *Gujarat economy: the way ahead*. Ed. by Sudha V. Menon. Hyderabad: ICFAI University, 2009. pp. 89–98. HML, SPIESRL.

Joshi, Sujan. *Agriculture in Gujarat progress and potential*. Gandhinagar: Helios Enprint, 2000. p. 216. AAUL.

Joshi, V.H. Operation flood: constraints and potentialities in Saurashtra. In *Resources, institutions and strategies*. Ed. by Martin Doornbos and K.N. Nair. New Delhi: Sage, 1990. pp. 97–115. HML.

Joshi, V.R. *Regulated markets in Gujarat.* Nadiad: Kaira District Co-operatives Union, 1971. p. 407. HML, SPIESRL, SPUL.

Kachroo, P. *Outstanding agriculture practices in Madras, Andhra Pradesh, Gujarat & Punjab*. New Delhi: Indian Council of Agriculture Research, 1964. p. 102. AAUL.

Kashyap, S.P. Irrigation induced agricultural growth, occupational diversification and poverty alleviation: experience of a prosperous district in Gujarat. In *Growth, employment and poverty change and continuity in rural India.* Ed. by G.K. Chadha and Alakh N. Sharma. New Delhi: Vikas, 1997. pp. 243–262. IIML.

Kashyap, S.P. *Prospects of 'Gujarat-67' Cotton: as an import substitute.* Ahmedabad: Balgovind, 1969. p. 150. AAUL, GVL, IIML, IRMAL, SGUL.

Kolavalli, Shashi, et al. Joint management in medium irrigation systems in Gujarat: two cases. In *Strategic change in Indian irrigation.* Ed. by Mark Svendsen and Ashok Gulati. New Delhi: Macmillan, 1995. pp. 291–336. SPUL.

Koppa, Gurulingappa G. Public-private partnership for irrigation system management: opportunities and challenges case study of water users cooperatives in Gujarat and Karnataka. In *Public private partnership*. Ed. by Ramesh G. and Vishnuprasad Nagadevara. New Delhi: Routledge, 2010. pp. 282–306. GVL.

Kumar, Ashok. Farm forestry in the tribal tract of Gujarat. In *Trends in tree sciences.* Ed. by P.K. Khosla and R.N. Sehgal. Solan: Indian Society of Tree Scientists, 1988. pp. 35–41. CEEL.

Kurien, V. Development of dairy technology in India. In *Changing scenario in farming practices policies and management*. Ed. by Kalyan Singh Kushwaha. Udaipur: Kushwaha Farm Book Series, 1999. pp. 156–172. AAUL.

Lal, R.B. *Role of minor forest produce in tribal life and culture*. Ahmedabad: Tribal Research and Training Institute, 1986. p. 148. TRTIL.

Lobo, Lancy and Kumar, Shashikant. *Land acquisition, displacement and resettlement in Gujarat: 1947–2004*. Los Angeles: Sage, 2009. p. 303. CSSL, IRMAL, UML.

Luke, A.K. Prosepects of brackish water fish farming in Gujarat. In *Brackish water aquaculture development in India.* Ed. by V.K. Srivastava, B.H. Dholakia and S. Vathsala. New Delhi: Concept, 1987. pp. 59–67. GVL.

Mahadevia, Darshini. Impact of structural adjustment programme on land and water resources of Gujarat: the impact of globalisation. In *Sustainable agriculture and food security.* Ed. by Vandana Shiva and Gitanjali Bedi. New Delhi: Sage, 2002. pp. 121–157. CEEL.

Makwana, N.H. Community forestry development in Gujarat. In *Environment planning and management in India.* Ed. by R.K. Sapru. New Delhi: Ashish, 1990. pp. 81–88. CEEL.

Mann, R.S. Problems of Bhils regarding the forest. In *Indian tribes in transition.* Ed. by N.N. Vyas and R.S. Mann. Jaipur: Rawat, 1980. pp. 113–128. CSSL, SPIESRL.

Mathur, Niti and Kashyap, S.P. Agriculture development in Gujarat: problems and prospects. In *Dynamics of development in Gujarat*. Ed. by Indira Hirway, S.P. Kashyap and Amita Shah. New Delhi: Concept, 2002. pp. 238–267. CSSL, EDIL, GIDRL, GVL, HML, SPUL, UML.

Mehta, Niti. *Development in agriculture: a comparative analysis of the growth components across two states*. New Delhi: Allied, 2011. p. 194. AERCL, CSSL.

Mehta, Niti and Arya, Anita. Krishi rath: an innovative approach, towards rural development. In *Rural development: under decentralized governance*. Ed. by M.R. Biju. New Delhi: Concept, 2012. pp. 346–364. CSSL.

Mehta, Sanatbhai. WTO agreement and agriculture in Gujarat. In *WTO agreement and Indian agriculture hoda, anwarul.* Delhi: Social Science, 2002. pp. 177–192. SPUL.

Mishra, P.K. Managing a programme of seed supply to Gujarat farmers: groundnut seed for 1988 kharif season. In *Public administration in India: case studies*. Ed. by M.C. Gupta and Kamal Nayan Kabra. New Delhi: Gyan, 1999. pp. 131–148. SPUL.

Mishra, R.R. *Effects of land reforms in Saurashtra.* Bombay: Vora, 1961. p. 240. SPIESRL, SPUL.

Mishra, Rudra Narayan. Dairy farming as an option for strengthening livelihoods: a case of poor and landless tribal households. In *Tribal development in Western India*. Ed. by Amita Shah and Jharna Pathak. New Delhi: Routledge, 2014. pp. 202–240. CSSL.

Mitra, Sudipta. *Gir forest and the saga of the Asiatic lion.* New Delhi: Indus, 2005. p. 254. CEEL, CSSL.

Nagabrmam D. Farmers' organisation for irrigation management: some experiences from the Mahi Kadana project. In *India: irrigation management partnerships*. Ed. by M.V.K. Sivamohan. Hyderabad: Booklinks, 1994. pp. 107–121. CSSL.

Naik, D.G. Economics of milk marketing in Gujarat. In *Milk pricing and marketing practices*. Ed. by Dilip Shah. Pune: Maricheemalee, 1987. pp. 253–261. CSSL, HML.

Nanavati, Arti and Patel, B.C. Inter-district vacation in agricultural productivity in Gujarat: 1970–71–1984–85. In *Agriculture, rural development and Panchayati raj: regional level strategies and policies.* Ed. by V.S. Mahajan. New Delhi: Deep & Deep, 1996. pp. 500–528. AAUL, SPIESRL.

Nand, Brahma. Tenures in Gujarat. In *Village communities and land tenures in Western India under colonial rule.* Ed. by Brahma Nand. New Delhi: Manohar, 2009. pp. 149–158. HML, SPUL.

Narayan, Shankar. Joint management of Gir national park. In *People and protected areas: towards participatory conservation in India*. Ed. by Ashish Kothari, Neena Singh and Saloni Suri. New Delhi: Sage, 1996. pp. 212–225. CSSL, SETUL.

Pandey, C.N. and Jethva, Bharat. *Status of vultures in Gujarat: a comprehensive statewide survey of vulture nests and population.* Gandhinagar: Gujarat Ecological Education and Research (Geer) Foundation, 2005. p. 42. CEEL.

Parikh, R.G. Food crops in Gujarat (1948). In *Dissertation in economics 1921–1971.* Ed. by C.H. Shah. Bombay: University of Bombay, 1974. pp. 143–145. SPIESRL.

Parthasarathy, R. Comparing Gujarat with Andhra Pradesh: reforms in irrigation management and people's participation. In *Users in water management: the Andhra model and its replicability in India.* Ed. by Rakesh Hooja, Ganesh Pangare and K.V. Raju. Jaipur: Rawat, 2002. pp. 282–302. SPUL.

Parthasarathy, R. Role of irrigation in the growth story of Gujarat. In *High growth trajectory and structural changes in Gujarat agriculture*. Ed. by R.H. Dholakia and S.K. Datta. Ahmedabad: Indian Institute of Management, 2010. pp. 140–164. AAUL.

Parthasarthy R. Role of irrigation in the growth story of Gujarat. In *High growth trajectory and structural changes in Gujarat agriculture.* Ed. by Ravindra H. Dholakia and Samar K. Datta. New Delhi: Macmillan, 2010. pp. 114–135. AAUL, EDIL, GVL, IIML, IRMAL.

Patel, A.D. Agricultural economics of Borsad taluka (1936). In *Dissertation in economics 1921–1971.* Ed. by C.H. Shah. Bombay: University of Bombay, 1974. pp. 134–137. SPIESRL.

Patel, Bimal, et al. Reforming urban land management in Gujarat. *In India infrastructure report 2009 land: a critical resource for infrastructure.* New Delhi: Oxford, 2009. pp. 176–189. CSSL, IIML.

Patel, Gunwant. *Gujarat's agriculture.* Ahmedabad: Overseas, 1977. p. 363. AAUL, AERCL, HML, SPIESRL, SUL, TRTIL.

Patel, K.N. and Gulati, O.T. Farmers' participation from micro to macro: the Anklav subminor in the Mahi project, Gujarat. In *India: irrigation management partnerships*. Ed. by M.V.K. Sivamohan. Hyderabad: Booklinks, 1994. pp. 123–139. CSSL.

Patel, Mohan. Agricultural development and environment: a case study of Kutch. In *Economic reforms and development*. Ed. by Raj Kumar Sen. New Delhi: Deep & Deep, 2003. pp. 73–79. HML.

Patel, S.M. et al. *Impact of the milk cooperatives in Gujarat*. Allahabad: United, 1977. p. 191. IRMAL.

Patel, U.M., Patel, D.B. and Shekh, A.M. *Comprehensive district agricultural plan (C-DAP): Panchamal district.* Anand: Anand Agricultural University, 2013. p. 182. AAUL.

Pathak, Jharna. Agroforestry in tribal areas: moving towards sustainable agriculture?. In *Tribal development in Western India*. Ed. by Amita Shah and Jharna Pathak. New Delhi: Routledge, 2014. pp. 161–201. CSSL.

Pathak, Mahesh and Shah, V.D. Five decades of Gujarat agriculture: some replications. In *High growth trajectory and structural changes in Gujarat agriculture.* Ed. by Ravindra H. Dholakia and Samar K. Datta. New Delhi: Macmillan, 2010. pp. 15–28. AAUL, EDIL, GVL, IIML, IRMAL.

Pathak, Mahesh and Singh, P.K. Gujarat's agriculture and the Sardar Sarovar Project. In *Gujarat: perspectives of the future*. Ed. by R. Swaminathan. New Delhi: Academic, 2008. pp. 333–357. CSSL, EDIL, GIDRL, GVL, IIML, IRMAL, SETUL, SPIESRL.

Pathak, Mahesh T., Desai, Mahendra D. and Charan, A.S. Development of agriculture in the backward regions of Gujarat: facts and issues. In *Economic development of backward regions problems and prospects.* Ed. by H.M. Patel, V.S. Vyas and M.T. Pathak. Vallabh Vidyanagar: Sardar Patel University, 1974. pp. 100–138. GVL.

Pathak, Mahesh T., Desai, Mahendra D. and Patel, Haribhai F. *Agricultural development in Gujarat.* Anand: Sardar patel University, 1979. p. 308. SPIESRL.

Pawar, J.R. Tribal agriculture in Northern Gujarat. In *Agro-economic problems of tribal India.* Ed. by M.L. Patel. Bhopal: Progress, 1972. pp. 54–64. CSSL, GUL, GVL, HML, SPIESRL, SPUL.

Punalekar, S.P. Gender market segmentation and marginalization in urban Gujarat. In *Social work practice religion philosophical foundations*. Ed. by Chhaya Patel. Jaipur: Rawat, 1999. pp. 276–310. CSSL.

Ranade, C.G., et al. *Performance of integrated milk co-operatives: a study of selected co-operative dairies in Gujarat and Maharashtra*. New Delhi: Concept, 1988. p. 139. HML.

Randhawa, M.S. et al. *Farmers of India: Madhya Pradesh, Rajasthan, Gujarat, Maharashtra.* Vol. 4. New Delhi: Indian Council of Agricultural Research, 1968. pp. 165–248. AERCL, SPIESRL.

Rastogi, S.K. and Dholakia, R.H. Linkages of agricultural exports and infrastructure development in Gujarat. In *High growth trajectory and structural changes in Gujarat agriculture*. Ed. by R.H. Dholakia and S.K. Datta. Ahmedabad: Indian Institute of Management, 2010. pp. 167–187. AAUL.

Rastogi, Siddhartha K. and Dholakia, Ravindra. Linkages of agricultural exports and infrastructure development in Gujarat. In *High growth trajectory and structural changes in Gujarat agriculture.* Ed. by Ravindra H. Dholakia and Samar K. Datta. New Delhi: Macmillan, 2010. pp. 136–151. AAUL, EDIL, GVL, IIML, IRMAL.

Rizvi, S.M.H. and Bhatt, D.A. Impact of hybrid cotton on the cropping pattern of Amod taluka, district Bharuch (Gujarat). In *Geography and rural development.* Ed. by R.N.P. Sinha. New Delhi: Concept, 1992. pp. 81–96. GVL.

Row, S.V.L.N. Agricultural taxation in Gujarat. In *Tax structure and economic development in India.* Ed. by M.L. Kantha Rao. New Delhi: Criterion, 1989. pp. 136–155. GVL, SPIESRL.

Roy, Ramashray. *Bureaucracy and development: case study of Indian agriculture.* New Delhi: Manas, 1975. p. 176. CSSL.

Rutten, Mario. Access of big farmers to land and agricultural trade in Central Gujarat. In *Capitalist development: critical essays.* Ed. by Ghanshyam Shah. Bombay: Popular, 1990. pp. 230–252. CSSL, IIML.

Sah, D.C. Crop commercialization and migration: evidences from Sardar Sarovar Project. In *Land reforms in India.* Vol. 8: *performance and challenges in Gujarat and Maharashtra.* Ed. by Ghanshyam Shah and D.C. Sah. New Delhi: Sage, 2002. pp. 404–439. CEEL, CSSL, GIDRL, GVL, HML, IIML, SETUL, SPUL, UML.

Sah, D.C. Livelihood struggle: agriculture in tribal Gujarat. In *Tribal issues in India.* Ed. by D.C. Sah and Yatindra Singh Sisodia. Jaipur: Rawat, 2004. pp. 39–57. CEEL, CSSL, GVL, HML, TRTIL.

Samvatsar, Swati and Diwanji, V.B. *Floral diversity assessment & conservation: with reference to Sardar Sarovar Project.* Dehra Dun: Bishen Singh, 2007. p. 670. GIDEL.

Sardar Patel University. *Some aspects of long term agricultural finance: a study of two areas in Gujarat.* Vallabh Vidyanagar: Sardar Patel University, 1969. p. 222. GVL.

Sarin, Madhu and Khanna, Renu. Women organise for wasteland development: a case study of SARTHI in Gujarat. In *Women and wasteland development in India.* Ed. by Andrea M. Singh and Neera Burra. New Delhi: Sage, 1993. pp. 129–172. CSSL, GVL.

Satish, S. and Sundar, A. *People's participation and irrigation management.* New Delhi: Commonwealth, 1990. pp. 9–42. CEEL.

Saxton, W.T. *Plants of Northern Gujarat.* Dehra Dun: Bishen Singh, 1978. p. 115. GIDEL.

Saxton, W.T. and Sedgwick, L.J. *Plants of Northern Gujarat.* Calcutta: Superintendent printing, 1916. p. 323. SPIESRL.

Sen, Sucharita and Mallik, Chinmoyee. Understanding Gujarat's agricultural growth in a liberalizing environment: signs of a redefined margin?. In *Poverty amidst prosperity: essays on the trajectory of development in Gujarat.* Ed. by Atul Sood. Delhi: Aakar, 2012. pp. 88–127. CSSL, IRMAL, MICAL.

Shah, Amita and Pattnaik, Itishree. High growth agriculture in Gujarat: an enquiry into inclusiveness and sustainability. In *Growth or development: which way is Gujarat going?* Ed. by Indira Hirway, Amita Shah and Ghanshyam Shah. New Delhi: Oxford, 2014. pp. 225–269. CSSL.

Shah, C.H., Shah, Vimal and Iyengar, Sudarshan. *Agricultural growth and equity: a micro-level experience.* New Delhi: Concept, 1991. p. 235. CSSL, GIDRL.

Shah, D.R. *Economic analysis of Cooperative dairy farming in Gujarat.* Bombay: Somaiya, 1985. p. 169. IRMAL, TRTIL.

Shah, Dilip. Milk pricing: a case study of urban co-operative dairy of Baroda. In *Milk pricing and marketing practices of cooperative dairy industry in Gujarat.* Ed. by Dilip Shah. Pune: Maricheemalee, 1987. pp. 115–132. CSSL, HML.

Shah, Dilip. Performance and problems of Gujarat cooperative milk marketing federation. In *Milk pricing and marketing practices of cooperative dairy industry in Gujarat.* Ed. by Dilip Shah. Pune: Maricheenalee, 1987. pp. 180–212. CSSL, HML.

Shah, Dilip. Rural energy system and agriculture: alternative scenarios for Gujarat. In *Random reflections on rural-development.* Jaipur: ABD, 2012. pp. 91–122. CEPTL.

Shah, Dilip. Social forestry: an approach to sustainable rural development: an experience of Gujarat. In *Random reflections on rural development.* Jaipur: ABD, 2012. pp. 280–292. CEPTL.

Shah, Dilip, ed. *Milk pricing and marketing practices of cooperative dairy industry in Gujarat.* Pune: Maricheemalee, 1987. p. 286. CSSL, HML.

Shah, Ghanshyam. Caste and land reforms in Gujarat. In *Land reforms in India.* Vol. 8: *performance and challenges in Gujarat and Maharashtra.* Ed. by Ghanshyam Shah and D.C. Sah. New Delhi: Sage, 2002. pp. 127–143. CEEL, CSSL, GIDRL, GVL, HML, IIML, SETUL, SPUL, UML.

Shah, Ghanshyam and Sah, D.C., ed. *Land reforms in India.* Vol. 8: *performance and challenges in Gujarat and Maharashtra.* New Delhi: Sage, 2002. p. 520. CEEL, CSSL, GIDRL, GVL, HML, IIML, SETUL, SPUL, UML.

Shah, J.M. Mechanism of pricing policies. In *Milk pricing and marketing practices of cooperative dairy industry in Gujarat.* Ed. by Dilip Shah. Pune: Maricheenalee, 1987. pp. 35–45. CSSL, HML.

Shah, M.P. Aphids in Gujarat. In *Oilseed production: constraints and opportunities.* Ed. by H.C. Srivastava and S. Bhaskaran. New Delhi: Oxford and IBH, 1985. pp. 423–426. IIML, SPIESRL.

Shah, Parmesh and Mane, P.M. Participatory-approaches to agricultural training-Aga Khan Rural Support Programme (India) AKRSP, Ahmedabad, Gujarat. In *Sustainable agriculture: NGOs, GOs and the rural poor.* Ed. by John Farrington and S. Satish. Hyderabad: Booklinks, 1995. pp. 122–164. CSSL.

Shah, Tushaar. Farmer organistion for lift irrigation: irrigation companies and tubewell co-operatives of Gujarat. In *Catalysing co-operation: design of self-governing organisations.* New Delhi: Sage, 1996. pp. 121–147. CSSL, IIML.

Shah, Tushaar. Transforming ground water markets in to powerful instruments of small farmer development: lessons from Punjab, Uttar Pradesh and Gujarat. In *Alternatives in rural developments.* Ed. by D.R. Shah. New Delhi: Sterling, 1990. pp. 197–242. AAUL, GVL, HML, TRTIL.

Shah, Tushar and Bhattacharya, Saumindra. Farmer organisation for lift irrigation: companies and tubewell cooperatives of Gujarat. In *Cooperative management of natural resources.* Ed. by Katar Singh and Vishwa Ballabh. New Delhi: Sage, 1996. pp. 156–175. AAUL, CSSL, GVL, HML, IIML.

Shah, U.M. Crop insurance in Gujarat. In *Crop insurance in India.* Ed. by S.L. Tripathi and C. Dinesh. Pune: Vaikunth Mehta National Institute of Cooperative Management, 1987. pp. 79–86. GVL, HML.

Shah, V.D. Rapid assessment of impact of NWDPRA in Gujarat. In *Glimpses of Indian agriculture: macro and micro aspect.* Ed. by R.S. Deshpande, et al. New Delhi: Academic, 2008. pp. 431–440. HML, IIML.

Shah, V.M. Crop insurance in Gujarat. In *Crop insurance in India.* Ed. by S.L. Tripathi and C. Dinesh. Pune: Vaikunth Mehta National Institute of Crops, 1987. pp. 79–87. GVL.

Sharan, Girija, ed. *Energy use in rural Gujarat.* Calcutta: Oxford and IBH, 1987. p. 186. GIDRL.

Sharma, Kailash, Ballabh, Vishwa and Pandey, Ajay. Analysis of farm forestry in Gujarat. In *Farm forestry in South Asia*. Ed. by N.C. Saxena and Vishwa Ballabh. New Delhi: Sage, 1995. pp. 277–296. CSSL, TRTIL.

Sharma, Usha. Problems and prospects of agricultural development in Saurashtra region. In *Economy of Saurashtra: problems and prospects*. Ed. by D.T. Lakdawala, et al. Bhavnagar: Bhavnagar University, 1990. pp. 70–74. GUL.

Sharma, Ushaben. *Analysis of course cereal prices in Gujarat.* Ahmedabad: Sardar Patel institute of economic & social research, 1980. p. 113. SPIESRL.

Sharma, Vijay Paul and Thaker, Hrima. Livestock development in Gujarat in 2000s: an assessment. In *High growth trajectory and structural changes in Gujarat agriculture.* Ed. by Ravindra H. Dholakia and Samar K. Datta. New Delhi: Macmillan, 2010. pp. 95–113. AAUL, EDIL, GVL, IIML, IRMAL.

Shashidharn, E.M. Civil society, organisation and irrigation management in Gujarat, India. In *Water for food and rural development*. Ed. by Peter P. Mollinga. New Delhi: Sage, 2000. pp. 247–265. HML.

Shelat, Kirit N. *What ails our agriculture?. the Gujarat experience.* Ahmedabad: Shree Bhagwati, 2007. p. 171. AAUL, AERCL, SPIESRL.

Shiyani, R.L. and Pandya, R.H. Sustainable relationship between forest and agriculture: a case of the Gir wildlife santuary. In *Sustainable development and earthcare*. Ed. by K.V. Sundaram, Mrityunjay Jha and P.S. Tiwari. New Delhi: Concept, 2009. pp. 73–89. HML.

Shrimal, Mohan Lall. Saurastra land reforms. In *Land reforms promise and performance*. New Delhi: Metropolitan, 1985. pp. 78–87. HML, IIML.

Shukla, Rohit. *Forest and tribal life: study of a micro-region: socio-cultural traits sustaining tribal ecology, a case study of Danta taluka, Banaskantha district, North Gujarat*. New Delhi: Concept, 1990. p. 141. IRMAL.

Siddiqi, Idris M., Khan, L.U. and Mohmmad Ali. Agriculture in Western states: Gujarat. In *Agricultural Development in India: an analytical state-wise study.* Bombay: Popular, 1989. pp. 114–120. GUL, IIML, SPUL.

Singh, Bhanwar. *Agrarian structure, technological change and poverty: microlevel evidence*. New Delhi: Agricole, 1985. p. 259. CSSL, SPIESRL.

Singh, Giriraj, et al. Forest protection by "Jungle Bachao Groups" in Panchmahals district, Gujarat. In *Joint forest management and community forestry in India: an ecological and institutional assessment.* Ed. by N.H. Ravindranath, K.S. Murali and K.C. Malhotra. New Delhi: Oxford, 2000. pp. 135–149. CEEL, CSSL, GIDEL.

Singh, H.S. *Gir Lion.* Ahmedabad: Pugmark Qmulus Consortium, 2007. p. 320. CEEL.

Singh, R.S. and Shah, K.P. Scope of farm machineries and equipment based agri-business activities in Gujarat. In *Agribusiness potential of Gujarat state (seminar proceedings) 2011*. Nagpur: Indian Society of Agricultural Marketing, 2011. pp 154–171. SPIESRL.

Singh, Sukhpal. High value crops and Gujarat's agricultural growth: cases of castor and psyllium (ISABGOL). In *High growth trajectory and structural changes in Gujarat agriculture.* Ed. by Ravindra H. Dholakia and Samar K. Datta. New Delhi: Macmillan, 2010. pp. 51–68. AAUL, EDIL, GVL, IIML, IRMAL.

Sinha, Shailendra. Gujarat: a forest poor state. In *Social forestry and tribal development*. Ed. by Desh Bandhu and R.K. Garg. New Delhi: Indian Environmental Society, 1986. pp. 70–79. CSSL.

Skutsch, Margaret M. Success of mixed motives: stove and forestry programmes in Gujarat. In *Managing rural development.* Ed. by Hein Streefkerk and T.K. Moulik. New Delhi: Sage, 1991. pp. 191–208. CSSL, SPIESRL.

Srivastava, R.L., Arya, Ranjana and Tewari, V.P. Potential of Jatropha cultivation in arid and semi-arid areas of Rajasthan and Gujarat. In *Resource management towards sustainable agriculture and development.* Ed. by R.K. Behl, J. Kubat and T. Kleynhans. Jodhpur: Agroblos, 2010. pp. 243–252. AAUL.

Sundar, Nandini, Jeffery, Roger and Thin, Neil. *Branching out: joint forest management in India.* New Delhi: Oxford, 2001. p. 289. CSSL.

Thakkar, Ramesh. Flying beauty. In *Art, culture and natural history of Kutch.* Ed. by S.K. Bhowmik. Vadodara: Government Press, 1976–77. pp. 126–129. CSSL, TRTIL.

Thakore, G.D. Agricultural credit through co-operatives. In *Winners and losers: styles of development and change in an Indian region.* Ed. by S. Devadas Pillai and Chris Baks. Bombay: Popular, 1979. pp. 380–386. CSSL, HML, SPIESRL.

Vadodaria, M.P., Maisuria, I.M. and Patel, J.R. Integrated management of cotton bollworms in Gujarat. In *Ecological agricultural and sustain-able development.* Vol. 2. Ed. by G.S. Dhaliwal and N.S. Randhawa. Chandigarh: Center for Research in Rural & Industrial Development, 1998. pp. 281–285. SPIESRL.

Vaishnav, M.N. Role of social forestry in the rural development of Gujarat. In *Geography and rural development.* Ed. by R.N.P. Sinha. New Delhi: Concept, 1992. pp. 113–118. GVL.

Vaishnav, M.N. Social forestry in rann of Katchh. In *Social forestry for rural development.* Ed. by P.K. Khosla and R.K. Kohli. Solan: Indian Society of Tree Scientist, 1988. pp. 40–46. CEEL.

Valentina, G. Market infrastructure for small and marginal farmers: a case of Rajkot district Gujarat. In *Rural resources and development initiatives.* Ed. by B.S. Vasudeva Rao and G. Rajanikanth. India: Associated, 2007. pp. 304–341. HML.

Van, Dorsten F. Impact of Amul on the milk economy of the Kheda district. In *Resources institutions and strategies.* Ed. by Martin Doornbos and K.N. Nair. New Delhi: Sage, 1990. pp. 57–76. HML.

Wadhva, Kiran. Land market in urban fringe areas: a case study of Ahmedabad. In *Urban fringe land markets on economic analysis.* New Delhi: Concept, 1983. pp. 110–186. HML.

Weber, Steven A. *Plants and Harappan subsistence: an example of stability and change from Rojdi.* New Delhi: Oxford and IBH, 1991. p. 200. GIDEL.

Journal Articles

Acharya, B.V. Mechanisation and agricultural production trends in Gujarat. *South Gujarat University Journal.* 5, 1976. pp. 129–133. GVL.

Acharya, B.V. and Pandya, Kiran. Inter district variations of agricultural production, productivity and area in Gujarat state. *Anvesak.* 21, 2, 1991. pp. 113–127. CEPTL, CSSL, IRMAL, SPIESRL.

Acharya, S., Patel, J.B. and Tikka, B.S. Commercial exploitation of heterosis through cytoplasmic genetic male sterility system in pigeon pea-Gujarat tur hybrid–1. *Gujarat Agricultural University Research Journal.* 33, 1–2, 2008. pp. 12–20. AAUL.

Adhvaryu, J.H., Patel, Arun S. and Patel, H.F. Environmental impact of Dantiwada irrigation project in Gujarat. *Artha-Vikas*. 18, 1 and 2, 1982. pp. 30–44. CSSL, GIDRL, GVL, HML.

Agrawal, Nand Kishor. From deficit to surplus fodder and fuel success in Sakwa village in South Gujarat. *Wastelands News*. 14, 3, 1999. pp. 43–44. IRMAL.

Agrawal, S.B., et al. Marketed surplus of milk in different agro-climatic zones of Gujarat and Maharashtra. *Indian Journal of Dairy Science*. 62, 1, 2009. pp. 43–47. AAUL, IRMAL.

Agro-Economic Research Centre. Flow of credit to small and marginal framer's in Gujarat: a case study in Panchmahals district. *Agricultural Situation in India*. 60, 4, 2003. pp. 197–201. EDIL, IIML, SPIESRL.

Agro-Economic Research Centre. Production and marketing of mangoes in Gujarat. *Agricultural Situation in India*. 39, 12, 1985. pp. 949–952. SPIESRL.

Agro-Economic Research Centre. Returns to bt. cotton vis-à-vis traditional cotton varieties in Gujarat state. *Agricultural Situation in India*. 66, 2, 2008. pp. 89–94. IIML, SGUL, SPIESRL.

Agro-Economic Research Centre. Review of state agricultural policy in Gujarat. *Agricultural Situation in India*. 61, 5, 2004. pp. [ ]. SPIESRL.

Akula, Baby, Shekh, A.M. and Parmar, R.S. Estimation of variability in Wheat production levels in middle Gujarat using simulation model. *Journal of Agrometeorology*. 7, 2, 2005. pp. 208–213. IRMAL.

Ambegaoker, K.N. Baroda cotton act and its scientific implication. *Rural India*. 4, 6, 1941. pp. 293–294. SGUL.

Amin, H.D., Telang, B.M. and Singh, J.D. Good future for date-palm cultivation in Gujarat. *Indian Farming*. 26, 1, 1976. pp. 7–10. GVL, SGUL.

Ant Ram and Ashok Kumar. Trends and acreage response of groundnut in Gujarat. *Anvesak*. 20, 1–2, 1990. pp. 135-[ ]. SPIESRL.

Arora, S.P. Status of sodium and potassium and N.S. ratio in different feeds and fodders of Kaira district of Gujarat. *Indian Journal of Dairy Science*. 56, 3, 2003. pp. 182–184. AAUL.

Arya, Anita. Agro-processing in Gujarat: role of contract farming and co-operatives. *Anvesak*. 35, 2, 2005. pp. 17–28. CSSL, GIDRL, SPIESRL.

Arya, Anita. Extent of competitiveness in regulated markets of Kheda district. *Anvesak*. 21, 2, 1991. pp. 129–143. CEPTL, CSSL, SPIESRL.

Arya, Anita. Groundnut marketing in Gujarat. *Indian Journal of Agricultural Marketing*. 8, 1, 1994. pp. 54–60. AAUL, IRMAL.

Arya, Anita. Spatial integration of regulated markets in Kheda district of Gujarat. *Indian Journal of Agricultural Marketing*. 5, 2, 1991. pp. 207–209. AAUL.

Arya, Anita. Stability of agricultural prices in Gujarat. *Anvesak*. 21, 1, 1991. pp. 109–124. CEPTL, CSSL, IRMAL, SPIESRL.

Ashwar, B.K., Jacob, Ninan and Soni, M.C. Attitude of dairy farmers towards dairy farming in North Gujarat. *Indian Journal of Dairy Science*. 64, 2, 2011. pp. 168–175. AAUL, IRMAL.

Babaria, C.H. Economic feasibility of irrigated fodder crops versus high yielding crops in Gujarat. *Artha-Vikas*. 10, 1, 1974. pp. 93-[ ]. HML.

Badreshia, R.L. and Patel, P.G. Studies on split application of nitrogen to hybrid maize in summer season under South Gujarat conditions. *Gujarat Agricultural University Research Journal*. 12, 2, 1987. pp. 48–49. AAUL, GVL.

Bagdi, G.L, Samra, J.S. and Kumar, V. Adoption of soil and water conservation technologies by the farmers of Sardar Sarovar Project catchment in Gujarat State. *Indian Journal of Soil Conservation*. 29, 1, 2001. pp. 65-[ ]. GIDRL.

Bagi, A.S. and Vyas, K.N. Morphology of the skin of Surati buffalo as compared to that of the other breeds of the buffalo and the Ok and its role in the moregulation. *Gujarat Agricultural University Research Journal.* 9, 1, 1983. pp. 52–56. AAUL, GVL.

Bagle, B.G. and Singh, A.K. Knowledge and adoption of ber cultivation in Panchmahals District of Gujarat. *Rural India*, 66, 12, 2003. pp. 248-[ ]. SGUL.

Bahudur, Rai and Kavi, D. Land problems of Gujarat. *Indian Journal of Agricultural Economics*. 3, 1, 1948, pp. 27–40. SGUL.

Bajpai, Gita. Problems of agrarian economy in the Baroda state. *Journal of the M.S. University of Baroda*. 24, 1, 1975. pp. 73–82. GVL.

Balooni, Kulbhushan and Singh, Katar. Role of non-governmental organisations in promoting social forestry in Gujarat. *Journal of Tropical Forestry*. 10, 1, 1994. pp. 8–18. IRMAL.

Bandhanial, K.A., Patel, B.K. and Jadeja, G.C. Estimation of avoidable losses in wagad cotton (gossypium hirsutam) in Gujarat. *Gujarat Agricultural University Research Journal.* 18, 2, 1993. pp. 126–127. GVL.

Bapat, M.T. Bovine population of Gujarat. *Khadi Gramodyog*. 18, 5, 1972. pp. 324–331. GVL, SGUL, TRTIL.

Bapat, M.T. and Purohit, S.D. Working of small farmers development agency in state of Gujarat and Rajasthan. *Artha-Vikas*. 21, 1–2, 1985. pp. 42–55. AAUL, GIDRL, GVL, HML.

Barmeda, J.N. Agrarian classes and the growth of tenancy in Gujarat. *Indian Journal of Agricultural Economics*. 6, 2, 1951. pp. 78–103. IIML, UML.

Barwe, V.K., Dhingra, M.M. and Tomar, S.S. Factors affecting age at first calving and its genetic and phenotypic relationships with other reproductive traits in Gir Cows. *Indian Journal of Dairy Science*. 49, 2, 1996, pp. 100–104. AAUL.

Bhaiya, Shantilal R. Escalation cultivation cost over a decade: a case study of Paddy cultivation in Gujarat. *Vishleshan.* 35, 4, 2010. pp. 30–40. CSSL, IIML.

Bhaiya, Shantilal R. and Chauhan, D.J. Economics of area, production and yield of Rice in Gujarat: district wise analysis. *Artha-Vikas*. 47, 2, 2011. pp. 55–72. CSSL.

Bhaiya, Shantilal R. and Chauhan, D.J. Economics of Paddy cultivation in Gujarat. *Artha-Vikas*. 46, 1, 2010, pp. 1–16. CSSL.

Bhalala, M.K., Jetani, K.L. and Zofair, S.M. SWOT analysis of Sakhi mandals operating in Banaskantha district of North Gujarat. *Gujarat Agricultural University Research Journal.* 36, 2, 2011, pp. 137–138. AAUL.

Bhalani, P.A. Biology and seasonal incidence of cauliflower head borer, hellula undalis fabricius under Junagadh (Gujarat state) condition. *Gujarat Agricultural University Research Journal.* 9, 2, 1984. pp. 63–66. AAUL, GVL.

Bhalani, P.A. and Parsana, G.J. Estimation of losses due to pod fly, melanagromyza obtusa malloch in pigeonpea under Junagadh (Gujarat) condition. *Gujarat Agricultural University Research Journal.* 17, 1, 1991. pp. 49–53. GVL.

Bhandari, M.C. Credit support for integrated rural development programme: a case study of Surat and Panchmahals districts. *Indian Journal of Agricultural Economics*. 39, 3, 1984. pp. 276–282. AAUL, CSSL, GIDRL, HML, IIML, TRTIL, UML.

Bhangale, P.B., et al. Study of effects of some climatic factors on physiological responses in Gir and crossbred lactating Cows. *Indian Dairyman*. 43, 3, 1990, pp. 282–286. AAUL.

Bharodia, R.K. and Talati, G.M. Seasonal incidence of tetranychus neocaledonicus andre in Gujarat state. *Gujarat Agricultural University Research Journal.* 10, 1, 1984. pp. 64–65. AAUL, GVL.

Bharpoda, T.M., Patel, H.P. and Patel, J.J. Evaluation of economic threshold levels for helicoverpa armigrea 'H 6' cotton (gossypium hirsutum) in Central Gujarat region. *Indian Journal of Agricultural Science*. 69, 4, 1999. pp. 304–305. GVL.

Bhatia, Bela. Official drought relief measures: a case study of Gujarat. *Social Action*. 38, 2, 1988. pp. 138–161. CSSL.

Bhat, S.S. Vegetable growing in Baroda. *Rural India*. 6, 9, 1943, pp. 361–373. SGUL.

Bhatt, Sonal. Household milk producers' economy in Gujarat: a case study of Valasan village of Anand district in Gujarat. *Indian Dairyman*. 60, 12, 2008, pp. 59–65. AAUL, IRMAL, SGUL.

Bhatt, Sonal. Impact of agricultural extension on farmers: a study of Krishi Mahotsav in Dehevi village of Central Gujarat. *Agricultural Situation in India.* 67, 12, 2011. pp. 699–712. IIML.

Bhatt, Sonal. Nature of agricultural land lease contracts: a study of three villages in Anand district. *Agricultural Situation in India.* 66, 2, 2008. pp. 63–69. IIML, SGUL, SPIESRL.

Bhatt, V.K., Patel, P.T. and Bhatt, R.K. Effect of methods and dates of sowing on yield of green kharif under North Gujarat Condition. *Indian Journal of Horticulture*. 64, 4, 2007, pp. 475–476. AAUL.

Bhavsar, B.K., Dhami, A.J. and Kodagali, S.B. Monthly variations in freezability and fertility of Mehsana Buffalo Semen. *Indian Dairyman*. 42, 2, 1989. pp. 246–250. AAUL.

Biradar, U.S. Factors affecting peak yield and days to attain peak yield in Surti Buffaloes. *Indian Dairyman*. 43, 1, 1990, pp. 32–34. AAUL.

Brahmbhatt, B.M. and Patel, A.S. Role of moisture conservation practices for semi-arid condition of Gujarat. *Gujarat Agricultural University Research Journal.* 8, 2, 1983. pp. 58–66. AAUL, GVL.

Brahmbhatt, D.M. Working of a farmers' service society in Gujarat: case study of a tribal area in Panchmahals district. *Artha-Vikas*. 14, 1, 1978. pp. 63–78. CSSL, GIDRL, GVL, HML.

Brahmbhatt, D.M., Patel, V.C. and Patel, H.F. Integrated dryland agricultural development programme in Gujarat. *Artha-Vikas.* 10, 1, 1974. pp. 38–54. GVL, HML, SGUL.

Brahmbhatt, R.M. and Patel, A.S. Soil and nutrient losses in run off water from loamy sand soil of middle Gujarat. *Gujarat Agricultural University Research Journal.* 9, 1, 1983. pp. 1–4. AAUL, GVL.

Butani, P.G. and Kapadia, G.N. Natural enemies of cotton bollworms in Saurashtra region of Gujarat. *Gujarat Agricultural University Research Journal.* 22, 1, 1996. pp. 131–133. GVL.

Chand, Faqir. I.D.A credits for J&K and Gujarat. *Agricultural Situation in India.* 33, 4, 1978. pp. 229-[ ]. SPIESRL.

Chand, Faqir. Planning commission approves irrigation projects for Gujarat. *Agricultural Situation in India.* 36, 3, 1981. pp. 186-[ ]. SPIESRL.

Chandra, Ram, et al. Influence of sowing time on growth and yield of plantago ovata forsk, under Middle Gujarat. *Indian Journal of Horticulture*. 63, 4, 2006, pp. 424–427. AAUL.

Chaturvedi, Vaibhav and Bazaz, Amir Bashir. Meeting food crop demand in a changing climate: a case of Mehsana district in North Gujarat. *Agricultural Situation in India*. 66, 5, 2009. pp. 257–264. IIML, IRMAL, SPIESRL.

Chaudhari, M.K. and Patel, N.M. Prediction of area under castor crop in the major castor growing districts of Gujarat state. *Gujarat Agricultural University Research Journal*. 19, 1, 1993. pp. 116–119. GVL.

Chauhan, N.B. Adoption of watershed management technology by beneficiaries in watershed area of Kheda district. *Rural India*. 66, 6–7, 2003. pp. 115–116. GVL.

Chauhan, V.S., et al. Yield prediction model of rice in Bulsar district of Gujarat. *Journal of Agrometeorology*, 11, 2, 2009. pp. 162-[ ]. IRMAL.

Chawla, H.L. Economics of tubewell irrigation in Gujarat. *Agricultural Situation in India*. 39, 7, 1984. pp. 505–507. SPIESRL.

Chawla, H.L. and Sharma, Chandar Dhar. Economics of tubewell irrigation in Gujarat. *Agricultural Situation in India*. 39, 4, 1984. pp. 233-[ ]. SPIESRL.

Chawla, H.L. and Sharma, Chandar Dhar. $172 million IDA credit for Gujarat irrigation. *Agricultural Situation in India*. 39, 4, 1984. pp. 238-[ ]. SPIESRL.

Chinchmalatpure, Anil R., Nayak, A.K. and Gururaja Rao, G. Land use planning of the bara tract area under Sardar Sarovar canal command of Gujarat. *Indian Farming*. 60, 1, 2010. pp. 15–18. IIML.

Chinchmalatpure, Anil R., Nayak, A.K. and Gururaja Rao, G. Suitability assessment for some crops on salt affected soils of Gujarat. *Indian Journal of Soil Conservation*. 29, 2, 2001. pp. 138-[ ].GIDRL.

Chopada, M.C., Sahu, D.D. and Kacha, H.L. Verification of medium range rainfall forecast under South Saurashtra agro climatic zone, Gujarat. *Journal of Agrometeorology*. 13, 1, 2011. pp. 65–67. IRMAL.

Choudhary, K.M. Crop insurance scheme for hybrid-4 cotton in Gujarat: field problems and prospects. *Artha-Vikas*. 17, 1–2, 1981. pp. 137–153. GIDRL, GVL, HML, SGUL.

Choudhary, Mahaveer, Patel, R.B. and Vejapara, V.P. Crisis management level of farmers of drought areas in Gujarat state. *Indian Journal of Social Research*, 48, 4, 2007. pp. 335–339. IRMAL.

Chua, Cathy. Development of capitalism in Indian agriculture: Gujarat, 1850–1900. *Economic and Political Weekly*. 21, 48, 1986. pp. 2092–2099. CEPTL, CSSL, GUL, IIML, IRMAL, SGUL, SPIESRL, TRTIL, UML.

Dalal, Bharat C. and Maharaja, Madhukar A. Marketing credit for fertilizers in the Gujarat state with special reference to the role of cooperatives in the distributive system. *Artha-Vikas*. 4, 1, 1968. pp. 109–122. HML.

Dalwadi, M.R. and Trivedi, B.S. Evaluation of methods for determining available N.P and K from sugarcane growing soils of South Gujarat. *Journal of the Gujarat Society of Agronomy and Soil Science*. 2, 2, 1999. pp. 71–73. AAUL.

Dani, N.I and Patel, R.B. Post Harvest disease of the Chiku fruit in Ahmedabad market and their control. *Journal of the Gujarat Research Society*. 46/47, 154/155, 1984/85. pp. 36–40. GVL.

Dantwala, M.L. Food deficit and commercial crops of Gujarat. *Artha Vijnana*. 3, 1, 1961. pp. 19–23. GVL, UML.

Das, A. and Maliwal, G.L. Effect of mulching on the yield of rainfed cotton in Bhal zone of Gujarat. *Gujarat Agricultural University Research Journal.* 21, 2, 1996. pp. 112–117. AAUL, GVL.

Das, N.C. and Khunt, K.A. Setting research priority for livestock sector in Gujarat. *Agriculture Economics Research Review*. 21, 2, 2008. pp. 73–81. AAUL, IRMAL.

Das, R.K. and Vyas, K.N. Distribution of the thickness cornification and papillation of epidermis, solitary lymph nodules, elastic fibres and melanin pigment in the prepuce of the Surati Buffalo. *Gujarat Agricultural University Research Journal.* 15, 1, 1989. pp. 62–69. GVL.

Das, Sevak, et al. Effect of weather parameters on pest disease of Okra during summer season in middle Gujarat. *Journal of Agrometeorology*. 13,1, 2011. pp. 38–42. IRMAL.

Dastur, R.H. and Gopani, D.D. Effect of spacing on the growth and yield of cotton in South Gujarat (Surat): with four text-figures. *Indian Journal of Agricultural Science*. 22, 2, 1952. pp. 113–138. GVL.

Dave, P.K. Game theoretic approach to farm decisions under uncertainty: a study of cotton producers of Gujarat. *Vishleshan*. 9, 2 and 3, 1983. pp. 109–128. CSSL, GIDRL, IRMAL.

Dave, P.K. and Bharadwaj, V.P. Some policy implications of a crop insurance scheme for small farmers of Gujarat. *Anvesak*. 11, 2, 1981. pp. 361–370. SPIESRL.

Dave, V.J. Economics of export oriented horticultural crops-chiku (SAPOTA) in Gujarat: a case study in Valsad district. *Artha-Vikas*. 34, 2,1998. pp. 90–92. AAUL, GIDRL, IRMAL.

Desai, B.M. Analysis of cropping pattern of farm families, Surat district. *Indian Journal of Agricultural Economics*. 32, 1, 1977. pp. 78–91. AAUL, CEPTL, CSSL, IIML, TRTIL, UML.

Desai, B.M. Economics of resource use on sample farms of Central Gujarat. *Indian Journal of Agricultural Economics.* 28, 1, 1973. pp. 71–85. AAUL, GIDRL, IIML, IRMAL, SGUL, UML.

Desai, B.M. Level and pattern of investment in agriculture: a micro cross-section analysis of a progressive and a backward area in Central Gujarat. *Indian Journal of Agricultural Economics.* 24, 4, 1969. pp. 70–79. SPIESRL, UML.

Desai, Bhupat M. and Namboodiri, N.V. Developing agriculture in Gujarat: a strategic perspective for ninth plan. *Economic and Political Weekly*. 32, 13, 1997. pp. A-31-A-40. CEPTL, CSSL, GIDRL, IIML, IRMAL, MICAL, SGUL, SPIESRL, UML.

Desai, D.K. and Patel, N.T. Improving growth of foodgrains productivity in the Western region of India. *Indian Journal of Agricultural Economics*. 38, 4, 1983. pp. 539–556. CSSL, UML.

Desai, D.R. and Patel, G.A. Impact of modern farming technology on rural employment in Saurastra. *Indian Journal of Agricultural Economics*. 25, 3, 1970. pp. 33–39. SPIESRL, UML.

Desai, H.B., Desai, M.C. and Patel, D.C. Study of animal feed resources and feeding practices of dairy animals in Valsad district. *Gujarat Agricultural University Research Journal.* 13, 2, 1988. pp. 58–64. AAUL, GVL.

Desai, H.B., Desai, M.C. and Purohit, L.P. Note on proximate composition of cattle feeds of Panchmahals. *Gujarat Agricultural University Research Journal.* 9, 1, 1983. pp. 74–86. AAUL, GVL.

Desai, H.B., Desai, M.C. and Purohit, L.P. Note on trace element content in cattle feeds of Panchmahals. *Gujarat Agricultural University Research Journal.* 9, 2, 1984. pp. 75–81. AAUL, GVL.

Desai, H.B., Desai, M.C. and Purohit, L.P. Survey of cattle feeds and feeding practices in Banaskantha District. *Gujarat Agricultural University Research Journal.* 11, 1, 1985. pp. 35–43. GVL.

Desai, H.B., Patel, J.S. and Shukla, P.C. Note on sulphur content of some fodders of Banaskantha district. *Gujarat Agricultural University Research Journal.* 14, 1, 1988. pp. 76–78. GVL.

Desai, H.B., et al. Animal nutrition survey in tribal area of Dang district. *Gujarat Agricultural University Research Journal.* 8, 2, 1983. pp. 102–110. AAUL.

Desai, H.B., et al. Note on proximate composition of concentrates used for cattle and buffaloes in Surat. *Gujarat Agricultural University Research Journal*. 5, 1, 1979. pp. 48–49. AAUL, GVL.

Desai, Hashmukh G. Dairy farming in South Gujarat: problems and remedies. *Indian Journal of Dairy Science*. 64, 2, 2011, pp. 162–167. AAUL, IRMAL.

Desai, I.D. and Mudaliar, S.D. Studies on the expansive soil of South Gujarat region. *South Gujarat University Journal.* 4, 1975. pp. 80–90. GVL.

Desai, J.K. Cattle problems of Gujarat, Saurashtra and Kutch. *Indian Journal of Agricultural Economics*. 8, 2, 1953. pp. 44–59. HML, IIML, UML.

Desai, K.B., Patel, M.R, and Patel, D.U. Gujarat vari-1 a new variety for South Gujarat. *Gujarat Agriculture University Research Journal.* 6, 2, 1981. pp. 109–110. AAUL, GVL.

Desai, M.B. Problems of agriculture in Gujarat. *Journal of the Gujarat Research Society.* 22, 2/86, 1960. pp. 93–104. GVL.

Desai, M.B. and Mehta, R.S. Green revolution in agriculture in Gujarat. *Journal of the M.S. University of Baroda*. 20, 2, 1971. pp. 1–18. GVL.

Desai, Mahendra D. Small farmers' development agency: experience in Surat district. *Economic and Political Weekly*. 9, 31, 1974. 1245–1255. CSSL, GUL, HML, IRMAL, SGUL, SPIESRL, UML.

Desai, Mahendra D. Small Farmer's development agency programme in the Surat district: an evaluation. *Artha-Vikas.* 10, 1, 1974. pp. 12–26. GVL, SGUL.

Desai, Mahendra D. Tenancy abolition and the emerging pattern in Gujarat. *Artha-Vikas.* 8, 2, 1972. pp. 45–52. GVL, HML, SGUL.

Desai, N.D. and Raman, S. Irrigation requirement of summer groundnut in Gujarat. *Indian Farming.* 42, 10, 1993. pp. 15–25. IIML.

Desai, N.K. Problems of mixed farming: study of a Charotar farm. *Indian Journal of Agricultural Economics*. 16, 3, 1961. pp. 46–49. IIML, UML.

Desai, R.M., Patel, K.G. and Trivedi, B.S. Effect of sulphur application on yield, it's uptake and different forms of sulphur in vertisols of South Gujarat under different cropping sequences. *Journal of the Society Agronomy and Soil Science*. 6, 1–2, 2006–07. pp. 12–16. AAUL.

Desai, R.M., et al. Response of summer groundnut (arachis hypogaea L) to dates of sowing, planting geometry and levels of phosphorus under South Gujarat conditions. *Gujarat Agricultural University Research Journal.* 16, 1, 1990. pp. 17–22. GVL.

Desai, S.S., Chovatia, R.S. and Virendrasingh. Effect of different plant growth regulators and micronutrients on fruit characters and yield of tomato CV-Gujarat Tomato-3 (GT-3). *Asian Journal of Horticulture*. 7, 2, 2012, pp. 546–549. AAUL.

Desai, S.T. Green Gujarat tree plantation campaign by milk producers of dairy cooperatives. *Indian Dairyman*. 62, 3, 2010. pp. 70–73. IRMAL.

Dhandhalya, M.G. and Shiyani, R.L. Assessment of yield gaps and prioritizing of production constraints: a regional analysis of major cereal crops in Saurashtra. *Journal of Rural Development*. 26, 4, 2007. pp. 577–597. CSSL, IIML.

Dhandhalya, M.G. and Shiyani, R.L. Economic viability and marketing efficiency of semi-rabi bajra: a case study of Saurashtra region in Gujarat. *Economic Affairs*. 54, 1–2, 2009, pp. 1–9. AAUL.

Dhandhalya, M.G. and Shiyani, R.L. Major crops research priority in Saurashtra region of Gujarat state framework and strategies for sustainable agricultural development. *Indian Journal of Social Research*. 49, 4, 2008. 357–368. IRMAL.

Dhandhalya, M.G. and Shiyani, R.L. Production potentials, yield gaps and research prioritization of production constraints in major oilseeds crops of Saurashtra region. *Indian Journal of Agricultural Research*. 43, 1, 2009. pp. 18–25. AAUL.

Dhandhalya, M.G. and Shiyani, R.L. Yield gaps: constraints prioritization and potentials of cotton production in Saurashtra region. *Agricultural Situation in India*. 63, 1, 2006. pp. 39–46. IIML.

Dhandhalya, M. G, Shiyani, R.L. and Visawadia, H.R. Organic groundnut farming for development of sustainable agriculture in Saurashtra region of Gujarat State. *Journal of Agricultural Development and Policy*. 20,1–2, 2008. pp. 102-[ ]. IRMAL.

Dhandhalya, M.G., Shiyanni, R.L. and Vishawadia, H.R. Organic wheat farming for sustaible agriculture in Saurashtra region of Gujarat state. *Indian Journal of Agricultural Marketing*. 24, 1, 2010. pp. 132–140. AAUL, IRMAL.

Dholakia, H.L. Forests of Gujarat. *Journal of the Gujarat Research Society*. 3, 2, 1941. pp. 94–107. GVL.

Dholakia, Ravindra H. Exports of agri-products from Gujarat: problems and prospects. *Vikalpa: The Journal of Decision Makers*. 28, 4, 2003. pp. 41–51. EDIL, IRMAL.

Dholakia, Ravindra H. and Iyengar, Sudarshan. Project appraisal for minor irrigation tanks: a study of Panchmahals. *Vishleshan*. 6, 1, 1981. pp. 22–33. CSSL, GIDRL.

Dinesh Kumar, M., Singhal, Lokesh and Rath, Pabitra. Value of groundwater: case studies in Banaskantha. *Economic and Political Weekly*. 39, 31, 2004. pp. 3498–3503. BUL, CEPTL, CSSL, EDIL, IIML, IRMAL, MICAL, SGUL, SPIESRL, UML.

Divyabhanusinh. Junagadh state and its Lions: conservation in princely India, 1879–1947. *Conservation and Society*. 4, 4, 2006. pp. 522–540. CSSL.

Dixit, Anita. Agriculture in a high growth state: Case of Gujarat (1960–2006). *Economic and Political Weekly*. 44, 50, 2009. 64–71. BUL, CEPTL, CSSL, EDIL, IIML, IRMAL, MICAL, SGUL, SPIESRL, SUL, UML.

Dodia, J.F., Korat, D.M. and Patel, H.M. Natural enemies of rice pests in Nawagam region of Gujarat. *Indian Farming*. 46, 2, 1996. pp. 23–24. GVL, IIML.

Dodia, J.F., Patel, M.C. and Patel, H.M. Determination of economic threshold level for sogatella furcifera (Horv) in Gujarat. *Gujarat Agricultural University Research Journal*. 22, 1, 1996. pp. 61–66. GVL.

Dodia, J.F., Yadav, D.N. and Patel, R.C. Management of fruit sucking moth, othries fullonia Cl. (Lepidoptera: Noctuidae) in citrus orchards at Anand (Gujarat). *Gujarat Agricultural University Research Journal*. 11, 2, 1986. pp. 72–73. GVL.

Dodia, J.F., et al. Determination of economic threshold level for rice leaf folder cnaphalocrocis medinalis guen in Gujarat. *Gujarat Agricultural University Research Journal*. 22, 2, 1997. pp. 51–56. AAUL, GVL.

Donde, W.B. IDA credit for irrigation projects in Gujarat and Maharastra. *Agricultural Situation in India.* 35, 3, 1980. pp. 187-[ ]. SPIESRL.

Dubey, D.D., Sharma, O.P. and Shaila, P.K. Characterisation and classification of salt affected soils of South Mehsana, Gujarat. *Current Agriculture.* 7, 3–4, 1983. pp. 129–137. AAUL.

Dudhat, B.L. and Khunt, K.A. Growth and projection of gap between the demand and supply of quality seeds in Gujarat state. *Agricultural Marketing.* 49, 3, 2006. pp. 48–55. IRMAL.

Dudhatra, M.G., Kalyansundaram, N.K. and Patel, B.J. Mixed cropping of Bajra Mung and Castor in North West Gujarat. *Gujarat Agricultural University Research Journal.* 18, 1, 1992. pp. 7–12. AAUL, GVL.

Farmer, Mayur J. and Patel, Bharti K. Comparative analysis of traditional vs mechanized farm power in state of Gujarat. *Vishleshan.* 25, 4, 2000. pp. 52–57. IIML, IRMAL.

Fatteh, U.G., Patel, A.T. and Patel, P.S. Hybrids revolutionise castor production in Gujarat. *Indian Farming.* 38, 1, 1988. pp. 25–36. IIML.

Fatteh, U.G., Patel, K.M. and Patel, A.T. Production technology for Mustard in Gujarat. *Indian Farming.* 38, 5, 1988. pp. 20–21. IIML.

Fulsounder, A.B. and Shukla, P.C. Correlative studies between quantitative and biological estimation of aflatoxins extracted from cattle feeds and their ingredients of Gujarat state. *Gujarat Agricultural University Research Journal.* 3, 2, 1978. pp. 74–77. AAUL, GVL.

Fulsounder, A.B. and Shukla, P.C. Qualitative studies on the aflatoxins in cattle feeds of Gujarat state. *Gujarat Agricultural University Research Journal.* 3, 2, 1978. pp. 78–81. AAUL, GVL.

Gajja, B.L., Chand, Khem and Parashad, R. Consequences of land heterogeneity on agricultural productivity, income and employment in the Kakrapar left bank canal command area, Gujarat State. *Current Agriculture.* 25, 1–2, 2001. pp. 27–35. AAUL.

Gajja, B.L., Chand, Khem. and Singh, Y.V. Impact of land irritability classes on crop productivity in canal command area of Gujarat: an economic analysis. *Agricultural Economic Research Review.* 19, 1, 2006. pp. 83–94. AAUL, IIML, IRMAL.

Gajja, B.L., Gupta, I.C. and Parashad, R. Role of land irritability classes in sustainable agricultural production system in Mahi right bank canal command area of Gujarat. *Current Agriculture.* 22, 1–2, 1998, pp. 39–53. AAUL.

Gajja, B.L. and Sharma, Vijay Paul. Farm economic efficiency level and conjunctive use of surfaces and groundwater in tobacco crop in Mahi right bank canal command area Gujarat. *Journal of Agricultural Development and Policy.* 4, 1 and 2, 1993. pp. 1–9. IRMAL.

Gajja, B.L., Sharma, Paul, and Parshad, R. Effect of land degradation on agricultural producation and income in Ukai-Kakrapar canal-command area in Gujarat. *Indian Journal of Agricultural Sciences.* 66, 5, 1996. pp. 306–308. AAUL, GVL.

Gajja, B.L., et al. Productivity variation and land irritability class in Kakrapar canal command area in Gujarat state. *Indian Journal of Agricultural Economics.* 49,4, 1994. pp. 609–616. IRMAL, UML.

Gandhi, G.M. and Varshney, A.K. Research support in Amelioration of social forestry programme in Kachchh. *Indian Forester.* 117, 5, 1991. pp. 395–402. IIML.

Gandhi, Maullik. Free diversity of Gandhinagar city, Gujarat, India. *Indian Forester.* 137, 9, 2011. pp. 1103–1108. CEPTL, GIDEL.

Gandhi, Vasant P. and Patel, N.T. Pesticides and the environment: a comparative study of farmer awareness and behaviour in Andhra Pradesh, Punjab and Gujarat. *Indian Journal of Agricultural Economics*. 52, 3, 1997. pp. 519–529. AAUL, CEPTL, CSSL, GIDRL, IRMAL, UML.

Garg, M.R., Bhanderi, B.M. and Sherasia, P.L. Mineral status of feeds and fodders in Dahod and Panchmahal district of Gujarat. *Indian Journal of Dairy Science*. 58, 5, 2005. pp. 341–446. AAUL, IRMAL.

Garg, M.R., Sherasia, P.L. and Bhanderi, B.M. Economic evaluation of feeding bypass protein feed on milch animals in Vadodara district of Gujarat. *Indian Journal of Dairy Science*, 58,6,2005. pp. 420–425. IRMAL.

Garg, M.R., et al. Mapping of certain mineral in feeds and fodders in the Mehsana district of Gujarat State. *Indian Journal of Dairy Science*. 52, 2, 1999. pp. 69–77. AAUL.

Garg, M.R., et al. Mineral status of feeds and fodders in Kaira district of Gujarat. *Indian Journal of Dairy Science*. 53, 4, 2000. pp. 291–297. AAUL.

George, P.C. and Govindan, A. Potato cycles in the Ahmedabad market: a harmonic analysis. *Agricultural Situation in India*. 30, 8, 1975. pp. 569–573. SPIESRL.

Ghetiya, L.V. and Butani, P.G. New record of aphis gossypii glover as a pest of coriander in Gujarat. *Gujarat Agricultural Research Journal*. 20, 2, 1995. pp. 179-[ ]. AAUL.

Ghosh, P.K. and Sojitra, V.K. Groundnut and pigeonpea intercropping: a risk-avoiding and remunerative practice for rainfed farming in the Saurastra region of Gujarat. *Indian Farming*. 46, 12, 1997. pp. 28–20. IIML.

Gondalia, V.K. and Patel, G.N. Economic evaluation of investment on Aonla (Emblica Officinalis G) in Gujarat. *Agricultural Economics Research Review*. 20, 2, 2007. pp. 385–394. IIML.

Gondalia, V.K. and Patel, G.N. Marketing of Aonla (Emblica Officinalis G.) in Gujarat. *Indian Journal of Agricultural Marketing*. 21, 2, 2007. pp. 114–124. AAUL, IRMAL.

Gondalia, V.L., Khunt, K.A. and Vekariya, S.B. Impact and progress of crop insurance programme in Gujarat state. *Agricultural Situation in India*. 66, 1, 2008. pp. 19–24. IIML, IRMAL, SPIESRL, SGUL.

Gopani, D.D. and Patel, C.H. Patan-sarson-66: a new variety for Gujarat. *Indian Farming*. 19, 5, 1969. pp. 26–28. IIML.

Goswami, K.V. and Singh, S.B. Cost-benefit analysis of afforestation in deep ravines of Gujarat. *Indian Journal of Agricultural Economics*. 31, 1, 1976. pp. 48–55. IIML, IRMAL, UML.

Govande, G.K. Improved varieties of pulses and lesser millets for Gujarat. *Indian Farming*. 11, 5, 1950. pp. 194–196. GVL.

Govande, G.K. New strains of pulses and millets in Baroda state. *Indian Farming*. 11, 4, 1950. pp. 153–154. GVL.

Guha, Amalendu. Raw cotton of Western India: output, transportation and marketing, 1750–1850. *Indian Economic and Social History Review*. 9, 1, 1972. pp. 1–42. CSSL.

Guha, G.S. Planning for difficult land and water regimes: a case of the Pancmahal region of Gujarat. *Anvesak*. 21, 2, 1991. pp. 145–149. CEPTL, CSSL, SPIESRL.

Guha, G.S. and Mathur, Niti. Spatial analysis of agro-processing sector in India. *Anvesak*. 24, 2, 1994. pp. 81–124. SPIESRL.

Gujarat, Government of. Crop insurance in Gujarat state. *Artha-Vikas*. 17, 1–2, 1981. pp. 201–208. GIDRL.

Gumber, Anil K. Occupational mobility of displaced families: a study of the Panam irrigation project in Gujarat. *Anvesak*. 19, 1–2, 1989. pp. 151–155. CEPTL, IRMAL, SPIESRL.

Gururaja Rao, G., Nayak, A.K. and Chinchmalctpure, Anil R. Field of dill (Anethum graveolens) on saline black soils of different unirrigated farm sites of Bhal area in Gujarat. *Indain Journal of Agricultural Science*. 71, 11, 2001. pp. 711–712. GVL.

Gururaja Rao, G., Singh, Ravender and Bhargava, G.P. Species diversity on salt affected soils under canal command areas and in Bhal region in Gujarat state. *Indian Forester*. 121, 12, 1995. pp. 1143–1150. IIML.

Hadwani, G.J., Gandhi, A.P. and Patel, M.S. Available boron in calcareous soils of Saurashtra. *Gujarat Agricultural University Research Journal*. 17, 2, 1992. pp. 147–150. GVL.

Halyal, K.G. Study of the impact of key village scheme in Gujarat state. *Gujarat Agriculture University Research Journal*. 7, 1, 1981. pp. 70–71. AAUL.

Halyal, K.G. and Patel, A.U. Study of some factors affecting the rate of adoption of some improved animal husbandry practices in the village around Anand Gujarat state. *Gujarat Agricultural University Research Journal*. 8, 2, 1983. pp. 84–90. AAUL, GVL.

Handa, B.K. Agricultural quality of ground-water in Kutch. *Indian Journal of Agricultural Science*. 36, 5, 1966. pp. 233–238. GVL.

Hardiman, David. Politicisation and agitation among dominant peasants in early twentieth century India: some notes. *Economic and Political Weekly*. 11, 8, 1976. pp. 365–371. CEPTL, CSSL, GUL, IIML, SGUL, SPIESRL, UML.

Hardiman, David. Well irrigation in Gujarat: systems of use, hierarchies of control. *Economic and Poltical Weekly*. 33, 25, 1998. pp. 1533–1544. CEPTL, CSSL, GIDRL, IIML, IRMAL, MICAL, SGUL, SPIESRL, UML.

Hirway, Indira. Critique of target group approach: a study in Gujarat. *Indian Journal of Agricultural Economics*. 39, 3, 1984. pp. 457–465. AAUL, CSSL, GIDRL, GVL, HML, IIML, IRMAL, TRTIL, UML.

Hirway, Indira. Some aspects of the functioning of the schemes for the poor: a study of poultry farming scheme in Gujarat. *Indian Journal of Labour Economics*. 28, 3, 1985. pp. 249–261. GIDRL, IIML.

Hirway, Indira. Trend in agricultural wages in Gujarat. *Indian Journal of Agricultural Economics*. 28, 3, 1973. pp. 65–72. AAUL, GIDRL, IIML, IRMAL, SGUL, UML.

Ilango, P. and Tripathi, S.L. Fertiliser distribution in Gujarat: Case study. *Cooperative Perspective*, 25,4,1991. pp. 35–52. IRMAL.

Iyengar, Sudarshan. Common property land resources in Gujarat: some findings about their size, status and use. *Wastelands News*, 5,1,1989. pp. 23–37. IRMAL.

Iyengar, Sudarshan. Common property land resources in Gujarat: some findings about their size, status and use. *Economic and Political Weekly*. 24, 25, 1989. pp. A-67-A-77. CEPTL, CSSL, IIML, IRMAL, SGUL, SPIESRL, UML.

Jadav, K.S., Patel, G.N. and Darji, V.B. Price behaviour of Brinjal in Middle Gujarat. *Artha-Vikas*. 47, 2, 2011. pp. 73–82. CSSL.

Jadav, N.B., Gorfad, P.S. and Parmar, G.M. Impact of frontline demonstrations on groundnut in Jamanagar district of Gujarat. *Gujarat Agricultural University Research Journal*. 34, 2, 2009. pp. 130–133. AAUL.

Jagadeeshawara, K., Patel, H.L. and Naik, K.V. Adoption of agricultural technologies among different categories of farmers in Kheda District. *Gujarat Journal of Extension Education*. 8, 9, 1997–98. pp. 14–18. AAUL.

Jain, Alpesh., Desai, H.K. and Upadhyay, K.G. Sensoric profile of market Shrikhand sold in Gujarat State. *Indian Journal of Dairy Science*. 56, 5, 2003. pp. 285–291. AAUL.

Jain, Amit and Rathod, Raju M. Distribution and retailing trends in rural markets a study in villages of Gujarat. *Indian Journal of Marketing*, 35,9, 2005. pp. 17–20 IRMAL.

Jain, Sunder Singh. Groundnut development programme in Gujarat. *Agricultural Situation in India*. 42, 2, 1987. pp. 105–127. SPIESRL.

Jani, Gaurang. Economic development and exploitation of tribals sugarcane harvesting labourers of South Gujarat. *Adivasi Gujarat*. 7, 1, 1997. pp. 55–57. CSSL, GVL, TRTIL.

Jani, Gaurang and Ganguly, Varsha. Problem of land alienation among tribals of Gujarat. *Adivasi Gujarat*. 10, 2, 2000. pp. 45–86. CSSL, GVL, TRTIL.

Jayaraman, T.K. Analysis of overdues of primary agricultural co-operative societies: a case study of Mahi-Kadana project in Gujarat state. *Indian Journal of Agricultural Economics*. 33, 3, 1978. pp. 21–30. AAUL, CEPTL, CSSL, GIDRL, HML, IIML, IRMAL, TRTIL, UML.

Jayaraman, T.K. Assessment of credit facilities in Mahi-Kadana command area. *Vishleshan*. 3, 4, 1977. pp. 319–329. CSSL.

Jayaraman, T.K. Consumption of fertilizers in irrigation projects under uncertainties: a case study from Gujarat state. *Margin*. 14, 4, 1982. pp. 41–49. CSSL, GIDRL, HML, UML.

Jayaraman, T.K. Cooperative credit in irrigated agriculture: a case study of an irrigation project in Gujarat. *Margin*. 11, 4, 1979. pp. 32–41. GIDRL, HML, SGUL, UML.

Jayaraman, T.K. Determinants of cropping patterns in command area of an irrigation project: An empirical investigation of Mahi-Kadana irrigation project. *Vishleshan*. 7, 2, 1981. pp. 120–132. CSSL.

Jayaraman, T.K. Evaluation of agricultural extension in the Mahi-Kadana irrigation project. *Indian Journal of Agricultural Economics*. 34, 4, 1979. pp. 40–48. CSSL, UML.

Jayaraman, T.K. Farmers' organizations in surface irrigation projects: two empirical studies from Gujarat. *Economic and Political Weekly*. 16, 38, 1981. pp. A-89-A-98. CEPTL, CSSL, GUL, IIML, IRMAL, SGUL, SPIESRL, UML.

Jayaraman, T.K. Labour absorption in irrigated agriculture: some empirical evidences from a surface irrigation project in Gujarat state. *Margin*. 14, 2, 1982. pp. 40–45. CSSL, GIDRL, HML, SGUL, UML.

Jayaraman, T.K. and Savdasia, V.B. Econometric model of relationship between inputs and aggregate agricultural production in Gujarat state, 1961–62 to 1973–74. *Margin*. 9 and 10, 4 and 1, 1977. pp. 20–32. GIDRL, HML, SGUL, UML.

Jhala, R.C., et al. Population dynamics of some insect pest of Chiku in South Gujarat. *Gujarat Agricultural University Research Journal*. 11, 2, 1986. pp. 69–71. GVL.

Johnson, Derek. Wealth and waste: contrasting legacies of fisheries development in Gujarat since 1950s. *Economic and Political Weekly*. 36, 13, 2001. pp. 1095–1102. BUL, CEPTL, CSSL, EDIL, GIDRL, IIML, IRMAL, MICAL, SGUL, SPIESRL, UML.

Jose, V.T. and Shah, A.H. Bionomics of the spider mite (Tetranychus Macfarlanei Banker and Pitchard) injurious to cotton in Gujarat. *Gujarat Agricultural University Research Journal.* 13, 2, 1988. pp. 12–18. AAUL, GVL.

Joshi, B.L., Pitha, M.S. and Vachhani, J.H. Gujarat gram 2-a bold seeded desi rainfed variety for Gujarat. *Indian Farming.* 54, 4, 2004. pp. 7–8. IIML.

Joshi, D.M. and Joshi, H.U. Occurrence of banana mosaic in South Gujarat area and its host-range. *Gujarat Agricultural University Research Journal.* 1, 2, 1976. pp. 105–110. GVL.

Joshi, G.N. Agricultural and economic development in Gujarat. *Anvesak.* 16, 2, 1986. pp. 57–83. CEPTL, GIDRL, SPIESRL.

Joshi, P.K. and Shiyani, R.L. Adoption of improved chickpea varieties evidences from tribal regions of Gujarat. *Indian Journal of Agricultural Economics.* 55, 2, 2000. pp. 159–171. GVL, UML.

Joshi, S.I. and Chhaya, N.D. 'Gholva' net of Onjal (Macchiwad) in South Gujarat. *South Gujarat University Journal*. 5, 1976. pp. 126–128. GVL.

Joshi, S.N. Agricultural development perspective Gujarat. *Anvesak.* 25, 1, 1995. pp. 1–52. GIDRL, IRMAL, SPIESRL.

Joshi, S.N. Cropping pattern changes in Gujarat. *Anvesak.* 26, 2, 1996. pp. 1–18. CSSL, GIDRL, IRMAL, SPIESRL.

Joshi, S.N. Horticultural development perspective in Gujarat. *Anvesak*. 29, 2, 1999. pp. 7–19. CSSL, GIDRL, IRMAL, SPIESRL.

Joshi, S.N. Influence of rainfall on area and production of lead crops in some selected districts of Gujarat. *Anvesak*. 29, 1, 1999. pp. 1–14. CSSL, GIDRL, IRMAL, SPIESRL.

Joshi, S.N. Managing rainfed areas in Gujarat. *Anvesak*. 30, 1, 2000. pp. 7–15. CSSL, GIDRL, SPIESRL.

Joshi, S.N. Research in states: Gujarat. *Indian Farming.* 17, 11, 1968. pp. 34–36. IIML.

Jotani, K.L., Chanda, D.N. and Tank, P.R. Inducing maturity and spawning of tiger prawn (penaeus monodon fabricius) in captivity through eyestalk ablation at the experimental shrimp hatchery at Okra(Gujarat).*Gujarat Agricultural University Research Journal.* 25, 1, 1999. pp. 85–89. AAUL, GVL.

Kaiwar, Vasant. Property structures, demography and the crisis of the agrarian economy of colonial Bombay presidency. *Journal of Peasant Studies*. 19, 2, 1992. pp. 255–300. CSSL.

Kalathiya, K.V., Dave, S.K. and Katrodia, J.S. Existing farming and cultural practices of coconut cultivation followed by the growers in Valsad district(South Gujarat). *Gujarat Agricultural University Research Journal.* 26, 2, 2001. pp. 50–57. GVL.

Kalathiya, K.V., Dave, S.K. and Katrodia, J.S. Personal and socio-economic characteristics of the coconut growers in Valsad district(South Gujarat). *Gujarat Agricultural University Research Journal.* 25, 2, 2000. pp. 39–45. GVL.

Kalyanasundaram, N.K. Micronutrient studies on tobacco grown in goradu soil of Gujarat. *Gujarat Agricultural University Research Journal.* 7, 1, 1981. pp. 66-[ ]. AAUL.

Kalyansundram, N.K. and Ramakrishnayya, B.V. Note on micronutrient status of tobacco varieties grown in goradu soil of Gujarat. *Indian Journal of Agricultural Sciences*. 51, 1, 1981. pp. 60–62. GVL.

Kamani, M.R. and Vyas, H.N. Bionomics of sugarcane top borer tryporyza nivella fabricius under Junagadh condition. *Gujarat Agricultural University Research Journal.* 10, 2, 1985. pp. 23–26. AAUL, GVL.

Kanani, P.R., Kher, A.O. and Savaliya, V.J. Adoption of indigenous practices of groundnut cultivation by groundnut growers in South Saurashtra zone. *Gujarat Journal of Extension Education*. 8, 9, 1997–98. pp. 6–10. AAUL.

Kanani, P.R., Waghmare, S.K. and Shiyani, R.L. Training needs of the tribal farmers in Gujarat. *Gujarat Agricultural University Research Journal.* 17, 2, 1992. pp. 61–66. GVL.

Kandya, A.K., et al. Application of geographic information system in identification of fire-prone area: a feasibility study in parts of Junagadh (Gujarat). *Indian Forester.* 124, 7, 1998. pp. 531–536. IIML.

Kant, Rajni and Pandey, S.D. Breeding preferences of anopheles culicifacies in the Rice agro-ecosystem in Kheda district, Gujarat. *Indian Journal of Malariology*. 36, 3–4, 1999. pp. 53–60. CSSL.

Kant, Rajni, Pandey, S.D. and Sharma, S.K. Mosquito breeding in relation to aquatic vegetation and some physico-chemical parameters in Rice fields of Central Gujarat. *Indian Journal of Malariology*. 33, 1, 1996. pp. 30–40. CSSL.

Kant, Rajni, et al. Species diversity and interspecific associations among mosquitoes in rice agro-ecosystem of Kheda district, Gujarat. *Indian Journal of Malariology*. 35, 1, 1998. pp. 22–30. CSSL.

Kantawala, T.C. Irrigation in Gujarat. *Journal of the Gujarat Research Society,* 6, 3, 1944. pp. 115–126. GVL.

Kapadia, C.A. Animal life of Gujarat. *Journal of the Gujarat Research Society.* 13, 1, 1951. pp. 1–18. GUL, SPUL.

Kapadia, G.A. Study of rainfall of twenty stations of Sorath district in Saurashtra. *Journal of the Gujarat Research Society.* 18, 2, 1956. pp. 114–129. GVL.

Kapadia, M.N. Biology of sesamum leaf roller and capsule borer antigastra catalaunalis (duponchel) in Gujarat. *Gujarat Agricultural University Research Journal.* 22, 2, 1997. pp. 144–146. AAUL, GVL.

Kapadia, M.N. Biology of spodoptera litura (fabricius) as a part of castor in Gujarat. *Gujarat Agricultural University Research Journal.* 22, 2, 1997. pp. 141–143. AAUL, GVL.

Kapadia, M.N. Occurrence and distribution of different parasites of opisina arenosella walker under Mahuva condition of Gujarat. *Gujarat Agricultural University Research Journal.* 12, 2, 1987. pp. 17–21. AAUL, GVL.

Kapadia, M.N. Record of three false wireworms infesting groundnut in Gujarat. *Gujarat Agricultural University Research Journal*. 19, 2, 1994. pp. 128–129. AAUL.

Kapadia, M.N. and Mittal, V.P. Biology of parasierola nephantidis muesebeck and its important in the control of opisina arenosella walker under Mahuva(Gujarat state) conditions. *Gujarat Agricultural University Research Journal.* 12, 1, 1986. pp. 29–34. AAUL, GVL.

Karla, Jessica P. and Sandhyakiran, G. Physico-chemical properties of forest soil of Chhotaudepur division. *Indian Forester.* 130, 9, 2004. pp. 1031–1039. GIDEL, IIML.

Khatri, T.J. Preharvest forecasting of groundnut yield in Gujarat utilizing eye estimate and rainfall veriables. *Gujarat Agriculture University Research Journal.* 7, 1, 1981. pp. 73-[ ]. AAUL.

Khatri, T.J., Patel, R.M. and Mistry, P.D. Analysis of crop weather for an early forecast of groundnut yield in Junagadh district of Gujarat. *Indian Journal of Agricultural Sciences.* 52, 3, 1982. pp. 182–185. GVL.

Khatri, T.J., Patel, R.M. and Mistry, P.D. Crop weather analysis for preharvest forecasting of groundnut yield in Surat and Bulsar district of Gujarat state. *Gujarat Agricultural University Research Journal.* 9, 1, 1983. pp. 29–32. AAUL, GVL.

Kher, A.O. and Jha, P.N. Note on sources of credit in Kodinar taluka of Gujarat. *Gujarat Agricultural University Research Journal*. 4, 2, 1979. pp. 52–54. AAUL.

Khunt, K.A. and Antani, K.L. Impact of weather and economic factors on acreage and production fluctuation of cotton in Gujarat state. *Agricultural Situation in India.* 46, 4, 1991. pp. 203–210. GVL, IIML.

Khunt, K.A., Gajipara, H.M. and Kakadia, B.H. Marketing of Kesar Mango in Saurashtra region of Gujarat state. *Indian Journal of Agricultural Marketing*. 15, 1, 2001. pp. 47–54. AAUL, IRMAL.

Khunt, K.A., Gajipara, H.M. and Vekariya, S.B. Price behaviour of major vegetables in Gujarat state. *Indian Journal of Agricultural Marketing*. 20, 1, 2006. pp. 28–37. AAUL, IRMAL.

Khurody, D.N. Retrospect and prospect of the dairy industry in Anand area. *Indian Dairyman*. 8, 11, 1955. pp. 237–242. AAUL.

Kochar, Anjini. Constraints on the development of consumer demand based rural household manufacturing units in arid regions: Kutch district Gujarat. *Indian Journal of Agricultural Economics*. 38, 3, 1983. pp. 347–353. CEPTL, GIDRL, UML.

Korat, D.M., Patel, N.C. and Pathak, A.R. Impact of transplanting period on pest incidence and yield of rice in Middle Gujarat. *Gujarat Agricultural University Research Journal.* 25, 1, 1999. pp. 63–67. AAUL, GVL.

Koshiya, D.J., Bharodia, R.K. and Talati, G.M. Laboratory evaluation of some insecticides for the control of leaf weevil, cyrtozemia dispar pascoe (Curculionidae coleoptera) infesting soyabean in Gujarat. *Gujarat Agricultural University Research Journal.* 3, 2, 1978. pp. 90–91. AAUL, GVL.

Krishna Rao, B., et al. Determination of crop coefficient and optimum irrigation schedules for bidi tobacco and pearl millet crops in central Gujarat. *Journal of Agrometeorology.* 14, 2, 2012. pp. 123–129. IRMAL.

Kuchhadiya, D.B., Shiyani, R.L. and Dixit, S.K. Analysis of growth and technological development of oilseeds in Gujarat. *Agricultural Situation in India.* 47, 3, 1992. pp. 175–178. IIML.

Kuchhadiya, D.B., Shiyani, R.L. and Thumar, B.L. Cost benefit analysis of Garlic crop in Jamnagar district of Gujarat state. *Agricultural Situation in India*. 47, 4, 1992. pp. 261–263. GVL.

Kulkarni, Madhav N. and Despande, Sagar. Estimation of the datum transformation parameters between WGS-84 and Everest ellipsoid for Gujarat region of Western India. *International Journal of Geoinformatics*. 2, 3, 2006. pp. 17–20. IRMAL.

Kunjadia, C.D., Patel, C.B. and Patel, M.B. Life history of sugarcane whitefly (Aleurolobus barodensis mask) under South Gujarat condition(Aleyrodidae: homoptera). *Gujarat Agricultural University Research Journal.* 19, 1, 1993. pp. 157–158. AAUL, GVL.

Lal, R.B. From farm to factory. *Adivasi Gujarat.* 4, 2, 1982. pp. 24–93. CSSL, GVL, SPUL, TRTIL.

Lenin, V., Bagle, B.G. and Dhandar, D.G. Factors constraining horticultural development in Panchmahals district of Gujarat. *Journal of Rural Development*. 26, 2, 2007. pp. 293–305. CSSL, GIDRL, IIML, IRMAL.

Lunagaria, M.M., et al. Validation of precis baseline simulation for Middle Gujarat agroclimatic zone. *Journal of Agrometeorology*. 13, 2, 2011. pp. 92–96. IRMAL.

Madappa, P.P., Patel, K.V. and Patel, N.T. Investment decisions pumpsets: a case study of a Saurashtra village. *Economic and Political Weekly*. 5, 1, 1970. pp. 21–25. CSSL, IRMAL, SGUL, SPIESRL, UML.

Madiman, S.G. and Desai, N.K. Cost of producing milk in Anand area 1950–51. *Indian Journal of Agricultural Economics*. 6, 2, 1951. pp. 33–46. IIML, UML.

Makwana, Manish and Parmar, Himanshu. Economics of production, marketing and feeding composition of fodder crops in Gujarat state. *Vishleshan*. 37, 1 and 2, 2012. pp. 33–44. CSSL.

Mali, Kiran P., et al. Evaluation of contribution of forestry sector to economy: application of forest resource accounting in Gujarat, India. *Journal of Social and Economic Development*. 13, 2, 2011. pp. 207–225. GIDRL, IRMAL, SPIESRL.

Maliwal, G.L. and Timbadia, N.K. Salinity, sodicity and boron status of soil and well waters of inland area Amreli district (Gujarat). *Gujarat Agricultural University Research Journal*. 16, 1, 1990. pp. 50–52. GVL.

Mandalia, V.K. Twenty-Five years of agriculture in Gujarat. *Rural India*. 38, 10–11, 1974. pp. 179–184. IIML.

Mandalia, V.K. and Charan, A.S. Study of development of hybrid-4 cotton in Gujarat and its production economics. *Indian Journal of Agricultural Economics*. 29, 3, 1974. pp. 154–162. GIDRL, IRMAL, UML.

Mane, P.M. (Success story on) Participatory strengthening of agriculture by tribals of Bharuch Gujarat. *Rural India*. 53, 13, 1990. pp. 259–264. GVL.

Manivel, P. Participatory evaluation of in station large-seeded groundnut trial in Gujarat. *Indian Farming*. 55, 12, 2006. pp. 10–12. IIML.

Manivel, P., Rajgopal, K. and Chondran, K. Groundnut in Saurashtra region of Gujarat. *Indian Farming*. 53, 5, 2003. pp. 9-[ ]. IIML.

Maraviya, R.B., Gupta, S.K. and Patel, J.C. Analysis of rainfall data for crop planning under dryland agriculture at Rajkot. *Gujarat Agricultural University Research Journal*. 17, 1, 1991. pp. 93–102. GVL.

Marsonia, P.F., Patel, M.S. and Koria, R.G. Status and distribution pattern of different forms of Sulphur in some profiles of calcareous soils of dry farming areas of Saurashtra and adjoining tract. *Gujarat Agricultural University Research Journal*. 11, 2, 1986. pp. 44–51. GVL.

Mathur, Niti and Kashyap, S.P. Agriculture in Gujarat: problems and prospects. *Economic and Political Weekly*. 35, 35 and 36, 2000. pp. 3137–3146. BUL, CEPTL, CSSL, GIDRL, IIML, IRMAL, MICAL, SGUL, SPIESRL, UML.

Mayani, V.V., Patel, J.C. and Dave, R.M. Cultivation problems of major kharif crops in dry farming area of Rajkot district. *Gujarat Agricultural University Research Journal*. 12, 2, 1987. pp. 44–47. AAUL, GVL.

Meena, R.L., Yadav, R.K. and Khajanchi, Lal. Growth, yield attributes and seed cotton yields as influenced by intercrops and nutrient management under saline black soils of Gujarat. *Indian Journal of Agricultural Sciences*. 79, 4, 2009. pp. 273–276. AAUL, IRMAL.

Mehta, Lyla. Drought diagnosis: dryland blindness of planners. *Economic and Political Weekly*. 35, 27, 2000. pp. 2439–2445. CEPTL, CSSL, IIML, IRMAL, MICAL, SGUL, SPIESRL, UML.

Mehta, M.B. Problems of creation of common property resources in semi-arid and saline areas: a case study of Kachch district in Gujarat(India). *Indian Forester*. 125, 1, 1999. pp. 105–110. IIML.

Mehta, Niti. Liberalised era and technical efficiency in agriculture: variations in Gujarat and West Bengal. *Indian Journal of Agricultural Economics.* 66, 2, 2011. pp. 214–229. CSSL, GIDRL, GVL, IIML, IRMAL, UML.

Menat, D.M. and Patil, R.G. Boron content in irrigation waters of some talukas of Mehsana and Sabarkantha district of North Gujarat. *Gujarat Agricultural University Research Journal.* 21, 2, 1996. pp. 122–124. AAUL, GVL.

Mewara, R.C. and Pandya, R.D. Knowledge and adoption level of Tomato growers regarding value added techniques in Navasari. *Rural India.* 70, 9, 2007. pp. 164–169. AAUL, GVL.

Minhas, J.S., Patel, P.K. and Gadewar, A.V. Dangs: a potential area for growing seed potatoes in Gujarat. *Indian Farming.* 38, 7, 1988. pp. 33–38. IIML.

Mishra, Ashok, Gohel, V.R. and Patel, J.G. Extent of seed transmission of urdbean leaf crinkle virus in Gujarat. *Gujarat Agricultural University Research Journal.* 19, 2, 1994. pp. 130–132. AAUL.

Mishra, Deepti, Mudgal, Manish and Chakradhar, B. Assessment of ground water quality of Bhavnagar region, Gujarat. *Journal of Scientific and Industry Research.* 68, 11, 2009. pp. 964–966. IRMAL.

Mishra, Nupur. BT cotton in India: two narratives and a few lessons. *Indian Journal of Public Administration.* 59, 4, 2013. pp. 789–803. CSSL.

Misra, V.N. Growth of crop output in Gujarat: a component analysis. *Anvesak.* 1, 1, 1971. pp. 1–15. CSSL, IRMAL, SPIESRL.

Misra, V.N. Labour market in agriculture: a study of Gujarat districts. *Indian Journal of Agricultural Economics.* 25, 3, 1970. pp. 8–15. IRMAL, SPIESRL, UML.

Misra, V.N. Some economic factors and population pressure in crop output growth in Gujarat: an inter-district analysis. *Artha Vijnana.* 16, 4, 1974. pp. 419–440. CSSL, GVL, HML, SGUL, UML.

Misra, V.N. and Gupta, B.L. Productivity wages and its determination in Gujarat agriculture: an inter-district analysis. *Indian Journal of Agricultural Economics.* 29, 3, 1974. pp. 22–33. GIDRL, IRMAL, UML.

Misra, V.N. and Radhakrishnan, R. Econometric models for acreage response: a study of Groundnut and Bajra in Gujarat. *Anvesak.* 1, 2, 1971. pp. 165–174. CSSL, IRMAL, SPIESRL.

Modak, Shrikant. Groundnut economy of Gujarat. *Economic and Political Weekly.* 21, 13, 1986. pp. A-38-A-44. CEPTL, CSSL, GUL, IIML, IRMAL, SGUL, SPIESRL, UML.

Modi, J.M., Mehta, K.G. and Gupta, Rajendra. Isabgol: a dollar earner of North Gujarat. *Indian Farming.* 23, 10, 1974. pp. 17–19. GVL, SGUL.

Modi, R.J., Patel, N.B. and Chauhan, H.D. Dairy animal housing pattern in rural area of milk shed of Gujarat. *Indian Journal of Dairy Science.* 63, 1, 2010. pp. 46–49. IRMAL.

Mody, S.K., et al. Serum mineral bioprofile of goat in North Gujarat. *Gujarat Agricultural University Research Journal.* 35, 1, 2010. pp. 49–50. AAUL.

Mohamed, K.H. Preliminary observation on the biology and fisheries of the thread-fin, polydactlus indicus shaw in the Bombay and Saurastra waters. *Indian Journal of Fisheries.* 11, 1, 1955. pp. 164–179. SGUL.

Mondal, B.K. Special forest privilege and its role on forest development: a case study in Gujarat(India). *Indian Forester.* 119, 6, 1993. pp. 441–445. IIML.

More, P.G. and Inamdar, J.A. Brief thesis entitled "a contribution to the flora of Parnera hill, Pardi and Udwada area in South Gujarat. *South Gujarat University Journal.* 2–3, 1973–1974. pp. 67–76. GVL.

Mori, J.D. and Patel, A.S. Note on potential and economics of one-year crop sequence under Saurashtra conditions. *Gujarat Agricultural University Research Journal.* 2, 1, 1976. pp. 67–68. GVL.

Moses, S.T. Fisheries of the Gujarat coast. *Journal of the Gujarat Research Society.* 4, 2, 1942. pp. 61–82. GVL.

Moses, S.T. Pisciculture as a means of combating weed nuisance in tanks with special reference to Dabhoi tank. *Journal of the Gujarat Research Society.* 7, 2–3, 1945. pp. 70–74. GUL.

Moses, S.T. Problem of tank management in Gujarat. *Journal of the Gujarat Research Society.* 14, 2, 1952. pp. 85–90. GUL.

Motiramani, D.P., Patel, J.C. and Giri, J.D. Evaluation of phosphorimeter for estimation of phosphorus availability of Bhal and coastal soils in Gujarat state. *Gujarat Agricultural University Research Journal.* 16, 1, 1990. pp. 53–56. GVL.

Motwani, V.T. Rust-resistant wheat varieties for Saurashtra. *Indian Farming.* 111, 9, 1953. pp. 21–22. GVL.

Mulchandani, L.H., Patel, M.M. and Maliwal, G.L. New record of grasshopper from Gujarat. *Gujarat Agricultural University Research Journal.* 18, 2, 1993. pp. 124–125. GVL.

Muralidharan, C.M. and Patel, G.M. Inventory and species composition of grasshopper fauna in different ecosystems of North Gujarat. *Gujarat Agricultural University Research Journal.* 33, 1–2, 2009. pp. 27–33. AAUL.

Muralidharan, C.M., Patel, G.M. and Patel, J.K. Nature extent of damage and crop losses due to some economic species of grasshoppers in North Gujarat. *Indian Journal of Agricultural Science.* 77, 10, 2007. pp. 698–700. IRMAL.

Muralidharan, C.M., Sodagar, N.N. and Vaghasia, V.R. Survey, distribution, extent of damage field behaviour and biology of red palm weevil, rhynchophorus ferrugineus Oliv on date groves of Kachchh(Gujarat). *Gujarat Agricultural University Research Journal.* 25, 2, 2000. pp. 9–14. GVL.

Mute, S.B. and Haria, N.H. Response of cotton to phosphorus in Gujarat farmer's fields. *Arth-Vikas.* 25, 1 and 2, 1989. pp. 64–71. GIDRL, HML.

Nagda, R.K., Jain, L.S. and Tailor, S.P. Incidences and factors affecting reproductive disorders in Surti buffaloes. *Indian Journal of Dairy Science.* 59, 6, 2006. pp. 414–416. AAUL.

Naik, G.D., Parmar, G.D. and Khunt, K.A. Acreage dynamics in relation to price and non-price parameters: a study of South Gujarat. *Agricultural Situation in India.* 52, 8, 1995. pp. 545–550. IIML.

Naik, Gopal and Pandit, Parag. Status of fruits and vegetables sector in India and Gujarat: emerging opportunities and challenges. *Agricultural Situation in India.* 58, 4, 2001. pp. 125–137. IIML, IRMAL.

Naik, K.N. Problems of Gujarat agriculture. *Journal of the Gujarat Research Society.* 11, 1, 1949. pp. 25–28. GUL.

NAIP Team. Marketing strategy for Banana pseudostem based production in Gujarat. *Indian Journal of Agricultural Marketing.* 24, 3, 2010. pp. 184–189. AAUL, IRMAL.

Nanavati, Arti and Patel, B.C. Inter-district variation in agricultural productivity in Gujarat. *Productivity.* 35, 2, 1994. pp. 314–322. HML, IRMAL, SPUL.

Narain, P., Saksena, Asha and Bhargava, P.N. Risk management in dryland agriculture: a case study at Jamnagar, Gujarat. *Indian Farming.* 40, 10, 1991. pp. 52–56. GVL.

Narala, Anuradha and Zala, Y.C. Technical efficiency of rice farms under irrigated conditions in Central Gujarat. *Agricultural Economics Research Review*. 23, 2, 2010. pp. 375–381. IRMAL.

Narala, Anuradha, Patel, G.N. and Zala, Y.C. Economic analysis of integrated pest management (IPM) technology in cotton production in Vadodara district of Gujarat. *Artha-Vikas*. 45, 1, 2009. pp. 33–48. CSSL.

Narayan, N.L. Baroda wool-grading and marketing experiment. *Indian Farming*. 8, 1, 1947. pp. 26–28. GVL.

Narayana, E. and Patel, J.C. Productivity of sunflower as influenced by phasic water and fertility management under South Gujarat conditions. *Gujarat Agricultural University Research Journal*. 23, 1, 1997. pp. 9–11. AAUL, GVL.

Nath, Abhay. Sensory process of tribal farmers inhabiting saline black soils in Gujarat. *Rural India*, 65, 1, 2002. pp. [ ]. SGUL.

Nayak, A.K., Gururaja Rao, G. and Chinchmalatpure, Anil R. Dill: a potential crop for salt-affected black soils of Bhal region in Gujarat. *Indian Farming*. 50, 7, 2000. pp. 40–41. IIML.

Nilakantan, Rahul and Datta, Samar K. Impact of groundwater recharge structures in Saurashtra and Katch. *Artha Vijnana*. 55, 2, 2013. pp. 198–209. CSSL, UML.

Padmaiah, M., Ramanjaneyulu, G.V. and Patel, K.S. Past and present experiences of farmers of Ranole village in Northern Gujarat: a case study. *Asian-Agri-History*. 7, 2, 2003. pp. 161–166. AAUL.

Palande, S.R. Co-operative cotton sale organisation in Baroda state. *Rural India*. 5, 3, 1942. pp. 131–132. SGUL.

Palkhiwala, A.B. and Shah, R.K. Possibilities of reclamation of saline and alkali soils of arid salines of Saurashtra. *Indian Journal of Agricultural Research*. 9, 1 and 2, 1975. pp. 77–82. AAUL.

Pande, M.B., Desai, H.B. and Shukla, P.C. Blood status of Mehsani buffaloes of Surat district. *Gujarat Agricultural University Research Journal*. 4, 1, 1978. pp. 36–39. AAUL, GVL.

Pande, V.C., et al. Incentives for soil and water conservation on farm in ravines of Gujarat: policy implications for future adoption. *Agricultural Economics Research Review*. 24, 1, 2011. pp. 109–118. IRMAL.

Pande, V.C., et al. Afforestation on community land in the semiarid tropics of Gujarat: an economic analysis. *Indian Forester*. 125, 2, 1999. pp. 212–218. IIML.

Pandey, Rakesh. Water-harvesting concept: an experience in Eastern Panchmahals. *Journal of Rural Development*. 17, 4, 1998. pp. 633–650. CSSL, GIDRL.

Pandey, V. and Gupta, B.R.D. Effect of distribution of agro-climatic element on sorghum (Sorghum bicolor) yield at Surat. *Indian Journal of Agricultural Science*. 59, 9, 1989. pp. 582–586. GVL.

Pandey, V., Patel, H.R. and Patel, V.J. Impact assessment of climate change on wheat yield in Gujarat using CERES wheat model. *Journal of Agrometeorology*. 9, 2, 2007. pp. 149–157. IRMAL.

Pandey, V., et al. Irrigation water requirement and production potentials of major crops over Narmada canal command area in Gujarat. *Journal of Agrometeorology*. 10, 2, 2008. pp. 314–320. IRMAL.

Pandey, Vyas. and Patel, A.T. Agroclimatic appraisal of Khedbrahma. *Gujarat Agricultural University Research Journal*. 13, 1, 1987. pp. 21–27. GVL.

Pandey, Vyas and Patel, R.R. Agroclimatic classification of arid and semi-arid region of Gujarat state on the basis of humid and moist periods. *Gujarat Agricultural University Research Journal*. 13, 1, 1987. pp. 17–20. GVL.

Pandey, Vyas and Patel, R.R. Agroclimatic study for dry farming of Banaskantha. *Gujarat Agricultural University Research Journal.* 11, 1, 1985. pp. 30–34. GVL.

Pandey, Vyas and Patel, R.R. Water harvesting potentials in some areas of North Gujarat an agroclimatic approach. *Gujarat Agricultural University Research Journal.* 14, 1, 1988. pp. 23–26. GVL.

Pandey, Vyas, Patel, V.J. and Patel, H.R. Impact assessment of climate change on maize cultivars in Middle Gujarat agro climatic region using CERES maize model. *Journal of Agrometeorology.* 10, 2, 2008. pp. 292–295. IRMAL.

Pandit, B.R., et al. Phytosociological studies of tropical dry deciduous forest in Gujarat, India. *Journal of Tropical Forestry*. 12, 2, 1996. pp. 54–58. IRMAL.

Pandya, A.J., Thakar, P.N. and Sharma, R.S. Important constraints plugging dairy development in Gujarat state and the remedial measures. *Indian Dairyman*. 51, 5, 1999. pp. 21–26. AAUL.

Pandya, H.V. and Shah, A.H. Study on egg parasitism of rice yellow stem borer in Gujarat. *Gujarat Agricultural University Research Journal.* 21, 1, 1995. pp. 197–199. GVL.

Pandya, H.V., Shah, A.H. and Purohit, M.S. Assessment of avoidable losses due to inspect pets of paddy under South Gujarat condition. *Gujarat Agricultural University Research Journal.* 14, 2, 1989. pp. 42–47. AAUL.

Pandya, P.R., Talpada, P.M. and Vashi, D.R. Chemical composition of the haulmes of different groundnut varieties of Gujarat. *Gujarat Agricultural University Research Journal.* 19, 1, 1993. pp. 127–130. AAUL, GVL.

Parakhia, A.M., Akbari, L.F. and Vaishnav, M.V. Occurrence of a new leaf spot of groundnut in Gujarat. *Gujarat Agricultural University Research Journal.* 22, 2, 1997. pp. 158–159. AAUL, GVL.

Parakhia, B.K. and Patel, M.S. Note on iron availability as affected by some important soil properties in medium-black calcareous soils of Saurashtra. *Indian Journal of Agricultural Sciences*. 51, 2, 1981. pp. 132–134. GVL.

Parikh, Dilip, Vora, Amrish J. and Alagh, Yoginder K. Redefining Gujarat's irrigation potential: a model. *Economic and Political Weekly*. 28, 26, 1993. pp. A-45-A-47. CEPTL, CSSL, IIML, IRMAL, SGUL, SPIESRL, UML.

Parikh, R.G. Food crops of Gujarat. *Journal of the Gujarat Research Society.* 11, 1, 1949. pp. 6–15. GUL.

Parmar, B.D. Spatial wage-differentials in agriculture: a case of Saurashtra region. *Indian Journal of Labour Economics*. 28, 1 and 2, 1985. pp. 115–126. IIML.

Parmar, B.D. Trends in agricultural wages in Saurashtra region. *Indian Journal of Industrial Relations*. 21, 4, 1986. pp. 479–489. SPUL.

Parmar, G.D., Naik, G.D. and Patel, K.S. Marketing of mango: a case study of South Gujarat. *Vishleshan.* 16, 1, 1991. pp. 30–36. IIML, IRMAL.

Parmar, G.D., Naik, G.D. and Patel, K.S. Selling of chiku and price received by chiku growers from different purchasing agencies in South Gujarat(RP 232–2). *Indian Cooperative Review.* 27, 2, 1989. pp. 202–209. IRMAL, SGUL.

Parmar, G.D., Khunt, K.A. and Desai, D.B. Marketing of vegetables in South Gujarat. *Indian Journal of Agricultural Marketing*. 8, 2, 1994. pp. 258–263. IRMAL.

Parmar, G.D., et al. Acreage dynamics in relation to price and non-price parameters: study of South Gujarat. *Agricultural Situation In India.* 52, 8, 1995. pp. 545–550. IRMAL.

Parmar, G.D., et al. Economic performance of the pulses in South Gujarat. *Agricultural Situation in India.* 48, 10, 1994. pp. 721–724. IIML.

Parmar, H.C., Zala, Y.C. and Arya, J.S. Comparative economics of milk productions: a case study of Vadodara district of Gujarat. *Indian Journal of Dairy Science*. 63, 5, 2010. pp. 408–413. AAUL.

Parmar, K.H., et al. Effect of different regimens on fertility and plasma profile of micro minerals in postpartum anestrus Surati buffaloes. *Gujarat Agricultural University Research Journal*. 38, 1, 2013. pp. 39–44. AAUL.

Parmar, R.S., Vaishnav, P.R. and Dixit, S.K. Relationship between rainfall and groundnut productivity of Junagadh district in Gujarat state. *Journal of Agrometeorology*. 9, 1, 2007. pp. 63–67. AAUL.

Parthasarthy, R. Impact of tractor use on agricultural employment in Gujarat. *Indian Journal of Labour Economics*. 35, 2, 1992. pp. 132–141. CSSL, IIML.

Parthasarthy, R. Participatory irrigation management programme in Gujarat: institutional and financial issues. *Economic and Political Weekly*. 35, 35 and 36, 2000. pp. 3147–3154. BUL, CEPTL,, CSSL, IIML, IRMAL, MICAL, SGUL, SPIESRL, UML.

Patel, A.A. and Sharma, B.M. Impact of drought prone areas programme in Banaskantha district of Gujarat state. *Gujarat Agricultural University Research Journal*. 10, 2, 1985. pp. 34–36. AAUL.

Patel, A.G., Yadav, D.N. and Patel, R.C. Natural enemies of agrotis spp from Gujarat. *Gujarat Agricultural University Research Journal*. 17, 1, 1991. pp. 130–131. GVL.

Patel, A.J. and Antani, K.L. Contribution of Banas dairy in milk marketing and processing in Banaskantha district of Gujarat. *Indian Journal of Agricultural Marketing*. 12, 3, 1998. pp. 103–104. IRMAL.

Patel, A.J., et al. Resource use efficiency and returns to scale in production of castor in Gujarat. *Gujarat Agricultural University Research Journal*. 33, 1–2, 2009. pp. 50–54. AAUL.

Patel, A.S. Development of agriculture in Gujarat: a crop pattern aspect. *Artha-Vikas*. 33, 1 and 2, 1997. pp. 1–44. AAUL, CSSL, GIDRL, IRMAL.

Patel, A.S. Emerging agrarian social structure of a Gujarat village. *Artha-Vikas*. 18, 1 and 2, 1982. pp. 14–29. CSSL, GIDRL, GVL, HML.

Patel, A.S. Invensive fodder cropping for milk production in Gujarat. *Indian Dairyman*. 23, 1, 1971. pp. 6–11. SGUL.

Patel, A.S. Some institutional and systemic constraints in farming efficiency in the SAT of Gujarat. *Artha-Vikas*. 15, 2, 1980. pp. 41–64. CEPTL, CSSL, GIDRL, HML, SGUL.

Patel, A.S. Yield differential in irrigated and unirrigated areas: a case study of deshi cotton in Gujarat. *Artha-Vikas*. 15, 2, 1979. pp. 91–98. CEPTL, CSSL, GIDRL, GVL, HML, SGUL.

Patel, A.S. and Sutaria, M.H. Response of hybrid pearl-miliet to N.P. and K in different agro-climatic zones of Gujarat. *Indian Journal of Agricultural Sciences*. 42, 11, 1972. pp. 1024–1027. GVL.

Patel, A.S., Patel, H.F. and Shishodia, A.K. Agricultural productivity performance in Gujarat-II. *Artha-Vikas*. 34, 1, 1998. pp. 43–66. CSSL, GIDRL, IRMAL.

Patel, A.S., Patel, H.F. and Shishodia, A.K. Economics of Banana crop in Gujarat. *Artha-Vikas*. 34, 2, 1998. pp. 1–35. AAUL, CSSL, GIDRL, IRMAL.

Patel, A.S., Patel, H.F. and Shishodia, A.K. Performance of agriculture in Gujarat-I. *Artha-Vikas*. 32, 1, 1996. pp. 19–41. CSSL, GIDRL, IRMAL.

Patel, A.S., Patel, H.F. and Shishodia, A.K. Prospects of horticultural crops in Gujarat: a case study of mango. *Artha-Vikas*. 33, 1 and 2, 1997. pp. 129–156. AAUL, CSSL, GIDRL, IRMAL.

Patel, A.V. and Parmar, M.T. Note on response of different groundnut varieties to row spacing and land management practice during under season Middle Gujarat. *Gujarat Agricultural University Research Journal.* 14, 2, 1989. pp. 86–87. AAUL.

Patel, Arun S. Agricultural development in Gujarat: performance and future strategy. (*Gujarat-2010: challenges and opportunities*). *Anvesak.* 31, 1–2, 2001. pp. 35–68. CSSL, GIDRL.

Patel, Arun S. Economics of water use in Dantiwada canal command area. *Anvesak.* 16, 2, 1986. pp. 1–13. GIDRL, SPIESRL.

Patel, Arun S. Factor determining the level of fertiliser use: a study in two district of Gujarat state. *Artha-Vikas.* 7, 1, 1971. pp. 22–39. GVL, HML.

Patel, Arun S. Growth pattern of agriculture in Gujarat: an aspect of non-foodgrain economy. *Artha-Vikas.* 36, 1, 2000. pp. 20–44. CSSL, GIDRL, IRMAL.

Patel, Arun S. Irrigation: its employment impact in the command areas of medium irrigation projects in Gujarat. *Indian Journal of Agricultural Economics.* 36, 4, 1981. pp. 20–30. AAUL, CEPTL, CSSL, GIDRL, GVL, HML, IIML, IRMAL, SGUL, TRTIL, UML.

Patel, Arun S. Well irrigation and farm economy: a micro level study in Gujarat. *Artha-Vikas.* 24, 1 and 2, 1988. pp. 21–41. CSSL, GIDRL, HML.

Patel, Arun S. and Patel, H.F. Income and employment impact of canal irrigation in Gujarat: a study of watrak panam and Fatewadi project area. *Agricultural Situation in India.* 44, 2, 1989. pp. 107–113. IIML, IRMAL.

Patel, Arun S. and Patel, H.F. Irrigation practices and efficiency of water use: a study of Machhu-irrigation project area in Gujarat. *Agricultural Situation in India.* 38, 7, 1983. pp. 459–466. IIML, IRMAL.

Patel, Arun S., Bagchi, Dilip and Patel, Vithal G. Problem of groundnut oil in Gujarat. *Agricultural Situation in India.* 29, 6, 1974. pp. 401–408. GVL, IIML, SPIESRL.

Patel, Arun S., Modhwadia, M.M. and Dodia, A.M. Performance of groundnut 'M-13' in Gujarat. *Indian Farming.* 30, 5, 1981. pp. 8-[ ]. IIML.

Patel, B.B. Price spread and farmer's share: oil and groundnut in Gujarat. *Economic and Political Weekly.* 6, 29, 1971. pp. 1435–1440. CSSL, GUL, HML, IRMAL, SGUL, SPIESRL, UML.

Patel, B.D. and Patel, G.M. First record of new species of white grubs in Gujarat. *Gujarat Agricultural University Research Journal.* 25, 1, 2000. pp. 110–112. GVL.

Patel, B.D. and Patel, G.M. First record of new species of white grubs in Gujarat. *Gujarat Agricultural University Research Journal.* 25, 1, 1999. pp. 110–111. AAUL.

Patel, B.K., Raj, M.F. and Shah, P.G. DDT and HCH residues in dairy milk of Gujarat. *Gujarat Agricultural University Research Journal.* 15, 1, 1989. pp. 70–76. GVL.

Patel, B.R., Raman, S. and Mehta, H.D. Response of summer groundnut to sprinkler irrigation in South Gujarat. *Journal of the Gujarat Society of Agronomy and Soil Science.* 4, 1–2, 2004. pp. 48–49. AAUL.

Patel, B.R., et al. Unusual case of disephalus distomus male monster in Meshana buffalo. *Gujarat Agricultural University Research Journal.* 38, 1, 2013. pp. 45–46. AAUL.

Patel, B.S. Cattle wealth and milk production in Gujarat. *Journal of the Gujarat Research Society.* 7, 2–3, 1945. pp. 64–69. GUL, GVL.

Patel, B.S., Patel, R.C. and Patel, M.S. Note on effectiveness of light trap for the control of Gujarat hairy caterpillar amsacta spp. *Gujarat Agricultural University Research Journal.* 7, 1, 1981. pp. 47–48. AAUL.

Patel, Bhikhabhai. Impact of collection of subsidiary forest products on life style of tribals and their price value: an evaluation study. *Adivasi Gujarat*. 15, 1, 2005. pp. 35–78. CSSL, GVL, TRTIL.

Patel, C.C. Soil erosion due to August 1968 foods in South Gujarat. *Agricultural Situation in India*. 25, 5, 1970. pp. 487–491. IRMAL, SPIESRL.

Patel, C.C., Patel, N.C. and Patel, J.R. Natural control of Gujarat hairy caterpiller, amsacta moorei butler with bio and microbial agent in Middle Gujarat. *Gujarat Agricultural University Research Journal*. 21, 1, 1995. pp. 54–58. GVL.

Patel, C.K., Patel, P.T. and Patel, R.N. Effect of physiological age and nitrogen on seed potato production in North Gujarat. *Gujarat Agricultural University Research Journal*. 35, 1, 2010. pp. 23–27. AAUL.

Patel, C.L., Ahir, N.J. and Naik, B.M. Production economics of summer rice cultivation in South Gujarat. *Journal of the Gujarat Society of Agronomy and Soil Science*. 2, 2, 1999. pp. 85–86. AAUL.

Patel, C.L., Patel, H.S. and Patel, H.C. Optimum spacing for three rice varieties under South Gujarat condition. *Gujarat Agricultural University Research Journal*. 8, 2, 1983. pp. 125–126. AAUL, GVL.

Patel, C.L., Patel, H.S. and Patel, R.B. Optimum seed rate and spacing for summer green gram under South Gujarat condition. *Gujarat Agricultural University Research Journal*. 9, 2, 1984. pp. 6–9. AAUL, GVL.

Patel, D.A. Growth of groundnut in Gujarat state. *Indian Journal of Agricultural Economics*. 21, 4, 1966. pp. 223–226. GIDRL, UML.

Patel, D.A. Hybrid seed enterprise of the Gujarat state cooperative marketing society. *Indian Cooperative Review*. 7, 1, 1969. pp. 37–46. HML, IRMAL.

Patel, D.A., Singh, P.K. and Desai, M.M. Economic evaluation of gobar gas plants in Mehsana district of Gujarat state. *Agricultural Situation in India*. 48, 1, 1993. pp. 17–23. GVL.

Patel, G.A. and Shah, R.L. Agriculture in Gujarat state. *Agricultural Situation in India*. 22, 7, 1967. pp. 767–774. GVL, IIML, IRMAL.

Patel, G.A. and Shah, R.L. Characteristics of use of irrigation water in Gujarat. *Artha-Vikas*. 10, 1, 1974. pp. 70–87. GVL, HML, SGUL.

Patel, G.A. and Shah, R.L. Cultivation of hybrid bajra in Gujarat state. *Artha-Vikas*. 5, 1, 1969. pp. 81–94. HML, SGUL.

Patel, G.F., Patel, S.T. and Patel, S.K. Occurrence of stem end rot of mango fruit in Gujarat. *Gujarat Agricultural University Research Journal*. 11, 1, 1985. pp. 59–60. GVL.

Patel, G.J. Fertilizer management for bidi tobacco in Gujarat. *Arth-Vikas*. 25, 1 and 2, 1989. pp. 114–120. GIDRL, HML.

Patel, G.M., Muralidharan, C.M. and Patel, J.K. Nature, extent of damage and crop losses due to some economic species of grasshoppers in North Gujarat. *Indian Journal of Agricultural Sciences*. 77, 10, 2007. pp. 698–700. AAUL.

Patel, G.N. and Agarwal, N.L. Growth and instability in production of groundnut in Saurashtra region of Gujarat. *Agricultural Situation in India*. 49, 3, 1994. pp. 171–176. IIML.

Patel, G.N., Patel, R.H. and Desai, M.M. Benefit cost appraisal and marginal analysis of summer groundnut in Kheda district of Gujarat. *Agricultural Situation in India*. 41, 8, 1986. pp. 635–640. GVL, IIML, IRMAL, SPIESRL.

Patel, G.N., Patel, R.M. and Desai, M.M. Credit requirements and gap on small and marginal bidi tobacco farms in Central Gujarat. *Indian Cooperative Review*. 26, 2, 1988. pp. 121–127. HML.

Patel, G.R. Zinc, iron and manganese availability in paddy soils of South Gujarat. *Gujarat Agriculture University Research Journal.* 7, 1, 1981. pp. 68–69. AAUL.

Patel, G.R. and Dangarwala, R.T. Availability of iron, manganese and zinc in paddy soils of South Gujarat. *Gujarat Agricultural University Research Journal.* 9, 2, 1984. pp. 29–35. AAUL, GVL.

Patel, Gunvant. How Gujarat tackles problems of production. *Productivity.* 6, 2–3, 1965. pp. 364–367. IRMAL.

Patel, Gunwant A. Cotton seed production programme in Gujarat. *Indian Farming.* 20, 2, 1970. pp. 18–20. IIML.

Patel, Gunwant A. and Pathak, J.H. Hybrid bajra: cause of break-through in bajra production in Gujarat state. *Anvesak.* 4, 1, 1974. pp. 91–98. IRMAL, SPIESRL.

Pate, H.F. Growth pattern of fertilizer consumption in Gujarat. *Artha-Vikas.* 22, 1 and 2, 1986. pp. 39–52. CSSL, GIDRL, GVL, HML.

Patel, H.F., Desai, M.D. and Pathak, M.T. Technical coefficients in Gujarat agriculture. *Artha-Vikas.* 15, 1, 1979. pp. 27–55. CEPTL, GIDRL, GVL, HML, SGUL.

Patel, H.G. and Upadhyay, K.G. Characterization of barundi sold in selected cities of Gujarat. *Indian Journal of Dairy Science.* 54, 6, 2001. pp. 344–348. AAUL.

Patel, H.M. and Jhala, R.C. Studies on host range, host preference and population dynamics of whitefly, bemisia tabaci (Gennadius) in South Gujarat, India. *Gujarat Agricultural University Research Journal.* 17, 2, 1992. pp. 76–81. GVL.

Patel, H.M., Bafna, A.M. and Patel, Z.N. Growth and yield of rabi castor as influenced by INM grown on vertic ustrochrepts of South Gujarat. *Gujarat Agricultural University Research Journal.* 37, 1, 2012. pp. 26–29. AAUL.

Patel, H.R. and Shekh, A.M. Yield gap and trend analysis of wheat using CERES wheat model in three districts of Gujarat state. *Journal of Agrometeorology.* 8, 1, 2006. pp. 28–39. IRMAL.

Patel, H.R., Shekh, A.M. and Venkatesh, H. Status of present day weather forecasting to the farmers: a case study of Middle Gujarat region. *Annals of Agricultural Research.* 19, 3, 1998. pp. 285–289. AAUL.

Patel, H.R., Yadav, S.B. and Rao, V.U.M. Impact of projected climate change on wheat and maize in Middle Gujarat agro climatic zone. *Journal of Agrometeorology.* 14, 2, 2012. pp. 134–137. IRMAL.

Patel, I.S. and Rote, N.B. Seasonal incidence of sucking pest complex of cotton under rainfed condition of South Gujarat. *Gujarat Agricultural University Research Journal.* 21, 1, 1995. pp. 127–129. GVL.

Patel, I.S. and Singh, P.K. Area and yield responses of bajra crop in Gujarat state. *Indian Journal of Agricultural Marketing.* 8, 1, 1994. pp. 87–95. AAUL, IRMAL.

Patel, I.S. and Singh, P.K. Estimates of bajara production in Gujarat state. *Artha-Vikas.* 27, 1 and 2, 1991. pp. 53–66. AAUL, CSSL, GIDRL, HML.

Patel, J.C. Landless tribal agricultural labourers and human rights. *Adivasi Gujarat.* 13, 1, 2003. pp. 36–39. CSSL, GVL, TRTIL.

Patel, J.G. and Patel, A.J. New leaf blight disease of chiku incited by pestalotia sapota in Gujarta. *Gujarat Agricultural University Research Journal.* 7, 1, 1981. pp. 41–42. AAUL, GVL.

Patel, J.M. and Patel, M.V. Contribution of underground irrigation waters towards sulphur concentration in soils of Banaskantha district. *Gujarat Agricultural University Research Journal.* 36, 1, 2011. pp. 22–24. AAUL.

Patel, J.M., Patel, N.V. and Patel, B.T. Delineation of sulphur deficient soil in Banaskantha district (Gujarat). *Gujarat Agricultural University Research Journal.* 37, 1, 2012. pp. 23–25. AAUL.

Patel, J.P. and Shukla, P.C. Note on effect feeding seaweed to growing Surti male buffalo calves. *Gujarat Agricultural University Research Journal*. 4, 1, 1978. pp. 62–63. AAUL.

Patel, J.P. et al. Response of wheat to N, P.K. and Zn application on farmer's field in Kutch district in Gujarat. *Gujarat Agricultural University Research Journal.* 10, 1, 1984. pp. 8–12. AAUL, GVL.

Patel, J.R., Shekh, A.M. and Ratanpara, H.C. Seasonal incidence and effect of minimum temperature and pressure on the population of mango hopper amritodus atkinsoni leth in Middle Gujarat. *Gujarat Agricultural University Research Journal.* 20, 1, 1994. pp. 5–8. AAUL, GVL.

Patel, K.A. Impact of risk variables on the yield of cotton in Kheda district, 1970–71 to 1979–80. *Artha-Vikas*. 18, 1 and 2, 1982. pp. 58–66. CSSL, GIDRL, GVL, HML.

Patel, K.A. Yield instability in Indian agriculture: a mateorological analysis. *Artha-Vikas.* 21, 1–2, 1985. pp. 23–41. GIDRL.

Patel, K.C., Ramani, V.P. and Patel, K.P. Available sulphur status in soils of Gujarat. *Gujarat Agricultural University Research Journal.* 22, 1, 1996. pp. 127–130. GVL.

Patel, K.G. and Vyas, H.N. Biology of green lacewing chrysopa (=Chrysoperla) scelestes bank (Neuroptera: chrysopidae) an important predator in Gujarat. *Gujarat Agricultural University Research Journal.* 11, 1, 1985. pp. 18–23. GVL.

Patel, K.P., et al. Distribution of micronutrients and sulphur in profiles of some soil series in Amdavad district. *Gujarat Agricultural University Research Journal*. 23, 2, 1998. pp. 106–109. GVL.

Patel, K.P., et al. Status of micronutrient cautions in soils of Gujarat. *Gujarat Agricultural University Research Journal.* 22, 2, 1997. pp. 136–140. AAUL.

Patel, K.R. and Mistry, P.D. Effect of periods moisture availability on groundnut crop in the Saurashtra region in Gujarat. *Indian Journal of Agricultural Sciences*. 51, 4, 1981. pp. 266–270. AAUL, GVL.

Patel, K.R. and Mistry, P.D. Estimation of useful rain for groundnut crop in Saurashtra region. *Gujarat Agricultural University Research Journal.* 7, 2, 1982. pp. 97–101. GVL.

Patel, K.R., Joshi, R.S. and Patel, B.S. Use of open pan evaporimeter in scheduling irrigation for wheat crop in South Gujarat. *Gujarat Agricultural University Research Journal.* 8, 2, 1983. pp. 51–54. AAUL, GVL.

Patel, K.R., Vashi, R.D. and Damame, H.S. Studies on intercrop cultivation with sugarcane in South Gujarat region. *Gujarat Agricultural University Research Journal.* 10, 1, 1984. pp. 13–17. GVL.

Patel, M.C. and Waghmare, S.K. Extent of water utilization and its management aspect by tribal and non tribal farmers in command area of Surat district. *Gujarat Journal of Extension Education*. 8, 9, 1997–98. pp. 42–45. AAUL.

Patel, M.G. and Patel, J.R. Relation between inspect damage and yield of Indian mustard sown on different dates in Gujarat. *Indian Journal of Agricultural Science.* 67, 4, 1997. pp. 157–158. AAUL, GVL.

Patel, M.K. Economics of seeds processing: a case of cotton in Gujarat. *Artha-Vikas*. 20, 1 and 2, 1984. pp. 65–82. CSSL, GIDRL, GVL, HML.

Patel, M.K., Fatteh, U.G. and Patel, V.J. Effect of nitrogen and its time of application on yield of castor GAUCH-1 (Ricinus Communis L.) under irrigated condition in North Gujarat. *Gujarat Agricultural University Research Journal.* 17, 1, 1991. pp. 27–29. GVL.

Patel, M.K., Fatteh, U.G. and Patel, V.J. Effect of spacing and sowing time on the yield of irrigated castor under North Gujarat conditions. *Gujarat Agricultural University Research Journal.* 17, 1, 1991. pp. 119–121. GVL.

Patel, M.L., Gami, R.C. and Patel, P.V. Balance of total nitrogen, available phosphorus and potash in vertisols of Gujarat under intensive cropping and fertilizer constraints. *Gujarat Agricultural University Research Journal.* 15, 1, 1989. pp. 1–10. GVL.

Patel, M.M. Characterisation of saline sodic soil series of package districts, Surat Bulsar and reclamation study. *South Gujarat University Journal.* 2–3, 1973–1974. pp. 121–123. GVL.

Patel, M.M. and Rajani, H.F. Nutritive value and cooking quality of Gujarat rice varieties. *Indian Farming.* 17, 3, 1967. pp. 34–38. IIML.

Patel, M.N. and Chaudhari, M.K. Prediction of area under castor crop in the major castor growing districts of Gujarat. *Gujarat Agricultural University Research Journal*. 19, 1, 1993. pp. 116–119. AAUL.

Patel, M.N., et al. Direct and residual effect of phosphorus in rice-wheat sequence under South Gujarat condition. *Indian Journal of Agronomy*. 42, 1, 1997. pp. 18–21. AAUL.

Patel, M.P., Patel, H.C. and Patel, R.G. Response of pam to various seed rates and spacing under clayey soils of South Gujarat. *Gujarat Agricultural University Research Journal.* 13, 2, 1988. pp. 46–50. AAUL, GVL.

Patel, M.R. and Singh, S.B. Investment pattern and cost analysis of electrical and dieselised pumps used for lift irrigation in Mehsana district (Gujarat). *Indian Journal of Agricultural Economics*. 31, 3, 1976. pp. 211–218. GIDRL, IRMAL, UML.

Patel, M.S., Hadvani, G.J. and Yadav, B.S. Effect of soil depth, irrigation depth and irrigation interval on growth, yield and nutrient uptaken in wheat (Triticum aestivum) on a clay soil in Gujarat. *Indian Journal of Agricultural Sciences.* 62, 12, 1992. pp. 800–804. AAUL, GVL.

Patel, M.S., Patel, K.P. and George, V. Micronutrients status of Mahi-Kadana command area of Gujarat. *Gujarat Agricultural University Research Journal.* 21, 1, 1995. pp. 171–175. GVL.

Patel, N.C. and Patel, Z.G. Performance of safflower under different irrigation scheduling in South Gujarat. *Annals of Agricultural Research*. 14, 1,1993. pp. 109–110. AAUL.

Patel, N.L. and Singh, S.P. Dynamics of growth in some agroforestry tree species under South Saurashtra region of Gujarat. *Indian Forester*. 122, 7, 1996. pp. 570–576. IIML.

Patel, N.P. and Karelia, G.N. Effect of N, P, K, and Zn on the grain yield of bajra under rainfed condition on farmers, fields in Mehsana district of Gujarat. *Gujarat Agricultural University Research Journal.* 20, 1, 1994. pp. 19–22. AAUL, GVL.

Patel, N.P., Karelia, G.N. and Upadhyay, S.M. Response of mustard to N, P and K under irrigated condition on farmer's fields in Mehsana district of Gujarat. *Gujarat Agricultural University Research Journal.* 17, 2, 1992. pp. 1–3. GVL.

Patel, N.T. Impact of inputs' and outputs' price change on the profitability of the cultivation of paddy and wheat in Dascroi taluka of Gujarat. *Vishleshan*. 5, 2–3, 1979. pp. 162–172. CSSL, GIDRL, IIML.

Patel, P.G. and Patel, N.P. Response of cotton varies/Hybrids to NPK fertilizers in different cotton zones of Gujarat. *Arth-Vikas*. 25, 1 and 2, 1989. pp. 72–113. GIDRL, HML.

Patel, P.G., Patel, B.P. and Patel, B.D. Influence of spacing sowing time and fertility levels on yield of wheat under irrigated condition of South Gujarat. *Gujarat Agricultural University Research Journal.* 13, 1, 1987. pp. 48–49. GVL.

Patel, P.I., Patel, R.H. and Desai, M.S. Heterosis and combing ability of grain sorghum (Sorghum bicolor) at different location in Gujarat. *Indian Journal of Agricultural Sciences.* 60, 6, 1990. pp. 382–386. AAUL, GVL.

Patel, P.K. and Vaishnani, N.L. Seed production of Gujarat castor hybrid – 3. *Indian Farming.* 26, 4, 1976. pp. 18–21. SGUL.

Patel, P.K., Dholaria, S.J. and Karkar, B.R. 'MT-67–52' a promising sesamum for Gujarat. *Indian Farming.* 30, 10, 1981. pp. 19–20. GVL, IIML.

Patel, Premji M. Integrated approach to institutional finance for agriculture: a case study of three co-operative societies in Sabarkantha district of Gujarat. *Indian Journal of Agricultural Economics.* 43, 3, 1988. pp. 390–397. AAUL, CSSL, GIDRL, HML, IIML, SGUL, TRTIL, UML.

Patel, Premji M. Inter-district variation in agricultural prices in Gujarat. *Indian Journal of Regional Science.* 19, 1, 1987. pp. 17–23. CEPTL, CSSL, GIDRL.

Patel, P.T., Sonani, V.V. and Patel, G.G. Effect of FYM and N levels on rice grown in the Bhal tract of Gujarat. *Journal of the Gujarat Society of Agronomy and Soil Science.* 4, 1–2, 2004. pp. 30–32. AAUL.

Patel, R.B. Aspergillus rot of mango fruits in Gujarat. *Journal of the Gujarat Research Society.* 34, 1/133, 1972. pp. 84–85. GVL.

Patel, R.B. and Rao, P.S. Post harvest diseases of the gauva fruits in Ahmedabad market and their control. *Journal of the Gujarat Research Society.* 46–47, 154/155, 1984–85. pp. 41–46. GVL.

Patel, R.C., et al. Management of Gujarat hairy caterpillar, amsacta moorei but. by ultra violet light trap. *Gujarat Agricultural University Research Journal.* 12, 2, 1987. pp. 59–61. AAUL, GVL.

Patel, R.G., Patel, H.C. and Patel, M.P. Effect of nipping and levels of phosphorus on yield and economics of gram in clay soils of South Gujarat. *Gujarat Agricultural University Research Journal.* 15, 1, 1989. pp. 77–78. GVL.

Patel, R.G., Patel, R.B. and Patel, H.C. Crop weed competition in summer groundnut under clayey soils of South Gujarat. *Gujarat Agricultural University Research Journal.* 14, 1, 1988. pp. 52–54. GVL.

Patel, R.G., Patel, T.D. and Patel, H.C. Response of arhar to various dates and methods of sowing under South Gujarat conditions. *Gujarat Agricultural University Research Journal.* 13, 2, 1988. pp. 71–72. AAUL, GVL.

Patel, R.G., Yadav, D.N. and Dodia, J.F. On the occurrence of systole albipennis walker (Hymenoptera: eurytomidae) infesting fennel in Gujarat. *Gujarat Agricultural University Research Journal.* 12, 1, 1986. pp. 51–53. AAUL, GVL.

Patel, R.H. and Parmar, G.D. Potentiality of increasing farm income and its complementarily with dairy enterprise in cotton zone of Surat district in Gujarat. *Agricultural Situation in India.* 52, 11, 1997. pp. 751–758. IIML, IRMAL.

Patel, R.H., Asodiya, P.S. and Bhatt, B.K. Impact of PACS finance on marginal and small farmers' economy of Panchmahal district of Middle Gujarat. *Artha-Vikas.* 46, 1, 2010. pp. 33–45. CSSL.

Patel, R.J. Cess on commercial crops: a case for Gujarat. *Vishleshan.* 6, 3, 1980. pp. 60–62. CSSL, GIDRL.

Patel, R.J. and Bhatt, Mahesh P. Investment on agricultural research in Gujarat. *Indian Journal of Agricultural Economics.* 32, 3, 1977. pp. 232–238. AAUL, CSSL, IRMAL, TRTIL, UML.

Patel, R.J. and Gabani, L.J. Economic analysis of hybrid bajra seed production and marketing in Gujarat. *Indian Journal of Agricultural Economics*. 28, 4, 1973. pp. 85–92. IRMAL, UML.

Patel, R.J. and Kuchhadiya, D.B. Economic analysis of lift irrigation on Saurashtra farms. *Vishleshan*. 3, 4, 1977. pp. 331–336. CSSL, GIDRL.

Patel, R.J. and Solanki, H.S. Economics of production and employment in cumin in Mehsana district of Gujarat state. *Vishleshan*. 4, 3, 1978. pp. 220–229. CSSL, GIDRL, IIML.

Patel, R.J., Patel, T.D. and Patel, R.H. Response of mustard varieties to time of N application and thinning under Middle Gujarat conditions. *Journal of the Gujarat Society of Agronomy and Soil Science*. 2, 2, 1999. pp. 93–94. AAUL.

Patel, R.J. and Thumar, B.L. Economic analysis of bullock draught power of Saurashtra farms. *Artha-Vikas*. 13, 2, 1978. pp. 44–57. GIDRL, HML.

Patel, R.M. Contribution of technological changes to outturn of bajri crop: Gujarat state. *Vishleshan*. 7, 3 and 4, 1981. pp. 219–225. CSSL, GIDRL, IIML.

Patel, R.R., Patel, J.R. and Sonani, V.V. Effect of inoculation N and P fertilization on yield and yield attributes of greengram var. Gujarat-1 (Vigna Radiata(L.) Wilczek). *Gujarat Agricultural University Research Journal*. 14, 1, 1988. pp. 17–22. GVL.

Patel, R.S., Patel, M.M. and Saxena, Alok. Industrial method of bypass protein and normal cattle feed production of Panchmahal dairy. *Indian Dairyman*. 62, 12, 2010. pp. 72–78. AAUL.

Patel, R.S., et al. Industrial method of Ghee making at Panchmahal dairy, Godhra. *Indian Dairyman*. 58, 8, 2006. pp. 49–56. AAUL.

Patel, S.K.J. Is agriculture a paying occupation? an inquiry in the Bhal region. *Journal of the Gujarat research Society*. 8, 1, 1946. pp. 16–25. GUL.

Patel, S.M. and Pandey, Madhav. Production economics of cotton in Gujarat (RP 242–2). *Indian Cooperative Review*. 14, 3, 1977. pp. 213–228. IRMAL, SGUL.

Patel, Sejal B. Costs and returns of production of cotton and its competing crops in Bharuch district: a micro study of Vagra taluka. *Vishleshan*. 38, 3 and 4, 2012. pp. 45–61. CSSL.

Patel, T.D. and Patel, Z.G. Yield and yield attributes of summer groundnut as affected by sowing time, spacing and phosphorus level in South Gujarat. *Gujarat Agricultural University Research Journal*. 14, 1, 1988. pp. 49–51. GVL.

Patel, T.D., Patel, Z.G. and Patel, H.C. Investigation on the optimum spacing for different varieties at sesamum grown in summer season under South Gujarat conditions. *Gujarat Agricultural University Research Journal*. 13, 2, 1988. pp. 1–3. AAUL, GVL.

Patel, U.K., et al. Cultural management of soil and rainwater in rainfed cotton G. Cot -11 G. Herbaceum L. using various improved cultural practice in black cotton soils of Middle Gujarat. *Gujarat Agricultural University Research Journal*. 14, 2, 1989. pp. 25–29. AAUL.

Patel, V.A. and Vaishnav, M.U. Assessment of losses in groundnut due to rust and 'tikka' leaf spots in Gujarat. *Gujarat Agricultural University Research Journal*. 12, 2, 1987. pp. 52–53. AAUL, GVL.

Patel, V.B. and Thakkar, K.A. Adoption behaviour of the tribal farmers of Sabarkantha district towards improved animal husbandry practices. *Gujarat Agricultural University Research Journal*. 37, 1, 2012. pp. 62–64. AAUL.

Patel, V.J. Forestry-scope and approach tribal migrants as farm. *Adivasi Gujarat*. 3, 2, 1980. pp. 54–62. CSSL, SPIESRL.

Patel, V.J. Improved wheat varieties 'J1–7' and GAU V1–10 (J-24) for Gujarat. *Gujarat Agricultural University Research Journal.* 2, 1, 1976. pp. 61–64. AAUL, GVL.

Patel, V.J. and Patel, C.B. Biology of tur pod fly, melanagromyza obtusa malloch under South Gujarat condition. *Gujarat Agricultural University Research Journal.* 18, 1, 1992. pp. 67–69. AAUL, GVL.

Patel, V.J., Joshi, N.V. and Kikani, B.K. Varietal trials on wheat (Triticum Aestivum L.) in Gujarat. *Indian Journal of Agricultural Sciences.* 42, 4, 1972. pp. 289–291. GVL.

Patel, V.K., et al. Anti darkening treatments and packaging on physico-chemical changes in whole and sliced fruits on frozen aonla CV: Gujarat aonla-1. *Asian Journal of Horticulture.* 7, 2, 2012. pp. 423–428. AAUL.

Patel, V.M. Impact of the milk co-operatives in Gujarat. *Indian Dairyman,* 39, 6, 1987. pp. 293-[ ]. SGUL.

Patel, Vithalbhai. Agricultural wages in Bharuch district of Gujarat. *Agricultural Situation in India.* 38, 4, 1983. pp. 207-[ ]. SPIESRL.

Patel, Vyas and Patel, A.T. Agroclimatic appraisal of Khed brahma. *Gujarat Agricultural University Research Journal.* 13, 1, 1987. pp. 21–28. GVL.

Patel, Yatin and Joshi, P.N. Floristic inventory in the Banni region of Bhuj taluka, Kachh district, Gujarat, India. *Indian Forester.* 137, 9, 2011. pp. 1114–1121. CEPTL, GIDEL.

Patel, Z.N. and Patel, J.C. Evaluation of diagnostic techniques for appraising salinity of Bhal-Nal soils of Gujarat using various dilute aqueous extracts. *Gujarat Agricultural University Research Journal.* 17, 2, 1992. pp. 26–30. GVL.

Patel, Z.N. and Patel, J.C. Rapid appraisal of salinity for Bhal-Nal soils of Gujarat using chloride content. *Current Agriculture.* 13, 1–2, 1989. pp. 67–71. AAUL.

Pathak, Mahesh and Singh, P.K. Frontiers of agricultural development in Gujarat. *Agricultural Situation in India.* 64, 11, 2008. pp. 537–546. IIML, IRMAL, SGUL, SPIESRL.

Pathak, Mahesh, Desai, Mahendra D. and Charan, A.S. Development of agriculture in the backward regions of Gujarat: facts and issues. *Artha-Vikas.* 9, 1–2, 1973. pp. 100–138. GVL, HML, SGUL.

Pathak, Mahesh, Patel, H.F. and Shah, V.D. Assessing the existing training and testing facilities of farm machinery in Gujarat. *Artha Vikas.* 38, 2, 2002. pp. 36–44. CSSL, IRMAL, SGUL.

Pathak, Pravin G. Regional development in the perspective of allied agricultural activities: a case study of Gujarat. *Anvesak.* 26, 1, 1996. pp. 1–49. CSSL, IRMAL, SPIESRL.

Pati, B.P. and Vijayan, S. Mortality in Asiatic Lions (Panthera Leo Persica) in Gir sanctuary and national park Gujarat: a case for population stabilisation. *Indian Forester.* 128, 10, 2002. pp. 1159–1161. GIDEL, SGUL.

Pati, B.P., Belim M. Hanif and Pathak, B.J. Rescue and health status of big carnivores in and around Gir protected area Gujarat. *Indian Forester.* 128, 10, 2002. pp. 1133–1144. GIDEL, IIML, SGUL.

Patra, B.K. and Sahu, D.D. Use of agrometeorological indices for suitable sowing time of wheat under South Saurashtra agroclimatic zone of Gujarat. *Journal of Agrometeorology.* 9, 1, 2007. pp. 74–80. IRMAL.

Pokharna, S.S., et al. Crop production forecasting in Gujarat using remote sensing and meteorological data. *Artha-Vikas.* 35, 1, 1999. pp. 38–47. AAUL, CSSL, GIDRL, IRMAL.

Prajapati, B.H., Khatri, T.J. and Upadhyay, S.M. Estimate of optimum plot size from uniformity data of mustard for North Gujarat. *Gujarat Agricultural University Research Journal.* 18, 2, 1993. pp. 35–39. AAUL, GVL.

Prajapati, B.H., et al. Optimum size and shape of plot for yield experiment on mustard under North Gujarat condition. *Gujarat Agricultural University Research Journal.* 38, 1, 2013. pp. 32–35. AAUL.

Prajapati, D.B., et al. Gujarat chilli: a high yielding cultivar of spice chilli for North Gujarat.*Gujarat Agricultural University Research Journal.* 38, 1, 2013. pp. 1–5. AAUL.

Prajapati, K.B. Effect of exercise on sexual behaviour of Mehsana buffalo bulls in different seasons. *Indian Journal of Dairy Science.* 52, 2, 1999. pp. 100–103. AAUL.

Prajapati, K.B., et al. Association of milk vein measurements, escutcheon length and skin fold thickness with milk production in Mehsana buffaloes. *Indian Journal of Dairy Science.* 46, 4, 1993. pp. 180–181. AAUL.

Prajapati, M.P. and Patel, L.R. Studies on physiological variations in frenchbean (Phaseolus Vulgaris L.) as influenced by weed control methods and nitrogen level under North Gujarat conditions. *Gujarat Agricultural University Research Journal.* 26, 2, 2001. pp. 12–17. GVL.

Prajapati, M.P., et al. Studies on physiological variations in frenchbean as influenced by integrated weed management and nitrogen levels under North Gujarat conditions. *Indian Journal of Agricultural Research.* 26, 2, 2001. pp. 12–16. AAUL.

Prasad, C. and Bhatia, P.C. Mahua as livelihood support for tribal regions. *Indian Farming.* 60, 8, 2010. pp. 10–16. GVL.

Purohit, M.L. Imbalances in food consumption and nutrition in Kutch district of Gujarat. *Agricultural Economics Research Review.* 10, 1, 1997. pp. 127–131. IIML.

Purohit, M.S., Holer, G.H. and Shah, A.H. Preliminary observation on the egg parasitoids of rice stem borer (Scirpophaga incertulas walker) under hot weather condition in Gujarat. *Gujarat Agricultural University Research Journal.* 18, 1, 1992. pp. 128–131. GVL.

Purohit, M.S., Shah, A.H. and Raman, S. Chemical control of Rice stem borer scirpophaga incertulas walker in Gujarat. *Gujarat Agricultural University Research Journal.* 13, 2, 1988. pp. 23–27. AAUL, GVL.

Purohit, M.S., Shah, A.H. and Raman, S. Yield losses in rice due to stem borer (Scripophaga incertulas walker) in Gujarat. *Gujarat Agricultural University Research Journal.* 15, 1, 1989. pp. 91–93. GVL.

Rabari, P.M. and Patel, R.C. Housefly breeding intensity in various media during different seasons: a study around Anand campus. *Gujarat Agricultural University Research Journal.* 2, 2, 1977. pp. 87–91. AAUL, GVL.

Rafique, A. Preparation and evaluation of spawn for the cultivation of pleurotus in Gujarat. *Journal of Scientific & Industrial Research.* 57, 3, 1998. pp. 143–147. EDIL.

Rai, A.B., Patel, K.G. and Jhala, R.C. Chemical control of mealybug, coccidohystrix insolita(Green) infesting pigeonpea in South Gujarat area. *Gujarat Agricultural University Research Journal.* 17, 2, 1992. pp. 72–75. GVL.

Rai, A.B., Shah, A.H. and Patel, R.N. Biology of oligonychus indicus (Acari: Tetranychidae) infating sorgham in South Gujarat. *Gujarat Agricultural University Research Journal.* 15, 1, 1989. pp. 47–52. GVL.

Rai, A.B., Shah, A.H. and Patel, R.N. Biology of oligonychus mangiferus (Tetranychidae: acarina), a pest of mango in Gujarat. *Gujarat Agricultural University Research Journal.* 14, 1, 1988. pp. 5–10. GVL.

Rai Bahadur, C.D. Land problems of Gujarat. *Indian Journal of Agricultural Economics.* 3, 1, 1948. pp. 27–40. IIML, UML.

Rajak, Sujeet, Sharma, Arpita and Ananthan, P.S. Market survey of shrimp feed in Gujarat. *Indian Journal of Marketing.* 36, 3, 2006. pp. 15–20. IRMAL.

Rajani, M.J. Physico-chemical characteristic of black cotton soils of Bharuch district of Gujarat state, India. *Vidya.* 16, 1, 1973. pp. 1–9. SGUL.

Ram, Ant and Kumar, Ashok. Trends and acreage response of groundnut in Gujarat. *Anvesak.* 20, 1–2, 1990. pp. 135–141. CEPTL, CSSL, IRMAL.

Ramachandran, V. and Krishna, P.V. Gujarat cooperatives in fertilizer distribution and marketing (RP 225–3). *Indian Cooperative Review.* 11, 4, 1974. pp. 493–503. IRMAL.

Ramani, V.P., Patel, K.C. and George, V. Status of micronutrient cautions in soils of Gujarat. *Gujarat Agricultural University Research Journal.* 22, 2, 1997. pp. 136–140. GVL.

Ramesh, D., Shah, R.L. and Patel, G.A. Measurement of size of farm and efficiency some alternative approaches: the Bhal tract (Gujarat state). *Indian Journal of Agricultural Economics.* 23, 1, 1968. pp. 70–78. AAUL, UML.

Rana, K. and Verma, Raja. Prediction of wheat yield in Gujarat from temperature and total precipitation. *Gujarat Agricultural University Research Journal.* 7, 1, 1981. pp. 74-[ ]. AAUL.

Ranade, Rahul and Dinesh Kumar, M. Narmada water for groundwater recharge in North Gujarat: conjunctive management in large irrigation projects. *Economic and Political Weekly.* 39, 31, 2004. pp. 3510–3513. BUL, CEPTL, CSSL, EDIL, GIDRL, IIML, IRMAL, MICAL, SGUL, SPIESRL, UML.

Ranjana, Arya, Lohara, R.R. and Meena, R.L. Establishment and biomass yield of salvadora persica with different treatments in the little rann of Kachchh. *Current Agriculture.* 36, 1–2, 2012. pp. 41–45. AAUL.

Ranjana, Arya., Lohara, R.R. and Meena, R.L. Performance of exotic acacia spp on highly saline black salty clay soil in the little rann of Kuchchh. *Current Agriculture.* 34, 1–2, 2010. pp. 69–74. AAUL.

Rankja, N.J., et al. Estimation of cotton yield based on weather parameters of Banaskantha district in Gujarat state. *Journal of Agrometeorology.* 12, 1, 2010. pp. 47–52. IRMAL.

Rao, Darsi V.S. and Parmar, G.D. Cost of production of milk in the urban area with special reference to Surat city of Gujarat state. *Gujarat Agricultural University Research Journal.* 16, 1, 1990. pp. 27–32. GVL.

Rao, Madhav V. Anand pattern: a model for dairy development in India. *Indian Dairyman.* 41, 11, 1989. pp. 582–595. AAUL.

Rao, V.M. Village lease markets for agricultural land: some approaches for analysis. *Economic and Political Weekly.* 9, 26, 1974. pp. A-55-A-62. CSSL, IRMAL, SGUL, SPIESRL, UML.

Rao, V.S. and Parmar, G.D. Comparative study of costs and returns for different categories of milk producer in Surat city. *Gujarat Agricultural University Research Journal.* 15, 2, 1990. pp. 37–42. AAUL.

Rawal, P.P., Jani, S.M. and Khandar, R.R. Foliar diseases of groundnut in Gujarat. *Indian Farming.* 32, 4, 1982. pp. 17–20. GVL, IIML.

Rawale, Kishor. Post harvest handling and marketing of mango in Gujarat. *Agricultural Marketing*. 47, 1, 2004. pp. 36–41. IRMAL.

Reddy, T.V.R. and Patel, I.C. Characteristics of agricultural extension-officers in Gujarat. *Indian Journal of Social Work*. 32, 4, 1972. pp. 429–435. GVL, TRTIL.

Rizvi, S.M.H. Social forestry in Gujarat. *Journal of the M.S. University of Baroda*. 29, 2, 1980. pp. 17–28. GVL.

Roy, Devparna. Of choices and dilemmas: bt. cotton and self identified organic cotton farmers in Gujarat. *Asian Biotechnology and Development Research*. 12, 1, 2010. pp. 51–79. IRMAL.

Rutten, Mario. Social profile of agricultural entrepreneurs: economic behaviour and life-style of middle-large farmers in Central Gujarat. *Economic and Political Weekly*. 21, 13, 1986. pp. A-15-A-23. CEPTL, CSSL, IIML, IRMAL, SGUL, SPIESRL, UML.

Sadaria, S.G., et al. Irrigation and nutrient requirement of garlic (Allium sativum) under South Saurashtra region in Gujarat. *Indian Journal of Agricultural Science*. 67, 9, 1997. pp. 402–403. AAUL, GVL.

Sah, D.C. and Ranade, C.G. Bio-fertilisers in Indian agriculture: a case study of Gujarat. *Economic and Political Weekly*. 18, 13, 1983. pp. A-32-A-43. CEPTL, CSSL, GUL, IRMAL, SGUL, SPIESRL, UML.

Sah, D.C. and Shah, Amita. Efficiency of fertilizer use: demand for soil testing services in Gujarat. *Indian Journal of Agricultural Economics*. 47, 3, 1992. pp. 459–467. AAUL, CEPTL, CSSL, HML, IIML, IRMAL, SGUL, UML.

Sah, D.C. and Shah, Amita. Inefficiency and efficacy of soil testing services: a case study of Gujarat. *Artha Vijnana*. 37, 1, 1995. pp. 77–100. AAUL, CSSL, GVL, HML, IRMAL, UML.

Sahu, D.D. and Sastry, P.S.N. Assessment of methods of estimating reference crop evapotranspiration (ET.) in Gujarat region. *Gujarat Agricultural University Research Journal*. 18, 2, 1993. pp. 105–108. AAUL, GVL.

Sahu, D.D. and Sastry, P.S.N. Phenophasic and seasonal water requirement of major kharif crops in different agroclimatic zones of Gujarat state. *Gujarat Agricultural University Research Journal*. 18, 2, 1993. pp. 28–34. AAUL, GVL.

Saini, G.R. and Sharma, Chand Dhar. Production and marketing of mangoes in Gujarat. *Agricultural Situation in India*. 39, 12, 1985. pp. 949-[ ]. SPIESRL.

Sandhu, G.S. Custom hiring in Gujarat: some finding. *Agricultural Situation in India*. 29, 10, 1975. pp. 759-[ ]. SPIESRL.

Sanghvi, P.S. Land problems and reforms in Saurashtra. *Journal of the University of Bombay*. 24, 4, 1956. pp. 22-[ ]. GVL.

Sardar Patel University, Vallabh Vidyanagar, Gujarat. Review of state agricultural policy in Gujarat. *Agricultural Situation in India*. 61, 5, 2004. pp. 295–314. SGUL.

Sarin, Madhu. Process documentation by a self-initiated forest protection group in Gujarat. *Wastelands News*. 10, 3, 1995. pp. 18–21. IRMAL.

Sarup, Shanti and Pandey, R.K. Inter-district growth analysis of groundnut in Gujarat. *Margin*. 18, 2, 1986. pp. 77–84. CSSL, GIDRL, SGUL, UML.

Savalia, S.G., Mehta, P.M. and Patel, M.L. Evaluation of soil availability parameters for predicting yield and P uptake by wheat in deep black soil of South Gujarat. *Journal of Agricultural Research*. 5, 1, 1994. pp. 85–90. AAUL.

Savalia, S.G. and Patel, M.L. Availability of native soil phosphorus in black soil of South Gujarat. *Gujarat Agricultural University Research Journal*. 17, 2, 1992. pp. 31–36. GVL.

Savalia, S.G., Patel, M.L. and Mehta, P.M. Survey of capacity, intensity and rate of release factors of soil phosphorous in different subgroups of soil of South Gujarat. *Gujarat Agricultural University Research Journal*. 19, 2, 1994. pp. 15–19. AAUL.

Sejalia, A.S., et al. On the biological aspects of tetranychus macfarlanei (Acari: tetranychidae) infesting okra (Abelmoschus esculentus) in South Gujarat. *Gujarat Agricultural University Research Journal*. 19, 1, 1993. pp. 32–37. AAUL, GVL.

Selvarajan, S. and Singh, N.P. Production and resource use planning Mahi right bank canal command zone 1 Gujarat. *Journal of Indian Water Resources Society*. 4, 1, 1998. pp. 11–17. IRMAL.

Sen, N.L., Kikani, K.P. and Kapadia, M.N. Studies on barrenness in coconut in Gujarat. *Gujarat Agricultural University Research Journal*. 10, 2, 1985. pp. 10–15. AAUL, GVL.

Shah, A.C. Note on supply of co-operative agricultural credit in Gujarat. *Journal of the Gujarat Research Society*. 22, 2/86, 1960. pp. 158–160. GVL.

Shah, A.H. and Patel, G.M. Record of chlumetia transversa walker as a new pest of mango in South Gujarat. *Agriculture and Agro-Industries Journal*. 11, 9, 1978. pp. 10-[ ]. IIML.

Shah, A.H., Jhala, R.C. and Patel, G.M. Occurrence of waxy scale, ceroplastes actiniformis green, on mango in South Gujarat. *Indian Journal of Agricultural Science*. 56, 1, 1986. pp. 67–68. AAUL, GVL.

Shah, A.H., Patel, G.M. and Jhala, R.C. Occurrence of mango flea weevil rhynchaenus mangiferae marshal in Gujarat and its relative damage in important varieties of mango. *Gujarat Agricultural University Research Journal*. 8, 2, 1983. pp. 127–128. AAUL, GVL.

Shah, A.H., Patel, M.B. and Patel, G.M. Record of coccinellid predator (Serangium earcesetosum sci.) of sugarcane whitefly in South Gujarat. *Gujarat Agricultural University Research Journal*. 12, 1, 1986. pp. 63–64. AAUL, GVL.

Shah, A.H., Purohit, M.S. and Patel, G.M. Afidentula minima gorham (Coccinellidae, coleoptera), a new pest of fingermillet and its intensity of damage in South Gujarat. *Gujarat Agricultural University Research Journal*. 10, 1, 1984. pp. 62–63. AAUL, GVL.

Shah, A.H., et al. Chemical control of rice yellow stem borer, scirpophaga incertuals and its carryover in Gujarat. *Gujarat Agricultural University Research Journal*. 21, 2, 1996. pp. 37–40. AAUL.

Shah, Amita. Levels of liquidity and farmer's perceptions: lessons from watershed projects in Gujarat. *Artha Vijnana*. 39, 4, 1997. pp. 457–472. GIDRL, UML.

Shah, Amita. Livestock under the frequent drought situation in Gujarat: evidence and issues. *Agricultural Economics Research Review*. 14, [ ], 2001. pp. 84–92. IIML, IRMAL.

Shah, Amita. Low cost options for watershed development in dry land agriculture: implications for employment. *Indian Journal of Labour Economics*. 37, 2, 1994. pp. 229–236. CSSL.

Shah, Amita. Management of protected areas: exploring an alternative in Gir. *Economic and Political Weekly*. 42, 27 and 28, 2007. pp. 2923–2930. BUL, CEPTL, CSSL, EDIL, IIML, IRMAL, MICAL, SGUL, SPIESRL, SUL, UML.

Shah, Amita. Moisture-yield interaction and farmers' perceptions: lessons from watershed projects in Gujarat. *Artha Vijnana*. 39, 4, 1997. pp. 457–472. AAUL, CSSL, EDIL, GIDRL, IRMAL, UML.

Shah, Amita. Promoting small water harvesting structures in dryland regions: a case study of the farm ponds scheme in Gujarat. *Agricultural Economics Research Review*. 14, 1, 2001. pp. 47–64. AAUL, IIML, IRMAL.

Shah, Amita and Sah, D.C. Dryland farming under the changing source environment: a case study of Gujarat. *Artha Vijanana*. 35, 3, 1993. pp. 241–269. AAUL, CSSL, GIDRL, GVL, UML.

Shah, Amita and Sah, D.C. Efficiency of fertilizer use: demand for soil testing services in Gujarat. *Indian Journal of Agricultural Economics*. 47, 3, 1992. pp. 459–467. GIDRL, UML.

Shah, C.H. Basic approach to development of agriculture with illustration from Gujarat. *Journal of the Gujarat Research Society*. 22, 2/86, 1960. pp. 105–113. GVL.

Shah, C.H. Impact of tenancy reform on level of technology (Gujarat and Maharashtra). *Artha-Vikas*. 8, 2, 1972. pp. 19–40. GVL, HML, SGUL.

Shah, D.B. et al. Estimation of minimum and maximum air temperature using models data over Gujarat. *Journal of Agrometeorology*. 14, 2, 2012. pp. 111–118. IRMAL.

Shah, Esha. Local and global elites join hands: development and diffusion of bt cotton technology in Gujarat. *Economic and Political Weekly*. 40, 43, 2005. pp. 4629–4639. BUL, CEPTL, CSSL, EDIL, GIDRL, IIML, MICAL, SGUL, SPIESRL, UML.

Shah, Ghanshyam. Kheduts in Gujarat. *Seminar*. 352, 1988. pp. 32–38. CSSL, GIDRL, GVL, IRMAL, UML.

Shah, J.P. and Trivakaran, G.A. Status and distribution of halophytes in Kuchchh district: a review. *Current Agriculture*. 36, 1–2, 2012. pp. 29–36. AAUL.

Shah, Jignesh and Dave, Darshana. Regional trends and pattern in milk production and drivers for future growth in Gujarat state. *Agricultural Economics Research Review*. 23, 2, 2010. pp. 295–302. IIML, IRMAL.

Shah, Jignesh and Meena, P.C. Social transition in dairying: a case study from Anand district of Gujarat. *Journal of Rural Development*. 30, 3, 2011. pp. 307–319. IRMAL.

Shah, N.R. Emerging problems of agricultural marketing: a case study of mustard in Gujarat. *Agricultural Situation in India*. 54, 5, 1997. pp. 247–250. IIML, IRMAL.

Shah, N.R. Prospects of increasing oilseeds and pulses production in Gujarat. *Agricultural Situation in India*. 45, 2, 1990. pp. 143-[ ]. SPIESRL.

Shah, Navin R. Groundnut development programme in Gujarat. *Artha-Vikas*. 22, 1 and 2, 1986. pp. 22–38. AAUL, CSSL, GIDRL, GVL, HML.

Shah, P.G., Raj, M.F. and Talati, J.G. Chlorinated pesticide residues in milk samples from Banaskantha district of Gujarat. *Gujarat Agricultural University Research Journal*. 18, 1, 1992. pp. 85–89. AAUL, GVL.

Shah, R.L. and Patel, G.A. Bhal tract: Gujarat state. *Indian Journal of Agricultural Economics*. 23, 1, 1968. pp. 70–78. GIDRL, TRTIL, UML.

Shah, R.L. and Patel, G.A. Measuring benefit due to contour bunding in Panchmahals district of Gujarat state. *Indian Journal of Agronomy*. 15, 4, 1970. pp. 410–414. AAUL.

Shah, R.M., Chandel, K.P.S. and Pant, K.C. Sabarmati: a new promising mung variety for Gujarat. *Indian Farming*. 34, 9, 1984. pp. 25–26. GVL.

Shah, R.M., Pathak, A.R. and Patel, R.S. ICCC. 4: a new high-yielding gram for Gujarat. *Indian Farming*. 35, 6, 1985. pp. 29–32. IIML.

Shah, Tushaar. Sustainable development of groundwater resource: lessons from Junagadh district. *Economic and Political Weekly*. 27, 10 and 11, 1992. pp. 515–520. CEPTL, CSSL, IIML, IRMAL, SGUL, SPIESRL, UML.

Shah, Tushar and Modak, Shrikant. Impact of NDDB's oilseeds project on farmers of Saurashtra. *Economic and Political Weekly*. 19, 38, 1984. pp. 1671–1676. CEPTL, CSSL, GUL, IIML, IRMAL, SGUL, SPIESRL, UML.

Shah, U.M. Crop insurance in Gujarat: case study. *Cooperative Perspective.* 22, 1 and 2, 1987. pp. 79–86. IRMAL.

Shah, V.B. and Maharaja, M. Crop insurance scheme in Gujarat. *Artha-Vikas.* 17, 1–2, 1981. pp. 125–136. GIDRL, GVL, HML, SGUL.

Shah, V.D. Constraints in fertilizer consumption. *Arth-Vikas.* 25, 1 and 2, 1989. pp. 13–26. GIDRL, HML.

Shah, V.D. and Patel, H.F. Impact of minimum support prices on agricultural economy in Gujarat. *Artha-Vikas*. 40, 2, 2004. pp. 39–53. CSSL.

Shaha, S.K. and Dasgupta, S.K. Fitting pearsonian system of curve to flowering frequencies in cotton at Kovilpatti, Coimbatore and Surat. *Indian Journal of Agricultural Sciences.* 44, 12, 1974. pp. 796–799. GVL.

Shaheen, F.A. and Shiyani, R.L. Energy costs and groundwater withdrawals: results from an optimal control model for North Gujarat. *Indian Journal of Agricultural Economics*. 62, 1, 2007. pp. 64–79. BUL, CSSL, GIDRL, IIML, UML.

Shaikh, A.S. and Zala, Y.C. Production performance and economic appraisal of broiler farms in Anand district of Gujarat. *Agricultural Economics Research Review*. 24, 2, 2011. pp. 317–323. IRMAL.

Shaikh, A.S. and Zala, Y.C. Study on marketing of broiler in Anand district of Gujarat. *Indian Journal of Agricultural Marketing.* 25, 2, 2011. pp. 18–26. IRMAL.

Sharan, Girja. Agro-mechanical technology in Gujarat. *Indian Journal of Agricultural Economics.* 39, 2, 1984. pp. 203–213. AAUL, CEPTL, CSSL, GIDRL, IIML, IRMAL, SGUL, TRTIL, UML.

Sharma, Diwakar and Gavali, Deepa. Protected areas in Gujarat prospects and perspectives. *Indian Forester*. 132, 10, 2006. pp. 1292–1302. GIDEL, IRMAL.

Sharma, P.S. Study of variability of rainfall and cropping pattern in Gujarat state. *Agricultural Situation In India.* 19, 8, 1964. pp. 715–721. GVL, HML.

Sharma, U.S. Strategy for agricultural extension: need to strengthen organizational set-up: a study of Gujarat. *Journal of Rural Development*. 7, 5, 1988. pp. 601–615. CSSL, GVL, IIML, IRMAL, SGUL.

Sharma, Urmila and Yadav, D.N. Sunnhemp-crotalaria juncea linn: a reservoir for entomophages at Anand (India). *Gujarat Agricultural University Research Journal.* 23, 1, 1997. pp. 44–48. AAUL, GVL.

Sharma, Usha. Impact of public price policy on the price-level coarse cereals in Gujarat. *Vishleshan.* 7, 2, 1981. pp. 106–111. CSSL, GIDRL, IIML.

Sharma, Ushaben. Adoption of new seed technology and factors associated with it in Gujarat. *Anvesak*. 10, 1, 1980. pp. 41–60. CEPTL, CSSL, IRMAL.

Sharma, Ushaben. Contribution of HYVs to cereal output yield and area in Gujarat. *Indian Journal of Agricultural Economics*. 36, 1, 1981. pp. 79–81. AAUL, CEPTL, CSSL, GIDRL, GVL, HML, IIML, IRMAL, SGUL, UML.

Shekh, A.M., Patel, H.R. and Patel, G.G. Validation of cropgro peanut model in Middle Gujarat agroclimate region. *Journal of Agrometeorology.* 14, 2, 2012. pp. 154–157. IRMAL.

Shenoy, G.V. and Raju, K.V. Effectiveness of cattle insurance under IRDP: analysis of evidence from Pune and Surat district. *Journal of Rural Development.* 8, 4, 1989. pp. 341–358. GVL, IIML.

Sherasia, P.L., Garg, M.R. and Bhanderi, B.M. Assessment of nutritional status of dairy cows in Jamnagar district. *Indian Journal of Dairy Science*. 63, 3, 2010. pp. 209–215. AAUL.

Shinoda, Takashi. Nomadic cattle herders and customary rights for grazing in North Gujarat, India. *Anvesak.* 43, 1, 2013. pp. 1–19. CSSL, SPIESRL.

Shiyani, R.L. Growth and instability of inland fish production in Gujarat: spatio temporal analysis. *Artha Vijnana.* 44, 2, 2002. pp. 189–198. GIDRL, IRMAL, UML.

Shiyani, R.L. and Hiremath, Deepa B. Analysis of vulnerability indices in various agro-climatic zones of Gujarat. *Indian Journal of Agricultural Economics.* 68, 1, 2013. pp. 122–137. AAUL, UML.

Shiyani, R.L. and Joshi, M.V. Growth rates variability in dairying activities in Saurashtra region. *Indian Dairyman.* 41, 11, 1989. pp. 554–557. AAUL, SGUL.

Shiyani, R.L., Kakadia, B.H. and Tarpara, V.D. Impact of drought on Saurashtra agriculture. *Agricultural Situation in India.* 60, 2, 2003. pp. 75–80. IIML.

Shiyani, R.L. and Kuchhadiya, D.B. Marketing of vegetables in South Saurashtra zone of Gujarat. *Indian Journal of Agricultural Marketing.* 12, 1–2, 1998. pp. 156–160. IRMAL.

Shiyani, R. L, Kuchhadiya, D.B. and Patel, M.V. Economic impact of drip irrigation technology on cotton growers of Saurashtra region. *Agricultural Situation in India.* 56, 7, 1999. pp. 407–412. IIML.

Shiyani, R.L. and Pandya, H.R. Diversification of agriculture in Gujarat: a spatiotemporal analysis. *Indian Journal of Agricultural Economics.* 53, 4, 1998. pp. 627–639. AAUL, IRMAL, UML.

Shiyani, R.L. and Pandya, Maurvi N. Total factor productivity changes of oilseed crops in Gujarat. *Agricultural Situation in India.* 49, 12, 2003. pp. 791–798. EDIL, IIML, IRMAL.

Shiyani, R.L., Patel, R.D. and Kuchhadiya, D.B. Economics of buffalo milk production in Kheda district of Gujarat state. *Indian Dairyman.* 42, 1, 1989. pp. 1–6. AAUL.

Shiyani, R.L., et al. Adoption of improved chickpea varieties Kribhco experience in tribal region of Gujarat, India. *Agricultural Economics,* 27, 1, 2002. pp. 33–39. IRMAL.

Shome, Surashree. Neighbours of the global village small farmers from Gujarat. *Productivity.* 44, 1, 2003. pp. 21–25. IRMAL.

Shrotriya, G.C. and Lakhani, K.G. Some considerations for stimulating fertilizers consumption in Gujarat state. *Arth-Vikas.* 25, 1 and 2, 1989. pp. 34–43. GIDRL, HML.

Shukla, D.C., et al. Balbesiosis in Kankrej cows at Chharodi farm. *Gujarat Agricultural University Research Journal.* 8, 2, 1983. pp. 115–116. GVL.

Shukla, Nimisha. Status of common property resource (CPR) land in Gujarat. *Artha-Vikas.* 44, 1 and 2, 2008. pp. 1–23. CSSL.

Shukla, P.C., Desai, H.B. and Desai, M.C. Sheep nutrition survey in Banaskantha district. *Gujarat Agricultural University Research Journal.* 13, 1, 1987. pp. 31–40. GVL.

Shukla, P.C., et al. Proximate and trace eliminate contents of some samples of cattle feeds of Mehsana district. *Gujarat Agricultural University Research Journal.* 7, 2, 1982. pp. 127–131. AAUL, GVL.

Shukla, Tara. Production and productivity in agriculture in Gujarat. *Artha Vijnana.* 7, 1, 1965. pp. 47–53. GVL, UML.

Shukla, Tara. Trends in capital formation in agriculture in Gujarat. *Journal of the Gujarat Research Society.* 23, 2/90, 1961. pp. 144–147. GVL.

Silori, C.S., Geevan, C.P. and Dixit, A.M. Livestock population vis a vis common property land resources trends from Gujarat. *Indian Forester.* 132, 10, 2006. pp. 1303–1314. GIDEL, IRMAL.

Singh, A.P. Unique terrestrial ecosystem of white mangrove (avicennia officinalis Linn) in Kachchh desert of Gujarat state. *Indian Forester.* 128, 1, 2002. pp. 95–98. GIDEL, IIML.

Singh, Baldev. Economics of irrigation: a regional perspective: a case study of a DPAP district, Surendranagar. *Indian Journal of Agricultural Economics*. 33, 4, 1978. pp. 231–239. AAUL, CSSL. GIDRL, UML.

Singh, Baldev. Productivity and resource structure: a case study of agricultural development of Gujarat. *Indian Journal of Agricultural Economics*. 35, 3, 1980. pp. 34–50. AAUL, CEPTL, CSSL, HML, IIML, IRMAL, SGUL, TRTIL, UML.

Singh, Baldev. Role of credit in agricultural development: a case study of a backward Indian district, Surendranagar. *Anvesak*. 7, 1, 1977. pp. 15–32. CSSL, SPIESRL.

Singh, D.V., Tripathi, V.N. and Dave, A.S. Factors affecting sexual maturity traits in Mehsana buffaloes. *Indian Journal of Dairy Science*. 48, 6, 1995. pp. 442–443. AAUL.

Singh, D.V., Tripathi, V.N. and Dave, A.S. Genetic and phenotypic parameters of body measurement taints in Mehsana buffaloes. *Indian Journal of Dairy Science*. 50, 2, 1997. pp. 83–87. AAUL.

Singh, D.V., et al. Field progeny testing in Mehsana buffaloes in their native tract. *Indian Journal of Dairy Science*. 47, 9, 1994. pp. 744–748. AAUL.

Singh, H.B., Pande, V.C. and Patel, A.P. Crop diversification for conservation and sustainable production on marginal tends of Mahi river in Gujarat. *Gujarat Agricultural University Research Journal.* 23, 2, 1998. pp. 97–100. GVL.

Singh, H.S. Appropriate silviculture models under the joint forest management: Gujarat state. *Indian Forester.* 123, 6, 1997. pp. 477–483. IIML.

Singh, Katar. Analysis and evaluation of planning and implementation of integrated rural development programme in Sabarkantha district of Gujarat. *Indian Journal of Agricultural Economics*. 39, 3, 1984. pp. 419–426. AAUL, CEPTL, CSSL, GIDRL, GVL, HML, IIML, TRTIL, UML.

Singh, Katar. Co-management of canal irrigation: case study in Gujarat. *Journal of Indian Water Resources Society*. 14, 1–4, 1994. pp. 26–33. IRMAL.

Singh, Katar and Ranjana. New strategy for increasing oilseeds production: lessons from Saurashtra experience with groundnuts. *Indian Journal of Agricultural Economics.* 37, 3, 1982. pp. 380–385. GIDRL, UML.

Singh, Katar, et al. Effect of canal irrigation on water logging and soil salinity in the Mahi right bank canal command area in Gujarat. *Ecology: Environment, Ecology and Energy Conservation.* 9, 11, 1995. pp. 1–7. IRMAL.

Singh, O.P. Analysis of major oilseeds production in Gujarat, India. *Economic Affairs*. 47, 4, 2002. pp. 234–242. AAUL.

Singh, O.P. Hydrological and farming system impacts of agricultural water management interventions in North Gujarat, India. *Indian Journal of Agricultural Economics.* 68, 3, 2013. pp. 292–312. AAUL, CSSL, UML.

Singh, O.P. Variation in land utilisation pattern and operational holdings: a case study of Gujarat state. *Rural India*. 63, 5, 2000. pp. 109–119. GVL.

Singh, O.P., et al. Virtual water trade in dairy economy: irrigation water productivity in Gujarat. *Economic and Political Weekly*. 39, 31, 2004. pp. 3492–3497. BUL, CEPTL, CSSL, EDIL, IIML, IRMAL, MICAL, SGUL, SPIESRL, UML.

Singh, P.K. Sustainable agricultural development in Gujarat: a perspective. *Vishleshan*. 28, 3, 2003. pp. 30–37. CSSL, IIML, IRMAL.

Singh, P.K. and Chauhan, D.J. Rural and agricultural credit in India and Gujarat: some aspects. *Artha-Vikas*. 45, 1, 2009. pp. 75–88. CSSL.

Singh, P.K. and Marakana, G.G. Inter regional disparities in the distribution of draught animals in Gujarat state. *Gujarat Agricultural University Research Journal.* 17, 2, 1992. pp. 102–106. GVL.

Singh, P.K. and Patel, H.F. Growth performance and prospects of seafood exports from Gujarat: econometric study. *Artha-Vikas*. 31, 1, 1995. pp. 10–18. CSSL, IRMAL.

Singh, P.K., Kakadia, B.H. and Patel, V.M. Marketing of potato in a major potato producing area in Gujarat. *Indian Journal of Agricultural Marketing.* 7, 2, 1993. pp. 179–185. AAUL.

Singh, R.V. and Deora, B.S. Frequency analysis of water deficit for crop planning in Gujarat. *Journal of Agrometeorology.* 10, 2, 2008. pp. 184–187. IRMAL.

Singh, Ravender and Kundu, D.K. Soil salinity effect on germination of wheat (Triticum aestivum), castor (Ricinus communis), safflower (Carthamus tinctorus) and dill seed (Anethum graveolens) in vertic ustochrpt of Bhal region of Gujarat. *Indian Journal of Agricultural Sciences.* 70, 6, 2000. pp. 459–461. GVL.

Singh, S.B. and Goswami, K.V. Cost-benefit analysis of afforestation in deep ravines of Gujarat. *Indian Journal of Agricultural Economics*. 31, 1, 1976. pp. 48–55. GIDRL, UML.

Singh, Sanjay and Singh, A.K. Genetic diversity in Mahuva under semi-arid ecosystem of Gujarat. *Indian Journal of Agricultural Sciences*. 75, 8, 2005. pp. 519–523. AAUL.

Singh, Sanjay, Singh, A.K. and Apparao, V.V. Genetic diversity in chironji under semi arid ecosystem of Gujarat. *Indian Journal of Agricultural Science.* 76, 11, 2006. pp. 695–698. IRMAL.

Singh, Sanjay, Singh, A.K. and Joshi, H.K. Prolonging storability of Indian gooseberry under semi arid ecosystem of Gujarat. *Indian Journal of Agricultural Science.* 75, 10, 2005. pp. 647–650. IRMAL.

Singh, Sanjay, Singh, A.K. and Joshi, H.K. Standardization of maturity indices in Indian gooseberry under semi arid conditions of Gujarat. *Indian Journal of Agricultural Science.* 76, 10, 2006. pp. 591–595. IRMAL.

Singh, Sanjay., Singh, A.K. and Joshi, H.K. Storage behaviour of Indian gooseberry (Emblica officinalis) cultivars under semi-arid eco system of Gujarat. *Indian Journal of Agricultural Sciences.* 73, 10, 2003. pp. 530–533. AAUL, GVL.

Singh, S.V., et al. Scope and suitability of potato genotypes for industrial processing for French fries in Gujarat and Western Uttar Pradesh. *Indian Journal of Agricultural Science*. 75, 12, 2005. pp. 781–785. IRMAL.

Singh, Sukhpal. Agricultural marketing infrastructure: case of cold storage industry in Gujarat. *Productivity.* 39, 4, 1999. pp. 668–671. IRMAL.

Singh, Sukhpal. Food security and sustainability under the internationalisation of agriculture in Gujarat state, India. *Journal of Rural Reconstruction.* 31, 2, 1998. pp. 69–84. IRMAL.

Singh, Sukhpal. Managing marketing: co-operative in horticultural business in South Gujarat. *Indian Journal of Agricultural Marketing*. 11, 1 and 2, 1997. pp. 73–82. AAUL, IRMAL.

Singh, Sukhpal. Marketing infrastructure and agro-processing development: case study of Gujarat. *Indian Journal of Agricultural Marketing.* 10, 2, 1996. pp. 1–9. AAUL, IRMAL.

Singh, Sukhpal. Marketing of liquid milk: a case study of Ahmedabad milk market. *Indian Journal of Agricultural Economics*. 62, 3, 2007. pp. 440–447. AAUL, CSSL, IIML, UML.

Sinha, Bitapi C. and Sinha, Sataya Priya. Impact of religious tourism of Gir national park, Gujarat, India. *Indian Forester*. 134, 5, 2008. pp. 667–673. CEPTL, GIDEL, IIML, IRMAL.

Sivasubramanian, M.N. Biogas plants in Gujarat. *Changing Villages*. 4, 5, 1982. pp. 38–48. GVL.

Solanki, J.V. and Shukla, R.K. Electrophoretic haemoglobin types in jersey cattle in Gujarat state. *Gujarat Agricultural University Research Journal*. 3, 1, 1977. pp. 29–32. GVL.

Somani, V.J. Socio-economic development of tribals through crossbred cows in Surat district of Gujarat state in India. *Vishleshan*. 32, 4, 2007. pp. 5–27. CSSL, IIML.

Souri, R.D. Rural reconstruction in Baroda. *Indian Farming*. 1, 11, 1940. pp. 552–555. GVL.

Sreenivasan, P.S. Agricultural bio-climatology of Gujarat. *Indian Farming*. 23, 7, 1973. pp. 28–29. GVL, IIML, SGUL.

Srivastava, A.K. Change in physical and chemical properties of soil in irrigated eucalyptus plantation in Gujarat state. *Indian Forester*. 119, 3, 1993. pp. 227–231. IIML.

Srivastav, Asheem K. Strategy for wasteland afforestation in Gujarat. *Indian Forester*. 118, 9, 1992. pp. 623–629. IIML.

Srivastava, R.L., et al. Initial performance of tissue culture raised bamboos in Rajasthan and Gujarat. *Indian Forester*. 134, 7, 2008. pp. 916–922. CEPTL, GIDEL, IRMAL.

Subbi Reddy, C. and Shah, C.B. Performance of high yielding Virginia rumer groundnut cultivars in summer season in Gujarat state. *Gujarat Agricultural University Research Journal*. 10, 2, 1985. pp. 83–84. AAUL, GVL.

Subbi Reddy, C. and Shah, Z.G. Studies on varietal behaviour of Spanish bunch groundnut cultivars in summer season in Gujarat state. *Gujarat Agricultural University Research Journal*. 11, 1, 1985. pp. 55–56. GVL.

Sud, Nikita. From land to the tiller to land liberalisation the political economy of Gujarat's shifting land policy. *Modern Asian Studies*. 41, 3, 2007. pp. 603–637. IRMAL.

Suryavanshi, B. Landholders and land tenure in Panchmahal district during the nineteenth century A.D. *Journal of Indian History*. 61, 1–3, 1983. pp. 197–218. GVL.

Tailor, S.P., Kothari, M.S. and Meena, R.K. Comparison of single and multi trait selection in Surti buffaloes. *Indian Journal of Dairy Science*. 63, 2, 2010. pp. 146–149. AAUL.

Talati, G.M. and Upadhyay, V.R. Status of shoot fly Atherigona approximata malloch as a pest of bajra pennisetum typhoides crop in Gujarat state. *Gujarat Agricultural University Research Journal*. 4, 1, 1978. pp. 30–35. AAUL, GVL.

Talati, Jayesh and Shah, Tushaar. Institutional vacuum in Sardar Sarovar project: framing 'rules-of-the-game'. *Economic and Political Weekly*. 39, 31, 2004. pp. 3504–3509. BUL, CEPTL, CSSL, EDIL, IIML, IRMAL, MICAL, SGUL, SPIESRL, UML.

Tewari, D.D. Domestication of non-timber forest products (NTFPs): a case of bamboo farming in Kheda district Gujarat, India. *Indian Forester*. 127, 7, 2001. pp. 788–798. GIDEL, IIML, SGUL.

Tewari, D.D. Historical policy review of success of castor revolution in Gujarat, India. *Journal of Human Ecology*. 38, 3, 2012. pp. 213–222. CSSL.

Thakar, K.P. and Patel, D.A. Marketing of carrot in Patan district of North Gujarat. *Gujarat Agricultural University Research Journal*. 35, 1, 2010. pp. 40–44. AAUL.

Thaker, D.N. and Sabnis, S.D. Further exploration of the Kwant range forests, Chhotaudepur division, Gujarat state, India. *Journal of the M.S. University of Baroda*. 19–20, 3, 1970–71. pp. 35–48. GVL.

Thakur, D.S. Foodgrain marketing efficiency: a case study of Gujarat. *Indian Journal of Agricultural Economics*. 29, 4, 1974. pp. 61–73. AAUL, GIDRL, IRMAL, SGUL, SPIESRL, SPUL, UML.

Thakur, D.S. Impact of dairy development through milk co-operatives: a case study of Gujarat. *Indian Journal of Agricultural Economics*. 30, 3, 1975. pp. 83–89. GIDRL.

Thanki, K.V. and Patel, J.R. Seasonal incidence of shoot-and-fruit borer (Leucinodes orbonalis) on eggplant (Solanum melongena) in Gujarat. *Indian Journal of Agricultural Sciences*. 58, 11, 1988. pp. 867–865. AAUL, GVL.

Thumar, R.K. and Kapadia, M.N. Biology and population dynamics of sugarcane, whitefly, aleurolobus barodensis maskeel under Junagadh of Gujarat condition. *Gujarat Agricultural Research Journal*. 20, 2, 1995. pp. 103–107. AAUL.

Trivedi, A.B. *Agriculture in Kathiawar*. *Journal of the University of Bombay*. 10, 1, 1941. pp. 89–117. HML.

Trivedi, B.S., Gami, R.C. and Padhiyar, G.H. Studies on relationship between EC at different soil: water rations and ECE in soil of South Gujarat. *Gujarat Agricultural University Research Journal*. 20, 2, 1995. pp. 30–34. AAUL.

Trivedi, H.P. Rural development in perspective of agricultural sector in Gujarat. *Artha-Vikas*. 44, 1 and 2, 2008. pp. 38–56. CSSL.

Trivedi, Meena and Sharma, D.K. Knowledge and adoption of ber cultivation in Panchmahals districts of Gujarat. *Rural India*. 66, 12, 2003. pp. 248–251. GVL.

Trivedi, P.M. Soil of Gujarat. *Journal of the Gujarat Research Society*. 3, 1, 1941. pp. 8–22. GVL.

Tuteja, K.L. Agricultural technology in Gujarat: a study of exotic seeds and saw gins, 1800–50. *Indian Historical Review*. 17, 1–2, 1991. pp. 136–151. GVL.

Tyagi, S.N., et al. Pictorial floritic diversity of grasses and associated vegetation from three grass lands of Randhikpur forest range, Dahod, Gujarat. *Indian Forester*. 136, 12, 2010. pp. 1581–1592. CEPTL, GIDEL, IRMAL.

Udaybhansinhji. Land reforms legislation and its implementation in the erstwhile Saurashtra state. *Indian Journal of Agricultural Economics*. 17, 1, 1962. pp. 134–140. GIDRL, UML.

Ullah, Shaukat. Status of vegetation and agricultural productivity pargana haveli Ahmedabad. *Studies in History*. 14, 2, 1998. pp. 313–324. GVL.

Upadhyay, S.M. Rural urban inequalities in consumption expenditure on milk and milk products in Amreli district (Gujarat). *Indian Journal of Dairy Science*. 52, 5, 1999. pp. 298–302. AAUL.

Upadhyay, S.M., Dixit, S.K. and Pandya, H.R. Analysis of consumption pattern in rural and urban sectors of Amreli district (Gujarat). *Gujarat Agricultural University Research Journal*. 25, 2, 2000. pp. 53–61. GVL.

Upadhyay, S.M., et al. Optimum plot size for summer paddy in the Navsari zone of Gujarat. *Gujarat Agricultural University Research Journal*. 19, 2, 1994. pp. 92–97. AAUL.

Vaghanshi, J.B., Patel, H.C. and Patel, J.C. Response of summer groundnut (Arachis hypoyaey L) var GG-2 to soil amendments, biological and chemical source of nitrogen and phosphorus under South Gujarat condition. *Gujarat Agricultural University Research Journal.* 24, 1, 1998. pp. 83–86. GVL.

Vaghela, D.T. and Krishnakumar, P.K. Contamination of trace metals in the coastal water along Veraval coast, Gujarat. *Gujarat Agricultural University Research Journal.* 34, 2, 2009. pp. 116–119. AAUL.

Vaidya, V.B. Validation of astro-meterological rainfall forecast for Gujarat. *Asian Agri-History.* 13, 3, 2009. pp. 181–188. AAUL.

Vaidya, V.B., et al. Rainfall probability analysis for crop planning in Gujarat state. *Journal of Agrometeorology.* 10, 1, 2008. pp. 186–188. IRMAL.

Vaishnav, H.A. Forest protection initiatives in Panchmahals district, Gujarat. *Wastelands News.* 11, 1, 1995. pp. 49–53. IRMAL.

Vasani, M.R., Kuchhadiya, D.B. and Shiyani, R.L. Cost and returns of buffalo milk production in Rajkot district of Saurashtra. *Indian Dairyman.* 44, 6, 1992. pp. 270–273. AAUL.

Vasvelia, S.P., Patel, R.G. and Raman, S. Response of mustard (Brassica Juncea L.) to varying irrigation schedules, row spacings and levels of nitrogen in lowland condition of South Gujarat. *Gujarat Agricultural University Research Journal.* 17, 1, 1991. pp. 85–86. GVL.

Vavadia, L.D., Shah, A.H. and Pandya, H.V. Chemical control of rice yellow stem borer, scirpophaga incertulas (WlK.) and its carryover in Gujarat. *Gujarat Agricultural University Research Journal.* 21, 2, 1996. pp. 37–40. GVL.

Vekariya, S.B. and Shiyani, R.L. Differential impact of uben irrigation project on farmers of South Saurashtra zone: a case study. *Artha-Vikas.* 36, 2, 2000. pp. 45–61. CSSL.

Vekariya, S.B. and Shiyani, R.L. Impact of an irrigation project on groundnut production in South Saurashtra of Gujarat. *Agriculture Economics Research Review.* 12, 1, 1999. pp. 7–14. AAUL, IRMAL.

Venkatesh, H., Patel, H.R. and Shekh, A.M. Appraisal of monsoon rainfall at Anand, Gujarat. *Gujarat Agricultural University Research Journal.* 22, 1, 1996. pp. 72–80. GVL.

Verma, A.K. Degradation of forests due to fallacious yield regulation and harvesting: a case study from Vyara forest division of Gujarat, India. *Indian Forester.* 128, 8, 2002. pp. 835–845. IIML, SGUL.

Verma, A.K. Estimation of regeneration loss due to forest fire in South Gujarat forests. *Indian Forester.* 125, 5, 1999. pp. 445–451. IIML.

Verma, A.K. Local demands of forest produce and working plan: a case study of Vyara forest division in Gujarat. *Indian Forster.* 127, 8, 2001. pp. 855–864. GIDEL, IIML, SGUL.

Verma, Balvir. Soil conservation in ravine areas of Gujarat. *Indian Farming.* 21, 11, 1972. pp. 37–38. SGUL.

Verma, Balvir and Patel, A.P. Erosion studies on soils of the Mahi ravines in Gujarat. *Indian Journal of Agricultural Sciences.* 39, 6,1969. pp. 515–522. GVL.

Verma, D.P.S. Some controversial issues of agroforestry programme of Gujarat state. *Journal of Rural Development.* 13, 1, 1994. pp. 9–20. CSSL, IIML.

Verma, D.P.S. Some dimensions of benefits from community forestry: a case study regarding the flow of benefits from the Dhanori village woodlot. *Indian Forester.* 114, 3, 1988. pp. 109–127. IIML.

Verma, D.P.S. Women and forestry: tale of six Harijan women of Ganeshpura. *Indian Forester.* 115, 11, 1989. pp. 780–788. IIML.

Verma, H.M. and Thakkar, R.M. Leakage in hybrid bajra programme in Gujarat. *Economic and Political Weekly.* 7, 53, 1972. pp. A-176-A-179. CSSL, IRMAL, SPIESRL, UML.

Vijayan, S. and Pati, B.P. Impact of changing cropping pattern on man-animal conflicts around Gir P.A. with specific reference to Talala taluka. *Indian Forester.* 127, 10, 2001. pp. 1121–1133. GIDEL, IIML.

Visawadia, H.R., Fadadu, A.M. and Tarpara, V.D. Comparative analysis of production and marketing of bt cotton and hybrid cotton in Saurashtra of Gujarat state. *Agriculture Economics Research Review.* 19, 2, 2006. pp. 293–300. AAUL, IRMAL.

Visawadia, H.R., Vekariya, S.B. and Shiyani, R.L. Comparison of regulated and unregulated markets for vegetables in Saurashtra region of Gujarat state. *Indian Journal of Agricultural Marketing.* 21, 3, 2007. pp. 85–99. AAUL, IRMAL.

Visawadia, H.R., Fadadu, A.M. and Tarpara, V.D. Comparative analysis of production and marketing of bt cotton and hybrid cotton in Saurashtra region of Gujarat state. *Agricultural Economic Research Review.* 19, 2, 2006. pp. 293–300. IIML.

Vivekanandan, P. Comprehensive crop insurance scheme: administrative models for Gujarat. *Cooperative Perspective.* 25, 3, 1990. pp. 24–26. IRMAL.

Vyas, H.G., Joshi, D.P. and Patel, K.C. Natural incidence of milky disease of white-grubs in Gujarat. *Indian Journal of Agricultural Sciences.* 56, 3, 1986. pp. 213–215. GVL.

Vyas, R.V., Yadav, D.N. and Patel, R.J. Studies on mass production of bacillus popilliae var. holotrichiae-a promising pathogen of white grub in Gujarat. *Gujarat Agricultural University Research Journal.* 17, 1, 1991. pp. 30–37. GVL.

Vyas, S.P. Amaranthus: an additional cash crop for arid Gujarat. *Indian Farming.* 60, 4, 2010. pp. 17–18. GVL, IIML, IRMAL.

Vyas, S.P., Yadav, M.S. and Sudhakar, N. Comparative performance of cenchrus setigerus genotypes in arid region of Gujarat. *Indian Forester.* 129, 10, 2003. pp. 1222–1224. IIML.

Vyas, V.S. Structural change in agriculture and the small sector. *Economic and Political Weekly.* 11, 1 and 2, 1976. pp. 24–31. CEPTL, CSSL, GUL, IIML, IRMAL, SGUL, SPIESRL, UML.

Vyas, V.S. and Chaudhary, K.M. Economics of dairy farming in Mehsana district. *Artha-Vikas.* 7, 2, 1971. pp. 20–40. HML.

Vyas, V.S., Tyagi, D.S. and Misra, V.N. New agricultural strategy and small farmers: a case study in Gujarat. *Economic and Political Weekly.* 4, 13, 1969. pp. A-49-A-53. CSSL, IRMAL, SPIESRL, UML.

Wankhede, N.P. Response of cotton to fertilizers in relation to control of weeds in South Gujarat. *Indian Journal of Agronomy.* 15, 4, 1970. pp. 397–399. AAUL.

Yadav, D.N. and Patel, R.C. Egg parasitism of heliothis armigera (HB) (Lepidoptera: noctuidae) in Gujarat. *Gujarat Agricultural University Research Journal.* 7, 1, 1981. pp. 19–22. AAUL, GVL.

Yadav, D.N., Patel, R.C. and Patel, D.S. Seasonal abundance of heliothis armigera on different host plants at Anand(Gujarat). *Gujarat Agricultural University Research Journal.* 11, 2, 1986. pp. 32–35. GVL.

Yadav, D.N., Patel, R.R. and Patel, R.C. Natural enemies of groundnut leafminer, aproaerema modicella Deventer (Lepidoptera: Gelechiidae) and their impact on its infestation at Anand(Gujarat). *Gujarat Agricultural University Research Journal.* 13, 1, 1987. pp. 13–16. GVL.

Yadavendra, I.P. and Hadwani, G.J. Protein content of chickpea genotgpes grown at different locations in Gujarat. *Indian Journal of Agricultural Sciences.* 55, 11, 1985. pp. 663–664. AAUL, GVL.

Zala, Y.C. and Gondaliya, V.K. Study on marketing of paddy in Middle Gujarat state. *Indian Journal of Agricultural Marketing.* 25, 1, 2011. pp. 1–9. IRMAL.

Zala, Y.C. and Parmar, G.D. Marketed surplus price relationship in paddy production in South Gujarat. *Indian Cooperative Review.* 26, 3, 1989. pp. 264–268. HML, IRMAL.

Zala, Y.C., et al. Socio-economic analysis of tribal farms of Middle Gujarat. *Artha-Vikas.* 47, 2, 2011. pp. 1–19. CSSL.

Working Papers, Reports and Other Materials

Acharrya, Akash and Joshi, Vidyut. *Addressing agricultural power subsidy: a case study of North Gujarat.* Surat: Centre for Social Studies, 2005. p. 39. Working Paper 2. CSSL, SPIESRL.

Adhvaryu, J.H. Irrigation efficiency and water utilization in Gujarat: some empirical evidence. In *Seminar on development of Gujarat: problems & prospects, 24–26 August, 1981.* Ahmedabad: Sardar Patel Institutee of Economic & Social Research, 1981. pp. 1–18. CSSL.

Adhvaryu, J.H. Irrigation efficiency and water utilization in Gujarat: some empirical evidence. In *Gujarat economy: problems and prospects.* Ed. by D.T. Lakdawala. Ahmedabad: Sardar Patel Institutee of Economic & Social Research, 1982. pp. 261–272. GIDRL, GUL, IIML.

Adhvaryu, J.H. *Studies in to the economics of farm management in the A.D.P. region of Surat and Bulsar. (Gujarat state).* Anand: Sardar Patel University, 1968. p. 35. SPIESRL.

Adhvaryu, J.H. and Parikh, Gokul O. *Studies into the economics of farm management in the I.A.D.P. region of Surat and Bulsar (Gujarat state).* Anand: Sardar Patel University, 1969. p. 42. SPIESRL.

Ahmed, Sara. *Who participates? the case of rural women, an NGO and joint forest management in Gujarat.* Anand: Institute of Rural Management, 1995. p. 23. IRMA Working Paper No. 83. GIDRL, IRMAL.

Arul, M.J. *Participatory management of forests.* Anand: Institute of Rural Management, 1998. p. 21. Working Paper 119. CSSL.

Arya, Anita and Mehta, Niti. *Performance of Gujarat economy: an analysis of growth and instability.* Ahmedabad: Sardar Patel Institutee of Economic & Social Research, 2011. p. 30. Working Paper 7. CSSL.

Asokan, S.R. and Arya, Anita. Agribusiness of Potatoes in Gujarat. In *Agribusiness potential of Gujarat state (Seminar proceeding) 2011.* Nagpur: Indian Society of Agricultural Marketing, 2011. pp. 111–120. SPIESRL.

Asopa, V.N. and Tripathi, B.L. *Irrigation agriculture in Gujarat: problems and prospects.* Ahmedabad: Indian Institute of Management, 1975. p. 154. GIDRL, IIML, IRMAL.

Asopa, V.N. and Tripathi, B.L. *Water co-operatives for utilization of irrigation potential in Gujarat.* [ ]: [ ], 1976. p. 59. Seminar Series XIII. GVL.

Babaria, C.H. *Economics of soil testing service in Gujarat*. Vallabh Vidyanagar: Sardar Patel University, 1982. p. 251. SPUL.

Babaria, C.H. Problems of water harvesting and management in Saurashtra. In *Economy of Saurashtra: problems and prospects*. Ed. by D.T. Lakdawala, et al. Bhavnagar: Bhavnagar University, 1990. pp. 118–125. GUL.

Balooni, Kulbhushan and Singh, Katar. *Economics of farm forestry: a case study in Shankerpura village, district Panchmahal, Gujarat*. Anand: Institute of Rural Management, 1994. p. 34. Working Paper 61. CSSL, GIDRL, IRMAL.

Bambal, P.J. *Nargol (Bulsar district, Gujarat) economic profile of a fishing village*. Vallabh Vidyanagar: Agro-Economic Research Centre, 1968. p. 107. Indian village Study No. 4. AERCL.

Bapat, Madhukar. *Intensive pulse development programme in Gujarat: a case study of Panchmahals and Bharuch district*. Vallabh Vidyanagar: Agro-Economic Research Centre, 1987. p. 162. AERC Research Study No. 73. AERCL, GIDRL, SPUL.

Bapat, Madhukar. *Working of small farmers development agency in Gujarat: a case study of Bharuch district.* Vallabh Vidyanngar: Agro-Economic Research Centre, Sardar Patel University, 1983. p. 114. AERC Research Study No. 61. AERCL, GIDRL, SPUL.

Bapna, S.L. *Green revolution and problems of marketing: a study of production and marketing of Bajra in three districts of Gujarat*. Vallabh Vidyanagar: Agro-Economic Research Centre, 1972. p. 217. Research Study No. 25. AERCL.

Bapna, S.L. and Rao, K.R. *Supply and price outlook for crops: a study based on preharvest market information in Gujarat.* Ahmedabad: Indian Institute of Management, 1984. p. 276. CMA Monograph No. 115. IIML.

Basant, Rakesh. *Indigenous knowledge and technology diffusion: a case of agro-mechanical technology in Gujarat, India*. Ahmedabad: Gujarat Institute of Development Research, 1988. p. 31. GIDR Working Paper No. 16. GIDRL, IRMAL.

Basant, Rakesh. *Trends in agro-mechanical technology in Gujarat: a district level analysis.* Ahmedabad: Gujarat Institute of Area Planning, 1987. p. 169. GIDR Working Paper No. 12. GIDRL.

Baviskar, B.S. *Dairy development in a tribal area in Gujarat.* Hague, Netherland: ISS, 1986. p. 47. IRMAL.

Bhagat, M.G. and Dasgupta, Subhachari. *Developing adivasis and small farmers.* Bombay: National Institute of Bank Management, 1975. p. 103. CSSL.

Bharwada, Charul and Mahajan, Vinay. *Changing nature of pastoralism: development, pastures and Maldharis of Gujarat.* Surat: Centre for Social Studies, 2006. p. 130. Monograph. CSSL.

Bhatia, Bela. *Lush fields and parched throats: the political economy of groundwater in Gujarat.* Helsinki: United Nations University, World Institute for Development Economics Research, 1992. p. 84. UNU/WIDER Working Paper No. 100. GIDRL.

Biswas, C.R. Dairy development in Saurashtra. In *Economy of Saurashtra: problems and prospects*. Ed. by D.T. Lakdawala, et al. Bhavnagar: Bhavnagar University, 1990. pp. 90–97. GUL.

Bokil, Milind S. *Weaving carpets for development designs: a study of Gujarat Khet Vikas Parishad.* Ahmedabad: Gujarat Khet Vikas Parishad, 1992. p. 54. GIDRL.

Brahmbhatt, D.M. *Decentralised planning in agriculture and rural development: a case study of Bharuch district in Gujart*. Vallabh Vidyanagar: Agro-Economic Research Centre, 1996. p. 111. Research Study No. 99. AERCL, GIDRL, IRMAL, SPUL.

Brahmbhatt, D.M. *Economic profile of the Kadana irrigation project and its command area*. Vallabh Vidyanagar: Agro-Economic Research Centre. 1976. p. 308. Research Study No. 45. AERCL, SPUL, UML.

Brahmbhatt, D.M. *Production and marketing of mangoes in Gujarat*. Vallabh Vidyanagar: Agro-Economic Research Centre, 1984. p. 233. AERC Research Study No. 63. GIDRL, IRMAL, SPIESRL.

Brahmbhatt, D.M. *Socio-economic profile of action research programme area in Mahi Kadana irrigation project*. Vallabh Vidyanagar: Agro-Economic Research Centre, 1987. p. 134. Research Study No. 72. AERCL, SPUL.

Brahmbhatt, D.M. *Socio-economic profile of action research programme area in Mahi Kadana irrigation project*. Vallabh Vidyanagar: Agro-Economic Research Centre, 1988. p. 296. Research Study No. 79. AERCL, SPUL.

Brahmbhatt, D.M. and Bapat, M.T. *Transforming tribal agriculture can evaluation of the leap forward project of the Gujarat state fertilizers company limited*. Vallabh Vidyanagar: Agro-Economic Research Centre, 1976. p. 156. Research Study No. 48. AERCL, SPIESRL, SPUL.

Brahmbhatt, D.M. and Bapat, M.T. *Working of farmer's service societies in Gujarat: two case studies of tribal areas in Gujarat*. Vallabh Vidyanagar: Agro-Economic Research Centre, 1978. p. 89. Research Study No. 52. AERCL, CSSL, SPUL.

Brahmbhatt, D.M., Patel, V.M. and Dave, V.J. *National rural development programme in Gujarat: a case study of Kheda district*. Vallabh Vidyanagar: Agro-Economic Research Centre, 1987. p. 155. Research Study No. 75. AERCL.

Charan, A.S. and Rao, S.V.L.N. Irrigation water rates in Gujarat: some issues and suggestions for policy. In *Gujarat economic association, conference papers, Vallabh Vidyanagar*. Ed. by D.T. Lakadawala and B.B. Patel. [ ]: [ ], 1985. pp. 1–6. GIDRL.

Choudhary, K.M. *Evaluation of intensive cotton district programme & aerial spraying scheme in Baroda district Gujarat*. Vallabh Vidyanagar: Agro-Economic Research Centre, 1981. p. 254. AERC Research Study No. 57. AERCL, GIDRL, IRMAL, SPIESRL.

Choudhary, K.M. *4 p plan-crop insurance scheme for hybrid-4 cotton in Gujarat*. Anand: Sardar Patel University, 1977. p. 137. Research Study No. 51. AERCL, SPIESRL.

Choudhary, K.M. and Sevak, R.D. *Drought prone area programme: a case study of the Banaskantha district in Gujarat (kharif 1972–73)*. Vallabh Vidyanagar: Agro-Economic Research Centre, 1973. p. 97. Research Study No. 32. AERCL.

Choudhary, K.M., Bapat, M.T. and Gupta, D.P. *Assessment of cooperative farming societies in Gujarat and Rajasthan (a few case studies)*. Vallabh Vidyanagar: Agro-Economic Research Centre, 1972. p. 377. AERCL.

Choudhary, K.M., et al. *Assessment of co-operative farming societies in Gujarat and Rajasthan (a few case studies)*. Vallabh Vidyanagar: Agro-Economic Research Centre, 1967. p. 412. Research Study No. 13. AERCL, CSSL, GVL.

Choudhary, Kameshwar. *Organisational reorientation for protected area management: the case of Gir forest in Gujarat*. Anand: Institute of Rural Management, 2001. p. 37. IRMA Working Paper No. 157. GIDRL, IRMAL, SPIESRL.

Dadi, M.M. Occupational structure and productivity levels in districts of Gujarat. In *Gujarat economic association conference papers, Baroda*. Ed. by V.S. Vyas, Pravin Visaria and A.R. Desai. Ahmedabad: Balgovind, 1971. pp. 79–86. GIDRL, IIML.

Dalal, B.C., Desai, J. and Maharaja, M.H. Integrated marketing of agricultural inputs – Gujarat. In *Seminar on coordinated marketing and use of fertilisers and other inputs*. Proceedings of the seminar. New Delhi: Fertiliser Association of India, 1971. pp. 343–351. HML.

Dalvi, M.K. and Shukla, Rohit. *Evaluation of Gujarat social forestry programme.* Ahmedabad: Sardar Patel Institute of Economics and Social Research, 1988. p. 311. Monograph Series 14. CSSL, IRMAL, SPIESRL.

Datta, Samar K. *Collective action, leadership and success in agricultural cooperatives: a study of Gujarat and West Bengal*. Ahmedabad: Indian Institute of Management, 1992. p. 369. IRMAL.

Datta, Samar K. *Fisheries sector development for Gujarat: proceedings of an experience sharing workshop organized by the fisheries commissionerate, government of Gujarat.* Ahmedabad: Indian Institute of Management, 2001. p. 274. IIML.

Datta, Samar, Nilkantan, Rahul and Chakrabarti, Milindo. *Towards evolving an agricultural policy matrix in a federal structure: the post WTO scenario in India*. New Delhi: Allied, 2010. pp. 54–56. AERCL.

Dave, V.J. *Co-operative marketing societies in Gujarat: reason for success and failure: case studies in Ahmedabad and Navsari districts*. Vallabh Vidyanagar: Agro-Economic Research Centre, 2004. p. 159. Research Study No. 125. AERCL.

Dave, V.J. *Economics of export oriented horticultural crop chiku (Sapota): a case study in Valsad district.* Anand: Sardar Patel University, 1998. p. 197. Research Study No. 126. AERCL, GVL, IRMAL.

Dave, V.J. *Economic viability of small and marginal farms in rainfed agriculture: a case study of Bhavnagar district in Gujarat*. Vallabh Vidyanagar: Agro-Economic Research Centre, 1994. p. 134. AERC research Study No. 92. AERCL, GIDRL, IRMAL, SPIESRL.

Dave, V.J. *Evaluation of fish farmer's development agencies in Gujarat.* Vallabh Vidyanagar: Agro-Economic Research Centre, 1997. p. 180. Research Study No. 105. AERCL, GVL, IRMAL.

Dave, V.J. *Flow of credit to small and marginal farmers in Gujarat: a case study in Panchmahals district*. Vallabh Vidyanagar: Agro-Economic Research Centre, 2002. p. 93. Research Study No. 118. AERCL, GIDRL, IRMAL.

Dave, V.J. *Role of co-operative credit in the development of different size group of farmers in Gujarat: a case study in Rajkot district.* Vallabh Vidyanagar: Agro-Economic Research Centre, 1999. p. 132. AERC Research Study No. 111. AERCL, GIDRL, GVL, IRMAL.

Deolalikar, Anil B. *Direct and indirect effects of irrigation: the case of Matar taluka in Gujarat state, India 1965–66 to 1974–75.* Ahmedabad: Gujarat Institute of Area Planning, 1985. p. [ ]. GIDRL.

Department of Agricultural Economics, M.S. University. *Changing farm production and organization in development agriculture: a case study of the impact of the development effort in agriculture in a district in Gujarat state(Report for the year 1967–68).* Baroda: M.S. University, 1967–68. p. 118. SPIESRL.

Desai, B.M. *Command area of the Dantiwada project socio-economic survey of three Banaskantha village in Gujarat*. Vallabh Vidyanagar: Agro-Economic Research Centre, 1964. p. 194. Research Study No. 5. AERCL.

Desai, B.M. *Economics of resource use on sample farms of Central Gujarat.* New York: Cornell University, 1973. p. 17. Occasional Paper No. 70. SPIESRL.

Desai, B.M. *Evaluation of some aspects of hybrid maize programme in Dahod taluka (Panchmahals district Gujarat)*. Vallabh Vidyanagar: Agro-Economic Research Centre, 1967. p. 55. Research Study No. 12. AERCL, SPUL.

Desai, B.M. *Relationship of consumption and production in changing agriculture: a study in Surat district, India*. Ahmedabad: CMA-IIMA, 1975. p. 44. Occasional Paper No. 80. IIML.

Desai, B.M. and Desai, D.K. *Farm production credit management in changing agriculture, Baroda district, Gujarat.* Ahmedabad: Indian Institute of Management, 1971. p. [ ]. Monograph No. 22. GIDRL.

Desai, B.M. and Desai, D.K. *Potentialities for mobilizing investible funds in developing agriculture*. Ahmedabad: Indian Institute of Management, 1971. p. 123. CMA Monograph No. 25. CSSL, IRMAL.

Desai, B.M. and Desai, M.D. *New strategy of agricultural development in operation: a case study of the Kaira district in Gujarat*. Vallabh Vidyanagar: Agro-Economic Research Centre, 1968. p. 160. Research Study No. 15. AERCL, CSSL, SPUL.

Desai, Babubhai D. *Socio-economic study of the milk producers of South Gujarat.* Surat: Centre for Social Studies, 1979. p. 25. CSSL.

Desai, D.B. *Socio-economic bench mark survey of Matar taluka phase II.* Ahmedabad: Department of Sociology, Gujarat University, [ ]. p. 82. GIDRL.

Desai, D.K. and Gopinath, C. *Impact of farm tractorization on productivity and employment, Gujarat state.* Ahmedabad: Indian Institute of Management, 1973. p. [ ]. GIDRL.

Desai, D.K. and Gopinath, C. *Impact of farm tractorization productivity and employment(Gujarat state).* Ahmedabad: Centre for Management in Agriculture, Indian Institute of Management, 1975. p. 271. IRMAL.

Desai, D.K. and Patel, D.A. *Management in seed industry: a case study on hybrid Bajra seed in Gujarat state.* Ahmedabad: Indian Institute of Management, 1968. p. 127. IIML.

Desai, Gunvant, Singh, Gurdev and Sah, D.C. *Impact of scarcity on farm economy and significance of relief operations.* Ahmedabad: Centre for Management in Agriculture (IIM), 1979. p. 140. CMA Monograph 84. IIML.

Desai, Gunvant M. *Growth of fertilizer use in Indian agriculture: past trends and future demand.* New York: State College of Agriculture and Life Science, [ ]. p. 148. CSSL.

Desai, Gunvant M., et al. *Cultivators experience of high yielding varieties of cotton: a micro study in Gujarat.* Ahmedabad: Indian Institute of Management, 1978. p. 174. CMA Monograph No. 77. IIML, IRMAL.

Desai, M.B. *Report on an enquiry into the working of the Bombay tenancy and agricultural lands act, 1948 (As amended up to 1953) in Gujarat (Excluding Baroda district).* Bombay: Indian Society of Agricultural Economics, 1958. p. 202. CSSL, SPIESRL.

Desai, M.B. *Tenancy abolition and the emerging pattern in Gujarat.* Baroda: M.S. University, 1971. p. 195. SPIESRL.

Desai, M.B. and Verma, S.K. *Changing farm production and organisation in developing agriculture: case study of impact of the development effort in agriculture in a district in Gujarat.* Baroda: M.S. University, 1978. p. 501. GIDRL.

Desai, M.D. *Employment, income and levels of living of agricultural labourers: a study in the Surat district, Gujarat, 1969–1970.* Vallabh Vidyanagar: Agro-Economic Research Centre, 1974. p. 15. Research Study No. 30 (Supplement). AERCL.

Desai, M.D. *Green revolution and problems of marketing: a study of production and marketing of Bajra in three districts in Gujarat*. Anand: Sardar Patel University, 1972. p. 251. SPIESRL, SPUL.

Desai, M.D. *Saving and investment in an agriculturally prosperous area: a case study of Surat district in Gujarat.* Vallabh Vidhayanagar: Agro-Economic Research Centre, 1975. p. 91. Research Study No. 40. IIML, SPUL.

Desai, M.D. *Saving and investment in an agriculturally prosperous area: a study in the Surat district, Gujarat.* Vallabh Vidyanagar: Agro-Economic Research Centre, 1976. p. 186. Research Study No. 47. IIML, SPUL.

Desai, M.D. and Karanth, K.S. *Study of pilot cooperative farming societies in Gujarat and Rajasthan.* Vallabh Vidyanagar: Agro-Economic Research Centre, 1964. p. 261. Research Study No. 7. AERCL.

Desai, N.B. *Report on the administrative survey of the Surat district.* Bombay: Indian Society of Agricultural Economics, 1958. p. 356. IIML.

Dharap, V.S. *Study of the hybrid bajra programme in the Ahmedabad district Gujarat (Kharif 1968–69).* Vallabh Vidyanagar: Agro-Economic Research Centre, 1969. p. 85. Research Study No. 19. AERCL.

Dharap, Vinayak S. and Maharaja, Madhukar, H. *Enquiry into the implementation of farm plans in Bardoli taluka: a study in an I.A.D. district in Gujarat.* Vallabh Vidyanagar: Agro-Economic Research Centre, 1967. p. 66. Research Study No. 14. AERCL.

Dholakia, Ravindra H. *Exports of agri-products from Gujarat: problems and prospects.* Ahmedabad: Indian Institute of Management, 2002. p. 22. IIM Working Paper No. 9. GIDRL, IIML.

Dholakia, Ravindra H., Ed. *Frontiers of agricultural development in Gujarat.* Ahmedabad: Centre for Management in Agriculture, Indian Institute of Management, 2007. p. 224. CMA Publication No. 226. CSSL, GVL, IIML.

Dinesh Kumar, Singh, Katar and Singh, Om Prakash. *Study of water-saving and energy-saving micro irrigation technologies in Gujarat.* Anand: India Natural Resource Economic and Management Foundation, 2004. p. 53. Research Report No. 2. CEEL.

Dobriyal, Kusum and Ballabh, Vishwa. *Comparative study of joint forest management in West Bengal and Gujarat.* Anand: Institute of Rural Management, 1995. p. 16. IRMA Working Paper No. 79. CSSL, GIDRL, IRMAL.

Dutta, Rajeshree. *Some aspects of land use planning in Gujarat.* Vallabh Vidyanagar: Agro-Economic Research Centre, 1993. p. 113. Research Study No. 88. AERCL, SPIESRL.

Dutta, Rajeshree A. Analysis of trends in operational land holdings in Gujarat. Vallabh Vidyanagar: Agro-Economic Research Centre, 1997. p. 114. AERC Research Study No. 103. AERCL, GIDRL, SPIESRL, SPUL.

Dutta, Rajeshree A. *State budgetary resource and agriculture development in Gujarat.* Vallabh Vidyanagar: Agro-Economic Research Centre, 2009. p. 62. AERCL.

Dutta, Rajeshree and Bhaiya, Shantilal R. *Rural non-farm employment in Gujarat.* Vallabh Vidyanagar: Agro-Economic Research Centre, 2004. p. 147. Research Study No. 124. AERCL.

Dutta, Rajeshree and Verma, H.M. *Oilseeds development perspective under liberalised economy.* Vallabh Vidyanagar: Agro-Economic Research Centre, 1998. p. 93. Research Study No. 107. AERCL, GVL.

Dutta, Rajeshree, Verma, H.M. and Patel, C.F. *Evaluation of management of seed supply in oilseeds and pulses in Gujarat.* Vallabh Vidyanagar: Agro-Economic Research Centre, 2000. p. 111. AERC Research Study No. 113. AERCL, GIDRL, IRMAL, SPIESRL.

Dutta, Rajeshree A., Makwana, Manish and Parmar, Himanshu. *Pre and post harvest losses in Gujarat.* Vallabh Vidyanagar: Agro-Economic Research Centre, 2013. p. 81. AERCL.

Faldu, D.G. Agriculture in Gujarat (Business session-1). In *Seminar on agricultural and rural financing issues & prospects. May 18–19, 1992.* Ahmedabad: National Productivity Council, 1992. pp. 1–12. SPIESRL.

Forest Department, Government of Gujarat. Role of forestry in development of state. In *Gujarat-2010: challenges and opportunities*. By Government of Gujarat. Ahmedabad: Sardar Patel Institutee of Economic & Social Research, 2001. pp. 603–616. Seminar volume. CSSL, EDIL, IRMAL, SGUL, SPIESRL

Gandhi, Rohit. Agriculture and allied services. In *Gujarat-2010: challenges and opportunities*. By Government of Gujarat. Ahmedabad: Sardar Patel Institutee of Economic & Social Research, 2001. pp. 118–127. Seminar volume. CSSL, EDIL, IRMAL, SGUL, SPIESRL.

Gandhi, Rohit. Gujarat agriculture sector. In *Gujarat-2010: challenges and opportunities*. By Government of Gujarat. Ahmedabad: Sardar Patel Institutee of Economic & Social Research, 2001. pp. 101–117. Seminar volume. CSSL, EDIL, IRMAL, SGUL, SPIESRL.

Gandhi, Vasant P. and Namboodiri, N.V. Cotton revolution in Gujarat: the impact of Bt technology. In *Frontiers of agricultural development in Gujarat*. Ed. by Ravindra H. Dholakia. Ahmedabad: Centre for Management in Agriculture, Indian Institute of Management, 2007. pp. 56–76. CMA Publication No. 226. CSSL, GVL, IIML.

Gandhi, Vasant P. and Namboodiri, N.V. *Fruit and vegetable marketing in India: consolidated study of wholesale markets in Ahmedabad, Chennai and Kolkata.* Ahmedabad: Indian Institute of Management, 2006. p. 40. CMA Publication Series No. 221. IIML.

Gandhi, Vasant P. and Namboodiri, N.V. *Improving irrigation management in India: a study of participatory irrigation management in the states of Andhra Pradesh, Gujarat and Maharashtra*. New Delhi: Allied, 2011. p. 128. CMA Publication No. 237. AERCL.

Gandhi, Vasant P. and Namboodiri, N.V. *Marketing of fruits and vegetables in India: a study of the wholesale markets in Ahmedabad area*. Ahmedabad: Indian Institute of Management, 2006. p. 57. IIML.

Ghatak, Ram Narayan and Singh, Katar. *Economics of tube-well irrigation: a case study in Hardoi district of Uttar Pradesh and Kheda district of Gujarat.* Anand: Institute of Rural Management, 1994. pp. 1–12. Working Paper 67. SPIESRL.

Gujarat Agriculture University. *Agroclimatology of Anand and rainfall analysis of Middle Gujarat zone*. Anand: Gujarat Agriculture University, 1985–86. p. [ ]. AAUL.

Gujarat, Government of. Gujarat 2010 challenges and opportunities. In *Gujarat-2010 challenges and opportunities (seminar volume)*. By Government of Gujarat. Ahmedabad: Sardar Patel Institutee of Economic & Social Research, 2001. pp. 617–621. CSSL, EDIL, IRMAL, SGUL, SPIESRL.

Gumber, Anil and Visaria, Pravin. *Agricultural growth, social overheads and diversification of economic activities: a study of inter-village differentials in Matar taluka of Gujarat.* Ahmedabad: Gujarat Institute of Area Planning, 1992. p. 49. Working Paper No. 39. CSSL, GIDRL.

Gupta, Dipankar. *Scarcity and market dependence in Damka: a portrayal of kisans in an a typical village.* Surat: Centre for Social Studies, 1979. p. 40. CSSL.

Hardiman, David. Politics of forest reservation: the Dangs, 1947–1992. In *International seminar on Gujarat society, development and deprivation, 6–9 December 1994.* Surat: Centre for Social Studies, 1994. pp. 1–9. CSSL.

Hashim, S.R. and Dadi, M.M. Population pressure size distribution of land holdings and land productivity: an analysis of interregional variations in Gujarat. In *Gujarat economic association conference papers, Baroda*. Ed. by V.S. Vyas, Pravin Visaria and A.R. Desai. Ahmedabad: Balgovind, 1971. pp. 65–78. GIDRL.

Hirway, Indira. *District agricultural profile: Sabarkantha district*. Gandhinagar: Government of Gujarat, 1988. p. 83. CSSL.

Hogle, Homer. *Influence of agriculture extension in selected villages of Kaira district (Gujarat, India)*. Michigan: University of Michigan, 1972. p. 175. Comparative education dissertation series. AAUL, AERCL.

Indian Society of Agricultural Economics (ISAE). *Co-operative farming in Gujarat: study into the working of co-operative farming societies in Gujarat*. Bombay: ISAE, 1959. p. 138. GIDRL.

Institute of Rural Management, Anand. *Oilseeds development: problems and prospects Saurashtra region, Gujarat state (1979–1981)*. Anand: Institute of Rural Management, 1981. p. [ ]. IRMAL.

Institute of Rural Management, Anand. *Study on the development of horticulture in the state of Gujarat.* Anand: Institute of Rural Management, 1992. p. 211. IRMAL.

Iyengar, Sudarshan. *Common property land resources in Gujarat: some findings about their size, status and use*. Ahmedabad: Gujarat Institute of Area Planning, 1988. p. 150. Working Paper No. 18. GIDRL, IRMAL.

Iyenger, Sudarshan. *Estimating cost of irrigation for a region: a case study of Matar taluka, Gujarat, India.* Ahmedabad: Gujarat Institute of Area Planning, 1984. p. 69. GIDRL.

Iyengar, Sudarshan. Pesticides use pattern among cotton cultivators in Gujarat: discussant's comments. In *Frontiers of agricultural development in Gujarat*. Ed. by Ravindra H. Dholakia. Ahmedabad: Centre for Management in Agriculture, Indian Institute of Management, 2007. pp. 103–108. CMA Publication No. 226. CSSL, GVL, IIML.

Jadeja, Priya, Parmar, D.S. and Shingi, Prakash M. *Rural consumers: an empirical profile.* Ahmedabad: Centre for Management in Agriculture, Indian Institute of Management, 2003. p. 130. CMA Monograph No. 210. IIML.

Jain, J.P., et al. *Impact of milk supply schemes on the rural economy in milk collection areas of Dudhsagar dairy Mehsana, Gujarat*. New Delhi: ICAR, 1977. p. 210. IRMAL.

Jain, Pankaj S. Voluntary organisations and public systems: a case study of cattle camps in Gujarat. Anand: Institute of Rural Management, 1989. p. 38. IRMAL.

Jaisani, B.G. *Economics of tobacco production in Middle Gujarat.* Anand: Gujarat Agricultural University, 1987. p. 47. IRMAL.

Jakasaniya, M.S., Patel, A.J. and Shekh, A.M. *Comprehensive district agricultural plan (C-DAP): Panchamal district.* Anand: Anand Agricultural University, 2013. p. 178. AAUL.

Jangam, Priti and Zala, Y.C. Comparative advantage of India in agricultural export: analysis of major crops of Gujarat. In *Agribusiness potential of Gujarat state (Seminar proceeding) 2011*. Nagpur: Indian Society of Agricultural Marketing, 2011. pp. 283–292. SPIESRL.

Jhala, B.K. Social forestry in tribal areas of Gujarat. In *Social forestry in tribal development*. Ed. by N.N. Vyas. Udaipur: MLV Tribal Research and Training Institute, 1981. pp. 23–29. CSSL.

Jhala, M.L. *Terms of trade for agriculture: a case study of Gujarat*. Vallabh Vidyanagar: Agro-Economic Research Centre, 1989. p. 82. AERC Research Study No. 82. AERCL, GIDRL, IRMAL, SPIESRL.

Jhala, R.C. and Patel, D.N. Impact of weather parameters on emergence of fruit flies, dacus cilialus and bactrocera cucurbitate from the fruits of cucurbits, small ground and bitter ground at Anand in Gujarat. In *Agro meteorological services for farmers*. Ed. by Vyas Pandey. Anand: Anand Agriculture University, 2010. pp. 236–251. AAUL.

Jhala, R.C. and Sisodiya, Dilip B. Impact of weather parameters on catches of melon fly, bactrocera cucubitate in parapheromore baited trap installed in cucurbits cultivation at Anand. In *Agro meteorological services for farmers in Gujarat*. Ed. by Vyas Pandey. Anand: Anand Agriculture University, 2010. pp. 326–334. AAUL.

Jodha, N.S. *Some aspects of co-operative short term agricultural finance: a study in three areas in Gujarat*. Vallabh Vidyanagar: Agro-Economic Research Centre, 1973. p. 80. Research Studies No. 26. AERCL, SPUL.

Jodha, N.S. *Some aspects of long term agricultural finance: a study of two areas in Gujarat*. Vallabh Vidyanagar: Agro-Economic Research Centre, 1969. p. 225. AERCL.

Joshi, Sujan. *Agriculture in Gujarat: progress and potential*. Gandhinagar: S.N. Joshi, 2000. p. 216. IRMAL.

Joshi, V.R. *Regulated markets in Gujarat*. Nadiad: Kaira District Cooperative Union, 1971. p. 407. IRMAL.

Joshi, Vidyut and Acharya, Akash. *Addressing agriculture power subsidy: a case study of North Gujarat*. Surat: Centre for Social Studies, 2002. p. 91. CSSL.

Kansaria, M.V. and Patel, M.S. Agroclimatic zones, types of soil and special area problems in Saurashtra region: solution. In *Economy of Saurashtra: problems and prospects*. Ed. by D.T. Lakdawala, et al. Bhavnagar: Bhavnagar University, 1990. pp. 60–69. GUL.

Khakhar, K.K. Entitlement and deprivation: a conceptual analysis with special reference to marine fisheries of Gujarat. In *International seminar on Gujarat society, development and deprivation, 6–9 December 1994*. Surat: Centre for Social Studies, 1994. pp. 1–12. CSSL.

Khanpara, V.D., Solanki, R.M. and Mathukia, P.K. Resource conservation in arid and semi-arid regions of Gujarat. In *National symposium on new paradigms in agronomic research at Navsari Agriculture University*. Navsari: Indian Society of Agronomy, 1955. pp. 226–247. AAUL.

Khatu, K.K., Jayaraman, B. and D'Souze, A.R. *Land use in Gujarat: status and strategy for conservation*. Baroda: Operation Research Group, 1981. p. 139. GIDRL.

Kolhatkar, V.V. *Inquiry in to the effects of the working of the tenancy legislation in the Baroda district of Bombay state*. Baroda: M.S. University, 1958. p. 54. IIML.

Krishnan, M., Lakra, W.S. and Biradar, R.S. Production potential of seaweed culture in Gujarat. In *Agribusiness potential of Gujarat state (Seminar proceeding) 2011*. Nagpur: Indian Society of Agricultural Marketing, 2011. pp. 78–85. SPIESRL.

Krishnaswamy, M.S. *Reported on the problem of delay in agricultural administration in Gujarat state*. Ahmedabad: Centre for Management in Agriculture, 1978. p. 107. AAUL, IRMAL.

Krishnaswamy, M.S. and Prakash, Hari. *Report on the problems of delay in agriculture administration in Gujarat state.* Ahmedabad: Indian Institute of Management, 1976. p. 108. GIDRL.

Kuchadiya, D.B., Shiyani, R.L. and Thumar, B.L. Economic analysis of crop yield and product price variability in Saurashtra region of Gujarat state. In *Economy of Saurashtra: problems and prospects.* Ed. by D.T. Lakdawala, et al. Bhavnagar: Bhavnagar University, 1990. pp. 86–89. GUL.

Kuchhadiya, D.B., et al. *Economic analysis of groundnut production in Saurashtra region of Gujarat.* Junagadh: Gujarat Agricultural University, 1996. p. 86. IRMAL.

Kumar, B.L. Oilseeds and pulses in Indian agriculture: a review of development policy and production performance. Ahmedabad: Gujarat Institute of Development Research, 2001. p. 66. GIDR Working Paper No. 126. GIDRL.

Kumar, B.L. *Production and transfer of goods and services in Matar taluka region: a case study of impact of irrigation.* Ahmedabad: Gujarat Institute of Area Planning, 1984. p. [ ]. GIDRL.

Kumar, B.L. *Successful experiment in group farming.* Ahmedabad: Gujarat Institute of Area Planning, 1979. p. 75. GVL.

Kumari, Nutan and Tilavat, Ashish. Frozen fruits and vegetables-prospects and opportunities in Gujarat. In *Agribusiness potential of Gujarat state (Seminar proceeding)2011.* Nagpur: Indian Society of Agricultural Marketing, 2011. pp. 258–266. SPIESRL.

Lal, R.B. *From farm to factory.* Ahmedabad: Gujarat Vidyapith, 1992. p. 69. TRTIL.

Lalitha, N. and Ramaswami, Bharat. Pesticides use pattern among cotton cultivators in Gujarat. In *Frontiers of agricultural development in Gujarat.* Ed. by Ravindra H. Dholakia. Ahmedabad: Centre for Management in Agriculture, Indian Institute of Management, 2007. pp. 77–98. CMA Publication No. 226. CSSL, GVL, IIML.

Maharaja, Modhukar. *Economic of cotton cultivation: a study in a selected region of Sabarkantha district in Gujarat.* Vallabh Vidyanagar: Agro-Economic Research Centre, 1966. p. 123. Research Study No. 10. SPUL.

Makadia, J.J., Ahir, N.J. and Patel, K.S. Economics and marketing of cashew plantation in Valsad district of South Gujarat. In *Agribusiness potential of Gujarat state (Seminar proceeding) 2011.* Nagpur: Indian Society of Agricultural Marketing, 2011. pp. 68–77. SPIESRL.

Malavia, D.D., Padmani, D.R. and Jadav, K.V. Crop sequence research in Saurashtra region. In *Crop sequence research in Gujarat agriculture.* Ed. by N.M. Patel, et al. Anand: Gujarat Agriculture University, 1997. pp. 108–115. AAUL.

Malavia, D.D., et al. Integrated nutrient management for pealmillet wheat crop sequence of South Saurashtra region of Gujarat. In *Crop sequence research in Gujarat university.* Ed. by N.M. Patel, et al. Anand: Gujarat Agriculture University, 1997. pp. 2–3. AAUL.

Mankad, Madhubhai K. Scientists show the way to turn adversities of nature in opportunities-discussant's comments. In *Frontiers of agricultural development in Gujarat.* Ed. by Ravindra H. Dholakia. Ahmedabad: Centre for Management in Agriculture, Indian Institute of Management, 2007. pp. 153–154. CMA Publication No. 226. CSSL, GVL, IIML.

Manoharan, S.S. *Burnt sugarcane phenomenon in South Gujarat: dilemma of capacity utilisation in cooperative sugar factories.* Anand: Institute of Rural Management, 1989. p. 20. IRMAL.

Mathur, D.P. and Gupta, V.K. *Management in small poultry farms: study in Maharstra and Gujarat regions*. Ahmedabad: Indian Institute of Management, 1978. p. 144. IIML, IRMAL.

Mathur, Niti. *Decadal growth of Gujarat's agriculture and perspective*. Ahmedabad: Agro-Climatic Regional Planning Unit, Planning Commission, 1997. p. [ ]. ARPU Technical Paper No. 28. GIDRL, IRMAL.

Meenakshi. Exports potential of agricultural commodities of Gujarat state. In *Agribusiness potential of Gujarat state (Seminar proceeding)2011*. Nagpur: Indian Society of Agricultural Marketing, 2011. pp. 253–257. SPIESRL.

Mehta, A.N., et al. *Agromeoteorology of pigeonpea*. Anand: Gujarat Agriculture University, 1995. p. 40. Report 1992–95. AAUL.

Mehta, Atul and Soni, N.V. *Comprehensive district agricultural plan, C-DAP: Panchamal district*. Anand: Anand Agricultural University, 2013. p. 396. AAUL.

Mehta, Niti. Agro-climatic features and irrigation development in Gujarat and West Bengal. *In Development in agriculture: a comparative analysis of the growth components across two states*. New Delhi: Allied, 2011. pp. 18–40. Sardar Patel Institutee of Economic & Social Research Monograph No. 26. IIML.

Mehat, Niti. Cropping pattern and changes during liberalization period: Gujarat. *In Development in agriculture: a comparative analysis of the growth components across two states*. New Delhi: Allied, 2011. pp. 42–52. Sardar Patel Institutee of Economic & Social Research Monograph No. 26. IIML.

Mehta, Niti. Growth analysis of the crop sector: growth analysis for Gujarat. *In Development in agriculture: a comparative analysis of the growth components across two states*. New Delhi: Allied, 2011. pp. 90–110. Sardar Patel Institutee of Economic & Social Research Monograph No. 26. IIML.

Mehta, Niti. Input use pattern and changes in technical efficiency in Gujarat agriculture. *In Development in agriculture: a comparative analysis of the growth components across two states*. New Delhi: Allied, 2011. pp. 156–164. Sardar Patel Institutee of Economic & Social Research Monograph No. 26. IIML.

Mehat, Niti. *Liberalised era and technical efficiency in agricultural: variations in Gujarat and West Bengal*. Ahmedabad: Sardar Patel Institutee of Economic & Social Research, 2011. pp. 214–229. Reprint Series 03, Vol. 66, No. 2. SPIESRL.

Mehta, Niti. *Performance of crop sector in Gujarat during high growth period: some explorations*. Ahmedabad: Sardar Patel Institutee of Economic & Social Research, 2012. pp. 195–204. Reprint Series 05, Vol. 20, No. 2. SPIESRL.

Mehta, Niti. *Productivity and resource structure: underlying dimensions of agricultural development in Gujarat*. Ahmedabad: Sardar Patel Institutee of Economic & Social Research, 2012. p. 45. Working Paper 11. CSSL, MICAL, SPIESRL.

Mehta, V.M., Patel, P.R. and Raval, I.K. *Study of students at agriculture colleges in Gujarat*. Junagadh: Agriculture Economic Section College of Agriculture, 1965. p. 84. AAUL.

Misra, V.N. Regional variations in agricultural growth in Gujarat: 1949–50 to 1968–69. In *Gujarat economic association, conference papers, Baroda*. Ed. by V.S. Vyas, Pravin Visaria and A.R. Desai. Ahmedabad: Balgovind, 1971. pp. 41–64. GIDRL, IIML.

Moulik, T.K. and Srivastava, U.K. *Bio-gas plants at the village level: problems and prospects of Gujarat*. Ahmedabad: Indian Institute of Management, 1975. p. 149. GIDRL.

Namboothiri, N.V. and Desai, Gunvant M. Demand versus supply factors in growth of fertilizer use: Gujarat's experience. In *Strategic issues in future growth of fertilizer use in India*. Ed. by Gunvant M. Desai and A. Vaidyanathan. New Delhi: Indian Council of Agricultural Research, 1994. pp. 137–166. Collection of papers USAID. CSSL.

Narayanamurthy, S.G. Irrigation water management: a case study of the Dantiwada project. In *National seminar on water management: the key to development agriculture: held under the auspices of Indian national science academy, New Delhi, 28–30 April 1986.* New Delhi: Agricole, 1988. pp. 309–334. IIML.

Painuly, J.P., Parikh, Jyoti K. and Shah, D.R. *Rural energy system and agriculture: alternative scenarios for Gujarat.* Bombay: Indira Gandhi Institute of Development Research, 1991. p. 35. IGIDR Discussion Paper No. 66. GIDRL, IRMAL.

Pandey, C.N., et al. *Medicinal plants of Gujarat.* Gandhinagar: Gujarat Ecological Eduction and Research, 2005. p. 410. CEEL, EDIL.

Pandey, Vikash N. and Jain Pankaj. *Village woodlots in Gujarat: an experiment in social forestry.* Anand: Institute of Rural Management, 1991. p. 32. IRMA Working Paper No. 17. GIDRL, IRMAL.

Pandor, G.A. *Socio-economic conditions of adiwasi small farmers of Surat district.* Surat: Centre for Social Studies, 1979. p. 86. CSSL.

Parikh, Gokul O. *District agriculture profile Panchmahals.* Ahmedabad: Sardar Patel Institutee of Economic & Social Research, 1988. p. [ ]. SPIESRL.

Parikh, Gokul O. *Economic and social survey of agricultural labourers in Gujarat state.* Ahmedabad: Sardar Patel Institutee of Economic & Social Research, 1985. p. 267. CSSL, GIDRL.

Parikh, N. and Thirumalai, S. *Bhadkad: social and economic survey of a village: a comparative study (1915 and 1955).* Bombay: Indian Society of Agricultural Economics, 1957. p. 71. CSSL.

Parmar, M.T. and Gandhi, A.P. *Dryland agricultural research 1971–81: all India co-ordinated research project for dryland agriculture.* Targhada: Main Dry Farming Research Station, Gujarat Agricultural University, 1981. p. 73. GIDRL.

Parmar, R.S., et al. Statistical investigation on the relationship between rainfall and groundnut productivity in Gujarat state. In *Agro meteorological services for farmers.* Ed. by Vyas Pandey. Anand: Anand Agriculture University, 2010. pp. 117–125. AAUL.

Parthasarathy, R. *Use of bullocks and tractors in agriculture in Gujarat: implications for employment and output, 1983–84.* Ahmedabad: Gujarat Institute of Area Planning, 1991. p. 19. Working Paper No. 37. CSSL, GIDRL, IRMAL.

Patel, A.S. *Agricultural development: facts and dilemma: a case study of a Kheda village.* In *Rural development and rural poor, 26–28 February 1987.* Surat: Centre for Social Studies, 1987. pp. 273–291. CSSL.

Patel, A.S. Participation of difference groups in the development process: a case study of milk producer's co-operative in a Kheda village. In *Gujarat economy: problems and prospects.* Ed. by D.T. Lakdawal. Ahmedabad: Sardar Patel Institutee of Economic & Social Research, 1983. pp. 335–350. Monograph Series No. 10. GUL.

Patel, A.S. and Patel, H.F. *Recent trends in the cost of cultivation in Gujarat.* Anand: Sardar Patel University, 1989. p. 37. Research Study No. 83. AERCL, GIDRL, IRMAL, SPIESRL, SPUL.

Patel, A.S. and Jodha, N.S. *Economic relationship between crop farming and dairying in a developing area. APL 480 micro level study of South Gujarat.* Vallabh Vidyanagar: Agro-Economic Research Centre, 1979. p. 175. Research Study No. 53. AERCL, GIDRL.

Patel, A.S. and Shah, N.R. Economics of scale in agriculture: a case study of Kaira district in Gujarat. In *Gujarat economic association conference papers,* Nadiad, 1976. pp. 47–62. GIDRL.

Patel, A.T., et al. Agronomic studies on hybrid castor for rainfed cultivation in North Gujarat semi-arid region. In *Maximising crop production in rainfed and problem areas: proceedings of the national seminar on "integrated management approach for maximising crop production in rainfed and problem area" held at IARI New Delhi, on February 26–28, 1986.* New Delhi: Indian Society of Agricultural Sciences, 1989. pp. 207–210. IIML.

Patel, Arun, Patel, Chandrakant and Pancholi, Ravindra. *Development of forest settlement in Gujarat: an evaluation.* Ed. Chandrakant Upadhyaya. Ahmedabad: Tribal Research and Training Institute, Gujarat Vidyapith, 2006. p. 223. Series 439. TRTIL.

Patel, Arun and Patel, H.F. Water rates policy for GWRDC tubewells in Gujarat. In *Gujarat economic association conference papers,* Vallabh Vidyanagar. Ed. by D.T. Lakdawala and B.B. Patel. Ahmedabad: Gujarat Economic Association & GLI, 1985. pp. 1–6. GIDRL.

Patel, Arun and Patel, J.B. Market led extension: challenges, opportunities and marketing extension service. In *Agribusiness potential of Gujarat state (seminar proceeding) 2011.* Nagpur: Indian Society of Agricultural Marketing, 2011. pp. 32–36. SPIESRL.

Patel, Arun S. Agricultural development in Gujarat: performance and future strategy. In *Gujarat-2010: challenges and opportunities.* By Government of Gujarat. Ahmedabad: Sardar Patel Institutee of Economic & Social Research, 2001. pp. 73–100. Seminar volume. CSSL, EDIL, IRMAL, SGUL, SPIESRL.

Patel, Arun S. *Fertiliser use in Gujarat: a micro view, a study of Baroda and Junagadh District.* Vallabh Vidyanagar: Department of Economics, Sardar Patel University, 1973. p. 68. GIDRL.

Patel, Arun S. *Growth pattern of agriculture in Gujarat: an aspect of non-foodgrain economy.* Anand: Sardar Patel University, 1998. p. 35. Working Paper No. 8. SPIESRL.

Patel, Arun S. *Review of state agriculture policy in Gujarat.* Anand: Agro-Economic Research Center, 2006. p. 110. AERCL, GIDEL, SPIESRL.

Patel, Arun S. *Review of state agriculture policy in Gujarat Part-I.* Vallabh Vidyanagar: Agro-Economic Research Centre, 2004. p. 85. Research Study No. 128. AERCL.

Patel, Arun S. *Review of state agriculture policy in Gujarat post WTO scenario.* Vallabh Vidyanagar: Agro-Economic Research Centre, 2004. p. 36. Research Study No. 128. AERCL.

Patel, Arun S. and Brahmbhatt, D.M. *Action research programme an interim evaluation: a case study of Mahi Kadana irrigation project.* Vallabh Vidyanagar: Agro-Economic Research Centre, 1991. p. 159. Research Study No. 86. AERCL, SPUL.

Patel, B.B. Impact of irrigation on labour absorption and labour market adjustments in agriculture in Matar taluka of Gujarat, India. Ahmedabad: Gujarat Institute of Area Planning, 1985. p. [ ]. GIDRL.

Patel, C.K., et al. Comparison of different crop sequences under North Gujarat condition. In *Crop sequence research in Gujarat agriculture.* Ed. by N.M. Patel, et al. Anand: Gujarat Agriculture University, 1997. pp. 49–51. AAUL.

Patel, Chhotabhai J. *Study on likely agriculture developments of the command area of the Kadana dam.* Fertilizernagar: Gujarat State Fertilizers, 1970. p. 140. AAUL.

Patel, G.J. *Economics of tobacco production in Middle Gujarat (1984–85)*. Anand: Gujarat Agriculture University, 1985. p. 51. Research bulletin No. 11. IRMAL, SPIESRL.

Patel, G.N. *Trends in input: output prices and their impact on income from foodgrain crops in Gujarat*. Anand: Gujarat Agriculture University, 1997. p. 52. IRMAL.

Patel, Girish and Patel, S.K. *Comprehensive district agricultural plan (C-DAP): Panchamal district*. Anand: Anand Agricultural University, 2013. p. 190. AAUL.

Patel, H.F. Integrated dry land agricultural development programme: a case study of Rajkot taluka in Gujarat. Vallabh Vidyanagar: Agro-Economic Research Centre, 1973. p. 107. AERC Research Study No. 27. AERCL, GIDRL.

Patel, H.F. and Dave, V.J. *Participatory irrigation management in Gujarat: a study in Mahesana, Anand and Bhavnagar district*. Vallabh Vidyanagar: Agro-Economic Research Centre, 2006. p. 137. Research Study No. 131. AERCL.

Patel, H.L. *Report on an evaluative study on training of women in agriculture in Gujarat*. Anand: Gujarat Agricultural University, Extension Education Institute, [ ]. p. [ ]. GIDRL.

Patel, H.R. and Pandey, Vyas. Climate changes and its impact on wheat and maize yield in Gujarat. In *International conference on challenges and opportunities in agro meteorology*. Ed. by S.D. Attri, L.S. Rathore and S.K. Dash. New Delhi: Indian Meteorological Society, 2009. pp. 99-[ ]. AAUL.

Patel, H.R. and Shekh, A.M. Crop sequence and weather: a case study of Middle Gujarat agro-climatic zone. In *Crop sequence research in Gujarat agriculture*. Ed. by N.M. Patel, et al. Anand: Gujarat Agriculture University, 1997. pp. 143–145. AAUL.

Patel, Himmat. *Transportation of agricultural products in Gujarat*. Vallabh Vidyanagar: Agro-Economic Research Centre, 1993. p. 97. AERC Research Study No. 87. AERCL, GIDRL, GVL, IRMAL.

Patel, J.R., et al. Effect of fertility levels on the productivity and economics of different crops sequence under irrigated condition of Middle Gujarat. In *Crop sequence research in Gujarat University*. Ed. by N.M. Patel, et al. Anand: Gujarat Agriculture University, 1997. pp. 7–11. AAUL.

Patel, K.V. and Krishna Swamy, M.S. Problems of tribal agriculture in the context of dry farmings: a case study of selected village in the Panchmahals district of Gujarat. In *Rural development for weaker section*. Bombay: T.R. Sundaram, 1974. pp. 70–88. Seminar Series XII. IIML, SGUL.

Patel, M.D., et al. *Study of economic potentialities of five acre family farming in Charotar tract of Gujarat, Bombay State*. Anand: Institute of Agriculture, 1958. p. 39. GUL.

Patel, M.R., et al. Studies on groundnut based sequence in South Saurashtra agro climatic zone. In *Crop sequence research in Gujarat University*. Ed. by N.M. Patel, et al. Anand: Gujarat Agriculture University, 1997. pp. 43–44. AAUL.

Patel, N.M., et al., ed. *Crop sequence research in Gujarat agriculture*. Anand: Gujarat Agriculture University, 1997. p. 161. AAUL.

Patel, Navneet M. *Changes in levels of energy use in agriculture with changes in levels*. Ahmedabad: Gujarat Institute of Area Planning, [ ]. p. [ ]. GIDRL.

Patel, Navneet M. *Effect of rainfall and rainy days on yields of major crops in Matar for 1965–66 and 1974–75*. Ahmedabad: Gujarat Institute of Area Planning, [ ]. p. [ ]. GIDRL.

Patel, Navneet M. *Growth of irrigation and it's effect on dairy development in Matar taluka*. Ahmedabad: Gujarat Institute of Area Planning, 1985. p. [ ]. GIDRL.

Patel, Navneet M. *Impact of changes in the levels of irrigation and technology on the energy requirement and availability for agriculture production in Matar taluka.* Ahmedabad: Gujarat Institute of Area Planning, 1985. p. [ ]. GIDRL.

Patel, P.R., et al. Studies on the fertiliser requirement of green gram in light soils of North Gujarat semi arid region. In *Maximising crop production in rainfed and problem areas: proceedings of the national seminar on "integrated management approach for maximising crop production in rainfed and problem area" held at IARI New Delhi, on February 26–28, 1986.* New Delhi: Indian Society of Agricultural Sciencs, 1989. pp. 204–206. IIML.

Patel, R.M. *Ankodia (Baroda district, Gujarat) economic life in a tobacco village*. Vallabh Vidyanagar: Agro-Economic Research Centre, 1964. p. 219. Indian Village Studies No. 3. AERCL.

Patel, R.M. *Economic profile of marginal farmers and labourers: a study in the Borsad taluka of Gujarat*. Vallabh Vidyanagar: Agro-Economic Research Centre, 1972. p. 139. Research Study No. 24. AERCL.

Patel, R.M. *Some reflections on integrated dry land agricultural development: a case study of Rajkot taluka, Gujarat*. Vallabh Vidyanagar: Agro-Economic Research Centre, 1988. p. 94. AERC Research Study No. 77. AERCL, GIDRL, IRMAL, SPUL.

Patel, R.M. *Working of fair price shops in Gujarat and Rajasthan: with special reference to Ahmedabad and Jaipur cities*. Vallabh Vidyanagar: Agro-Economic Research Centre, 1965. p. 60. Research Study No. 6. AERCL.

Patel, R.M. and Patel, H.F. *Integrated dryland agricultural development programme: a case study of Rajkot taluka in Gujarat 1972–73*. Vallabh Vidyanagar: Agro-Economic Research Centre, 1974. p. 217. Research Study No. 34. AERCL.

Patel, R.M., Sevak, R.D. and Choudhary K.M. *Economic of dairy enterprise in Gujarat*. Vallabh Vidyanagar: Agro-Economic Research Centre, 1985. p. 179. Research Study No. 65. AERCL.

Patel, S.M. and Pandey, M.K. *Production economics of V-797 and CO-2 cotton in Gujarat state.* Ahmedabad: ICM, 1980. p. 99. IRMAL.

Patel, S.M., et al. *Impact of the milk cooperatives in Gujarat.* Ahmedabad: ICM, 1975. p. 182. IRMAL.

Patel, Sujata. *'Anand Pattern': a socio-historical analysis of its origin and growth.* The Hague: Institute of Social Studies, 1986. p. 49. Working paper-series on Dairy aid and development No. 29. CSSL.

Patel, V.C. *Consumption pattern in rural Gujarat: a study of four villages in Anand taluka.* Vallabh Vidyanagar: Agro-Economic Research Centre, 1973. p. 55. Research Study No. 31. AERCL, GVL.

Patel, V.C. *Jambua (Panchmahals district Gujarat) change in socio-economic life of a tribal village*. Vallabh Vidyanagar: Agro-Economic Research Centre, 1980. p. 208. Resurvey of Indian village No. 3. AERCL.

Patel, V.C. and Desai, M.C. *Factors affecting milk supply to cooperative dairies in Gujarat: a study of Amul and Dudhsagar dairies*. Vallabh Vidyanagar: Agro-Economic Research Centre, 1976. p. 44. Research Study No. 46. AERCL.

Patel, V.G. *Economics of pulses production and identification of constraints in raising their production in Gujarat.* Vallabh Vidyanagar: Agro-Economic Research Centre, 1999. p. 58. AERC Research Study No. 110. AERCL, GIDRL, GVL, IRMAL, SPIESRL.

Patel, V.G. *Economic viability of small and marginal farms in irrigated agriculture: a study of Panchmahals district in Gujarat*. Vallabh Vidyanagar: Agro-Economic

Research Centre, 1994. p. 62. AERC Research Study No. 93. AERCL, GIDRL, IRMAL.

Patel, V.J. *New strategy for high density agroforestry*. Surendrabag Kardej: Jivrajbhai Patel Agroforestry Centre, 1988. p. 121. CSSL.

Patel, V.J. *Wasteland development through agro-forestry*. Vadodara: Gujarat Energy Development Agency, 1986. p. [ ]. GIDRL.

Patel, V.M. *Emerging problems of agricultural marketing: a case study of Banana in Gujarat*. Vallabh Vidyanagar: Agro-Economic Research Centre, 1996. p. 104. AERC Research Study No. 100. AERCL, GIDRL, GVL.

Patel, V.M. *Emerging problems of agricultural marketing: a case study of tomato in Gujarat*. Vallabh Vidyanagar: Agro-Economic Research Centre, 1995. p. 115. AERC Research Study No. 96. AERCL, GIDRL, GVL, IRMAL.

Pathak, Jharna. *Agroforestry in tribal areas of Gujarat: move towards sustainable agriculture?* Ahmedabad: Gujarat Institute of Development Research, 2011. p. 43. Working Paper No. 203. CSSL, SPIESRL.

Pathak, Jharna. *Dose the system of rice intensification outperform conventional system?: a case study of Gujarat*. Ahmedabad: Gujarat Institute of Development Research, 2010. p. 35. Working Paper Series No. 196. CSSL.

Pathak, Mahesh. *Evaluation of comprehensive district agriculture planes (C-DAPs) of 3 districts of Gujarat*. Vallabh Vidyanagar: Agro-Economic Research Centre, 2011. p. 59. Research Study No. 138. AERCL.

Pathak, Mahesh and Patel, H.F. Agricultural development in Gujarat: problems and prospects. In *Gujarat economy: problems and prospects*. Ed. by D.T. Lakdawala. Ahmedabad: Sardar Patel Institutee of Economic & Social Research, 1982. pp. 211–224. GIDRL, GUL, IIML.

Pathak, Mahesh and Patel, H.F. Agricultural development in Gujarat: problems and prospects. In *Seminar on development of Gujarat: problems & prospects, 24th-26th August, 1981*. Ahmedabad: Sardar Patel Institutee of Economic & Social Research, 1981. pp. 1–17. CSSL.

Pathak, Mahesh and Shah Navin R. *Block level plan (Thasra taluka Kheda district Gujarat)*. Vallabh Vidyanagar: Agro-Economic Research Centre, 1981. p. 154. Research Study No. 56. AERCL.

Pathak, Mahesh and Shah, V.D. *Agro-economic research for agriculture policy (Gujarat and Rajasthan experience: 1980–2004)*. Anand: Sardar Patel University, 2004. p. 90. Research Study No. 127. AERCL, SPIESRL.

Pathak, Mahesh, Patel, Arun and Patel, Haribhai. *Economics of tubewell irrigation in Gujarat*. Vallabh Vidyanagar: Agro-Economic Research Centre, 1985. p. 205. AERC Research Study No. 67. AERCL, GIDRL.

Pathak, Mahesh, Patel, H.F. and Shah, V.D. *Assessing the existing training and testing facilities of farm machinery in Gujarat*. Vallabh Vidyanagar: Agro-Economic Research Centre, 2001. p. 70. AERC Research Study No. 117. AERCL, GIDRL, IRMAL, SPIESRL.

Pathak, Mahesh, Shah, V.D. and Jhala, M.L. *Impact of fertilizer price hike on Gujarat agriculture*. Vallabh Vidyanagar: Agro-Economic Research Centre, 1993. p. 83. Research Study No. 89. AERCL, IRMAL.

Pathak, Mahesh J., Patel Haribhai F. and Dutta, Rajeshree A. *Inter-district variations in agricultural development in Gujarat 1949–50/1991–92*. Vallabh Vidyanagar: Agro-Economic Research Centre, 1994. p. 88. Research Study No. 94. AERCL, GIDRL.

Pathak, Mahesh T. and Patel, Haribhai F. *Inter-district variations in agricultural development in Gujarat 1949–50 and 1978–79*. Vallabh Vidyanagar: Agro-Economic Research Centre, 1982. p. 79. Research Study No. 59. AERCL.

Pathak, Mahesh T. and Shah, Navin R. *Block level plan (Balasinor taluka Kheda district)*. Vallabh Vidyanagar: Agro-Economic Research Centre, 1979. p. 55. Research Study No. 54. AERCL.

Pathak, Mahesh T. and Singh, P.K. Frontiers of agricultural development in Gujarat. In *Frontiers of agricultural development in Gujarat*. Ed. by Ravindra H. Dholakia. Ahmedabad: Centre for Management in Agriculture, Indian Institute of Management, 2007. pp. 14–32. CMA Publication No. 226. CSSL, GVL, IIML.

Pathak, Mahesh T., Desai, Mahendra D. and Charan, A.S. Development of agriculture in the backward regions of Gujarat: facts and issues. In *Economic development of backward regions problems & prospects. (Proceedings of an all-India seminar on the development of backward regions with special reference to Gujarat)*. Ed. by H.M. Patel, et al. Vallabh Vidyanagar: Sardar Patel University, 1974. pp. 100–138. GIDRL, GUL, HML.

Pathak, Mahesh T., Desai, Mahendra D. and Patel, H.F. *Some aspects of agricultural development in Gujarat 1949–50/1974–75*. Vallabh Vidyanagar: Agro-Economic Research Centre, 1977. p. 92. Research Study No. 49. AERCL.

Pathak, Mahesh T., Desai, Mahendra and Patel, Haribhai F. *Agricultural development in Gujarat 1949–50 – 1974–75*. Vallabh Vidyanagar: Agro-Economic Research Centre, Sardar Patel University, 1979. p. 308. Research Study No. 49-B. AERCL, CSSL, GIDRL, SPUL.

Pattnaik, Itishree, et al. *Agricultural extension service through Krishi Mahotsav in Gujarat: a preliminary assessment*. Ahmedabad: Gujarat Institute of Development Research, 2012. p. 55. GIDR Occasional Paper Series No. 2. CSSL, GIDRL.

Poffenberger, Mark, ed. *Community forest economy and use patterns: participatory rural appraisal (PRA) methods in South Gujarat, India*. New Delhi: SPWD, 1992. p. 79. IRMAL.

Punalekar, S.P. *Agricultural profile of Dangs district*. Surat: Centre for Social Studies, 1989. Various. CSSL.

Rajaram, N. Village milk cooperatives in Kheda district: a sociological analysis. In *International Seminar on "Gujarat Society", 17–20 December 1986*. Surat: Centre for Social Studies, 1986. pp. 1–47. CSSL.

Raju, G., Vaghela, Raju and Raju, Manju S. *Development of people's institutions for management of forests*. Ahmedabad: Viksat, 1993. p. 172. CSSL.

Rao, G.G., Singh, Ravendra and Bhargava, G.P. *Vegetation types in Bhal area, Mahi right bank and Ukai-Kakrapar commands of Gujarat*. Anand: Central Soil Salinity Research Institute, 1997. p. 49. AAUL.

Rathore, S.S. and Patel, D.M. Gujarat. In *Advances in agronomy in India*. Ed. by R.K. Pandey and Apurba Sarkar. Meerut: Loyal, 1995. pp. 19–31. AAUL.

Ray, S.S. *Cotton production estimation and condition assessment in Surendranagar district, Gujarat*. Anand: Gujarat Agriculture University, 1994. p. 19. IRMAL.

Sah, D.C. *Farmers' response to soil testing services in Gujarat: a diagnostic analysis*. Ahmedabad: Gujarat Institute of Area Planning, 1990. p. [ ]. IRMAL.

Sah, D.C. *MID-term evaluation of shree niketan rural development project*. Surat: Centre for Social Studies, 1994. p. 96. CSSL.

Sah, D.C. and Mehta, Kartik. *Impact of GCOGF on summer groundnut in Kheda*. Anand: National Dairy Development Board, 1985. p. 17. Oilseeds and vegetable oil project. CSSL.

Sah, D.C. and Prasad, Vishnu. *Impact of GCOGF on rapeseed-mustard in Mehsana.* Anand: National Dairy Development Board, 1985. p. 18. Oilseeds and vegetable oil project. CSSL.

Sah, D.C. and Shah, Amita. *Farmers' fertilizer practices and soil-testing services: evidence from Gujarat.* Ahmedabad: Gujarat Institute of Development Research, 1995. p. 15. Working Paper No. 67. Also In *strategic issues in future growth of fertilizer use in India.* Ed. by Gunvant M. Desai and A. Vaidyanathan. New Delhi: Indian Council of Agricultural Research, 1994. pp. 167–184. Collection of papers USAID. CSSL, GIDRL.

Sah, D.C. and Shah, Amita. *Soil testing facilities and activities in Gujarat.* Ahmedabad: Gujarat Institute of Area Planning, 1990. p. 77. CSSL, GIDRL.

Sanjiv, Kumar. Status and comparison of poultry sector of Gujarat with other states of the country. In *Agribusiness potential of Gujarat state (Seminar proceeding) 2011.* Nagpur: Indian Society of Agricultural Marketing, 2011. pp. 121–128. SPIESRL.

Sarabhai, Kartikeya V., et al. *People's involvement in wildlife management: an approach to joint sanctuary management of the Shoolpansehwar wildlife sanctuary, Gujarat.* Ahmedabad: Viksat, 1991. p. 112. IRMAL.

Sardar Patel Institutee of Economic & Social Research. *Agricultural growth and potential in Gujarat.* Ahmedabad: Sardar Patel Institutee of Economic & Social Research, 1985. p. 171. GIDRL.

Sardar Patel Institutee of Economic & Social Research. *Study on impact of agricultural lands celing act on economic conditions of surplus land-allottees in Gujarat.* Ahmedabad: Sardar Patel Institutee of Economic & Social Research, 1990. p. 202. SPIESRL.

Sathyapalan, Jyothis. *Impact of dry land salinity on agriculture and drinking water: a study from the coastal Gujarat.* Hyderabad: Centre for Economic and Social Studies, 2010. p. 94. CESS Monograph 14. CSSL.

Satpath, Swetapadma D. and Sudarshan Naidu, N.T. Study on feasibility of farmer's market in Ahmedabad for vegetable. In *Agribusiness potential of Gujarat state(Seminar proceeding)2011.* Nagpur: Indian Society of Agricultural Marketing, 2011. pp. 129–143. SPIESRL.

Saxena, Rakesh. *Joint forest management in Gujarat: policy and managerial issues.* Anand: Institute of Rural Management, 2000. pp. p. 21. Working Paper 149. GIDRL, IRMAL, SPIESRL.

Saxena, Rakesh. *Status and utilisation of draught animal power in Gujarat.* Anand: Institute of Rural Management, 1995. p. 14. Working Paper No. 93. CSSL, IRMAL.

Sevak, R.D. *Cost of milk production in Gujarat: a case study of Mehsana district.* Vallabh Vidyanagar: Agro-Economic Research Centre, 1986. p. 147. Research Study No. 68. AAUL, AERCL, GIDRL, IRMAL, SPUL.

Sevak, R.D. *Drought prone area programme: a case study of the Banaskantha district in Gujarat (Rabi and summer 1972–73).* Vallabh Vidyanagar: Agro-Economic Research Centre, 1975. p. 123. Research Study No. 38. AERCL, SPIESRL, SPUL, UML.

Sevak, R.D. *Drought prone area programme: a case study of the Banaskantha district in Gujarat.* Vallabh Vidyanagar: Agro-Economic Research Centre, 1973. p. 92. Research Study No. 29. AERCL, SPIESRL, SPUL.

Sevak, R.D. and Brahmbhatt, D.M. *Performance of hybrid bajri in Gujarat 1966–67 to 1976–77.* Vallabh Vidyanagar: Agro-Economic Research Centre, 1980. p. 147. Research Study No. 55. AERCL, GIDRL, IRMAL, SPIESRL.

Shah, Amita. *Changing interface between agriculture and livestock: a study of livelihood options under dry land farming systems in Gujarat*. Ahmedabad: Gujarat Institute of Development Research, 2006. p. 24. Working Paper No. 170. CSSL, IRMAL, SPIESRL.

Shah, Amita. Cotton revolution in Gujarat: the impact of bt technology-discussant's comments. In *Frontiers of agricultural development in Gujarat*. Ed. by Ravindra H. Dholakia. Ahmedabad: Centre for Management in Agriculture, Indian Institute of Management, 2007. pp. 99–103. CMA Publication No. 226. CSSL, GVL, IIML.

Shah, Amita. *Moisture yield interactions and farmers' perceptions: lessons from watershed projects in Gujarat*. Ahmedabad: Gujarat Institute of Development Research, 1997. p. 28. Working Paper No. 86. CSSL, GIDRL, IRMAL.

Shah, Amita. *Promoting small water harvesting structures in dryland regions: a case study of the farm ponds scheme in Gujarat*. Ahmedabad: Gujarat Institute of Development Research, 2000. p. 36. Working Paper No. 115. GIDRL.

Shah, Amita. *Who benefits from watershed development?: evidences from Gujarat*. Ahmedabad: Gujarat Institute of Development Research, 2000. p. 27. IRMAL.

Shah, Amita and Sah, D.C. *Farm information centres of GSFC: an evaluation*. Ahmedabad: Gujarat Institute of Area Planning, 1989. p. 136. CSSL.

Shah, B.R. Gujarat agriculture: prospects and problems. In *Frontiers of agricultural development in Gujarat*. Ed. by Ravindra H. Dholakia. Ahmedabad: Centre for Management in Agriculture, Indian Institute of Management, 2007. pp. 33–46. CMA Publication No. 226. CSSL, GVL, IIML.

Shah, C.H. *Agricultural growth and equity: micro level experience, second resurvey of Matar taluka, 1994, 95*. Ahmedabad: Gujarat Institute of Area Planning, 1985. p. [ ]. GIDRL.

Shah, C.H. *Note on measurement of irrigation*. Ahmedabad: Gujarat Institute of Area Planning, 1985. p. [ ]. GIDRL.

Shah, Dilip R. Frontiers of agricultural development in Gujarat-discussant's comments. In *Frontiers of agricultural development in Gujarat*. Ed. by Ravindra H. Dholakia. Ahmedabad: Centre for Management in Agriculture, Indian Institute of Management, 2007. pp. 47–51. CMA Publication No. 226. CSSL, GVL, IIML.

Shah, N.C. and Shukla, Rohit. Some tentative implications of drought-proneness to agriculture and level of living. In *Gujarat economy problems and prospects*. Ed. by D.T. Lakdawala. Ahmedabad: Sardar Patel Institutee of Economic & Social Research, 1983. pp. 319–334. Monograph 10. IIML.

Shah, N.R. *Emerging problems of agricultural marketing: a case study of mustard in Gujarat*. Vallabh Vidyanagar: Agro-Economic Research Centre, 1995. p. 73. AERC Research Study No. 98. AERCL, GIDRL, IRMAL.

Shah, N.R. *Prospects of increasing oilseed and pulse production in Gujarat*. Vallabh Vidyanagar: Agro-Economic Research Centre, 1990. p. 81. AERC Research Study No. 84. AERCL, GIDRL, IRMAL, SPIESRL, SPUL.

Shah, N.R. *Study of the hybrid bajra programme in the Kaira district Gujarat (Summer 1967–68)*. Vallabh Vidyanagar: Agro-Economic Research Centre, 1969. p. 96. Research Study No. 18. AERCL.

Shah, Navin R. *Groundnut development programme in Gujarat*. Vallabh Vidyanagar: Agro-Economic Research Centre, 1988. p. 67. AERC Research Study No. 69. AERCL, GIDRL, IRMAL, SPUL.

Shah, Niresh C. *Impact of irrigation on consumption*. Ahmedabad: Gujarat Institute of Area Planning, 1985. p. [ ]. GIDRL.

Shah, Tushaar. Collective action on village commons: community fodder farms in Kheda district, Gujarat. Anand: Institute of Rural Management, 1989. p. 31. IRMA Case Study No. 5. GIDRL, IRMAL.

Shah, Tushaar. *Cooperative organisations in Indian oilseed systems: a study of the role of grofed in groundnut system of Gujarat*. Anand: Institute of Rural Management, 1986. p. 122. IRMAL.

Shah, Tushaar. *Farmer attitudes towards foot-and-mouth disease control: conceptual issues and empirical analyses from Kheda*. Anand: Institute of Rural Management, 1992. p. 27. Working Paper 30. CSSL, SPIESRL.

Shah, Tushaar. *Managing conjunctive water use in canal commands: lessons from the analyses of the Mahi right bank canal, Gujarat*. Anand: Institute of Rural Management, 1988. p. 24. IRMA Research Paper No. 3. GIDRL, SPIESRL.

Shah, V.D. Fertilizer consumption in Gujarat. Vallabh Vidyanagar: Agro-Economic Research Centre, 1989. p. 89. AERC Research Study No. 80. AERCL, GIDRL, IRMAL, SPUL.

Shah, V.D. *Impact of national watershed development project for rainfed areas (NWDPRA) in Gujarat: a rapid assessment*. Vallabh Vidyanagar: Agro-Economic Research Centre, 1999. p. 68. AERC Research Study No. 112. AERCL, GIDRL, IRMAL.

Shah, V.D. *Production and utilisation pattern of milk at the rural producer's level in Gujarat*. Vallabh Vidyanagar: Agro-Economic Research Centre, 1998. p. 173. Research Study No. 108. AERCL, IRMAL, SPUL.

Shah, V.D. *Repayment of minor irrigation loans of and development bank in Gujarat.* Vallabh Vidyanagar: Agro-Economic Research Centre, 1986. p. 190. Research Study No. 70. GVL, SPUL.

Shah, V.D. *Returns to bt cotton vis-à-vis traditional cotton varieties in Gujarat state*. Vallabh Vidyanagar: Agro-Economic Research Centre, 2007. p. 112. Research Study No. 134. AERCL.

Shah, V.D. and Patel, H.F. *Impact of minimum support prices on agricultural economy in Gujarat.* Vallabh Vidyanagar: Agro-Economic Research Centre, 2003. p. 129. Research Study No. 123. AERCL, SPIESRL.

Shah, V.D. and Patel, V.G. *Impact of national watershed development project for rainfed areas (NWDPRA) in Gujarat*. Vallabh Vidyanagar: Agro-Economic Research Centre,1996. p. 176. AERC Research Study No. 102. AERCL, GIDRL, IRMAL.

Shah, V.D., Makwana, Manish and Sharma, Shreekant. *Economics of production processing and marketing of fodder crops in Gujarat*. Vallabh Vidyanagar: Agro-Economic Research Centre, 2011. p. 164. Research Study No. 144. AERCL.

Sharan, Girja. *Agricultural mechanization in Gujarat.* Ahmedabad: Indian Institute of Management, 1982. p. [ ]. IIM Working Paper No. 421. GIDRL, IIML.

Sharan, Girija. Engineering the agriculture in extremely arid areas like Kutch. In *Agricultural development paradigm for the Ninth plan under new economic development*. Ed. by Bhupat M. Desai. New Delhi: Oxford, 1997. pp. 388–398. CMA Monograph No. 179. CSSL, GUL.

Sharan, Girija. Technology to improve agriculture and home comforts in Kutch. In *Frontiers of agricultural development in Gujarat*. Ed. by Ravindra H. Dholakia. Ahmedabad: Centre for Management in Agriculture, Indian Institute of Management, 2007. pp. 112–124. CMA Publication No. 226. CSSL, GVL, IIML.

Sharan, Girija and Chokshi, S.N. *Rasulia dug well: an irrigation scheme.* Ahmedabad: Centre for Management in Agriculture, Indian Institute of Management, 1976. p. 53. CMA Monograph No. 65. CSSL.

Sharan, Girija, et al. *Design and development of packaging for Tomato in Gujarat.* Ahmedabad: Indian Institute of Management, 2000. p. 36. IRMAL.

Sharma, A.K., et al. *25 years research on soil and water conservation in ravine lands of Gujarat*. Vasad: CSWCRII, 1981. p. 197. IRMAL.

Sharma, Kailash C., Ballabh, Vishwa and Pandey, Ajay. *Analysis of farm forestry in Gujarat.* Anand: Institute of Rural Management, 1991. p. 21. WP-10. IRMAL.

Sharma, Ushaben. *Analysis of coarse cereal prices in Gujarat.* Ahmedabad: Sardar Patel Institutee of Economic & Social Research, 1980. p. [ ]. GIDRL.

Sharma, Usha S. Performance and prospects of Gujarat agriculture. In *Gujarat economy: problems and prospects.* Ed. by D.T. Lakdawala. Ahmedabad: Sardar Patel Institutee of Economic & Social Research, 1982. pp. 225–260. GIDRL.

Sharma, Usha S. Agricultural planning in Gujarat sixth plan appraisal. In *Seminar on development of Gujarat: problems & prospects, 24th-26th August, 1981.* Ahmedabad: Sardar Patel Institutee of Economic & Social Research, 1981. pp. 1–18. CSSL.

Sharma, Usha S. Performance and prospects of Gujarat agriculture. In *Gujarat economy: problems and prospects.* Ed. by D.T. Lakdawala. Ahmedabad: Sardar Patel Institutee of Economic & Social Research, 1982. pp. 225–260. GIDRL, GUL, IIML.

Sharma, Usha S. Performance and prospects of Gujarat agriculture. In *Seminar on development of Gujarat: problems & prospects, 24th-26th August, 1981.* Ahmedabad: Sardar Patel Institutee of Economic & Social Research, 1981. pp. 1–41. CSSL.

Shekh, A.M., Patel, P.C. and Modi, R.J. *Comprehensive district agriculture plan (C-DAP): Anand district.* Anand: Anand Agricultural University, 2013. p. 242. AAUL.

Sheikh, A.S., et al. Productivity, economics and soil fertility as influenced by crop sequence in North Gujarat. In *Crop sequence research in Gujarat agriculture*. Ed. by N.M. Patel, et al. Anand: Gujarat Agriculture University, 1997. pp. 45–48. AAUL.

Shenoy, G.V., et al. System study on cattle insurance scheme in Gujarat and Maharashtra. Anand: Institute of Rural Management, 1987. p. 111. IRMAL.

Sheth, R.H. Irrigation potential availability for Saurashtra region from Sardar Sarovar (Narmada project). In *Economy of Saurashtra: problems and prospects*. Ed. by D.T. Lakdawala, et al. Bhavnagar: Bhavnagar University, 1990. pp. 107–108. GUL.

Shibin, T.S. and Lad, Yogesh A. Overview of infrastructural support for agribusiness in Gujarat. In *Agribusiness potential of Gujarat state (Seminar proceeding) 2011.* Nagpur: Indian Society of Agricultural Marketing, 2011. pp. 193–204. SPIESRL.

Shingi, Prakash M. *Charcoal production and marketing in Gujarat.* Bangkok: FAO, 1993. p. 70. IRMAL.

Shingi, Prakash M. and Seetharaman, S.P. *Production route to woodfuel energy: a case study of Gujarat's social forestry programme.* Ahmedabad: Centre for Management in Agriculture(IIM), 1989. p. 49. IIML.

Shingi, Prakash M., et al. *Area irrigated in Gujarat: 1984–85.* Ahmedabad: Centre for Management in Agriculture, Indian Institute of Management, 1991. p. [ ]. IIM CGSF data centre data series working paper 2. GIDRL.

Shingi, Prakash M., et al. *Area under bajra in Gujarat: 1976–77 to 1985–86.* Ahmedabad: Centre for Management in Agriculture, Indian Institute of Management, 1991. p. [ ]. IIM CGSF data centre data series working paper 9. GIDRL, IIML.

Shingi, Prakash M., et al. *Area under fodder cultivation in Gujarat: 1975–76 to 1980–81.* Ahmedabad: Indian Institute of Management, Centre for Management in Agriculture, 1991. p. [ ]. IIM CGSF data centre data series working paper 7. GIDRL, IIML.

Shingi, Prakash M., et al. *Area under fodder cultivation in Gujarat: 1981–82 to 1985–86.* Ahmedabad: Indian Institute of Management, Centre for Management in Agriculture, 1991. p. [ ]. IIM CGSF data centre data series working paper 6. GIDRL, IIML.

Shingi, Prakash M., et al. Area under jower in Gujarat: 1976–77 to 1985–86. Ahmedabad: Indian Institute of Management, Centre for Management in Agriculture, 1991. p. [ ]. IIM CGSF data centre data series working paper 10. GIDRL, IIML.

Shingi, Prakash M., et al. *Climate and geographical distribution of sheep and goat population in Gujarat.* Ahmedabad: Indian Institute of Management, Centre for Management in Agriculture, 1991. p. [ ]. IIM CGSF data centre data series working paper 5. GIDRL, IIML.

Shingi, Prakash M., et al. *Density of cattle population in Gujarat.* Ahmedabad: Indian Institute of Management, Centre for Management in Agriculture,1991. p. [ ]. IIM CGSF data centre data series working paper No. 1. GIDEL, GIDRL, IIML.

Shingi, Prakash M., et al. *Normal rainfall and pattern of variation in Gujarat.* Ahmedabad: Indian Institute of Management, Centre for Management in Agriculture, 1991. p. [ ]. IIM CGSF data centre data series working paper 3. GIDRL, IIML.

Shingi, Prakash M., et al. *Rainfall pattern in Gujarat: 1971 to 1990.* Ahmedabad: Indian Institute of Management, Centre for Management in Agriculture, 1991. p. [ ]. IIM CGSF data centre data series working paper 8. GIDRL, IIML.

Shingi, Prakash M., et al. *Sheep and goat population in Gujarat.* Ahmedabad: Indian Institute of Management, Centre for Management in Agriculture, 1991. p. [ ]. IIM CGSF data centre data series working paper 4. GIDRL, IIML.

Shingi, Prakash M. et al. *Strategic planning for development of westelands: a GIS study of Junagadh district.* Ahmedabad: Centre for Management in Agriculture, 1994. p. [ ]. IIML.

Shiyani, R.L., Joshi, P.K. and Bantilan, M.C.S. Impact of chickpea research in Gujarat patancheru, international crops research institute for the semi-arid tropics. Junagadh: Gujarat Agricultural University. 2001. p. [ ]. ICRISAT Impact Series No. 9 GIDRL.

Shroff, J.C., et al. Development of weather based models for predicting outbreak of pest of okra in Middle Gujarat region. In *Agro meteorological services for farmers.* Ed. by Vyas Pandey. Anand: Anand Agriculture University, 2010. pp. 282–288. AAUL.

Shukla, Rohit. Forestry and environmental concerns of Gujarat. In *Gujarat-2010: challenges and opportunities*. By Government of Gujarat. Ahmedabad: Sardar Patel Institutee of Economic & Social Research, 2001. pp. 587–602. Seminar volume. CSSL, EDIL, IRMAL, SGUL, SPIESRL.

Shukla, Rohit and Dalvi, Rohit. *Evaluation of Gujarat: social forestry programme.* Ahmedabad: Sardar Patel Institutee of Economic & Social Research, 1988. p. 312. SPIESR Monograph Series No. 14. GIDRL, SPIESRL.

Shukla, Rohit and Shah, N.C. Some tentative implications of drought proneness to agriculture and levels of living. In *Gujarat economy: problems and prospects*. Ed. by D.T. Lakdawala. Ahmedabad: Sardar Patel Institutee of Economic & Social Research, 1983. pp. 319–334. Monograph Series No. 10. GUL.

Shukla, Rohit and Shah, N.C. Some tentative implications of drought proneness to agriculture and levels of living. In *Seminar on development of Gujarat: problems &*

prospects, 24th-26th August, 1981. Ahmedabad: Sardar Patel Institutee of Economic & Social Research, 1981. pp. 1–17. CSSL.

Singh, Baldev and Sharma, U.S. Agriculture and animal husbandry. In *Gujarat economy in 2001 A.D.: a study in perspective*. Ahmedabad: Sardar Patel Institutee of Economic & Social Research, 1980. pp. 159–200. GUL.

Singh, Baljeet. Production potential and its realisation of important fruit and vegetable crops of Gujarat. In *Agribusiness potential of Gujarat state (Seminar proceeding) 2011.* Nagpur: Indian Society of Agricultural Marketing, 2011. pp. 52–67. SPIESRL.

Singh, Gurudev. Farming contracts, experience and role of government-discussant's comments. In *Frontiers of agricultural development in Gujarat*. Ed. by Ravindra H. Dholakia. Ahmedabad: Centre for Management in Agriculture, Indian Institute of Management, 2007. pp. 155–159. CMA Publication No. 226. CSSL, GVL, IIML.

Singh, H.S. *Wildlife of Gujarat: wildlife and protected habitats of Gujarat state.* Gandhinagar: Gujarat Ecological Education and Research, 1998. p. 123. GIDRL.

Singh, Katar A. Holistic strategy for promoting growth and development of agribusiness in Gujarat. *In Agribusiness potential of Gujarat state (seminar proceedings) 2011.* Nagpur: Indian Society of Agricultural Marketing, 2011. pp. [ ]. SPIESRL.

Singh, Katar and Ballabh, Vishwa. *Afforestation of village common lands: a case study of Aslali village woodlot in Gujarat*. Anand: Institute of Rural Management, 1989. p. 28. IRMA Case Study No. 4. GIDRL, IRMAL.

Singh, Katar and Durgaprasad, P. *Study of milk animals scheme of IRDP & its linkages with dairy development programme in Amreli district, Gujarat*. Anand: Institute of Rural Management, 1987. p. 90. IRMAL.

Singh, Katar, et al. *Impact of milk animals programme of IRDP in Sabarkantha district, Gujarat.* Anand: Institute of Rural Management, 1984. p. 212. GIDRL, IRMAL.

Singh, Narendra, Patel, K.S. and Laua, A.K. Production and export performance of fresh vegetables from Gujarat state: constraints and emerging issues. *In Agribusiness potential of Gujarat state(seminar proceedings) 2011.* Nagpur: Indian Society of Agricultural Marketing, 2011. pp. 267–282. SPIESRL.

Singh, P.K. *Building up of an efficient marketing system to obviate the need for large scale state intervention in Gujarat*. Vallabh Vidyanagar: Agro-Economic Research Centre, 2004. p. 130. Research Study No. 126. AERCL.

Singh, R.P. *Features of traditional farming systems in two villages of Gujarat.* Patancheru: ICRISAT, 1982. p. 34. IRMAL.

Singh, S.B. and Patel, G.J. *Economics of tobacco production in Middle Gujarat.*Anand: Gujarat Agriculture University, 1983. p. 54. IRMAL.

Singh, Sonal, Patel, Sandip and Shibin, T.S. Agricultural infrastructure projects support for the production of agribusiness in Gujarat. In *Agribusiness potential of Gujarat state (seminar proceeding) 2011.* Nagpur: Indian Society of Agricultural Marketing, 2011. pp. 144–153. SPIESRL.

Singh, Sukhpal. *Agricultural development in Gujarat: problems and prospects.* Anand: Institute of Rural Management, 1997. p. 84. IRMAL.

Singh, Sukhpal. Contract farming for agricultural development in Gujarat: evidence and issues. In *Frontiers of agricultural development in Gujarat*. Ed. by Ravindra H. Dholakia. Ahmedabad: Centre for Management in Agriculture, Indian Institute of Management, 2007. pp. 125–152. CMA Publication No. 226. CSSL, GVL, IIML.

Singh, Sukhpal and Saxena, Rakesh. *Agricultural development in Gujarat: problems and prospects.* Anand: Institute of Rural Management, 1997. p. 84. IRMAL.

Skutsch, Margaret M. *Not-so-social forestry in Gujarat, India*. Enschede: Twente Univ of Tech, 1987. p. 50. VOK Working Paper No. 27. IRMAL.

Sood, Ankita and Ray, C.N. *Contract farming as an institutional innovation in agriculture development*. Ahmedabad: CEPT University, 2010. p. 27. Working Paper No. 49. CSSL.

Soparkar, Farhin N. Export potential of cumin from Gujarat. In *Agribusiness potential of Gujarat state (seminar proceeding) 2011*. Nagpur: Indian Society of Agricultural Marketing, 2011. pp. 218–233. SPIESRL.

Srivastava, Akhil. Production potential and trade value of important commercial crops of Gujarat state. In *Agribusiness potential of Gujarat state (seminar proceeding) 2011*. Nagpur: Indian Society of Agricultural Marketing, 2011. pp. 104–110. SPIESRL.

Srivastava, U.K., et al. *Management of marine fisheries: an analysis of problems in harvesting and processing: micro study in Gujarat state*. Ahmedabad: Indian Institute of Management, 1979. p. 287. CMA Monograph No. 80. IRMAL.

Sudarshan Naidu, N.T. Critical analysis contract farming rules of Gujarat state. *In Agribusiness potential of Gujarat state(seminar proceedings) 2011*. Nagpur: Indian Society of Agricultural Marketing, 2011. pp. 17–31. SPIESRL.

Sudha, Bela R., Navalawala, Bhasita and Sodhi, Harpreet. Venture capital assistance(VCA) and project development facility(PDF) under small farmer's agri-business consortium (SFAC) scheme by Gujarat government. In *Agribusiness potential of Gujarat state (seminar proceeding) 2011*. Nagpur: Indian Society of Agricultural Marketing, 2011. pp. 37–51. SPIESRL.

Swain, Mrutyunjay and Kapadia, Kalpana. *Problems and prospects of oilseeds in Gujarat: special reference to groundnut*. Vallabh Vidynagar: Agro-Economic Research Centre, 2013. p. 116. AERCL.

Swain, Mrutyunjay, Kalamkar, S.S. and Kapadia, Kalpana M. *State of Gujarat agriculture 2011–2012*. Vallabh Vidyanagar: Agro-Economic Research Centre, 2012. p. 40. AERC Report No. 146. AERCL.

Tewari, D.D. *Economics and management of non-timber forest products: a case study of Gujarat, India*. New Delhi: Oxford, 1998. p. 164. CMA Monograph No. 175. AERCL, GIDRL.

Thakar, Himanshu N. *Planning components of agriculture produce regulated market in Gujarat*. Ahmedabad: CEPT, 1982. p. 142. IRMAL.

Thaker, K.R., et al. Economics of rice based crop sequence for Middle Gujarat. In *Crop sequence research in Gujarat agriculture*. Ed. by N.M. Patel, et al. Anand: Gujarat Agriculture University, 1997. pp. 56–58. AAUL.

Thakor, R.F. and Joshi, P.J. Participatory irrigation management: an impact study of Mehasana district of Gujarat State. In *Extension strategies for agriculture and rural development*. Ed. by Ashok K. Singh. Delhi: Daya, 2010. pp. 365–369. AAUL.

Thomas, P. and Ballabh, Vishwa. *Forestry and economic development: lessons from the tribal belt of Eastern Gujarat*. Anand: Institute of Rural Management, 1996. p. 15. WP-104. CSSL, GIDRL, IRMAL.

Trivedi, Y.A. and Upadhyay, H.N. Gujarat fisheries 2010: opportunities and challenges. In *Gujarat-2010: challenges and opportunities*. By Government of Gujarat. Ahmedabad: Sardar Patel Institutee of Economic & Social Research, 2001. pp. 128–147. Seminar volume. CSSL, EDIL, IRMAL, SGUL, SPIESRL.

Tyagi, D.S. and Misra, V.N. *Significance of the new strategy of agricultural development for small farmers: acrossectional study of two areas of Gujarat*. Vallabh Vidyanagar: Sardar Patel University, 1969. p. 95. HML.

Upadhyay, P.N., et al. Effect of manuring in pearl millet-wheat crop sequence under Middle Gujarat conditions. In *Crop sequence research in Gujarat University*. Ed. by N.M. Patel, et al. Anand: Gujarat Agriculture University, 1997. pp. 18–20. AAUL.

Vadodaria, M.P., et al. Integrated management of cotton bollworms in Gujarat. In *Ecological agriculture and sustainable development.* Vol. 2. Chandigarh: Centre for Research in Rural & Industrial Development, 1998. pp. 281–285. Proceedings of international conference on ecological agriculture. CSSL.

Vaidya, T.K. Irrigation and water potential in Saurashtra. In *Economy of Saurashtra: problems and prospects.* Ed. by D.T. Lakdawala, et al. Bhavnagar: Bhavnagar University, 1990. pp. 109–117. GUL.

Van Dorsten, F. *Milk marketing and rural dairy development: a comparison of the impact of the Delhi milk scheme and the Mehsana district co-operative milk producers' union (Dadhsagar dairy).* The Hague: Institute of Social Studies, 1986. p. 100. Working paper-series on dairy aid and development No. 22. CSSL.

Van Dorsten, Frank. *Impact of Amul on the milk economy of Kheda district (Gujarat).* Netherlands: ISS, 1986. p. 43. IRMAL.

Van Koppen, Barbara, Parthasarthy, R. and Safiliou, Constantina. *Poverty dimensions of irrigation management transfer in large-scale canal irrigation in Andra Pradesh and Gujarat, India.* Sri Lanka: International Water Management Institute, 2002. p. 26. IWMI Research Report No. 61. GIDRL.

Vaswani, L.K., Venkatakrishnan, V. and Upadhyay, Ravindra. Marketing of horticulture products: a case study of cooperatives in South Gujarat. In *Agriculture-market linkages: evaluating and evolving a conceptual framework in Indian context.* Mumbai: Department of Economic Analysis and Research, 2003. pp. 15–39. Occasional Paper No. 28. IIML.

Vyas, V.S. Economy efficiency on small farms of Central Gujarat. *In Seminar on problem of small farmers.* Bombay: Indian Society of Agricultural Economics, 1968. pp. 60–75. Seminar Series – VII. GUL, SPUL.

Vyas, V.S. *Study of wheat prices in the states of Gujarat and Rajasthan (1948–49 to 1960–61).* Vallabh Vidyanagar: Agro-Economic Research Centre, 1963. p. 64. Ad-hoc Resarch Studies No. 1. AERCL.

Vyas, V.S. and Choudhary, K.M. *Economic of dairy farming in Mehsana district of Gujarat State: report of a survey.* Vallabh Vidyanagar: Centre for Studies in Economics of Dairying, 1971. p. 416. SPUL.

Vyas, V.S. and Maharaja, M.H. *Factors affecting marketable surplus and marketed supplies: a study in two regions of Gujarat and Rajasthan.* Vallabh Vidyanagar: Agro-Economic Research Centre, 1966. p. 78. AERCL.

Vyas, V.S., Srivastava, D.C. and Dharap, V.S. *Pace & pattern of marketing of groundnut in Saurashtra region of Gujarat.* Anand: Sardar Patel University, 1969. p. 134. SPIESRL.

Vyas, V.S., Tyagi, D.S. and Misra, V.N. *Significance of the new strategy of agricultural development for small farmers: a cross-sectional study of two areas of Gujarat.* Vallabh Vidyanagar: Agro-Economic Research Centre, 1969. p. 95. AERCL, IRMAL, SPUL.

Wadhwa, D.C. *Agrarian legislation in India (1793–1966)* Vol. 1. Bombay: Gokhale Institute of Politics and Economic, 1972. pp. 151–227. SPIESRL.

World Wide Fund for Nature. *Focus on some conservation issues of Gujarat.* Baroda: Gujarat State Office, [ ]. p. 30. CSSL.

14

Poverty

Books/Chapter in Books

Arora, S.L. Some experiences of involving the rural poor for self-employment: a case study of Nanded (Gujarat). In *Planning development and disparities in rural India.* Ed. by Ashok Kumar. New Delhi: Commonwealth, 1990. pp. 210–221. IIML.

Batra, S.L. *Land reforms in Gujarat: distribution of ceiling surplus land among rural poor.* New Delhi: Gyan Sagar, 1999. p. 128. GIDRL.

Bhatt, Anil. *Poverty tribals and development: a rehabilitation approach.* New Delhi: Manohar, 1990. p. 93. IIML.

Bhatt, Anil. Vansda. In *Poverty, tribals and development: a rehabilitation approach.* New Delhi: Manohar, 1990. pp. 20–27. IIML.

Breman, Jan. *Poverty regime in village India: half a century of work and life at the bottom of the rural economy in South Gujarat.* New Delhi: Oxford, 2007. p. 458. CSSL, GIDRL, GVL, IRMAL.

Desai, Anjana. Geographical study of poverty on space: tribal communities of Dangs district in South Gujarat. In *Regional planning and rural development.* Ed. by L.R. Singh. Allahabad: Technical, 1986. pp. 261–272. TRTIL.

Dutta, Shyam S. Partnership for urban poverty reduction: a review experience. In *Poverty and vulnerability in a globalilsing metropolis Ahmedabad.* Ed. by Amitabh Kundu and Darshini Mahadevia. New Delhi: Manak, 2002. pp. 237–267. CEPTL, CSSL.

Ghosh, Archana, Sami, Ahmad S. and Maitra, Shipra. *Basic services for urban poor: a study of Baroda, Bhilwara, Sambalpur and Siliguri.* New Delhi: Concept, 1995. p. 305. CSSL, SPIESRL.

Hirway, Indira. *Abolition of poverty in India: with special reference to target group approach in Gujarat.* New Delhi: Vikas, 1986. p. 284. CSSL, GIDRL, IRMAL, SPUL.

Iyenger, Sudarshan. Gujarat. In *Poor in a hostile society: glimpses of changing poverty scenario in India.* Ed. by V.M. Rao. New Delhi: Vikas, 1998. pp. 108–145. GVL, SPIESRL.

Jani, B.M. Experiments and experiences of planning for reduction of poverty: a study of Gujarat and Rajasthan. In *Development experiences in the Indian economy: inter-state perspectives.* Ed. by P.R. Brahmananda and V.R. Panchamukhi. Delhi: Bookwell, 2001. pp. 459–472. CSSL, IIML.

Kohli, Atul. *Poverty amid plenty in the new India.* New Delhi: Cambridge University press, 2012. p. 180. SPIESRL.

Kundu, Amitabh and Mahadevia, Darshini. Globalisation, poverty and vulnerability. In *Poverty and vulnerability in a globalising metropolis Ahmedabad.* Ed. by Amitabh

Kundu and Darshini Mahadevia. New Delhi: Manak, 2002. pp. 1–29. CEPTL, CSSL.

Kundu, Amitabh and Mahadevia, Darshini, ed. *Poverty and vulnerability in a globalising metropolis Ahmedabad*. New Delhi: Manak, 2002. p. 372. CEPTL, CSSL.

Lobo, Lancy and Das, Biswaroop. *Poor in urban India: life in the slums of a Western Indian city.* Jaipur: Rawat, 2001. p. 203. CSSL.

Mittal, Nidhi. Growth with limited outcomes: poverty and inequality in Gujarat. In *Poverty amidst prosperity: essays on the trajectory of development in Gujarat*. Ed. by Atul Sood. Delhi: Aakar, 2012. pp. 147–162. CSSL, IRMAL, MICAL.

Murty, G.V.S.N. and Shah, Niresh. Poverty, inequality and level of living in Gujarat. In *Gujarat economy: problems and prospects.* Ed. by D.T. Lakdawala. Ahmedabad: Sardar Patel Institute of Economic & Social Research, 1982. pp. 89–128. GIDRL.

Pathak, Jharna. Creating new options for the poor: a case of Gujarat. In *Democratic governance and human development*. Ed. by Yatindra Singh Sisodia. Jaipur: Rawat, 2013. pp. 283–307. CSSL.

Pichholiya, K.R. Economic activities of urban poor: a case study of Ahmedabad. In *Development programmes for urban poor.* Ed. by Girish K. Misra and M.K. Narain. New Delhi: Indian Institute of Public Administration, 1989. pp. 128–145. SGUL.

Ray, C.N. *Livelihoods for the urban poor: a case study of Umeed programme in Ahmedabad.* Ahmedabad: Centre for Urban Equity, 2010. p. 62. CEPTL.

Ray, C.N. *Politics of rural development: the case of anti-poverty programme in West Bengal & Gujarat*. Jaipur: Rawat, 1994. p. 171. CSSL, GIDRL.

Rutten, Mario. Elite attitudes towards the poor: Patidar entrepreneurs in rural Central Gujarat. In *Other Gujarat: social transformations among weaker section.* Ed. by Takashi Shinoda. Mumbai: Popular, 2002. pp. 260–283. ASL, CEEL, CSSL, EDIL, GIDRL, SETUL, SPIESRL.

Schenk-Sandbergen, Loes Ch. People of Dhobi talav: poverty and solidarity. In *Winners and losers: styles of development and change in an Indian region*. Ed. by S. Devadas Pillai and Chris Baks. Bombay: Popular, 1979. pp. 171–201. CSSL, SPIESRL.

Shah, Amita. Poverty and natural resources: understanding the dynamics in the context of dryland regions in Western India. In *New development paradigms & challenges for Western & Central India.* Vol. 1. Ed. by R. Parthasarthy and Sudarshan Iyengar. New Delhi: Concept, 2006. pp. 82–109. CSSL, EDIL, GIDRL.

Shah, Amita and Sajitha, O.G. Poverty and livelihood among tribals: status, opportunities and strategies. In *Tribal development in Western India.* Ed. by Amita Shah and Jharna Pathak. New Delhi: Routledge, 2014. pp. 26–57. CSSL.

Shah, Kirtee. Housing for the urban poor in Ahmedabad: an integrated urban development approach. In *Indian city: poverty, ecology and urban development*. Ed. by Alfred de Souza. New Delhi: Manohar, 1983. pp. 145–170. CSSL, TRTIL.

Shah, N.C. Poverty: its concept and incidence in Gujarat. In *Dynamics of development in Gujarat.* Ed. by Indira Hirway, S.P. Kashyap and Amita Shah. New Delhi: Concept, 2002. pp. 439–457. CSSL, EDIL, GIDRL, GVL, HML, IRMAL, SPUL, UML.

Sharma, Usha. Prospects for rural poverty alleviation: experience of Gujarat state. In *Essays on regional science regional development and planning.* Ed. by C.R. Pathak. Kharagpur: Regional Science Association, 1998. pp. 229–240. IIML.

Sood, Atul, ed. *Poverty amidst prosperity: essays on the trajectory of development in Gujarat.* Delhi: Aakar, 2012. p. 286. CSSL, IRMAL, MICAL.

Spodek, Howard. Struggle and development: a history of coping with poverty. In *Poverty and vulnerability in a globalising metropolis Ahmedabad.* Ed. by Amitabh Kundu and Darshini Mahadevia. New Delhi: Manak, 2002. pp. 207–236. CEPTL, CSSL.

Vakil, C.N. *Poverty, planning and inflation*. Bombay: Allied, 1978. p. 316. CSSL.

Journal Articles

Bharti, Madhu. Impact of poor urban services on health and asset creation: a case study of Ahmedabad. *Social Action*. 56, 2, 2006. pp. 155–171. CEPTL, CSSL.

Bhatt, Mahesh and Chawda, V.K. Haunts of hunger and disease: a study of Ahmedabad. *Indian Journal of Labour Economics.* 15, 1–2, 1972. pp. 116–146. SPIESRL.

Chauhan, Uttara and Lal, Niraj. Public-private partnerships for urban poor in Ahmedabad: a slum project. *Economic and Political Weekly*. 34, 10 and 11, 1999. pp. 636–642. CEPTL, CSSL, IIML, IRMAL, MICAL, SGUL, SPIESRL, UML.

Dantwala, M.L. Profile of poverty and unemployment in 12 villages. *Indian Journal of Agricultural Economics*. 30, 2, 1975. pp. 1–17. SPUL, UML.

Hirway, Indira. Critique of target group approach: a study in Gujarat. *Indian Journal of Agricultural Economics*. 39, 3, 1984. pp. 289–297. CSSL, UML.

Jhabwala, Renana and Jumeni, Usha. Ahmedabad 2001 planning for the poor: a focus on self-employed women. *Nagarlok.* 20, 4, 1988. pp. 74–96. SPIESRL.

Krishna, Anirudh, et al. Falling into poverty in a high-growth state: escaping poverty and becoming poor in Gujarat villages. *Economic and Political Weekly*. 38, 49, 2003. pp. 5171–5179. BUL, CEPTL, CSSL, EDIL, GIDRL, IIML, IRMAL, MICAL, SGUL, SPIESRL, UML.

Krishna, Anirudh, et al. Why growth is not enough household poverty dynamics in Northeast Gujarat, India. *Journal of Development Studies.* 41, 7, 2005. pp. 1163–1192. BUL, GIDRL.

Kumar, B.L. People's perceptions of poverty, development and change: insights from re-survey of a Gujarat village. *Man & Development*. 19, 4, 1997. pp. 124–136. CSSL, GIDRL, GVL, IRMAL, UML.

Mahadevia, Darshini. Information of employment and incidence of poverty in Ahmedabad. *Indian Journal of Labour Economics*. 41, 3, 1998, pp. 514–530. AAUL.

Masavi, M.I. and Naik, T.B. Poverty among Kolghas of Gujarat. *Khadi Gramodyog.* 28, 11, 1982. pp. 496–503. GVL, TRTIL.

Patel, M.S. Short profile of poverty in a tribal area. *Adivasi Gujarat.* 1, 1, 1978. pp. 54-[ ]. SPIESRL.

Patel, Tara. Some reflections on the beggar problem in Ahmedabad. *Sociological Bulletin*. 8, 1, 1959. pp. 5–15. CSSL, HML, TRTIL.

Pathak, Mahesh T. and Shah, Navin R. Dimensions of poverty and unemployment: a case study in Gujarat. *Artha-Vikas*. 16, 1, 1980. pp. 21–40. CEPTL, CSSL, GIDRL, HML, SGUL.

Radhakrishna, R., Parikh, Bhanumati K. and Shah, N.C. Levels of living, poverty and liquor consumption: a study of Ahmedabad slums. *Anvesak*. 12, 1, 1982. pp. 57–84. CEPTL, CSSL, GIDRL.

Sarma, Atul and Radhakrishna, R. Unemployment and poverty in Gujarat: a case for intervention. *Artha-Vikas*. 16, 1, 1980. pp. 1–20. CEPTL, CSSL, GIDRL, HML, SGUL.

Shah, Ghanshyam and Desai, Kiran. Globalization and the poor: a study of Gujarat. *IASSI Quarterly*. 29, 2, 2010. pp. 43–67. BUL, CSSL, IIML.

Shah, N.C. Temporal estimates of incidence of poverty in rural Gujarat. *Vishleshan*. 6, 1, 1980. pp. 48–54. CSSL, GIDRL, IIML.

Unni, Jeemol and Uma Rani. Gender, informality and poverty. *Seminar*. 531, 2003. pp. 27–33. CSSL, MICAL, UML.

Vaidya, Chetan. Role of community savings and loan association, Baroda in meeting credit needs of urban poor. *Nagarlok*. 27, 1, 1995. pp. 33–37. SPIESRL.

Vansiya, Yogesh N. and Patel, Manish R. Rural poverty in South Gujarat region: a critical study. *VNSGU Journal of Humanities & Social Sciences*. 2, 2, 2010. pp. 95–116. CSSL, SGUL.

Working Papers, Reports and Other Materials

Basu, D.N., Vaidya, C.V. and Maskara, J.D. Provision of basic services for the urban poor: an overview for the state of Gujarat. In *Seminar on development of Gujarat: problems & prospects, 24th-26th August, 1981*. Ahmedabad: Sardar Patel Institute of Economic & Social Research, 1981. pp. 1–22. CSSL.

Bhatt, Anil. *Rehabilitation approach to poverty alleviation: a study of BAIF's tribal development project in Vansda*. Ahmedabad: Public System Group, Indian Institute of Management, 1987. p. 92. CSSL, IIML.

Commerce Research Bureau. *Report on an integrated programme for eradication of extreme poverty in village: Vani (Ahmedabad district Gujarat)*. Bombay: Shri Sadguru Seva Sangh Trust, 1972. p. 48. SPIESRL.

Commerce Research Bureau. *Report on an integrated programme for eradication of extreme poverty in village: Dhrumath, Surendranagar district, Gujarat*. Bombay: Shri Sadguru Seva Sangh Trust, 1971. p. 48. SPIESRL.

Desai, B.M., et al. *Rural development for rural poor: Dharampur project*. Vol. I and II. Ahmedabad: Indian Institute of Management, 1976. p. 171. and p. 193. CMA Monograph No. 63. CSSL, IIML, TRTIL.

Hirway, Indira. *Economic development and poverty alleviation in Gujarat*. Ahmedabad: Gandhi Labour Institute (GLI), 1992. p. [ ]. GIDRL.

Iyengar, Sudarshan. Locating and describing poverty in Gujarat: an exploration. In *Gujarat-2010: challenges and opportunities*. By Government of Gujarat. Ahmedabad: Sardar Patel Institute of Economic & Social Research, 2001. pp. 271–285. Seminar volume. CSSL, EDIL, IRMAL, SGUL, SPIESRL.

Iyengar, Sudarshan and Visaria, Pravin. *Voluntary agencies, lending institutions and the rural poor in Gujarat: an overview of six case studies*. Ahmedabad: Gujarat Institute of Area Planning, 1989. p. 29. Working Paper No. 22. CSSL, GIDRL, IRMAL.

Joshi, Rutul and Sanga, Prashant. *Land reservations for the urban poor: the case of town planning: schemes in Ahmedabad*. Ahmedabad: Centre for Urban Equity, 2009. p. 13. Working Paper No. 4. CEPTL.

Joshi, Satyakam. *Organizing and managing a large scale survey research in the slum localities of Surat*. Surat: Centre for Social Studies, 1993. p. [ ]. Seminar on urban poor in India, 10–11 February 1993. CSSL.

Kumar, B.L. *Development and change in poverty and living standards in a Gujarat village.* Ahmedabad: Gujarat Institute of Development Research, 1997. p. 46. Working Paper No. 87. CSSL, GIDRL, IRMAL.

Kumbhar, B.L. *Rural poor in Gujarat: ameliorative measures and results: a review.* Ahmedabad: Gujarat Institute of Area Planning, [ ]. p. [ ]. GIDRL.

Lobo, Lancy. *Problems and coping mechanisms of people in a Surat slum*. Surat: Centre for Social Studies, 1993. p. [ ]. Seminar on urban poor in India, 10–11 February 1993. CSSL.

Mahadevia, Darshini. *Development dichotomy in Gujarat.* New Delhi: Research Foundation for Science, Technology and Ecology, 1998. p. 71. CEPTL, CSSL.

Mahadevia, Darshini. *Poverty and vulnerability in Ahmedabad.* Ahmedabad: Oxfam, 1997. p. 70. SPIESRL.

Murty, S.N. and Shah, Niresh. Poverty, inequality and levels of living in Gujarat. In *Gujarat economy problems and prospects.* Ed. by D.T. Lakdawala. Ahmedabad: Sardar Patel Institute of Economic & Social Research, 1983. pp. 89–128. Monograph-10. GUL, IIML.

National Institute of Urban Affairs. *Status of urban poor in Surat: a benchmark study.* New Delhi: Author, 2002. p. 20. CSSL.

Pandya, H.R. and Bhatt, B.D. Income generation through poverty alleviation programme in Junagadh district. In *Agricultural finance-problems and prospects.* Ed. by D.B. Kuchhadiya and R.L. Shiyani. Junagadh: Department of Agricultural Economics, 1997. pp. 94–98. SPIESRL.

Patel, Girish. *Public interest litigation and the poor in Gujarat*. Ahmedabad: Girish Patel Sanman Samiti, 2009. p. 131. CSSL.

Shah, Amita. *Estimates of BPL-households in rural Gujarat: measurement, spatial pattern and policy imperatives*. Ahmedabad: Gujarat Institute of Development Research, 2007. p. 30. CSSL, GIDRL, IRMAL.

Shah, Amita and Sajitha, O.G. *Poverty and livelihood among tribals in Gujarat: status, opportunities, and strategies.* Ahmedabad: Gujarat Institute of Development Research, 2008. p. 34. Working Paper No. 187. CSSL, SPIESRL.

Shah, M.N. Is urbanization in Gujarat poverty induced? In *Gujarat economic association conference papers, Baroda*. Ed. by V.S. Vyas, Pravin Visaria and A.R. Desai. Ahmedabad: Balgovind, 1971. pp. 153–164. GIDRL, IIML.

Shah, Rajesh, Jagtap, Meena and Vyas, Swati. *Life and living of urban poor Ahmedabad, Gujarat.* Ahmedabad: Vikas Centre for Development, 1995. p. [ ]. SPIESRL.

UNNATI Organisation for Development Education. Impact of structural adjustment programme (SAP) on the poor household economy of Gujarat. Bangalore: Action Aid, [ ]. p. [ ]. GIDRL.

Urban Affairs, National Institute of. *Status of urban poor in Surat: a benchmark study.* New Delhi: National Institute of Urban Affairs, 2002. p. 51. CSSL.

Van Koppen, Barbar, et al. *Poverty dimensions of irrigation management transfer in large-scale canal irrigation in Andhra Pradesh and Gujarat, India*. Colombo: International Water Management Institute (IWMI), 2002. p. 26. IRMAL.

Vyas, V.S., et al. *Rural development for rural poor: Dharampur project.* Ahmedabad: Indian Institute of Management, [ ]. p. [ ]. UML.

15

Education, Human Development

Books/Chapter in Books

Bhagavan, Manu. *Sovereign spheres: princes, education and empire in colonial India.* New Delhi: Oxford, 2003. p. 219. CSSL.

Budhdev, Pravina V. Development of girls education in Gujarat state (India). In *Education India: the next millennium*. Ed. by Marmar Mukhopadhyay, et al. New Delhi: Institute of Education, Rural Studies and Development, 1998. pp. 258–270. HML.

Desai, Chitra. *Girls' school education and social change*. Bombay: R.R. Sheth, 1976. p. 288. CSSL.

Desai, D.M. Gujarat. In *Education of teachers in India Vol-2.* Ed. by S.N. Mukerji. New Delhi: S. Chand, 1968. pp. 42–61. GVL, SPUL.

Desai, I.P. Education of the scheduled castes and scheduled tribes in Gujarat. In *Social context of education: essays in honour of Professor J.P. Naik*. Bombay: Allied, 1978. pp. 244–253. CSSL, GVL.

Desai, I.P. Western educated elites and social change in India. In *Social structure and change.* Vol. I, *theory and method – evaluation of the work of M.V. Srinivas*. Ed. by A.M. Shah, B.S. Baviskar and E.A. Ramaswamy. New Delhi: Sage, 1996. pp. 79–103. CSSL, SGUL.

Desai, K.G. Educational psychology Gujarat: development of psychological tests in Gujarat. In *Bunch of current Indian studies (a study of functional economics of areas and ideas).* Ed. by M.R. Sinha. Bombay: Indian Institute of Asian Studies, 1969. pp. 83–87. GUL, SPIESRL, SUL.

Ghosh, Sourindra. Analysis of state of education in Gujarat. In *Poverty amidst prosperity: essays on the trajectory of development in Gujarat.* Ed. by Atul Sood. Delhi: Aakar, 2012. pp. 180–198. CSSL, IRMAL, MICAL.

Gupta, S. Mahatma Gandhi (1869–1948) basic tenets of basic education. In *Education in India*. Delhi: Shipra, 2005. pp. 169–185. SUL.

Heredero, J.M. *Education for development: social awareness, organization and technological innovation*. New Delhi: Manohar, 1989. p. 144. CSSL.

Hirway, Indira and Mahadevia, Darshini. Human development and gender development in Gujarat: some Issues. In *Gujarat: perspectives of the future*. Ed. by R. Swaminathan. New Delhi: Academic, 2008. pp. 152–194. CSSL, EDIL, GIDRL, GVL, IIML, IRMAL, SETUL, SPIESRL.

Iyengar, Sudarshan. Education in Gujarat: a review. In *Growth or development: which way is Gujarat going?* Ed. by Indira Hirway, Amita Shah and Ghanshyam Shah. New Delhi: Oxford, 2014. pp. 477–516. CSSL.

Iyengar, Sudarshan. Mainstreaming Nai talim: concept, scope and issues. In *Perspectives on Nai talim.* Ed. by S.V. Prabhath. New Delhi: Serials, 2010. pp. 77–108. AAUL, CSSL, SPUL.

Jeremiah, M.S. *Deteriorating quality of higher education: owing to poverty of resources.* Jaipur: ABD, 1998. p. 184. SPUL.

Joshi, Satyakam and Desai, Kiran. Overview of effectiveness of the Nai talim organizations in Gujarat with reference to their role in social change. In *Perspectives on Nai talim.* Ed. by S.V. Prabhath. New Delhi: Serials, 2010. pp. 181–209. AAUL, CSSL, SPUL.

Joshi, Uma, et al. Corporate social responsibilities: glimpses of Vadodara corporates. In *Prism of lifelong education.* Ed. by Rameshwari Pandya. New Delhi: Concept, 2013. pp. 160–172. IIML.

Joshi, Vidyut. Century of tribal education in Gujarat. In *Education reformat different levels*. Ed. by P.R. Panchmukhi. Bombay: Himalaya, 1989. pp. 197–225. SUL.

Joshi, Vidyut. Century of tribal education in Gujarat. In *Reforms towards equality and relevance: studies in educational reform in India volume-III.* Ed by P.R. Panchamukhi. Bombay: Himalaya, 1989. pp. 75–96. GVL.

Karandikar, C.M. Managing resources through cluster resource center (CRC) at primary school level in Gujarat. In *Management of primary education a challenge.* Ed. by Sneha Joshi, N. Pradhan and Ashutosh Biswal. Vadodara: Good Companions. 2000, pp. 338–343. HML.

Khirwadkar, Anjali, Tomar, Archana and Saharasbuddhe, Milina. Managing teachers at primary education level in Baroda: some issues. In *Management of primary education a challenge.* Ed. by Sneha Joshi, N. Pradhan and Ashutosh Biswal. Vadodara: Good Companions. 2000. pp. 116–122. HML.

Mehta, Anjal. Management of Gujarati language instructional process at the Nagar Prathamik Schools of Baroda. In *Management of primary education a challenge.* Ed. by Sneha Joshi, N. Pradhan and Ashutosh Biswal. Vadodara: Good Companions, 2000. pp. 254–260. HML.

Mehta, Hansa. *My reminiscences of student days in Baroda college.* Baroda: Butala, 1981. pp. 170–174. SPIESRL.

Mehta, Sushila. Student movement in Gujarat. In *Student power in India.* Ed. by G.S. Mansukhani. New Delhi: Oxford, 1975. pp. 18–44. HML.

Misra, P.N. Quantification of optimal role of government expenditure on education for regional development in Gujarat. In *Education and regional development.* Ed. by Jandhyala B.G. Tilak. New Delhi: Yatan, 1986. pp. 196–212. GVL.

Mukhopadhyay, Marmar. Self regulation the key to institution building Indian institute of management Ahmedabad. In *Leadership for institute building in education.* Delhi: Shipra, 2012. pp. 178–190. CSSL, SUL.

Pandey, V.C. Distance education development in India: B.R. Ambedkar Open University (BRAOU). In *Technology and development of distance education.* Ed. by V.C. Pandey. Delhi: Isha, 2005. pp. 203–238. GVL.

Pandor, G.A. Participation of scheduled tribes in education. In *Winners and losers: styles of development and change in an Indian region.* Ed. by S.Devadas Pillai and Chris Baks. Bombay: Popular, 1979. pp. 387–404. CSSL, SPIESRL.

Pandya, Rameshwari and Chokshi, Shridha. Health education: a success story from Gujarat. In *Prism of lifelong education.* Ed. by Rameshwari Pandya. New Delhi: Concept, 2013. pp. 88–111. IIML.

Parmar, A.V. Study of democratic in educated tribal and non-tribal youth of South Gujarat. In *Challenges of education*. Ed. by Hemlata Talesra, Maneesha Shukla and Uma Shanker Sharma. Delhi: Authors Press 2003. pp. 354–363. HML.

Parmar, A.V. Study of social values in educated tribal and non-tribal youth of South Gujarat. In *Agenda for education: design and direction*. Ed. by Hemlata Talesra, et al. New Delhi: Kanishka, 2004. pp. 202–209. HML.

Patel, B.B. and Alagh, Raksha. Education and health care strategies for Gujarat in the context of emerging global opportunities and challenges. In *Gujarat: perspectives of the future*. Ed. by R. Swaminathan. New Delhi: Academic Foundation, 2008. pp. 299–331. CSSL, EDIL, GIDRL, GVL, IIML, IRMAL, SETUL, SPIESRL.

Patel, Narottambhai. *Social transformation through Nai talim: Nai talim in Gujarat philosophy and development*. Ahmedabad: Gujarat Vidyapith, 2002. p. 317. TRTIL.

Patel, Narottambhai and Dabhi, Jasangbhai. Gujarat Nai talim sangh and development of Nai talim in Gujarat. In *Perspectives on Nai talim*. Ed. by S.V. Prabhath. New Delhi: Serials, 2010. pp. 158–166. AAUL, CSSL, SPUL.

Patel, Sarjoo and Shukla, Maneesha. Value of education: a study of parents of children studying in Vadodara municipal corporation primary schools. In *Managing educational challenges a global view*. Ed. by Hemlata Talesra, et al. Delhi: Authors Press. 2002. pp. 325–334. HML.

Patel, Tara. *Development of education among tribal women*. Delhi: Mittal, 1984. p. 198. GUL, SPUL, TRTIL.

Rudolph, Hoeber and Rudolph, Lloyd I. Parochialism and cosmopolitanism in university government: the environments of Baroda University. In *Education and politics in India: studies in organization, society, and policy*. Ed. by Susanne Hoeber Rudolph and Lloyd I. Rudolph. Delhi: Oxford, 1972. pp. 207–272. CSSL.

Saiyadain, Mirza S., Murthy, Nirmala and Singh, J.P. *Challenges in adult education: an impact study in Gujarat*. Delhi: Macmillan, 1990. p. 151. GIDRL, IIML, SPIESRL.

Sen, N.B. Gujarat and its basic education. In *Advancement of learning in independent India*. Ed. by N.B. Sen. New Delhi: New Book Society of India. 1967. pp. 7–16. AAUL, HML.

Shah, Dilip and Jani, Sudhir. Basic education in rural higher education: a study of gram vidyapiths of Gujarat. In *Perspectives on Nai talim*. Ed. by S.V. Prabhath. New Delhi: Serials, 2010. pp. 167–180. AAUL, CSSL, SPUL.

Shah, Ghanshyam. Education and backward castes in Gujarat. In *Education and the disprivileged*. Ed. by Sabyasachi Bhattacharya. Hyderabad: Orient, 2002. pp. 255–269. CSSL.

Shah, Ghanshyam, et al. *Tribal education in Gujarat*. Surat: Centre for Social Studies, Delhi: Ajanta, 1985. p. [ ]. CSSL, GIDRL, SPUL.

Shah, Ghanshyam., Joshi, Vidyut and Patel, Tara. *Tribal education in Gujarat*. Delhi: Ajanta, 1985. p. 142. CSSL, SPIESRL.

Shah, K.R. and Lakdawala, D.T. Cost, size and location of colleges in Gujarat. In *Essays on economics of human resources*. Ed. by K.R. Shah. Rohtak: Spellbound, 1938. pp. 142–458. CSSL, GVL.

Shah, Vimal. Educational problems of scheduled caste and scheduled tribe school and college students in India. New Delhi: Allied, 1982. p. 421. CSSL.

Shah, Vimal P. and Patel, Tara. *Who goes to college?: scheduled caste/tribe post-metric scholars in Gujarat*. Ahmedabad: Rachana, 1977. p. 219. CSSL, GIDRL, GUL, SGUL, SPIESRL, SPUL, TRTIL.

Shetty, Anitha D. University-industry: the scenario at MSU. In *Agenda for education: design and direction*. Ed. by Hemlata Talesra, et al. New Delhi: Kanishka, 2004. pp. 91–111. HML.

Shukla, M.M. Administration of education in the state and the Union Territories: Gujarat. In *Administration of education in India*. Ed. by S.N. Mukerji and K.L. Shrimali. Baroda: Acharya, 1962. pp. 353–371. SUL.

Shukla, M.M. Gujarat. In *Education in India*. Ed. by S.N. Mukerji. Baroda: Acharya, 1962. pp. 353–371. GUL, SGUL, SPUL, SUL.

Sinha, Ratnawali. Mainstreaming the marginalized: status of tribal education and development in Gujarat. In *Tribal education: implications for development*. Ed. by S.N. Chaudhary. New Delhi: Concept, 2012. pp. 269–291. CSSL, TRTIL.

Taj, Haseem. Sarva Shiksha Abhiyan (SSA) an approach to universal elementary education (UEE). In *Current challenges in education*. New Delhi: Neelkamal, 2008. pp. 28–43. SUL.

Talmaki, Rekha K. Tribal communities and their status in Valod(South Gujarat). In *Prism of lifelong education*. Ed. by Rameshwari Pandya. New Delhi: Concept, 2013. pp. 59–75. IIML.

Trivedi, Parimal. Globalization of education: threat or opportunity lessons from innovations at Gujarat University. In *Higher education: quality and management*. Ed. by Paul Khurana and P.K. Singhal. New Delhi: Gyan, 2010. pp. 185–190. HML.

Vakil, R.N., Kulinchandra, Y. and Patel, P.G. *School education in Gujarat: present status and future scenario*. Ahmedabad: R.N. Vakil Hiran Charitable Trust, 2006. p. 80. SPIESRL.

Vakil, Rashu. Education 2010. In *Gujarat: perspectives of the future*. Ed. by R. Swaminathan. New Delhi: Academic Foundation, 2008. pp. 213–219. CSSL, EDIL, GIDRL, GVL, IIML, IRMAL, SETUL, SPIESRL.

Virani, F.B. Human resource development: Gujarat gas company limited experience. In *HRD in the new economic environment*. Ed. by T.V. Rao, et al. New Delhi: Tata McGraw-Hill, 1994. pp. 142–150. HML.

Visaria, Leela. Schooling of tribal children: current scenario and challenges. In *Tribal development in Western India*. Ed. by Amita Shah and Jharna Pathak. New Delhi: Routledge, 2014. pp. 84–128. CSSL.

Journal Articles

Acharya, B.V. Supply of graduates from South Gujarat University. *Artha-Vikas*. 6, 2, 1970. pp. 93–106. HML.

Ardeshana, V.R. and Kher, A.O. Constraints faced by the teachers in teaching at the collage of agriculture, Junagadh. *Gujarat Agricultural University Research Journal*. 17, 2, 1992. pp. 67–71. GVL.

Baranda, Bachubhai. Study of educated unemployed tribal youth. *Adivasi Gujarat*. 15, 1, 2005. pp. 79–89. CSSL, GVL, TRTIL.

Bhal, J.D. Study of the vocabulary in Gujarati pupils of standard VI in Saurashstra. *Indian Educational Review*. 16, 2, 1981. pp. 71–71. IIML.

Bhatt, R.G. and Dharaiya, R.K. Investigation into the efficacious of teaching learning process in the morning and evening classes conducted by the various schools of Gujarat University. *Vidya: The Journal of Gujarat University*. 19, 2, 1976. pp. 61–70, SGUL.

Chandra, Arvind and Khurana, Kanwal. Reasons for attending adult education classes: a research study among women in Baroda. *Indian Journal of Adult Education*. 32, 2, 1971. pp. 15–20. AAUL.

Dabhi, Manjula L. Globalization and its impact on higher education in Gujarat. *Vishleshan*. 36, 1, 2011. pp. 36–47. CSSL, IIML.

Dashora, Kamini B. Problems of tribal education in Gujarat. *Third Concept*. 22, 253, 2008. pp. 48–52. CSSL.

Desai, Devang J. and Patel, Pankajray. Satisfaction survey for parents a study with special reference to a primary school in Vapi, Gujarat. *Indian Journal of Marketing*. 36,10, 2006. pp. 30–38. IRMAL.

Desai, Rohit, Kotak, Rekha and Dave, Alka. Why do girls drop out?: a case study of Sayla taluka in Gujarat. *Anvesak*. 29, 1, 1999. pp. 15–25. CSSL, GIDRL, IRMAL.

Dholakia, Jitendra. Some aspects of unemployment among the educated in Gujarat. *Artha-Vikas*. 6, 2, 1970. pp. 79–87. HML.

Dyer, Caroline. Operation blackboard. *Seminar*. 436, 1995. pp. 29–31. CSSL, GVL, MICAL, UML.

Jones, Dawn E. and Jones, Rodney E. Scholars' rebellion: educational interests and agitational politics in Gujarat. *Journal of Asian Studies*. 36, 3, 1977. pp. 457–476. CSSL.

Joshi, S.D. Educational problems of the scheduled castes and scheduled tribes of Baroda District. *Journal of the M.S. University of Baroda*. 24, 2, 1980. pp. 187–194. GVL.

Joshi, V.H. Problem of supply of graduates from Saurashtra University. *Artha-Vikas*. 6, 2, 1970. pp. 88–92. HML.

Kapadia, K.M. Progress of education in Navsari taluka. *Sociological Bulletin*. 8, 1, 1959. pp. 16–68. CSSL.

Kothari, V.N. Likely supply of graduates from the M.S. University of Baroda during 1969–70 to 1973–74. *Artha-Vikas*. 6, 2, 1970. pp. 101–104. HML.

Kumar, J. and Bhatia, H. Human development goals for Gujarat. *Vishleshan*. 33, 2, 2008. pp. 44–53. CSSL, IIML.

Lakdawala, D.T. and Shah, K.R. Cost, size and location of colleges in Gujarat. *Anvesak*. 4, 1, 1974. pp. 23–41. CEPTL, IRMAL, SPIESRL.

Lakdawala, D.T. and Shah, K.R. Financing of universities in Gujarat. *Economic and Political Weekly*. 10, 20, 1975. pp. 795–801. CEPTL, CSSL, GUL, IRMAL, SGUL, SPIESRL, TRTIL, UML.

Mazumdar, B.N., Desai, C.A. and Shah, N.C. Study of timed vital capacity and maximum expiratory flow rate in medical students of Gujarat. *Journal of the M.S. University of Gujarat*. 24, 3, 1975. pp. 27–30. GVL.

Mehta, Prayag. Social background of secondary school pupils in Surat. *Journal of the Gujarat Research Society*. 22, 1/85, 1960. pp. 46–52. GVL.

Menon, Sujata. Emergence of school education for girls in British Gujarat: 1949–1901. *Anvesak*. 34, 2, 2004. pp. 27–36. CSSL, GIDRL.

Minama, G.L. Plea for rationalizing post-matric scholarship for tribals. *Adivasi Gujarat*. 1, 2, 1978. pp. 16–19. CSSL, GVL, SPIESRL, TRTIL.

Naik, J.P. Quick appraisal of the national adult education programme in Gujarat. *Indian Journal of Adult Education*. 40, 2, 1979. pp. 1–5. GVL.

Padia, Darshana. Efforts for human development in Gujarat: via the prism of DHDR. *Anvesak*. 43, 1, 2013. pp. 21–32. CSSL.

Pandya, Dhaval J. Growth, trends and pattern of higher education in South Gujarat: a case study of Veer Narmad South Gujarat University, Surat. *VNSGU Journal of Humanities & Social Sciences*. 2, 1, 2010. pp. 178–189. CSSL.

Pandya, R. and Kapoor, Richer. Evaluation of adult education programme in Baroda City. *Indian Journal of Adult Education*. 66, 3–4, 2005. pp. 28–43. AAUL.

Parekh, K.M. Meeting basic needs: some issues in elementary education in Gujarat. *Vishleshan*. 9, 1, 1983. pp. 93–100. CSSL, GIDRL.

Parlikar, Kalpana. Status of home science at school level in Gujarat. *Journal of Indian Education*. 14, 2, 1988. pp. 40–43. GVL.

Parthasarthy, R. Problems of research and education in Gujarat Agricultural University. *Agricultural Situation in India*. 42, 5, 1987. pp. 403–406. GVL, IIML, IRMAL, SPIESRL.

Patel, Arunbhai and Pancholi, Ravindrabhai. Human development in relation to the tribal and non-tribal areas of Gujarat. *Adivasi Gujarat*. 15, 1, 2005. pp. 29–34. CSSL, GVL, TRTIL.

Patel, Bhikhabhai S. Evaluative study of the model residential schools. *Adivasi Gujarat*. 12, 1, 2002. pp. 6–104. CSSL, GVL, SPIESRL, TRTIL.

Patel, Bhikhabhai S. Evaluative study of the model residential schools (Gradually). *Adivasi Gujarat*. 13, 1, 2003. pp. 1–135. CSSL, GVL, TRTIL.

Patel, Bhikhabhai S. Evaluative study of the model residential schools. *Adivasi Gujarat*. 12, 2, 2002. pp. 1–126. CSSL, GVL, SPIESRL, TRTIL.

Patel, Ila. Gender ideology in adult literacy primers in Gujarat. *Trends in Social Science Research*. 3, 2, 1996. pp. 87–96. CSSL.

Patel, Niranjana N. Educational facilities as could be made available to the children of tribal communities through the Balwadi scheme as being operated in the state: an evaluation study. *Adivasi Gujarat*. 15, 1, 2005. pp. 90–104. CSSL, GVL, TRTIL.

Patil, Asha. and Saini, Chaman. Women entrepreneurs: a study of the marketing strategies adopted by women entrepreneurs of Baroda city. *Indian Journal of Adult Education*. 69, 3, 2008. pp. 47–52. AAUL.

Punalekar, S.P. Structural constraints in tribal education: a case study of tribal community in South Gujarat. *Indian Journal of Social Science*. 6, 1, 1993. pp. 19–30. IIML.

Raina, B.L. Continuing education programme in M.S. University of Baroda, Gujarat: a study. *Indian Educational Review*. 29, 3–4, 1994. pp. 117–129. IIML.

Reddy, K.N. University finances: a case study of the M.S. University of Baroda. *Vishleshan*. 4, 1, 1978. pp. 5–24. CSSL, GIDRL, IIML.

Sahoo, P.R. and Dwivedi, T.N. Adult education in a slum of Baroda city (Navapura Study). *Indian Journal of Adult Education*. 40, 8, 1979. pp. 35–41. SGUL.

Shah, B.V. Education and social change among tribals in India. *Sociological Bulletin*. 28, 1–2, 1979. pp. 25–45. CSSL.

Shah, B.V. Gujarat college students and selections of bride. *Sociological Bulletin*. 11, 1 and 2, 1962. pp. 121–140. CSSL.

Shah, B.V. Gujarati college students and caste. *Sociological Bulletin*. 10, 1, 1961. pp. 41–60. CSSL, HML.

Shah, K.R. and Agrawal, Sarita. Financing of secondary education in Gujarat. *Journal of Educational Planning and Administration*. 17, 3, 2003. pp. 299–33. GIDRL, IRMAL.

Shah, P.G. Physical norms of students in Gujarat. *Journal of the Gujarat Research Society*. 19, 3/75, 1957. pp. 218–225. GVL.

Shah, Ramesh B. Gujarat: 2010 challenges and education. (*Gujarat-2010: challenges and opportunities*). *Anvesak.* 31, 1–2, 2001. pp. 110–123. CSSL, GIDRL.

Shah, Vimal. Tribal education in Gujarat. *Vanyajati.* 14, 3, 1966. pp. 109–112. CSSL, TRTIL.

Sharan, Girija. Non-formal education among workmen: an experiment in Ahmedabad. *Economic and Political Weekly.* 15, 35, 1980. pp. M-74-M-84. CEPTL, CSSL, GUL, IIML, IRMAL, SGUL, SPIESRL, UML.

Sheth, Suchitra and Haeems, Nina. 'Sisters under the skin': events of 2002 and girls' education in Ahmedabad. *Economic and Political Weekly.* 41, 17, 2006. pp. 1708–1712. BUL, CEPTL, CSSL, EDIL, IIML, IRMAL, MICAL, SGUL, SPIESRL, SUL, UML.

Shukla, Jaykumar R. Student's strike in the Gujarat College, Ahmedabad-1929. *Vidya: The Journal of Gujarat University.* 20, 1, 1977. pp. 80–97. SGUL.

Sindhi, Swaleha A. Socio-economic transformation via education in Gujarat. *Third Concept.* 26, 312, 2013. pp. 25–28. CSSL.

Singh, Satvir. Study of preparatory science examination results of the M.S. University of Baroda for Year 1974–75. *Indian Educational Review.* 16, 4, 1981. pp. 65–71. IIML.

Unnikrishnan, Praseetha. Integrated education for the disabled children in Ahmedabad city. *Social Action.* 57, 1, 2007. pp. 74–83. CEPTL, CSSL, GVL, IIML.

Vaisahnav, B.S. Macro study of a rural high-school of Gujarat. *Indian Journal of Social Research.* 15, 1, 1974. pp. 56–58. CEPTL.

Vamdatt, Daxa A. Place of English in the post-graduate teaching of economics: a case study of Gujarat. *Vishleshan.* 2, 3, 1976. pp. 262–268. GIDRL, IIML.

Veena, D.R. 'Pattern of education for economic development': an experience of a developing region-'Gujarat'. *Journal of Gujarat Research Society.* 38, 3/146, 1976. pp. 29–62. GVL.

Veena, D.R. Supply of manpower by educational levels in Gujarat: an analysis in extrapolation: trend and transaction approach. *Anvesak.* 6, 2, 1976. pp. 127–140. CSSL.

Veena, Dhan Raj. Pattern of education and economic development: a case study of Gujarat. *Anvesak.* 3, 1–2, 1973. pp. 177–188. SPIESRL.

Vyas, G.N. Serological studies for Gujarat region. *Journal of the Gujarat Research Society.* 19, 3/75, 1957. pp. 232–241. GVL.

Waghmare, S.K. and Patel, H.N. Characteristic of the students of dairy science collage, Anand. *Gujarat Agricultural University Research Journal.* 1, 1, 1975. pp. 70–74. GVL.

Yadav, M.S., Biswal, B.N. and Menon, M.B. Correspondence education in the M.S. University of Baroda: a proposal. *Journal of the M.S. University of Baroda.* 25–26, 2, 1976–77. pp. 97–106. GVL.

Working Papers, Reports and Other Materials

Acharya, B.V. and Bhatt, P.K. *Development of finance of a growing University: a case study of South Gujarat University.* Surat: South Gujarat University, 1993. CSSL.

Amin, N.B. and Madan, P.J. University and industry. In *Profiles of a growing city: the city of Baroda.* Ed. by K.N. Reddy, et al. Baroda: M.S. University, 1971. pp. 9–11. Souvenir: 2nd Gujarat Economic conference, 2–3 January 1971. CSSL.

Desai, D.M. Perspectives on the M.S. University of Baroda. In *Profiles of a growing cit: the city of Baroda*. Ed. by K.N. Reddy, et al. Baroda: M.S. University, 1971. pp. 67–72. Souvenir: 2nd Gujarat Economic conference, 2–3 January 1971. CSSL.

Desai, Dhanwant M. *Some problems of education in the Gujarat state*. Baroda: M.S. University, 1967. p. 64. CSSL, SPUL.

Desai, I.P. *Distribution of primary school in the tribal taluka of Bharuch & Panchmahal Districts*. Surat: Centre for Regional Development Studies, 1976. p. 32. CSSL, SPIESRL.

Desai, I.P. *Distribution of primary school in the tribal taluka of Valsad & Surat Districts*. Surat: Centre for Regional Development Studies, 1977. p. 33. CSSL.

Desai, I.P. *Profile of education among the scheduled tribes in Gujarat*. Surat: Centre for Social Studies, 1974. p. 69. CSSL, IRMAL.

Desai, I.P. and Pandore, G.A. *Scheduled caste and tribe high school students in Gujarat. January 1973-July 1974*. Surat: Centre for Regional Development Studies, 1974. p. 281. CSSL, GIDRL.

Desai, I.P. and Shah, B.V. *Scheduled caste and tribe high school and college students in Gujarat*. Surat: Centre for Regional Development Studies, 1975. Summary of findings. p. 94. CSSL, IRMAL.

Desai, Kiran. *Review study of a vocational training centre (Vivekananda Gramin Tekniki Kendra)*. Surat: Centre for Social Studies, 2003. p. 112. CSSL.

Desai, P.K. Education in Ahmedabad. In *Ahmedabad*. Ahmedabad: Rotary Club, 1940. pp. 43–57. CSSL.

Education Department, Government of Gujarat. Challenges and opportunities in education sector. In *Gujarat-2010: Challenges and opportunities*. by Government of Gujarat. Ahmedabad: Sardar Patel Institute of Economic & Social Research, 2001. pp. 363–372. Seminar volume. CSSL, EDIL, IRMAL, SGUL, SPIESRL.

Gandhi, R.D. *Disparities in literacy rates in the rural area of Gujarat*. Ahmedabad: Gujarat Institute of Area Planning, 1978. Data Bank Project Publication No. 3. CSSL.

Gujarat Council of Primary Education Gandhinagar. *Role of village education committee (VEC)/mother teacher association (MTA)/parent teacher association (PTA) in school improvement*. Ahmedabad: Sardar Patel Institute of Economic & Social Research, 2003. p. 89. SPIESRL.

Gujarat, Government of. *Report of the commission on modernization of university acts*. Gandhinagar: Education and Labour Department, Government of Gujarat, 1970–71. p. [ ]. CSSL.

Gujarat, Government of. Technical education: Gujarat state vision-2010. In *Gujarat-2010: challenges and opportunities*. By Government of Gujarat. Ahmedabad: Sardar Patel Institute of Economic & Social Research, 2001. pp. 348–353. Seminar Volume. CSSL, EDIL, IRMAL, SGUL, SPIESRL.

Hirway, Indira and Mahadevia, Darshini. *Gujarat human development report 1999*. Ahmedabad: Mahatma Gandhi Labour Institute, 1999. p. 332. CSSL, SPIESRL.

Hirway, Indira and Mahadevia, Darshini. *Gujarat human development report 2004*. Ahmedabad: Mahatma Gandhi Labour Institute, 2004. p. 353. CSSL, IIML.

Jadeja, Y.D. *Primary education in Surat district*. Surat: Centre for Regional Development Studies, 1970. p. 34. CSSL.

Joshi, Vidyut. Century of tribal education in Gujarat. In *Tribal Education in Gujarat*. By Centre for Social Studies. Delhi: Ajanta, 1985. pp. 19–49. CSSL, GUL.

Joshi, Vidyut. Primary education in Gujarat in 21st century. In *Gujarat-2010: challenges and opportunities*. By Government of Gujarat. Ahmedabad: Sardar Patel Institute of Economic & Social Research, 2001. pp. 354–362. Seminar Volume. CSSL, EDIL, IRMAL, SGUL, SPIESRL.

Joshi, Vidyut and Trivedi, Vimal. *Privatisation of higher education: issues and problems, with special reference to South Gujarat.* Surat: Centre for Social Studies, 2003. p. 68. CSSL.

Kropac, Michael. *Dalit empowerment and vocational education: an impact study*. New Delhi: Indian Institute of Dalit Studies, 2007. p. [ ]. Working Paper Series, Vol. II, No. 03. CSSL.

Kumar, B.L. *Schools and schooling in tribal Gujarat: the quality dimension*. Ahmedabad: Gujarat Institute of Development Research, 2004. p. 33. Working Paper No. 150. CSSL, GIDRL, IRMAL.

Kumar, B.L. *Tribal education in Gujarat: an evaluation of educational incentives schemes.* Ahmedabad: Gujarat Institute of Development Research, 2004. p. 48. Working Paper No. 145. CSSL, GIDRL, IRMAL, TRTIL.

Lakdawala, D.T. and Shah, K.R. *Optimum utilization of educational expenditure in Gujarat.* Ahmedabad: Sardar Patel Institute of Economic & Social Research (SPIESR), 1978. p. 269. Monograph Series 5. GIDRL, SPUL, UML.

Lal, Rash Bihari. *Wastage and stagnation in primary education among the tribals: a case study in four tribal development blocks of Gujarat.* Ed. Vimal Shah. Ahmedabad: TRTI, 1978. p. 54. Series-27. TRTIL.

Mathew, Thomas. *Adult education programme in Gujarat organization and administration.* Ahmedabad: Sardar Patel Institute of Economic & Social Research, 1984. p. 39. TRTIL.

Mehta, S.S. *Evaluation of "human resources development programme"of IFFCO, Kalol.* Ahmedabad: Gandhi Labour Institute, 1986. Various pages. CSSL.

Mukunda Das, V. *Adult education in Gujarat: a study report*. Anand: Institute of Rural Management, 1989. p. 103. IRMAL.

Pancholi, R.R. and Vahoniya, D.M. *Monitoring and evaluation of tribal ashram schools scheme: with special reference to Gujarat*. Ed. by C.B. Upadhyay. Ahmedabad: Gujarat Vidyapith, 2011–12. p. 75. TRTIL.

Parikh, Gokul O. *Adult education programme in Gujarat: a study of Community involvement*. Ahmedabad: Sardar Patel Institute of Economic & Social Research, 1985. p. 144. GIDRL, TRTIL.

Parikh, R.D. *Non-urban graduates in Gujarat*. Ahmedabad: Gujarat University, 1965. p. 66. CSSL, HML.

Pasricha, Prem, Pagedar, Rajani M. and Gajjar, Jagdishchandra. *Adjustment inventory for college students.* Baroda: M.S. University, 1964. Guidance and counseling series No. 12. CSSL.

Patel, Bhikhabhai S. *Evaluative study of the model residential schools, for scheduled tribes in Gujarat State.* Compil. by Siddharaj Solanki. Ahmedabad: Gujarat Vidyapith, 2000–2001. p. 254. Serise-369. TRTIL.

Patel, Harbans. *Non-enrolment of tribal girls in schools: a study on ten villages in Poshina region.* Surat: Centre for Social Studies, 1985. p. 41. CSSL.

Patel, Tara. *Education among tribal women in Gujarat.* Ahmedabad: Gujarat University, 1983. p. 241. CSSL, GIDRL, SPIESRL.

Patel, Tara. Education among tribal women in Gujarat. *In Tribal education in Gujarat*. By Centre for Social Studies. Delhi: Ajanta, 1985. pp. 50–81. CSSL, GUL.

Phadke, J.K. and Shukla, R.C. *Educational waste: a study in drop-outs among schedule tribe college students in Vyara*. Vyara: Institute of Tribal Development and Research Arts and Commerce College, 1980. p. 66. CSSL.

Photre, Vinayak K., Dabhi, Jesangbhai and Patel, Narottambhai. *Social transformation through Nai talim study of the present status of Nai talim institutions in Gujarat report-5*. Ahmedabad: Gujarat Vidyapith, 2001. p. 89. TRTIL.

Pisupati, Rupa. *Human resource management practices in Anand taluka panchayat, Kheda district, Gujarat.* Anand: Institute of Rural Management, 1996. p. 30. Working Paper No. 106. CSSL, IRMAL, SPIESRL.

Punalekar, S.P. *Certified school in Baroda: a profile of their perspective, programmes and emergent needs. III parts*. Surat: Center for Social Studies, 1985. p. 34., p. 48. and p. 50. CSSL.

Punalekar, S.P. Social stratification and educational inequalities: a case of tribals from Maharashtra, Gujarat and Rajasthan villages. In *Tribal Education in Gujarat*. by Centre for Social Studies. Delhi: Ajanta, 1985. pp. 82–117. CSSL, GUL.

Punalekar, S.P. and Ranadive Jyoti. *Tribal education: an inter-state study.* Surat: Centre for social studies, 1984. p. 229. CSSL, SETUL.

Quraishi, Mansooruddin A. *Muslim education and learning in Gujarat (1297–1758)*. Baroda: M.S. University, 1972. p. 328. CSSL, HML, SETUL.

Rami, Gaurang. *Status of primary education: a case study of the Dangs district in Gujarat.* Surat: Department of Economics, South Gujarat University, 2011. Working Paper 02. CSSL.

Rangarajan, T. *Research project on educational standards in Gujarat.* Ahmedabad: Vikram A. Sarabhai, 1986. p. 113. IIML.

Rangarajan, T. *Research project on educational standards in Gujarat: progress report II.* Ahmedabad: Vikram A. Sarabhai, 1985. p. 55. IIML.

Ratnawali. *Education and health needs assessment of some of the villages of Bharuch district.* Surat: Centre for Social Studies, 2007. p. 86. CSSL.

Raval, Govindbhai and Raval, Sumatibahen. *Social transformation through Nai talim success story series of Nai talim institution of Gujarat: Vishwamangalam Anera.* Ahmedabad: Gujarat Vidyapith, 2001. p. 82. TRTIL.

Sarma, Atul, Shah, Vimal P. and Parikh, Bhanumati K. *Adult education programme in Gujarat: an appraisal.* Ahmedabad: Sardar Patel Institute of Economic & Social Research, 1979. p. 118. Monograph Series 7. CSSL, GVL, SPIESRL.

Sarma, Atul, et al. *Adult education programme in Gujarat, revisited*. Ahmedabad: Sardar Patel Institute of Economic & Social Research (SPIESR), 1981. p. 146. GIDRL.

Shah, B.V. *Field studies in the sociology of education: the report on Gujarat*. New Delhi: National Council of Educational Research and Training, 1979. p. 603. CEEL.

Shah, B.V. *Social change and college student of Gujarat*. Baroda: M.S. University, 1964. p. 231. CSSL, GVL, HML, SGUL.

Shah, B.V. and Thaker, J.D. *Scheduled caste and scheduled tribe college students in Gujarat*. Vallabh Vidyanagar: Sardar Patel University. 1978, p. 330. CSSL, SGUL.

Shah, B.V. and Thaker, J.D. *Scheduled caste and scheduled tribe college students in Gujarat, a research study*. Vallabh Vidyanagar: Sardar Patel University, 1977. p. 357. CSSL.

Shah, B.V. and Thaker, J.D. *Educational problems of scheduled caste and scheduled tribe college students in Gujarat-1973, a research study.* Vallabh Vidyanagar: Sardar Patel University, 1973. p. 541. CSSL.

Shah, Ghanshyam. *Mid-day meals scheme in Gujarat: an evolution*. Surat: Centre for Social Studies, 1988. p. 166. CSSL.

Shah, Ghanshyam. Evaluation of mid-day meals scheme: an interim report. Surat: Centre for Social Studies, 1987. p. 34. CSSL.

Shah, Ghanshyam. Profile of education among the scheduled tribes in Gujarat. *In Tribal education in Gujarat.* By Centre for Social Studies. Delhi: Ajanta, 1985. pp. 1–18. CSSL, GUL.

Shah, K.R. Review of educational expansion in the districts of Gujarat, (1960–1965–66). In *Gujarat Economic Association conference papers, Baroda.* Ed. by V.S. Vyas, Pravin Visaria and A.R. Desai. Ahmedabad: Balgovind, 1971. pp. 87–101. GIDRL, IIML.

Shah, K.R. and Lakdawala, D.T. *Optimum utilization of educational expenditure in Gujarat.* Ahmedabad: Sardar Patel Institute of Economic & Social Research, 1978. p. 269. CSSL, GVL.

Shah, K.R. and Srikantiah, S. Equity issues involved in higher education: a study of the M.S. University. In *Gujarat economy: problems and prospects.* Ed. D.T. Lakdawala. Ahmedabad: Sardar Patel Institute of Economic & Social Research, 1982. pp. 509–532. GIDRL.

Shah, K.R. and Srikantiah, S. Equity issues involved in higher education: a study of the M.S. University, Baroda. In *Gujarat economy: problems and prospects*. Ed. by D.T. Lakdawal. Ahmedabad: Sardar Patel Institute of Economic & Social Research. 1983. pp. 509–532. Monograph Series No. 10. GUL.

Shah, K.R. and Srikantiah, S. Equity issues involved in higher education: a study of the M.S. University, Baroda. In *Seminar on Development of Gujarat problems & prospects, 24th-26th August, 1981.* Ahmedabad: Sardar Patel Institute of Economic & Social Research, 1981. pp. 1–49. CSSL.

Shah, K.R. and Veena, D.R. Educating the poor and backward: a study of Gujarat. In *Gujarat Economy: problems and prospects.* Ed. by D.T. Lakdawala. Ahmedabad: Sardar Patel Institute of Economic & Social Research, 1983. pp. 563–580. Monograph Series-10. GUL, IIML.

Shah, K.R. and Veena, D.R. Educating the poor and backward: a study of Gujarat. In *Seminar on Development of Gujarat problems & prospects, 24th-26th August, 1981*. Ahmedabad: Sardar Patel Institute of Economic & Social Research, 1981. pp. 1–23. CSSL.

Shah, K.R. and Veena, D.R. Educating the poor and backward: a study of Gujarat. In *Gujarat economy: problems and prospects.* Ed. D.T. Lakdawala. Ahmedabad: Sardar Patel Institute of Economic & Social Research, 1982. pp. 563–580. GIDRL.

Shah, Maya. *Economic factors explaining variations in literacy rates in areas: a case study of Gujarat.* Baroda: M.S. University, 1981. p. 55. CSSL, SPIESRL.

Shah, Navalbhai. *Social transformation through Nai talim success story series of Nai talim institutions of Gujarat. Adivasi Seva Samiti Shamalaji.* Ahmedabad: Gujarat Vidyapith, 2001. p. 84. TRTIL.

Shah, Ramesh B. Gujarat: 2010 challenges and education. In *Gujarat-2010: challenges and opportunities*. By Government of Gujarat. Ahmedabad: Sardar Patel Institute of Economic & Social Research, 2001. pp. 338–347. Seminar volume. CSSL, EDIL, IRMAL, SGUL, SPIESRL.

Shah, Vimal. Assessment of education among the scheduled casts in Gujarat. In *Removal of untouchability (proceeding of a Seminar).* Ed. by Vimal P. Shah. Ahmedabad: Gujarat University, 1980. pp. 1–12. CSSL, SPIESRL.

Shah, Vimal. Educational development of the tribals in Gujarat. In *Gujarat economy: problems and prospects.* Ed. D.T. Lakdawala. Ahmedabad: Sardar Patel Institute of Economic & Social Research, 1982. pp. 533–546. GIDRL.

Shah, Vimal P. Educational development of the tribals in Gujarat. In *Gujarat Economy: problems and prospects.* Ed. by D.T. Lakdawala. Ahmedabad: Sardar Patel Institute of Economic & Social Research, 1983. pp. 533–546. Monograph Series-10. IIML, GUL.

Shah, Vimal P. Educational development of the tribals in Gujarat. In *Seminar on development of Gujarat problems & prospects, 24–26 August, 1981.* Ahmedabad: Sardar Patel Institute of Economic & Social Research, 1981. pp. 1–10. CSSL.

Shah, Vimal P. Social class, awareness and educational attainment of tribals. In *Tribal Education in Gujarat.* By Centre for Social Studies. Delhi: Ajanta, 1985. pp. 118–140. CSSL, GUL.

Shah, Vimal P. *Social context of tribal education in Gujarat.* Ahmedabad: Gujarat University, 1981. p. 151. CSSL, IRMAL.

Shah, Vimal P. and Patel, Tara. *Social contexts of tribal education in Gujarat.* Ahmedabad: Gujarat University, 1981. p. 87. CSSL, SETUL, SPIESRL.

Shah, Vinod K. *Impact of teacher's training.* Ahmedabad: Sardar Patel Institute of Economic & Social Research, 2003. p. 137. SPIESRL.

Shah, Vipin. *Financing of higher education in Gujarat.* Anand: N.S. Patel Arts College, 2002. p. 85. Research Project report. CSSL.

Sharan, Girja. Centrally planned education programme and a micro level experiment in Gujarat-some lessons. In *Gujarat economy: problems and prospects.* Ed. by D.T. Lakdawala. Ahmedabad: Sardar Patel Institute of Economic & Social Research, 1982. pp. 581–588. GIDRL.

Sharma, Atul, Shah, Vimal and Parikh Bhanumati K. *Adult education programme in Gujarat: an appraisal.* Ahmedabad: Sardar Patel Institute of Economic & Social Research. 1979. p. 118. SGUL.

Sharma, Girja. Centrally planned education programme and a micro level experiment in Gujarat-some lessons. In *Gujarat Economy: problems and prospects.* Ed. by D.T. Lakdawala. Ahmedabad: Sardar Patel Institute of Economic & Social Research, 1983. pp. 581–588. Monograph Series-10. GUL, IIML.

Sharma, Girja. Centrally planned education programme and a micro level experiment in Gujarat-some lessons. In *Seminar on Development of Gujarat Problems & Prospects, 24th-26 August, 1981.* Ahmedabad: Sardar Patel Institute of Economic & Social Research, 1981. pp. 1–10. CSSL.

Shylendra, H., Uma Rani and Patel, Mukesh R. Human development through "micro trickle-down": case of a development intervention in a backward village of Gujarat. by SWDF. Anand: Institute of Rural Management, 2000. p. 14. IRMA Working Paper No. 136 GIDRL, IRMAL, SPIESRL.

Spodek, Howard. Alternative education for working class women the 'SEVA' academy of Ahmedabad, India. *International Seminar on Gujarat Society, Development and Deprivation, 6–9 December 1994.* Surat: Centre for Social Studies, 1994. pp. 1–19. CSSL.

Srikantiah, S. and Shah, K.R. Equity issues involved in higher education: a study of the M.S. university Baroda. In *Gujarat Economy: problems and prospects.* Ed. by D.T. Lakdawala. Ahmedabad: Sardar Patel Institute of Economic & Social Research, 1983. pp. 509–532. Monograph Series-10. IIML.

Vashi, D.G. *Enquiry into physical norms of Gujarat university students.* Ahmedabad: Gujarat University, 1960. p. 156. SPUL.

Veena, D.R, Bhatnagar, R.R. and Shah, Ila A. Growth pattern of education in Gujarat. In *Seminar on Development of Gujarat Problems & Prospects, 24–26 August, 1981*. Ahmedabad: Sardar Patel Institute of Economic & Social Research, 1981. pp. 1–44. CSSL.

Visaria, Leela and Mathew, Thomas. Adult education programme in Gujarat fourth evaluation. Ahmedabad: Sardar Patel Institute of Economic & Social Research, 1983. p. 55. GIDRL.

Visaria, Leela and Mathew, Thomas. *Adult education programme in Gujarat forth evaluation.* Ahmedabad: Sardar Patel Institute of Economic & Social Research, 1983. p. 209. SPIESRL.

Visaria, Leela and Patel, H.T. Adult education programme in Gujarat: an in-depth study. Ahmedabad: Sardar Patel Institute of Economic & Social Research, 1984. p. 68. CSSL, GIDRL.

16

Trade, Transport

Books/Chapter in Books

Arasaratnam, Sinnappah. *Maritime India: in the seventeenth century*. Delhi: Oxford, 1994. pp. 54–89. SETUL.

Arunachalam, B., Edward, Mary R. and Pendse, Sahin S. *Navigational hazards, landmarks and early charting: special study of Konkan and South Gujarat*. Mumbai: Maritime History Society, [ ]. p. 130. UML.

Bajpai, Gita. Broach in the nineteenth century: changing profile under colonial rule. In *Ports and their hinterlands in India (1700–1950)*. Ed. by Indu Banga. New Delhi: Manohar, 1992. pp. 213–226. SETUL.

Banga, Indu, ed. *Ports and their hinterlands in India (1700–1950)*. New Delhi: Manohar, 1992. p. 385. SETUL.

Batra, Satkartar. *Ports of Gujarat: West coast of India*. Adipur: Kandla Commercial, 1968. p. 176. *GVL, TRTIL.

Batra, Satkartar. *Ports of Gujarat (west coast of India)*. Kandla: Kandla Commercial (Weekly). 1963. p. 176. HML, SPUL, SUL.

Bid, Poorni, Nanavaty, Reema and Patel, Neeta. Women, water and transportation: mapping the interplay Banaskantha, Gujarat, India. In *Balancing the load: women*, gender and transport. Ed. by Priyanthi Fernando and Gina Porter. London: Zed, 2002. pp. 169–185. CSSL, GVL.

Brooze, Frank. External dynamics of port city morphology: Bombay 1815–1914. In *Ports and their hinterlands in India (1700–1950)*. Ed. by Indu Banga. New Delhi: Manohar, 1992. pp. 245–272. SETUL.

Commissariat, M.S. *Mandelslo's travels in western India*, A.D. 1638–39. London: Oxford, 1931. p. 115. CSSL.

Dani, Laxmidas. ed. *Gujarat vepari mahamandal*. Ahmedabad: Author, 1962. p. 244. *GVL.

Dasgupta, Arun. Gujaratis and Europeans in Asian trade (1500–1624). In *Essays in honour of Prof. S.C. Sarkar*. New Delhi: People's, [ ]. pp. 200–216. HML.

Dasgupta, Ashin. Ship-owning merchants of Surat, C. 1700. In *Asian merchants and businessmen in the Indian ocean and the China sea*. Ed. by Denys Lombard and Jean Aubin. New Delhi: Oxford, 2000. pp. 105–112. HML.

Dasgupta, Uma. Broker in Mughal Surat, C. 1740. In *World of the Indian ocean merchant*. New Delhi: Oxford, 2001. pp. 399–409. HML.

Dasgupta, Uma. Crisis in Surat, C. 1730–32. In *World of the Indian ocean merchant*. New Delhi: Oxford, 2001. pp. 361–368. HML.

Dasgupta, Uma. Merchant of Surat, C. 1700–1750. In *World of the Indian Ocean merchant*. New Delhi: Oxford, 2001. pp. 315–341. HML.

Dasgupta, Uma. Note on the ship-owning merchant of Surat, C. 1700. In *World of the Indian Ocean merchant*. New Delhi: Oxford, 2001. pp. 342–350. HML.

Dasgupta, Uma. Pieter Phoonses of Surat, C. 1730–1740. In *World of the Indian Ocean merchant*. New Delhi: Oxford, 2001. pp. 410–420. HML.

Dasgupta, Uma, ed. *World of the Indian Ocean merchant, 1500–1800: Collected essays of Ashin Das Gupta*. New Delhi: Oxford, 2001. p. 511. HML.

Dossal, Marian. Knowledge for power: the significance of Bombay revenue survey, 1811–1827. In *Ports and their hinterlands in India (1700–1950)*. Ed. by Indu Banga. New Delhi: Manohar, 1992. pp. 227–243. SETUL.

Dupont, Veronique. Role of trade and traders in small-scale industrial development: the example of a textile-printing centre in Gujarat. In *Webs of trade: dynamics of business communities in western India*. Ed. by Philippe Cadene and Denis Vidal. New Delhi: Manohar, 1997. pp. 108–135. CSSL, HML.

Emma, Tarlo. Genesis and growth of a business community: a case study of Vaghri street traders in Ahmedabad. In *Webs of trade*. Ed. by Cadene Philippe and Vidal Denis. New Delhi: Manohar, 1997. pp. 53–84. CSSL, HML.

Gopal, Surendra. *Commerce and crafts in Gujarat: 16th and 17th centuries*. New Delhi: Indian Council of Historical Research, 1975. p. 289. CSSL, SGUL.

Goswami, Chhaya. *Call of the sea: Kachchhi traders in Muscat and Zanzibar, c.1800–1880*. Hyderabad: Orient Blackswan, 2011. p. 343. CSSL, HML.

Hariharan, K.V., ed. *So I rest on my oars: collection of writings and speeches 1947–1970 of M.A. Master*. Bombay: M.A. Master Memorial Trust, 1970. p. 756. GVL.

Jha, Murari Kumar. Social world of Gujarati merchants and their Indian Ocean networks in the seventeenth century. In *South Asian diaspora: transnational networks and changing identities*. Ed. by Rajesh Rai and Peter Reeves. London: Routledge, 2009. pp. 28–44. CSSL.

Karnik, V.B. Ahmedabad experiment. In *Indian trade unions: a survey*. Bombay: P.C. Manaktala, 1966, pp. 91–107. CSSL, SPUL.

Latey, Salil. and Vaidya, B.C. Railway transport in Vadodara: a historical perspective. In *Geography of transport development in India*. Ed. by B.C. Vaidya. New Delhi: Concept, 2003. pp. 273–282. HML.

Maloni, Ruby. *European merchant capital and the Indian economy: a historical reconstruction based on Surat factory records 1630–1668*. New Delhi: Manohar, 1992. p. 463. CSSL.

Masihi, Edwin J. *Trade union leadership in India: a sociological perspective*. Delhi: Ajanta, 1985. p. 240. CSSL.

Masselos, Jim. Changing definitions of Bombay: city state capital city. In *Ports and their hinterlands in India (1700–1950)*. Ed. by Indu Banga. New Delhi: Manohar, 1992. pp. 273–316. SETUL.

Mehta, M.J. Business environment and urbanization: Ahmedabad in the 19th century. In *Studies in urban history*. Ed. by J.S. Grewal and Indu Banga. Amritsar: Guru Nanak Dev University, 1978, pp. 123–134. CSSL, HML.

Mehta, Shirin. Mahajans and the business communities of Ahmedabad. In *Business communities of India: a historical perspective*. Ed. by Dwijendra Tripathi. New Delhi: Manohar, 1984. pp. 173–183. CSSL, HML, SPUL.

Mookherjee, Surya. Union response to textiles restructuring: experience in Gujarat. In *Indian textiles: an intersectoral perspective*. Eds. by S.S. Mehta and Vinod Shanbhag. New Delhi: Oxford, 1990. pp. 132–143. CSSL.

Moosvi, Shireen. Gujarat ports and their hinterland: the economic relationship. In *Ports and their hinterlands in India (1700–1950)*. Ed. by Indu Banga. New Delhi: Manohar, 1992. pp. 9-[ ]. SETUL.

Moreland, W.H. and Geyl, P. Description of Gujarat trade. In *Jahangir's India: the remonstrantie of francisco pelsaert*. Delhi: Idarah-I-Adabiyat-I Delli, 1972. pp. 19–20. IAD Oriental Series No. 8. SPUL.

Nightingale, Pamela. *Trade and empire in Western India, 1784–1806*. Cambridge: Cambridge University press, 1970. p. 264. CSSL, SPIESRL.

Pearson, M.N. *Merchants and rulers in Gujarat: the response to the Portuguese in the sixteenth century*. New Delhi: Munshiram Manoharlal, 1976. p. 178. ASL, CSSL, SETUL.

Ray, Aniruddha. Cambay and its hinterland: early eighteen century. In *Ports and their hinterlands in India (1700–1950)*. Ed. by Indu Banga. New Delhi: Manohar, 1992. pp. 22-[ ]. SETUL.

Rutten, Mario. Access of big farmers to land agricultural trade in Central Gujarat. In *Capitalist development: critical essays. felicitation volume in honour of Prof. A.R. Desai*. Ed. by Ghanshyam Shah. Bombay: Popular, 1990. pp. 230–247. CSSL.

Sharma, G.D. Ports of Gujarat in the nineteenth century: trading networks and commercial practices. In *Ports and their hinterlands in India (1700–1950)*. Ed. by Indu Banga. New Delhi: Manohar, 1992. pp. 199–211. SETUL.

Shresthova, Sangita., Barve, Rekha and Chokshi, Paulomi. My daily oddyssey: transportation in the lives of SEWA bank clients Ahmedabad India. In *Balancing the load*. Ed. by Priyanthi Fernando and Gina Porter. London: Zed, 2002. pp. 200–224. CSSL, GVL.

Simpson, Edward. Sailors that do not sail: Hinduism, anthropology and parochialism in the Indian Ocean. In *Journeys and dwellings: Indian ocean themes in South Asia*. Ed. by Helene Basu. Hyderabad: Orient Longman, 2008. pp. 90–120. CSSL.

Singh, Dilbagh and Rajshirke, Ashok B. Merchant communities in Surat: trade, trade practices and institutions in the late eighteenth century. In *Ports and their hinterlands in India (1700–1950)*. Ed. by Indu Banga. New Delhi: Manohar, 1992. pp. 181–198. SETUL.

Singh, O.P. *Surat and its trade in the second half of the 19th century*. Delhi: University of Delhi. 1977. p. 223. CSSL, GUL, HML.

Solanki, K.D. *History of shipping in Gujarat*. Mumbai: Bhartiya Vidya Bhavan, 1998. p. 642. ASL.

Tambs-Lyche, Harald. Indian Ocean trade and the merchant castes: India's west coast, 1500–1800. In *Journeys and dwellings: Indian Ocean themes in South Asia*. Ed. by Helene Basu. Hyderabad: Orient Longman, 2008. pp. 125–146. CSSL.

Tod, James. *Travels in Western India: embracing a visit to the sacred mounts of the Jains, and the most celebrated shrines of Hindu faith between Rajpootana and the Indus, with an account of the ancient city of Nehrwalla*. Indian Reprint. Delhi: Oriental, 1971. p. [ ]. CSSL.

Tripathi, Dwijendra. Business and the princely states: the case of Baroda. In *States and business in India: a historical perspective*. Ed. by Dwijendra Tripathi. New Delhi: Manohar, 1987. pp. 275–301. HML.

Tripathi, Dwijendra and Mehta, M.J. Class character of the Gujarati business community. In *Business communities of India: a historical perspective*. Ed. by Dwijendra Tripathi. New Delhi: Manohar, 1984. pp. 151–171. CSSL.

Tripathi, Dwijendra and Mehta, Markrand. *Business houses in Western India: a study in entrepreneurial response, 1850–1956*. New Delhi: Manohar, 1990. pp. 37–54. SPUL.

Journal Articles

Bauss, Rudy. Textiles, bullion and other trades of Goa: commerce with Surat, other areas of India, Luso-Brazilian Ports, Macau and Mozambique, 1816–1819. *Indian Economic and Social History Review*. 34, 3, 1997. pp. 275–288. CSSL, IIML, UML.

Bhatt, R.D. and Amin, P.R. Commercial vehicle traffic characteristics on Ahmedabad-Vadodara section of N.H. 8. *Indian Highways*. 18, 10, 1990. pp. 19–40. CEPTL.

Development Resource Centre. Grassroots merchants of illicit goods in Gujarat. *Seminar*. 504, 2001. pp. 46–49. CSSL, IIML, MICAL, UML.

Dholakia, Ravindra H. Exports of agri-products from Gujarat: problems and prospects. *Vishleshan*. 29, 1, 2004. pp. 1–18. CSSL, IIML.

Gekonge, John Makana. Determinants of regional transport generation by various development activities: a case study of Bharuch district in Gujarat state-India. *Anvesak*. 30, 1, 2000. pp. 17–38. CSSL, GIDRL.

Gekonge, John Makana. Freight transport generation by various disaggregated land-use development patterns of the developing regional areas: a case study of Bharuch district in Gujarat state, India. *Indian Journal of Regional Science*. 33, 1, 2001. pp. 85–97. CSSL, GIDRL.

Gekonge, John Makana. Regional changes in transport demand and development of strategy planning: a case study of Bharuch District in Gujarat State, India. *Indian Journal of Regional Science*. 41, 2, 2009. pp. 17–29. CSSL, GIDRL.

Gopal, Surendra. Gujarati shipping in the seventeenth century. *Indian Economic and Social History Review*. 8, 1, 1971. pp. 31–39. CSSL, UML.

Heston, Alan. Note on Camel carts and other informal urban transport in Gujarat. *Anvesak*. 12, 2, 1982. pp. 83–98. CEPTL, CSSL, GIDRL.

Joshi, G.N. Domestic terms of trade and income distribution: a comparative study of Gujarat and India. *Vishleshan*. 23, 4, 1998. pp. 207–211. IIML, IRMAL.

Joshi, G.N. Domestic terms of trade and income distribution: a comparative study of Gujarat and India. *Vishleshan*. 13, 3, 1987. pp. 159–168. CSSL, GIDRL.

Kamdar, V.P., Shah, J.D. and Shah, D.P. Comparative study of economic analysis of bye passes around cities on national highway in Gujarat. *Indian Highways*. 18, 8, 1990. pp. 23–28. CEPTL.

Kanhere, Usha. White collar trade unionism: bank officers' trade unions in Ahmedabad. *Sociological Bulletin*. 35, 2, 1986. pp. 73–94. TRTIL.

Mahadevia, Darshini, Joshi, Rutul and Datey, Abhijit. Ahmedabad's BRT system. *Economic and Political Weekly*. 48, 48, 2013. pp. 56–64. CSSL, SPIESRL, SUL, UML.

Mathew, K.S. Trade economy on coastal Gujarat in the sixteenth century. *Journal of the Oriental Institute*. 34, 3–4, 1985. pp. 201–216. GVL.

Nayak, K.C. and Shah, J.D. Study of trattie delay and economic lossat selected level crossings on national highways in Gujarat. *Indian Highways*. 12, 5, 1984. pp. 18–27. CEPTL.

Nayyar, A.K. Management of city: transport in Ahmedabad. *Nagarlok*. 11, 1, 1979. pp. 79–89. CEPTL.

Oonk, Gijsbert. Gujarati business communities in East Africa: success and failure stories. *Economic and Political Weekly*. 40, 20, 2005. pp. 2077–2081. BUL, CEPTL, CSSL, EDIL, GIDRL, IIML, IRMAL, MICAL, SGUL, SPIESRL, UML.

Pandya, P.C. and Joshi, A.P. Laboratory and field study of anti stripping agents: with aggregates of Gujarat state, failing in stripping value in bituminous road work. *Indian Highways*. 14, 6, 1986. pp. 17–38. CEPTL.

Pearson, M.N. Brokers in western Indian port cities their role in servicing foreign merchants. *Modern Asian Studies*. 22, 1, 1988. pp. 455–472. CSSL.

Shah, A.R., Bhatt, H.K. and Shah, H.J. Micro level study of road accidents on NH 8A and 8B passing through Rajkot-Kandla section. *Indian Highways*. 21, 4, 1993. pp. 35–40. CEPTL.

Shah, V.K. Economies of scale in passenger transportation: a case study of Gujarat state road transport corporation. *Anvesak*. 7, 2, 1977. pp. 207–214. CEPTL, CSS, IRMAL, SPIESRL.

Shivanand Swamy, H.M., Patel, V.L. and Patel, L.M. Planning for public transport system in Ahmedabad. *Nagarlok*. 26, 1, 1994. pp. 41–69. CEPTL, SPIESRL.

Thakkar, Jyoti D. Note on the level and structure of Gujarat's interregional trade. *Anvesak*. 1, 1, 1971. pp. 143–154. IRMAL, SPIESRL.

Working Papers, Reports and Other Materials

Bajpai, Gita. Urban growth in Central Gujarat: a case study of Baroda city in the second half of the 19th century. In *Studies in trade and urbanization in western India*. Ed. by V.K. Chavda. Baroda: M.S. University, 1985. Series No. 9. pp. 111–124. CSSL.

Chavda, V.K. Currency in Gujarat. In *Studies in trade and urbanization in Western India*. Ed. by V.K. Chavda. Baroda: M.S. University, 1985. pp. 155–161. Series No. 9. CSSL.

Dey, Kushankur. From traditional 'dukandaari' to modern retailing: a study on Aditya Birla retail in Gujarat. In *Agribusiness potential of Gujarat state (Seminar Proceeding) 2011*. Nagpur: Indian Society of Agricultural Marketing, 2011. pp. 172–192. SPIESRL.

Mathew, K.S. Trade and trading centres in the early 16th century Gujarat. In *Studies in trade and urbanization in western India*. Ed. by V.K. Chavda. Baroda: M.S. University, 1985. pp. 13–26. Series No. 9. CSSL.

Munshi, Sunil. Geographer's view concerning the study of urban history of Surat. In *Studies in trade and urbanization in Western India*. Ed. by V.K. Chavda. Baroda: M.S. University, 1985. pp. 75–83. Series No. 9. CSSL.

Nanavati, Arti. Road, transportation and communication in Gujarat. Ahmedabad: D.T. Lakdawala Memorial Trust, 2000. p. 45. Occasional Paper Series 6. CSSL, GIDRL.

Panda, Haribandhu and Pundir, R.S. *Problems and possible solutions for better traffic management: a case Study of Vadodara-Ahmedabad section of national highway eight*. Anand: Institute of Rural Management, 2002. p. 49. Research Paper 19. SPIESRL.

Patel, Arjun, et al. Socio-economic study, Gujarat: port development Gujarat (PODEG). Surat: Centre for Social Studies, 2003. p. 102. CSSL.

Rajgopal. Administrative arrangements for rural marketing: a study across three states. Anand: Institute of Rural Management, 1995. p. [ ]. Working Paper 84. CSSL.

Transportation and Housing, Dept. of challenges and opportunities in the transport sector. In Gujarat-2010 challenges and opportunities (seminar volume). By Government of Gujarat. Ahmedabad: Sardar Patel Institute of Economic & Social Research, 2001. pp. 495–496. CSSL, EDIL, IRMAL, SGUL, SPIESRL.

17

Health, Well Being

Books/Chapter in Books

Acharya, Akash. Micro health insurance: NGO experience in Gujarat. In *Health dynamics and marginalized communities*. Ed. by Mohammad Akram. Jaipur: Rawat, 2007. pp. 266–276. CSSL, GIDRL.

Anker, Richard and Anker, Martha. *Reproductive behaviour in households of rural Gujarat: Social economic and community factors*. New Delhi: Concept, 1982. p. 140. GIDRL.

Bhatia, Bela. Health care utilization by the tribals of Dang district. In *Demography of tribal development*. Ed. by Ashish Bose, U.P. Sinha and R.P. Tyagi. Delhi: B.R., 1990. pp. 205–212. CSSL, GVL.

Das, Mitoo. Disease and illness and their ethno medical treatment among the Rathwas of Suskal, Gujarat. In *Tribal health and medicines*. Ed. by A. K. Kalla and P.C. Joshi. New Delhi: Concept, [ ]. pp. 283–300. HML.

Das, N.P. and Shah, Urvi. Reproductive health services remain missing at the grassroots level: evidence from a time-use study of service providers in rural Gujarat. In *Migration, health and development*. Ed. by S. Lahiri, B. Paswan and K.C. Das. Jaipur: Rawat, 2011. pp. 351–383. CSSL, GVL.

De, Jayasree and Patel, Dharmendra. Urban air pollution and human health in Vadodara. In *Explorations in applied geography*. Ed. by Ashok Dutt, H.N. Misra and Meera Chatterje. New Delhi: Prentice Hall, 2008. pp. 121–136. HML.

Gandotra, M.M. and Das, Narayan. Infant mortality: an analysis of recent births in Gujarat. In *Infant mortality in India*. Ed. by Anrudh K. Jain and Pravin Visaria. New Delhi: Sage, 1988. pp. 275–295. CSSL, GIDRL.

Gulhati, Ravi, et al. *Strengthening voluntary action in India: health-family planning, the environment and women's development*. Delhi: Konark, 1995. pp. 9–47. CEEL.

Haque, M. Body-built and nutritional status of three tribes in Gujarat. In *Tribal health: socio-cultural dimensions*. Ed. by Buddhadeb Chaudhuri. New Delhi: Inter-India, 1986. pp. 119–122. CSSL, GIDRL, GVL.

Hardiman, David. Knowledge of the Bhils and their systems of healing. In *Adivasis in colonial India: survival, resistance and negotiation*. Ed. by Biswamoy Pati. Hyderabad: Orient Blackswan, 2011. pp. 293–315. CSSL.

Hirway, Indira. *Denial of maternity benefits to women workers: a study of the factory sector in Gujarat*. New Delhi: Oxford, 1986. p. 151. CSSL.

India. Ministry of Health and Family Welfare. In *Diarrhoea in rural India: West Zone*. New Delhi: Vision, 1990. pp. 3–8 and pp. 21–79. CSSL.

Joshi, Archana, Dhapola, Mrinalika and Pelto, Pertti J. Gynaecological problems: perceptions and treatment-seeking behaviours of rural Gujarati women.

In *Reproductive health in India: New evidence*. Ed. by Michael A. Koenig, et al. Jaipur: Rawat, 2008. pp. 133–158. CSSL.

Joshi, Sandhya. *Child survival, health and social work intervention*. New Delhi: Concept, 1996. p. 250. CSSL.

Kolay, Swapan Kumar. Determinants of nutritional status among the Dhodias in coastal region of Gujarat. In *Tribal health and nutrition*. Ed. by S.N. Chaudhary. Jaipur: Rawat, 2012. pp. 145–161. CSSL.

Kshatriya, Gautam and Kapoor, A.K. Demographic structure and health care practices of Dhodia tribal population of district Valsad, Gujarat. In *Social dimensions of health*. Ed. by Ajit K. Dalal and Subha Ray. Jaipur: Rawat, 2005. pp. 107–135. CSSL.

Mahadevia, Darshini. Health for all in Gujarat: Is it achievable? In *Dynamics of development in Gujarat*. Ed. by Indira Hirway, S.P. Kashyap and Amita Shah. New Delhi: Concept, 2002. pp. 340–371. CSSL, EDIL, GIDRL, GVL, HML, IRMAL, SPUL, UML.

Mehta, D.C. and Shah, M.H. Measurement of mortality in rural Gujarat under sample registration. In *Studies on Mortality in India*. Ed. by K.E. Vaidyanathan. Tamilnadu: Gandhigram Institute of Rural Health & Family Planning, 1972. pp. 55–70. SPIESRL.

Patel, B.B. Evaluation of the working of the schemes of maternity benefits, group life insurance for landless agricultural labourers, and old-age pension schemes in Gujarat. In *Social security for unorganized labour*. Ed. by B.B. Patel. New Delhi: Oxford, 1993. pp. 139–149. CSSL.

Patel, Vinubhai M. and Mavalankar, Dileep. Primary health care under Panchayat raj in Gujarat: perceptions of health services staff. In *Participatory pathways*. Ed. by Rajiv Balkrishnan. South Asia: Darling Kindersley, 2007. pp. 79–92. HML.

Rajaram, N., et al. Health and nutritional status of women. In *Profile of women in Gujarat*. Ed. by Parul Dave. Baroda: M.S. University, 2005. pp. 121–177. GVL.

Rajyaguru, H.M. Need for co-ordinating delivery of maternal and child health services in district head quarters: the case of Baroda city. In *Population policy in India*. Ed. by M.M. Gandotra and Narayan Das. Bombay: Blackie, 1984. p. 86. HML, SPIESRL.

Ramani, K.V., et al. Managing urban health through public-private partnership: a study of Ahmedabad city. In *Strategic issues and challenges in health management*. Ed. by K.V. Ramani, Dilip Mavalankar and Dipti Govil. London: Sage, 2008. pp. 173–184. GIDRL.

Ratnawali. Reproductive health: perception and practices among the tribal womens of Gujarat. In *Studies on bio-medical anthropology: profiles of health cultures*. Ed. by R.K. Mutatkar, Ajit Danda and Vikas Bhatt. New Delhi: Aryan, 2010. pp. 83–96. CSSL.

Ray, C.N. Economic liberalisation and the utilisation of health services in Ahmedabad. In *Issues in urbanisation: study of Ahmedabad city*. Ed. by Jan Hesselberg. Jaipur: Rawat, 2002. pp. 184–221. SPIESRL.

Sah, D.C. and Kazi, Babasaheb. Changing health perceptions and practices: Malaria in tribal and non-tribal rural Surat. In *Tribal issues in India*. Ed. by D.C. Sah and Yatindra Singh Sisodia. Jaipur: Rawat, 2004. pp. 157–172. CEEL, CSSL, GVL.

Satia, J.K. Scaling-Up for child survival: Key issues. In *Managing rural development: health and energy programmes in India*. Ed. by Hein Streefkerk and T.K. Moulik. New Delhi: Sage, 1991. pp. 38–49. CSSL, HML, IIML, SETUL, SPIESRL.

Shah, Ghanshyam. *Public health and urban development: Plague in Surat.* Delhi: Sage, 1997, p. 317. CEPTL, CSSL, GIDRL.

Shah, Ghanshyam. Plague, the poor and health services. *In Public health and the poverty of reform: the South Asian predicament.* Ed. by Imrana Qadeer, Kasturi Sen and K.R. Nayar. New Delhi: Sage, 2001. pp. 459–475. CSSL.

Shah, Neha. Health status of the tribal population. In *Tribal development in Western India*. Ed. by Amita Shah and Jharna Pathak. New Delhi: Routledge, 2014. pp. 129–160. CSSL.

Sharma, Sandeep. Rich state with poor health: disappointing status of public health in Gujarat. In *Poverty amidst prosperity: essays on the trajectory of development in Gujarat*. Ed. by Atul Sood. Delhi: Aakar, 2012. pp. 199–213. CSSL, IRMAL, MICAL.

Sinha, Bakshi D. and Menon. P.S.K. *Environmental sanitation: health and Panchayati raj*. New Delhi: Concept, 1996. p. 134. CSSL, SPIESRL.

Sinha, Harshit. *Leprosy in India: a study in medical geography*. Jaipur: Rawat, 2000. p. 259. CSSL.

Streefland, Pieter H. Management and utilisation of immunisation and oral rehydration therapy in rural Gujarat. In *Managing rural development: health and energy programmes in India.* Ed. by Hein Streefkerk and T.K. Moulik. New Delhi: Sage, 1991. pp. 50–78. CSSL, HML, IIML, SETUL, SPIESRL.

Streefkerk, Hein and Moulik, T.K., ed. *Managing rural development: health and energy programmes in India*. New Delhi: Sage, 1991. p. 225. CSSL, HML, IIML, SETUL, SPIESRL.

Van der Veen, Klaas W. Government and private health care: two competing institutions. In *Managing rural development: health and energy programmes in India.* Ed. by Hein Streefkerk and T.K. Moulik. New Delhi: Sage, 1991. pp. 79–94. CSSL, HML, IIML, SETUL, SPIESRL.

Van der veen, Klass W. Socio-cultural aspects of medical care in Valsad District, Gujarat state. In *Social and cultural context of medicine in India.* Ed. by Giri Raj Gupta. New Delhi: Vikas,1981. pp. 168–193. Main currents in Indian sociology-IV. CSSL, IIML, SPIESRL.

Visaria, Leela. Health situation in Gujarat. In *Growth or development: which way is Gujarat going?* Ed. by Indira Hirway, Amita Shah and Ghanshyam Shah. New Delhi: Oxford, 2014. pp. 434–476. CSSL.

Visaria, Leela. Regional variations in female autonomy and fertility and contraception in India. In *Girls' schooling, women's autonomy and fertility change in south Asia.* Ed. by Roger Jeffery and Alaka M. Basu. New Delhi: Sage, 1996. pp. 235–268. CSSL.

Zwart, Frank de. Constant flux of personnel: some ideas on personnel transfers in bureaucracy. In *Managing rural development: health and energy programmes in India.* Ed. by Hein Streefkerk and T.K. Moulik. New Delhi: Sage, 1991. pp. 114–125. CSSL, HML, IIML, SETUL, SPIESRL.

Journal Articles

Acharya, Akash. Access and utilization of health care services in urban low-income settlements in Surat. *VNSGU Journal of Humanities & Social Sciences.* 1, 2, 2009. pp. 64–87. CSSL, SGUL.

Acharya, Akash and Kent Ranson, M. Health care financing for the poor: community-based health insurance schemes in Gujarat. *Economic and Political Weekly.* 40, 38, 2005. pp. 4141–4150. BUL, CEPTL, CSSL, EDIL, GIDRL, IIML, IRMAL, MICAL, SGUL, SPIESRL, UML.

Banthia, Jayant and Dyson, Tim. Smallpox and the impact of vaccination among the Parsees of Bombay. *Indian Economic and Social History Review.* 37, 1, 2000. pp. 27–51. CSSL, IIML, UML.

Bharti, Madhu. Impact of poor urban service on health and asset creation: a case study of Ahmedabad. *Social Action.* 56, 2, 2006. pp. 153–171. BUL, CSSL, GVL, IIML.

Bhat, Nimita and Patel Ashvin. Surat epidemic, 1994: was it Plague. *Radical Journal of Health.* 2, 4, 1996. pp. 201–212. CSSL.

Bhati, P.G., et al. Socio-economic aspects of Malaria in Kheda district, Gujarat. *Indian Journal of Malariology.* 33, 4, 1996. pp. 200–208. CSSL.

Bhatt, R.M. Biting rhythms of Malaria vector anopheles culicifacies in Kheda district, Gujarat. *Indian Journal of Malariology.* 28, 2, 1991. pp. 91–97. CSSL.

Bhatt, R.M. and Kohli, V.K. Biting rhythms of some anophelines in Central Gujarat. *Indian Journal of Malariology.* 33, 4, 1996. pp. 180–190. CSSL.

Bhatt, R.M., Sharma, R.C. and Kohli, V.K. Inter specific associations among anophelines in different breeding habitats of Kheda district, Gujarat. Part I: Canal irrigated area. *Indian Journal of Malariology.* 27, 3, 1990. pp. 167–172. CSSL.

Bhatt, R.M., Srivastava, H.C. and Pujara, P.K. Biology of Malaria vectors in Central Gujarat. *Indian Journal of Malariology.* 31, 2, 1994. pp. 65–76. CSSL.

Bhatt, R.M., et al. Resting of mosquitoes in outdoor pit shelters in Kheda district, Gujarat. *Indian Journal of Malariology.* 26, 2, 1989. pp. 75–81. CSSL.

Bhatt, R.M., et al. Seasonal prevalence of anophelines in Kheda district, Gujarat. *Indian Journal of Malariology.* 28, 1, 1991. pp. 9–18. CSSL.

Bhatt, R.N., et al. Inter specific associations among anophelines in different breeding habitats of Kheda district Gujarat: Part II: Non-Canal area. *Indian Journal of Malariology.* 30, 2, 1993. pp. 91–100. CSSL.

Chauhan, Naresh. Areas of infant mortality-performance of Gujarat: a comparative study. *Vishleshan.* 37, 1 and 2, 2012. pp. 27–32. CSSL.

Chowdhury, Renuka. Report of campaign against female foeticide in Vadodara. *Social Welfare.* 54, 3, 2007. pp. 17–19. GVL.

Das, Biswaroop. Perceptions beliefs and practices related to health hygiene diseases and cure in rural India study of three village in South Gujarat. *Man & Development,* 26, 4, 2004. pp. 1–22. CSSL, IRMAL, UML.

Desai, Anjana and Prajapati, Avantika. Drinking water-borne diseases in an urban environment: case of Ahmedabad. *Journal of Region, Health and Health Care.* 3, 2, 1998. pp. 1–10. CSSL.

Gautam, A.S., et al. Microscopic diagnosis of Malaria in Kheda district of Gujarat. *Indian Journal of Malariology.* 29, 2, 1992. pp. 83–87. CSSL.

Ghosh, B. Differential rates of achievements in PHC areas in mass vasectomy campaign in Gujarat. *Demography India.* 5, 1–2, 1972. pp. 60–70. SGUL.

Hardiman, David and Raje, Gauri. Practices of healing in tribal Gujarat. *Economic and Political Weekly.* 43, 9, 2008. pp. 43–50. BUL, CEPTL, CSSL, EDIL, IIML, IRMAL, MICAL, SGUL, SPIESRL, SUL, UML.

Hari Kumar, R., et al. Diet and nutritional situation of the population in the severely drought affected areas of Gujarat. *Journal of Human Ecology.* 18, 4, 2005. pp. 319–325. CSSL.

Iyengar, Sudarshan and Bhargava, Ashok. Primary health care and family welfare programme in rural Gujarat. *Economic and Political Weekly*. 22, 27, 1987. pp. 1087–1092. CEPTL, CSSL, IIML, IRMAL, GUL, SGUL, SPIESRL, TRTIL, UML.

Jhala, C.I. Health survey of families residing in Sankdisheri, Ahmedabad. *Journal of the Gujarat Research Society*. 25, 3/99. 1963. pp. 234–236. GVL.

Kanchan, Rolee. Primary health services: their adequacy and accessibility in Vadodara district. *Journal of Region, Health and Health Care*. 2, 1, 1997. pp. 13–19. CSSL.

Karmakar, P., et al. Micro in vitro assessment of plasmodium falciparum sensitivity to chloroquine and mefloquine in Gujarat. *Indian Journal of Malariology*. 27, 1, 1990. pp. 37–42. CSSL.

Kent Ranson, M. Helping members of a community-based health insurance scheme access quality inpatient care through development of a preferred provider system in rural Gujarat. *National Medical Journal of India*. 19, 5, 2006. pp. 274–282. CSSL.

Khader, Vijay and Patel, Geetha H. Chemical analysis of deep fat fried snacks (Chevda and Ganthia) commonly consumed in Gujarat. *Indian Journal of Nutrition and Dietetics*. 19, 3, 1982. pp. 87–95. SGUL.

Mahadevia, Darshini. Health for all in Gujarat: Is it achievable? *Economic and Political Weekly*. 35, 35 and 36, 2000. pp. 3193–3204. BUL, CEPTL, CSSL, GIDRL, IIML, IRMAL, MICAL, SGUL, SPIESRL, UML.

Matzger, Helen and Moench, Marcus. Ground water availability for drinking in Gujarat: quantity, quality and health dimensions. *Economic and Political Weekly*. 29, 13, 1994. pp. A-31-A-41. CEPTL, CSSL, IIML, IRMAL, MICAL, SPIESRL, UML.

Mavalankar, Dileep and Patel, Vinubhai M. Primary health care under Panchayati raj in Gujarat: perceptions of health services staff. *Social Change*. 28, 1, 1998. pp. 54–69. CSSL, IRMAL, UML.

Mehta, Chamanlal M. and Vora, D.D. Health of Gujarati children at birth analysis of the new born for the years 1928–1942 (Report of a special investigation conducted under the Auspices of the society). *Journal of the Gujarat Research Society*. 7, 2 and 3, 1945. pp. 41–45. GUL.

Mehta, Jivraj N. Hospitalisation in Gujarat. *Journal of the Gujarat Research Society*. 9, 2, 1947. pp. 73–81. GUL.

Mehta, Jivraj N. Medical and health problems of Maha-Gujarat. *Journal of the Gujarat Research Society*. 10, 3, 1948. pp. 151–155. GUL.

Mehta, P.M. Health and hygiene in Gujarat. *Journal of the Gujarat Research Society*. 2, 4, 1940. pp. 220–230. GUL, GVL.

Mohan, P.V.T. Krishna. Is anaemia a public health problem in Gujarat?: an investigation Using NFHS-2 Data. *Demography India*. 32, 2, 2003. pp. 171-[ ]. GIDRL.

Nagabrahmam, D. Health, social system and interventions: evidences and experiences from Gujarat. *Journal of Rural Development*. 13, 4, 1994. pp. 537–542. CSSL, IIML, IRMAL.

Nagpal, B.N. Morphological variations in natural populations of anopheles stephensi Liston 1901 collected from Kutch (Gujarat). *Indian Journal of Malariology*. 27, 1, 1990. pp. 25–35. CSSL.

Nanda, Mandira. Indigenous health practices among the Kolaghas of Gujarat. *Journal of the Anthropological Survey in India*. 52, 4, 2003. pp. 101–109. GVL.

Nanda, Satyajeet and Pramanik, Aparimita. Media, exposure, gender stereotype and contextual stigma perceptions about HIV and AIDS: evidence from Gujarat, India. *Journal of Health Management*. 12, 4, 2010. pp. 461–481. CSSL.

Negi, R.S. Incidence of sickle-cell trait in South Gujarat. *Bulletin of the Anthropological Survey of India.* 17, 4, 1968. pp. 423–426. GVL.

Negi, R.S. Poradic occurrence of sickle-cell trait in peninsular Gujarat. *Bulletin of the Anthropological Survey of India.* 17, 4, 1968. pp. 375–377. GVL.

Pandey, I.M., Ban Jerome. and Liyanage, Shantha. Managing mental health sector in Gujarat: an overview of strategic priorities. *Vikalpa.* 29, 1, 2004. pp. 1–13. GVL.

Pandya, A.P. and Mehta, N.R. Survey of haematophagous arthropods in Surat District, Gujarat: a general account. *South Gujarat University Journal.* 4, 1975. pp. 101–107. GVL.

Pandya, A.P. and Mehta, N.R. Survey of haematophagous arthropods in Surat District, Gujarat, India II additional Records. *South Gujarat University Journal.* 6, 1977. pp. 124–127. GVL.

Pandya, A.P. and Niyogi, A.K. Survey of sandflies (Diptera, Psychodidae Phlebotominae) in Kala-Azar and Non-Kala-Azar villages (Baroda, Brouch, Kaira and Panch-Mahal) District of Gujarat state, India. *Journal of the M.S. University of Baroda.* 19–20, 3, 1970–71. pp. 29–34. GVL.

Pandya, H.G., Shah, C.C. and Naik, K.G. Vitamin contents of some fruits and vegetables of Gujarat. *Journal of the Gujarat Research Society.* 9, 2, 1947. pp. 96–103. GUL.

Pant, C.S. and Srivastava, H.C. Distribution of three genetic markers and Malaria in other backward castes of Kheda district, Gujarat. *Indian Journal of Malariology.* 34, 1, 1997. pp. 42–46. CSSL.

Pant, C.S., et al. Frequency of ABO blood groups, sickle-cell haemoglobin, G-6-PD deficiency and their relation with Malaria in scheduled castes and scheduled tribes of Kheda district, Gujarat. *Indian Journal of Malariology.* 29, 4, 1992. pp. 235–239. CSSL.

Patel, Jigisha and Somani, Vipul. Fertility behavior of tribal women: a case of South Gujarat. *VNSGU Journal of Humanities & Social Sciences.* 4, 1, 2013. pp. 25–37. CSSL.

Patel, Ramanlal. Incidence of neurosis among school going Gujarati boys and girls. *Journal of the Gujarat Research Society.* 12, 2, 1950. pp. 80–87. GUL.

Patel, Sangita V., et al. Sexual behaviour among persons living with HIV/AIDS in Gujarat. *Indian Journal of Social Work.* 73, 2, 2012. pp. 177–194. CSSL.

Pathak, J.D. Report of the health centres maintained by Gujarat research society. *Journal of the Gujarat Research Society.* 10, 3, 1948. pp. 156–169. GUL.

Prasad, Purendra. Health care access and marginalized social spaces: Leptospirosis in South Gujarat. *Economic and Political Weekly.* 35, 41, 2000. pp. 3688–3694. BUL, CEPTL, CSSL, GIDRL, IIML, IRMAL, MICAL, SGUL, SPIESRL, UML.

Prasad, Purendra. Narratives of sickness and suffering: a study of Malaria in South Gujarat. *Sociological Bulletin.* 54, 2, 2005. pp. 218–237. CSSL, IIML, IRMAL.

Prasad, Purendra N. Healing in South Gujarat: conceptions, practices and restricted medical pluralism. *Indian Anthropologist.* 37, 1, 2007. pp. 13–28. CSSL.

Puri, Mukesh. Human development a supplementary nutrition schemes for reducing the infant mortality rate in Gujarat. *Administrator.* 45,1, 2002. pp. 52–56 IRMAL.

Ranson, Michael Kent, Jayaswal, Rupal and Mills, Anne J. Strategies for coping with the costs of inpatient care: a mixed methods study of urban and rural poor in Vadodara district, Gujarat, India. *Health Policy and Planning.* 27, 4, 2012. pp. 326–338. IRMAL.

Ratnawali. Supplementary nutrition to women and children: a situational analysis of Anganwadis in tribal areas of Gujarat. *Social Change.* 40, 3, 2010, pp. 319–343. CEPTL, CSSL, UML.

Raval, P.N. and Desai, N.R. Status of gender-differentials in Gujarat in population (2001 Census) health, education and employment. *Vishleshan.* 35, 3, 2010. 20–37. CSSL, IIML.

Ravi Priya, Kumar. Healing as facilitated by socio-centric health beliefs: a study of earthquake affected rural Kachchh. *Eastern Anthropologist.* 60, 2, 2007. pp. 217–232. CSSL.

Sethna, Suresh M. Need for a nutritional survey of Gujarat. *Journal of the Gujarat Research Society.* 2, 4, 1940. pp. 213–219. GVL.

SEWA-Rural Team. Infant mortality rate: Issues and experience. (*Gujarat-2010: Challenges and Opportunities*). *Anvesak.* 31, 1–2, 2001. pp. 153–159. CSSL.

SEWA-Rural Research Team. Study of sensitivity of P. Falciparum to chloroquine in a rural area of Bharuch district, Gujarat. *Indian Journal of Malariology.* 33, 3, 1996. pp. 126–130. CSSL.

Shah, B.K., Shah, V.N. and Shah, C.J. Residency training programme in a tertiary care hospital of Gujarat: appraisal by residents. *Journal of Health Management.* 12, 1, 2010. pp. 65–71. CSSL.

Shah, Ghanshyam. Diseases, doctors and urban public health system: a study of Surat city. *IASSI Quarterly.* 14, 1–2, 1995. pp. 115–139. GIDRL, IIML.

Shah, N.C. Lung function (Mechanical) tests in normal healthy subjects of Baroda. *Journal of the M.S. University of Baroda.* 31–32, 3, 1982–83. pp. 35–38. GVL.

Shah, P.G. Physical fitness of the Gujarati speaking population. *Journal of the Gujarat Research Society.* 1, 1, 1939. pp. 6–13. GUL.

Sharma, R.C. and Gautam, A.S. Studies on outbreak of Malaria in Muliad village of Kheda district, Gujarat. *Indian Journal of Malariology.* 27, 3, 1990. pp. 157–162. CSSL.

Sharma, R.C., Malviya, V.S. and Bhati, P.G. Economic loss due to Malaria in Kheda district, Gujarat. *Indian Journal of Malariology.* 27, 3, 1990. pp. 149–155. CSSL.

Sharma, R.C., et al. Relapse pattern of plasmodium vivax in Kheda district, Gujarat. *Indian Journal of Malariology.* 27, 2, 1990. pp. 95–99. CSSL.

Sharma, V.P., Sharma, R.C. and Gautam, A.S. Bio-environmental control of Malaria in Nadiad, Kheda district, Gujarat. *Indian Journal of Malariology.* 23, 2, 1986. pp. 95–117. CSSL.

Shastri, D.K. Medical science in ancient Gujarat. *Journal of the Gujarat Research Society.* 7, 2–3, 1945. pp. 77–87. GVL, GUL.

Sinha, Harshit. Spatial and epidemiological aspects of Plague in India: a case study of Mamla village and Surat city. *Journal of Region, Health and Health Care.* 2, 1, 1997. pp. 21–30. CSSL.

Sinha, Tara, et al. Barriers to accessing benefits in a community-based insurance scheme: lessons learnt from SEWA insurance, Gujarat. *Health Policy and Planning.* 21, 2, 2006. pp. 132–142. CSSL.

Srivastava, H.C. Treehole breeding of Mosquitoes in Nadiad, Kheda district (Gujarat). *Indian Journal of Malariology.* 26, 3, 1989. pp. 161–165. CSSL.

Srivastava, H.C., et al. Studies on plasmodium vivax relapse pattern in Kheda district, Gujarat. *Indian Journal of Malariology.* 33, 4, 1996. pp. 173–179. CSSL.

Thawani, Madhu and Garg, Priti. Bringing down maternal mortality rate: the Gujarat model. *Nagarlok.* 43, 4, 2011. pp. 60–73. CSSL.

Trivedi, D.H., Shah, D.N. and Joshi, G.D. Episode of xerophthalmia in a small village of Baroda. *Journal of the M.S. University of Baroda.* 24, 3, 1980. pp. 143–152. GVL.

Trivedi, M.J. Sanitary and health survey of a Gujarat village-Bareja. *Journal of the Gujarat Research Society*. 2, 4, 1940. pp. 243–253. GUL, GVL.

Visaria, Leela. PPP: the Gujarat experience. *Seminar*. 604, 2009. pp. 34–37. CSSL, GVL, IIML, MICAL, UML.

Visaria, Leela and Bhatt, Meera. Public provisioning of health and decentralization in Gujarat. *Economic and Political Weekly*. 46, 49, 2011. pp. 59–66. BUL, CEPTL, CSSL, EDIL, IRMAL, SPIESRL, SUL, UML.

Vyas, Rajendra T. Blindness in Gujarat. *Journal of the Gujarat Research Society*. 23, 3/91, 1961. pp. 245–253. GVL.

Working Papers, Reports and Other Materials

Acharya, Akash. *Access and utilization of health care services in urban low-income settlements in Surat, India*. Surat: Centre for Social Studies, 2008. p. 29. Working Paper No. 5. CSSL.

Acharya, Akash. *Health status, health needs and health care-seeking behaviour of people living in 22 slums of Surat city*. Surat: Centre for Social Studies, 2006. p. 84. Report. CSSL.

Amin, Avni, Fatula, Emily and Grenon, Marie-Claude. *Men's perceptions of illnesses of the Nether area: Evidence from qualitative studies conducted in the Santrampur taluka of Panchmahals district, Gujarat*. Godhara: SARTHI, 1996. p. 43. Working Paper No. 3. CSSL.

Bhargava, Ashok. *Immunization campaign in a rural area in Kachchh, Gujarat, 1986–87.1988*. p. 23. GIDR Working Paper No. 15. GIDRL.

Bhat, Ramesh, et al. *Mental health care pilots in Gujarat: processes, outcomes and leaning*. Ahmedabad: Centre for Management in Agriculture, 2007. p. 224. IIML.

Centre for Environmental Planning and Technology. *Rural health care system in Gujarat: perspective for the next decade*. Ahmedabad: CEPT University, [ ]. p. 151. GIDRL.

Chatterjee, Mirai. Health for all in Gujarat. In *Gujarat-2010: Challenges and opportunities*. By Government of Gujarat. Ahmedabad: Sardar Patel Institute of Economic & Social Research, 2001. pp. 378–386. Seminar Volume. CSSL, EDIL, IRMAL, SGUL, SPIESRL.

Clerk, S.H. *Respiratory morbidity in trap workers: a case study in Jhagadia taluka, Bharuch district, Gujarat state*. Ahmedabad: Gandhi Labour Institute, 1989. p. 59. CSSL.

Coutinho, Lester, Bisht, Suman and Raje, Gauri. *Vaccines, targets and reports: some perceptions and practices of the immunization programme in Gujarat and Uttar Pradesh*. Delhi: Centre for Development Economics, 1997. p. 44. Working Paper No. 4. CSSL.

Dave, Parul and Majithia, Vanita. *Perceived by functionaries in implementation of tribal health and welfare services in Panchmahal, Gujarat*. Baroda: M.S. University, 1982. p. 44. CSSL.

Dave, Parul and Tavkar, Nivedita. *Child care amongst the tribals of Limkheda, Panchmahals, Gujarat*. Baroda: Department of Child Development, M.S. University, 1983. p. 23. CSSL.

Dave, Parul, Divakaran, Meena and Majithia, Vanita. *Nutritional status of under fives in Limkheda, Panchmahals, Gujarat*. Baroda: M.S. University, 1983. p. 35. CSSL.

Deodhar, Seema, Prakash, Tripti and Purandare, Vasanti. *Preliminary health needs assessment survey of Hazira*. Pune: Foundation for Research in Community Health, 2000. p. 75. CSSL.

Desai, Mahesh D. *Engineering aspects of so called Plague in Surat (1994)*. Surat: Centre for Social Studies, 1995. p. 53. CSSL.

Gandotra, M.M. *Determinants of infant mortality: an analysis or recent births in Gujarat.* Ahmedabad: Gujarat Institute of Area Planning, 1984. p. 25. Seminar Paper. CSSL.

Grenon, Marie-Claude and Mawji, Tazeem. *Women's perceptions of sexually transmitted diseases: evidence from qualitative studies conducted in the Santrampur taluka of Panchmahals district, Gujarat*. Godhra: Sarthi, 1996. p. 24. Working Paper No. 1. CSSL.

Grenon, Marie-Claude, Fatula, Emily and Khanna, Renu. *Validation of local herbal plants traditionally used for STDs in women and men: evidence from qualitative studies conducted in the Santrampur taluka of Panchmahals district, Gujarat*. Godhra: Sarthi, 1997. p. 31. Working Paper No. 5. CSSL.

Health and Family Welfare, Department of, Government of Gujarat. Gujarat 2010-Chaalenges and opportunities key paper on Gujarat: vision 2010, challenges and opportunities. *In Gujarat-2010: Challenges and opportunities*. By Government of Gujarat. Ahmedabad: Sardar Patel Institute of Economic & Social Research, 2001. pp. 423–426. Seminar Volume. CSSL, EDIL, IRMAL, SGUL, SPIESRL.

Health Promotion in South-East Asia. *Anubhav: experiences in health and community development*. New Delhi: Voluntary Health Association of India, [ ]. p. 31. CEEL.

International Institute for Population Science. *National family health survey: MCH and family planning, Gujarat. 1993*. Bombay: Author, 1995. p. 308. CSSL.

International Institute for Population Science. *National family health survey: Gujarat. 1998–99*. Bombay: Author, 2001. p. 314. CSSL.

International Institute for Population Science. *National family health survey (NFHS-3) Gujarat. 2005–06*. Bombay: Author, 2008. p. 122. CSSL.

International Institute for Population Science. *Reproductive and child health project: District level household survey-2002, Gujarat: Ahmedabad*. Vadodara: Centre for Operations Research and Training (Cort), 2003. p. 69. GIDRL.

International Institute for Population Science. *Reproductive and child health: District level household survey-2004, Gujarat: Amreli*. Vadodara: Centre for Operations Research and Training (Cort), 2004. p. 67. GIDRL.

International Institute for Population Science. *Reproductive and child health: District level household survey-2004, Gujarat: Anand*. Vadodara: Centre for Operations Research and Training (Cort), 2004. p. 67. GIDRL.

International Institute for Population Science. *Reproductive and child health project: District level household survey-2002, Gujarat: Banaskantha*. Vadodara: Centre for Operations Research and Training (Cort), 2003. p. 73. GIDRL.

International Institute for Population Science. *Reproductive and child health: District level household survey-2004, Gujarat: Bharuch*. Vadodara: Centre for Operations Research and Training (Cort), 2004. p. 67. GIDRL.

International Institute for Population Science. *Reproductive and child health: District level household survey-2004, Gujarat: Bhavnagar*. Vadodara: Centre for Operations Research and Training (Cort), 2004. p. 66. GIDRL.

International Institute for Population Science. *Reproductive and child health: District level household survey-2004, Gujarat: Dahod.* Vadodara: Centre for Operations Research and Training (Cort), 2004. p. 67. GIDRL.

International Institute for Population Science. *Reproductive and child health project: District level household survey-2002, Gujarat: Gandhinagar.* Vadodara: Centre for Operations Research and Training (Cort), 2003. p. 71. GIDRL.

International Institute for Population Science. *Reproductive and child health project: District level household survey-2002, Gujarat: Jamnagar.* Vadodara: Centre for Operations Research and Training (Cort), 2003. p. 68. GIDRL.

International Institute for Population Science. *Reproductive and child health project: District level household survey-2002, Gujarat: Junagadh.* Vadodara: Centre for Operations Research and Training (Cort), 2003. p. 69. GIDRL.

International Institute for Population Science. *Reproductive and child health project: District level household survey-2002, Gujarat: Kachchh.* Vadodara: Centre for Operations Research and Training (Cort), 2003. p. 70. GIDRL.

International Institute for Population Science. *Reproductive and child health: District level household survey-2004, Gujarat: Kheda.* Vadodara: Centre for Operations Research and Training (Cort), 2004. p. 66. GIDRL.

International Institute for Population Science. *Reproductive and child health project: District level household survey-2002, Gujarat: Mahesana.* Vadodara: Centre for Operations Research and Training (Cort), 2003. p. 69. GIDRL.

International Institute for Population Science. *Reproductive and child health: District level household survey-2004, Gujarat: Dahod.* Vadodara: Centre for Operations Research and Training (CORT), 2004. p. 67. GIDRL.

International Institute for Population Science. *Reproductive and child health: District level household survey-2004, Gujarat: Narmada.* Vadodara: Centre for Operations Research and Training (Cort), 2004. p. 67. GIDRL.

International Institute for Population Science. *Reproductive and child health: District level household survey-2004, Gujarat: Navsari.* Vadodara: Centre for Operations Research and Training (Cort), 2004. p. 67. GIDRL.

International Institute for Population Science. *Reproductive and child health: District level household survey-2004, Gujarat: Panchmahals.* Vadodara: Centre for Operations Research and Training (Cort), 2004. p. 67. GIDRL.

International Institute for Population Science. *Reproductive and child health project: District level household survey-2004, Gujarat: Patan.* Vadodara: Centre for Operations Research and Training (Cort), 2004. p. 67. GIDRL.

International Institute for Population Science. *Reproductive and child health: District level household survey-2004, Gujarat: Porbandar.* Vadodara: Centre for Operations Research and Training (Cort), 2004. p. 67. GIDRL.

International Institute for Population Science. *Reproductive and child health project: District level household survey-2002, Gujarat: Rajkot.* Vadodara: Centre for Operations Research and Training (Cort), 2003. p. 71. GIDRL.

International Institute for Population Science. *Reproductive and child health project: District level household survey-2002, Gujarat: Sabarkantha.* Vadodara: Centre for Operations Research and Training (Cort), 2003. p. 71. GIDRL.

International Institute for Population Science. *Reproductive and child health project: District level household survey-2002, Gujarat: Surat.* Vadodara: Centre for Operations Research and Training (Cort), 2003. p. 69. GIDRL.

International Institute for Population Science. *Reproductive and child health project: District level household survey-2002, Gujarat: Surendranagar*. Vadodara: Centre for Operations Research and Training (Cort), 2003. p. 69. GIDRL.

International Institute for Population Science. *Reproductive and child health project: District level household survey-2002, Gujarat: Dangs*. Vadodara: Centre for Operations Research and Training (Cort), 2003. p. 71. GIDRL.

International Institute for Population Science. *Reproductive and child health: District level household survey-2004, Gujarat: Vadodara*. Vadodara: Centre for Operations Research and Training (Cort), 2004. p. 66. GIDRL.

International Institute for Population Science. *Reproductive and child health: District level household survey-2004, Gujarat: Valsad*. Vadodara: Centre for Operations Research and Training (Cort), 2004. p. 67. GIDRL.

Iyengar, Sudarshan and Sinha, Ratnawali. *Mapping of reproductive healthcare seeking behaviour of women and service provisions in selected tribal areas in Gujarat*. Surat: Centre for Social Studies, 2004. p. 78. CSSL.

Jain, Anrudh, et al. *Impact of family planning program inputs on use of contraceptives in Gujarat state, India*. Ahmedabad: Gujarat Institute of Development Research, 1992. p. 24. Working Paper No. 43. CSSL, GIDRL.

Javadekar, P.A. Mental morbidity in a semi-slum area in Baroda. In *Gujarat economic association conference papers (Key Papers)*. Ed. by D.T. Lakadawala and B.B. Patel. Vadodara: [ ], 1982. pp. 43–50. GIDRL.

Jhaveri, Ketan. *Clinical aspects of suspected plague, observed during Surat epidemic of 1994*. Surat: Centre for Social Studies, 1994. p. 16. CSSL.

Kazi, Babasaheb. *Benchmark study on sexual behaviour among three target groups in Surat city*. Surat: Centre for Social Studies, 1999. p. 43. CSSL.

Kazi, Babasaheb. *Situation analysis of sexual health in Surat*. Surat: Centre for Social Studies, 1999. Draft report. p. 34 and p. 47. CSSL.

Khan, M.E. and Prasad, C.V.S. *Health financing in India; a case study of Gujarat and Maharashtra*. Baroda: Operations Research Group, 1985. p. 137. GIDRL.

Khanna, Renu, Mehta, N.R. and Bhatt, Anil. *Voluntary effort in community health: review of the community health project of SEWA-Rural (An Abridged report)*. Jhagadia: Society for Education, Welfare and Action-Rural, 1991. p. 240. CSSL, SETUL.

Kumar, B.L. *Primary health care in Gujarat: evidence on utilization, mis-matches and wastage*. Ahmedabad: Gujarat Institute of Development Research, 2004. p. 38. Working Paper No. 149. CSSL, GIDRL, IRMAL.

Lal, Ras Bihari. *Health and sanitation programme in a tribal block*. Ahmedabad: Gujarat Vidyapith, 1967. p. 17. IIML.

Lobo, Lancy and Kazi, Babasaheb. *Ethnography of Malaria in Surat: validation study*. Surat: Centre for Social Studies, 1997. p. 103. CSSL.

Lobo, Lancy, Prasad, Purendra N. and Kazi, Babasaheb. *Ethnography of Malaria in Surat District: a component of Malaria control and resource project supported by DFID (Non-Tribal Village Study)*. Surat: Centre for Social Studies, 1999. p. 14. CSSL.

Lobo, Lancy, Prasad, Purendra N. and Kazi, Babasaheb. *Ethnography of Malaria in Surat District: a component of Malaria control and resource project supported by DFID through British council division*. Surat: Centre for Social Studies, 1998. p. 50. CSSL.

Lobo, Lancy, et al. *Ethnography of Malaria in Surat district. (Composite Report-1995–2000)*. Surat: Centre for Social Studies, 2000. p. 78. CSSL.

Mankodi, Kashyap. *Treatment and default in the Tuberculosis control programme in Valsad District*. Surat: Centre for Social Studies, 1982. p. 85. CSSL.,

Medico Friend Circle. *Carnage in Gujarat: a public health crisis*. Pune: Medico Friend Circle, 2002. p. 53. CSSL.

Panda, Smita Mishra and Lund, Ragnhild. *Environmental hazard's women's work and health in rural Kutch, Gujarat, India*. Anand: Institute of Rural Management, 2003. p. 26. Working Paper-177. IRMAL, SPIESRL.

Patel, B.B. and Alagh, Raksha. Major issues in health in Gujarat. In *Gujarat economy: problems and prospects*. Ed. by D.T. Lakdawala. Ahmedabad: Sardar Patel Institute of Economic & Social Research, 1983. pp. 589–626. Monograph Series-10. GIDRL, GUL, IIML.

Patel, B.B. and Alagh, Raksha. Major issues in health in Gujarat. In *Seminar on development of Gujarat problems & prospects, 24th-26 August, 1981*. Ahmedabad: Sardar Patel Institute of Economic & Social Research, 1981. p. 71. CSSL.

Patel, C.C. Water: Scarce and valuable resource. In *Gujarat-2010: challenges and opportunities*. By Government of Gujarat. Ahmedabad: Sardar Patel Institute of Economic & Social Research, 2001. pp. 451–471. Seminar Volume. CSSL, EDIL, IRMAL, SGUL, SPIESRL.

Patel, Ishwarbhai. Sanitation. In *Gujarat-2010: challenges and opportunities*. By Government of Gujarat. Ahmedabad: Sardar Patel Institute of Economic & Social Research, 2001. pp. 427–450. Seminar Volume. CSSL, EDIL, IRMAL, SGUL, SPIESRL.

Patel, K.N. Health sector in Gujarat: Current status, vision 2010 and future strategy. In *Gujarat-2010: challenges and opportunities*. By Government of Gujarat. Ahmedabad: Sardar Patel Institute of Economic & Social Research, 2001. pp. 387–422. Seminar Volume. CSSL, EDIL, IRMAL, SGUL, SPIESRL.

Pool, Robert. *Food avoidances and the hot/cold syndrome: a case study in rural Gujarat, India*. Amsterdam: University of Amsterdam, Department of South and South Asian Studies, Anthropology Sociology Centre, 1984. p. 79. Working Paper No. 39. CSSL, GIDRL.

Prasad, Purendra N. and Lobo, Lancy. *Leptospirosis epidemic in South Gujarat: a preliminary study*. Surat: Centre for Social Studies, 1999. p. 49. CSSL.

Rajaram, N., et al. *Health status of women in Gujarat*. Vadodara: M.S. University, 1999. p. 142. CSSL, SETUL.

Ratnawali. *Estimating community prevalence rate of sickle cell anemia among tribal population of Gujarat: a bio anthropological study in Warli tribe*. Surat: Centre for Social Studies, 2012. p. 99. CSSL, TRTIL.

Ratnawali. *Rural health services at cross-roads: insights from Gujarat*. Surat: Centre for Social Studies, 2009. p. 42. Working Paper No. 8. CSSL, GIDRL.

Sarvodaya Planning and Training Centre, Vanasthali-Kanjod. *Health plan for Valod taluka*. Vanasthali-Kanjod: Author, 1978. p. 53. CSSL.

SEWA-Rural Team. Infant mortality rate: issues and experience. In *Gujarat-2010: challenges and opportunities*. By Government of Gujarat. Ahmedabad: Sardar Patel Institute of Economic & Social Research, 2001. pp. 373–377. Seminar Volume. CSSL, EDIL, IRMAL, SGUL, SPIESRL.

Shah, Ghanshyam. *Public health-urban society interface: a study of pneumonic Plague in Surat*. Surat: Centre for Social Studies, 1996. p. 239. CSSL.

Shah, S.M. Evaluation of the integrated child development services project in Chhota Udepur (Gujarat): a case study. In *Gujarat economy: problems and prospects*. Ed.

by D.T. Lakdawala. Ahmedabad: Sardar Patel Institute of Economic & Social Research, 1983. pp. 627–640. Monograph Series-10. IIML.

Shariff, Abusaleh. *Factors affecting child health: search for maternal education effects in rural Gujarat.* Ahmedabad: Gujarat Institute of Development Research, 1993. p. 29. Working Paper No. 47. CSSL, GIDRL, IRMAL.

Shroff, Preeti and Acharya, Shrawan. *Factors affecting utilization of primary health care centres in rural areas: a micro level study of PLTC Por, Taluka Vadodara.* Ahmedabad: School of Planning, 2000. p. 20. Working Paper-16. CEPTL.

Sinha, Ratnawali and Iyengar, Sudarshan. *Working of Anganwadis selected tribal talukas of Valsad district.* Surat: Centre for Social Studies, 2005. p. 52. CSSL.

Subramanian, Ashok. *Profile of voluntary health effort in Gujarat.* Ahmedabad: Indian Institute of Management, 1984. p. [ ]. IIM Working Paper No. 509. GIDRL, IIML.

Visaria, Leela. *Sex differentials in nutritional status in a rural area of Gujarat: an interim report.* Ahmedabad: Gujarat Institute of Area Planning, 1987. p. 36. Working Paper No. 7. CSSL, GIDRL, IRMAL.

Visaria, Leela. *Two immunization campaigns in a rural area of Kachchh, Gujarat: an assessment.*, March 1988. p. 23. GIDR Working Paper No. 19. GIDRL.

Visaria, Leela, Barua, Alka and Mistry, Ramkrishna. *Medical abortion: some exploratory findings from Gujarat.* Ahmedabad: Gujarat Institute of Development Research, 2006. p. 28. Working Paper No. 166. CSSL, SPIESRL.

Visaria, Leela, Visaria, Pravin and Jain, Anrudh. *Consistency between estimates of contraceptive prevalence rates based on service statistics and surveys in Gujarat state, India.* Ahmedabad: Gujarat Institute of Development Research, 1992. p. 39. Working Paper No. 42. CSSL, GIDRL.

Visaria, Leela, et al. *Medical abortion: Some exploratory findings from Gujarat.* Ahmedabad: Gujarat Institute of Development Research, 2006. p. 28. GIDRL, IRMAL.

18

History, Geography, Archaeology

Books/Chapter in Books

Ad-Dabir, Abdullah Muhammad al-Makki al-Asafi, al-ulughkhani Hajji. *Zafar Ul walih BI muzaffar wa alihi: an Arabic history of Gujarat (English Translation)* Vol. 1. Baroda: Oriental Institute, 1970. p. 474. SPUL.

Ajithprasad, P. Palaeolithic cultural sequence in the Sakhi Valley, Gujarat. In *River valley cultures of India*. Ed. by K.K. Chakravarty and G.L. Badam. New Delhi: Aryan, 2005. pp. 183–198. HML.

Allan, J., Haig, T. Wolseley and Dodwell, H.H. Gujarat, Malwa and Khandesh. In *Cambridge shorter history of India*. Ed. by H.H. Dodwell. New Delhi: S. Chand, 1969. pp. 299–319. SPUL.

Allchin, Bridget, Goudie, Andrew and Hegde, Karunarkara. *Prehistory and palaeogeography of the great Indian desert*. London: Academic, 1978. p. 370. GVL.

Amin, J.P. Some rare sculptures of Khambhat. In *New dimensions of indology (Dr. Praveen Chandra Parikh Felicitation volume)*. Ed. by Dinesh Chandra, Mahendra R. Trivedi and Balaji Ganorkar. Delhi: Bhartiya Vidya, 1997. pp. 227-[ ]. GVL.

Andaya, Leonard Y. Gujarati legacy in Southeast Asia. In *Gujarat and the sea*. Ed. by Lotika Varadarajan. Vadodara: Darshak Itihas Nidhi, 2011. pp. 385–404. AAL, CSSL, GIDRL.

Antunes, Luis Frederico Dias. Banias and the foreign trade of Diu (18th century). In *Gujarat and the sea*. Ed. by Lotika Varadarajan. Vadodara: Darshak Itihas Nidhi, 2011. pp. 599–612. AAL, CSSL, GIDRL.

Bagchi, Tilak. Nature, man and crafts of Kachchh. In *Portrait of anthropological research*. Ed. by Debabrata Mandal, Tilak Bagchi and Asok Mukhopadhyay. New Delhi: Sarup, 2008. pp. 427–436. HML.

Bajpai, Gita. Some preliminary ideas on the agrarian roots of nationalism in Gujarat: case study of select district in South Gujarat in the Nineteenth century. In *Regional roots of India nationalism*. Ed. by Makrand J. Mehta. New Delhi: Criterion, 1990. pp. 80–105. GVL.

Bakshi, S.R. and Sharma, S.K. Affairs of Gujarat and Malwa. In *Great Moghuls*. Ed. by S.R. Bakshi and S.K. Sharma. New Delhi: Deep & Deep, 1999. pp. 135–150. GVL.

Bayley, Edward Clive. *History of Gujarat: local Muhammadan dynasties*. Ed. by Nagendra Singh. New Delhi: S. Chand, 1970. p. 541. ASL, CSSL, IRMAL, SETUL.

Beveridge, H., tr. *Akbar Nama of Abu-l-Fazl*. Vol. III. Delhi: Rare & Low Price, 1973 and 1993. p. 1274. CSSL, SPUL.

Beveridge, H., tr. Arrival of the Shahinshah at Ahmedabad, the uplifting of the banners of conquest and the victory over Muhammad Husian M. In *Akbar Nama of Abu-l-Fazl*. Vol. III. Delhi: Rare & Low Price, 1973 and 1993. pp. 72–89. CSSL, SPUL.

Beveridge, H., tr. Expedition of the Shahinshah for the second time to Gujarat and his return with victory. In *Akbar Nama of Abu-l-Fazl*. Vol. III. Delhi: Rare & Low Price, 1973 and 1993. pp. 59–71. CSSL, SPUL.

Beveridge, H., tr. Forms the design of taking the fort of Surat. In *Akbar Nama of Abu-l-Fazl*. Vol. III. Delhi: Rare & Low Price, 1973 and 1993. pp. 24–31. CSSL, SPUL.

Beveridge, H., tr. March of the sacred army of the Shahinshah from Ahmedabad to the port of cambay and his beholding the sea. In *Akbar Nama of Abu-l-Fazl*. Vol. III. Delhi: Rare & Low Price, 1973 and 1993. pp. 13–16. CSSL, SPUL.

Beveridge, H., tr. Return of the Shahinshah cortege to Agra after the conquest of Gujarat. In *Akbar Nama of Abu-l-Fazl*. Delhi: Rare & Low Price. 1973 and 1993. pp. 48–54. CSSL, SPUL.

Beverideg, H., tr. Sending of M. Khan to quell the disturbances in Gujarat. In *Akbar Nama of Abu-l-Fazl*. Vol. III Delhi: Rare & Low Price, 1973 and 1993. pp. 607–615. CSSL, SPUL.

Bhargava, G.S. Probing in Kutch. In *After Nehru: India's new image*. New Delhi: Allied, 1966. pp. 256–279. SPUL.

Bhatt, Usha. Women organizations and national awareness in India: a case study of Jyotisangh, Ahmedabad, 1934–1947. In *Regional roots of Indian nationalism.* Ed. by Makrand Mehta. New Delhi: Criterion, 1990. pp. 203–213. GVL.

Bhowmik, S.K. Hundred years of the Kutch museum, Bhuj. In *Art, culture and natural history of Kutch.* Ed. by S.K. Bhowmik. Vadodara: Government Press, 1976–77. pp. 1–12. CSSL, TRTIL.

Bhowmik, S.K., ed. *Art, culture and natural history of Kutch.* Vadodara: Government Press, 1976–77. p. 235. Bi-Lingual. CSSL, TRTIL.

Bird, James. *Political and statistical history of Gujarat*. Delhi: J. Jetley, 1835. p. 427. TRTIL.

Bird, James, tr. *Medieval Gujarat: its political and statistical history.* New Delhi: Academic, 1980. p. 427. BVL, CSSL, IRMAL.

Bird, James, tr. *Political and statistical history of Gujarat*. New Delhi: Asian Educational Services. 2005. p. 427. AAL.

Briggs, H.G. *Cities of Gurjarashtra: their topography and history illustrated in the journal of a recent tour with accompanying documents*. Bombay: Times press, 1849. p. 408. ASL.

Bukhari, Mahmud., Tirmizi, S.A.I. and Chand, Tara. *Tarikh-I-Salatin-I-Gujarat*. Bombay: Asia, 1964. p. 47. GUL, GVL.

Campbell, James M. *History of Gujarat: ancient, medieval, modem: Gazetteer of the Bombay presidency,* Vol. 1. Bombay: Vintage, 1989. p. 594. CSSL, HML.

Campbell, James M. *History of Gujarat: ancient, medieval, modem.* Haryana: Saraswati, 1896. p. [ ]. BVL.

Carswell, John. Gujarat, the deccan, China and the Islamic world. In *Gujarat and the sea*. Ed. by Lotika Varadarajan. Vadodara: Darshak Itihas Nidhi, 2011. pp. 297–314. AAL, CSSL, GIDRL.

Chakrabarti, Dilip K. *Archaeology of ancient Indian cities*. Delhi: Oxford, 1995. p. 296. CSSL.

Chandra, Sudhir. From Gujaratni *asmita* to Gujaratni *rashtriya asmita*: a comparative note on regional and panindian nationalism during the late nineteenth century. In *Regional roots of Indian nationalism*. Ed. by Makrand J. Mehta. New Delhi: Criterion, 1990. pp. 39–64. GVL.

Chaturvedi, Vinayak. *Peasant pasts: history, politics, and nationalism in Gujarat.* Ranikhet: Permanent Black, 2007. p. 307. CSSL.

Chaube, J. *History of Gujarat kingdom 1458–1537.* New Delhi: Munshiram Manoharlal, 1975. p. 320. ASL, GVL, SETUL, SUL, UML.

Chavda, Vijay Singh. *Modern Gujarat*. Ahmedabad: New Order Book, 1982. p. 276. HML, SPIESRL.

Chitalwala, Y.M. Archaeological work in Kutch. In *Art, culture and natural history of Kutch.* Ed. by S.K. Bhowmik. Vadodara: Government Press, 1976–77. pp. 80–84. CSSL, TRTIL.

Chitalwala, Y.M. Harappan and post-harappan settlement patterns in the Rajkot district of Saurashtra. In *Essays in Indian protohistory*. Ed. by D.P. Agrawal and Dilip K. Chakrabarti. Delhi: B.R., 2012. pp. 113–121. SPUL.

Church, Sally K. Gujarat in a 13th century Chinese source: zhao rugua's chapter on Gujarat in Zhu fan Zhi. In *Gujarat and the sea*. Ed. by Lotika Varadarajan. Vadodara: Darshak Itihas Nidhi, 2011. pp. 353–384. AAL, CSSL, GIDRL.

Commissariat, M.S. *History of Gujarat: including a survey of its chief architectural monuments and inscriptions.* 3 Vols. Bombay: Longman, 1938. p. 620. BVL, CSSL, GVL, HML, SUL, UML.

Commissariat, M.S. *History of Gujarat: with a survey of its monuments and inscriptions.* Vol. 2. Bombay: Longman, 1957. p. 592. ASL, CSSL.

Commissariat, M.S. *Imperial Mughal framers in Gujarat. Bombay:* University of Bombay, 1940. p. 56. ASL.

Commissariat, M.S. *Mandelslo's travels in Western India*, A.D. 1638–9. London: Humphrey, 1931. p. 115. CSSL.

Commissariat, M.S. *Studies in the history of Gujarat: the Thakkar Vassonji Madhavji lectures of the University of Bombay for the year 1930–31*. Ahmedabda: Saraswati, 1935 and 1987. p. 157. BVL, CSSL, GUL, HML, SETUL, SUL.

Copland, Ian. *British raj and the Indian princes: paramountcy in Western India, 1857–1930.* Hyderabad: Orient Longman, 1987. p. 345. CSSL.

Craig, Jennifer. Evidence of Gujarat in the Philippines: historical and archaeological sources of Sufi-Islam. In *Gujarat and the sea*. Ed. by Lotika Varadarajan. Vadodara: Darshak Itihas Nidhi, 2011. pp. 425–438. AAL, CSSL, GIDRL.

Cunningham, Alexgnder. Kachh. In *Ancient geography of India*. Varasani: Indological, 1963. pp. 254–256. GUL.

Cunningham, Alexgnder. Saurashtra. In *Ancient geography of India*. Varasani: Indological, 1963. pp. 273–274. GUL.

Curtis, William Eleroy. City of Ahmedabad. In *India under Britisher*. New Delhi: Srishti, 2009. pp. 126–133. GUL.

Dar, Muhammed Ibrahim. *Literary and cultural activities in Gujarat under the Khaljis and the sultanate*. Bombay: Bazm-Ilshaat Ismal Yusuf College, 1959. p. 62. Bazm-i-Isha'at Series No. 1. GUL.

Dasgupta, Ashin. *Indian merchants and the decline of Surat c.1700–1750*. Wiesbaden: Franz Steiner Verlag, 1979. p. 305. CSSL, HML, IIML.

Dasgupta, Ashin. Merchants of Surat, c.1700–50. In *Elites in south Asia.* Ed. by Edmund Leach and S.N. Mukherjee. Cambridge: Cambridge University press, 1970. pp. 201–222. CSSL. GVL, SPIESRL.

Daya, Dalpatram. *Bhut nibandh: an essay, descriptive of the demonology and other popular superstitions of Guzerat*. Tr. by Alexander Kinloch Forbes. Bombay: Bombay Gazette Press, 1849. p. 95. (Reprint Gurgaon: Vintage, 1990.) CSSL.

Desai, Anjana and Sengupta, Smita. Problems of changing land use pattern in the urban fringe: the case of Ahmedabad. In *Perspectives in urban geography volume nine: rural-urban fringe*. Ed. by C.S. Yadav. New Delhi: Concept, 1987. pp. 355-[ ].GVL.

Desai, Govindbhai H. *Prevention of fragmentation and consolidation of holdings in the Baroda State: Being a collection of legislative measures adopted by His Highness Maharaja Sayaji Rao Gaekwad*. Baroda: Pustakalaya Sahayak Sahakari Mandal, 1934. p. 149. CSSL.

Desai, H.P. and Gandhi, Pankaj. *Glimpses of Gujarat (geography, demography and government policies)* Vol. 1–2. (development, culture, industry and tourism). Jaipur: ABD, 2007. p. 253. AAL.

Desai, Madhavi. *Study of Bardoli: being a history of the Bardoli satyagraha at 1928 and its sequel*. Ahmedabad: Navjivan, 1929. p. 249. SETUL.

Desai, Shambhuprasad Harprasad. *Junagadh and Girnar*. Junagadh: Prabhas, 1972. p. 65. CSSL, *GVL.

Desai, Z.A. Arabic and Persian inscriptions of Gujarat. In *Epigraphic resources in Gujarat*. Ed. by Ramlal Parikh and Rasesh Jamindar. Baroda: Butala, 1981. pp. 10–19. ASL, HML.

Desai, Ziyauddin. Written Persian sources of the history of Gujarat. In *Dr. H.G. Shastri felicitation volume (essay on Sanskrit literature Indian history, culture and archaeology)*. Ed. by P.C. Parikh, Bharati Shelat and Thomas Parmar. Ahmedabad: Dr. H.G. Shastri Felicitation volume committee, 1994. pp. 59–65. SPUL.

Devare, Hema. Gujarat's maritime connections with Southeast Asia as seen through the textile trade. In *Gujarat and the sea*. Ed. by Lotika Varadarajan. Vadodara: Darshak Itihas Nidhi, 2011. pp. 483–496. AAL, CSSL, GIDRL.

Devendra, Somasiri. "Sailing on a string and a prayer": the ORU culture in Srilanka and the Indian ocean. In *Gujarat and the sea*. Ed. by Lotika Varadarajan. Vadodara: Darshak Itihas Nidhi, 2011. pp. 109–132. AAL, CSSL, GIDRL.

Dhanju, Jaspal Kaur. *Economy and society of Northern Gujarat circa 1750–1850*. New Delhi: Khama, 1995. p. 319, ASL.

Dharaiya, R.K. *Gujarat in 1857*. Ahmedabad: Gujarat University, 1970. p. 180. CSSL, GUL, GVL, SGUL.

Dharaiya, R.K. Maitraka – Kalin Gujarat: a reappraisal. In *Dr. H.G. Shastri felicitation volume (essay on sanskrit literature Indian history, culture and archaeology)*. Ed. by P.C. Parikh, Bharati Shelat and Thomas Parmar, Ahmedabad: Dr. H.G. Shastri Felicitation volume committee, 1994. pp. 118–110. SPUL.

Dharaiya, R.K. Nationalism and constructive activities in Gujarat: the role of Jugatram Davc. In *Regional roots of India nationalism*. Ed. by Makrand Mehta. New Delhi: Criterion, 1990. pp. 252–258. GVL.

Dhavalikar, M.K. Core and periphery: Harappans in Gujarat. In *Gujarat and the sea*. Ed. by Lotika Varadarajan. Vadodara: Darshak Itihas Nidhi, 2011. pp. 253–264. AAL, CSSL, GIDRL.

Divekar, V.D. Western India. In *Cambridge economic history of India*. Vol. 2: c.1757-c. 1970. Ed. by Dharma Kumar. Hyderabad: Orient Longman, 1982. pp. 332–352. CSSL.

Dobbin, Christine. Competing elites in Bombay city politics in the mid nineteenth century 1852–83. In *Elites in south Asia.* Ed. by Edmund Leach and S.N.

Mukherjee. Cambridge: Cambridge University press, 1970. pp. 79–94. CSSL, GVL, SPIESRL.

Dosabhai, Edalji. *History of Gujarat: from the earliest period to the present time*. New Delhi: Asian Educational Services, 1986. p. 345. AAL, CSSL, HML, SPUL, SUL.

Dosabhai, Edalji. *History of Gujarat from the earliest period to the present times*. Ahmdabad: United printing, 1894. p. 345. ASL, CSSL.

Douglas, James. *Bombay and Western India*. 2v. Delhi: K.K., 1985. p. 472 and p. 414. CSSL.

Dumasia, Naoroji M. *Dharampur*. Bombay: Times Press, 1928. p. 80. SUL.

Dumasia, Naoroji M. *Jamnagar: a sketch of its ruler and its administration*. Bombay: Time Press, 1927. p. 260. CSSL.

Fairservis, Walter A. *Roots of ancient India*. London: University of Chicago, 1975. pp. 267–273. GVL.

Fawcett, Charles. *English factories in India*.Vol. III (New Series) *Bombay, Surat and Malabar coast*. Oxford: Clarendon Press, 1954. p. 436. CSSL.

Forbes, Alexander Kinloch. Râs-Mâlâ: hindu annals of western India: with particular reference to Gujarat. New Delhi: Heritage, 1973. p. 715. ASL, CSSL.

Foster, William. *Voyage of Thomas Best to the East Indies 1612–14*. New Delhi: Munshiram Manoharlal, 1997. p. 316. SETUL.

Foster, William, ed. *Voyage of Nicholas Downtown to the east India 1614–15: as recorded in contemporary narratives latter*. New Delhi: Munshiram Manoharlal, 1997. p. 224. SETUL.

Frost, Honor. From Ugarit to India via Dilmun and Lothal: stone anchors undersea and in sacred contexts. In *Gujarat and the sea*. Ed. by Lotika Varadarajan. Vadodara: Darshak Itihas Nidhi, 2011. pp. 79–88. AAL, CSSL, GIDRL.

Fukazawa, H. Western India. In *Cambridge economic history of India*. Vol. 2: c.1757-c.1970. Ed. by Dharma Kumar. Hyderabad: Orient Longman, 1982. pp. 185–206. CSSL.

Furber, Holden. *Bombay presidency in the mid eighteenth century*. Bombay: Asia, 1965. p. 76. CSSL, GVL.

Gaur, A.S., Sundaresh and Tripathi, Sila. Ancient anchorage systems in India with reference to the Gujarat coast. In *Gujarat and the sea*. Ed. by Lotika Varadarajan. Vadodara: Darshak Itihas Nidhi, 2011. pp. 89–106. AAL, CSSL, GIDRL.

Gaur, Aniruddh Singh. *Harappan maritime legacies of Gujarat*. New Delhi: Asian, 2000. p. 287. SPUL.

Gense, J.H. and Banaji, D.R., ed. *Gaikwads of Baroda: English documents,* 10 Vols. Bombay: D.B. Taraporevala, 1940. Various pages. CSSL.

Ghosh, Suresh Chandra. *Peninsula of Gujarat in the early nineteenth century*. New Delhi: Sterling, 1977. p. 163. GUL, GVL, HML, SPUL, SUL.

Gillion, Kenneth L. *Ahmedabad: a study in India urban history*. London: Cambridge University Press, 1968. p. 195. CSSL, GVL, SETUL, SPUL, SUL.

Gopal, Surendra. *Commerce and crafts in Gujarat: 16th and 17th Centuries*. New Delhi: Peoples, 1975. p. 289. CSSL, SETUL, SPIESRL.

Goswami, Chhaya. Khojas: a historical overview of the settlements overseas. In *Gujarat and the sea*. Ed. by Lotika Varadarajan. Vadodara: Darshak Itihas Nidhi, 2011. pp. 627–650. AAL, CSSL, GIDRL.

Govinden, P.C. *Kathiawar directory. 3 Parts.* 2 Vol. Rajkot: [ ], 1921. p. 764. SETUL.

Gupchup, Vijay V. *Bombay: social change 1813–1857*. Bombay: Popular, 1993. p. 352. SGUL.

Gupta, Hari Ram. *Kutch affair*. Delhi: U.C. Kapur, 1969. p. 522. SUL.

Hall, Kenneth R. 15th-century Gujarat cloth trade with Southeast Asia's Indonesian archipelago. In *Gujarat and the sea*. Ed. by Lotika Varadarajan. Vadodara: Darshak Itihas Nidhi, 2011. pp. 439–466. AAL, CSSL, GIDRL.

Hardiman, David. Baroda: the structure of a 'progressive' state. In *People, princes and paramount power: society and politics in the Indian princely state*. Ed. by Robin Jeffrey. Delhi: Oxford, 1978. pp. 107–135. CSSL.

Hardiman, David. *Histories for the subordinated*. Ranikhet: Permanent Black, 2006. p. 392. CSSL, IIML, SPUL, UML.

Hardiman, David. *Peasant nationalists of Gujarat Kheda district 1917–1934*. Delhi: Oxford, 1981. p. 309. ASL, CSSL, GUL, IIML, IRMAL, SPUL, SUL, UML.

Hardiman, David. Penetration of merchant capital in pre-colonial Gujarat. In *Capitalist development: critical essays. felicitation volume in honour of Prof. A.R. Desai*. Ed. by Ghanshyam Shah. Bombay: Popular, 1990. pp. 29–44. CSSL, IIML.

Hardiman, David. Quit India movement in Gujarat. In *Indian nation in 1942*. Ed. by Gyanendra Pandey. Calcutta: Centre for Studies in Social Sciences, 1988. pp. 77–122. GVL, SPUL.

Haynes, Douglas. From avoidance to confrontation?: a contestatory history of merchant-state relations in Surat, 1600–1924 social relations in South Asia. In *Contesting power: resistance and every day*. Ed. by Douglas Haynes and Gyan Prakash. Delhi: Oxford, 1991. pp. 239–289. CSSL, SETUL.

Haynes, Douglas E. *Small town capitalism in Western India: artisans, merchants and the making of the informal economy, 1870–1960*. New Delhi: Cambridge University press, 2012. p. 344. CSSL.

Hiromu, Nagashima. Factories and facilities of the East India companies in Surat: locations, building characteristics and ownership. In *Asian port cities, 1600–1800: local and foreign cultural interactions*. Ed. by Haneda Masahi. Japan: Kyoto University Press, 2009. pp. 192–228. CSSL.

Jamindar, Rasesh. Post-independence epigraphical discoveries in Gujarat. In *Epigraphic resources in Gujarat*. Ed. by Ramlal Parikh and Rasesh Jamindar. Baroda: Butala, 1981. pp. 20–35. ASL, HML.

Jamindar, Rasesh. Kaccha-a museum by itself. In *Art, culture and natural history of Kutch*. Ed. by S.K. Bhowmik. Vadodara: Government Press, 1976–77. pp. 25–34. CSSL, TRTIL.

Jamindar, Rasesh. Some observations on the ksatrapa epigraphs from Kaccha. In *Art, culture and natural history of Kutch*. Ed. by S.K. Bhowmik. Vadodara: Government Press, 1976–77. pp. 92–107. CSSL, TRTIL.

Jani, Mudrika. Historical background of Bhuj. In *Arts, culture and natural history of Kutch*. Ed. by S.K. Bhowmik Vadodara: Government Press, 1976–77. pp. 67–73. CSSL, TRTIL.

Jani, S.V. Baroda state-Saurashtra relation. In *New dimensions of indology (Dr. Praveen Chandra Parikh felicitation volume)*. Ed. by Dinesh Chandra, Mahendra R. Trivedi and Balaji Ganorkar. Delhi: Bhartiya Vidya, 1997. pp. 302-[ ]. GVL.

Jhaveri, Krishanlal Mohanlal. *Gujaratis: the people their history and culture*. 5vols. New Delhi: Cosmo. 2002. Various. GUL.

Jhote, Ratnamanirao. *Ahmedabad and other places of interest in Gujarat*. Ahmedabad: Gujarat Vidya Sabha, [ ]. p. 51. HML.

Johnson, Gordon. Chitpavan brahmins and politics in Western India in the late nineteenth and early twentieth centuries. In *Elites in south Asia*. Ed. by Edmund

Leach and S.N. Mukherjee. Cambridge: Cambridge University press, 1970. pp. 95–118. CSSL, SPIESRL.

Joshi, Mahipatram H. and Trivedi, Hariprasad M., ed. *Important states of India*. Idar: Mahipatram H.Joshi, 1946. p. 204. HML.

Joshi, Satyakam. Merger process of princely state Vansda in South Gujarat. In *Making of the Indian union: merger of princely states and excluded areas*. Ed. by Sajal Nag, Tejimala Gurubg and Abhijit Choudhury. New Delhi: Akansha, 2007. pp. 355–362. CSSL.

Kamath, M.V. and Kher, V.B. *Story of militant but non-violent trade unionism: a biographical and historical study*. Ahmedabad: Navjivan, 1993. p. 412. CSSL.

Kamerkar, Mani. *British paramountcy: British Baroda relations 1818–1848*. Bombay: Popular, 1980. p. 253. CSSL.

Kansara, T.P. Importance of ancient seal and other ancient collections of the Kutch museum. In *Art, culture and natural history of Kutch*. Ed. by S.K. Bhowmik. Vadodara: Government Press, 1976–77. pp. 88–91. CSSL, TRTIL.

Kapadia, Aparna. Alexander Forbes and the making of a regional history. In *Idea of Gujarat: history, ethnography and text*. Ed. by Edward Simpson and Aparna Kapadia. Hyderabad: Orient Blackswan, 2010. pp. 50–65. AAL, ASL, BUL, CEPTL, CSSL, GIDRL, IRMAL, MICAL, SETUL.

Katani, Hiroyaki. Western Indian in historical transition (seventeenth to early twentieth century) In *Structure of the case in seventeenth to nineteenth century Western Indian: the rural in the Deccan and the urban coast in coastal Gujarat*. New Delhi: Manohar, 2002. pp. 63–85. HML.

Khan, Ali Muhammad. *Mirat-i-Ahmadi: a history of Gujarat in Persian*. Baroda: Oriental Institute. 1928. p. [ ]. HML.

Khan, Ali Muhammad. *Mirat-I-Ahmadi: a Persian history of Gujarat*. Tr. by M.F. Lokhandwala. Baroda: Oriental Institute, 1965. p. 946. Gaekward's Oriental Series No. 146. CSSL, HML.

Khan, Ali Mohammed. *Political and statistical history of Gujarat*. New Delhi: Asian Educational Services, 2005. p. 427. HML.

Khan, Ali Muhammad. *Political and statistical history of Gujarat*. Tr. by James Bird. London: Oriental Translation Fund of Great Britain and Ireland, 1835. p. 427. TRTIL.

Khan, Mohammad Afzal. Iranis and commerce: a case study of Shaista Khan in Gujarat and Bengal. In *Medieval India research in the history of India*. Ed. by B.L Bhadani. New Delhi: Manohar, 2012. pp. 227–234. GVL.

Khan, Mohammed Ali. *Medieval Gujarat, its political and statistical history*. based on Mohammed Ali Khan's Mirat-i-Ahmadi transcribed in 1822 by Narsain Dass of the Kait tribe at Ahmedabad. Tr. By James Bird. New Delhi: Academic Books, 1980. p. 427. CSSL.

Khare Randhir. *Dangs: journeys into the heartland*. New Delhi: Harper Collins, 2000. p. 358. SETUL.

Khare, Randhir. *Kutch: triumph of the spirit*. New Delhi: Rupa, 2004. p. 245. CSSL.

Khare, Yogesh P. and Mehta, Ashish J. Sea level change and seashore settlement. In *Gujarat and the sea*. Ed. by Lotika Varadarajan. Vadodara: Darshak Itihas Nidhi, 2011. pp. 33–48. AAL, CSSL, GIDRL.

Khatri, Javed. Diu fisherfolk community: culture and language. In *Gujarat and the sea*. Ed. by Lotika Varadarajan. Vadodara: Darshak Itihas Nidhi, 2011. pp. 525–536. AAL, CSSL, GIDRL.

Khobrekar, V.G. *Disturbances in Gujarat, 1857–1864*. Baroda: Baroda Record Office, 1962. p. 348. SETUL.

Kolff, Dirk H.A. *Naukar, rajput and sepoy: the ethnohistory of the military labour market in Hindustan, 1450–1850*. Cambridge: Cambridge University press, 1990. p. 217. CSSL.

Kondo, Osamu. Japan and the Indian ocean at the time of the Mughal empire, with special reference to Gujarat. In *Indian Ocean: explorations in history, commerce and politics*. ed. by Satish Chandra. New Delhi: Sage, 1987. pp. 174–190. CSSL.

Kothari, Rita. Memories and movements: borders and communities in Banni, Kutch, Gujarat. Hyderabad: Orient Blackswan, 2013. p. 181. MICAL, SETUL.

Krishnan, Gauri Parimoo. Gujarati in spirit and form: unique textile from Gujarat from Southeast Asia in the collection of the Asian civilizations museum, Singapore. In *Gujarat and the sea*. Ed. by Lotika Varadarajan. Vadodara: Darshak Itihas Nidhi, 2011. pp. 467–482. AAL, CSSL, GIDRL.

Krishnan, K. and Dimri, Kiran. Exploration in the Lilka river basin in Saurashtra, Gujarat: a preliminary report. In *River valley cultures of India*. Ed. by K.K. Chakravarty and G.L. Badam. New Delhi: Aryan, 2005. pp. 199–204. HML.

Kumar, Raj. Ranjit Singh's army. In *Military system in India*. New Delhi: Common Wealth, 2004. pp. 68–87. SUL.

Lalit Kumar. Mystery of the shaking minarets of the mosque of Sidi Basir. In African elites in India. By Habshi Amarat; ed. by Kenneth X. Robbins and John Mcleod. Ahmedabad: Mapin, 2006. pp. 138–143. TRTIL.

Lalit Kumar. Some seals of Dang's chiefs of Gujarat. In *New dimensions of indology (Dr. Praveen Chandra Parikh felicitation volume)*. Ed. by Dinesh Chandra, Mahendra R. Trivedi. and Balaji Ganorkar. Delhi: Bhartiya Vidya, 1997. pp. 268-[ ]. GVL.

Leach, Edmund and Mukherjee, S.N. ed. *Elite in South Asia*. Cambridge: Cambridge University press, 1970. p. 266. CSSL, GVL, SPIESRL.

Leshnik, Lawrence S. Harappan "port" at Lothal: another view. In *Ancient cities of the Indus*. Ed. by Gregory L. Possehi. New Delhi: Vikas, 1979. pp. 203–211. CSSL.

Lokhandwala, M.F. *Zafar ul walih bi Muzaffar wa Alihi: an Arabic history of Gujarat*, Vol. I. Baroda: Oriental Institute, 1970. p. 474. Gaekwar's Oriental Series No. 152. CSSL, HML.

Lokhandwala, M.F. *Zafar Ul Walih bi Muzaffar Wa Alihi: an Arabic history of Gujarat*. Vol. 2. Baroda: Oriental Institute, 1974. p. 1055. Gaekward's Oriental Series No. 157. CSSL, HML.

Lunde, Paul. *Joao de Castro's* survey of the west coast of India (1538). In *Gujarat and the sea*. Ed. by Lotika Varadarajan. Vadodara: Darshak Itihas Nidhi, 2011. pp. 199–220. AAL, CSSL, GIDRL.

Majumdar, A.K., Succession state of the Delhi sultanate a Gujarat. In *Delhi Sultanate*. Ed. by R.C. Majumdar. Bombay: Bhartiya Vidya Bhavan, 1967. pp. 155–167. SUL.

Majumdar, Asoke Kumar. *Chaulukyas of Gujarat: a survey of the history and culture of Gujarat from the middle of the tenth to the end of the thirteenth century*. Bombay: Bharatiya Vidya Bhavan, 1956. p. 545. GUL, GVL, SPUL, SUL.

Majumdar, M.R. Historical and culture chronology of Gujarat. Baroda: M.S. University, 1960. p. 34. ASL, BVL.

Makki, Abdallah Muhammad and Denison, Ross E., ed. *Arabic history of Gujarat*. Vol. I. London: John Murray, 1910. p. 390, ASL.

Marianna, Postans. *Cutch or random sketches of Western India with legends and traditions*. New Delhi: Asian Educational Services, 2001. p. 283. MICAL.

Mathew, K.S. *Portuguese and the sultanate of Gujarat*. Delhi: Mittal, 1986. p. 263. HML.

Mayne, C. *History of the Dhvangadhra State*. Calcutta: Zhacker Spink, 1921. p. 359. SUL.

Mehta, Dinkar. Unique cave of Kutch. In *Dr. H.G. Shastri felicitation volume (essay on sanskrit literature Indian history, culture and archaeology)*. Ed. by P.C. Parikh, Bharati Shelat and Thomas Parmar. Ahmedabad: Dr. H.G. Shastri Felicitation Volume Committee, 1994. pp. 154–156. SPUL.

Mehta, Makrand. Gujarat and the sea: a study of the Jain overseas merchants in the ancient and medieval periods. In *Gujarat and the sea*. Ed. by Lotika Varadarajan. Vadodara: Darshak Itihas Nidhi, 2011. pp. 575–598. AAL, CSSL, GIDRL.

Mehta, Makrand. *Indian merchants and entrepreneurs in historical perspective: with special reference to shroffs of Gujarat: 17th to 19th centuries*. Delhi: Academic, 1991. p. 240. CSSL, SPIESRL, SPUL.

Mehta, R.N. Archaeological activities in Gujarat with special references to epigraphical finds. In *Epigraphic resources in Gujarat*. Ed. by Ramlal Parikh and Rasesh Jamindar. Baroda: Butala, 1981. pp. 40–47. ASL, HML.

Mehta, R.N. Place-names as recorded in epigraphs of Gujarat. In *Epigraphic resources in Gujarat*. Ed. by Ramlal Parikh and Rasesh Jamindar. Baroda: Butala, 1981. pp. 57–63. ASL, HML.

Mehta, R.N. Two singnet rings in the Bhuj museum. In *Art, culture and natural history of Kutch*. Ed. by S.K. Bhowmik. Vadodara: Government Press, 1976–77. pp. 85–87. CSSL, TRTIL.

Mehta, R.N. When Rabbit attacked a dog': origin of Ahmedabad. In *New dimensions of indology (Dr. Praveen Chandra Parikh felicitation volume)*. Ed. by Dinesh Chandra, Mahendra R. Trivedi. and Balaji Ganorkar. Delhi: Bhartiya Vidya, 1997. pp. 136-[ ]. GVL.

Mehta, Shirin. *Peasantry and nationalism: a study of the Bardoli satyagraha*. New Delhi: Manohar, 1984. p. 215. CSSL.

Mehta, Shirin. Socio-economic origins of a business community: the Bhatias of Kutch as overseas merchants. In *Gujarat and the sea*. Ed. by Lotika Varadarajan. Vadodara: Darshak Itihas Nidhi, 2011. pp. 613–626. AAL, CSSL, GIDRL.

Menon, V.P. Deccan and Gujarat state. In *Story of the integration of the Indian states*. By V.P. Menon. Delhi: Orient Longmans, 1961. pp. 190–200. CSSL, SPUL.

Menon, V.P. Saurashtra. In *Story of the integration of the Indian states*. By V.P. Menon. New Delhi: Orient Longmans, 1961. pp. 167–189. CSSL, SPUL.

Merh, Sukumar S. Changing land-sea relationship in the Ranns of Kachchh: a geoarchaeological perspective. In *Gujarat and the sea*. Ed. by Lotika Varadarajan. Vadodara: Darshak Itihas Nidhi, 2011. pp. 11–32. AAL, CSSL, GIDRL.

Mishra, V.B. *Gujarat prathiuras and their times*. Delhi: S. Chand, 1966. p. 150. SUL.

Misra, S.C. *Rise of Muslim power in Gujarat: a history of Gujarat from 1298 to 1442*. New Delhi: Munshiram Manoharlal, 1982. p. 252. CSSL, GUL, HML, SPIESRL, SUL.

Misra, S.C. Studies in the history of Gujarat. In *Studies in modern Indian history: regional survey*. Ed. by S.P. Sen. Calcutta: Institute of Historical Studies, 1969. pp. 63–71. GVL, SPUL.

Misra, S.C. and Rahman, M.L. *Mirat-I-Sikandiri: a history of Gujarat from the inception of the dynasty of the sultans of Gujarat to the conquest of Gujarat by Akbar of Shaikh Sikandar IBN Mohammad Urf Manjnu IBN Akbar*. Baroda: M.S. University, 1958. p. 249. Department of History Series No. 3. CSSL, GUL.

Mistri, Manibhai. Size of the missing main idol of the Sun temple at Modhera. In *Dr. H.G. Shastri felicitation volume (essay on Sanskrit literature Indian history, culture and archaeology)*. Ed. by P.C. Parikh, Bharati Shelat and Thomas Parmar. Ahmedabad: Dr. H.G. Shastri Felicitation volume committee, 1994. pp. 159–162. SPUL.

Momin, K.N. Route-indicators of the sultanate period in Gujarat. In *Aspects of Indian history and culture.* Ed. by C.E. Ramachandran and K.V. Raman. New Delhi: Books & Books, 1984. pp. 309–316. GVL.

Moreland, W.H. and Geyl, P. Burhanpur and Gujarat. In *Jahangir's India: the remonstrantie of francisco pelsaert*. Delhi: Idarah-I-Adabiyat-I Delli, 1972. pp. 37–43. IAD Oriental Series No. 8. SPUL.

Munshi, K.M. *Glory that was Gurjaradesa (the Maharaja Solanki millennial celebration volume) Part–III – the imperial Gurjaras*. Bombay: Bharatiya Vidya Bhavan, 1944. p. 284. GUL.

Munshi, K.M. *Glory that was Gurjaradesa.* Bombay: Bharatiya Vidya Bhavan, 1955. p. 505. GUL, HML, IIML, SUL.

Munshi, K.M. *Glory that was Gujaradesa, part I. pre-historic west coast*. Bombay: Bhartiya Vidya Bhavan, 1943. p. 136. ASL.

Munshi, K.M. *Somnath the shrine eternal.* Gujarat: Somnath Board of Trustees, 1951. p. 115. GVL, HML, SUL.

Murdeshwar, Anand K. Kutch state. In *Administrative problems relating to nationalisation*. Bombay: Popular, 1957. pp. 246–298. SUL.

Nanavati, J.M. *Ceilings in the temples of Gujarat.* Baroda: Government press, 1914. p. [ ]. BVL.

Nanji, Rukshana. Merchants and mariners: a review of early Parsi settlements on the coast of Western India, with special reference to Sanjan. In *Gujarat and the sea*. Ed. by Lotika Varadarajan. Vadodara: Darshak Itihas Nidhi, 2011. pp. 551–574. AAL, CSSL, GIDRL.

Nightingale, Pamela. *Trade and empire in Western India 1784–1806*. Cambridge: Cambridge University press, 1970. p. 264. CSSL, SPUL.

Osada, Toshiki. *Indu civilization: text and context*. New Delhi: Manohar, 2006. p. 269. CSSL, UML.

Ottolenghi, Roberto. Kutch and Kathiawar. In *Invincible traveller*. Ed. by Raj Thapar. Ghaziabad: Vikas, 1980. pp. 140–151. GUL.

Ovington, J. *Voyage to Surat: in the year 1689.* Ed. by H.G. Rawlinson. New Delhi: Asian Educational, 1994. [London: Oxford, 1929]. p. 313. CSSL.

Pandit, Sunderlal. Annexation of Surat. In *How India lost her freedom*. by Sunderlal Pandit. Bombay: Popular, 1970. pp. 190–192. CSSL, SPUL.

Pandya, Amrit. *New dynasties of Gujarat history*. Bombay: Oxford, 1950. p. [ ]. BVL.

Pandya, Amrit V. *New dynasties of medieval Gujarat.* Vallabh Vidyanagar: Swastik, 1969. p. 80. *GVL, TRTIL.

Pandya, G.B. *Gaikwads of Baroda: Maharaja Sayajirao II, A.D. 1821 to A.D. 1830.* selections from the Baroda residency records. Baroda: M.S. University, 1958. p. 267. CSSL, GVL.

Pandya, Kaushik. *Journey to the glorious Gujarat*. Ahmedabad: Akshara, 2007. p. [ ]. BUL.

Pandya, Maheshchandra. Role of dalit leaders during the Indian freedom struggle: a case study of Sabarkantha District. In *Regional roots of India nationalism*. Ed. by Makrand Mehta. New Delhi: Criterion, 1990. pp. 196–203. GVL.

Pandya, Suman. Harappan culture in Gujarat. In *Essays in Indian protohistory.* Ed. by D.P. Agrawal and Dilip K. Chakrabarti. Delhi: B.R., 1979. pp. 49–57. SPUL, TRTIL.

Pandya, Suman H. Chalcolithic personality of Gujarat: a survey. In *New dimensions of indology (Dr. Praveen Chandra Parikh feliciation volume).* Ed. by Dinesh Chandra, Mahendra R. Trivedi. and Balaji Ganorkar. Delhi: Bhartiya Vidya, 1997. pp. 174-[ ]. GVL.

Parekh, Shailesh. *Tagor in Ahmedabad*. Kolkata: Visva-Bharati, 2008. p. 111. SETUL.

Parekh, V.S. Daksinamurti sculptures from Gujarat. In *Aspects of Indian history and culture.* Ed. by C.E. Ramachandran and K.V. Raman. New Delhi: Books & Books, 1984. pp. 285-[ ]. GVL.

Parikh, P.C. Evolution of Brahmi into Nagari script in Gujarat: a brief survey. In *Dr. H.G. Shastri felicitation volume (essay on Sanskrit literature Indian history, culture and archaeology)*. Ed. by P.C. Parikh, Bharati Shelat and Thomas Parmar. Ahmedabad: Dr. H.G. Shastri Felicitation volume committee, 1994. pp. 51–55. SPUL.

Parikh, Pravin. Development of Brahmi script in Gujarat. In *Epigraphic resources in Gujarat*. Ed. by Ramlal Parikh and Rasesh Jamindar. Baroda: Butala, 1981. pp. 73–80. ASL, HML.

Parikh, R.G. Sidelights on the places and social & economic life of the people of Gujarat during the seventeenth century as recorded by the French travellers in India. In *Dr. H.G. Shastri felicitation volume (essay on Sanskrit literature Indian history, culture and archaeology)*. Ed. by P.C. Parikh, Bharati Shelat and Thomas Parmar, Ahmedabad: Dr. H.G. Shastri Felicitation volume committee, 1994. pp. 79–82. SPUL.

Parikh, Ramlal and Jamindar, Rasesh. *Epigraphic resources in Gujarat*. Baroda: Butala, 1981. p. 80. ASL, HML, SGUL.

Parmar, Ladhabhai Harji, Compli. *Rewakantha directory.* Vol. 1 and 2. Rajkot: Parmar Press, 1922. p. [ ]. SETUL.

Parmioo, Ratan. Sea voyages in the story of shripâla râsa from the Gujarat coast with supplementary notes from Shri Jagadu Charita. In *Gujarat and the sea*. Ed. by Lotika Varadarajan. Vadodara: Darshak Itihas Nidhi, 2011. pp. 509–524. AAL, CSSL, GIDRL.

Parwez, Mohammad. Process of integration of Junagarh. In *Making of the Indian union: merger of princely states and excluded areas*. Ed. by Sajal Nag, Tejimala Gurubg and Abhijit Choudhury. New Delhi: Akansha, 2007. pp. 146–158. CSSL.

Patel, Ambika S. *Iron technology in early historic India: a case study of Gujarat.* Delhi: Sandeep, 2007. p. 167. CEPTL.

Patel, Arjun. Process of integration of Baroda state with Indian union. In *Making of the Indian union: Merger of princely states and excluded areas*. Ed. by Sajal Nag, Tejimala Gurubg and Abhijit Choudhury. New Delhi: Akansha, 2007. pp. 30–35. CSSL.

Patel, G.D. Ahmedabad district. In *How India lost her freedom*. Bombay: Popular, 1970. pp. 22–38. CSSL, SPUL.

Patel, G.D. *Land problem of reorganized Bombay state.* Bombay: N.M. Tripathi, 1957. p. 466. GVL.

Patel, Sujata and Thorner, Alice., ed. *Bombay: mosaic of modern culture*. Bombay: Oxford, 1995. p. 235. CSSL.

Pearson, M.N. *Costal Western India: studies from the Portuguese records*. New Delhi: Concept, 1981. p. 149. CSSL.

Pereira, Jose Manuel Malhao. Indian Ocean and Chinese techniques of navigation: reflections on nautical information from early Portuguese sources. In *Gujarat and the sea*. Ed. by Lotika Varadarajan. Vadodara: Darshak Itihas Nidhi, 2011. pp. 181–198. AAL, CSSL, GIDRL.

Pillai, S. Devadas. Rajahs and prajas: *an Indian princely state, then and now*. Bombay: Popular, 1976. p. 133. ASL, CSSL, SPUL.

Pomey, Patrice. Comparative study of sewn boats from the Mediterranean, the Red sea and the Indian Ocean: the question of Gujarat. In *Gujarat and the sea*. Ed. by Lotika Varadarajan. Vadodara: Darshak Itihas Nidhi, 2011. pp. 133–146. AAL, CSSL, GIDRL.

Possehl, Geogory. Date of the Surkotada cemetery: a reassessment in light of recent archaelogical work in Gujarat. In *Face of Indian civilization*. Ed. by Jagat Pati Joshi. New Delhi; Aryan Book International, 1997. pp. 81–88. GVL.

Possehl, Gregory L. *Indu civilization in Saurashtra*. Delhi: B.R., 1980, p. 264. SPUL.

Possehl, Gregory L. Lothal: a gateway settlement of the Harappan civilization. In *Ancient cities of the Indus*. Ed. by Gregory L. Possehl. New Delhi: Vikas, 1979. pp. 212–218. CSSL.

Prajapati, Manibhai K. *Glorious history & culture of Anhilwad Patan (Gujarat)*. Patan: Satyam, 2009. p. 858. SGUL.

Prasad, Pushpa. Akbar and the Jains. In *Akbar and his India*. Ed. by Irfan Habib. Delhi: Oxford, 1997. pp. 97–108. SETUL.

Prasad, Pushpa. *Lekhapaddhati: documents of state and everyday life from ancient and early medieval Gujarat, 9th to 15th centuries*. New Delhi: Oxford, 2007. p. 245. CSSL, HML.

Rai, Govind Chandra. Finger rings and their development: Harappa-Mohenjodara culture in Studies.In *Studies in the development of ornaments and jewellery in proto-historical India*. Varnashi: Chwkhaba Sanskrit Series, 1964. pp. 131–134. SUL.

Rai, Govind Chandra. Foot ornaments and other pieces of jewellery: Harappa-Mohenjodara culture. In *Studies in the development of ornaments and jewellery in proto-historical India*. Varnashi: Chwkhaba Sanskrit Series, 1964. pp. 149–150. SUL.

Rai, Govind Chandra. Girdles-beads, spacers and terminal: Harappa-Mohenjodara culture. In *Studies in the development of ornaments and jewellery in proto-historical India*. Varnashi: Chwkhaba Sanskrit Series, 1964. pp. 139–143. SUL.

Rai, Govind Chandra. Neck and breast ornaments and their development: Harappa-Mohenjodara culture. In *Studies in the development of ornaments and jewellery in proto-historical India*. Varnashi: Chwkhaba Sanskrit Series, 1964. pp. 65–105. SUL.

Rai, Govind Chandra. Ornaments of the ears and their development: Harappa-Mohenjodara culture. In *studies in the development of ornaments and jewellery in proto-historical India*. Varnashi: Chwkhaba Sanskrit Series, 1964. pp. 34–37. SUL.

Rai, Govind Chandra. Ornaments of the head and their development: Harappa-Mohenjodara culture. In *Studies in the development of ornaments and jewellery in proto-historical India*. Varnashi: Chwkhaba Sanskrit Series, 1964. pp. 10–27. SUL.

Rai, Govind Chandra. Sequence of culture based on ornaments: Harappa-Mohenjodara culture. In *Studies in the development of ornaments and jewellery in proto-historical India*. Varnashi: Chwkhaba Sanskrit Series, 1964. pp. 214–219. SUL.

Rajgor, Dilip. Roman currency in Gujarat. In *New dimensions of indology (Dr. Praveen Chandra Parikh felicitation volume)*. Ed. by Dinesh Chandra, Mahendra R. Trivedi and Balaji Ganorkar. Delhi: Bhartiya Vidya, 1997. pp. 197-[ ]. GVL.

Rajyagor, S.B. *History of Gujarat*. New Delhi: S. Chand, 1982. p. 539. BUL, CSSL, HML, IIML, SPUL, SUL.

Rao, S.R. *Lothal and the Indus civilization*. Bombay: Asia, 1973. pp. 39–49. SPUL.

Rao, S.R. "Persian Gulf" seal from Lothal. In *Ancient cities of the Indus*. Ed. by Gregory Possehi. New Delhi: Vikas, 1979. pp. 148–150. CSSL.

Rao, S.R. Contacts between Lothal and Susa. In *Ancient cities of the Indus*. Ed. by Gregory Possehl. New Delhi: Vikas, 1979. pp. 174–175. CSSL.

Rao, S.R and Devkar, V.L. *Excavations at Amreli*. Baroda: Museum and Picture Gallery, 1966. p. 114. GVL, SUL.

Raval, R.L. Cultural perspectives of the emerging nationalism in the Nineteenth century Gujarat. In *Regional roots of Indian nationalism*. ed. by Makrand J. Mehta. New Delhi: Criterion, 1990. pp. 15–28. GVL.

Raval, R.L. Transition profile of Kutch (1809 to 1860). In *Art, culture and natural history of Kutch*. Ed. by S.K. Bhowmik. Vadodara: Government Press, 1976–77. pp. 35–58. CSSL, TRTIL.

Rawlinson, H.G. Foundation of the company and Hawkins mission to Surat. In *British beginnings in Western India 1579–1657*. Bombay: Clarendon Press, 1920. pp. 35–51. SPUL.

Rawlinson, H.G. Struggle with the Portuguese by sea 1612–35. In *British beginnings in Western India 1579–1657*. Bombay: Clarendon Press, 1920. pp. 89–99. SPUL.

Ray, Mihir Kumar. Paramountcy in action (ii) Baroda. In *Princely states and the paramount power 1858–1876*. by Mihir Kumar Ray. New Delhi: Rajesh, 1981. pp. 158–192. CSSL, SPUL.

Reddy, C.G.K. *Baroda dynamite conspiracy: the right to rebel*. New Delhi: Vision, 1977. p. 176. CSSL.

Richards, John F. *Mughal empire*. Cambridge: Cambridge University press, 1993. p. 320. CSSL, SETUL.

Rodrigues, Vitor Luis Gaspar. '*Easternisation*' of the Portuguese fleets in the Asian seas during the 16th century: causes and consequences. In *Gujarat and the sea*. Ed. by Lotika Varadarajan. Vadodara: Darshak Itihas Nidhi, 2011. pp. 221–250. AAL, CSSL, GIDRL.

Rushbrook Williams, L.F. *Black hills: Kutch in history and legend: a study in Indian local loyalties*. London: Weidenfeld and Nicolson, 1958. p. 276. CSSL, GIDEL, GUL, SETUL.

Saletore, Bhasker Anand. *Main currents in the ancient history of Gujarat*. Baroda: M.S. University, 1960. p. 73. BVL, CSSL, GUL, GVL, HML, SUL.

Sangar, Satya Prakash. *Indian textiles: in the seventeenth century*. New Delhi: Reliance, 1998. p. 236. SETUL.

Sankalia, H.D. *Archaeology of Gujarat (including Kathiawar)*. Bombay: Natwarlal, 1941. p. 268. BVL, GUL, GVL, SGUL.

Sankalia, H.D. *Indian archaeology today*. Delhi: Ajanta, 1979. p. 204. CSSL.

Sankalia, Hasmukh D. *Studies in the historical & cultural geography and ethnography of Gujarat*. Poona: Deccan College, 1949. p. 245. Deccan College Monograph Series No. 3. BVL, HML, SPUL.

Savalia, R.T. Antiquity of the prevalence of shakti worship in Gujarat. In *Dr. H.G. Shastri felicitation volume (essay on Sanskrit literature Indian history, culture and archaeology)*. Ed. by: Parikh, P.C., Shelat, Bharati. Parmar, Thomas. Ahmedabad: Dr. H.G. Shastri Felicitation volume committee, 1994. pp. 137–138. SPUL.

Schwatcts, Paul. *Printing on cotton at Ahmedabad India in 1678.* Ahmedabad: S.R. Bastikar, 1969. p. 28.*GVL.

Sen, S.P. State of affairs of the French company at Surat. *In French in India first establishment and struggle.* by S.P. Sen Calcutta: University of Calcutta, 1947. pp. 62–96. GVL.

Shah, Kunjlata N. Hind and Britannia the first patriotic novel in Gujarati language. In *Regional roots of Indian nationalism.* ed. by Makrand J. Mehta. New Delhi: Criterion, 1990. pp. 28–38. GVL.

Shah, Priyabala. In epigraphically resources of the temples of Gujarat. In *Epigraphic resources in Gujarat*. Ed. by Ramlal Parikh and Rasesh Jamindar. Baroda: Butala, 1981. pp. 36–39. ASL, HML.

Sharma, R.K. *History, archaeology and culture of the Narmada valley*. Delhi: Sharada, [ ]. p. 316. UML.

Shastri, H.G. Inscriptions of Gujarat: a brief survey. In *Epigraphic resources in Gujarat*. Ed. by Ramlal Parikh and Rasesh Jamindar. Baroda: Butala, 1981. pp. 1–9. ASL, HML.

Shastri, H.G. and Nanavati, Rajendra I. *Gujarat under the maitrakas of Valabhi.* Vadodara: University of Delhi, 2000. p. [ ]. BVL.

Sheikh, Samira. *Forging a region: sultans, traders, and pilgrims in Gujarat, 1200–1500.* New Delhi: Oxford, 2010. p. 265. AAL, CSSL, IIML, SPUL.

Shelat, Bharati. Eras used in the epigraphic records of Gujarat. In *Epigraphic resources in Gujarat*. Ed. by Ramlal Parikh and Rasesh Jamindar. Baroda: Butala, 1981. pp. 64–72. ASL, HML.

Shelat, J.M. Gujarat. In *Bhavan's book university: Akbar*. Bombay: Bharatiya Vidya Bhavan, 1964. pp. 120–142. SPUL.

Shinde, Vasant, Deshpande, Shweta and Deshpande, Sanjay. *Heritage sites of Gujarat: a gazetteer*. New Delhi: Aryan, 2011. p. 337. HML.

Shokoohy, Mehrdad. Sidi Sayyid-or Sidi Said-Masque in Ahmedabad. In *African elites in India.* by Habshi Amarat. Ed. by Kenneth X. Robbins and John Mcleod. Ahmedabad: Mapin, 2006. pp. 144–161. TRTIL.

Shukla, Jaykumar R. Student and Indian freedom struggle: a case study of Gujarat college students strike (Ahmedabad). In *Regional roots of Indian nationalism.* Ed. by Makrand Mehta. New Delhi: Criterion, 1990. pp. 164–173. GVL.

Siddiqi, Iqtidar Husain. Diplomatic relation between the rulers of Delhi and Gujarat during the Sixteenth century. In *Medieval India a miscellany,* Vol. 3. Ed. by Aligarh Muslim University. Bombay: Asia, 1975. pp. 113–126. GVL.

Siddiqui, Iqtidar Husain. Interstate relationship: the sultanates of Delhi and Gujarat. In *Composite culture under: the sultanate of Delhi*. Delhi: Primus, 2012. pp. 101–116. SPUL.

Sikandar Manjhu, Gujarati. *Mirati sikandari: a study in the medieval history of Gujarat*. Tr. By Fazlullah Lutfullah Faridi. (Bombay: Education Society's Press, 1899). Gurgaon: Vintage, 1990. p. 327. CSSL, IIML.

Simpson, Edward. Kutch and the sea. In *Gujarat and the sea*. Ed. by Lotika Varadarajan. Vadodara: Darshak Itihas Nidhi, 2011. pp. 537–548. AAL, CSSL, GIDRL.

Simpson, Edward. Making sense of the history of Kutch. In *Idea of Gujarat: history, ethnography and text*. Ed. by Edward Simpson and Aparna Kapadia. Hyderabad: Orient Blackswan, 2010. pp. 66–83. AAL, ASL, BUL, CSSL, CEPTL, GIDRL, IRMAL, MICAL, SETUL.

Simpson, Edward and Kapadia, Aparna, ed. *Idea of Gujarat: history, ethnography and text*. Hyderabad: Orient Blackswan, 2010. p. 268. AAL, ASL, BUL, CSSL, CEPTL, GIDRL, IRMAL, MICAL, SETUL.

Singh, Nagendra. ed., *Local Muhammadan dynasties Gujarat*. New Delhi: S. Chand, 1970. p. 541. CSSL, GVL, HML, SPIESRL.

Singhal, C.R. *Catalogue of the coin in the prince of Wales museum of Western India, Bombay the sultans of Gujarat*. Bombay: British India Press, 1935. p. 154. GVL.

Sonawane, V.H. Harappan and Harappan – affiliated chalcolithic settlements of Rupen, Saraswati and Banas river valleys of North Gujarat. In *River valley cultures of India*. Ed. by K.K. Chakravarty and G.L. Badam. New Delhi: Aryan, 2005. pp. 205–278. HML.

Sonawane, V.H. Sailing boats depicted in rock art at Chamardi in Gujarat. In *Gujarat and the sea*. Ed. by Lotika Varadarajan. Vadodara: Darshak Itihas Nidhi, 2011. pp. 499–508. AAL, CSSL, GIDRL.

Soundara Rajan, K.V. *Ahmedabad*. New Delhi: Archeological Survey of India, 1980. p. 71. SETUL.

Spodek, Howard. *Ahmedabad: shock city of twentieth-century India*. Hyderabad: Orient Blackswan, 2012. p. 330. AAL, CSSL, SETUL, SPUL, UML.

Spodek, Howard. *Urban-rural integration regional development: a case study of Saurashtra, India, 1800–1960*. Chicago: University of Chicago, 1976. p. 144. CSSL, SETUL, SGUL.

Srivastava, Ashirbadilal. Conquest of Gujarat, new administrative measures. In *Akbar the great,* Vol. I, Agra: Shiva Lal Agarwala, 1962. pp. 131–154. SPUL.

Srivastava, Ashirbadilal. Man Singh in Bihar, conquest of Orissa, Junagarh and Saurashtra. In *Akbar the great,* Vol. I. Agra: Shivalal Agrawala, 1962. pp. 370–383. SPUL.

Subrahamanayam, Sanjay. Mughal Gujarat and the Iberian world in the transition of 1580–1. In *Explorations in connected history: mughals and franks*. New Delhi: Oxford, 2005. pp. 42–70. SPUL.

Subramanian, Lakshmi. *Indigenous capital and imperial expansion: Bombay, Surat and West Coast*. Delhi: Oxford, 1996. p. 369. IIML.

Subramanian, Lakshmi. Power and the weave: weavers, merchants and rulers in eighteenth-century Surat. In *Politics and trade in the Indian Ocean world: essays in honour of Ashin Das Gupta*. Ed. by Rudrangshu Mukherjee and Lakshmi Subramanian. New Delhi: Oxford, 2003. pp. 52–82. CSSL, HML, SETUL.

Sundaresh, Gaur, A.S. and Tripathi, Sila. Maritime archaeology of the Okhamandal region, Gujarat. In *Gujarat and the sea*. Ed. by Lotika Varadarajan. Vadodara: Darshak Itihas Nidhi, 2011. pp. 63–78. AAL, CSSL, GIDRL.

Tarachand. *Some aspects of medieval Gujarat*. Delhi: Oriental, 1968. p. 150. SPUL.

Thakkar, Ramesh J. Handsome desert beast. In *Art, culture and natural history of Kutch*. Ed. by S.K. Bhowmik. Vadodara: Government Press, 1976–77. pp. 108–113. CSSL, TRTIL.

Thapar, Romila. *Somanatha: the many voices of a history*. New Delhi: Penguin, 2004. p. 260. CSSL, SETUL.

Thomaz, Luis Filipe F.R. Forgotten Portuguese document of the economic history of Gujarat. In *Gujarat and the sea*. Ed. by Lotika Varadarajan. Vadodara: Darshak Itihas Nidhi, 2011. pp. 315–350. AAL, CSSL, GIDRL.

Tirmizi, S.A.I. Muslim merchants of medieval Gujarat. In *Business communities of India: a historical perspective.* Ed. by Dwijendra Tripathi. New Delhi: Manohar, 1984. pp. 59–67. CSSL, HML, SPUL.

Tirmizi, S.A.I. *Some aspects of medieval Gujarat.* Delhi: Munshiram Manoharlal, 1968. p. 150. CEPTL, CSSL, GVL, GUL, HML, SUL.

Tripathi, Alok. Harappan ships and maritime spheres. In *Gujarat and the sea*. Ed. by Lotika Varadarajan. Vadodara: Darshak Itihas Nidhi, 2011. pp. 265–280. AAL, CSSL, GIDRL.

Trivedi, A.B. *Post-war Gujarat: an economic survey after world war II*. Bombay: Author, 1949. p. 289. CSSL, BVL, GVL.

Turab Vali, Mir Abu. *History of Gujarat*. Ed. by E. Denison Ross. Calcutta: Asiatic Society of Bengal, 1909. p. 110. ASL.

Vanina, Eugenia. *Urban crafts and craftsmen in medieval India: thirteenth-eighteenth centuries.* New Delhi: Munshiram Manoharlal, 2004. p. 196. SETUL.

Varadarajan, Lotika, Mankad, Rupal and Ajabia, Himanshu. Windows on Gujarat: an ethno-technological reconstruction. In *Gujarat and the sea*. Ed. by Lotika Varadarajan. Vadodara: Darshak Itihas Nidhi, 2011. pp. 155–178. AAL, CSSL, GIDRL.

Varadarajan, Lotika, ed. *Gujarat and the sea.* Vadodara: Darshak Itihas Nidhi, 2011. p. 653. AAL, CSSL, GIDRL.

Vasa, Pulin. Nani Rayan in Kachchh: archaeological evidences of shipping and trade in ancient India. In *Gujarat and the sea*. Ed. by Lotika Varadarajan. Vadodara: Darshak Itihas Nidhi, 2011. pp. 281–296. AAL, CSSL, GIDRL.

Verma, Susan. Archaeology of the early temples of Saurashtra. In *Archaeology as history in early south Asia.* Ed. by Himanshu Prabha Ray and Carla M. Sinopoli. New Delhi: Indian Council of Historical Research, 2004. pp. 411–425. GVL.

Verma, Tripta. *Karkhanas: under the Mughals from Akbar to Aurangzeb*. Delhi: Pragati, 1994. p. 181. SETUL.

Virji, Krishnakumari J. *Ancient history of Saurashtra: being a study of the Maitrakas of Valabhi V to VIII centuries A.D.* Bombay: Konkan Institute of Arts and Science, 1952. p. 354. Indian History and Culture Series. GUL, SGUL, SUL, UML.

Vora, K.H., Gaur, A.S. and Sundaresh. Archaeological sites along the Gujarat coast: proxoes to decipher the past shoreline. In *Gujarat and the sea*. Ed. by Lotika Varadarajan. Vadodara: Darshak Itihas Nidhi, 2011. pp. 49–62. CSSL, GIDRL.

Vora, P.K. Kutch yesterday and Kutch today. In *Art, culture and natural history of Kutch.* Ed. by S.K. Bhowmik. Vadodara: Government Press, 1976–77. pp. 59–63. CSSL, TRTIL.

Wadhwa, D.C. *Agrarian legislation in India: 1793–1966.* Vol. 1. Bombay: Orient Longman, 1973. p. 865. CSSL.

Watson, J.W. *History of Gujarat*. (Bombay: Government Central Press, 1876). New Delhi: Cosmo, 1983. p. 154. CSSL, HML, SPUL.

Weber, Thomas. Historiography and the Dandi march: the other myths of Gandhi's salt march. In *Facets of Mahatma Gandhi*. Vol. 1: *non-violence and satyagraha*. Ed. by Subrata Mukherjee and Sushila Ramaswamy. New Delhi: Deep & Deep, 1996. pp. 192–214. CSSL.

Weber, Thomas. *On the salt march: the historiography of Gandhi's march to Dandi.* New Delhi: Harper Collins, 1997. p. 594. SETUL.

Wilberforce-Bell, H. *History of Kathiawad: from the earliest times.* New Delhi: Ajay, 1980. p. 313. CSSL, SETUL, TRTIL.

Wood, John R. Rajkot: Indian nationalism in the princely context: the Rajkot satyagraha of 1938–9. In *People, princes and paramount power: society and politics in the Indian princely state.* Ed. by Robin Jeffrey. Delhi: Oxford, 1978. pp. 240–274. CSSL.

Wormser, Paul and Guillot, Claude. Gujarat and the Malay world, 15 th-17th centuries: trade and influence. In *Gujarat and the sea.* Ed. by Lotika Varadarajan. Vadodara: Darshak Itihas Nidhi, 2011. pp. 405–424. AAL, CSSL, GIDRL.

Yagnik, Achyut and Sheth, Suchitra. *Ahmedabad: from royal city to megacity.* Delhi: Penguin, 2011. p. 348. SETUL.

Yagnik, Achyut and Sheth, Suchitra. Shaping of modern Gujarat: Plurality, hindutva and beyond. New Delhi: Peiguin, 2005. p. 328. CSSL, EDIL, GIDRL IIML, MICAL, SETUL.

Zeuner, Frederick. *Stone age and pleistocene chronology in Gujarat.* Poona: Deccan College, 1950. p. 46. GVL.

Journal Articles

Afrozasultana and Rafiqasultana. Ethno-archaeological history of Gujarat. *Adivasi Gujarat.* 13, 1, 2003. pp. 40–47. CSSL, GVL, SPIESRL, TRTIL.

Bajpai, Gita. Colonial rule and the princely state of Baroda: a study in some aspects of the imperial connections in the second half of the nineteenth century. *Journal of Indian History.* 63, 1–3, 1985. pp. 239–253. GVL.

Bajpai, Gita. Some aspects of continuity and changes of the Baroda. *Journal of Indian History.* 58, 1–3, 1980. pp. 63–74. GVL, HML.

Bellasis, A.F. Old tombs in the cemeteries of Surat. *Journal of the Bombay Branch of the Royal Asiatic Society.* [ ], [ ], 1861. pp. 140–156. GVL.

Benjamin, N. Arab merchants of Bombay and Surat (c.1800–1840). *Indian Economic and Social History Review.* 13, 1, 1976. pp. 85–95. CSSL, IIML, UML.

Bhagat, Niranjan. Garavi Gujarat. *Seminar.* 470, 1998. pp. 47–51. CSSL, MICAL, UML.

Bhagia, Indra G. Interesting facets of two Tughlaq dynasty coins found recently in Gujarat. *Journal of the Numismatic Society of India.* 51, 1–2, 1989. pp. 29–32. HML.

Bhan, Kuldeep. Nageshwara: a matyre Harappan shell working site on the Gulf of Kutch, Gujarat. *Journal of the Oriental Institute.* 34, 1–2, 1984. pp. 67–80. GVL.

Bharucha, Atusha. History of the Western kshatrapas of Gujarat. *Journal of Oriental Institute.* 47, 3–4, 1998. pp. 289–296. GVL.

Biddulph, C.H. Silver coins of Surat mint with regional years later than the Forty-Ninth, or last, year of Shah Alam II. *Journal of the Numismatic Society of India.* 25, 1, 1963. pp. 115–129. HML.

Chaghatai, M.A. Muslim monuments of Ahmedabad: through their inscriptions. *Bulletin of the Deccan College Research Institute.* 3, 2, 1942. pp. 79–180. HML.

Chowdhary, S.N. Excavation of Buddhist stupa and vihara at Devni-mori near Shamalaji-North Gujarat. *Journal of the Oriental Institute.* 9, 4, 1960. pp. 451–458. GVL.

Commissariat, M.S. Brief history of the Gujarat saltanat. *Journal of the Bombay Branch Royal Asiatic Society*. 26, 74–75, 1921–23. pp. 99–157. GVL.

Das, Maya. Kachh and debajani. *Modern Review*. 93, 2, 1953. pp. 85–104. GVL.

Dasgupta, Arun A. and Pearson, M.N. Merchants and rulers in Gujarat: the response to the Portuguese in the sixteenth century. *Indian Economic and Social Histoey Review*. 15, 3, 1978. pp. 410-[ ]. HML.

Dasgupta, Ashin. Pieter Phoonsen of Surat, c.1730–1740. *Modern Asian Studies*. 22, 3, 1988. pp. 551–560. CSSL.

Dave, J.H. Somnath. *Bhavan's Journal*. 2, 1, 1955. pp. 98–110. GVL.

Dave, K.B. Ancient temples of Gujarat. *Journal of the Gujarat Research Society*. 5, 2, 1943. pp. 104–110. GVL.

Dave, Kanaiyalal R. Unique metal image of Sun from Gujarat. *Journal of the Oriental Institute*. 4, 4, 1955. pp. 405–406. GVL.

Desai, G.J, Some factual errors in the account of Surat (1746–48) given in the gazetteer of Surat District(1962). *South Gujarat University Journal*. 1, 1972. pp. 96–104. GVL.

Desai, G.J. Some factual errors in the account of Surat (1748–51) given in the gazetteer of Surat District(1962). *South Gujarat University Journal*. 2–3, 1973–1974. pp. 57–66. GVL.

Desai, Gunvant J. Composition and revenue estimates of Surat aththavisi paragnas according to different authorities of the eighteenth century. *South Gujarat University Journal*. 4, 1975. pp. 107–113. GVL.

Desai, T.M. Post-War planning in Bombay province-with special reference to British Gujarat. *Journal of the Gujarat Research Society*. 11, 1, 1949. pp. 16–20. GUL.

Desai, Z.A. Biscriptal Mughal inscription from Gujarat. *Journal of the Oriental Institute*. 35, 3–4, 1986. pp. 283–290. GVL.

Deshpande-Mukherjee, Arati. Shellfishing and shell crafts during the Harappan period in Gujarat. *Man and Environment*. 23, 1, 1998. pp. 63–80. HML.

Desoulieres, Alain. Mughal diplomacy in Gujarat (1533–1534) in Correia's 'Lendas da India'. *Modern Asian Studies*. 22, 3, 1988. pp. 433–454. CSSL.

Dhaky, M.A. Vyala figures of the temples of Gujarat. *Journal of the Gujarat Research Society*. 23, 4/92, 1961. pp. 293–298. GVL.

Divanji, P.C. Pre Historic Aryan settlements on the soils of Gujarat. *Journal of the Gujarat Research Society*. 8, 2 and 3, 1946. pp. 74–81. GUL.

Divanji, Prahlad C. Materials for the history of Gujarat of the Pre-Valabhi period. *Journal of the Gujarat Research Society*. 3, 1, 1941. pp. 1–7. GVL.

Frost, Marcia J. Coping with scarcity: wild foods and common lands: Kheda district (Gujarat, India), 1824/5. *Indian Economic and Social History Review*. 37, 3,2000. pp. 295–329. CSSL, GIDRL, HML, IIML, IRMAL, UML.

Gaudani, H.R. and Dhaky, M.A. Some newly discovered and less know Maru-Gurjar temples in Northern Gujarat. *Journal of the Oriental Institute*. 17, 2, 1967. pp. 149–156. GVL.

Giri, Kamal. Cultural life as depicted on Dabhoi gates, Gujarat. *Journal of the Oriental Institute*. 34, 3–4, 1985. pp. 181–192. GVL.

Goetz, H. Gupta sculptures from Northern Gujarat. *Journal of the Gujarat Research Society*. 14, 1, 1952. pp. 1–15. GUL.

Goetz, H. "Pretty" archaic style" in old Gujarat. *Journal of the Gujarat Research Society*. 8, 2 and 3, 1946. pp. 113–116. GUL.

Gyani, R.G. Archaeological work in Gujarat. *Journal of the Gujarat Research Society*. 8, 2 and 3, 1946. pp. 88–94. GUL.

Gyani, R.G. Coinage of Gujarat. *Journal of the Gujarat Research Society*. 1, 1, 1939. pp. 20–32. GUL.

Hardiman, David. Usury, dearth and famine in Western India. *Past & Present*. 152, 1996. pp. 113–156. CSSL.

Hashim, S.A. Gujarat potters of Baroda District. *Journal of the M.S. University of Baroda*. 24–25, 1, 1973–74. pp. 93–100. GVL.

Haynes, Douglas. Dynamics of continuity in Indian domestic industry: jari manufacture in Surat,1900–47. *Indian Economic and Social History Review*. 23, 2, 1986. pp. 127–149. CSSL, IIML, UML.

Haynes, Douglas E. From tribute to philanthropy: the politics of gift giving in a Western Indian city. *Journal of Asian Studies*. 46, 2, 1987. pp. 339–360. CSSL.

Hegde, Karunakara. Analytical examination of a metal image from Samalaji. *Journal of the Oriental Institute*. 12, 2, 1962. pp. 177–180. GVL.

Hegewald, Julia A.B. Aspects of Jaina temple architecture in Rajasthan and Gujarat. *South Asia Research*. 22, 2, 2002. pp. 107–122. HML.

Hirananda, S. Note on the work done by the archaelogical department Baroda State. *Journal of the Gujarat Research Society*. 2, 1, 1940. pp. 1–7. GUL.

Isaka, Riho. Gujarati intellectuals and history writing in the colonial period. *Economic and Political Weekly*. 37, 48, 2002. pp. 4867–4872. BUL, CEPTL, CSSL, EDIL, GIDRL, IIML, IRMAL, MICAL, SGUL, SPIESRL, UML.

Jaychandra, V. History of the Surastran ksatrapas re-examined. *Journal of the Gujarat Research Society*. 2, 2, 1940. pp. 101–111. GUL, GVL.

Jha, Murari Kumar. Indian merchant groups and the European traders competition and collaboration in 17th century Gujarat. *Journal of Indian Ocean Studies*. 12, 2, 2004. pp. 301-[ ]. HML.

Jha, Murari Kumar. Mughal state and the merchant groups at Surat in the 17th Century: hostility and mutual adjustment. *Indica*. 41, 2, 2004. pp. 103-[ ]. HML.

Joshi, Mrinal. Jaina women of Gujarat as seen through their inscriptions. *Journal of Gujarat Research Society*. 45, 3–4, 2010. pp. 25–33. CSSL.

Kajaria, D.T. Sea-Shore of Kutch-Mandvi. *Bhavan's Journal*. 21, 4, 1974. pp. 37–46. GVL.

Kooiman, Dick. Communalism and Indian princely states: a comparison with British India. *Economic and Political Weekly*. 30, 34, 1995. pp. 2123–2133. CEPTL, CSSL, IIML, IRMAL, MICAL, SGUL, SPIESRL, UML.

Majmudar, M.R. Newly discovered Buddha bronze from Bhuj(Kutch). *Journal of the Oriental Institute*. 7, 3, 1959. pp. 217–218. GVL.

Mallick, B.S. Currencies and their exchange value in seventeenth-century Gujarat and Bengal. *Indian Historical Review*. 7, 1–2, 1980–81. pp. 116–133. CSSL, HML, IIML.

Mallick, Binoy Shankar. English trade and indigenous finance in Bengal and Gujarat in the seventeenth century: a study of dadni system and the rate of interest. *Studies in History*. 2, 1, 1986. pp. 31–45. CSSL.

Maloni, Rubi. Europeans in seventeenth century Gujarat: presence and response. *Social Scientist*. 36, 3–4, 2008. pp. 64–98. CSSL, UML.

Mehta, M.J. British rule and the practice of sati in Gujarat. *Journal of Indian History*. 44, 2, 1966. pp. 553–560. GVL.

Mehta, M.J. Some aspects of Surat as trading centre in the 17th century. *Indian Historical Review*. 1, 2, 1974. pp. 247–261. GVL.

Mehta, Makrand. Gandhi and Ahmedabad, 1915–20. *Economic and Political Weekly*. 40, 4, 2005. pp. 291–299. CEPTL, CSSL, EDIL, IIML, IRMAL, MICAL, SGUL, SPIESRL, UML.

Mehta, Makrand. Gujarati business communities in East African diaspora: major historical trends. *Economic and Political Weekly*. 36, 20, 2001. pp. 1738–1747. BUL, CEPTL, CSSL, EDIL, GIDRL, IIML, IRMAL, MICAL, SGUL. SPIESRL, UML.

Mehta, Makrand. Leader and his milieu: Gandhi and Ahmedabad, 1915–20. *Indian Historical Review*. 12, 1–2, 1985–86. pp. 173–187. CSSL, IIML.

Mehta, Makrand and Dixit, Yatindra. Mahajans of Gujarat: Some questions relating to the problems of transition from ancient to medieval period. *India Past and Present*. 2, 2, 1985. pp. 229–239. HML.

Mehta, R.N. Early Mediaeval sculpture from Kashipura Sarar, district Baroda. *Journal of the Oriental Institute*. 8, 1, 1958. pp. 71–72. GVL.

Mehta, R.N. Stone-age sites in Valia taluka and Mangrol taluka of Barouch and Surat districts. *Journal of the Oriental Institute*. 17, 2, 1967. pp. 142–148. GVL.

Mehta, R.N. Vasravi: an Iron-Smelting site, taluka Mangrol, district Surat. *Journal of the Oriental Institute*. 9, 3, 1960. pp. 305–309. GVL.

Mehta, Shirin. Akbar as reflected in the contemporary Jain literature in Gujarat. *Social Scientist*. 20, 9–10, 1992. pp. 54–60. CSSL, UML.

Mehta, Shirin. Role of women in the peasant movement of Gujarat: a study in the Gandhian phase-1915–28. *Indian Historical Review*. 12, 1–2, 1985–86. pp. 164–172. CSSL, HML, IIML.

Mehta, Shirin M. Social and economic back ground of the Bardoli satyagraha. *Journal of Indian History*. 55, 3, 1977. pp. 159–166. GVL.

Mitra, Pranab Kumar. Surat in 17th century as seen by the foreign travellers. *Historical Review*. 1, 1, 1986. pp. 45–53. HML.

Modak, Cyril. Maharaja Bhaguatsinhjee of Gondal hands. *Modern Review*. 76, 1, 1944. pp. 53-[ ]. GVL.

Momin, K.N. Route-Indicators of the sultanate period in Gujarat. *Journal of the M.S. University of Baroda*. 32, 1, 1982–83. pp. 121–130. GVL.

Momin, K.N. Some sculptures of Vishnu from district, Kheda-Gujarat. *Journal of the M.S. University of Baroda*. 25–26, 1, 1976–77. pp. 93–96. GVL.

Munshi, K.M. Junagadh's integration and Somanath reconstruction. *Bhavan's Journal*. 47, 1, 2000. pp. 49–54. GVL.

Nagarch, B.L. Newly discovered temple and sculptures at Zalod, district Panchmahals, Gujarat. *Journal of the Oriental Institute*. 42, 3–4, 1993. pp. 161–166. GVL.

Nanavati, J.M. Problems of the chronology of Harappan sites in Gujarat. *Journal of the Oriental Institute*. 11, 4,1962. pp. 421–427. GVL.

Nanavati, J.M. Three Post-Gupta Sun images from Saurashtra. *Journal of the Gujarat Research Society*. 25, 100, 1963. pp. 295–296. GVL.

Nanavati, J.M. Unpublished ksatrapa inscription from Kutch. *Journal of the Oriental Institute*. 11, 3, 1962. pp. 237–238. GVL.

Nanavati, Rajendra J. Buddhist archaeology in Gujarat. *Journal of the Oriental Institute*. 46, 1–2, 1996. pp. 15–26. GVL.

Oonk, Gijsbert. Motor or millstone?: the managing agency system in Bombay and Ahmedabad, 1850–1930. *Indian Economic and Social History Review*. 38, 4, 2001. pp. 419–452. CSSL, GIDRL, HML, IIML, UML.

Padmaja, V.T. Three sakti pithas of Gujarat. *Journal of the Oriental Institute*. 35, 3–4, 1986. pp. 241–248. GVL.

Padmaja, V.T. Yantra worship in the shakta centres of Gujarat. *Journal of the Oriental Institute*. 34, 3–4, 1985. pp. 173–179. GVL.

Pandey, S.N. Archaeological evidences for the history of Somanatha temple. *Journal of the Oriental Institute*. 28, 3–4, 1979. pp. 139–144. GVL.

Pandey, S.N. Images of Nataraja from Somanatha temple. *Journal of the Oriental Institute*. 37, 3–4, 1988. pp. 329–332. GVL.

Pandya. Amrit V. Saurashtra before the dawn of history. *Journal of the Gujarat Research Society*. 12, 3, 1950. pp. 153–162. GUL, GVL.

Pandya. Amrit V. Saurashtra before the dawn of history-II. *Journal of the Gujarat Research Society*. 14, 1, 1952. pp. 16–21. GVL.

Parekh, V.S. Some sculptures from Masara, district Baroda. *Journal of the Oriental Institute*. 25, 1, 1975. pp. 78–82. GVL.

Parekh, V.S. and Trivedi, Vasantalal. Remarkable sadasivamurti from Dhamatvan (dist. Ahmedabad). *Journal of the Oriental Institute*. 28, 1, 1978. pp. 85–87. GVL.

Parikh, K.T. Two newly discovered bronzes of matrka Ambika Devi From Bhoral, district Banas-Kantha, North-Gujarat. *Journal of the M.S. University of Baroda*. 20–21, 1, 1971–72. pp. 41–44. GVL.

Parikh, R.T. New discovered sculpture of Matrka Vaishnvi from Tharad, district Banas-Kantha, North-Gujarat. *Journal of the M.S. University of Baroda*. 20–21, 1, 1971–72. pp. 39–40. GVL.

Paruck, F.D.J. Nahapana and the Shaka era in Gujarat. *Journal of the Gujarat Research Society*. 4, 3, 1942. pp. 149–168. GVL.

Prakash, S. Crop choice and peasant rationality in British Gujarat, 1850 to 1937. *Studies in History*. 1, 2, 1985. pp. 201–220. CSSL.

Rabitoy, Neil. Administrative modernization and the Bhats of British Gujarat, 1800–1820. *Indian Economic and Social History Review*. 11, 1, 1974. pp. 46–73. CSSL, HML, IIML, UML.

Ram, Sadhu. Interpretation of a uerse in the Junagadh inscription of Skandagupta. *Journal of the Oriental Institute*. 28, 3–4, 1979. pp. 90–91. GVL.

Rapp, Eueenludwig. Armenian epigraph at Ahmedabad. *Journal of the Oriental Institute*. 17, 1, 1967. pp. 22–25. GVL.

Rawal, R.K. Some aspects of the British impact of religion, culture and literature in Gujarat during the Nineteenth century. *Vidya: The Journal of Gujarat University* 20, 1, 1977. pp. 98–126. SGUL.

Ray, Indrani. European traders in Surat (1730–1750). *Calcutta Historical Journal*. 6, 1, 1981. pp. 15–29. HML.

Ray, Rajat Kant. Pedhis and mills: the historical integration of the formal and informal sectors in the economy of Ahmedabad. *Indian Economic and Social History Review*. 19, 3 and 4, 1982. pp. 387–396. CSSL.

Sandesara, B.J. Historical Sanskrit play depicting the conflict between sultan Mohammad II of Ahmedabad and king Gangadasa of Champaner. *Journal of the Oriental Institute*. 4, 2–3, 1955. pp. 193–204. GVL.

Sandesara, Bhogilal J. Fourteen century Sanskrit inscription from Anahilavad Patan, North Gujarat. *Journal of the Gujarat Research Society*. 12, 2, 1950. pp. 92–93. GUL, GVL.

Sankalia, H.D. “Ancient name of Kutch”. *Journal of the Oriental Institute*. 31, 2, 1981. pp. 183–184. GVL.

Sankalia, H.D. Brief summary of "studies in historical geography and cultural ethnography of Gujarat". *Journal of the Gujarat Research Society*. 7, 4, 1945. pp. 139–146. GUL.

Sankalia, H.D. Early mediaeval temples of Gujarat and treatises on architecture. *Journal of the Gujarat Research Society*. 3, 2, 1941. pp. 73–76. GVL.

Sastri, Hirananda. Pre-Mughal citrapata from Gujarat. *Indian Historical Quarterly*. 14, [ ], 1938. pp. 353–425. GVL.

Shah, Umakant P. Lothal-a port? *Journal of the Oriental Institute*. 9, 3, 1960. pp. 310–320. GVL.

Shah, V.P. and Mehta, R.M. Few early sculptures from Gujarat. *Journal of the Oriental Institute*. 1, 2, 1951. pp. 160–164. GVL.

Shamsul, Ulma and Modi, Jivanji Jamshedji. Anquetil du perron of Paris and Dastur Darab of Surat. *Journal of the Bombay Branch Royal Asiatic Society*. 24, 1915–1917. pp. 385–456. GVL.

Shankardass, Rani Dhavan. Spokesman for the peasantry: the case of Vallabhbhai Patel and Bardoli. *Studies in History*. 2, 1, 1986. pp. 47–69. CSSL.

Shastri, H.G. Text of the two copper-edicts from Vadnagar. *Journal of the Oriental Institute*. 17, 2, 1967. pp. 181–192. GVL.

Shastri, H.G. Two maitraka copper-edicts from Vadnagar. *Journal of the Oriental Institute*. 17, 1, 1967. pp. 59–63. GVL.

Shelat, Bharati. Amrtavarsini stepwell at Ahmedabad: an epigraphic overview. *Journal of the Gujarat Research Society*. 58, 1–2, 2013. pp. 16–19. CSSL.

Shelat, Bharati. Kaloli, copper-plates of rastrakutes dharavarsa Dhruvaraja(I) of the Laota branch of Gujarat, Asaka Sam. 744 (A.D. 822). *Journal of the Oriental Institute*. 47, 1–2, 1997. pp. 29–42. GVL.

Shrivastava, Lily. Four uninscribed die-struck coin of Vadnagar. *Journal of the Oriental Institute*. 46, 3–4, 1997. pp. 207–218. GVL.

Shrivastava, LiLy. Some interesting observation on the coins of Gujarat. *Journal of the Oriental Institute*. 39, 1–2, 1989. pp. 119–130. GVL.

Simpson, Edward. Changing perspectives of three Muslim men on the question of saint worship over a 10-Year period in Gujarat, Western India. *Modern Asian Studies*. 42, 2/3, 2008. pp. 377–403. CSSL, IRMAL.

Singh, Mahendra Pal. Custom and the custom house at Surat in the Seventeenth century. *Quarterly Review of Historical Studies*. 10, 2, 1970–71. pp. 80–90. GVL.

Sinha, Nandini. Early Maitrakas, landgrant charters and regional state formation in early medieval Gujarat. *Studies in History*. 17, 2, 2001. pp. 151–163. HML.

Sompura, Kantilal F. Decorative sculptures in the temples of Gujarat. *Journal of Indian History*. 55, 3, 1977. pp. 67–80. GVL, HML.

Sonawane, V.H. Archaeology of the Panchmahals. *Journal of the M.S. University of Baroda*. 27–28, 1, 1978–1979. pp. 115–122. GVL.

Sonawane, V.H. Four Kshatrapa coins from Mataria,(Panchmahals). *Journal of the M.S. University of Baroda*. 25–26, 1, 1976–77. pp. 83–84. GVL.

Sonawane, V.H. Pasupatinatha temple at Pavagadh. *Journal of the M.S. University of Baroda*. 29, 1, 1980. pp. 41–46. GVL.

Sonawane, V.H. Two rare sculptures of Gajendra Moksa from Gujarat. *Journal of the Oriental Institute*. 35, 1–2, 1985. pp. 127–130. GVL.

Spodek, Howard. "Manchesterisation" of Ahmedabad. *Economic Weekly*, 17, 11, 1965. pp. 438–490. HML, UML.

Srinivasan, Saradha. Geographical features as referred to in Dwaraka-Mahatmya. *Journal of the Oriental Institute*. 35, 3–4, 1986. pp. 229–234. GVL.

Sukheswala, R.N. Geological evolution of Maha-Gujarat. *Journal of the Gujarat Research Society*. 10, 2, 1948. pp. 53–79. GUL.

Thosar, H.S. Some unknown facts about the Rastrakutas of Gujarat. *Journal of the Oriental Institute*. 40, 1–2, 1990. pp. 75–82. GVL.

Torri, Michelguglielmo. Ethnicity and trade in Surat during the dual government era: 1759–1800. *Indian Economic and Social History Review*. 27, 4, 1990. pp. 377–404. CSSL, UML.

Torri, Michelguglielmo. In the deep blue sea: Surat and its merchant class during the diarchic era(1759–1800). *Indian Economic and Social History Review*. 19, 3 and 4, 1982. pp. 267–299. CSSL.

Torri, Michelguglielmo. Loch ness monster?: the Mahajans of Surat during the second half of the Eighteenth century. *Studies in History*. 13, 1, 1997. pp. 1–18. CSSL.

Torri, Michelguglielmo. Mughal nobles, Indian merchants and the beginning of British conquest in Western India: the case of Surat 1756–1759. *Modern Asian Studies*. 32, 2, 1998. pp. 257–315. CSSL.

Torri, Michelguglielmo. Social groups and the redistribution of commercial wealth: the customs houses of Surat (1759–1800). *Studies in History*. 1, 1, 1985. pp. 57–86. CSSL.

Torri, Michelguglielmo. Surat during the second half of the Eighteenth century: what kind of social order?: a Rejoinder to Lakshmi Subramanian. Modern Asian Studies. 21, 4, 1987. pp. 679–710. CSSL, HML.

Tripathi, Dwijendra. Birth, growth and death of firms in a proto-industrial economy: the experience of the Ahmedabad textile industry, 1858–1929. *Indian Historical Review*. 16, 1–2, 1989–1990. pp. 163–194. CSSL, IIML.

Trivedi, A.B. To the Kathiawar coast. *Journal of the Gujarat Research Society*. 4, 2, 1942. pp. 83–102. GVL.

Trivedi, P.M. Gujarat: highways of Aryan migration. *Journal of the Gujarat Research Society*. 1, 2, 1939. pp. 23–30. GUL.

Varma, Supriya. Changing settlement patterns in Kathiawar. *Studies in History*. 6, 2, 1990. pp. 137–161. CSSL.

Varma, Supriya. Villages abadoned: the case for mobile pastoralism in post-Harappan Gujarat. *Studies in History*. 7, 2, 1991. pp. 279–300. CSSL, GIDRL.

Vasavada, R.J. Evolving architectural traditions. *Seminar*. 470, 1998. pp. 52–57. CSSL, CEPTL, IRMAL, MICAL, UML.

Vyas, G.N. Serological study for Gujarat region. *Journal of the Gujarat Research Society*. 19, 3/75. 1957. pp. 232–241. GVL.

Wadia, D.N. Geological evolution of Gujarat. *Journal of the Gujarat Research Society*. 4, 4, 1942. pp. 215–219. GVL.

Wittmann, Cecila. Gold coins of the Chaulukyas of Gujarat: a reappraisal. *Journal of the Numismatic Society of India*. 40, 1 and 2, 1978. pp. 116–119. HML.

Working Papers, Reports and Other Materials

Acharya, Harinarayan Girdharlal. Natural history around Ahmedabad. In *Ahmedabad*. Ahmedabad: Rotary Club, 1940. pp. 97–115. CSSL.

Baroda State Press. *Baroda blue book*. Vol. X. Baroda: State Press, 1940. p. 112. CSSL.

Baroda State Press. *Baroda blue book*. Vol. IX. Baroda: State Press, 1938. p. 78. CSSL. (Ed. by R.V. Desai)

Bombay Presidency. *Gazetteer of Bombay presidency: Ahmedabad*. Vol. IV. Bombay: Government Central Press, 1879. p. 361. CSSL.

Bombay Presidency. *Gazetteer of the Bombay presidency*: *history of Gujarat*. Vol. I, *part I*. Bombay: Government Central Press, 1896. p. 594. CSSL, BVL.

Bombay Presidency. *Gazetteer of the Bombay presidency. Gujarat population: Musalmans and Parsis*, Vol. IX, part II. Bombay: Government Central Press, 1899. p. 287. CSSL.

Bombay Presidency. *Gazetteer of the Bombay presidency: Surat and Broach*, Vol. II-B. Bombay: Government Central Press, 1904. p. 66. CSSL.

Cama, J.C. History of Ahmedabad. In *Ahmedabad*. Ahmedabad: Rotary Club, 1940. pp. 3–21. CSSL.

Castellino, J. Ahmedabad and the B.B. & C.I. Rly. In *Ahmedabad*. Ahmedabad: Rotary Club, 1940. pp. 63–69. CSSL.

Commissariat, M.S. *Studies in the history of Gujarat: the Thakkar Vassonji Madhavji lectures of the University of Bombay for the year 1930–31*. Ahmedabad: Saraswati, 1987. p. 157. CSSL.

De, Aparajita. *Imagined geographies: geographical knowledge of self and others in everyday life: the case of Ahmedabad*. Surat: Centre for Social Studies, 2004. p. 73. CSSL.

Desai, Z.A. Arabic and Persian inscriptions of Gujarat. In *Epigraphical resources of Gujarat*. Ed. by Ramlal parikh And Rasesh Jamindar. Souvenir publication on the occasion of sixth congress of the epigraphical society of India, 9–11 March 1980. Ahmedabad: Gujarat Vidyapith, 1980. pp. 12–22. CSSL.

Enthoven, R.E., compil. *Imperial gazetteer of India: provincial series, Bombay presidency*, Vol. I. Reprint Edition. New Delhi: Usha, 1985. Original in 1909. p. 587. CSSL.

Fischer, Eberhard and Shah, Haku. *Vetra ne khambha-memorials for the dead: wooden figures and memorial slabs of Chodhri, Gamit and Vasava tribes, South Gujarat (India)*. Ahmedabad: Gujarat Vidyapith, 1973. p. [ ]. Monograph. CSSL.

Gaur, A.S. Sundaresh, and Vora, K.H. *Archaeology of bet Dwarka island: an excavation report*. New Delhi: Aryan Books, [ ]. p. 202. UML.

Gokhale, Balkrishna Govind. *Surat in the seventeenth century: a study in urban history of pre-modern India*. London: Curzon, 1979. p. 222. Scandinavian Insitute of Asian Studies, Monograph Series No. 28. CSSL, GUL.

Gujarat, Government of. *Gujarat state gazetteer. Part I & II*. Gandhinagar: Gujarat State, 1989. p. 607 and p. 628. CSSL.

Gujarat, Government of. *Gujarat state gazetteers: Amreli District*. Ahmedabad: Gujarat State, 1972. p. 628. CSSL.

Gujarat, Government of. *Gujarat state gazetteers: Bhavnagar District*. Ahmedabad: Gujarat State, 1969. p. 630. CSSL.

Gujarat, Government of. *Gujarat state gazetteers: Broach District*. Revised Edition. Ahmedabad: Gujarat State, 1961. p. 792. Revised edition of volume II of the original gazetteer of the Bombay presidency relating to Surat and Broach. CSSL.

Gujarat, Government of. *Gujarat state gazetteers: Gandhinagar district*. Gandhinagar: Government of Gujarat, 1980. p. 417. CSSL.

Gujarat, Government of. *Gujarat state gazetteers: Jamnagar district*. Ahmedabad: Gujarat State, 1970. p. 634. CSSL.

Gujarat, Government of. *Gujarat state gazetteers: Junagadh district*. Ahmedabad: Gujarat State, 1975. p. 848. CSSL.

Gujarat, Government of. *Gujarat state gazetteers: Kheda district*. Ahmedabad: Gujarat State, 1977. p. 841. CSSL.

Gujarat, Government of. *Gujarat state gazetteers: Kutch district*. Ahmedabad: Gujarat State, 1971. p. 623. CSSL.

Gujarat, Government of. *Gujarat state gazetteers: Mehsana district*. Ahmedabad: Gujarat State, 1975. p. 862. CSSL.

Gujarat, Government of. *Gujarat state gazetteers: Panchmahals district*.Ahmedabad: Gujarat State, 1972. p. 808. CSSL.

Gujarat, Government of. *Gujarat state gazetteers: Rajkot district.* Ahmedabad: Gujarat State, 1965. p. 633 and p. 224. With Supplement. CSSL.

Gujarat, Government of. *Gujarat state gazetteers: Sabarkantha district.* Ahmedabad: Gujarat State, 1974. p. 734. CSSL.

Gujarat, Government of. *Gujarat state gazetteers: Surat district*. Ahmedabad: Gujarat State, 1962. p. 1991. with supplement. CSSL.

Gujarat, Government of. *Gujarat state gazetteers: Surendranagar district.* Ahmedabad: Gujarat State, 1977. p. 730. CSSL.

Gujarat, Government of. *Gujarat state gazetteers: Vadodara district.* Ahmedabad: Gujarat State, 1979. p. 840. CSSL.

Gupta, Ashin Das. *Indian merchants and the decline of Surat c. 1700–1750.* Wlesbaden: Franz Steiner Verlag, 1979. p. 305. IIML.

Hardiman, David. State community and capital in Gujarat 1400–1900. In *International Seminar on "Gujarat Society", 17–20 December 1986*, Surat: Centre for Social Studies, 1986. pp. 1–30. CSSL.

Haynes, Douglas. Dynamics of continuity in Indian domestic industry: jari manufacture in Surat, 1900–1947. *International seminar on "Gujarat Society", 17–20 December 1986*, Surat: Centre for Social Studies, 1986. pp. 1–36. CSSL.

Jamindar, Rasesh. Post-Independence epigraphical discoveries in Gujarat. In *Epigraphical resources of Gujarat*. Ed. by Ramlal Parikh And Rasesh Jamindar. Souvenir publication on the occasion of sixth congress of the epigraphical society of India, 9–11 March 1980. Ahmedabad: Gujarat Vidyapith, 1980. pp. 23–41. CSSL.

Kshirsagar, Shiwaram K. *Indomitable Sardar and the triumph of Borsad*. Vallabh Vidhyanagar: Sardar Patel University, 1973. p. 251. SPUL.

Lakha, Salim. Ideology and class relations in early twentieth century India: the case of Ahmedabad. In *International seminar on "Gujarat Society", 17–20 December 1986,* Surat: Centre for Social Studies, 1986. pp. 1–34. CSSL.

Lal, R.B. *Tribal village in the shadow of polo-nagari archeological remains: Dungri Garasias.* Ahmedabad: Gujarat Vidyapith, 1979. p. 27. TRTIL.

Majmudar, M.R. *Gujarat: its art heritage illustrated with 60 art – plates in monochrome and 11 in colour and with a map*. Bombay: University of Bombay, 1968. p. 168. Thakkar Vassonji Madhavji Lecture Series. GUL.

Master, Framroz Sorabji, compil. *Palanpur agency directory.* Vol. I. Ahmedabad: Praja Bandhu, 1908. p. 748. CSSL, SETUL.

Mehta, M.J. Khatapatras as a source of urban history. In *Studies in trade and urbanization in Western India*. Ed. by V.K. Chavda. Baroda: M.S. University, 1985. Series No. 9. pp. 179–184. CSSL.

Mehta, R.N. Archaeological activities in Gujarat with special referencs to epigraphical finds. In *Epigraphical resources of Gujarat.* Ed. by Ramlal parikh And Rasesh Jamindar. Souvenir publication on the occasion of sixth congress of the epigraphical society of India, 9–11 March 1980. Ahmedabad: Gujarat Vidyapith, 1980. pp. 46–54. CSSL.

Mehta, R.N. *Excavation at devnimori: a report of the excavation conducted from 1960 to 1963*. Baroda: M.S. University, 1966. p. 197. CSSL.

Mehta, R.N. Highlights on Baroda. In *Profiles of a growing city: the city of Baroda*. Ed. by K.N. Reddy and others. Baroda: M.S. University, 1971. pp. 107–114. Souvenir: 2nd Gujarat Economic conference, 2–3 January 1971. CSSL.

Mehta, R.N. Place-Names as recorded in epigraphs of Gujarat. In *Epigraphical resources of Gujarat. Ed. by Ramlal parikh And Rasesh Jamindar*. Souvenir publication on the occasion of sixth congress of the epigraphical society of India, 9–11 March 1980. Ahmedabad: Gujarat Vidyapith, 1980. pp. 63–69. CSSL.

Misra, S.C. and Mathew, K.S., eds. *General chronicle of the events in the Kingdom of Gujarat which is called Cambay*. Baroda: M.S. University, 1981. p. 94. Department of History Series No. 7. CSSL.

Munshi, K.M. *Early Aryans in Gujarat*. Bombay: University of Bombay, 1941. p. 120. Thakkar Vassanji Madhavji Lecture Series. BVL, GUL, GVL, HML, SPUL.

Munshi, Sunil. Geographer's view concerning the study of urban history of Surat. In *Studies in trade and urbanization in Western India*. Ed. by V.K. Chavda. Baroda: M.S. University, 1985. pp. 75–83. Series No. 9. CSSL.

Pandor, G.A. and Shah, R.J., ed. *Sayajirao III: the men and his times*. Vadodara: M.S. University, 1997. p. [ ]. Seminar procceeding. CSSL.

Parikh, Pravin C. Development of Brahmi script in Gujarat, In *Epigraphical resources of Gujarat.* Ed. by Ramlal Parikh and Rasesh Jamindar. Souvenir publication on the occasion of sixth congress of the epigraphical society of India, 9–11 March 1980. Ahmedabad: Gujarat Vidyapith, 1980. pp. 82–90. CSSL.

Prakash, Om. Dutch source material on the history of Surat in the 17th century. In *Studies in trade and urbanization in Western India*. Ed. by V.K. Chavda. Baroda: M.S. University, 1985. pp. 173–178. Series No. 9. CSSL.

Prakash, Om. Trade and urbanization in Gujarat in the early 17th century: a Dutch account. In *Studies in trade and urbanization in Western India*. Ed. by V.K. Chavda. Baroda: M.S. University, 1985. pp. 69–74. Series No. 9. CSSL.

Pramar, V.S. Effects of trade and urbanization on the architecture of Gujarat. In *Studies in trade and urbanization in Western India*. Ed. by V.K. Chavda. Baroda: M.S. University, 1985. pp. 85–93. Series No. 9. CSSL.

Rao, S.R. Lothal seals provide key to the decipherment of Indus script. In *Epigraphical resources of Gujarat*. Ed. by Ramlal parikh And Rasesh Jamindar. A souvenir publication on the occasion of sixth congress of the epigraphical society of India, 9–11 March 1980. Ahmedabad: Gujarat Vidyapith, 1980. pp. 54–62. CSSL.

Ray, Aniruddha. Brief history of the city of Cambay from the 16th century to the early century. In *Studies in trade and urbanization in Western India*. Ed. by V.K. Chavda. Baroda: M.S. University, 1985. pp. 27–67. Series No. 9. CSSL.

Ray, Aniruddha. French at Surat, 1693–1701. In *Portuguese, Indian ocean and European bridgeheads 1500–1800*. Ed. by Pius Malekandathil and Jamal Mohammed. Kerala: Institute for Research in Social Science, 2001. pp. 587–615. HML.

Saletore, B.A. *Main currents in the ancient history of Gujarat*. Baroda: M.S. University, 1960. p. 73. CSSL.

Shah, Priyabala. Epigraphical resources of the temples of Gujarat. In *Epigraphical resources of Gujarat*. Ed. by Ramlal parikh And Rasesh Jamindar. Souvenir publication on the occasion of sixth congress of the epigraphical society of India, 9–11 March 1980. Ahmedabad: Gujarat Vidyapith, 1980. pp. 42–45. CSSL.

Shashtri, H.G. Incriptions of Gujarat: a brief survey. In *Epigraphical resources of Gujarat*. Ed. by Ramlal Parikh and Rasesh Jamindar. Souvenir publication on the occasion of sixth congress of the epigraphical society of India, 9–11 March 1980. Ahmedabad: Gujarat Vidyapith, 1980. 1–p. 11. CSSL.

Shelat, Bharti. Eras used in the epigraphic records of Gujarat. In *Epigraphical resources of Gujarat*. Ed. by Ramlal Parikh and Rasesh Jamindar. Souvenir Publication on the Occasion of sixth congress of the epigraphical society of India, 9–11 March 1980. Ahmedabad: Gujarat Vidyapith, 1980. pp. 70–81. CSSL.

Sompura, Kantilal F. *Structural temples of Gujarat, up to 1600 AD*. Ahmedabad: Gujarat University, 1968. p. 536. Thesis Publication Series. SGUL.

Standing, Eswin Martimer. Indian twilight: Ahmedabad 1921–1922. Ahmedabad: Bharati Sarabhai Charity Trust, 2009. p. 231. SETUL.

Subbarao, Bendapudi. *Baroda through the ages: Being the report of an excavation conducted in the Baroda area 1951–52*. Baroda: M.S. University, 1953. p. 130. M.S. University Archaeological Series No. 1. CSSL, GVL.

Watson, J.W. *Statistical account of Junagadh: Being the Junagadh contribution to the Kathiawar portion of the Bombay gazetteer*. Bombay: Bombay Gazette Steam, 1884. p. 160. CSSL.

Watson, J.W. *Statistical account of Nawanagar: Being the Nawanagar contribution to the Kathiawar portion of the Bombay gazetteer*. Bombay: Education Society, 1884. p. 62. CSSL.

White, W.U. Electric supply in Ahmedabad. In *Ahmedabad*. Ahmedabad: Rotary Club, 1940. pp. 81–96. CSSL.

Year Index (1835 to 1960)

Author Index

Keyword Index